INDEX TO THE COURT BOOKS OF

THE STATIONERS' COMPANY,

1679–1717

INDEX TO
THE COURT BOOKS OF
THE STATIONERS' COMPANY,
1679–1717

Alison Shell and Alison Emblow

General Editor: Robin Myers

BIBLIOGRAPHICAL SOCIETY

2007

Copyright Alison Shell and Alison Emblow
and The Bibliographical Society, 2007

Published by The Bibliographical Society
and Oxford University Press

ISBN 978 0948170 15 7

A CIP record for this book is available
from the British Library

Designed and typeset by David Chambers

Printed and bound in the United Kingdom
by Cambridge University Press

CONTENTS

FOREWORD

Court Books E, F and G cover the years when the country was still haunted by the spectres of revolution and civil war and Charles II was attempting to subdue the City livery companies by replacing their charters and interfering in their elections. The end of Court Book F minutes the internal politics surrounding the expiry of the Printing Act in 1695, which spelt the end of the Company's statutory powers over the book trade as it moved into a period of stability at the start of Court Book G.

There are useful but varied indexes to Court Books B to D, 1576 to 1687, too disparate in method ever to be reduced to a single uniform sequence. With the completion of the microfilming of the entire archive (1554 to 1920s), we began to consider further indexing, at least to the end of the seventeenth century, although only intended for in-house use. Alison Shell and Alison Emblow had helped me with preparations for the microfilm in their vacations and were admirably equipped for a job which we supposed could be done comfortably within the year. The Stationers' Company's Educational Trust made them a grant and they set to work, Alison Shell leading the way with E and F, Alison Emblow following with G.

The task turned out to be inordinately protracted. There were all sorts of snags, not the least being the primitive state of computer technology in 1987. Alison Shell, at my ill-advised suggestion, keyed her chronological lists into an Amstrad; but the software, as we found out too late, had no alphabetizing facility, nor were there any sort of conversion programmes in existence at that time; the printer, using fan-fed paper, could only produce a few pages at a time. So her work stayed locked up on a number of 3½ inch disks – we were offered some advice, but no-one seemed able to do anything for us. In the meantime, Alison Emblow, starting a few months later, took warning and wisely decided to revert to the time-honoured method of 6 by 3½ inch index cards for Court Book G, before keying them into her slightly more up-to-date computer – it was long-winded, but safe.

There matters rested until Robin Alston offered to publish the index as a Bibliographical Society Occasional Paper. By this time technology had advanced enough for Elisabeth Leedham-Green to convert the disks laboriously into ASCII which Robin Alston could put into a continuous alphabetical index and print out, codes and all, making it accessible and usable but not yet in a state to publish to the world. Checking and revising ought now to have begun but by this time, both editors were in post, married and living at a distance from Stationers' Hall. More time passed and the Occasional Papers ceased . . . .

But it is an ill wind, as the saying is, and we discovered that the endless delays were a blessing in disguise when the Bibliographical Society agreed to publish the index as a monograph with David Chambers, a superb book editor, to oversee its transformation. Other improvements were now thought of – Alison Emblow collated the entire index with the so-called Wast Books or draft minutes and searched for discrepancies which might, in the turbulent 1680s and early '90s, be significant. With the rapid advance of the internet, Alison Shell was able to identify a great many of the works mentioned in the court books by making web searches in the English Short Title Catalogue on-line. Alison Shell's introductory account of the inner workings of the Court, set in the context of the Company itself and of the wider political scene, and her far-reaching Bibliography and list of abbreviations make it clear how far the project has advanced from a mere name and subject index. 'Indexers tell a different story from historians', as Alison Shell puts it, 'they stress continuity', and as such, the Index to the Court Books 1697–1717 will add a new dimension to book trade and other historical studies in addition to being an essential and, surprisingly, readable reference tool.

Stationers' Hall, August 2005　　　　　　　　　　　　　Robin Myers

ACKNOWLEDGEMENTS

The division of responsibility between the authors was as follows: Alison Shell wrote the introduction to this volume and indexed Court Books E and F; Alison Emblow indexed Court Book G, collated the whole index with the surviving draft minutes, and brought the whole index into final form. Both editors would like to pay tribute here to the General Editor, Robin Myers, who – among so many other services to book trade history – devised the project's parameters, and has supervised the work from instigation to completion. Her learned enthusiasm has been a constant delight to the authors.

As the Foreword explains, this project first begun in the late 1980s as an in-house index at Stationers' Hall. Since then it has metamorphosed several times, and its completion has been exceptionally protracted. The Editors would like to thank the various officers of the Bibliographical Society who have been involved with the project – most recently Mirjam Foot – for their patience during the process, as well as for a grant of £200 towards reproduction expenses in the early stages of the project. Funds for reproduction were also granted by Durham University. The Worshipful Company of Stationers generously funded the scholarly work in its initial stages, from its Educational Trust for the Training of Young People and from a bequest made by the late Wilfrid Hodgson. Many individual Company employees deserve our gratitude: the trustees of the Archive and Library Trust, the Hon. Librarian Keith Fletcher, Elisa Civale, and several Past Masters, especially the late George Mandl, the late Charles Rivington, the late Allan Thompson and Christopher Rivington (happily still with us). David Chambers has been an endlessly cheerful and facilitating production editor; David Lee has provided wise guidance on the process of indexing. Early in the project, the index was rescued from some antiquated software by the combined efforts of Robin Alston and Elisabeth Leedham-Green. The late Don McKenzie and the late Michael Treadwell took an inspirational interest in the project; Arnold Hunt and Giles Mandelbrote provided invaluable scholarly advice throughout; Anna Greening and Julian Pooley gave us the benefit of their palaeographical expertise. Don and Marjorie Emblow kindly checked index entries against photocopies; John Arnold, Editor of *Stationers' News*, supplied photographs. In the absence of footnores to the Index itself, Bridget Wright of the Royal Library, Windsor Castle, should be credited with throwing light on the career of Samuel Carr. Finally, Paul Nash has done a splendid job with the final revisions to the text.

INTRODUCTION
COURT BOOKS E–G, 1679–1717

This index gives detailed access to the entries in the three Court Books of the Stationers' Company which cover the period between 1679 and 1717, conventionally designated as Court Books E, F and G. The Court was not only the main regulatory body of the Stationers' Company, but the point of official intersection between the Company and wider political and financial spheres, within and outside London; and its duties were correspondingly diverse. Hence, the Court minutes cover a wide range of material, relevant to many types of historical endeavour.

Formal arrangements of the Court[1]

Typically, courts took place at least once a month, though they met more frequently – sometimes even daily – at times of crisis. Special courts like election courts, at which Company officers were voted into position, or pension courts, at which Company pensioners and other needy individuals received charitable handouts, are designated as such in the minutes, but were also used as a forum for discussing other kinds of Company business. The Court comprised the Master, the Upper and Under Warden, and the Assistants, a body of twelve to fifteen senior and influential members of the Company; the Clerk, a servant of the Court, took minutes. In addition to those mentioned above, attenders at court would have included those who had been summoned by the Beadle – most commonly to be bound, freed or cloathed, or to answer charges brought against them by another member of the Company – and those who wanted to petition the court.[2]

Functions of the Court

The Court was the official channel through which orders from the Lord Mayor

---

1. For a recent account of livery company administration, see Joseph P. Ward, *Metropolitan Communities: Trade Guilds, Identity, and Change in Early Modern London* (Stanford: Stanford University Press, 1997), ch.4.

2. On the Beadle's role, Court etiquette, penalties for non-attendance and misbehaviour, and the quarter-courts (which, unlike the Courts of Assistants, were general assemblies of Company members held for the purpose of collecting quarterage), see *The Orders, Rules, and Ordinances, Ordained, Devised, and Made by the Master and Keepers or Wardens and Commonalty of the Mystery or Art of Stationers* (1692: facsimile reprint, London: Harrison & Co., n.d.), pp.4–6.

of London were received, and it acted as the main representative body of the Stationers' Company in all legal matters, seeing to the appointment of attorneys when proceeding against those transgressing Company regulations, and considering counsel's opinions on lawsuits.[3] Part of the Court's job, as for all livery companies at this date, was also to lobby Parliament on matters affecting members' interests, such as the ratification and extension of the Company's regulatory powers, the repeal of unfavourable legislation and the restriction of competition; when bills with relevance to the Company's concerns were being drafted, it would appoint committees to wait on the House of Commons.[4] Though the House of Lords approached the Court on one occasion with an order to search for a pamphlet on the Jacobite conspiracy, the Company had most to do with the House of Commons or with individual members of Parliament.[5] An example of the direct, almost informal relationship that could prevail between the Company and members of the government was Lord Pembroke's intervention in his role as Lord Privy Seal in a question of the English Stock, requesting the Company to allow Awnsham Churchill to print an interlineary Latin/English Aesop.[6]

Just as the Court was the essential intermediary between the government and the ordinary Stationer, it was also the means for presenting Company members with communications from the Crown such as Charles II's mandate on press control and James II's commission on licensing, or with ecclesiastical dignitaries' interventions in the licensing process.[7] In the early years of this period, before the lapse of the Licensing Act in 1695, it was also the Court's job to keep the Company informed of developments in the Act that might affect it, such as the clause passed in April 1693 whereby letter founders and press makers needed to tell the Company what they were making.[8] The end of Court Book F, from January to May 1697, shows the Court seeking legal advice as to whether paper to be used for printing rather than resale was taxable under the Paper Act, and

3. Liber A, the Company's record of mayoral precepts, &c. (described in Myers, p.52) is referred to in the Court Books on a number of occasions: see index under 'Liber A'.

4. See Jeremy Boulton, 'London 1540–1640', ch.10 in Peter Clark (ed.), *The Cambridge Urban History of Britain*, vol.II, 1540–1840 (Cambridge: Cambridge University Press, 2000), p.341.

5. 9 March 1695/6, F240r.

6. 11 June 1694, F209r. See also 2 August 1697, F265r; 4 October 1697, F268r; 28 October 1697, F270r. As Michael Treadwell points out, the Court's apparent refusal to discuss it may have been a tactical mistake: '1695–1995', p.10.

7. 20 June 1681, E113r; 22 May 1685, F36r (see also 22 August 1685, F43r, where Robert Midgely tells the Court that he has been authorised to license books under the new Licensing Act, and where the Archbishop of Canterbury refuses to license prognostications).

8. 10 April 1693, F186v.

preparing to defend a test case. The names of people who were to keep members of the book trade informed of these developments, and solicit money from them to cover legal fees, are listed in the minutes together with the regions they were to cover.[9]

Censorship questions, especially in the earlier part of the period covered by this index, also came within the Company's purview and were potentially of intense interest outside Company boundaries. They were, however, only one part of the Court's disciplinary function. The maintenance of discipline within the Company and the book trade was an area where the boundaries between internal and external Company business were especially fluid, needing to be re-assessed in relation to each specific offence. Those found guilty of illegal printing of any kind were summoned before the Court, and in practice, illegal printing resolved into two main categories: subversive material, which the government had an interest in suppressing; and the printing of books to which one had no title.[10] The English Stock, a joint stock company trading from Stationers' Hall, monopolised a small list of very popular books, including almanacks, primers, children's ABCs and other school books, catechisms and psalters, and determined who should be responsible for printing them.[11] Throughout this period, both outsiders and those of standing within the Company were tempted to encroach on this market by printing illicit copies of these

9. Summarised from: 12 January 1696/7, F254r; 19 March 1696/7, F257v; 22 March 1696/7, F257v; 1 April 1697, F260r; 3 May 1697, F261v. See 'Acts of Parliament: Paper Act'. For the Court's response to a request from the House of Commons that they should consider the possibility of supplying all England with stamped paper and parchment, see 4 June 1694, F207v-208r. The Paper Act is briefly described in Plomer, 1668-1725.

10. See index under 'Printing, Seditious', and 'Printing, Illegal'.

11. No scholarly list has ever been compiled of the items which formed part of the English Stock from year to year, though lists were compiled for various purposes at the time (cf. 3 May 1686, f.55r; 1 September 1690, F142r; and the Stock account books). See Robin Myers, 'The Financial Records of the Stationers' Company, 1605-1811', in Robin Myers & Michael Harris (eds), *Economics of the British Booktrade, 1605-1939* (Cambridge/ Alexandria, VA: Chadwyck-Healey, 1985), pp.1-31; Cyprian Blagden, 'The English Stock of the Stationers' Company: An Account of its Origins', *The Library*, 5th ser., 10 (1955), pp.163-185. On the complex relationship between the Company and the English Stock, see also Robin Myers, 'George Hawkins (1705-1780): Bookseller and Treasurer of the English Stock of the Stationers' Company', pp.113-129 in Robin Myers & Michael Harris (eds.), *The Stationers' Company and the Book Trade, 1550-1990* (Winchester: St Paul's Bibliographies, 1997). With regard to almanacks, see index under 'Almanacks'; Cyprian Blagden, 'The Distribution of Almanacks in the Second Half of the 17th Century', *Studies in Bibliography*, 11 (1958), pp.107-116; and Bernard Capp's *Astrology and the Popular Press: English Almanacs, 1500-1800* (London: Faber & Faber, 1979), ch.2, which makes extensive use of the Court Books. Capp's book is reviewed at length by Michael Harris in *Publishing History*, 8 (1980), pp.87-104.

books.[12] More rarely, the court had to act where it detected wrong-doing on the part of its own officials or their subordinates, and safeguard against this happening in future;[13] while as a means of forestalling dispute, it sometimes officially recorded the re-assignment of a book's copyright.[14]

That Court minutes were prescriptive as well as archival in importance is illustrated in the Court's attitude to byelaws. These had to be passed by an assembly of the entire Stationers' Company, but it was the Court that saw to their printing, and the Court Books recorded them whether they afterwards appeared in print or not.[15] The important byelaws of 1678 fall just outside this period, but the subsequent set concerning printing of names, the Renter Wardens, property, the power to search, schoolbooks, patent rights and the livery are written in full in the minutes of 17 August 1681.[16] The 'Rules and Ordinances Concerning Letter Patents', first written out at 1 August 1681 and followed by the 'Counsel's Opinion Concerning English Stock', were engrossed at 5 October 1681 with some alterations, and on 5 December 1681 it was ordered that they should be hung in the hall.[17] A byelaw concerning the entry of names in registers, in a move to suppress seditious literature, was resolved upon at an assembly of the Company on 6 December 1682.[18] Further byelaws about fines for comprinting, the clerk, the renter wardens, the choice of livery, searching and apprentices were transcribed into the minutes for 14 May 1694.[19]

The Court's crucial role in regulating internal affairs can also be seen in orders relating to book-keeping and archival duties. From past officials the Court demanded papers relating to Company business, and where Company and private affairs were mingled in a single document, as may have been the case with 'Martin's Callendar Booke', the Clerk was ordered to copy out the relevant

12. Enormous variation is discernible in the ways offenders were disciplined, but the case of George Calvert shows that it could sometimes affect one's career within the Company (see index under his name).

13. e.g. an exact table of fees being drawn up in response to the case of the clerk's man who elicited extortionate fees for binding and freeing apprentices (G122v, 6 August 1705).

14. See index under 'Assignments'. It was especially common to use the Court as a means of negotiating block rates for the re-assignment of books felt to be of little or no value.

15. 2 August 1680, E102v; 4 September 1682, E157r. See index under 'Byelaws'.

16. E125r (transcribed in Arber I, pp.20–24). For the 1678 byelaws, see Blagden, ch.IX.

17. E117v (Counsel's Opinion E122r); E131r. The differences between the two versions are as follows: (i) Clause No.6 in the first, about the distribution of £200 from the English Stock to the poor of the Company (E118v) is reworded in the second (E132v) and also mentioned in the preamble (E131r). (ii) The second has a clause about the Assistants laying out profits for the benefit of the Company (E132v). There are notes at the beginning of the first version, referring the reader to the second.

18. E161v (Wing 0411).   19. F205r.

portions.[20] Sometimes the court ruled that regulations were to be copied out separately for the greater convenience of Company officials.[21] It was the Court, too, who decided when the system of accounts and registers needed reforming or keeping up to the mark. This period sees the institution of the Clerk's Wast Register, regular reports on auditing the Wardens' and Renter Wardens' accounts, a perennial anxiety that books should be kept up to date, and a similar concern, manifested in the committees of December 1691, that the Wardens', Stock-keepers' and Treasurer's accounts should be as accurate as possible.[22] Incidental archival information emerges from the Court's decisions, such as the fact that there was a special chest for miscellaneous papers, and that the Clerk's books were kept in a room behind the Court Room.[23]

What also emerges is the tight control, both physical and intellectual, that the Company attempted – at least intermittently – to keep over its documents. There is a Court order in July 1695 for a catalogue of all Company documents, and in April 1682 it was ordered that no English Stock account books should be removed from the Hall without permission.[24] Whenever Clerks were changed the books were always transferred from the past Clerk to his successor by Court order;[25] the list of books entered in Court Book E is of the greatest importance in this context.[26] The current Clerk was not, though, the only one to write in the

20. 3 January 1680/1, E106r; 7 March 1680/1, E107v; 5 October 1696, F250r; Martin's book (which cannot be identified with any of the surviving documents in the Company archives) at 7 February 1680/1, E106v. See also the table of the Clerk's fees for various duties, 26 March 1697, F258v. On 4 July 1698 (G10v) Ambrose Isted's widow was required to deliver up all writings in her custody which related to the Company.

21. For example the order that the Oxford Articles should be entered into a book for the Stock-keepers' use: G30r (4 September 1699).

22. Clerk's Wast Register, 4 April 1687, F81v. However, only one volume was compiled: see Myers, p.25. Committees which discuss accounts: 7 December 1691, F162v; 22 December 1691, F163v. See index under 'Clerk', 'Cheque Book', 'Register Book', 'Renter Wardens', 'Wardens' Accounts', and Myers, 'Financial Records', p.15. Myers has commented, though, that it took the Company nine years to bring themselves to act on the advice of a 1692 committee that an accountant should be appointed to regularize the Stock accounts: 'Financial Records', p.20, referring to F182b and G90a.

23. 5 October 1696, F250r, & 21 June 1700, G41r; 3 April 1693, F186r.

24. 1 July 1695, F227r; 3 April 1682, E151r. However, Myers describes the frequent discrepancy between theory and practice in the case of Stock accounts: 'Financial Records', pp.11–12.

25. 1 August 1681, E117v; 5 December 1692, F183r; cf. 5 October 1696, F250v. Some dilatoriness is visible in a Court order of 2 May 1698 (G7r) by which John Garrett, the last clerk but one, is ordered to deliver all counterparts of leases in his custody to the present clerk.

26. 30 March 1681, E108v. The list is signed for by John Garrett, and includes books of court orders; registers of copies; Wardens' accounts; apprentice registers; apprentice calendars; registers of freemen and liverymen; book of fines; 2 books of entry of

Court Books; in an entry of 1702, for instance, it was ordered that the Court Book should be delivered to a former Clerk, John Lilly, to enter the record of a lawsuit.[27] The Court regularly expressed concern that entries in all records should be kept up to date, and in the Court Books and elsewhere, it seems likely that several entries were copied up at a time; this may explain the pronounced variations in handwriting visible between one set of entries and another in Court Book G, even where the same person was probably responsible for both.[28] Finally, it was the first of the Clerks within this period, John Lilly, who anticipated the present editors by instituting an index for the Court books.[29]

The Court oversaw the internal management of the Company by electing officers: those who served generally for a year, the Master, the Upper Warden, the Under Warden, the two Renter Wardens and the Stock-keepers for the Court, the livery and the yeomanry, and the servants of the Company whose annual re-election tended to be routine, such as the Clerk, the Treasurer and the Beadle.[30] Court Assistants – members of the Court with no designated office – were chosen from among senior livery members, and calls to the Assistantship were under-taken at irregular intervals whenever the Court felt its numbers were running low.[31] From those who were unable or unwilling to serve in the higher Company offices, the Renter Wardens collected fines in lieu of service, a constant feature of Court business;[32] they also saw to the collections of fines from those lower down the hierarchy who were admitted to the freedom or the livery of the Company, and monitored the collection of quarterage, a subscription levied on all members of the Company. Any committees appointed to look at issues in

seizures; English Stock account books; register of plate, and of money lent out in bonds; register of S.C. leases; the Lord Mayor's precept book (Liber A); and a book containing a copy of Norton's will.

27. 6 July 1702, G77r. See below, 'Handwriting and Layout'. A rhyme doodled in Court Book D may suggest that apprentices were employed to copy up court minutes.

28. See below, p.43.

29. See 7 July 1701, G62r; 5 July 1714, G220r. Lilly's abstracts survive in an early 18th-century recension, at the beginning of the 'Index to the Court Books to 1775' (see Myers, p.77, and p.40 below).

30. There were three elections during the year. The Stock-keepers and Treasurer were elected in early March; the Clerk, Beadle, Renter Wardens and other Company officers in late March; and the Master and Wardens in late June/early July, at the beginning of the Company's year (see Myers (ed.), *Stationers' Company*, p.250). Elections to the minor Company offices are not consistently recorded, but those appointed in this way include the porter, the cook, the bargemaster and the bargemaster's mate.

31. Cyprian Blagden, 'The Stationers' Company in the Eighteenth Century', *Guildhall Miscellany*, 10 (1959), pp.36–53, discusses election to the court in this period, and the question of Renter Wardenships and seniority (pp.42–43). See also below, p.27, for an example of individuals being elected onto the Court as a reward for efforts in suppress-ing illegal printing.

32. See index under 'Fees and Fines'.

more detail drew their membership from among the Assistants, almost without exception, and commonly included the most senior Company officials. Through election dinners the Court arranged for the socialising which was so important a part of life in all Livery companies; and by seeing to the construction of stands on public occasions and the maintenance of the barge which carried Stationers' Company members at the celebrations for the annual inauguration of the Lord Mayor of London, it kept up the public face of the Company and provided opportunities for internal networking.[33] Apprentices were bound, turned over and freed at courts, and courts were also the occasion on which freemen summoned to the livery were cloathed; the names of the individuals concerned were listed in the court minutes.[34]

A number of financial matters came within the Court's remit. It considered and oversaw the public sealing of bonds entered into by the Company; ordered the payment of bills incurred by the Company; authorised the defrayal of travel and other costs incurred by those pursuing Company interests; and recorded any bequests of money or plate which members had made to the Company. Especially – though not exclusively – through quarterly pension courts, it fulfilled the charitable functions so central to the Company's purpose: receiving petitions from the badly-off, allotting, re-allocating and administering pensions in cases of general hardship among Company members and their dependents, and making one-off charitable donations in response to specific needs.[35] It passed a number of regulations to do with the English Stock, and administered a number of routine Stock affairs such as the re-assignment of shares and the determination of dividends.[36] It appointed auditors of accounts drawn up by the Under-Warden, the Renter Wardens and the Treasurer.[37] Individual members of the Company, and those involved with it in some other capacity, had *ad hoc* financial dealings

33. See Kenneth Nicholls Palmer, *Ceremonial Barges on the River Thames: A History of the Barges of the City of London Livery Companies and of the Crown* (London: Unicorn, 1997), pp.126–127; Michael Osborne, *The State Barges of the Stationers' Company, 1680–1850* (London: Stationers' Company, 1972).

34. On apprenticeship within London livery companies, see Christopher Brooks, 'Apprenticeship, Social Mobility and the Middling Sort, 1550–1800', ch.2 in Jonathan Barry & Christopher Brooks (ed.), *The Middling Sort of People: Culture, Society and Politics in England, 1550–1800* (Basingstoke: Macmillan, 1994).

35. See W. Craig Ferguson, 'The Stationers' Company Poor Book, 1608–1700', *The Library*, 5th ser., 31 (1976), pp.37–51. Pension courts are not always described as such in the minutes, and could also cover ordinary Court business. For an example of a charitable donation, see G215v, 1 February 1713/4 (Thomas Parkhurst's bequest of Bibles and psalms to the poor of the Stationers' Company).

36. See index under 'English Stock: Shares' and 'English Stock: Dividends'. On the number and reallocation of Stock shares, see Blagden, 'Stationers' Company in the 18th Century', p.41.

37. See Myers, 'Financial Records of the Stationers' Company', pp.14–15, 20.

with it. Two examples may help to illustrate the range of such dealings. Robert Stephens was granted the lease in 1702 of four warehouses he had built on Company land; and in 1715, Nahum Tate, co-author with Nicholas Brady of the metrical psalms which became one of the English Stock's biggest earners, asked to borrow £30 from the Company on the assignment to them of his salary as Poet Laureate.[38] Matters concerning the maintenance of Stationers' Hall, relationships with the Hall's neighbours and the buying, selling, renting and upkeep of Company and English Stock property were also routed through the court, as were requests to rent out the Hall for a variety of gatherings, ranging from concerts to funerals.[39]

Content of the Court Books

The Court's priorities determine what one is likely to find in the records. They can be an excellent source of biographical information about individual Company members, especially those who served on the Court, held other Company offices or were elected to a share of the English Stock. For instance, we learn of Thomas Bassett that he demanded Court membership, causing the Court to consider stopping money out of his next dividend; that he was on the list of loyal Court Assistants presented to the Crown in 1684; that he was a member of Benjamin Harris's partnership for printing the proceedings of the Westminster Parliament in 1685; that he was elected Under Warden in 1687 and Upper Warden in 1691 and 1693, though incapacitated from serving as such by 1694, and bankrupt by 1696, causing the Court to get rid of his £320 share in the English Stock.[40] The aggregate of Company members on the Court, and serving on committees, gives an indication as to the balance of power at any one time between the various trades represented among members.[41] For those interested in

38. 2 November 1702, G83r; 4 July 1715, G230v. On Robert Stephens's career, see Plomer 1668–1725, p.281; Blagden, pp.167, 179 & 183; Leona Rostenberg, 'Robert Stephens, Messenger of the Press: An Episode in 17th-Century Censorship', *Papers of the Bibliographical Society of America*, 49 (1955), pp.131–152; and below. Stephens did not practise as a printer, and other sources of income may therefore have been important to him. Tate and Brady's 'New Version of the Psalms' first appeared in 1696. See Christopher Spencer, *Nahum Tate* (New York: Twayne, 1972), ch.8. The *ODNB* entry for Tate comments on his propensity for running into debt. For the complex history of the Company's involvement with the 'New Version of the Psalms', see the 'Account of Dr Brady's and Mr Tate's Psalms', 1706 to 1764 (Stationers' Company archives, described on p.73 of Myers), and index under 'Tate, Nahum', 'Brady, Nicholas', 'Psalms: Tate & Brady's Psalms'.

39. e.g. 20 December 1701, G66v; 1 June 1702, G71v. See index under 'Stationers' Company: Hall', 'Treasurer/ Warehousekeeper', and 'English Stock: Property'.

40. See index under his name.

41. See Treadwell, 'Printers', who tends to reinforce Blagden's contention that the printers lost ground to the booksellers in 17th- and 18th-century Courts.

topics rather than people – the Company's dealings with the government and the City of London, the presses at Oxford and Cambridge, or activity of other kinds in the book trade outside London – it is an equally necessary source. But the records are, inevitably, most exhaustive when considering the internal workings of the Company: the day-to-day operation and safeguarding of the English Stock, the rotation of administrative duties, the role of Company officials such as the Beadle, and matters of internal husbandry such as accommodation and relations with neighbours.

Potentially as intriguing as the records themselves is the question of what got left out. On the whole, the doings of committees remain unrecorded until their members report back to the general court, though there are exceptions to this rule.[42] One also needs to consider the limits of reportage in the minutes for general courts. At this period, there were probably three versions of Court orders: the rough notes taken by the Clerk during meetings; the version of these notes which was copied into a quarto vellum volume, or 'wast book', to be passed by the Master or Court; and the final version written up in the folio Orders of the Court. The final version, as well as having undergone three stages of simplification, is – as Robin Myers puts it – 'the most stylised and innocuous, with controversial or sensitive matters omitted or tactfully smoothed over'.[43] Where more than one version survives, the differences between these are consistently interesting as revealing the rhetorical processes by which official versions of events are arrived at. [44] More occasionally, they are of factual significance: when John Boileau, Bureau and Bernard are reported for dealing in scandalous books in September 1684, only the draft records hint that works by the author Henri Arnauld may be the reason for the complaint.[45] While this index is based on the official version of events, the letter 'W' before an item in an entry is intended to alert scholars to where the draft minutes are significantly different.

* * * * *

42. For example 27 December 1684, F27v.

43. Myers, pp.42–43.

44. The Wast Books for this period have been lost, but miscellaneous draft minutes 1690–1698 and addendum draft minutes 1682–1692 are preserved in the Stationers' Company archives: Series 1, Box F, and Addendum to Series 1. See below, pp.47–48, for details of coverage in the index; Sidney Hodgson, 'Papers and Documents Recently Found at Stationers' Hall', *The Library*, 4th ser., 25 (1945), pp.23–36; and Myers, pp.44, 112, 205. As she explains, the Addendum to Series 1 was rediscovered too late to be included on the Stationers' Company microfilm.

45. 1 Sep 1684, F23r & W.

The introduction so far has attempted a brief overview of the general duties of the Stationers' Company Court during the late seventeenth and early eighteenth centuries, and the more important of the specific issues and trends recorded in the period covered by Court Books E–G will be discussed below. They show the Company adopting both proactive and reactive stances towards government interventions of various kinds: conspicuously the various attempts to control its membership made under Charles II and James II, and the new problems created by the lapse of the Licensing Act in 1695, solved in part by the subsequent passing of the 1710 Copyright Act. These are to be seen against the background of the Court's sustained drive to regulate Company membership and hierarchy, campaigning against those on the fringes of the trade as part of a wider intolerance of seditious and illegal printing, and to try and protect the English Stock against the encroachments of the university presses at a period when these were moving towards greater autonomy.

Quo Warranto proceedings

To those tracing ideological fluxes and developments in the final decades of the seventeenth century, particularly during the last years of the Stuarts, the activities of the Stationers' Company are of obvious interest: both because of the part it played in the mechanisms of government censorship, and because it was itself subject to political purging. The Court Books give eloquent testimony to one of the most important political events ever to shake the Company's constitution, the Crown's various *quo warranto* proceedings against City livery companies. Charles II in the last years of his reign, and James II during his short period of rule, both felt it desirable to establish control over parliament by means of withdrawing the existing charters of parliamentary corporations, and replacing them by new ones allowing a greater degree of monarchical intervention; and they made considerable use of this type of writ as a way of inducing corporations to surrender their charters, and petition for new ones by which the Crown would be entitled to remove objectionable individuals.[46] Several provincial towns complied, changing the membership of their corporations in accordance with the Crown's wishes. Because of the City of London's general tactical importance, it was a prime target for similar action;[47] and the Whiggish sympathies of many Londoners, combined with their hostile behaviour during the trial of

46. Robert H. George, 'The Charters Granted to English Parliamentary Corporations in 1688', *English Historical Review*, 55 (1940), pp.47–56, describes the differences between Charles' policy and his brother's.

47. See Jennifer Levin, *The Charter Controversy in the City of London, 1660–1688, and its Consequences* (London: Athlone, 1969), p.23. On support for Whigs in the City, see Robert Beddard, 'The Unexpected Whig Revolution of 1688', in Robert Beddard (ed.), *The Revolutions of 1688* (Oxford: Clarendon, 1991), pp.11–101.

Shaftesbury, had made Charles II particularly conscious of the need to subdue London. At all times, though, the Crown was primarily interested in controlling membership and had little wish to interfere in the internal workings of corporations.[48]

A *quo warranto* against the City of London charter was launched on 21 December 1681, the day of the Common Council elections at which freemen could vote. Eighteen months later the charter was declared defective by the Court of King's Bench, whose membership had recently been massaged to ensure that its verdicts would be acceptable to the Crown.[49] The City prepared a petition of submission, and its Common Council voted to accept a new charter specifying that all mayors, sheriffs, Justices of the Peace and other officers should be subject to royal approval. In effect, this changed the status of those holding the higher offices: instead of elected representatives, they became commissioners whose position was dependent on the Crown. Whigs and Dissenters were purged from livery companies, and in the 1685 election, four Tory aldermen were returned to Parliament. Till 1688, London continued to be governed without a charter, but by a Royal commission.[50]

It was in early 1684 that writs of *quo warranto* were issued against all City livery companies, with the intention of ensuring that the chief officers were loyal, and keeping religious dissenters from positions of influence.[51] When the Stationers' Company received a subpoena to this effect on 26 March 1684, the Assistants and Clerk immediately surrendered their positions to the Master and Wardens.[52] The Company's petition to the Crown was drawn up the very next day; in it, the Company promised that elections to the Court of Assistants and other posts should be approved by the Crown, and that their control of the press would be tightened; they also took the opportunity to apologise for 'evill members of the Company' and to request that the Company's rights over certain books should be continued. On 7 April they drew up a new list of Assistants to be presented to the Crown, and ten days later a warrant for a new charter was issued from Windsor.[53] Possibly the first company to obtain their new charter,

---

48. The narrative in this and the succeeding paragraph is drawn from the following sources, except where otherwise specified: John Miller, *Charles II* (London: Weidenfeld & Nicolson, 1991), ch.13; Maurice Ashley, *James II* (London: J.M. Dent, 1977), pp.206–207; Ronald Hutton, *Charles the Second, King of England, Scotland and Ireland* (Oxford: Clarendon, 1989), pp.419–420; and Blagden, pp.166–172.

49. Alfred F. Havighurst, 'The Judiciary in the Reign of Charles II', *Law Quarterly Review*, 66 (1950), pp.62–78, 229–252 (ref. pp.244–245).

50. Levin, *Charter Controversy*, p.55.

51. See index under 'City of London', 'Crown', 'Livery' and 'Lord Mayor'.

52. 26 March 1684, F11v. For an account of how these proceedings affected Court Assistants, see Treadwell, 'Printers', p.35.

53. 27 March 1684, F12v; & 7 April, F13v. See George, 'Charters', p.54.

the Stationers certainly received ironic praise for being early in a contemporary satirical ballad.[54] When the charter had been approved, the Master informed the 'assembly' on 27 May that the King was continuing the old privileges of Letters Patent and granting some new ones. As Cyprian Blagden has pointed out, this broadened the Company's remit to an unprecedented degree – at least on paper.[55] The new charter and the Company's address to the Crown were read, and the letter was copied out in full.[56] Twelve months later, in May 1685, the Company was to negotiate a list of loyal Stationers with the Lord Mayor and aldermen, whose areas of concern at this period frequently overlapped with and were subservient to the Crown's.[57]

The next phase of the Crown's action was to come in October 1687, when the new monarch James II sent out an order *via* the Lord Mayor, displacing the current Master and Wardens together with many of the Assistants, and restoring others displaced in 1684.[58] This order was supplemented by another, in which several liverymen were also displaced and others restored. Elections to replace the officials took place on 12 October, and as part of the minutes for 17 October a hyperbolical address of thanks to the Crown is copied out, in which the King is asked to 'vouchsafe to pardon our honest Ambition to throw ourselves downe at your sacred Feet.'[59] During the turbulent year of 1688, when James II and his court were driven into exile, the Court of Aldermen took over the duty of regulating Stationers' Company membership.[60] On 1 March an order came from them that seven Assistants and 46 liverymen should be displaced; and the Court resolved that, in future, only members of the book trade would be called to the Livery.[61] Various liverymen were restored by an order of the Court of Aldermen in October, and in November the pre-*quo warranto* Assistants were summoned to a meeting which ended in declaring that the Company had made no surrender of its new charter – they had, after all, gained by the change.[62] Subsequently,

---

54. 'A New Song, in Praise of the Loyal Company of Stationers': excerpted in Blagden, 'Charter Trouble', pp.371–2.   55. 'Charter Trouble', p.375.

56. 27 May 1684, F14v. The word 'assembly' is used since without Assistants there could not be a Court. See also Blagden, pp.166–169; George Kitchin, *Sir Roger L'Estrange: A Contribution to the History of the Press in the Seventeenth Century* (London: Kegan Paul, 1913), pp.325–327; and the index under his name.

57. Blagden, p.171.

58. 3 October 1687, F89v. James II's further alterations reflected his policy of friendliness towards Catholics and Dissenters: see Levin, *Charter Controversy*, p.57.

59. F90v; F93r.

60. For London's reaction to the 1688 Revolution, see Tim Harris, 'London Crowds and the Revolution of 1688', in Eveline Cruickshanks (ed.), *By Force or By Default? The Revolution of 1688–1689* (Edinburgh: John Donald, 1989).

61. F97v.

62. Blagden, 'Charter Trouble', p.376; Treadwell, 'The Stationers and the Printing Acts', pp.768–9.

new officials were elected.[63] What Blagden describes as the 'final tidying up' took place in June 1690. It was announced on the 2nd that the *quo warranto* had just been reversed by an Act of Parliament, and on the 5th, in resolution of a dispute over precedence which had arisen, the Assistants appended a rare list of signatures to the day's minutes in Court Book F.[64]

Hierarchy and status

Even in less trying circumstances, questions of status and precedence were emotive ones.[65] It was routine for Court members to pay substantial fines to preserve their seniority if they were passed over for Company offices, or did not wish to hold them. In addition, it is not uncommon at this period for an Assistant to query his place on the Court, a practice which seems to have been found understandable and acceptable. The Court, though, did react angrily to the cases of John Starkey and Giles Sussex. Both these men, feeling that their positions as senior liverymen ought to have guaranteed them places on the Court of Assistants which they had not yet been offered, tried to gain them by trying to win favour within the Company and appealing to the Court of Aldermen as an outside arbitrator. The Court consistently vetoed their applications, and on one occasion was even provoked into listing in full the reasons why it did not want Sussex as an Assistant. Nevertheless, Sussex's petition had a dramatic result when the Master and Wardens were committed to Newgate for contempt of the Court of Aldermen.[66]

At the other end of the Stationers' Company hierarchy, the Court Books record the bindings and freedoms of apprentices which took place at court. Folio 90v in Court Book G, where a note of these is squeezed into a corner, suggests that such records must sometimes have been an afterthought; since they were recorded separately, for them to be mentioned in the Court Books at all is a kind of double entry.[67] Masters are often disciplined for having bound their apprentices

63. 11 October 1688, F108r; 27 November 1688, F109v. The recruitment of new Assistants at the beginning of February 1689 was actually undertaken according to the old byelaws: Blagden, 'Charter Trouble', p.376.

64. F135r & F135v. See Blagden, pp.171–172.

65. Cf. Ward, *Metropolitan Communities*, pp.83–85.

66. See index under Starkey's and Sussex's names, and 'Assistants'. On the Starkey case, see Treadwell, 'Printers on the Court', p.33. Starkey's pronounced Whig sympathies may not have helped his case: see Melinda S. Zook, *Radical Whigs and Conspiratorial Politics in Late Stuart England* (University Park: Pennsylvania, 1999), pp.11, 18, 28. On the Sussex case, see Blagden, 'Stationers' Company in the 18th Century', p.43: the article is valuable too for its discussion of the changes in Company hierarchy at this period.

67. Details of an apprentice's trade, father, master's name etc. are given in the Memorandum Books, to which the following volumes are effectively indexes: 'Apprentices

by 'foreign' indentures – those from outside the Stationers' Company – as a way of exceeding the stipulated number of apprentices and getting extra labour.[68] The abuses to which this and related practices could lead are detailed in the summary of the Free Workmen Printers' petition in the minutes of 5 March 1687/8.[69] A general tightening-up on printers, booksellers, bookbinders and other book dealers who operated outside the Stationers' Company can be observed as far back as the minutes of 10 June 1684, which summarise a petition from the Company to the Lord Mayor concerning the translation to the Stationers of freemen from other City companies.[70] Many such individuals were summoned to subsequent courts and freed there. Some years later, the Court decreed that masters' trades and places of residence should be recorded in the Apprentice Registers.[71]

Control over printing

This is only part of the attempt made during this period to control those on the fringes of the book trade. In August 1688, three widows were summoned for unlicensed printing: but since the Court granted two of the widows leave to continue printing for the Company for the rest of the year, and suggested the possibility of applying for licences, the occasion may simply demonstrate a failure to build consideration of a widow's position into the system.[72] Marginalisation was, however, frequently a prelude to more dubious dealings, as is reflected in the Company's crackdown on foreign booksellers in September 1684

Bound, Turned Over, Free and Cloathed, 1640–1748' (Stationers' Company archives, pressmark I B 19); Apprentice Register, 7 August 1666–6 March 1727 (S.C. pressmark I C 28); Master and Apprentice Calendars, 5 March 1654–7 September 1692, 2 May 1670–18 July 1697, 4 April 1687–10 February 1718 (S.C. pressmarks I C 32–34). All these dates are approximate and as given in Myers. D. F. McKenzie used the Court Books to supplement and clarify the Memorandum Books when compiling his three-volume *Stationers' Company Apprentices*, Volumes 2 and 3 of which relate to the period covered by Court Books E–G (1641–1700 & 1701–1800, Oxford: Oxford Bibliographical Society, 1974–1978).

68. Some of these cases are listed in the index under 'Foreign Indentures'. James Smallshaw actually pays the fine himself before being freed (7 February 1698/9, G20r).

69. F99r.

70. F16v. For issues of translation, see under 'London, City of: Lord Mayor'.

71. 4 November 1706, G136r. The Court issued orders from time to time that the apprentice registers should be kept up to date: see index under 'Apprentices'.

72. 6 August 1688, F104v (Widows Holt, Thompson and Flesher). On the anomalous position of women in the book trade, see Bell, 'Women and the Opposition Press'. The activities of Elizabeth Blair, the widow Mallett and 'Button and his Mother' demonstrate that widows were also involved in activities more straightforwardly describable as counterfeit or seditious printing: see index under their names. On women printers, publishers and booksellers, see Maureen Bell, 'A Dictionary of Women in the London Book Trade, 1540–1730', MLS (Master in Library Studies) dissertation, University of

for traffic in scandalous books.[73] There were complaints throughout the period about hawkers, stall-booksellers and petty chapmen. In May 1688, it was emphasized that even though many of them had lately been made free of the Company, this was a one-off measure. Subsequently, between October and December 1690, the Court negotiated with the Bishop of London to withdraw and discontinue hawkers' licences, and read a draft Act to be presented to Parliament concerning the suppression of hawkers.[74]

Anonymous printing, more likely than anything else to blur the distinction between the respectable and the seditious end of the book trade, was perhaps most prevalent towards the beginning of this period. The case of Richard Janeway, prosecuted under the Company byelaws for selling an anonymous pamphlet, demonstrates that the Company could take a serious view of it. Janeway, however, hit back by listing the various seditious books he had sold and who had commissioned them, and by doing so, gave rise to a new byelaw designed to suppress anti-Government pamphlets.[75] Similarly, when Benjamin Harris petitioned in December 1685 concerning the damasking of Henry Care's *English Liberties*, a controversial Whig book found at his house, he twisted the Court's arm by suggesting that he had printed similar matter in partnership with members of the court, and the court promised to 'doe him what favour they could at the Secretaries of State'.[76] In his study of the Warden's Accounts of the

Loughborough, 1983, introduction; C.J. Mitchell, 'Women in the 18th-Century Book Trades', in *Writers, Books and Trade: An 18th-Century English Miscellany for William B. Todd*, ed. O.M. Brack, jnr. (New York: AMS, 1994), pp.25–75.

73. 1 September 1684, F23r (concerning the booksellers John Boileau, Barnardi, Bernard and Bureau). On French immigrant booksellers, see Julian Roberts, 'The Latin Trade', ch. 6 in John Barnard & D. F. McKenzie with Maureen Bell (eds), *The Cambridge History of the Book in Britain: Volume IV, 1557–1695* (Cambridge: Cambridge University Press, 2002), pp.168–169.

74. 7 May 1688, F101v; 8 October 1690, F144r; special committee on 15 October 1690, F145r; 1 December 1690, F146v.

75. 1 March 1681/2, E146r; 3 April 1682, E150r; 2 October 1682, E158r; 4 October 1682, E159r; 6 November 1682, E159v; 6 December 1682, E161v–162r, and index under Janeway's name.

76. 7 December 1685, F47r, and index under Harris's name; see also Stationers' Company archives, Series 1, Box A, folder 3, and the draft minutes for 7 December 1685. In a separate petition, Harris claimed that the book was already entered to him, and that it was going to be sold for waste paper anyway. In a memorandum written at the Court, he confesses to printing the 'Proceedings of the Westminster Parliament before that at Oxford' in partnership with other court members, though of Court members present on this occasion, only Thomas Bassett figures on Harris's list. The item itself is impossible to identify from these details, but the context identifies it as controversial. For Harris's biography, see David Knott, 'The Booksellers and the Plot: Luttrell Pamphlets in the University of London Library', *The Book Collector*, 23 (1974), pp.194–206. For *English Liberties*, see Zook, *Radical Whigs*, pp.81–82. For references to other named seditious items printed in this period, *A Raree-Show* and *Monmouth Routed*, see 11 April 1681, E110r, and 3 August 1685, F42r. For *Monmouth Routed*,

Stationers' Company in the late seventeenth century, John Hetet has described how some senior Company members, having seized unlicensed books, sold them on at enhanced rates; these episodes may hint at a similar kind of complex double dealing.[77] As Sir Roger L'Estrange argued at the time, the fact that the Stationers often had an interest in violating printing regulations could make them untrustworthy policemen.[78]

They are also two symptoms, among many to be found in the earlier portion of these Court minutes, of the age's exceptional political tension and volatility. Court Book E begins in the midst of the Popish Plot and tracks the first years of the Monmouth Rebellion, while Court Book F covers the period of the Exclusion Crisis and the 1688–9 Revolution. Famously, this was a time when political controversy brought about a publishing boom. Parliament's failure to renew the 1662 Licensing Act at the height of this period, between 1679 and 1685, meant that control of the press was, as Melinda Zook has put it, 'under no other restrictions than the haphazard restraints of royal prerogative'.[79] The political dialogues through which the first Whigs and Tories defined themselves led to an outpouring of broadsides, news-sheets, pamphlets and other printed material which can only have benefited Stationers on one level.[80] But its production and distribution involved so many individuals who were not Stationers that this aspect was of serious concern to the Company hierarchy – arguably more worrying to most of them than its often subversive content. In retrospect, the productivity of this period has been seen as demonstrating how the book trade was growing out of the Company's control – even during times when the Licensing Act was in force, there was widespread disregard of licensing even for

see Stationers' Company archives, Series 1, Box A, folder 6. For *A Raree-Show*, see Miller, *Charles II*, p.357; Hutton, *Charles II*, pp.407–408; B.J. Rahn, 'A Ra-Ree Show – a Rare Cartoon: Revolutionary Propaganda in the Treason Trial of Stephen College', in Paul J. Korshin (ed.), *Studies in Change and Revolution: Aspects of English Intellectual History, 1640–1718* (London: Scolar, 1972), pp.77–98. For documents relating to College, see also Stationers' Company archives, Box Q, folder 1. To 'damask' a book was to print over it in such a way as to make it unreadable.

77. 'The Warden's Accounts of the Stationers' Company', in Robin Myers & Michael Harris (eds), *The Economics of the British Book Trade, 1605–1939* (Cambridge/ Alexandria, VA: Chadwyck-Healey, 1985), pp.37–59. See also index under 'Licensing Act'; and for examples in the period immediately prior to that covered here, J. Walker, 'The Censorship of the Press During the Reign of Charles II', *History: The Journal of the Historical Association*, n.s. 35 (1950), pp.219–238.

78. *Considerations and Proposals in Order to the Regulation of the Press* (1663), discussed in Siebert, *Freedom*, pp.256–257.

79. Zook, *Radical Whigs*, p.26. For the Licensing Act, see below, pp.35 ff.

80. On the question of how early one can use the term 'Whig', see Zook, *Radical Whigs*, p.xii, and Mark Knights, *Politics and Opinion in Crisis, 1678–81* (Cambridge: Cambridge University Press, 1994), pp.108–112. On the possible number of printed items in circulation between 1679 and 1681, see W.G. Mason, 'The Annual Output of Wing-Listed Titles, 1649–1684', *The Library*, n.s. 39 (1974), pp.219–220; Knights, *Politics*, p.168.

uncontroversial publications, while the contemporary over-supply of printers meant that many would have found it financially worthwhile to risk being involved in the production of anti-government material.[81] But as far as they were able, Charles II and James II both took a strong line on radical and oppositional printing throughout their reigns, and not without success; the eventual renewal of the Licensing Act in 1685 saw to it that the number of books printed in 1686 was the lowest for a decade.[82]

The Company's government-sponsored role in suppressing seditious literature means that the Court Books are a good means of tracking printers and publishers with radical Whig and dissenting sympathies, such as Henry Care, Benjamin Harris, Langley and Jane Curtis and Francis Smith.[83] But the Company was only one of many agencies for press control, and the day-to-day division of responsibility between them, the Crown, the Secretaries of State and Sir Roger L'Estrange, appointed Surveyor of the Press in 1663, was not always clear.[84] L'Estrange's appearances in the Court Books are sometimes a prelude to lengthy and involved dialogues between him and the Company over particular cases: when James Deane, who commissioned Widow Mallett to print the ballad 'Monmouth Routed', subsequently informed on her to L'Estrange, he appears to have referred the question of her disciplining to the Court, who agreed to remit her prosecution – but only if L'Estrange agreed.[85] Robert Stephens, the Messenger of the Press, also appears at Court on several occasions during his term of office, usually demanding payment for having searched out illegal presses: in many cases, though not always, associated with seditious material. However, informing on these was by no means restricted to Stephens. In May 1693 Henry Hills asked the Court for a certificate proving that he had searched out one Downing's illegal press, in order to claim the Government reward; and in March 1683/4, various people were called onto the Court by order of the Crown as a reward for stamping out seditious printing.[86] The Customs House was a channel through

81. Blagden, pp.165, 170; Bell, 'Women and the Opposition Press', pp.55–56; 'Walker, 'Censorship', pp.225–226.

82. Zook, *Radical Whigs*, p.142. However, Richard L. Greaves believes that efforts to curb the press were 'feeble and largely ineffective': *Secrets of the Kingdom: British Radicals from the Popish Plot to the Revolution of 1688–9* (Stanford: Stanford University Press, 1992), p.40 (see also p.51).

83. James Sutherland, *The Restoration Newspaper and its Development* (Cambridge: Cambridge University Press, 1986), pp.175, 191; Bell, 'Women and the Opposition Press'; Zook, *Radical Whigs*, pp.27–29. For accounts of radical publishing at this date, see Greaves, *Secrets of the Kingdom*, esp. pp.15–20, 40–51, and Neil Keeble, *The Literary Culture of Nonconformity in Later Seventeenth-Century England* (Leicester: Leicester University Press, 1987), ch.3.

84. For a discussion of their respective roles, see Siebert, *Freedom*, pp.250–260.

85. 3 Aug 1685, F42r.

86. 8 May 1693, F188r (Henry Hills II); 3 March 1683/4, F9v. See Blagden, p.157; and cf. his 'Charter Trouble', p.370.

which seditious material and illegal importations of Stock books could enter the country, and in 1695 the Court negotiated with the Customs House Commissioners for leave to view all books about to be imported.[87] A rare case of illegal exportation came to light in the case of Mayo, Baldwin, Hinch and Palmer, whose empire of illegal printing involved the export of presses and type to the Colonies.[88]

The English Stock

Despite the occasional importation of books on the English Stock's list or which impinged on its monopoly, the Stock was mainly threatened in this period through comprinting, the domestic printing of items to which one had no title.[89] Almanacks seem to have been a particularly tempting target for this; Robin Myers has discussed the Company's court orders against almanack pirates, and – after the 1711 Stamp Act came into force – payments made for information leading to the prosecution of offenders.[90] Motives for illicitly printing copies of profitable books are, of course, easy to find; but it may also be legitimate to read between the lines, and guess that the lack of access to this type of regular work for most Stationers' Company members must have created considerable ill feeling. Certainly, the rights of the Company to Stock books did not go uninterrogated. In 1714, for instance, a challenge from Jacob Tonson made the Company look into their right to print schoolbooks.[91] In addition, questions of overlap with the Stock came up on a number of occasions: for instance, when George Sawbridge printed a book including a calendar.[92] On another occasion, the Court was asked to allow an ABC to be printed in a spelling book; they agreed, eliciting payment for the privilege.[93]

The English Stock, in normal times something of a goldmine for its shareholders, went through a number of financial vicissitudes during this period: in part because of the continued threat of clandestine comprinting, but also because

87. 1 July 1695, F227v, and 5 August 1695, F230r. See index under 'Customs House'.

88. See index under 'Mayo, John'. See also 3 August 1685, F42r, and 22 December 1685, F49r, where Godfrey Head is disciplined for having cast type for a Quaker to send to Pennsylvania.

89. On the importation of Stock books, see 2 March 1690/1, F150v, and 10 October 1707, G146r. The latter incident was taken seriously enough for a special, private court to be called.

90. 'Introduction: Searching the Stationers' Company Records for Printing History', *JPHS*, 21 (1992), pp.5–12. For action of various kinds against almanack and other pirates, see index under 'Almanacks' and 'Printing, Illegal'; and Capp, *Astrology*, pp.240–1.

91. 7 June 1714, G219r .

92. 5 February 1704/5, G114v, & 5 March 1704/5, G116v (George Sawbridge II).

93. 7 August 1704, G110v.

this was a time when its dealings with Oxford proved a financial drain.[94] The Stock-keepers set up a committee in February 1686/7 to peruse a catalogue of the Company's books to check on comprinting and decide which needed altering; a year previously, they had called for the money due to printers and paper suppliers.[95] In July 1690 the straitened state of the Stock was gradually becoming apparent in a debate as to how it could be supplied with paper, and by February 1692/3 measures were discussed to counter its lack of financial resources; it was even suggested that the number of shares should be increased to provide an injection of cash, though this idea was rejected.[96] The fact that over these years dividends were delayed, and (as discussed below) not paid at all in 1692, is a measure of the seriousness of the problem. One can see a marked contrast with the Court's earlier sense that dividends were a priority, on one occasion even going into debt to finance them – admittedly a self-interested attitude, given that the Court would have comprised most of the Stock's largest shareholders.[97] Though these were the worst years, problems occasionally recrudesced in subsequent decades. In 1713, for instance, a series of promissory notes were made out to Thomas Guy in order to get money to pay the printers for the English Stock, with a promise that he would be reimbursed before any dividends were paid.[98]

The Stock-keepers usually held separate committees, so whenever they impinged upon general Courts it may be a sign that the issue in question was one of exceptional financial impact.[99] Conversely, matters concerning the actual books within the English Stock seem to have been resolved by general Courts as much as by the Stock-keepers: for instance, in 1706 there is an order for the correction of the classical authors on the list.[100] Assigning different portions of a book to different printers, partly to discourage piracy, was a common practice and called for careful organisation: there is an unusual list of the printers who kept the standing formes for different signatures in the minutes for 7 June 1680, while in 1702 the Court orders the printers to deliver the parts of an impression all together.[101]

94. For the following narrative, see Michael Treadwell, '1695–1995: Some Tercentenary Thoughts on the Freedom of the Press', *Harvard Library Bulletin*, n.s. 7 (1996), pp.3–19; and index under 'English Stock: Accounts'.

95. 7 February 1686/7, F71r; 1 February 1685/6, F50v.

96. 5 July 1690, F138r; 6 February 1692/3, F183v.

97. 19 December 1688, F111v.

98. 24 April 1713, G209r. Blagden, pp.190–191.

99. There are references to separate committees at (e.g.) F124v and F164r. However, there is only one volume of Stock Board minutes, covering 1755–56, until 1869 when minutes began to be kept regularly (Myers, p.74).

100. 2 December 1706, G136v.

101. E100v (for psalters, unspecified format and 12°; Child's Guide; primer; Cambr[idge] primer; ABC; horn book); G71v (1 June 1702).

General Courts were also asked to decide whether to buy shares in new companies whose areas of interest were similar to the English Stock's, or impinged upon it.[102]

Company finance

Financial matters discussed at Court at this period were, of course, not limited to the English Stock. Pensions for the poorer members of the Company and their relicts and dependants, one of the original *raisons d'être* of the Company and Stock, were thought sufficiently important to have a Court designated for their distribution; together with election Courts, they tend to be the only Courts given specific titles at this period. One-off charitable payments, or loans to aspiring printers from named charities such as the Tyler Bequest, could in contrast be dealt with at any Court. Other financial outgoings which the Court oversaw included expenditure upon the fabric of the Hall, or upon the barge and other Company property, and the honouring of expired bonds taken out by the Company – which, more often than not, were met by taking out new ones.[103] Though incoming money from quarterage, rent and fines did not under normal circumstances pass through the Court, and only appeared in the minutes when there was some difficulty or delay over payment, bequests of money and plate always did; very few of these matters run on for more than one Court.[104] The Court also considered requests for financial help from outside; throughout the 1690s, for instance, the Lord Mayor and Aldermen delivered petitions to the Court, asking for subscriptions from individual Company members and from the English Stock to defray various Crown expenses, usually military and naval.[105] It betrays the often anxious state of the English Stock during these years that the Court always firmly refused the latter request, even where it granted the former. Either the Stock Board kept no minutes at this date or none survive, so despite the distinction drawn between the two in these petitions, it has always been a painful task to tease out the finances of the English Stock from the general Company finances. A sign of their interdependence is that, when the Stock was doing badly, everything from dividends to dinners was liable to be postponed or cancelled.[106]

102. For example 1 November 1689, F125v (patent right for making paper).

103. See index under 'Stationers' Company: Hall', '... Barge', '... Property', '... Bonds'.

104. Exceptions include the frequent, sometimes acrimonious debates with the London parish of St Faith's over charitable donations: see index under 'Lamb's Charity', 'Norton's Bequest', 'St. Faith's', 'St. Austin's'.

105. See 'London, City of: Lord Mayor'.

106. See Blagden, 'English Stock', p.178, and Myers, 'Financial Records', p.3. For dividends, see footnote 36; for dinners, see 7 October 1689, F124r (the minutes stress that though the Stock partners bear the charges of dinners, cutting back on them will help the Company in general).

Oxford and Cambridge

The disputes, the negotiations and – perhaps most of all – the agreements between the Company and Oxford and Cambridge contributed towards this in large part.[107] The printing privileges possessed by the two ancient universities had the potential to be a constant aggravation to the Company.[108] While there could be little objection to the University presses printing learned texts for which there was limited demand, the Company did feel under threat whenever the universities attempted to keep their presses moving by printing popular books. Their history of buying Oxford off by a covenant of forbearance – an annual payment for not printing privileged books – was interrupted in the early 1670s, just previous to the beginning of Court Book E. John Fell and others at Oxford, to whom the University privileges had been leased, began to encroach on popular books as a way of subsidising learned ones, part of a wide-ranging attempt to put the University press on a new footing. They experienced difficulties with pricing and distribution of a kind which eventually forced them to abandon the attempt and come to an agreement with the Company, but the episode was a harbinger of other difficulties. Peter Parker and Thomas Guy, soon to become names of ill omen for the Court, first enter the story in 1678 as sublessees of the University's privilege.[109]

The Court Books of the subsequent period show a Company alarmed by Oxford's activity, and seeking to challenge the workings of its privilege as far as possible. But prolonged legal proceedings against Oxford in the early 1680s, first in Chancery and then in King's Bench, resulted only in an agreement in September 1685 which had much in common with the former covenants of forbearance. During this period, despite the Company's increasing dislike of dealing with Parker and Guy directly, their names become more prominent: especially once their appointment as university printers was retrospectively authorised by the University.[110] However, the University and the Stationers'

---

107. The following summary of the Company's dealings with Oxford and Cambridge is complementary to that given in Blagden, pp.197–199, 199–204. See the index entries under 'Oxford University', 'Cambridge University', 'Parker, Peter, & Guy, Thomas'. The history of both University presses has been covered extensively elsewhere: most recently, by David McKitterick in 'University printing at Oxford and Cambridge', ch.8 in Barnard, McKenzie and Bell (eds), *Cambridge History of the Book*, IV. For Oxford, see Harry Carter, *A History of the Oxford University Press*, vol.I (Oxford: Clarendon, 1975), and John Johnson & Strickland Gibson, *Print and Privilege at Oxford to the Year 1700* (London: Oxford University Press, 1966).

108. Carter, *History*, pp.21–22, 27, & ch.III, gives an account of how Oxford's printing rights were regularised. See also Johnson & Gibson, *Print and Privilege*, ch.1.

109. This was originally shared with Moses Pitt and William Leake. See Carter, *History*, ch.VIII; Johnson & Gibson, *Print and Privilege*, esp. ch.5.

110. See Johnson & Gibson, *Print and Privilege*, p.99, for the Company's refusal after the 1685 agreement to have any dealings with Parker and Guy except through the University.

Company might have found themselves in rare agreement that Parker and Guy had overstepped the mark, on the occasion in September 1684 when the Court became aware that Parker and Guy were printing 25,000 psalters in Oxford – though Parker and Guy counter-attacked by pointing to the Company's non-payment of rent.[111]

As John Johnson and Strickland Gibson comment, the 1685 agreement left plenty of opportunity for 'trouble in the offing'.[112] Parker and Guy's letter to the Company of May 1688, taking exception to the Stationers' complaints about them to the Crown, is symptomatic of the continuing edginess of the relationship between Oxford and the Company, but the next phase of dispute only erupted into the Court Books in September. Oxford were at this stage comprinting on the Company, because the latter were behindhand with their payments; consequently, a committee was appointed to consider the Treasurer's advice that under the circumstances, the Company did not need to pay up. The argument was potentially endless, and negotiations were delayed for a number of other reasons. When the Company appealed to the University for a decision the whole matter was referred back to Parker and Guy; and in the last months of James II's reign, the University itself was under threat from a *quo warranto* relating to its press, making its future position unclear.[113] But this was annulled after the change of monarch, and in March 1688/9 the Court approved a covenant that Parker and Guy were to be discharged their comprinting of Stationers' Company books, that the Company were to pay the rent arrears, and that Parker and Guy were to deliver the Company all the primers printed in Oxford for 9s 9d per ream, and pay the Company £180.

Parker and Guy, though, were soon to be dislodged.[114] Their lease came to an end in the spring of 1691, and they were ousted by a cohort of senior Stationers' Company officials, negotiating under their own names because of the University's distrust of the Company itself. By April 1691 a new agreement was beginning to be mooted, though the terms were not finalised till February 1691/2; the minutes claim that it 'had beene near twelve monethes defending' because of the misrepresentations of the Company which Parker and Guy had made to Oxford.[115] But if the Company had at last regained control over Oxford, the whole saga had involved them in considerable expense. November 1692 saw the

---

111. For the unease this created within the University, see Johnson & Gibson, *Print and Privilege*, pp.95–96. See also the dispute around this time over Godfrey Head's receiving an order to cast type for Oxford: 21 July 1685, F41r.

112. *Print and Privilege*, p.99.

113. For an account of the change in Parker and Guy's position within the University around this time, and see Johnson & Gibson, *Print and Privilege*, pp.101–103, 106.

114. See Johnson & Gibson, *Print and Privilege*, ch.VII.

115. 6 April 1691, F152r; 1 February 1691/2, F164v.

question of losses to the Company become prominent, with the Court's decision that the English Stock dividends should be deferred till February of next year – a real confession of failure for an organization where, as Robin Myers has noted, the payment of a large dividend 'tended to outweigh all considerations of solvency and trading common sense'.[116] When that date came, the situation was so far from having improved that it was suggested the number of shares in the Stock should be increased to provide short-term cash; and though this particular proposal was rejected as being contrary to byelaws, others were seriously discussed.[117] For several years afterwards, the Company's need to borrow money is a constant theme in Court minutes.[118]

This reflects the fact that matters did not improve after the new Oxford branch of the English Stock was set up as a separate entity, in a series of negotiations from April 1693. In April 1695 the court again ruled that there should be no dividend for the past year because of the charges of the new Stock, the losses sustained through comprinting, and the high price of paper. This decision was clearly not accepted without complaint, as in May a committee was appointed to settle a dispute arising from it; the same committee also settled the balance of payments between the English and Oxford Stock, and discussed the sale of the impressions of books sent from Oxford which the Company had been obliged to purchase at a fixed rate. In the eighteenth century, the Company weathered a further crisis when Benjamin Tooke, having just been sacked as Treasurer, refused to deliver £100 rent to Oxford: a situation which was partially solved by the Master, Captain William Phillipps, advancing the sum to the Company.

The position between the Company and Cambridge at this period was equally fraught, for different reasons. The story of George Sawbridge's double-dealing with the Company is only obliquely testified to by the Court Books – perhaps out of corporate embarrassment – but has been well told elsewhere.[119] Sawbridge, who had been the Treasurer of the English Stock from 1647, entered into a partnership with John Hayes, the printer at Cambridge, which he kept secret from the rest of the Company. In 1669, he secured the lease of the printing-house

116. Myers, 'Financial Records', p.1.

117. For this paragraph, see index under 'English Stock: Dividends', 'English Stock: Shares', 'English Stock: Tooke Affair', 'Oxford University', 'Oxford Stock', and 'Printers, Free Workmen'.

118. Treadwell, '1695–1995', p.12.

119. See, most recently, David McKitterick, *A History of Cambridge University Press. Volume One: Printing and the Book Trade in Cambridge, 1534–1698* (Cambridge: Cambridge University Press, 1992), ch.18, and *Volume Two: Scholarship and Commerce, 1698–1872* (Cambridge: Cambridge University Press, 1998), ch.6. A briefer account of the relationship between Cambridge and the Company in the late 17th century can be found in D.F. McKenzie, *The Cambridge University Press, 1696–1712*, 2 vols (Cambridge: Cambridge University Press, 1966), vol.I, introduction.

at Cambridge, making it possible for him to gain a double interest in the Press, as owner and as agent of the Company, and thus to gain a double profit for the work done by Hayes. Duplicitous though the arrangement was, it may have had advantages for the Company as well as for Sawbridge; Blagden points out how it prevented the 'continual bickering which went on at Oxford'.[120]

The swindle was discovered towards the end of Sawbridge's life, whereupon his appointment as Treasurer was curtailed and a standing committee appointed to disentangle the affair. He died in 1681, but the Company hardly attempted reform until his widow and son were also dead. Eventually, the remainder of the printing-house lease was assigned to the trustees of the English Stock, and articles of agreement were signed between the Company and Hayes in 1690 – Hayes being, at that point, a servant of the Stock and not of Cambridge. But the last years of the seventeenth century were, in any case, to see considerable changes to the status quo in Cambridge. A new press, set up under the control of the University rather than that of the Stationers, began work in the last months of 1698, thus hiving off most of Hayes's business apart from that conducted with the Stationers. The old press was becoming a liability to the Company, and Cambridge eventually took it over in 1707 after Hayes's death. Throughout this period and thereafter, the Company maintained an agreement with Cambridge that the University would not print a number of Stock books: a remnant of their empire in a period that saw irreversible moves towards autonomy on the part of both Universities.[121]

Provincial printing

Other evidence survives in the Court Books of the Company's attitude to provincial printing outside Oxford and Cambridge. In June 1686 a petition of other master printers was presented to the Court, alleging that three presses in York were printing Stock books.[122] It may have been a continuation of the same trouble that prompted the Court to take legal advice about regulating printing 'in York and elsewhere' in July 1688, or in March 1691/2 to ask the Wardens and Robert Stephens to visit York and seize all illegal books there.[123] In December 1685 the workmen printers complained about an illegal printing house at Chester, a grievance echoed nine years later in Ichabod Dawkes's petition against the 'Inconveniency' of the press at Chester, which suggested that

---

120. Blagden, 'Early Cambridge Printers', p.286.

121. Carter, *History*, dates the beginning of the present Oxford University Press to 1690.

122. 7 June 1686, F57v. See also the previous complaint at F47v (7 December 1685).

123. 2 July 1688, F103v; 7 March 1691/2, F166r. See also Blagden, pp.146, 154, 159. The 1662 Licensing Act had allowed printing in York.

many recent illegal pamphlets might have come from there; but though the Court agreed that one of the Secretaries of State should be informed, it is not till June 1697 that the Court Books record a Chester printer being prosecuted for printing illegal almanacks.[124]

Licensing Act to Copyright Act

As John Feather has commented, the lapse of the Licensing Act in 1695 had the effect of freeing printing from geographical restrictions;[125] but threats from the provinces were only one reason why the Court's main concern in the last decades of the seventeenth century was to keep the Act alive. The Act had come into force in 1662, drawing on earlier legislation that had fallen into abeyance during the Civil Wars. Except for the 1679–1685 hiatus discussed above, it had been renewed at various periods up till 1695, when it lapsed because Parliament was unable to agree on a bill that would have renewed the existing legislation: a sign, most of all, that parliamentary regulation of the book trade was an unwieldy business, though its cessation has often been seen as a landmark in the history of free speech.[126] The Act was very much in the interests of Company members: less for ideological reasons than because it stipulated that books had to be registered as part of the approval process, and gave them power to prohibit the importation of books which might affect their members' sales. A number of committees were set up to try and save the Act between 1680 and 1695, and others followed after the Act's expiration.[127] The Court also nominated deputations to wait upon various officials to help them draft the Acts,[128] and after the Act's lapse, petitioned Parliament on several occasions for a renewal. Between

---

124. See index under 'Chester'; McKitterick, *History of Cambridge University Press*, vol.II, p.52; and Treadwell, '1695–1995', p.18.

125. *The Provincial Book Trade in 18th-Century England* (Cambridge: Cambridge University Press, 1985), ch.1. 'Licensing Act' and 'Printing Act' are alternative terms.

126. The most recent account of this is given by Michael Treadwell in 'The Stationers and the Printing Acts at the End of the Seventeenth Century', ch.38 in Barnard, McKenzie & Bell (eds), *Cambridge History of the Book*, IV. See also Timothy Crist, 'Government Control of the Press After the Expiration of the Printing Act in 1679', *Publishing History*, 5 (1979), pp.49–77; Raymond Astbury, 'The Renewal of the Licensing Act in 1693 and its Lapse in 1695', *The Library*, 5th ser., 33 (1978), pp.296–322; Julian Hoppitt, *A Land of Liberty? England 1689–1727* (Oxford: Clarendon, 2000), pp.177, 181; Treadwell, '1695–1995'; Siebert, *Freedom*, ch.12. Havighurst, 'Judiciary', pp.235–237, describes the prosecutions following the lapse of the Licensing Act, and its replacement by a proclamation ordering all authors and publishers of anti-government libels to be arrested. On contemporary ideological opposition to censorship, see Keeble, *Literary Culture of Nonconformity* (1987), pp.97–98.

127. See index under 'Acts of Parliament: Copyright Act' and '... Licensing/Printing Act'.

128. 1 February 1680/1, E106v; 11 April 1695, F221v.

1695 and 1714, fifteen bills were brought into Parliament aimed at establishing control over what was printed, but all failed except the Copyright Act of 1710. This clarified issues of intellectual property, establishing rights to copies on a statutory basis, giving the authors some control over the reprinting of their works, and reviving the Stationers' Company register as a record of copy ownership; and it also required the deposition of works at libraries.[129]

It was primarily for reasons of copyright that the Company wanted a renewal of the Act. Entering books at Stationers' Hall was compulsory as long as the Licensing Act was on the statute books, and without it, there was no means of protecting copyright except by lengthy suits in Chancery.[130] Other parts of the old Licensing Act had, indeed, often been perceived as a burden for the average Stationer. From 1686 to 1694 Company members were repeatedly urged to deliver up, under the terms of the Act, three copies of every book printed for the three great libraries: Oxford, Cambridge and the King's Library in London. In November 1687 the Keeper of the King's Library renewed a demand made by his predecessor just over a year beforehand, stressing the 'late revived' Licensing Act, and requesting as well a copy of every book printed before the last Act's expiration; in response, it was ordered that a ticket ordering all printers to send copies to the Master should be printed and sent round by the beadle.[131] In February 1692/3 the pressure increased still further; papers were ordered to be delivered to all Company members requesting three copies not only of first editions but of reprints with additions, and threatening prosecution after the second warning.[132] Finally, in June 1694, the Master was desired by the Court to proceed on information in the Exchequer brought by the Attorney-General against several Stationers' Company members who had failed to comply with the regulations.[133]

But whatever the routine disadvantages of the Licensing Act, historians are right to point to its great symbolic significance for the Stationers' Company –

128. 1 February 1680/1, E106v; 11 April 1695, F221v.

129. Astbury, 'Renewal of Licensing Act', p.322; John Feather, 'The Book Trade in Politics: The Making of the Copyright Act of 1710', *Publishing History*, 8 (1980), pp.19–44. On the related topic of the 1712 Stamp Act, which affected newspapers and periodicals, see P.B.J. Hyland, 'Liberty and Libel: Government and the Press during the Succession Crisis in Britain, 1712–1716', *English Historical Review*, 101 (1986), pp.863–888.

130. However, Feather distinguishes between printers' and booksellers' petitions to Parliament, concerned to protect their property and their investments in copies, and the journeyman's need to protect his skills in an environment where the number of master printers would no longer be regulated: 'Book Trade in Politics', p.24.

131. 4 October 1686, F64v; 7 November 1687, F94r. The order was revived later: see 1 February 1691/2, F165r.

132. 6 February 1692/3, F183v.

133. 4 June 1694, F208r.

felt by both Stationers and others, since opposition to the Act often came from those who felt it gave the Stationers too much power.[134] Given this, and given the very evident concern with the issue in the Court Books as elsewhere in Company records, it is remarkable that the Stationers seem not to have lobbied for the Act's continuance in a unified and effective fashion. In his magisterial account of the Company in the 1690s, the late Michael Treadwell has gone further than anyone else towards establishing why, arguing that the high turnover of Court members through death or bankruptcy in the years immediately prior to the lapse of the Act further handicapped a Company which was already 'weak, debt-ridden and directionless'.[135] The Act's lapse has routinely been read as the point where the Company receded from high politics – in effect, stopped being important – and even if perspectives were different at the time, there is no doubt that it was a body-blow for the Company.

Yet one must issue a proviso to this. Though the Stationers' power over the printed word, and thus over the very history of thought, has come to have an awesome retrospective significance within a broadly liberal academy, we should not assume that a typical Stationer in late Stuart England would have felt this power particularly important, nor that it determined Company strategies. While many individual members of the Company certainly exhibited passionate political and religious convictions, the Company's support of the Act was practically rather than ideologically motivated. The power it gave them over censorship was never other than incidental to their main financial and social preoccupations, while the Copyright Act, when it came, was a partial solution to some of the problems which it was undoubtedly in their interests to fix. Minutes can be surprisingly emotional at times; as one reads through the Court Books, it is striking that, concerned though Court members were about the Licensing Act, the near-disasters to the English Stock seem to have troubled them more, while the *quo warranto* upheaval, striking at the roots of the Company's self-governance, was perhaps the episode they found most traumatic.

Even if the period covered by these Court Books marks the last time that the Stationers were serious political players on the national stage, one does need to ask how far this can legitimately be called a failure on the Company's part. After all, its political agency could never have been self-determining, ebbing and flowing as it did with the different attitudes to censorship manifested by the successive rulers and Parliaments of early modern England. Whatever the Stationers did or failed to do in the 1680s and 1690s, their prominence within the often draconian world of late Stuart press control could not have survived the change of regime. As the Stationers move into the eighteenth century, we see

134. Treadwell, 'Stationers and Printing Acts', p.771.

135. '1695–1995', pp.13–14 (quotation p.14); see also his 'Stationers and Printing Acts', p.772.

them settling – happily on the whole – into a more limited role which, as Michael Harris points out, is broadly in keeping with the trajectory followed by other City livery companies.[136]

Conclusion

Thus, for scholars of the Stationers' Company, the lapse of the Licensing Act has given a clear – though perhaps at some level a deceptive – focus to the change that all Livery companies were experiencing around this time. There is a consensus that by the early eighteenth century – certainly by the time Court Book G ends – City livery companies were experiencing an unstoppable decline in their control over trade. Jeremy Boulton has even remarked, 'Many livery companies became just another excuse for merry-making'.[137] When levelled at the Stationers this charge is hard to evade, even if distinctions between the crucial and the frivolous are proving increasingly problematic as our historical understanding of institutions becomes less and less functionalist. Now that feasting, for instance, has come to be seen as an important oligarchical mechanism which promoted cohesion and reinforced hierarchies through communal goodwill, the Company's pronounced interest in dinners, to which the Court Books bear extensive witness, need not be interpreted simply as a sign of decadence – the joys of networking, after all, are what has kept the Company alive to this day.[138] In an age which has seen the flowering of anecdotal history, it is hard even to dismiss the minutest of institutional pettinesses as unworthy of serious consideration. True, no scholar may ever look into how the irascible beadle Randall Taylor abused those travelling to Mortlake on the Company barge in 1688 – but it should be the job of an index to treat this regrettable incident on a par with seemingly weightier matters, and this is what the editors have tried to do.[139]

Indexers tell different stories from historians, ones which stress not failure but continuity. One gets a flavour of this by taking the first court minute indexed from Court Book E and setting it against the last one in Court Book G. At the court of 3 November 1679, three apprentices are freed, there is a discussion about charitable payments to be made to Company freemen and freemen's widows resident in the parish of St Faith's, a reward for Joseph Leigh's good services is agreed upon, and a prosecution is set in motion against a freeman's

---

136. 'Networks and Hierarchies: the Stationers' Company in the City of London', ch.10 in *The Stationers' Company: a History of the Later Years*.

137. 'London 1540–1700', pp.334–5. On the related issue of entrenched trading dynasties in the London livery companies, see Geoffrey Holmes and Daniel Szechi, *The Age of Oligarchy: Pre-Industrial Britain, 1722–1783* (London: Longman, 1993), p.154.

138. Ward, *Metropolitan Communities*, pp.95–96.

139. 6 Aug 1688, F105r.

newly married widow, seemingly relating to a dispute over the ownership of bonds. Thirty-eight years later, at the court of 6 May 1717, four apprentices are bound, one turned over and two freed, that year's auditors for the Renter Warden's accounts are chosen, Thomas Norman's request to fine for Renter Warden is disallowed, Richard Harbin is sworn onto the livery, and Thomas Varnam, in a signal example of string-pulling, gets elected as an Assistant because he is heir to Thomas Guy, who has expressed charitable intentions towards the Company. As so often, what attracts researchers outside the fields of genealogy and Company history are matters incidental to the internal regulation which organisations would have seen as their main business. But whether the user of this volume is interested in the operations of copyright and censorship, the policing of the book trade in London and the provinces, the minutiae of gossip or the advancement or regression of individual Company members, the current volume is, above all, a *vade mecum* for the institutional and human stories still to be unearthed in the archives of the Stationers' Company.

HISTORY OF THE PROJECT

Several indexes to early Court Books are available, but the scholar wishing to make use of them has a more haphazard experience than consulting a neat row of volumes on a library shelf. This is hardly surprising: the task of indexing and calendaring the Court Books has been undertaken piecemeal, during a time-span of over 70 years to date, and the earliest Court orders, like other early Stationers' Company records, preserve material in what can seem a random way.

With the publication of the present volume, the period 1576–1717 will be covered. Court minutes for the period 1576–1602 are to be found in Liber B, and were edited by W. W. Greg and E. Boswell in *Records of the Court of the Stationers' Company, 1576–1602 from Register B [i.e. Liber B]* (1930).[140] W. A. Jackson's *Records of the Court of the Stationers' Company, 1602–1640* (1957) follows on from this, drawing both on ff.79–183 of Liber A and on the earlier portion of Court Book C.[141] Both volumes were published, like the current one, by the Bibliographical Society. The remaining portion of Court Book C, from 1641 to 1655, and all of Court Book D, were indexed by Raylee Johnston for an MA thesis at Victoria University, Wellington, also providing a calendar of selected portions; this thesis is available on Section XII of the Stationers' Company microfilm, and completes the sequence up to the current undertaking. The present volume is the first index to be compiled after the widening of access to the Stationers' Company records that has been brought about by the Chadwyck-Healey microfilm; Court Books E–G can be found on reel 57 of this publication, and the microfilmed portion of the draft minutes on reel 100.

Abstracts, or calendars, of entries in the Court Books survive from the early eighteenth century onwards. Drawn up by the Clerks of the Company and containing the more frequently invoked portions of Court orders, they were intended for day-to-day use in a Company context, not scholarly purposes. For a full account of all indexes and abstracts included on the Stationers' Company microfilm, see Myers, section XII.

140. For Liber B, see Myers, p.24. The MS contains decrees and ordinances, 1576–1602, initially considered too sensitive for Arber to publish in his transcription of the early Registers.

141. For Liber A, see Myers, pp.52–53.

BIBLIOGRAPHICAL DESCRIPTION OF
COURT BOOKS

COURT BOOK E

Small folio, blind stamped reverse calf, head and tail bands. Four red labels on spine: (1) 'COURT BOOK LIBER E FROM 1674'; (2) 'TO 168[damaged]'; (3) 'E'; (4) 'BY LAWS ENGLISH STOCK'. Rebacked; some leaves loose; slightly browned; ink-stained on front fore-edge and covers. Page size: 31.5 × 20 cm. Red ruled; side heads. Stationers' Company muniment room pressmark (VI B 214) pencilled inside front cover. Note in another hand in red on recto of loose endpaper, directing reader to 131v onwards, where red crosses appear at intervals. Verso blank. Recto of flyleaf blank; on the verso, a note in a late 18th-century/early 19th-century hand and a pencil note by Cyprian Blagden. 171ff of Court orders. Verso of f.171 blank, followed by 3 blank ff., 1f. of caveats bound in upside down and 15 blank ff.

The volume contains:
1–94r: wast book for 1 March 1674/5 to 29 October 1679. Copied fair in Court Book D (except for Court of 29 October 1679) from f.244v to end. It follows straight on from the wast book for 1668–1674/5.
(NB: All discussion of Court Book E should be taken as meaning those leaves of the volume which do not have their contents duplicated in Court Book D; for discussion and indexing of the rest, see Johnston.)
94v–105: wast minutes from 3 November 1679 to 6 December 1680.
106–171: Apparently fair copy (i.e. Court Book) from 3 January 1680/1 to 25 June 1683.
1f. of caveats (unnumbered), dated between 3 May 1675 and 11 August 1679.

Court Book E, by virtue both of its format and of its composition, is an anomaly in the series of Court Books. The explanation is probably that half-way through its being filled up, the Company acquired a new wast book which has now been lost, and decided to use the remaining pages of Court Book E for a fair copy of Court minutes. See the description in Myers, pp.47–48.

COURT BOOK F

Folio, blind stamped reverse calf, head and tail bands. Two red labels on spine: (1) 'COURT BOOK 1683 TO 1697'; (2) 'F.' Binding somewhat collapsed, joints split. Page size: 36.5 × 23 cm. Red ruled; side heads. Stationers' Company muniment room pressmark (VI B 215) pencilled inside front cover. 4 blank ff., 267 ff. of minutes with verso of f.267 blank, 3 blank ff. The volume contains a fair copy of Court orders from 30 June 1683 to 28 October 1697. (NB: The actual foliation in the volume runs from ff.1–271, there being no f.244, 247 or 256. The folio numbers throughout this edition abide by the actual foliation.)

COURT BOOK G

Folio, blind stamped reverse calf, head and tail bands. Two red labels on spine, the first damaged: (1) 'COURT BOOK 169[7] TO 171[7]'; (2) 'G'. Rebacked in lighter calf. Page size: 38.2 × 26.9 cm. Red ruled; side heads. Stationers' Company muniment room pressmark (VI B 216) pencilled inside front cover. 2 blank ff., 250 ff. of minutes, 2 blank ff. The volume contains a fair copy of Court orders from 8 November 1697 to 6 May 1717. There is no f.12, 19, 37, 42, 48–53, or 174; f.75v is blank.

HANDWRITING AND LAYOUT[142]

The wast portion of Court Book E appears to be written by two individuals. Hand No.1 occurs at 1r–18v, 19v–38v (32r blank) and 40r-v, and Hand No.2 at 18v–19v, 39r (32r blank) and 41r–105v. Hand No. 2 may also be responsible for the caveats bound in at the end of the volume. If they are to be distinguished from each other, the pattern is consistent with John Lilly, the Stationers' Company clerk between 1673 and 1691, doing most of the writing and occasionally handing over to John Garrett, his assistant. The Court of 3 January 1680/1 (f.106r) signals the beginning of Court Book E as a fair copy of Court minutes, and also gives one the day (26 March 1681) on which Lilly resigned and Garrett took over. What is almost certainly Garrett's hand – it differs no more from Hand No.2 in the wast portion than is attributable to the different types of script – continues to the end of Court Book E and to f.176v of Court Book F. Here it ends abruptly, half-way through the minutes of 1 August 1692; it seems to have been standard practice to copy out the names and court orders passed, and then hand over to one's successor.

Hand No.3 takes over where Garrett leaves off and continues to 7 November 1692 (f.181r), the date on which Garrett proffered his resignation to the Court. From here to f.244v is a palaeographical puzzle. At least five different styles of handwriting are identifiable: Hand No.4 (ff.181r–187r), cursive in style; Hand No.5 (ff.187r–201v), an upright, large and formal court hand becoming more fluent under pressure; Hand No.6 (ff.202r–218r and ff.233r–244v), a compact,

142. In writing this section, the Editors have greatly benefited from the expertise of Anna Greening (who has supplied the detailed descriptions of hands), Robin Myers and Julian Pooley.

heavier formal hand; Hand No.7 (ff.218r–222r), an open hand similar to No. 4; and Hand No.8 (ff.222r–232v), a large, formal legal hand. As ever at this period, one must allow for the variations engendered by nibs, ink and the whims of copyists. Thus, it is not clear whether hands 4, 5, 7 and 8 belong to four different people, or fewer than four, or whether they were all styles of handwriting temporarily adopted by the Clerk at the time, Christopher Grandorge. Hand No.6, however, is the unusually distinctive one belonging to Nicholas Hooper, Beadle between 1674 and 1692. Its presence is explained by two Court orders of 6 July and 5 October 1696 (ff.245v, 250v). In the first, Hooper was requested to draw up the Court minutes which Grandorge had neglected to enter, but no dates of these are given; the second order reaffirms the first, with the added stipulation that he should copy out apprentice lists – though it is not made clear whether these are the lists in the Court Books or the Apprentice Registers. To complicate matters still further, the Court of 6 July also ordered Benjamin Tooke to officiate as Clerk while Grandorge was ill, and his duties might well have involved filling in any gaps in the minutes not covered by Hooper. Hooper is not mentioned in a third Court order of 1 March 1696/7 (f.255r) that the Court minutes for 3 February 1695/6–30 June 1696 should be copied up, but the minutes for those dates are again in his hand.[143] This sequence of orders and hands seems to indicate that persons other than the Clerk and his assistants copied up Court minutes, and that there could be a substantial time-lag between the Courts themselves and the copying up of their proceedings. Hand No.8, which runs from f.244v to the end of Court Book F, is probably that of Simon Beckley, appointed as Clerk in March 1697 and remaining in the post till 1723, long after the completion of Court Book G. The minutes in this hand date back to July 1696, but as the above description indicates, minutes often did pile up during Grandorge's term in office.

The beginning of Court Book G is clearly in the same hand as the end of Court Book F, but at f.38v (8 April 1700) it changes to a small hand, clumsy at first, which gains confidence over the next few months. From f.44v (9 September 1700) another, more fluent hand is contributing the side-headings and occasionally the apprentice lists; this copyist takes over completely on 7 April 1701 (f.58r). Judging by the different colours of ink and thicknesses of pen as well as the varying calligraphic styles, the minutes at this date were characteristically copied up four, five or more entries at a time. John Lilly was commissioned to engross the proceedings and judgement against Mr Randall of Newcastle in an official court hand; these include an official memorandum before the Queen's Bench ratifying the terms of the original charter.[144]

143. This is also true of the minutes immediately previous to these, dating back to 7 October 1695 (with the exception of a portion of 19 November 1695).
144. See G77r (26 June 1702), G72r–75r (July 1702).

Most court records follow a standard form, listing the date, the fact that the court was held at Stationers' Hall, and the names of master and wardens at the top, followed by the list of those Court Assistants attending. Each item on the agenda is given a different paragraph, with sub-headings in the margins. There are, however, some differences between the start and the end of the sequence. The name (if any) and date of the Court, together with side-headings, are written in the margin in Court Book E; the Master's name is written across the top of the minutes, and the Wardens' names head those of the Assistants, whose names are written in two columns underneath. The beginning of Court Book F marks a transition to writing the Court's place and date across the top of the minutes. Any designation relating to the Court is usually in the margin; Pension and Election Courts are the only ones at this stage in the Company's history to be consistently – if not invariably – distinguished in this manner. Assemblies, and meetings held after *quo warrantos* had technically removed the Master, Wardens and Assistants from office, are sharply distinguished from this general rule by the absence of names; in such cases the title of the assembly is written across the page.

ARRANGEMENT OF ENTRIES

Conventions adopted:

Specific references to Court Books are given by citing the date, the book (E, F or G), the leaf number and whether reference to an item begins on the recto or verso of the leaf. An entry comprises name, or subject; date; folio reference for the *start* of the entry; short description of entry.

Names:

The most commonly occurring (in the majority of cases, the most standard) spelling for a name has been the one used at the beginning of biographical main entries, but all forms of surnames found for that individual in the Court Books have been listed as alternatives and, where necessary, cross-referred. Though several alternative spellings of most Christian names exist in the original Court Books, these have been silently normalised in most cases, with widely divergent forms being indicated. Titles too have been normalised, and the index cross-refers surnames to titles (e.g. 'Villiers, George', to 'Buckingham'), following the way that aristocrats are most commonly referred to in the Court Books themselves.

Name-entries have been run together where it seems certain or possible that they refer to the same person, though future researchers should perhaps be wary of deceptive coherence or unwitting separation, especially in the case of very common surnames. In cases where – as commonly – surnames only are given in an entry, it has often been possible to work out the identity of the person from the unfolding narratives in the Court Books. In cases where this is less certain or where other entries are lacking, only the surname has been indexed. Fathers and sons sharing the same name have been designated 'snr' and 'jnr'; where this happens elsewhere, the entries have been placed in chronological sequence and the individuals have been differentiated by Roman numerals. Sometimes, in the case of very common names, fathers and sons form part of such a sequence; in such cases, both 'snr/jnr' and Roman numerals may be used for a particular individual. Wives and widows have their full names (where known) recorded in the main entry, but elsewhere are referred to as 'Mrs' or 'Widow', again in accordance with the original.

Material has been supplied to individual entries in three circumstances: where information is lacking in individual entries but present elsewhere in the Court Books; where the ESTC database sheds light on confusing or incomplete entries for published material; or where a well-known individual, not referred to by their full name in the Court Books themselves, is easily identifiable from the

45

ODNB or other standard reference works (e.g. Gilbert Ironside, Vice-Chancellor of Oxford, often referred to simply as 'Dr Ironside'). Though the biographical entries need to be read in the light of such sources as the British Book Trade Index, McKenzie's *Stationers' Company Apprentices* and Plomer, this is not a biographical dictionary; the decision was taken at an early stage not to normalise these entries in keeping with any outside source since there was a danger of suppressing new information by so doing.

Entries referring to books:

It is most common for the Court Books to list the title of a work without giving its author. Where the author of a book is given in the Court Books, the fullest details of that book are given under the name-entry for that author; in other cases, these are given under the title and cross-referred, even where the author is well-known (e.g. John Foxe), with authors' names supplied in square brackets. Different versions of titles or alternative titles are also cross-referred to the title most commonly given in the Court Books themselves (e.g. Foxe's *Acts and Monuments* to *Book of Martyrs*). Almanacks, catechisms, grammars and similar publications, though often associated with the name of a particular author, are cross-referred from the author's name to the entry for the type of book (e.g. William Lilly to 'Grammar').

Items have been checked against Wing and the ESTC database throughout. Thanks to recent advances in online searching, it has proved possible to identify with reasonable certainty several books for which the Court Books give only partial details. Where necessary, the index also records variation between the titles given in the Court Books and those appearing in print; printed titles are italicized, titles as given in the Court Books are in inverted commas. There are, though, several reasons why items mentioned in the Court Books may not appear at all in Wing or ESTC. The copyright of a book is not the same as its physical existence, and in some cases copyrighted books never got printed. Sometimes the very reason for an item being mentioned in the Court Books is that it was called in and destroyed; sometimes, deals involving books can be clinched between people who make no subsequent appearance on the title-pages of surviving editions, and may never have been involved in a work's actual publication. In addition, the Court Books seldom yield enough information to identify specific editions of standard Stock works (e.g. Psalms), or other often-reprinted texts with any precision.

Conventions:

This index is available on the computer at Stationers' Hall. Thus, in direct quotations from the Court Books, spelling has been modernized to aid the process of online searching, but original punctuation and capitalization has been retained.

Level of coverage:

Most entries follow a standard form and have been abbreviated without loss; many, though, are not standard at all. Bearing in mind the necessity to keep a large project down to a publishable size, the following limitations have been adhered to:

Though attempts have been made to summarise the more complex entries in calendar form, it should always be remembered that this index is a guide to the Court Books, not a substitute for them.

Attendance at English Stock meetings has not been recorded. Similarly, where a Court official is simply present at a meeting or serves on a committee during the period of his office, this has not been noted unless the minutes draw more specific attention to it in some way (e.g. his being added to a committee, or reporting from it). However, a partial index to committee membership and attendance at English Stock meetings in Court Book G forms part of the in-house version of this index at Stationers' Hall.

Relationship with draft minutes:

Two sets of draft minutes survive (see above, p.19) of which the specific dates are given below:

Draft minutes in Series 1, Box F, folder 13, on microfilm: 5 June 1690 (not minutes but order for Warden to pay Treasurer Tooke £10 for arm broken while on S.C.'s service); 13 June 1690 (not minutes but confirmation of receipt by Tooke of £10 from Warden Parkhurst); 22 December 1691; 27 September, 7 & 24 October and 11 November 1695; 15 October, 2 November and 7 December 1696; 5 July, 2 & 7 August, 28 September, 4, 16 & 28 October, 8 November, 6 & 22 December 1697; 7 February, 1 & 7 March 1697/8; 26 March, 13 & 18 April, 2 & 6 May, 6, 7 & 22 June 1698.

(NB: Draft minutes present in this folder whose dates fall outside the parameters of Court Books E–G have not been listed.)

Draft minutes 1682–1692, not on microfilm:

1682: 27 March, 3 April, 8 May, 24 & 26 June, 1 & 3 July, 7 August, 4 September, 4 & 6 October (the latter an alphabetical list of Assistants and livery, not Court minutes), 6 November, 4 December.

1682/3: 7 January, 4 & 5 February, 1, 3 & 7 March.

1683: 26 March, 2, 19 & 20 April, 7 May, 30 June, 2 July, 6 August, [n.d.] September, 8 October, 6 & 12 November, 19 & 20 December.

1683/4: 2 March.

1684: 26 March, 7 April, 27 May, 2, 16 & 25 June, 7 & 16 July, 4 August, 1 September, 6 October, 3 November, 3 & 27 December.

1684/5: 6 & 16 January, 1 February, 1 March.

1685: 26 March, 6 April, 6 & 20 May, 1 & 26 June, 6 July, 3 & 22 August, 7 & 12 September, 5 October, 2 November, 7 & 22 December.

1685/6: 7 February, 1 & 7 March.

1686: 26 March, 3 May, 7 June, 3 & 5 July, 2 August, 6 & 8 September, 4 & 11 October, 8 November, 6 & 20 December.

1686/7: none.

1687: 4 April, 2 & 30 May, 6 June, 1 August, 5 September, 3, 13 & 17 October, 7 November, 5 & 10 December.

1687/8: 9 January, 5 March.

1688: 2 April, 7 May, 15 & 25 June, 6 August, 4 September, 11 October, 3 November, 3 & 19 December.

1688/9: 1 & 4 March.

1689: 3 June, 1 & 6 July, 5 August, 9 September, 7 October, 1 & 4 November, 2 & 20 December.

1689/90: 3 February, 3 March.

1690: 26 March, 7 April, 5 May, 2 June, 7, 12 & 18 July, 1 & 25 September, 6 & 15 October, 3 November.

1690/1: 2 March.

1691: 4 & 6 April, 4 May, 8 June, 4 July, 7 & 23 September, 5 October, 2 November, 7 & 11 December (the latter a committee court).

1691/2: 1 February, 1 March.

1692: 26 March, 15 April, 2 May, 2, 4 & 6 July (the latter a committee of Master and Wardens), 1 August, 5 & 12 September, 3 October.

Those with a detailed interest in specific entries will inevitably want to look at both official minutes and drafts wherever these survive. Where a comparison of fair copy and draft yields substantive differences or amplifications, these are signalled with the occurrence of '(W)' and briefly described. Loose insertions in this sequence are listed in Myers, pp.206–212.

SELECT BIBLIOGRAPHY

(see also Abbreviations)

Astbury, Raymond. 'The Renewal of the Licensing Act in 1693 and its Lapse in 1695', *The Library*, 5th ser., 33 (1978), pp.296–322.

Bell, Maureen. 'A Dictionary of Women in the London Book Trade, 1540–1730', MLS (Master in Library Studies) dissertation, University of Loughborough, 1983.

Bell, Maureen. 'Women and the Opposition Press at the Restoration', in John Lucas (ed.), *Writing and Radicalism* (London: Longman, 1996), pp.39–60.

Blagden, Cyprian. 'The English Stock of the Stationers' Company: An Account of its Origins', *The Library*, 5th ser., 10 (1955), pp.163–185.

Blagden, Cyprian. 'Charter Trouble', *The Book Collector*, 6 (1957), pp.369–377.

Blagden, Cyprian. 'The English Stock of the Stationers' Company in the Time of the Stuarts', *The Library*, 5th ser., 12 (1957), pp.167–186.

Blagden, Cyprian. 'Early Cambridge Printers and the Stationers' Company', *Transactions of the Cambridge Bibliographical Society*, 2:4 (1957), pp.285–288.

Blagden, Cyprian. 'The Stationers' Company in the Civil War Period', *The Library*, 5th ser., 13 (1958), pp.1–17.

Blagden, Cyprian. 'The Distribution of Almanacks in the Second Half of the 17th Century', *Studies in Bibliography*, 11 (1958), pp.107–116.

Blagden, Cyprian. 'The Stationers' Company in the Eighteenth Century', *Guildhall Miscellany*, 10 (1959), pp.36–53.

Capp, Bernard. *Astrology and the Popular Press: English Almanacs, 1500–1800* (London: Faber & Faber, 1979).

Carter, Harry. *A History of the Oxford University Press*, vol. I (Oxford: Clarendon, 1975).

Crist, Timothy. 'Francis Smith and the Opposition Press in England, 1660–1688'. Unpublished PhD thesis, Cambridge, 1977.

Crist, Timothy. 'Government Control of the Press After the Expiration of the Printing Act in 1679', *Publishing History*, 5 (1979), pp.49–77.

Feather, John. 'The Book Trade in Politics: The Making of the Copyright Act of 1710', *Publishing History*, 8 (1980), pp.19–44.

Ferdinand, C. Y. 'Towards a Demography of the Stationers' Company, 1601–1700', *JPHS*, 21 (1992), pp.51–69.

Ferguson, W. Craig. 'The Stationers' Company Poor Book, 1608–1700', *The Library*, 5th ser., 31 (1976), pp.37–51.

Greg. W. W., & E. Boswell, *Records of the Court of the Stationers' Company, 1576–1602* (London: Bibliographical Society, 1930).

Greg, W. W. 'The Decrees and Ordinances of the Stationers' Company, 1576–1602.' *The Library*, 4th ser., 8:4 (1928), pp.395–425.

Hetet, John. 'The Wardens' Accounts of the Stationers' Company, 1663–79', in Robin Myers & Michael Harris (eds), *Economics of the British Book Trade, 1605–1939* (Cambridge/Alexandria, VA: Chadwyck-Healey, 1985), pp.32–59.

Jackson, W. A. *Records of the Court of the Stationers' Company, 1602–1640* (London: Bibliographical Society, 1957).

Johnson, John, & Strickland Gibson, *Print and Privilege at Oxford to the Year 1700* (London: Oxford University Press, 1966).

Kahl, William F. *The Development of London Livery Companies: An Essay and a Bibliography*. Boston: Baker Library, Harvard Graduate School of Business Administration, 1960).

Kitchin, George. *Sir Roger L'Estrange: A Contribution to the History of the Press in the Seventeenth Century* (London: Kegan Paul, 1913).

McKitterick, David. *A History of Cambridge University Press. Volume One: Printing and the Book Trade in Cambridge, 1534–1698* (Cambridge: Cambridge University Press, 1992); *Volume Two: Scholarship and Commerce, 1698–1872* (Cambridge: Cambridge University Press, 1998).

McKenzie, D. F. *The Cambridge University Press, 1696–1712: a Bibliographical Study*, 2 vols (Cambridge: Cambridge University Press, 1966).

McKenzie, D. F. *Stationers' Company Apprentices*, vols 2–3, for 1641–1700 & 1701–1800 (Oxford: Oxford Bibliographical Society, 1974–1978).

Mitchell, C. J. 'Women in the 18th-Century Book Trades', in O. M. Brack, jnr., ed. *Writers, Books and Trade: An 18th-Century English Miscellany for William B. Todd* (New York: AMS, 1994), pp.25–75.

Myers, Robin. 'The Financial Records of the Stationers' Company, 1605–1811', in Robin Myers & Michael Harris (eds), *Economics of the British Book Trade, 1605–1939* (Cambridge/Alexandria, VA: Chadwyck-Healey, 1985), pp.1–31.

Myers, Robin. 'George Hawkins (1705–1780): Bookseller and Treasurer of the English Stock of the Stationers' Company', in Robin Myers & Michael Harris (eds.), *The Stationers' Company and the Book Trade, 1550–1990* (Winchester: St Paul's Bibliographies, 1997), pp.113–129.

Myers, Robin. 'Introduction: Searching the Stationers' Company Records for Printing History', *JPHS*, 21 (1992), pp.5–12.

Myers, Robin. (ed.), *The Stationers' Company: A History of the Later Years, 1800–2000* (London: Stationers' Company, 2001).

Siebert, F. S. *Freedom of the Press in England, 1476–1776: The Rise and Decline of Government Control* (Urbana: University of Illinois Press, 1965).

Treadwell, Michael. 'Printers on the Court of the Stationers' Company in the 17th and 18th Centuries', *JPHS*, 21 (1992), pp.29–42.

Treadwell, Michael. 'Lists of Master Printers and the Size of the London Printing Trade, 1673–1723', in Robin Myers & Michael Harris (eds), *Aspects of Printing from 1600* (Oxford: Oxford Polytechnic Press, 1987), pp.141–170.

Treadwell, Michael. '1695–1995: Some Tercentenary Thoughts on the Freedoms of the Press', *Harvard Library Bulletin*, n.s. 7:1 (1996), pp.3–19.

Treadwell, Michael. 'The Stationers and the Printing Acts at the End of the Seventeenth Century', ch.38 in John Barnard & D. F. McKenzie with Maureen Bell (eds), *The Cambridge History of the Book in Britain: Volume IV, 1557–1695* (Cambridge: Cambridge University Press, 2002).

The Stationers' Company records have been catalogued and microfilmed: *The Records of the Stationers' Company, 1554–1920s*, 115 reels, Chadwyck-Healey, 1987. For the details of Robin Myers' index to the sequence, see 'Abbreviations'. The Court Books feature on reel 57 and the minutes from Series 1, Box F, on reel 100.

Two manuscript abstracts in the archives of the Stationers' Company were also consulted in the preparation of the current publication: the anonymous 'Index to the Court Books to 1775' and J. Noorthouck's 'Index to the Court Books to 1779', compiled in 1780. (See Blagden, p.259.)

ABBREVIATIONS

Arber   Edward Arber, ed. *A Transcript of the Registers of the Company of Stationers of London, 1554–1640 A.D.* 4 vols.(London: privately printed, 1875–1877; and Birmingham, 1894).

Blagden   Cyprian Blagden, *The Stationers' Company: A History, 1403–1959* (London: George Allan & Unwin, 1960).

ESTC   English Short-Title Catalogue.

JPHS   Journal of the Printing Historical Society.

Johnston   Johnston, R. P., 'The Court Books of the Stationers' Company, 1641–79: A Complete Index and Selected Entries.' Diss., University of Wellington, 1983. On the Stationers' Company microfilm.

Myers   Robin Myers, *The Stationers' Company Archive: An Account of the Records, 1554–1984* (St Paul's Bibliographies, Winchester/ Omnigraphics Inc., Detroit, 1990).

ODNB   H.C.G. Matthew & Brian Harrison, ed. *The Oxford Dictionary of National Biography ... from the Earliest Times to the Year 2000.* (Oxford: Oxford University Press, 2004).

Plomer   Henry R. Plomer *et al., A Dictionary of the Booksellers and Printers Who Were at Work in England, Scotland and Ireland from 1641 to 1667* (London: Bibliographical Society, 1907); [same title] ... *from 1668 to 1725* (London: Bibliographical Society, 1922); [same title] ... *from 1726 to 1775* (London: Bibliographical Society, 1932).

S.C.   Stationers' Company.

STC   *A Short-Title Catalogue of Books Published in England, Scotland, & Ireland, and of English Books Printed Abroad, 1475–1640,* compiled by A. W. Pollard and G. R. Redgrave, second edition revised by W. A. Jackson, F.S. Ferguson and Katharine F. Pantzer, 3 vols (London: Bibliographical Society, 1976–1991).

Wing   *Short-Title Catalogue of Books Printed in England, Scotland, Ireland, Wales, and British America and of English Books Printed in Other Countries, 1641–1700,* compiled by Donald Wing, second edition revised and edited by John Morrison, Carolyn W. Nelson *et al.,* 3 vols (New York: Modern Language Association of America, 1982–1994).

Opposite: Top: Court Books C to K (1603–1753) as they stand on the muniment shelves at Stationers' Hall (E is third from left, smaller format).
Bottom: Court Book F f1, a special court held in the Common Hall on Wednesday 6th day of December 1682 reinforcing the order for entering all publications in the register of copies

THE INDEX

ABBOTT, George   4 Jul 1709 G167v bound to Thomas Lingard, 7 years

ABBUTT, John   5 Aug 1706 G134r bound to William Crosse, 8 years

ABC   7 Jun 1680 E100v printing of Stock ABC assigned to Mrs White   1 Oct 1688 F107v George Croome confesses to printing 'ABC with Additions', a Stock book, and distributing all but c. 200   3 Nov 1690 F146r Wardens to search for and seize comprinted copies of ABC and type   7 Aug 1704 G110v Thomas Hodgkins permitted to print in his spelling book for Thomas Ballard on payment of 10s per 1000

ABHORRERS – see LETTER ABOUT ABHORRERS

ABINGTON, William   4 Jun 1683 E170v granted £50 from Tyler bequest

ABREE, James   6 Aug 1705 G122v bound to Ichabod Dawkes   6 Oct 1712 G204v freed by Ichabod Dawkes

ABRIDGEMENT OF THE BOOK OF MARTYRS – see BOOK OF MARTYRS

ACCIDENCE   7 Mar 1691/2 F166v Mrs Harris promises to give Roger Norton a full account of her printing his Accidence and Grammar

See also GRAMMARS

ACKESDEN, Thomas   4 Aug 1701 G63v freed by Robert Andrews

ACCOUNTANT   3 May 1703 G89r decision to employ one, to assist Stock-keepers in keeping accounts of English and Oxford Stocks   7 Jun 1703 G90r William Bowyer elected

ACCOUNTS – see CLERK, ENGLISH STOCK, MASTER AND WARDENS, RENTER WARDENS, WARDENS

ACTS AND MONUMENTS – see BOOK OF MARTYRS

ACTS OF PARLIAMENT

— DUTY UPON ALMANACKS   4 Jun 1711 G190v Bill before House of Commons for laying duty upon all almanacks   14 Jun 1711 G191v Act for duty on almanacks

— COPYRIGHT ACT   1 Mar 1706/7 G138v fees and charges for bill in Parliament for securing copyright to be paid to Jodrell, Clerk to House of Commons   4 Aug 1707 G144v committee to meet Members of the House of Commons to obtain Act for securing of property of books and copies   1 Mar 1707/8 G149v Clerk's bill for charges to be paid once an account of subscriptions relating to Copyright Act has been given   12 Apr 1708 G152r Henry Million to collect money subscribed in support of   7 Jun 1708 G153r committee to settle bills for   13 Jan 1709/10 G173v Sir Edward Northey's opinion concerning   6 Feb 1709/10 G175v attempt to make saving clause for S.C. part of Act   18 Apr 1710 G178v 'Act of Parliament for Encouragement of Learning by Vesting the Copies of Printed Books in Authors or Purchasers of Such Copies During the Term Therein Mentioned' read. Committee to consider proper method of keeping Register book   1 May 1710 G179r S.C. to pay £30 towards charges of Act, at suggestion of Warden John Baskett

— CORPORATION ACT   4 Jul 1685 F40r Master and Wardens take oath prescribed in the 'Act for Well Governing and Regulation of Corporations' made in 1673   2 Jul 1687 F85v Master and Wardens take oath prescribed in the 'Act for Well Governing and Regulation of Corporations' made in 1673   6 May 1689 F118r committee to look into new Act 'for the Settling [of] Corporations' and its consequences for S.C.   4 Nov 1689 F126v five members added to committee; any three to make a quorum with Master and Wardens; any member not attending to be fined 12d   2 Jun 1690 F135r Court revises its composition in response to 'An Act [of 20 May] for Reversing the Judgment in a *Quo Warranto* Against the City of London and Restoring the City of London to its Ancient Rights and Privileges'

— ACT FOR LOWERING INTEREST RATES 6 Sep 1714 G221r Elizabeth and Mary Hussey to be given notice that S.C. will not pay more than 5% interest on their £100 bonds in accordance with Act of Parliament for lowering of interest rates

— PAPER ACT 4 Jun 1694 F207v Court to tell House of Commons that it cannot as a corporation supply country with stamped paper and parchment but will allow S.C. members a parcel rate to encourage them to bring paper and parchment to be stamped 12 Jan 1696/7 F254r Corporation and English Stock to defray expenses of attendances and meetings re. proposed imposition of tax on paper and parchment 17 Mar 1696/7 F257r legal advice to be taken as to whether paper in the hands of printers is liable to duty under the present Act 19 Mar 1696/7 F257v case and Sir Bartholomew Shower's opinion read to Court, then to printers; second opinion demanded 22 Mar 1696/7 F258r committee's account of paper currently in S.C.'s warehouses expected by Wednesday next; then to be taken to Master, Wardens and Stock-keepers. Defaulting printers and booksellers given until next Wednesday to pay duty on paper and parchment 1 Apr 1697 F260r Court considers test case of a printer who had paper in his hands to be printed on, not to be sold. Members and non-members of S.C. dealing in paper to be asked to give money towards cost of test case 3 May 1697 F261v Clerk to draw up several fair copies of paper drawn up by John Lilly re. collecting moneys and send them out 13 Apr 1699 G24r Master and Wardens to attend Sir Theodore Jansenn with their case concerning the Act, the House of Commons having voted for a further duty to be laid on paper 7 Aug 1699 G28r doorkeeper of House of Commons to be paid fees for attendance in relation to the Act of Parliament for laying a duty upon paper 4 Sep 1699 G30r Clerk to be paid for attending Parliamentary sessions concerning the Act 23 Feb 1699/1700 G35v two papers of reasons against paper duty for MPs, and petition drawn up by paper makers, are read in court and a committee is ordered to prepare a digest. A clause about right and property of books to be referred to this committee 3 Jun 1700 G40r costs of suit against Robert Everingham, who acted on behalf of S.C., in respect of Act for laying a duty upon paper

— ACT AGAINST PEDLARS, HAWKERS AND PETTY CHAPMEN 1 Dec 1690 F146v draft of this approved by Court and half charges paid; Court to use its influence

— ACT FOR REGULATING THE PRESS 4 May 1713 G209v Clerk to take a copy of bill to be brought into House of Commons 14 May 1713 G210r Bill for regulating the press read

— LICENSING/PRINTING ACT 25 Aug 1680 E103r committee set up to deal with Act, to meet on Wednesdays and Fridays at 2pm; Treasurer to pay expenses 8 Nov 1680 E105r committee to attend to the business of the Act and consult when it thinks fit 1 Feb 1680/1 E106v committee to attend Sir William Jones, counsel, Sir Robert Atkins and Sir George Treby about the drafting of the Act 29 Jan 1684/5 F29r 'An Act for Preventing Abuses in Printing Seditious, Treasonable and Unlicensed Books and Pamphlets and for Regulating of Printing and Printing Presses' 22 May 1685 F37v committee appointed to revive the 1673-4 Printing Act 6 Jul 1685 F40v revived by new Parliament from 24 June for 7 years. Read to the Table 4 Oct 1686 F64v [Samuel] Carr, the Keeper of His Majesty's Library, demands a copy of all books printed in and about London under the terms of the Printing Act 7 Feb 1686/7 F70r David Mallett, Thomas Milbourne and Mrs Playford summoned for driving trade of printing contrary to the Act 15 Oct 1690 F145r heads and clauses concerning suppression of hawkers to be drawn up for a possible additional Act to improve the regulations surrounding the printing and selling of books 22 Oct 1690 F145r committee re. hawkers appoints sub-committee to draw up heads and clauses 1 Feb 1691/2 F165r Robert Stephens to list all printers in and about London stating which are not qualified according to the Act. Order requiring all members to send Master three copies of books for Crown and

Universities to be revived, printed and distributed   6 Feb 1692/3 F183v notices asking members to deliver to Master three copies of each book in accordance with Act to be delivered, with prosecution after second notice   10 Apr 1693 F186v type-founders, press-makers &c. to receive printed papers re. their obligation to tell Master and Wardens what they are engaged on   4 Sep 1693 F191r booksellers and printers neglecting to bring 3 copies of every printed or reprinted book to Master are to be prosecuted. Randall Taylor to have rent increased if he does not comply with this rule   4 Jun 1694 F208r Master to proceed against S.C. members who have not brought in three copies of every book for King's library and university libraries   24 Oct 1694 F214r Act nearly expired. Court leaves renewing of it to Master and Wardens   28 Jan 1694/5 F216v committee elected for this purpose   15 Feb 1694/5 F217v proposals to be offered to Parliament are read and agreed to with alterations; Treasurer to finance Master and Wardens   11 Apr 1695 F221v Court agrees to House of Commons' order to produce on 13 April charters, patents, orders of Court and registers, 1679-1682, in preparation of Bill for regulating printing and printing presses   11 Nov 1695 F234v Nicholas Hooper's bill for Acts, &c., written when S.C. was trying to continue the Printing Act, is referred to Master and Wardens   2 Dec 1695 F236v Clerk reads out copy of new Act and Court resolves itself into a committee   9 Mar 1695/6 F240v Court informed that the House of Commons will hear S.C.'s case on 11 Mar   5 Oct 1696 F250v committee appointed to consult with Vice-Chancellors of Oxford and Cambridge and other persons thought convenient   10 Jan 1698/9 G18v committee to consider Bill   6 Sep 1703 G94v Allen, Solicitor in Parliament, paid for his attendance concerning   20 Dec 1703 G100r committee appointed concerning   21 Mar 1705/6 G129v Robert Stephens, Messenger of the Press, who was employed by S.C. to attend at Custom House when Act of Parliament concerning printing was in force, allowed to discontinue this as Act no longer in force

See also ENGLISH STOCK

— ACT FOR RELIEF OF PRISONERS   5 Mar 1704/5 G116v for relief of poor prisoners for debts

— ACTS FOR IMPOSITION ON WINES   25 Jun 1691 F156r Lord Mayor requires S.C. to lend money to Crown upon this and East India goods

ACTON, Valentine   21 Mar 1712/13 G207v elected to Rebecca Fowler's pension

ADAMS, George   3 Jul 1710 G182r bound to Thomas Francklyne, 7 years

ADAMS, Jarvis   9 Apr 1711 G189v bound to Mary Knell, 7 years   3 Nov 1712 G205r turned over to John Walker

ADAMS, John   2 Jul 1716 G242r his son Thomas is bound to John Watts, 7 years

ADAMS, Sarah   6 Feb 1681/2 E143v deceased; her £40 share voted to Capt. Samuel Roycroft

ADAMS, Thomas (I)   2 Mar 1701/2 G67v freed by Job King

ADAMS, Thomas (II)   2 Jul 1716 G242r son of John, is bound to John Watts, 7 years

ADAMS, William   6 Feb 1681/2 E143v granted his mother's Christmas dividend on account of poverty despite her dying before the previous dividend day

ADAMSON, James (I)   4 Oct 1686 F64v elected to Livery   8 Nov 1686 F67r cloathed   1 Mar 1687/8 F97v expelled from Livery by order of Lord Mayor   11 Oct 1688 F108v restored to Livery   10 Apr 1693 F186v elected Assistant Renter Warden and summoned   4 Dec 1693 F196r competes unsuccessfully for share declined by Abel Swale   4 Jun 1694 F208r elected to the late Mrs Ibbottson's £40 share   11 Nov 1695 F234v deceased; William Richardson is elected to his £40 share

ADAMSON, James (II)   6 Oct 1712 G204r his apprentice Jasper Chaplin is freed

ADCOCK, Richard   7 Jun 1697 F263r freed by John Maynard

ADDISON, William   1 Jun 1702 G71v bound to William Botham, 7 years   12 Nov 1716 G244v freed by William Botham

ADLEY, William, snr – see following entry

ADLEY, William, jnr   4 Jun 1716 G240v son of William, is bound to Thomas Walker, 7 years

ADMIRAL JURISDICTION – see VIEW OF ADMIRAL JURISDICTION

AESOP'S FABLES   11 Apr 1681 E109v assigned by [Francis?] Egglesfeild to Samuel Mearne   18 Mar 1686/7 F79v in English; among books in catalogue annexed to Oxford agreement   11 Jun 1694 F209r Court to wait upon the Earl of Pembroke re. his desire for a Latin-English interlineary Aesop, discussed with Awnsham Churchill   1 Jul 1695 F227v Awnsham Churchill's request to print a beginners' Aesop in English and Latin referred to committee   2 Dec 1695 F236v agreement between Awnsham Churchill and S.C. read; consideration of it deferred   12 Dec 1695 F238r Awnsham Churchill is allowed to print 1000 without having to pay S.C. if he sticks to agreement and informs them of printers   2 Aug 1697 F265r Capt. John Churchill asks that he and his brother be allowed to print a new edition; Court asks to see previous agreement   6 Sep 1697 F267r Capt. John Churchill produces a 'writing which he called an Agreement' and Court order of 12 December 1695 is read   4 Oct 1697 F268r committee to negotiate with Awnsham Churchill; stipulated that it must be a volume worth 4s or more 'in Quires in money to Booksellers'   28 Oct 1697 F270r stipulation altered; now to be a quality to justify a price of 3s or over in quires to the booksellers   8 Nov 1697 G1r Awnsham Churchill to print in English and Latin

AGERTON, Thomas   10 Sep 1705 G123v bound to William Turner, 7 years

ALDERSEY, Abraham – see following entry

ALDERSEY, William   3 Dec 1711 G195v son of Abraham, is bound to John Williams, 7 years

ALIENS   5 Mar 1685/6 F52v committee resolves to apply to the Secretary of State re. unlicensed aliens selling books   14 Mar 1686/7 F78v Archbishop of Canterbury and Bishop of London to be entreated for leave to enter caveats against haberdashers and foreigners selling books   7 May 1688 F101v Robert Everingham summoned to answer a complaint that he has employed foreign journeyman printers

ALLAM/ALLAN/ALLUM, Matthew   3 Jun 1695 F226r William Long is bound to him   2 Nov 1713 G214v elected to cloathing   7 Dec 1713 G214v to be summoned to next Court to be cloathed   4 Jul 1715 G231r of Fleet Street, to be given notice by Clerk that he will be sued if he does not accept cloathing   6 Aug 1716 G242r Clerk to inform him that he will be proceeded against unless he takes cloathing at next Court   1 Oct 1716 G244r to be prosecuted for not accepting cloathing

ALLAN/ALLEN, Thomas   26 Mar 1683 E167v vintner; to lease a vault in S.C. court to be dug out at his own expense   2 Apr 1683 E168r committee to inquire what dimensions he proposes for vault   7 May 1683 E169v draft of lease to him presented to Court; Ambrose Isted and Henry Clarke ordered to examine it before next Court   4 Jun 1683 E170v Ambrose Isted and Henry Clarke report; Allen's lease is accordingly engrossed   1 Oct 1683 F4r lease sealed

See also ALLAM, ALLEN

ALLEN, [   ]   9 Mar 1695/6 F240v solicitor; gives Court notice that the House of Commons Committee for the Printing Act will hear S.C.'s case on 11 Mar   6 Sep 1703

G94v solicitor in Parliament; paid for acting on S.C.'s behalf   12 Jun 1704 G107r attorney; bill of £30 to be paid by Joseph Collyer   20 Dec 1704 G115v remainder of his bill to be paid   22 Jun 1705 G120v attorney, Lyllie's cousin, to be employed in S.C.'s suit against Benjamin Tooke

ALLEN, Edward   6 Aug 1716 G242v son of Samuel, is bound to John Fowler, 7 years

ALLEN, Henry (I)   3 Mar 1711/12 G197r Henry Allen turned over to him from Nathaniel Cliff

ALLEN, Henry (II)   3 Oct 1709 G171r bound to Nathaniel Cliff, 7 years   3 Mar 1711/12 G197r turned over from Nathaniel Cliff to Henry Allen

ALLEN, John   3 May 1697 F262r freed by Jacob Tonson

ALLEN, Robert   5 Jul 1697 F264v bound to Medriach Mead

ALLEN, Samuel   6 Aug 1716 G242v his son Edward is bound to John Fowler, 7 years
See also ALLAN

ALLESTREE, Henry   3 Dec 1705 G126r bound to Edmund Parker, 7 years

ALLESTREE, Thomas, snr – see following entry

ALLESTREE, Thomas, jnr   2 Jun 1712 G200v son of Thomas, is bound to Sarah Holt, 7 years   1 Apr 1717 G249v turned over from Sarah Holt to Richard Harbin

ALLETT, Thomas   6 Dec 1708 G159v bound to Henry Clements, 7 years

ALLOTT, Mrs   2 Aug 1686 F61v her executors have given Philip Briggs £3 charity for putting his son as apprentice to a saddle tree maker. She gives £30 towards putting out 5 boys and 5 girls as apprentices

ALLOWAY, Anne   22 Jun 1698 G9v elected to the late John Clifford's pension   28 Sep 1702 G80v elected to the late Rachael Herne's pension. Ursula Dikes given her pension

ALLIANCE OF DIVINE OFFICES   7 Oct 1689 F125r Roger Norton assigns Charles Broome [Hamon L'Estrange's] 'The Alliance of Divine Offices'

ALLUM – see ALLAM

ALMANACKS   1 Mar 1679/80 E97r Thompson fined for printing Welsh Almanack illegally, and agreement re. [Thomas] Jones's printing it to be sealed   6 Dec 1680 E105v to be printed with Marlow's type, bought at cost price. Those usually printed not to be removed from the printer without an order of the Table. Mrs Maxwell ordered to omit abuse of Benjamin Harris in future impressions of the Gadbury and Trigg almanacks   6 Mar 1681/2 E146v Treasurer to pay Ashbole £20 for Mrs Lilly, for the copy of her husband's almanack   3 Apr 1682 E150r Richard Janeway fined for printing illegally   8 May 1682 E153r Samuel Roycroft to print Sheet B of Saunders' Almanack for the year ensuing. John How submits suit between himself and S.C. re. counterfeit almanacks to Court; fined 20 nobles and legal fees   2 Jul 1683 F2r Ralph Holt complains that Samuel Roycroft is printing Sheet B of Saunders's Almanack with Marlow's type, which Holt bought from S.C.   4 Feb 1683/4 F8v Under Warden and Treasurer ordered to curtail George Larkin's printing of unlicensed almanacks and report to next Court   1 Mar 1683/4 F9r to be altered by Treasurer after the Archbishop of Canterbury's order that the feast of St Matthias is to be on February 24, not 25   7 Jul 1684 F20v Ralph Holt reminds Court of his dispute with Samuel Roycroft re. Sheet B of Saunders's Almanack; is allowed to print it for the year ensuing   30 Sep 1684 F24r new almanack to be printed for S.C. called 'Merlinus Rusticus', written by Henry Crabtree   3 Dec 1684 (W) King's request for himself and Council to receive almanacks from S.C. each year, rather than from Samuel Mearne, his bookbinder, granted   7 Sep 1685 F43v ordered that all almanacks are to be licensed by the Archbishop of Canterbury   7 Dec 1685 F47v John Gellebrand to be prosecuted for unlawfully printing a sheet almanack   11 Oct 1686 F65v S.C.'s almanack printed illegally by Henry Hills snr   8 Nov 1686 F66v committee to consider Henry Hills' printing of the Catholic Almanack   7 Nov 1687 F94v letter from John Gadbury re. his agreement with John Baker and Thomas Bassett over both his 1688 almanack and Raven's Almanack, claiming that he cast in the latter gratis as charity for poor of S.C.   6 Aug 1688 F104v Widow Flesher allowed to continue printing 1½ sheets of Galen's Almanack until she has disposed of her stock, and Widow Holt permitted to continue for one year printing the almanack formerly printed by her husband   3 Nov 1688 F109v Treasurer to publish advertisements against counterfeit almanacks   19 Dec 1688 F111v Treasurer is short of dividend money, since the national disturbance of carriers due to present troubles (Invasion of the Prince of Orange – W) has meant fewer almanacks going to chapmen   20 Dec 1688 F112r letter to Dr Gilbert Ironside, Vice-Chancellor of Oxford, re. differences between S.C. and Oxford over almanacks is read and approved   5 Sep 1690 F142v debate as to whether Robert Roberts should be fined for printing these illegally or if they should be given to other printers; agreed he should be fined   2 Mar 1690/1 F150r Henry Clarke's widow allowed to go on printing almanacks for S.C.   8 Jun 1691 F154v Joshua Coniers is discovered to have printed Dr John Partridge's 'Predictions and Prognostications', a Stock book   2 Nov 1691 F162r voted not to continue presenting them to Archbishop of Canterbury and Secretaries of State except for Ryder and Vellum, 2½ doz each   7 Aug 1693 F190r no more than 500 reams of almanacks and school books to be printed at Cambridge p.a. and sold to S.C. at 20s per ream   11 Nov 1695 F235v Benjamin Tooke indemnified against a 'sudden fall of Guineas', as he is likely to receive many for the almanacks he is printing   17 Oct 1696 F251r Robert Stephens discovers a press in Distaff Lane printing sheet almanacks for 1697; they had printed 20 reams in red before being raided   2 Nov 1696 F252r Treasurer to give credit for 1697 almanacks to partners desiring it, up to amount of dividends; to come out of next dividends   22 Jun 1697 F263r printer in Chester to be prosecuted for printing almanacks   16 Oct 1697 F269r Charles Browne and William Onley to be prosecuted for printing and binding counterfeit books and almanacks   28 Oct 1697 F270r Master outlines measures to discourage counterfeit almanacks   8 Nov 1697 G1r advertisement put in the Gazette, and letter sent to the country chapmen for preventing the printing and publishing of counterfeit almanacks, to be entered in Stock-keepers' books   6 Dec 1697 G2r advertisement to be put in the next Gazette to promote detection of counterfeit stitched almanacks   5 Dec 1698 G16v John Bradford to be proceeded against for printing S.C.'s almanack under the title of the 'Merchant's Speculum'   5 May 1701 G59v Bradford to be proceeded against for printing sham sheet almanack. Sheet almanack in imitation of Oxford sheet almanack to be printed at Cambridge by S.C.'s printer   2 Jun 1701 G60r opinion of Cooper concerning printing and publishing of sheet almanack; John Bradford to be prosecuted for printing and publishing   7 Sep 1702 G80r permission given for Pepper's Almanack to be printed by Charles Bertie and Cecil   1 Feb 1702/3 G85r almanack called the 'Tradesman's or Shopkeeper's Companion' printed by John Stephens without leave. Gardner denied permission to print French almanack in English   27 Mar 1703 G87r Farly not to print Exeter Almanack any longer in prejudice of the S.C. patent   6 Sep 1703 G94v committee to discuss a letter concerning almanacks with Dr John Gadbury   15 Nov 1703 G97v bill in Chancery to be brought against John Bradford of London and John Treadwell and Robert Wollame of Norwich concerning sham sheet almanacks   20 Nov 1703 G98r printed (illegally) by Benjamin Harris and his son. Special meeting of Court to discuss John Gellebrand's advertisement for Royal Almanack   22 Nov 1703 G98v printing of Royal Almanack by Gellebrand   6 Dec 1703 G99v Clerk to enquire whether Flood and Baker of Norwich are involved in selling and publishing sham almanacks   26 Jan 1703/4 G100v S.C.'s almanack printed by Wollame of Norwich   7 Aug 1704 G110v almanack called 'Raven's' or 'London Almanack' to be printed by Joseph Raven   5 Feb 1704/5 G114v Henry Eyres to be prosecuted for printing 'The Annalist', a sham almanack   10 Sep 1705 G123r small 'London Plate Almanack' to be engraved for 1706   4 Nov 1706 G135v 'The City and Country Remembrancer', a sham almanack, printed by George Croome and sold by Benjamin Bragg   6 Oct 1707 G145v Peter Parker, Charles Brown, Elizabeth Blair, Button and his mother and Gwillam to be prosecuted for printing and selling counterfeit almanacks and psalms   3 Nov 1707 G146v Joseph Collyer to deliver to Slater plates of an almanack 'seeing them first Defaced'; William Bowyer permitted to print Partridge's Almanack in French   3 May 1708 G152v John Rogers and Joseph Milbourne not to be proceeded against further for selling sham almanacks. S.C. books to be searched for an order of court concerning Thomas Jones's printing of the Welsh Almanack   22 Jun 1708 G153v John Rogers granted privilege of printing Welsh Almanack   5 Jul 1708 G155r John Rogers to have exclusive privilege of printing Welsh Almanack for 3 years   22 Dec 1708 G159v Benjamin Bragg and Samuel Farley to be made party to S.C.'s bill in Chancery for printing   7 Feb 1708/9 G160v George Croome summoned for printing sheet almanacks for Benjamin Bragg; on bond of £100 not to print any more of S.C.'s almanacks   7 Jul 1709 G168r Committee to meet concerning difference between S.C. and Dr Partridge relating to his almanack for the year ensuing   24 Jul 1709 G168v letter to Awnsham Churchill from Partridge concerning almanack read. Committee to consider the matter   3 Oct 1709 G171r advertisement read re. prohibiting printing of Partridge's Almanack, by an injunction granted by the Lord High Chancellor. To be printed and published in newspapers   5 Dec 1709 G172r Partridge's Almanack, a false almanack containing a calendar, printed and published, probably by Benjamin Harris. Master and Wardens to enquire into this   8 Dec 1709 G172v advertisement to be put in the 'Gazette' about Benjamin Harris printing Partridge's Almanack illegally   17 Dec 1709 G173r John Partridge's letter to a Member of Parliament touching his almanack for the year 1710 considered by Court. Committee to prepare an answer   4 Dec 1710 G185v injunction granted against Benjamin Harris for printing and advertisement to be put in newspapers concerning. Whaley [i.e. John Whalley?] to send over almanacks from Ireland to be printed by S.C.   5 Feb 1710/11 G186v bill in Chancery to be brought against Chester carrier for bringing almanacks imported from Ireland to Chester   14 May 1711 G191r Court to decide what to do to prevent resolution of Committee of House of Commons for laying duty on. Account of number printed and sold by S.C. for the past two years to be put before Lowndes   4 Jun 1711 G190v (minutes copied before those of 4 May) thanks to Master, Wardens and Clerk for service to S.C. concerning Bill in House of Commons for laying duty upon   14 Jun 1711 G191v Court to consider manner and number to be printed, given that they would have to be stamped as a result of the Act. Quartan books in almanacks to be allowed as formerly   10 Jul 1711 G192v Master and Wardens attended Commissioners of the Stamp Office re. stamping of almanacks, but told matter lay before Lord Treasurer   13 Aug 1711 G193r Master and Wardens applied to the Lord Treasurer to have almanacks printed before being stamped. Court decides that they should deliver paper to be stamped in accordance with the Act of Parliament. Master to treat with those to pay and receive duties for stamping almanacks. Sheet almanacks to be printed in red and black. Penny to be added to usual price besides the stamps   10 Sep 1711 G193v bond from S.C. to Crown of £3000 penalty for paying the stamp duties on   1 Jun 1713 G210r friend (John Sprint) of Partridge and John Darby has insisted that he should have £150 for his almanack. Agreed to give him £100 for this year and Sprint and Darby to agree on allowance for future years 7 Sep 1713 G213r time and manner of payment to Partridge, pursuant to the order of 1 June, is the responsibility of Richard Mount and Darby 1 Mar 1713/14 G216v bill in Chancery to be brought against Blisse of Exeter and others for printing 7 Jun 1714 G219r Thomas Norris to be summmoned before the Commissioners of the Stamp Office for printing and publishing 'Dr Partridge's prophecy' 4 Oct 1714 G222v Master, Wardens and Stock-keepers to decide what action to take over sheet almanack called 'Dublin's Calendar' 5 Mar 1714/15 G237v letter read from Dr Partridge's executors concerning the allowance to him for his almanack and order of 1 June 1713. Matter referred to Stock-keepers

— S.C.'s CALENDAR 8 Nov 1686 F66v Dorman Newman to be summoned for illegal printing of the calendar of the S.C. almanack 6 Dec 1686 F68v Newman refuses to give satisfaction re. calendar 5 May 1701 G61v bill in Chancery against Peter Parker and Edwards for illegally printing and publishing 7 Jul 1701 G61v Parker and Edwards served with a subpoena to answer a bill in Chancery for printing and publishing 4 May 1702 G70v complaint that Thomas Hodgkins has printed for John Taylor 'An Ephemerides of the Celestial Motions for Six Years' which contains S.C.'s calendar. Not permitted to print any more of the said books 14 Mar 1703/4 G104r George Parker examined concerning printing of S.C.'s calendar in the Ephemerides 5 Feb 1704/5 G114v complaint against Daniel Browne, William Davis, Thomas Slater and George Sawbridge for printing 5 Mar 1704/5 G116v printed by George Sawbridge

See also ACTS OF PARLIAMENT, EPHEMERIS/EPHEMERIDES, MERLIN REVIVED, MERLINUS LIBERATUS, MERLINUS RUSTICUS, PROGNOSTICATIONS

AMEN CORNER 3 Mar 1689/90 F130v Clerk to prepare draft lease of house there to Walter Davis as agreed on 3 Oct 1687, now he has repaired it 16 Jun 1691 F155v Nicholas Hooper to be let a house there until next Midsummer Day at £16 p.a. and after that as tenant at will 4 Jul 1692 F174r properties there not to have their leases renewed until they are within 3 years of expiry

See also HALL

AMEN COURT – see LONDON, CITY OF

AMERY, John 7 May 1685 (W) confirmed member of new Livery 3 Aug 1685 F42r fined as Assistant Renter Warden 2 Nov 1685 F45v competes unsuccessfully for Capt. William Phillipps's £80 share 1 Feb 1685/6 F50r elected to Adam Felton's £80 share 1 Mar 1685/6 F52r elected Stock-keeper for Yeomanry with William Whitwood 7 Nov 1687 F94r his £80 share to be disposed of unless he pays for it 11 Oct 1688 F108v restored to Livery 4 Oct 1697 F268v elected to the late Mrs Flesher's £160 share 1 Aug 1698 G11v order that if he does not pay for Livery share by next Court day it is to be disposed of 1 Oct 1711 G194v poor lunatic member of S.C. His petition read and given 20s from Poor Box via John Walthoe 4 Feb 1711/12 G196r ordered that mortgage on his £160 share should be paid off or share disposed of 3 Mar 1711/12 G196v mortgaged £160 share purchased by John Walthoe. Walthoe to pay him £5 for cloathing and £12 a year in four quarterly instalments and £5 at his death towards his burial

AMEY, Henry 7 Nov 1715 G234v son of John, is bound to John Stevens, 7 years

AMEY, John – see preceding entry

ANATOMY OF ... BODIES 7 Dec 1685 F48r by Dr Thomas Gibson; assigned by Thomas Flesher to Edward Jones

ANDERSON, William 6 Jun 1692 F171v private press discovered in his and Thomas Topham's house; landlord to be prosecuted

ANDERTON, [ ]   8 May 1693 F188r Robert Stephens given £5 for discovering Ander-ton's press

ANDERTON, Edward – see following entry

ANDERTON, Stephen   7 Nov 1715 G234v son of Edward, is bound to John Leake, 7 years

ANDREWES, Edward   4 Jun 1694 F208v son of Tobias Andrewes of Uppingham, Rutland, gentleman; bound to Benjamin Needham, 7 years

ANDREWES, Tobias – see preceding entry

ANDREWS, [ ]   4 Oct 1708 G157v Jones's letter to Andrews to be referred to Benjamin Harris committee

ANDREWS, Elizabeth (I)   25 Mar 1703 G86v deceased; Beatrice Turner is given her pension

ANDREWS, Elizabeth (II)   20 Dec 1705 G126r elected to Mary Muggs' pension   23 Dec 1714 G224r discharged from Poor Book because she has a place in St Bartholomew's Hospital. Elizabeth Proper is given her pension

ANDREWS, Henry   13 Apr 1702 G70r bound to Robert Elmes, 7 years

ANDREWS, James   5 Jul 1703 G92r bound to Henry Carter, 7 years

ANDREWS, Richard   1 Aug 1692 (W) his executrix frees Joseph Shotwell   12 Sep 1692 F179r deceased; his executor is master of the newly made freeman Joseph Shotwell of Clerkenwell, whose details the Lord Chamberlain needs

ANDREWS/ANDREWES, Robert   3 Feb 1684/5 F30r elected to Charles Harper's £40 share   7 May 1685 (W) confirmed member of new Livery   1 Mar 1686/7 F77r elected Stock-keeper for Yeomanry with Miles Flesher   5 Sep 1687 F87v elected to Christopher Wilkinson's £80 share   11 Oct 1688 F108v restored to Livery   26 Mar 1689 F115v fined for Assistant Renter Warden   4 May 1696 F242v elected as Assistant and summoned   8 Jun 1696 F243r sworn in as Assistant   3 Aug 1696 F246v elected to Thomas Parkhurst's £160 share   1 Mar 1697/8 G4r elected Stock-keeper for the Assistants   3 Jun 1700 G40v Thomas James is bound to him   4 Aug 1701 G63v his apprentice Thomas Ackesden is freed   4 Jul 1702 G77r elected Under Warden   18 Dec 1702 G84r receives William Rawlins's fine for Master   3 Jul 1703 G91v elected Under Warden   1 Jul 1704 G109r fined for Upper Warden   3 Jun 1706 G132r £100 of his or his friend's to be taken in by S.C. to repay William Richardson   6 Jul 1706 G133v elected Upper Warden   9 Feb 1707/8 G149r his apprentice Thomas James is freed   17 Jul 1708 G155v grant to and Articles of Agreement between Andrews, Capt. William Phillipps and Henry Mortlock and University of Oxford read   8 Nov 1708 G158v declines claim to Mrs Towse's £320 share   2 Jul 1709 G166v elected Master   24 Jul 1709 G168v letter asking to be excused office of Master by reason of his present indisposition   1 Aug 1709 G169v excused from office of Master on payment of usual fine of £10   6 Feb 1709/10 G175r elected to Robert Scott's £320 share. His £160 share disposed of to William Rogers

ANDREWS/ANDREW, Samuel   2 Aug 1703 G94r bound to Samuel Bridge   3 Feb 1706/7 G138r turned over from Samuel Bridge to Benjamin Beardwell   7 Aug 1710 G183r freed by Benjamin Beardwell

THE ANNALIST [i.e. 'The British Annalist', 1705?]   5 Feb 1704/5 G114v sham almanack printed by Henry Eyres

ANSON, Elizabeth   3 May 1697 F262r Elizabeth Robins is bound to her

ANSON, Staford   4 Aug 1690 F141v cloathed and promises payment of fine

ANTROBUS, William   3 May 1703 G89v bound to James Orme, 7 years   4 Mar 1705/6 G129r turned over from James Orme to John Matthews (scratched out)   6 Oct 1712 G204v freed by John Matthews

APOLLONIUS [of Perga]   2 Aug 1708 G156r Capt. Edward Darrell, Robert Knaplock, Richard Mount and Benjamin Walford to provide a better paper for

APPRENTICES   7 Sep 1685 F44r all turnovers to be entered in Apprentice Register   5 Mar 1687/8 F99r free workmen's petition read re. the various ways masters flout rules with regard to supernumerary apprentices; referred to committee. Clerk to produce list of particular offenders over binding apprentices at every Court day when apprentices are bound   4 Sep 1688 F107r journeymen printers complain that Bennett Griffin has taken supernumerary apprentices   7 Mar 1691/2 F166v Stephen Keyes is tendered cloathing when appearing at Court to bind an apprentice   13 Mar 1692/3 F184r committee to see what fines have been imposed for binding apprentices by foreign indentures; F185r Robert Everingham is fined for having bound Thomas Smith with foreign indentures   8 May 1693 F188r John Hippinstall comes in to free William Peirson and is fined 30s for having bound him with a foreign indenture   4 Sep 1693 F191r Thomas Hodgkins is refused leave to bind a third apprentice despite his alleging that one is sick and useless   9 May 1694 F204v Court agrees to free Henry Pointing after workmen printers, contrary to usual stance, ask that his foreign indenture be ignored   3 Feb 1695/6 F239r four bound – unspecified   2 Mar 1695/6 F240r blank where they were supposed to be filled in   6 Apr 1696 F242r eight bound – unspecified   4 May 1696 F242v five bound – unspecified   8 Jun 1696 F243r five bound – unspecified   3 Aug 1696 F248r five bound – unspecified   7 Sep 1696 F249r four bound – unspecified   5 Oct 1696 F250v Nicholas Hooper to enter all apprentices whom Christopher Grandorge has neglected to enter. Three bound – unspecified   17 Oct 1696 F251v two bound – unspecified   2 Nov 1696 F252r five bound – unspecified   7 Dec 1696 F253r five bound – unspecified   1 Feb 1696/7 F255r eight bound – unspecified   4 Nov 1706 G136r masters' trades and places of abode to be inserted in register book of apprentices   2 Mar 1712/13 G207r following complaint, ordered that no journeyman printer should have an apprentice bound to him until he has paid all his arrears of quarterage

See also PRINTERS

ARCHBISHOP OF CANTERBURY – see CANTERBURY, ARCHBISHOP OF

ARCHIVES   5 Oct 1696 F250v vouchers and Under Warden's papers are ordered to be put in the chest. Any S.C. papers ever delivered to a member or another to be noted, also who delivered them and why

ARDEN, John   6 Nov 1699 G33r cloathed   26 Mar 1700 G38r fined for First Renter Warden   6 Oct 1701 G64v elected to William Horton's £40 share   4 Feb 1705/6 G127v deceased; Richard Wilkins given his £40 share   3 Jun 1706 G132r bequest of £40 share to Thomas Asgall, an infant of about 12 or 13 years (sic). Payment of proceeds to his wife's executors delayed   4 Nov 1706 G136r Mrs Asgall, mother of Thomas Asgall, the legatee of Arden's £40 share, asks the Court to pay it to her son despite his being a child; agreed, on condition that she and her sureties can make out a bond to S.C. to that effect; Thomas Asgall to receive Arden's £40 share as his mother has provided an indemnity to S.C.

ARDEN, Mrs – see preceding entry

ARGALUS AND PARTHENIA   7 Apr 1690 F133r by Francis Quarles; assigned for the late Thomas Rookes by Thomas Burdikin to William Freeman

ARGENT, Mrs   5 Jul 1697 F264v deceased; disposal of her £80 share deferred until next Court day   2 Aug 1697 F265v William Hill elected to her £80 share

ARGYLL, Archibald Campbell, Marquis of   1 Sep 1684 F23r John Boileau is reported for dealing in scandalous books, including material relating to Argyll's case (W) 'Argiles Case'

ARIS, Samuel   5 May 1707 G142r turned over from William Sayes to Daniel Bridge   6 Sep 1708 G157v turned over from Daniel Bridge to Richard Janeway   5 Mar 1710/11 G188r freed by Richard Janeway

ARNAT/ARNOTT, John   7 Apr 1707 G141r bound to Edward Head, 7 years   6 Oct 1712 G204v turned over to Mary Head

ARNAULD [?the author Henri Arnauld]   1 Sep 1684 F23r John Boileau, Bureau and Bernard are reported for dealing in scandalous books (W) 'Arnauld'

ARNOTT – see ARNAT

ARNE, Thomas   18 Dec 1702 G84r John Price turned over to him from Henry Lloyd

ARNO, John, snr – see following entry

ARNO, John, jnr   8 Aug 1715 G232r son of John, is bound to John Williams, 7 years

ARNOLD, David   2 Jul 1694 F210v servant to Henry Kifft; freed

ARNOLD, John (I)   6 Aug 1694 F211v yeoman of Benson, Oxfordshire; his son Thomas is bound to Giles Sussex

ARNOLD, John, snr (II) – see following entry

ARNOLD, John, jnr (III)   4 Mar 1716/17 G248r son of John, is bound to John Sackfield, 7 years

ARNOLD, Ralph   5 Apr 1703 G88r bound to Richard Mount, 7 years   12 Nov 1711 G195r freed by Richard Mount; George Hales is bound to him   4 Mar 1716/17 G248r William Tricketts is bound to him

ARNOLD, Thomas   6 Aug 1694 F211v son of John Arnold of Benson, Oxfordshire, yeoman; bound to Giles Sussex   4 May 1702 G71r freed by William Sussex

ARNOLD, William   5 Dec 1698 G17r bound to Elizabeth Astley, 7 years   22 Dec 1715 G235v freed by Elizabeth Astley

ART OF WHEEDLING [i.e. Richard Head, *Proteus Redivivus: the Art of Wheedling*]   19 Dec 1683 F7r complaint re. Thomas Passenger's sale of this book deferred to next Court

ARTON, Rachel   27 Mar 1697 F260r deceased; Richard Fairbank voted to her pension

ASBURNE, Archibald, snr – see following entry

ASBURNE, Archibald, jnr   4 Sep 1704 G112r son of Archibald Asburne, freed by redemption on payment of 20s to Poor Box

ASGALL, Mrs   4 Nov 1706 G136r has given securities to indemnify S.C. in respect of payment of John Arden's £40 share to her son Thomas

ASGALL, Thomas   3 Jun 1706 G132r infant of about 12 or 13 years (*sic*). John Arden's £40 share bequeathed to him but payment deferred as Court would not permit money to be paid to an infant   4 Nov 1706 G136r to receive Arden's £40 share as his mother has provided an indemnity to S.C.

ASHBOLE, [   ]   6 Mar 1681/2 E146v to be paid £20 for Mrs Lilly, for the copy of her husband's almanack

ASHBURNE, Alexander   5 Sep 1698 G14v freed by William Horton

ASHFIELD, Thomas (I)   6 May 1706 G131v bound to Thomas Grover, 7 years

ASHFIELD, Thomas (II)   6 Oct 1707 G145v bound to William Gray, 7 years

ASHTON, [John]   9 Feb 1690/1 F148r Samuel Heyrick allowed to print 'The Trials of the Lord Preston and the Late [John] Ashton' in S.C. kitchen

ASHTON, Charles   13 Dec 1705 G126v Master of St John's College, Cambridge; signatory to Articles between S.C. and University

ASHURST, Samuel   5 May 1701 G59v bound to Oliver Elliston, 7 years   7 Apr 1712 G199r freed by John Baskett, cloathed   13 Apr 1713 G208v elected into Mrs Elliston's £40 share   26 Mar 1715 G227r fined for Renter Warden   4 Apr 1715 G227v Thomas Silvester is bound to him   1 Apr 1717 G249v elected to Daniel Midwinter's £80 share. His £40 share disposed of to Owen Lloyd

ASKEW, James   3 Mar 1706/7 G139r bound to John Saltmarsh, 7 years

ASSEMBLY'S CATECHISM – see CATECHISMS

ASSIGNMENTS   7 Nov 1681 E137v Robert Scott succeeds in negotiating a low assignment fee of 50s for books 'of little or no value' assigned to him by Mrs Martin. Samuel Mearne and Henry Herringman are ordered to be present at Robert Scott's entering of several books   5 Dec 1681 E140r Thomas Newcomb allowed to enter at a lower rate than usual 88 books 'of little value' assigned to him by George Thomason   4 Apr 1687 F81v Clerk to record assignments in registers consistently   3 Jul 1693 F190r Clerk to note time and place of assignment opposite original entry in the margin

See also CLERK

ASSISTANTS   20 Jun 1681 E113r six new Assistants appointed in accordance with mandate of the Crown   5 Sep 1681 E129r voted that no more should be called   3 Oct 1681 E130r confirmed that no more are to be called in. Seniority alone not to guarantee a place on the Court   3 Jul 1682 E155v to be fined 2s if they appear at dinner and not at Court   26 Mar 1684 F12r surrender of their places in connection with *quo warranto* proceedings   7 Apr 1684 F13v Master supervises drawing-up of list of Assistants loyal to the government, to be presented to the Crown   24 Apr 1684 F14r those submitted to Crown on 7 April are nominated in new Patent   27 May 1684 F15r new list confirmed   2 Jun 1684 F15v those on new list sworn in   3 Dec 1684 F26v to attend James Cokes's translation to the Weavers' Company   7 Sep 1685 F43v any Assistant to be fined 2s if absent from private Court without good reason   1 Feb 1685/6 F50v to dine with Sir Robert Jefferies, the Lord Mayor   11 Oct 1686 (W) all absent members to pay their forfeits as per order of 7 September 1685   5 Dec 1687 F95r Commission from Crown read to Court re. dispensing with the Oaths of Allegiance and Supremacy for S.C. officials; ordered to be entered in S.C. books. Precedence to be determined from the time that officials were called to be Assistants, rather than according to seniority on the Livery   1 Mar 1687/8 F98r proposal that S.C. members who are not printers, booksellers or bookbinders can become Assistants is vetoed   6 Aug 1688 F105v the whole Court, listed, have the Stock estate of St Martin's Ludgate conveyed to them in trust for S.C.   27 Nov 1688 F110r those who were dismissed as a result of the *quo warranto* proceedings of 26 Mar 1684 restored. All who have served or fined for office not obliged to serve or fine again   4 Feb 1688/9 F112v to take places according to seniority and under those who have served and fined for Wardens. Voted to call in new Assistants according to byelaws of S.C. and not according to the 'late new Patent'   1 Mar 1688/9 F113r old Assistants recalled into Court take their place   4 Mar 1688/9 F114r all Assistants who have served or fined as Master or Wardens to have precedence as formerly; rest to be dated from cloathing   26 Mar 1689 F116r committee to inquire into the order of precedence of those Assistants who have not served or fined as Master or Warden   6 May 1689 F116v committee report that precedence goes by Renter Wardenship and the call to the Livery which was closed on 10 Aug 1670. Members ranked. Voted re. the requests of Daniel Blague, Bennett Griffin and others to become Assistants that the Table is at present full   7 Oct 1689 F124r dispute for precedence between John Towse, Henry Herringman and John Bellinger traced back to confusion over *quo warranto*. Assistants to be paid 2s 6d for attendance at Court instead of dinners in view of S.C. debts   2 Dec 1689 F127v Bennett Griffin's renewed claim to a position on Court by right of seniority is rejected   3 Mar 1689/90 F130r Court inform John Starkey when he refuses Junior Assistant's place that precedence is according to when people come on Court   8 Apr 1690 F133v to have their usual fees for attending this Court even though it is a bye-Court   2 Jun 1690 F135r further Assistants to be elected in view of the Court's small size. Agreed to restore all those who had been Assistants on 5 May 1689   5 Jun 1690 F135v questions on precedent from time of re-election arise; Court recommends amicable agreement and works out order (signatures)   3 Nov 1690 F145v all Assistants not wearing gowns at next Court to be fined 12d   4 May 1691 F153r order for Assistants to sit in their gowns suspended until the beginning of winter   2 May 1692 F171r to give Master and Wardens advice re. Oxford printing materials &c.   18 Jul 1692 F174v Master and Wardens summoned to Guildhall re. not admitting Giles Sussex to Court   26 Jul 1692 F175r committee appointed to safeguard S.C. rights after mayoral order to elect Sussex to Court voted down   28 Jul 1692 F175v reasons why Sussex should not be admitted to the Court are copied out in full   1 Aug 1692 F176v proceedings in Sussex case to be entered in Register; Master and Wardens thanked for maintaining Court rights   7 May 1694 F203v William Thackery, William Whitwood, Bennett Griffin and Charles Harper elected new Assistants from call to Livery closed on 13 Jun 1670   5 Aug 1695 F230v Assistants to be fined 10s for charity out of dividend if they bring anyone to the feast on 10 August apart from their wives or one friend each   4 May 1696 F242r William Thackery dropped from Court. Any Assistant or Renter Warden who comes to Court after 11am to forfeit half crown dinner money to Poor Box. Five new Assistants elected: Samuel Sprint, Thomas Cockerell, John Place, Robert Andrews and Capt. Samuel Roycroft   8 Apr 1700 G38v four new ones elected   6 May 1700 G39r no new ones to be elected   3 May 1703 G89r give 5s each to Thomas Hopper for placing his brother as an apprentice   4 Oct 1703 G95v to wear gowns with foins only and no other gowns on penalty of one shilling   10 Feb 1703/4 G102r who appeared at a private court to have half a crown for attendance   4 Sep 1704 G112r Master and Wardens to take care of the standing for them on Thanksgiving Day   27 Sep 1704 G112r ordered that from Michaelmas Day to Lady Day all to sit in their gowns on all Court days   7 May 1705 G119v four more to be elected   3 Feb 1706/7 G137v four more to be elected   9 Feb 1707/8 G148v debate about chosing four new Assistants to be adjourned   1 Mar 1707/8 G149r eight more to be elected out of those who have held or fined for Renter Warden   3 May 1708 G152r three more elected   20 Jun 1713 G210v those coming to Pension Court after 10 o'clock to forfeit 1 shilling to Poor Box   14 Mar 1714/15 G226r six more to be elected. Clerk to prepare a list of such of Livery as have held or fined for Renter Warden   26 Mar 1715 G227r who arrive after sitting of Court to forfeit 1 shilling to Poor Box   5 Mar 1715/16 G237v those who signed notes to Thomas Guy to fund English Stock indemnified against the notes and all costs and charges

ASTBURY, John, snr – see following entry

ASTBURY, John, jnr   4 Aug 1712 G202v son of John, is bound to Thomas James, 7 years   14 Mar 1714 G226r turned over to Mary Head

ASTLEY, Elizabeth   5 Dec 1698 G17r William Arnold is bound to her   2 Jun 1701 G60v Rebecca Brimsmead is bound to her   22 Dec 1715 G235v her apprentice William Arnold is freed

ASTWOOD, [   ]   11 Apr 1681 E110r a printer; clears Francis Smith and Benjamin Harris of asking for 'A Raree-Show' [attr. Stephen College] to be printed

ASTWOOD, James   2 Dec 1700 G54r and John Darby snr; their apprentice William Smith is freed   5 May 1701 G59v Richard Marks is bound to him   7 Jul 1701 G62r his apprentice Bryan Mills is freed

ATKIN, John   9 Feb 1707/8 G148v printer; bill in Chancery to be brought against him   1 Mar 1707/8 G149r to be proceeded against to get an answer upon subpoena   4 Oct 1708 G157v John and Thomas Jones to be made party to S.C.'s bill in Chancery against Atkin and others

ATKINS/ATKYNS, John   7 Feb 1697/8 G3v bound to Jeremiah Wilkins   23 Mar 1704/5 G117r freed by Jeremiah Wilkins

ATKINS, Maurice   8 Nov 1703 G97r freed by Thomas Newborough   3 Nov 1707 G146v cloathed   3 Oct 1709 G171r Christopher Nowell turned over to him from Richard Sare   1 Oct 1711 G195r Robert Dodd turned over to him from Thomas Baker   7 Jul 1712 G201v Charles Motte is bound to him   1 Sep 1712 G203r Mary Bucktrout is bound to him   4 May 1713 G209v excused office of Renter Warden for one further year

ATKINS, Thomas   31 Aug 1716 G242v Richard Weedon turned over to him from Robert Harman

ATKINSON, Francis, snr – see following entry

ATKINSON, Francis, jnr   5 May 1712 G199v son of Francis, is bound to Elizabeth Grover, 7 years

ATKINSON, John   12 Apr 1708 G152r bound to John Hartley, 8 years   3 May 1714 G219r turned over to Christopher Bateman

ATKINSON, Thomas   6 Nov 1699 G33r bound to Jonathan Robinson, 7 years

ATTORNEY – see ALLEN, [   ]

ATTORNEY GENERAL   3 Aug 1702 G79v committee to obtain opinion re. case of Benjamin Tooke   5 Oct 1702 G81v opinion on Tooke read   12 Jul 1703 G92v opinion on Tooke   2 Aug 1703 G93v opinions on cases concerning Tooke
See also NORTHEY, Sir Edward

ATWOOD, [   ]   2 Oct 1699 G31v carpenter; to be paid 10s for attendance and viewing of S.C's houses

AUBREY, Thomas   4 Nov 1706 G136r bound to John Humphreys, 7 years

AUSTIN, Samuel   27 Mar 1703 G87v bound to Joseph Bush   1 Mar 1713/14 G216v freed by Joseph Bush   5 Apr 1714 G218r William Whitehead is bound to him   13 Jun 1715 G229v James Knowles is bound to him

AVE MARIA LANE   4 Jul 1681 E115v Roger Norton and John Towse desired to continue efforts to secure amelioration money for ground cut off in Ave Maria Lane   2 May 1698 G7v committee to treat with tenants in   6 Jun 1698 G8r report of committee read and agreed to   4 Jul 1698 G10v revival of committee to treat with tenants here and in Amen Corner

AYLMER, Brabazon, snr   7 Feb 1697/8 G3v his son Brabazon Aylmer is bound to him   1 Mar 1697/8 G4r elected Stock-keeper for Livery   5 Dec 1698 G17r requests that his son-in-law, Robert James, be excused from cloathing   1 Mar 1700/1 G56r elected Stock-keeper for Livery   2 Mar 1701/2 G67r elected Stock-keeper for Livery, his apprentice James Round is freed   4 May 1702 G71r John Herringman is bound to him   7 Jun 1703 G90r given thanks of Court and 3 guineas for his attendance in the warehouse after removal of Benjamin Tooke   6 Mar 1703/4 G103v elected to John Place's £160 share. His £80 share disposed of to Edward Jones   4 Jun 1705 G120v his apprentice Brabazon Aylmer is freed   4 Aug 1707 G144v his apprentice Thomas Quirke is freed   1 May 1710 G179v his £160 share, already assigned to Richard Mount, disposed of to Mount

AYLMER, Brabazon, jnr   7 Feb 1697/8 G3v bound to his father, Brabazon Aylmer   4 Jun 1705 G120v freed by Brabazon Aylmer

AYLWARD, John, snr – see following entry

AYLWARD, John, jnr   3 Jun 1695 F226r son of John Aylward; bound to William Barker

AYNGE, Alice   7 Jun 1714 G219v executrix of John Dowley, her bond of £500 paid off by bonds from Mrs Gretton and Mrs Dyer

AYRES, John   7 Apr 1701 G58v freed by John Newton

AYREY, James   5 Jul 1703 G92r bound to James Willshire, 7 years   5 Feb 1704/5 G115r turned over from James Willshire to William Sayes

AYSHFORD, Daniel – see following entry

AYSHFORD, John   9 Apr 1716 G239r son of Daniel, is bound to Richard Standfast, 7 years

B. N., Philomath – see OBSERVATIONS ON TIME

BABBINGTON, Randolph – see following entry

BABBINGTON, Samuel   5 Aug 1695 F231v son of the late Randolph Babbington of Runbury, Chester, yeoman; bound to Hannah Smith

BACK, John   6 Apr 1691 F152v summoned with Thomas James to next Court re. their printing a copy belonging to Joshua Coniers   8 Jun 1691 F154v he and Coniers accuse each other of comprinting; some of the register entries appear under Back's name   3 Dec 1694 F215r excused cloathing for 1 year   3 Feb 1695/6 F239r cloathed   6 Sep 1697 F267r Mathew Hatham is bound to him   6 Jun 1698 G8v his apprentice Arthur Bexworth is freed

BACKHOUSE, William   2 Jun 1701 G60v bound to George Shell

BACKWELL, Hugh   4 Feb 1716/17 G246v son of Robert, is bound to Hugh Meere, 7 years

BACKWELL, Robert – see preceding entry

BAGNALL, [   ]   4 Aug 1712 G202v turned over to Dryden Leach

BAGNALL, John   7 Feb 1708 G160v bound to Andrew Hind, 7 years   3 Jul 1710 G182r turned over to William Wise from Andrew Hind

BAILY/BAYLEY, John   7 Oct 1698 G15r bound to Isaac Cleave, 8 years   1 Dec 1707 G147v freed by Isaac Cleave

BAITEN, Thomas   1 Feb 1702/3 G85r bound to Adam Hampton, 7 years

BAKER   7 Mar 1697/8 G4r who serves S.C. with bread for a benefactor's gift to give a receipt quarterly to the Warden

BAKER'S ARITHMETIC [by Humphrey Baker]   1 Mar 1682/3 E165r assigned by Elizabeth Thomas, administratrix of Edward Thomas, to John Wright and William Thackery

BAKER, [ ] 6 Jun 1681 E113r bond to be delivered up to himself and John Low, Jonathan Edwin's securities, on payment of £40   3 Jun 1700 G40r payment of £100 due to him from S.C.   7 Jul 1701 G62r debt of £102 10s from S.C. paid   6 Dec 1703 G99v of Norwich; Clerk to enquire whether involved in selling and publishing of sham almanacks   20 Dec 1711 G196r Nahum Tate to be involved in prosecuting him for printing the 'New Version of Psalms' without Tate's permission

BAKER, Anthony   6 Dec 1697 G2r is bound to John Meekes

BAKER/BARKER, Bartholomew   6 Jun 1698 G8v bound to Benjamin Tooke snr, 7 years   9 Sep 1706 G134v freed by Benjamin Tooke   5 Jul 1708 G154v cloathed   4 Oct 1708 G158r of Bishopgate Street, stationer; Abraham Hemingway is bound to him   13 Jun 1715 G229v John Nortman is bound to him   7 Nov 1715 G234v his apprentice Abraham Hemingway is freed

BAKER, Charles   2 Oct 1699 G31v his apprentice William Bates is freed

BAKER, Humphrey – see BAKER'S ARITHMETIC

BAKER, Capt./Major John   20 Jun 1681 E113r Crown mandate that he should become an Assistant   4 Dec 1682 E161r fine of 12d for late arrival at Court remitted on his excuse that he was commanded to wait on the Lord Mayor   20 Apr 1683 E169r elected to Mrs White's £160 share which she surrendered in return for ready money   7 Apr 1684 F13v on list of loyal Assistants presented to the Crown   7 Jul 1684 F20v given leave to sue S.C. members who have had dealings in any of his books since 7 Oct 1681   7 May 1685 (W) confirmed as member of new Livery   4 Jul 1685 F39v competes unsuccessfully for Upper Warden. Fined for two years of Under Warden because of want of choice for Upper Warden   7 Sep 1685 F44r requests that John Cross be given 10s charity   1 Mar 1685/6 F52r elected Stock-keeper for Assistants with John Towse   26 Mar 1686 F54v pays 12d charity for being absent from Court with Master's leave   3 Jul 1686 F59r elected Upper Warden   5 Jul 1686 F60v William Cooper is elected Stock-keeper in his place since he is now Warden   21 Oct 1686 (W) Letter from Baker and John Bellinger requesting that Obadiah Blagrave give a bond of £1000 for carrying out his duties   2 Jul 1687 F85v ties with Ambrose Isted in vote for Upper Warden and elected in second ballot   7 Nov 1687 F94v agreement between John Gadbury, Thomas Bassett and Baker re. almanacks printed for charity; letter from him (W) requesting the charity for John Crosse   7 May 1688 F101r assigns Joseph Glanvill's 'An Earnest Invitation … to the Lord's Supper', 7th edn, to Joshua Phillipps and Joseph Watts   11 Oct 1688 F108v restored to Assistants   27 Nov 1688 F110v elected Upper Warden   26 Mar 1689 F116r deceased; Ambrose Isted elected Upper Warden in his stead and it is decided to dispose of his share at another Court   6 May 1689 F118r his Livery share disposed of to George Copping

BAKER, Major John – see BAKER, Capt. John

BAKER, John (I)   5 Feb 1693/4 F199r late of Quinton, Gloucestershire, clerk; his son William is bound to William Baker for seven years

BAKER, John (II)   2 Apr 1694 F202v servant to Brabazon Aylmer; freed   8 Nov 1697 G1v John Legg is bound to him

BAKER, John (III)   2 Mar 1701/2 G67v bound to Henry Playford, 7 years

BAKER, Mrs   20 Dec 1701 G66v deceased; disposal of her £80 share to be deferred until next monthly Court   9 Feb 1701/2 G67r her £80 share disposed of to Thomas Cockerell

BAKER, Nevinson   6 Oct 1707 G145v bound to William Taylor, 7 years

BAKER, St John   3 Jul 1699 G27v bound to Robert Battersby, 7 years   2 May 1709 G165r freed by Susanna Battersby   7 Apr 1712 G199r Gustavus Hackett is bound to him

BAKER, Thomas (I)   4 Sep 1699 G30v bound to John Jones, 7 years   6 May 1700 G39v bound to Robert Clavell, 7 years   9 Sep 1706 G134v apprentice of John Jones, freed by Robert Clavell   2 Oct 1710 G184v of Ludgate Street, bookseller; Robert Dodd is bound to him   1 Oct 1711 G195r Robert Dodd turned over from him to Maurice Atkins

BAKER, Thomas (II)   3 May 1708 G152v bound to John England, 7 years

BAKER, William (I)   4 Oct 1686 F64v elected to livery   8 Nov 1686 F67r cloathed   18 Jul 1690 F140v S.C. gives him bond for payment of £102 10s on 18 Jan 1690/1, with £200 penalty   9 Feb 1690/1 F149r competes unsuccessfully for Thomas Hodgkins's £40 share   4 May 1691 F153v elected Assistant Renter Warden   3 Aug 1691 F158v competes unsuccessfully for Thomas Cockerell's £40 share. Elected to Widow Satterthwait's £40 share   1 Aug 1692 F177r he and Freeman Collins to pay balance of Renter Wardens' accounts   5 Feb 1693/4 F199r William Baker jnr is bound to him for seven years   1 Oct 1694 F213v his apprentice Isaac Stanton is freed   7 Oct 1695 F233v competes unsuccessfully for the late Mrs Sawbridge's £80 share   2 Mar 1695/6 F239v placed in the Livery according to his seniority in freedom in the Haberdashers' Company, from which he was translated. His apprentice Thomas Bartlett is freed   3 Aug 1696 F246v elected to Robert Andrews's £80 share   3 Apr 1699 G24r Edne Bourne is bound to him   3 Mar 1700/1 G57r deceased; his apprentice William Baker is freed by his executor, Tooke   1 Dec 1701 G66r his apprentice Edward Brown is turned over to Robert Steel

BAKER, William (II)   5 Feb 1693/4 F199r son of the late John Baker of Quinton, Gloucestershire, clerk; bound to William Baker for seven years   3 Mar 1700/1 G57r freed by Tooke, executor of William Baker, deceased

BALDRY, John   1 Jun 1702 G71v Lorraine Whitledge is bound to him

BALDWIN, [ ]   22 Dec 1685 F48v petition of John Mayo, Baldwin, Simon Hinch and John Palmer

BALDWIN, Charles   2 Jul 1705 G121v bound to William Warter, 7 years

BALDWIN, Jonathan   6 Jul 1713 G212v freed by Elinor James

BALDWIN, Mrs   2 May 1709 G164v to explain why she had the Select Psalms printed without S.C.'s leave   6 Jun 1709 G165v to be summoned to next Court to explain why she had the Select Psalms printed   4 Jul 1709 G167r appears before Court to answer complaints; Master, Wardens and Stock-keepers to settle

BALDWIN, Richard (I)   6 Oct 1690 F144r fined 20s for having accepted Richard Humphrey as apprentice when turned over from Joseph Hutchinson, a foreigner   9 Feb 1690/1 F149r summoned to next Court for failing to enter a pamphlet   12 Sep 1692 F179r summoned to show why he should not be cloathed   6 Aug 1694 F211v Samuel Briscoe, his apprentice, is freed

BALDWIN, Richard (II)   2 Aug 1708 G156v bound to Robert Whitledge, 7 years   7 May 1716 G240r freed by Robert Whitledge

BALDWIN, Robert   6 Feb 1715/16 G236r freed by patrimony
See also BALDWYN

BALDWINE, Jonathan   22 Jun 1704 G108r bound to Samuel Smith, 7 years
See also BALDWIN, BALDWYN

BALDWYN, Richard   5 Dec 1692 F183r cloathed   4 Sep 1693 F191r Court questions John Gellebrand's right to assign to Baldwyn Bishop John Wilkins's 'Swift and Secret Messenger' [i.e. *Mercury: or The Secret and Swift Messenger*]
See also BALDWIN, BALDWINE

BALE, George   23 Mar 1679/80 E98r 25s of his money remaining in Taylor's hands to be made up to 40s, paid to Under Warden and discharged at 10s a quarter

BALES, John   6 Apr 1696 F242r servant to Edward Jones; freed

BALL, [ ]   7 Mar 1691/2 F166v Court refuses his request that Thomas Wall of Bristol's Livery fine, for which Wall is being sued, should be abated   26 Mar 1692 F167v pays Wall's Livery fine; Court abates £5 of it and order Warden to pay John Lilly's legal fees

BALLARD, [ ]   2 Dec 1706 G136v excused cloathing for twelve months

BALLARD, Samuel   3 Mar 1700/1 G57r freed by John Salisbury and John Nicholson   5 Jun 1710 G180r excused cloathing   6 Nov 1710 G185r bookseller; Aaron Ward is bound to him   3 Dec 1711 G195v to be summoned to next Court to take cloathing   4 Feb 1711/12 G196r summoned to take cloathing at next Court   3 Mar 1711/12 G197r cloathed

BALLARD, Thomas   4 Oct 1697 F268v freed by George Conyers   7 Aug 1704 G110v Thomas Hodgkins permitted to print ABC in Spelling Book for him

BALLDEN, Andrew – see following entry

BALLDEN, Gabriel   12 Nov 1711 G195r son of Andrew; bound to Robert Willoughby, 7 years

BALLETT, John, snr – see following entry

BALLETT, John, jnr   1 Jul 1695 F228r son of John Ballett snr of Westleton, Suffolk, tanner; bound to Stephen Keyes

BANDBRIDGE/BANDRIDGE, Jane   21 Jun 1700 G40v elected to Mary Boate's pension   20 Dec 1700 G54r elected to Elizabeth Goreing's pension   1 Mar 1707/8 G150r pensioner, deceased; Elizabeth Hope given her pension

BANKS/BANKES, Hammond   12 Jun 1704 G107v bound to Alexander Bosvile, 7 years   1 Oct 1711 G195r freed by Alexander Bosvile   1 Feb 1713/14 G216r John Rogers is bound to him

BANKS, William   4 Jul 1698 G11r bound to Thomas Yates, 7 years

BANNERS   3 Oct 1692 F180r banners and trophies to be repaired for Lord Mayor's Day   28 Oct 1697 F269r detailed account given of how they should be renovated for the Royal progress   7 Mar 1697/8 G4v herald painters to be paid for making banners and escutcheons   5 Sep 1715 G232v Robert Andrews reports of behalf of committee set up to view banners and trophies of S.C. that three of them are worn out. Banners to be provided by Master and Wardens for next Lord Mayor's Day

BARBER, Anthony   5 Mar 1704/5 G117r turned over from John Weekes, is freed by Alexander Boswell

BARBER, Daniel   20 Dec 1701 G66r elected to Thomasine Mann's pension   22 Jun 1702 G76r elected to Ann Desborough's pension

BARBER, John   1 Oct 1705 G124r cloathed. Robert Raikes is bound to him   4 Feb 1705/6 G127v William Newbould is bound to him   3 May 1708 G152v printer; Rowland Steevens is bound to him   27 Mar 1710 G177r fined for Assistant Renter Warden   6 Aug 1711 G193r George Cotton is bound to him   1 Oct 1711 G194v Edward Fowkes is bound to him   7 Apr 1712 G198v elected to Robert Stephens' £80 share   1 Dec 1712 G205r his apprentice Robert Raikes is freed

BARBER, Martha   24 Mar 1713/14 G217r elected to Magdalen Burrowse's pension. Isaac Lane is given her pension   27 Sep 1715 G233r deceased; Elizabeth Miller is given her pension

BARBER CHIRURGEONS' COMPANY 22 May 1685 F37v agrees to turn book-dealing members over to S.C.

See also LONDON, CITY OF: LIVERY COMPANIES

BARETT, Joseph 3 May 1680 E99v printer; cloathed

BARGE 1 Dec 1679 E95r committee to meet next Friday at 2 pm 5 Mar 1679/80 E97v ground for a barge house at Nine Elms to be viewed by a committee 18 Apr 1680 E99r Roger Norton and John Macock to audit accounts 7 Jun 1680 E100r £18 3s credit of barge account to be paid by Martin to Under Warden 26 Mar 1683 E167r dinner to be held on barge on 29 May every year in commemoration of Evan Tyler 7 Dec 1685 F47r shipwright's bill for work on the barge to be considered by the next Court, and Clerk in the meantime to compare with former bills 1 Feb 1685/6 F50r Sir Peter Vandeput, the owner of the S.C. barge house, voluntarily lowers his rent to £10 p.a. 12 Oct 1687 F91v to be trimmed before next Lord Mayor's Day 7 May 1688 F101r 29 May collation to be held at Chelsea. Master, Wardens and Assistants to be transported there by barge 6 Aug 1688 F105r Randall Taylor apologises for his behaviour on the barge on a trip to Mortlake, and asks for his £10 fine to be remitted 9 Sep 1689 F123r Court called re. its condition; agreed that Assistants and Livery who had not already contributed to repair should do so. Committee appointed to oversee this 12 Sep 1692 F179r bargemaster tells Court the barge has sprung a leak; ordered for her to be repaired 6 Nov 1693 F194v Master and Wardens to pay as much of the shipwright's bill for mending the barge as they think fit 12 Nov 1694 F214v Under Warden to pay shipwright's bill for mending barge 27 Sep 1695 (W) Master and Wardens to be responsible for looking after barge 7 Sep 1696 F249r bargemaster tells Court that the barge needs to be mended and to be launched next spring, and that he needs a new coat; Court agrees 5 Oct 1696 F250v Upper Warden tells Court that the barge committee agrees to her being repaired 7 Dec 1696 (W) Loftus to be paid £4 of £6 bill as Wardens had told him when they went to view barge 4 Oct 1697 F268v John Barrow [snr] says the barge needs to be blocked and launched next spring tide; committee to view her and negotiate with shipwright 6 Dec 1697 G2r Loftus the shipwright's bill for cleaning 5 Sep 1698 G14r in need of trimming; committee to examine 7 Oct 1698 G14v 15s paid for barge road by John Barrow [jnr] 10 Jan 1698/9 G18v complaint that Francis Charleton had damaged the barge; Barrow the bargemaster to fit barge house with a new lock to prevent any further damage 7 Feb 1698/9 G20r Master and Wardens to view damage to barge and barge house 6 Mar 1698/9 G21v John Simms presents committee's report that the barge and barge house are in a bad condition. Barrow the bargemaster to make clean at no charge to S.C. 7 Aug 1699 G28r Barrow has acquainted the Court that the barge wants mending. Master and Wardens to attend to this 2 Oct 1699 G31r Loftus's bill for mending 1 Jul 1700 G41r committee to raise subscription for new bottom 19 Jul 1700 G43r subscription for new bottoming raised; barge to be launched next spring tide 7 Oct 1700 G45v no member to be admitted to barge on Lord Mayor's Day unless wearing a gown 2 Jun 1701 G60v members who had contributed to building or repair to have free use of it for one day in the summer 6 Oct 1701 G65r in need of trimming 7 Sep 1702 G80r to be trimmed 5 Oct 1702 G81r no-one to be admitted to barge on Lord Mayor's Day without their Livery gowns 6 Sep 1703 G94v in need of trimming 4 Oct 1703 G95v bill for trimming to be paid. No-one to be admitted to barge on Lord Mayor's Day without their gowns 4 Sep 1704 G112r to be trimmed and launched next spring tide 2 Oct 1704 G112v continuance of former order for no boys, and no-one without gowns, to be admitted to barge on Lord Mayor's Day 10 Sep 1705 G123r to be repaired for Lord Mayor's Day 9 Sep 1706 G134v Master and Wardens to take care about launching 4 Nov 1706 G135v Loftus to be paid by

Warden for fitting up 1 Dec 1707 G147r shipwright to be paid for cleansing 4 Oct 1708 G158r to be launched and trimmed next spring tide. No members to be admitted to barge on Lord Mayor's Day except in gowns 3 Oct 1709 G171r to be trimmed and launched next spring tide 4 Dec 1710 G186r shipwright's bill for trimming it to be paid 1 Oct 1711 G194v to be trimmed next spring tide 5 Sep 1715 G232v new cloth to be provided by Master and Wardens for next Lord Mayor's Day 3 Oct 1715 G233v to be launched, viewed by Master and Wardens and cleaned 1 Oct 1716 G244r Master and Wardens to take care that it is trimmed and launched the next spring tide

BARGEMASTER (1682–1690 and 1692–1697, John Barrow snr; 1698–1708 John Barrow jnr; 1709–1717, Daniel Barrow. Annual elections have not been listed) 5 Mar 1679/80 E97v his salary and mate's reward to be referred 26 Mar 1680 E98v to be paid £4 and a sum for oars 5 Jul 1680 E102r to have a coat and silver badge with S.C. arms, to be returned when he relinquishes the post 2 Aug 1680 E102v goldsmith to be paid £4 18s 9d for bargemaster's badge 22 Sep 1680 E104r mate to have 40s salary paid quarterly 1 Aug 1681 E117v to have a new coat 4 Sep 1682 E157v to have a new coat 6 Oct 1684 F25r Under Warden to provide a new coat for bargemaster in time for Lord Mayor's Day 5 Oct 1685 F45r to have a new coat of S.C. livery with silver badge 7 Dec 1685 F46v orders concerning bargemaster, mate and watermen 26 Mar 1686 F54r complains he is 33s (W-30s) to the bad since he always pays watermen immediately and S.C. lowered pay after last time; deferred 7 Jun 1686 F58r paid 33s owing for watermen 21 Feb 1686/7 F72r to be paid for road-chain, anchor and cable 12 Oct 1687 F91v he and mate to have new coats and caps 2 Oct 1693 F192v to have a new coat for Lord Mayor's Day and take care that the barge's leak is mended 7 Oct 1695 F233v request for a new coat for Lord Mayor's Day turned down 7 Oct 1698 G14v to have a new coat against next Lord Mayor's Day. 15s paid by him for the barge road, to be reimbursed by the Warden 10 Jan 1698/9 G18v to serve Charleton with a summons to next Court day for damaging barge. To put a new lock on the barge house 6 Mar 1698/9 G21v Court ordered that he take care that the barge be made clean without charge to S.C. and kept in good order for the future 7 Aug 1699 G28r has acquainted Court that the barge needs mending 9 Sep 1700 G44v to receive new coat and breeches 5 Oct 1702 G81r to have a new coat 10 Sep 1705 G123r to ensure barge repaired for Lord Mayor's Day 7 Oct 1706 G135r to have new livery for next Lord Mayor's Day 4 Oct 1708 G158r to have new livery 3 Nov 1712 G205r bill to be paid by Master and Wardens 1 Oct 1716 G244r to have new livery for next Lord Mayor's Day

BARGEMASTER'S MAN 26 Mar 1686 F54r elected waterman 4 Apr 1687 F81v elected waterman

BARGEMASTER'S MATE 5 Mar 1679 E97v reward for bargemaster's mate to be referred 27 Mar 1682 E149r William Hill elected 26 Mar 1683 E166v William Hill elected 26 Mar 1684 F11v William Hill elected 26 Mar 1685 F32r William Hill elected 26 Mar 1686 F54r William Hill elected 4 Apr 1687 F81r Francis Charleton elected 26 Mar 1688 F116r Francis Charleton elected 26 Mar 1689 F116r Francis Charleton elected 26 Mar 1690 F131v Francis Charleton elected 26 Mar 1692 F168r Francis Charleton elected 27 Mar 1693 F185v Francis Charleton elected 26 Mar 1694 F201v Francis Charleton elected 26 Mar 1695 F219v Francis Charleton elected 26 Mar 1696 F241r Francis Charleton elected 26 Mar 1697 F259v Charleton elected 26 Mar 1698 G5v Francis Charleton elected 27 Mar 1699 G23r Francis Charleton elected 26 Mar 1700 G38r Thomas Charleton elected 26 Mar 1701 G57v Charleton junior elected 26 Mar 1702 G68v Charleton elected 27 Mar 1703 G87v Thomas Charleton elected 27 Mar 1704 G105r Francis Charleton elected   26 Mar 1705 G117v Thomas Charleton elected   26 Mar 1706 G130v Francis Charleton elected   26 Mar 1707 G140r Thomas Charleton elected   26 Mar 1708 G151r Thomas Charleton elected   26 Mar 1709 G163r Francis Charleton elected   27 Mar 1710 G177v Robert Charleton elected   26 Mar 1711 G189r Robert Charleton elected   26 Mar 1712 G198r Charleton elected   26 Mar 1713 G208r Thomas Charleton elected   26 Mar 1714 G217v Thomas Charleton elected   26 Mar 1715 G227r Thomas Charleton elected   26 Mar 1716 G238v Francis Charleton elected   26 Mar 1717 G248v Francis Charleton elected

See also BARGEMASTER

BARGEMASTER'S MATE'S MAN   26 Mar 1686 F54r elected waterman   4 Apr 1687 F81v elected waterman

BARK, John   2 Oct 1704 G112v his apprentice Matthew Hotham is freed

BARKER, Andrew   7 Jun 1697 F263r bound to Robert Pedmore

BARKER, Bartholomew – see BAKER, Bartholomew

BARKER, Christopher   7 Jun 1680 E100r printer, deceased; his widow to have 20s

BARKER, Mrs   3 Jan 1680/1 E106r paid 20s charity

BARKER, Ursula   1 Oct 1683 F3r admitted to the 40s pension of Widow Enderby, deceased   7 Mar 1686/7 F78r deceased; 20s paid to Henry Hills from Poor Box for her burial   23 Mar 1686/7 F80r Elizabeth Sabin elected into her 40s pension

BARKER, William   8 Apr 1695 F221r his apprentice Robert Williamson is freed   3 Jun 1695 F226r John Aylward jnr is bound to him   26 Sep 1712 G203v his apprentice John Vernon is freed   28 Sep 1709 G170v elected to Margaret Driver's pension   23 Mar 1710/11 G188v elected to Elizabeth Wells's pension

BARLOW, William   24 Mar 1713/14 G217r elected to Diana Battersby's pension. Samuel Wallsall given his pension

BARNARD, [   ]   6 Aug 1683 F3r upholsterer; bill to be paid

BARNARD, Henry   1 Aug 1692 (W) is freed by John Harris   12 Sep 1692 F179r of the Poultry and newly made free of John Harris; name sent to Lord Chamberlain

BARNARD, John   6 Jun 1698 G8v bound to William Lillingston, 7 years

BARNARDI, [   ]   1 Sep 1684 F23r reported for dealing in scandalous books (W) 'Obscene cards and keeping a rolling press'

BARNES, [   ] (I)   2 Oct 1699 G31v bricklayer; to be paid for viewing S.C.'s houses

BARNES, [   ] (II)   5 Jun 1710 G180r of Pall Mall; enquiry to be made as to whether he is a freeman of S.C.

BARNES, Edward   4 Oct 1714 G222v his son Thomas is bound to Thomas Teale, 7 years

BARNES, James   5 Mar 1704/5 G117r bound to John Hunter, 7 years

BARNES, Magdalen   5 Oct 1685 F45r given 5s charity in response to petition   22 Jun 1698 G9v deceased; John Lowndes to be given her pension

BARNES, Thomas   4 Oct 1714 G222v son of Edward, is bound to Thomas Teale, 7 years

BARNSLEY, Henry   9 Feb 1707/8 G148r bound to Thomas White, 7 years

BARRETT, Anne   26 Mar 1696 F241r ?deceased; Anne Harper to be given her pension

BARRETT, Benjamin   1 Sep 1712 G203r turned over from Richard Davis to William Shaw   2 Aug 1714 G221r freed by William Shaw

77

BARRETT, Philip 6 Jun 1698 G8v freed by Christopher Coningsby, cloathed 2 Nov 1702 G83r Robert Hurst is bound to him 3 Apr 1710 G178v stationer; John Coles is bound to him 26 Mar 1711 G189r excused from office of First Renter Warden for one year 26 Mar 1712 G198v excused from office of Assistant Renter Warden for one year 26 Mar 1713 G207v fined for First Renter Warden 6 May 1717 G250v Joshua Bradley is bound to him

See also BARETT

BARRISSE, Henry – see following entry

BARRISSE/BARRISTE, John 4 Jun 1694 F208v son of Henry Barrisse of Flitton, Northamptonshire, husbandman; bound to Robert Roberts 2 Jun 1701 G60v freed by Robert Roberts

BARROW, Daniel 26 Mar 1686 F54r elected waterman 4 Apr 1687 F81v elected waterman 1709–1717 bargemaster

BARROW, John, snr 1682–1690 and 1692–1697 bargemaster (though his election is not recorded for 1691, he is described as continuing in post in 1692)

BARROW, John, jnr 26 Mar 1686 F54r elected waterman 4 Apr 1687 F81v elected waterman 1698–1708 bargemaster

See also BARGE, BARGEMASTER

BARROW, Nathaniel 8 Jun 1691 F154v watchmaker in Cornhill; to be summoned for not paying quarterage arrears

BARTHOLOMEW, Isaac 7 Apr 1701 G58r freed by patrimony

BARTHOLOMEW, Richard 7 Apr 1701 G58r his son Isaac is freed by patrimony; arrears of quarterage paid

BARTLETT, Samuel 11 Nov 1695 F235v servant to Christopher Coningsby; freed

BARTLETT, Thomas 2 Mar 1695/6 F240r servant to William Baker; freed

BARTON, Edward 6 Jun 1681 E113r articles between him and S.C. re. psalms to be sealed

See also PSALMS

BARTON, George 7 Sep 1702 G80v bound to John Williams, 7 years

BARTON, William 7 Sep 1696 F248v deed produced whereby Barton or heirs are to be paid £10 if his version of the psalms has sold well; inquiry ordered as to payment 5 Oct 1696 F250v to be paid £10 for his psalms

See also PSALMS

BASKERVILE, Ann 26 Mar 1694 F201v deceased; Richard Fairbank elected to her pension

BASKERVILE/BASKERVILLE, Anthony 20 Dec 1689 F128v cloathed, promising payment of fine 1 Feb 1691/2 F165r John Towse succeeds in delaying legal proceedings against Baskervile for not paying his Livery fine for 6 months

BASKERVILE, John, snr – see following entry

BASKERVILE, John, jnr 1 Jul 1695 F228v son of John Baskervile, Clerkenwell, stationer; bound to Daniel Moggs

BASKETT/BASKET, John (I) 5 May 1690 F135r cloathed and promises payment of fine 2 Dec 1695 F237v Henry Symonds is bound to him 26 Mar 1696 F241r elected Renter Warden with Oliver Elliston 1 Apr 1697 F260v to speak to the cardmakers about money needed for a Paper Act test case 3 Jul 1699 G27v Henry Taylor is bound to him 7 Sep 1702 G80v Robert Hayes is bound to him 9 Sep 1706 G134v agreement with Oxford University over printing of Clarendon's History 7 Oct 1706 G135r elected Assistant 3 Feb 1706/7 G137v elected to Mrs Collins's £80 share. Requested that Capt. Edward Darrell be his senior in all the books 7 Apr 1707 G140v elected to Samuel Sprint's £160 share 1 Dec 1707 G147r committee to decide whether to take his Clarendon in folio 3 Dec 1707 G148r committee decides not to take any part of his impression of Clarendon in folio 9 Feb 1707/8 G148v report of committee re. taking his version of Clarendon in folio read and agreed to. Proposals re. impression in octavo debated and referred to Master, Wardens and Stock-keepers 26 Mar 1708 G151r further members added to committee to consider his proposals re. impression of Clarendon in octavo 30 Mar 1708 G151r committee decides not to take his octavo impression of Clarendon 12 Apr 1708 G151v Court agrees with decision of committee not to take his octavo impression of Clarendon 3 Jul 1708 G154r competes unsuccessfully for Under Warden 6 Sep 1708 G157r Clerk to attend him to obtain the answer of Mead and others. To be given first refusal on remaining books of Clarendon 2 Jul 1709 G166v elected Under Warden 7 Nov 1709 G172r his apprentice Robert Hayes is freed 1 May 1710 G179r at his own suggestion to pay £30 on S.C.'s behalf towards costs for obtaining Act of Parliament 1 Jul 1710 G181r elected Under Warden 31 Jan 1710/11 G186v his apprentice Richard Watkins is freed 10 Sep 1711 G194r committee to meet him and Williams re. ensuring English Stock is protected despite granting of Oxford Stock privileges to another 1 Oct 1711 G194v no agreement in meeting between Master and Baskett and Williams concerning English Stock 7 Apr 1712 G199r on making up the balance of his account to be paid £100 with interest in October. His apprentice Samuel Ashurst is freed 4 Aug 1712 G202v committee appointed to settle matter in difference between S.C. and himself and Williams re. printing at Oxford and English Stock 1 Sep 1712 G203r request for £50 more rent than was paid to Oxford, and liberty to print Psalms and to have the £30 p.a. paid to S.C. by Norton, in addition to £200 p.a. for printing 6 Oct 1712 G204r report read of committee who has met with him. Agreed he should be paid £200 p.a. on the same account as the S.C. had used to pay the University of Oxford; he in turn is to pay money to English Stock for printing Psalms 4 Jul 1713 G211r only person qualified to be elected Upper Warden. Fined for two years' Upper Warden 7 Dec 1713 G215r Robert Micklewright is bound to him 22 Dec 1713 G215v fined for Master to preserve seniority 5 Apr 1714 G218r John Brinckworth is bound to him 3 Jul 1714 G220r elected Master and took oath 6 Dec 1714 G224r Henry Davies is bound to him 2 Jul 1715 G230r elected Master by casting vote of Upper Warden 22 Dec 1715 G235v William Serjeant is bound to him 30 Jun 1716 G241r elected Master but excused 4 Feb 1716/17 G246v to be new trustee of S.C.'s property

See also the two following entries

BASKETT, John (II) 1 Nov 1714 G223r son of Master; freed by patrimony and cloathed

BASKETT, Thomas 1 Apr 1717 G249v son of John, is bound to John Williams, 7 years

BASSETT, John 12 Nov 1683 F5r elected to Henry Hills's £160 share after lengthy argument re. his suitability, occasioned by his collusion with John Starkey to force himself onto Court

BASSETT, Judith 3 May 1697 F262r freed by patrimony

BASSETT/BASSET, Mrs 6 Dec 1703 G99v widow of Thomas Bassett. Repayment of money secured by assignment of her husband's Assistant's share to William Rawlins to be recorded in S.C.'s books 2 Jun 1712 G200r deceased; her Assistant's share disposed of to Thomas Hodgkins

BASSETT, Richard   3 May 1697 F262r freed by William Crooke   4 Sep 1699 G30r cloathed

BASSETT/BASSET, Thomas   4 Dec 1682 E160v assigned one fifth of the 'History of France' [i.e. François Eudes de Mézeray, *A General Chronological History of France*] by William Cadman   3 Dec 1683 F6r to pay S.C. £8 out of his next dividend, 1/6 of the expenses which he and the five others demanding Court membership had cost the Company   19 Dec 1683 F7r Court considers his request for his dividend not to be stopped until his co-offenders are called to account   20 Dec 1683 F7v petition considered; ordered that the sequestration order be suspended and the dividend paid next dividend day   7 Apr 1684 F14r on the list of loyal Assistants presented to the Crown   29 Jan 1684/5 F29v with Simon Miller, to give a dinner to Court members or pay a penalty of £10   7 May 1685 (W) confirmed as member of new Livery   7 Dec 1685 F47v in Benjamin Harris's partnership for printing the proceedings of the Westminster Parliament   3 Jul 1686 F59v asks to fine for one year's Under Wardenship on account of being abroad   21 Feb 1686/7 F71v misunderstanding over the procedure for making complaints about Treasurer's orders; to negotiate with committee   4 Apr 1687 F81r among those appointed to audit Renter Wardens' accounts   2 Jul 1687 F85v elected Under Warden; voted that he should not be allowed to fine   7 Nov 1687 F94v agreement between John Gadbury, Capt. John Baker and Bassett re. almanacks printed for charity   5 Dec 1687 F94v to be summoned with Henry Harefinch to answer the complaint of Edward Brewster and Nathaniel Ranew. Orders of 12 Nov and 3 Dec read re. his reimbursing £8 upon admission to the Stock when he was fined for trying to join Court. To have £3 refunded to equalise his payment with those of Henry Mortlock, Thomas Parkhurst and William Miller   9 Jan 1687/8 F97r to be summoned to answer the complaint of Brewster and Ranew   5 Mar 1687/8 F99r maintains right to 'Turkish History' of which Brewster and Ranew claim a moiety; they are allowed to sue him   11 Oct 1688 F108v restored to Livery   4 Feb 1688/9 F112v re-elected Assistant   6 Jul 1689 F121r competes unsuccessfully for Upper Warden   4 Nov 1689 F126v to be added to the Corporation Act committee   2 Dec 1689 F127r competes unsuccessfully for the late Ralph Smith's £320 share   3 Feb 1689/90 F128v with Henry Mortlock, added to committee appointed to negotiate with Master re. Cambridge   11 Apr 1690 F133v requests that John Williams should not be considered for the position of Second Renter Warden because he lives out of town   5 May 1690 F135r chosen to audit Renter Wardens' accounts with William Rawlins   5 Jun 1690 F135v re-appointed Assistant   5 Jul 1690 F138v competes unsuccessfully for Upper Warden   7 Jul 1690 F139r elected to the late Dorothy Thrale's £320 share   9 Feb 1690/1 F148r chosen to audit Renter Wardens' accounts with John Bellinger   6 Apr 1691 F152v Master to supervise Clerk drawing up a mortgage of Bassett's £320 share to William Rawlins for £250   4 May 1691 F153v asks for 40s to be paid out of Poor Box for discharging William Birch out of Ludgate prison   4 Jul 1691 F156v elected Upper Warden   23 Jun 1692 F172v competes unsuccessfully for Upper Warden   4 Jul 1692 F174r to augment Oxford committee   26 Jul 1692 F175v to deliver all S.C. keys to Upper Warden   3 Apr 1693 F185v as a co-proprietor of the English Josephus, complains that Roger L'Estrange's new translation will affect his sales   1 Jul 1693 F189r elected Upper Warden   7 May 1694 F204r fails to appear as Upper Warden, so an assembly to approve revised ordinances cannot take place   9 May 1694 F204v his circumstances incapacitate him from serving as Upper Warden so Henry Mortlock is elected in his stead   20 Dec 1694 F216r William Rawlins is paid the dividend from Bassett's £320 share which is mortgaged to him   3 Aug 1696 F248r bankrupt; commissioners desire a catalogue of copies entered to him; granted on condition they pay the search fee. Court finds that his share has for a long time been mortgaged to William

Rawlins, now in the country; consideration deferred until Rawlins' return   7 Sep 1696
F248v bankrupt; Rawlins gives details of Bassett's assignment of his £320 share to
him   7 Dec 1696 F252v allowed to make second mortgage of £320 share up to full
value; S.C. discharged from all demands on share by commissioners of bankruptcy   22
Dec 1696 F254r discharge of his share by William Battersby, one of the commissioners
in bankruptcy, is approved   3 May 1697 F262r his apprentice John Doleman is
freed   13 Apr 1698 G6r share to be disposed of unless he can show cause to the
contrary, as mortgage payments not made to William Rawlins   2 May 1698 G7r
disposal of share in English Stock to be deferred to next General Court

BASSILL, Richard   2 Nov 1702 G83r Robert Harman is bound to him   6 Sep 1708
G157v bookseller; John Rayner is bound to him   5 May 1712 G199v his apprentice
Robert Harman is freed   6 May 1717 G250v Richard Longbotham is bound to him.
His apprentice John Rayner is freed

BATEMAN, Christopher   3 Jun 1689 F119r cloathed   1 Aug 1692 (W) his
apprentice John Hartley is freed   12 Sep 1692 F179r master of newly made freeman
John Hartley of Gray's Inn, whose details are sent to Lord Chamberlain   13 Apr 1702
G70r elected Assistant Renter Warden   3 May 1703 G89v his apprentice Thomas
Hodson is freed   12 Nov 1705 G125r buttery warehouse to be let to him   7 Apr 1707
G140v elected to Jasper Harmer's £40 share   6 Oct 1707 G145v bookseller; Stephen
Bateman, his son, is bound to him   1 Mar 1710/11 G187v elected Stock-keeper for
Yeomanry and sworn in   5 Mar 1710/11 G188r his apprentice Joshua Worrall is
freed   13 Apr 1713 G208v elected to John Overton's £80 share   3 May 1714 G219r
John Atkinson turned over to him

BATEMAN, John   4 Aug 1707 G144v bound to Daniel Midwinter, 7 years   7 Feb
1714/15 G225r freed by Daniel Midwinter

BATEMAN, Stephen (I)   17 Oct 1687 F93r elected Assistant Renter Warden   1 Mar
1687/8 F98r summoned to next Court to be nominated for Assistant   5 Mar 1687/8
F99r elected Assistant   2 Jul 1688 F103v to advise Christopher Wilkinson on laying
out £10 for William Jacob's relief   2 Jul 1688 F104r elected to the late Blanche
Pawlett's £40 share   6 Aug 1688 F106r tells Court that he and Wilkinson have laid out
£10 for Jacob's relief   12 Apr 1692 F169r elected to Richard Simpson's £80 share   7
Dec 1696 F252v competes unsuccessfully for the late Mary Felton's £160 share   5 Jul
1697 F264v elected to Mrs Frances Clarke's £160 share and sworn in

BATEMAN, Stephen (II)   6 Oct 1707 G145v bound to Christopher his father, 7
years

BATEMAN, William   26 Mar 1681 E108r to have £20 credit in English Stock and give
a bond to the Treasurer for its payment   4 Sep 1682 E157v petition for four more
years to repay his debt to Stock to be considered by Treasurer   6 Mar 1703/4 G103v
Henry Porton turned over to him (repeated under 3 Apr 1704)

BATERSBY, Katherine   26 Mar 1702 G69r freed by patrimony
See also BATTERSBY

BATES, Charles   6 Nov 1704 G113r Samuel Savage is bound to him   2 Dec 1706
G136v Samuel Savage turned over from him to Alexander Milbourne   4 Sep 1710
G183v of Pye Corner, bookseller; John Clerke is bound to him   4 Dec 1710 G185v to
be served with a copy of the Writ of Execution against Benjamin Harris

BATES, Richard   6 Sep 1714 G221v son of Thomas; bound to William Haddon, 7
years

BATES, Thomas – see previous entry

BATES, Timothy 4 Oct 1686 F64v elected to livery 8 Nov 1686 F67r cloathed 1 Mar 1687/8 F97v expelled from Livery by order of Lord Mayor 11 Oct 1688 F108v restored to Livery

BATES, William 2 Oct 1699 G31v freed by Charles Baker

BATESON, Mary 21 Mar 1694/5 F219r takes over Elizabeth Wright's pension 27 Sep 1699 G30v pensioner, deceased; Dina Sedgwick is given her pension

BATH AND WELLS, BISHOP OF – see KEN, Thomas

BATLEY, Jeremiah 4 Jul 1709 G167v bound to Thomas Guy, 7 years 3 Mar 1711/12 G197r turned over from Thomas Guy to Thomas Varnam

BATTERSBY, Diana 27 Sep 1698 G13v to receive the pension due to Thomas Egglesfeild, having provided for him 1 Mar 1713/14 G216v who used to clean the Hall, deceased 24 Mar 1713/14 G217r deceased; William Barlow is given her pension

BATTERSBY, Robert 7 Sep 1691 F160r cloathed; promises to pay half his Livery fine in six months and the other half in a year, his father being present 3 Jul 1699 G27v St John Baker is bound to him

BATTERSBY, Susanna 1 Mar 1707/8 G150r her son Winstanley is bound to her 2 May 1709 G165r her apprentice St John Baker is freed 5 Apr 1714 G218r John Walton is bound to her

BATTERSBY, William 22 Dec 1696 F254r assignee of commissioners for statute of bankruptcy against Thomas Bassett; discharge to S.C. of share approved

BATTERSBY, Winstanley 1 Mar 1707/8 G150r bound to Susanna, his mother, 7 years

See also BATERSBY

BATTERTON, [ ] [i.e. Betterton?] 5 Mar 1704/5 G117r the player, apprentice to Matthew Rhodes; query as to whether he is free of S.C.

BAUKIN, George 2 Jul 1709 G166v carpenter; employed in repairs to Morphew's house

BAWDEN, Thomas 5 Aug 1689 F122v Sarah Eversden is shortly to be married to him and so is due a bond from S.C. for £20 plus interest

BAXTER, [ ] 2 Dec 1706 G136v with Andrew Toake, to examine and correct all classical authors belonging to English Stock

BAXTER, Benjamin 9 Feb 1707/8 G149r bound to Emmanuel Matthews, 7 years

BAXTER, George 6 Aug 1705 G122v bound to Thomas Franklin

BAXTER, Robert 24 May 1710 G179v bound to Robert Hayes, 7 years

BAYLEY, John 1 Dec 1707 G147v freed by Isaac Cleave

BAYLEY, Richard, snr – see following entry

BAYLEY, Richard, jnr 12 Nov 1716 G244v son of Richard, is bound to Edward Davis, 7 years

BAYLEY, Thomas 4 Jul 1698 G11r bound to David Edwards, 7 years

BAYNAM, George 9 Sep 1700 G45r bound to John Wyatt, 7 years

BEACHAM – see BEAUCHAMP

BEADLE 1681–1691 Randall Taylor 5 Dec 1681 E140v to be paid £5 for cleaning the Common Hall and Court room 8 May 1682 E153v complaints about Randall Taylor give rise to a list of orders and rules for the Beadle 7 Aug 1682 E156v to be paid £6 for cleaning 6 Aug 1683 F3r to have a new gown 22 May 1685 F37r to deliver public notice of James II's commission re. licensing to all S.C. members   6 Jul 1685 F40v Warden to pay arrears of his salary due from Renter Warden   7 Nov 1687 F94r to deliver a ticket to all printers giving them notice to send a copy of every book they print for King's Library and universities   26 Mar 1690 F131v neglected to summon pensioners due to receive quarterly charity. To have his salary suspended until he does so   8 Jun 1691 F154v salary to be paid by Wardens instead of Renter Wardens   5 Oct 1691 F161r to place members in order of seniority on festival days   1692–1702 Nicholas Hooper   4 Jul 1692 F173r to provide a list of all S.C. members not free of the City to Town Clerk   7 Aug 1693 F190v Randall Taylor offered freedom now he no longer needs as Beadle to be disenfranchised from S.C.   2 Apr 1694 F202r henceforth to be paid out of quarterage   4 Jun 1694 F208r his bill for writing in several S.C. matters to be considered and a suitable sum paid   10 Sep 1694 F212r mayoral precept read checking that the Beadle has summoned all S.C. Livery to the election of sheriffs   26 Mar 1697 F258v committee to settle his fee   1 Apr 1697 F260v to tell those named to solicit for donations towards Paper Act test case of their duties   3 May 1697 F262r fees committee to inspect his bill and report   5 Jul 1697 F264v £10 due to him from Christopher Grandorge to be deducted out of the £24 p.a. due to him   2 Aug 1697 F265v £5 owed to the Beadle by Christopher Grandorge to be paid off, together with other debts to S.C. officials   4 Oct 1697 F268r table of fees read and authorised. To draw up accounts with Treasurer of all matters between them relating to S.C. before next Court   7 Mar 1697/8 G4v to give a list of the persons receiving the charity of a benefactor's gift of bread and money   5 Sep 1698 G14r accounts with S.C. to be made up by the Treasurer for the next Court day   4 Mar 1699/1700 G36v subpoenaed to appear as witness at Taunton Assizes   8 Apr 1700 G39r to ensure that no boys play in the S.C.'s garden nor pigeons be kept there   3 Jun 1700 G40v a new silver head to be made for the top of his staff   5 Aug 1700 G44r to have a new gown for 13 August   7 Oct 1700 G45v his quarterly bills to be entered into the Warden's instructions   5 Oct 1702 G81r Nicholas Hooper deceased; his eldest son to officiate until new Beadle chosen at Christmas   29 Jan 1702/3 G84v election postponed until 26 March   1703–1717 Henry Million   5 Apr 1703 G88r young Hooper paid for officiating as Beadle since his father's death   3 Jul 1704 G109v to be paid 40s for extraordinary service and for this year's attendance   5 Sep 1709 G170r list of fees for binding and making free to be prepared for next Court Day   4 May 1713 G209v Counsel's opinion to be sought concerning orders of Court that he should be disenfranchised so as to be a good witness for the S.C.   7 Nov 1715 G234r John England required to pay Beadle's fees incurred while suing him for non-payment of Livery fine

BEADLE, Rebecca   4 Mar 1688/9 F114r deceased; her £80 share voted to Richard Chiswell   5 Aug 1689 F122v her executors complain that Richard Chiswell still owes them for the share

BEALE, Edward   9 Sep 1706 G134v freed by James Dover

BEALE, William   5 Sep 1698 G14v bound to William Hensman   7 Jun 1708 G153v freed by William Hensman

BEAMONT, [   ]   26 Jan 1703/4 G100v brazier of Boston; defendant in S.C.'s bill in Chancery

BEARD, William   26 Mar 1697 F258v comes second in election of a Clerk to replace Christopher Grandorge

BEARDSWORTH, Thomas   2 Nov 1702 G83r bound to William Holland, 7 years

BEARDWELL, Benjamin   5 Feb 1693/4 F199r Josiah Hodges is bound to him for seven years   5 Feb 1699/1700 G35r James Edwards is bound to him   3 Mar 1700/1 G57r his apprentice Hedges [i.e. Hodges] is freed   7 Apr 1701 G58r cloathed; John

Shenton is bound to him   3 Dec 1705 G126r his apprentice Richard Mendall is freed. William Corke turned over to him   7 Oct 1706 G135r John Ogden is bound to him   3 Feb 1706/7 G138r Samuel Andrews turned over to him from Samuel Bridge   7 Aug 1710 G183r his apprentice Samuel Andrews is freed

BEARDWELL, Edward   1 Dec 1707 G147v bound to Abel Roper, 7 years

BEAUCHAMP/BEAUCHAMPE/BEACHAM, Gilbert   7 May 1694 F204r son of the late John Beacham of Kidderminster, Worcestershire; bound to John Miller   19 Jun 1701 G61r freed by Emmanuel Matthews and John Miller   4 Mar 1705/6 G128v purchased counterfeit psalters from James Drinkell and William Palmer and copies of 'The Compleat Schoolmistress' [i.e. *The First Book for Children, or the Compleat School-mistress*] from Gwillam at Bristol fair   1 Apr 1706 G130v committee to consider matter of counterfeit psalters and 'Compleat Schoolmistress' sold to him

BEAUCHAMP/BEACHAM, John   7 May 1694 F204r late of Kidderminster, Worcestershire; his son Gilbert is bound to John Miller

BEAUCHAMP, John   4 Sep 1699 G30v bound to Robert Limpany, 7 years

BEAVER, Samuel   2 May 1709 G165r bound to John Green, 7 years

BEAVER/BEVER/BEVOR, Thomas   1 Feb 1696/7 F255r re-summoned re. cloath-ing   3 May 1697 F261v cloathed and promises to pay fine at two six-monthly intervals   4 Oct 1697 F268v Thomas Smith is bound to him   4 May 1702 G70v Thomas Smith turned over from him   8 Nov 1703 G97r elected to John Richardson's £100 share (*sic*)   27 Mar 1704 G104v fined for First Renter Warden   3 Apr 1704 G106r Abraham Cotterell is bound to him   3 Oct 1709 G171r of Fleet Street, stationer; Joel Stephens is bound to him

BECKINGTON, John   8 May 1704 G106v bound to Andrew Mayhew, 7 years   2 Jul 1711 G192v freed by the widow of Andrew Mayhew

BECKLEY, Simon   1697–1717 Clerk   26 Mar 1697 F258v elected to replace Christopher Grandorge as Clerk from a field of six; apprised of duties, sworn in and ordered to give bond   5 Aug 1706 G134r Beckley and Bowyer to ensure that each tenant of Corporation produces a receipt for rent paid and that a rental be made   4 Jun 1711 G190v thanks of S.C. for service concerning bill in House of Commons for duty on almanacks

BEDCOCK, Joseph   7 Jun 1697 F263r bound to James Walker

BEDDER, Thomas   3 Nov 1712 G205r freed by patrimony

BEDDOW, John   27 Sep 1715 G233r replaces Jane Mawson in pension book

BEDFORD, Timothy   7 Nov 1698 G16r bound to Lawrence Hatsell, 7 years

BEDLAM   26 Mar 1690 F131r Mrs Billingsley petitions for charity since her husband Benjamin is detained there

BEESLEY, Charles, snr – see following entry

BEESLEY, Charles, jnr   4 Aug 1712 G202v son of Charles, is bound to Robert Gifford, 7 years

BELL, [   ]   29 Jul 1700 G43v a commissioner for the bankruptcy committee to deal with him about producing Norton's patents

BELL, [   ]   2 Aug 1714 G221r son of Thomas, is bound to Ichabod Dawkes, 7 years

BELL, Alexander   1 Sep 1712 G203r freed by Dryden Leach

BELL, Andrew   4 Mar 1694/5 F219r freed by Thomas Benskin   1 Jul 1695 F228v Hugh Montgomery is bound to him   11 Nov 1695 F235r elected to cloathing and

summoned   2 Dec 1695 F237r cloathed   4 Jul 1702 G77r his apprentice Hugh Montgomery is freed   4 Mar 1705/6 G129r Thomas Dryer is bound to him   26 Mar 1709
G163r excused from serving as Renter Warden   5 Mar 1710/11 G188r Thomas Dryer
turned over from him to Edmund Curll   5 May 1712 G199v elected Renter Warden   13
Apr 1713 G208v his apprentice Thomas Dryer is freed

BELL, Charles   7 May 1705 G120r bound to Aaron Rymes, 8 years

BELL, Edward   8 Jun 1696 F243r freed by John Grover   1 Apr 1706 G131r Charles
Round is bound to him

BELL, Richard   9 Apr 1711 G189v bound to Edmund Powell, 7 years   1 Oct 1716
G244r turned over from Edward [i.e. Edmund?] Powell to Thomas Sharpe

BELL, Thomas   2 Aug 1714 G221r his son (unnamed) is bound to Ichabod Dawkes, 7
years

BELLENGER – see BELLINGER

BELLINGER/BELLENGER, John   20 Jun 1681 E113r Crown mandate that he should
become an Assistant   5 Sep 1681 E129r elected to John Hancock's £80 share   6 Feb
1681/2 E143v elected to Thomas Newcomb's £160 share   7 Mar 1682/3 E166r failure
to dine with Lord Mayor to be considered at next Court   3 Dec 1683 F6r gives 20s to
Poor Box for his failure to dine with Sir William Pritchard, late Lord Mayor   1 Mar
1683/4 F9r elected Stock-keeper for Assistants with Edward Brewster   7 Apr 1684
F13v on the list of loyal Assistants presented to the Crown   5 Jul 1684 F19v chosen to
audit Warden's accounts with John Macock, Henry Herringman and Henry Clarke   1
Sep 1684 F23v tells Court that Peter Parker and Thomas Guy are printing 25,000
books of psalms in Oxford   2 Mar 1684/5 F31v elected Stock-keeper for Assistants
with Robert Scott   26 Mar 1685 F32r appointed with Robert Scott to audit Warden's
accounts   7 May 1685 (W) confirmed as member of new Livery   4 Jul 1685 F39v
fined for two years of Under Warden because of want of choice for Upper Warden.
Elected Upper Warden   6 Jul 1685 F40v Robert Clavell is elected Stock-keeper in his
place   2 Nov 1685 F45v elected to the late James Cotterell's £320 share on Master's
casting vote   3 Jul 1686 F58v elected Master when Herringman stands down. Fined
for second year of Upper Warden   21 Oct 1686 (W) letter from him and John Baker
requesting that Obadiah Blagrave give a bond for £1000 for carrying out his duties   2
Jul 1687 F85v competes unsuccessfully for Master   1 Aug 1687 F87v debate concerning precedence between Bellinger, John Towse and Henry Herringman referred to next
Court   5 Sep 1687 F88v Towse to pay a £5 fine and then take precedence of both
Herringman and Bellinger   5 Dec 1687 F96r to deliver up all papers concerning S.C.
to Under Warden   11 Oct 1688 F108v restored to Assistants   27 Nov 1688 F110v
among those chosen to audit Renter Wardens' accounts   1 Mar 1688/9 F113v elected
Stock-keeper for Assistants with Thomas Dring   6 Jul 1689 F121v among those chosen
to audit Warden's accounts   7 Oct 1689 F124r John Towse claims precedence over
Bellinger and Herringman and confusion discovered over order of 5 Sep 1687; deferred   3 Feb 1689/90 F129v elected Stock-keeper for Assistants with Henry Mortlock   1
Mar 1689/90 F129v elected Stock-keeper for Assistants with Henry Mortlock   5 May
1690 F134v to stand in for Master at a Court of Aldermen on 6 May   5 Jul 1690
F138r among those chosen to audit Warden's accounts   9 Feb 1690/1 F148r chosen
to audit Renter Wardens' accounts with Thomas Bassett   2 Mar 1690/1 F150v elected
Stock-keeper for Assistants with Christopher Wilkinson   6 Apr 1691 F152r gives his
name to agreement compiled with Oxford   4 Jul 1691 F156v among those chosen to
audit Renter Wardens' accounts. Competes unsuccessfully for Master   1 Feb 1691/2
F164v his part in concluding Oxford agreement is detailed   1 Mar 1691/2 F165v
elected Stock-keeper for Assistants with Christopher Wilkinson. Capt. John Williams

transfers the mortgage of his £160 share from Mrs Webb to Bellinger   7 Mar 1691/2
F166v indemnified by transfer of mortgage of Stock estate against engagement with
Oxford   2 May 1691/2 F170r declaration of trust re. Oxford from him, Master and
Henry Mortlock read and approved   23 Jun 1692 F172v competes unsuccessfully for
Master   6 Feb 1692/3 F184r asks that John Williams's £160 share be disposed of at
next Court to satisfy a debt to him of £150   1 Jul 1693 F189r competes unsuccessfully
for Master   3 Jul 1693 F189v elected Master when Henry Herringman is excused
because of ill health   6 Oct 1693 F193r seals and executes deed for new Stock at
Oxford and Cambridge with Henry Mortlock   2 Jul 1694 F210r augments drain committee negotiating with St Martin's Ludgate   6 Aug 1694 F211r deceased; executors
ordered to pay his share of the charge for the 1693 election day feast   6 May 1695
F222r Henry Mortlock elected to his £320 share when Bellinger's executrix Mrs
Johnson tells Court of his wife's remarriage

BELLINGER, Mrs – see preceding entry

BELSOE, Thomas   8 Nov 1703 G97r bound to Samuel Walker, 7 years

BEMBRIDGE/BENBRIDGE, William   4 Sep 1704 G112r bound to Thomas Crane, 7
years   6 Oct 1712 G204v freed by Thomas Crane

BENBOW, Benjamin   3 Jul 1710 G182r freed by Benjamin Motte

BENBRIDGE – see BEMBRIDGE

BENDIGLE, [ ]   6 Sep 1680 E103v schedule to be made of his goods in Taylor's
custody

BENEFACTORS   2 May 1681 E111r Lamb's bequest of 2s per week to St Faith's in
arrears   7 Mar 1682/3 E166r Clerk to draw up two tables of names of all benefactors,
to be hung in Hall and Court room   2 Apr 1683 E168r committee to inquire into
benefactors and their gifts and draw up a perfect table thereof   3 Feb 1689/90 F129r
committee to compile an accurate list of S.C. benefactors, pursuant on Court orders of
7 March 1682 and   2 April 1683   3 Mar 1689/90 F130v committee report that they
think the benefactors' list should be written in gold in wainscot panelling towards upper
end of hall   7 Jul 1690 F138v committee dealing with tabling the benefactors to be
enlarged   25 Sep 1690 F143r committee's list of benefactors approved and ordered to
be hung in the Hall   3 Nov 1690 F145v preface or title of list to be agreed upon at next
Court   1 Dec 1690 F146r list to be entitled 'The Names of the Benefactors of this S.C.'
and to be written out for painter, Trevett   7 Mar 1697/8 G4v committee to consider
how benefactor's gift of bread and money should be distributed. Baker who serves S.C.
with bread for the said charity to give a receipt

BENNET/BENNIT/BENNITT, Joseph   7 May 1685 (W) confirmed as member of new
Livery 26 Mar 1688 F99v excused Renter Wardenship for this year in response to a
letter from Sir Roger L'Estrange   26 Mar 1689 F115v elected Assistant Renter
Warden   6 May 1689 F117r excused First Renter Wardenship

See also BENNETT, BENNITT

BENNETT, [ ]   12 Nov 1694 F214v summons Mrs Redmaine over entering caveats
against Richard Busby's grammars, authorised to Bennett by Busby; deferred   3 Dec
1694 F215v gives further proof of title to Busby's works; entered to him with a salvo   1
Apr 1697 F260v to ask booksellers, printers and paper manufacturers of St Paul's
Churchyard for money towards Paper Act test case

BENNETT, Francis   3 Jul 1699 G27v bound to Robert Whitledge, 7 years   3 Mar
1706/7 G139r freed by Robert Whitledge

BENNETT, Isum   5 Aug 1706 G134r freed by William Cross

BENNETT, John (I)   4 Dec 1693 F196v John Hastings is bound to him

BENNETT, John (II)   6 Apr 1696 F242r servant to William Fryer; freed   2 Aug 1708 G156v John Miflin is bound to him   8 Nov 1708 G158v Richard Loader turned over to him from Elizabeth Thomas   6 Mar 1709/10 G176v Gunsmith, of Minories; Thomas Greaves is bound to him   5 Mar 1710/11 G188r John Miflin turned over from him to William Drewett

BENNETT, John (III)   4 May 1702 G71r bound to Adam Winch, 7 years

BENNETT/BENNET, Margaret   2 Apr 1694 F202v widow; Thomas Howlatt jnr is bound to her for seven years   6 Jul 1700 G43r Andrew Norman is bound to her   5 May 1701 G59r James Burnaby is bound to her   6 Mar 1703/4 G103v John Driver is bound to her   3 Nov 1707 G146v printer; Francis Reading is bound to her   6 Jun 1709 G165v Thomas Howlatt is freed by her   4 Jul 1709 G167v John Driver and Francis Reading turned over from her to Thomas Howlatt

BENNETT, Mary   7 Feb 1698/9 G2ov John Bowes is bound to her

BENNETT, Mrs   6 Feb 1709/10 G175r remarried; her £160 share disposed of to William Freeman

BENNETT, Robert, snr   6 Dec 1708 G159v of the Minories; his son Robert is bound to him for 7 years

BENNETT, Robert, jnr   6 Dec 1708 G159v bound to Robert, his father, 7 years

BENNETT/BENNET/BENNITT, Thomas   3 Jun 1689 F119r cloathed   7 Mar 1697/8 G5r William Ward is bound to him   2 Oct 1699 G31r elected to Mrs Bentley's £40 share   1 Mar 1699/1700 G36r elected Stock-keeper for Yeomanry   1 Mar 1700/1 G56r elected Stock-keeper for Yeomanry   26 Mar 1701 G57v elected Assistant Renter Warden   5 Oct 1702 G81r elected to Awnsham Churchill's £80 share   1 Mar 1702/3 G86r elected Stock-keeper for Livery   5 Apr 1703 G88r Henry Clements is bound to him   8 Nov 1703 G97r his apprentice Jonah Bowyer is freed   2 Mar 1703/4 G102v elected Stock-keeper for Livery   6 Mar 1703/4 G103v elected to Richard Simpson's £160 share. His £80 share disposed of to Robert Everingham   30 Jun 1704 G108v arbiter for S.C. in negotiations with Benjamin Tooke   5 Feb 1704/5 G114v matters in dispute between S.C. and Samuel Buckley to be referred to Bennett   1 Mar 1704/5 G116r elected Stock-keeper for Livery   7 May 1705 G119v to meet with Benjamin Tooke re. accounts of Tate and Brady's Psalms   4 Jun 1705 G120v elected Assistant. His apprentice William Ward is freed. Royston Meredith is bound to him   16 Oct 1705 G124v reference to bill of fare for Lord Mayor's Dinner when he was Renter Warden   1 Mar 1705/6 G128v elected Stock-keeper for Assistants   9 Sep 1706 G134v deceased   4 Nov 1706 G136r Royston Meredith turned over from him to Richard Wilkins   7 Apr 1707 G141r his late servant, Henry Clements, is freed

BENNETT, William   2 Oct 1699 G31v freed by William Fryer

See also BENNET, BENNITT

BENNITT, Thomas   4 May 1691 F153v appears with note in George Calvert's hand requesting to surrender his £160 share to Bennitt; voted that he cannot do so

See also BENNET, BENNETT

BENSKIN, Thomas   4 Mar 1694/5 F218v Andrew Bell, his apprentice, freed   11 Nov 1695 F235r cloathed   27 Mar 1704 G104v fined for First Renter Warden   6 Nov 1704 G113r Jonas Browne is bound to him   4 Feb 1705/6 G127r elected to Thomas Horne's £40 share

BENSON, Edward   1 Dec 1701 G66r bound to John Walthoe, 7 years

BENSON, John, snr – see following entry

BENSON, John, jnr   2 Mar 1712/13 G207r son of John, is bound to William Heathcott, 7 years   4 Jul 1715 G231r turned over from William Heathcott to James Read

BENSON, Robert   16 Jun 1684 F17v of Lincoln's Inn Fields and son of William Benson, a late member of S.C.; freed

BENSON, William   16 Jun 1684 F17v deceased; his son is freed

BENTLEY, Mrs   2 Oct 1699 G31r deceased; her £40 share disposed of to Thomas Bennett

BENTLEY/BENTLY, Richard (I)   25 Jun 1684 F18r of Covent Garden; is freed upon application to the Court   2 Nov 1685 F46r Bentley, Robert Scott and George Wells complain that Richard Royston has printed their 'Life of Dr Hammond' [by John Fell]   7 Dec 1685 F47v Wells, on his behalf, accuses Royston of printing their 'Life of Dr. Hammond'; deferred   1 Feb 1685/6 F50v Royston is allowed further time to discuss with Wells and Bentley   4 Oct 1686 F64v elected to livery   8 Nov 1686 F67r summoned re. cloathing   6 Dec 1686 F68v to be sued for refusal of cloathing and failure to attend Court to explain why   20 Dec 1686 F69v appears, apologises and is cloathed   1 Aug 1687 F87r assigned part of 'Three translations or books' (itemised) by Sir Roger L'Estrange   3 Apr 1693 F186r elected Assistant Renter Warden and summoned   10 Apr 1693 F186v fined for First Renter Warden   7 May 1694 F203r elected to the £40 share surrendered by Samuel Keeble   5 Jun 1699 G25v his apprentice Edmund Rumball is freed

BENTLEY, Richard (II)   8 Dec 1705 G126v Master of Trinity College, Cambridge; signatory to articles between S.C. and University

BERESFORD, John   5 May 1707 G142r bookbinder; John Lardner is bound to him
See also BERRESFORD, BERRISFORD

BERNARD, [   ]   1 Sep 1684 F23r reported for dealing in scandalous books (W) 'Gregorio Leti and Arnauld'

BERRESFORD, Edmond   8 Apr 1700 G39r John Phillips is bound to him

BERRESFORD, John   8 May 1704 G106v of Mark Lane, summoned to cloathing   7 Jul 1707 G143v his apprentice John Phillips is freed
See also BERESFORD, BERRISFORD

BERRISFORD, John   3 Nov 1701 G65r his apprentice Humphrey Jackson is freed   8 Nov 1703 G97r William James is bound to him   12 Jun 1704 G107r cloathed   5 Feb 1704/5 G115r his apprentice Joseph Harper is freed   6 Nov 1710 G185r bookbinder; William Green is bound to him   26 Mar 1713 G207v excused office of First Renter Warden for a further year   26 Mar 1714 G217r fined for First Renter Warden   7 Jun 1714 G219v Edward Safyer is bound to him   4 Jun 1716 G240v John Rogers is bound to him

BERRISFORD, Richard   4 Aug 1707 G144v bound to Thomas Willmer, 7 years
See also BERESFORD, BERRESFORD

BERRY, Francis   2 May 1715 G228v son of John, is bound to Richard Berry, 7 years

BERRY, John (I)   6 Nov 1704 G113r bound to Robert Podmore, 7 years

BERRY, John (II)   2 May 1715 G228v his son Francis is bound to Richard Berry, 7 years

BERRY, Richard   4 Aug 1707 G144v bound to Robert Podmore, 7 years   4 Feb 1711 G196v turned over from Robert Podmore to Andrew Parker   6 Sep 1714 G221v freed by Andrew Parker   2 May 1715 G228v Francis Berry is bound to him

BERSMANN, [Gregor]   18 Mar 1687/8 F79v his edition of Ovid among books in catalogue annexed to Oxford agreement

BERTIE, Charles   7 Sep 1702 G80r M.P. for Stamford, Lincs, with Mr Cecil; request for Pepper's Almanack to be printed is granted

BEST, James   3 Jul 1710 G182r bound to Richard Sare, 7 years

BEST, Richard   6 Aug 1711 G193r freed by patrimony

BETTENHAM, James   6 May 1700 G39v bound to William Bowyer, 7 years   9 Jun 1707 G142v freed by William Bowyer

BETTESWORTH/BETTSWORTH/BEXWORTH, Arthur   6 Jun 1698 G8v freed by John Back   9 Jun 1707 G142v bookbinder; cloathed, William Hinchcliffe is bound to him   4 Dec 1710 G185v to be served with a copy of the Writ of Execution against Benjamin Harris   2 Jun 1712 G200v elected Assistant Renter Warden   23 Jun 1712 G200v fined for Assistant Renter Warden   2 Mar 1712/13 G206v elected to Mrs Mills' £80 share   7 Sep 1713 G213v John Morley is bound to him   5 Apr 1714 G218r Henry Smith turned over to him from Samuel Clarke   5 Jul 1714 G220v his apprentice William Hinchcliffe is freed

BETTESWORTH/BETTSWORTH, Peter   9 Jun 1707 G142v bound to Thomas Franklin, 7 years   6 Aug 1716 G242v freed by Thomas Franklin   10 Sep 1716 G243r Robert Cole is bound to him

BETTY, William   9 Apr 1711 G189r bound to Richard Hyett, 7 years

BEVER – see BEAVER

BEVERLY, [ ]   7 Mar 1680/1 E107v Clerk to answer his demands re. rent in arrears from Bishop's bequest   2 May 1681 E111r to be entreated as City officer to halt proceedings against S.C. for rent

BEVOR – see BEAVER

BEXWORTH – see BETTESWORTH

BIBLES   1 Oct 1688 F107r Vice-Chancellor of Oxford petitions Crown re. S.C. and King's Printers encroaching on University printing of Bibles   24 Oct 1695 F234v agreement with Oxford mentions a quarto Bible to be begun on 1 January 1696   2 Nov 1702 G82v advertisement for sale of Bibles, psalms and common prayer books at Exeter to be investigated, as Court suspects they may be counterfeit

See also GREEK TESTAMENT, LATIN TESTAMENT

BICKERTON, Ralph – see following entry

BICKERTON, Ralph Weaver   12 Nov 1716 G244v son of Ralph; bound to Daniel Browne, 7 years

BICKERTON, Samuel   4 Jun 1705 G120v bound to Thomas Bradyll   9 Jun 1707 G142v apprentice to Thomas Bradyll, turned over to Thomas Bickerton

BICKERTON, Thomas   6 Aug 1705 G122v freed by George Sawbridge   9 Jun 1707 G142v Samuel Bickerton turned over to him   3 Aug 1713 G213r William Sarson turned over to him from George Strahan   3 Oct 1715 G233v Henry Crofts is bound to him

BIDDULPH, Charles   12 Nov 1705 G125r bound to Jeffrey Wale, 7 years

BIGGS, [ ]   4 Feb 1695/6 F217r carpenter; committee appointed to settle dispute about his bill   11 Nov 1695 F235v carpenter; Under Warden to pay him £10 for the remainder of his bill

BILLING, Jonathan   2 Mar 1701/2 G67v bound to Thomas James, 7 years

BILLING, Robert   5 Apr 1703 G88r freed by James Knapton

BILLINGSLEY, Benjamin   1 Mar 1687/8 F97v expelled from Livery by order of Lord Mayor

See also following entry

BILLINGSLEY, Mrs   3 Feb 1689/90 F128v wife of Benjamin; petitions on behalf of herself and husband, 'he lying in a distressed condition'   26 Mar 1690 F131r petition read re. her husband's payment of Livery fine, his present detainment in Bedlam and their children's need; given £5

BIRCH, William   4 May 1691 F153v in Ludgate; Thomas Bassett asks for 40s to be paid out of Poor Box for his discharge   26 Mar 1696 F241r competes unsuccessfully for Beadle   26 Mar 1697 F262v competes unsuccessfully for Beadle   8 May 1699 G24v petition to be referred to next Pension Court   21 Jun 1700 G40v elected to Anne Croome's pension

BIRD, Edward   2 Dec 1700 G54r bound to William Redmayne, 7 years

BIRD, John (I)   7 Nov 1709 G172r bound to John Nutt, 7 years

BIRD, John (II)   2 May 1715 G228v his son William is bound to Ichabod Dawkes, 7 years

BIRD, William (I)   7 Nov 1681 E138r arrears of legacy to be paid: £10 p.a. to St Paul's Cross for preachers

BIRD, William (II)   2 May 1715 G228v son of John; bound to Ichabod Dawkes, 7 years

BISSELL, James   1 Oct 1694 F213r allowed to defer cloathing for a year   7 Oct 1698 G15r to be summoned to next Court day to be cloathed   7 Feb 1698/9 G20r excused from cloathing for twelve months   7 Dec 1702 G83v summoned to take cloathing at next Court   5 Apr 1703 G88r summoned to take cloathing at next Court   3 May 1703 G89v elected to cloathing, Clerk to request an answer from him   4 Oct 1703 G96r cloathed   7 Jul 1707 G143v Clerk to call on him for his Livery fine   7 Dec 1713 G215r owing £5 in respect of Livery fine   7 May 1716 G239v elected Assistant Renter Warden   4 Jun 1716 G240r excused office of Renter Warden for a year

BLACKBURN, John   7 Oct 1706 G135r bound to Owen Lloyd, 7 years

BLACKBURNE, Edward, snr – see following entry

BLACKBURNE, Edward, jnr   7 Dec 1713 G215r son of Edward, is bound to Samuel Keeble, 7 years

BLACKWELL, [   ]   3 Jan 1680/1 E106r paid 7s 6d charity

BLADEN, John   5 Aug 1700 G44r bound to John Marshall, 7 years

BLADON, [   ], Dr   28 Mar 1680 E98v his psalters to be kept at Customs House by Awnsham Churchill until agreement is reached between Bladon and S.C.

BLAGRAVE, Mrs   7 Nov 1709 G171v deceased; her £80 share in English Stock disposed of to William Mount

BLAGRAVE, Obadiah   2 Mar 1684/5 F31v elected Stock-keeper for Livery with George Wells   7 May 1685 (W) confirmed as member of new Livery   1 Mar 1685/6 F52r elected Stock-keeper for Livery with Thomas Sawbridge snr   26 Mar 1686 F53v fined for First Renter Warden   4 Oct 1686 F64r elected to Samuel Lowndes's £80 share   21 Oct 1686 (W) letter from John Bellinger and John Baker requesting that he give a bond for £1000 for carrying out his duties. Fenn to be his surety   8 Nov 1686 (W) copy of bond to S.C. as Treasurer   6 Dec 1686 F68v counterpart of mortgage made out to S.C. for his service to be sealed   20 Dec 1686 F69v to be indemnified for signing bonds to Henry Hills on S.C.'s behalf   1 Mar 1686/7 F77r competes unsuccessfully for Warehousekeeper   30 May 1687 F83r voted £70 gratuity for acting as *pro tempore* Warehousekeeper; £50 debt to S.C. cleared and £20 given him   1 Mar 1687/8 F98r competes unsuccessfully for Treasurer. Summoned to next Court to be nominated for Assistant   5 Mar 1687/8 F99r elected Assistant

BLAGUE, Anne   22 Dec 1709 G173r widow of Daniel Blague, to be paid money for his funeral   4 Dec 1710 G186r Court rejects request for an annuity

See also BLAGUE, Daniel

BLAGUE, Daniel, snr – see following entry

BLAGUE, Daniel, jnr   26 Mar 1680 E98r son of Daniel Blague snr; freed by patrimony   12 Nov 1683 F5r competes unsuccessfully for Henry Hills's £160 share   7 Jan 1683/4 F8r competes unsuccessfully for Henry Herringman's £160 share   13 Oct 1687 F91v sworn in as Assistant   9 Jan 1687/8 F96v competes unsuccessfully for Edward Brewster's £160 share   6 May 1689 F117r desires to become an Assistant and is told that the Table is full at present (*sic*)   19 Nov 1695 F236r John Bullard, his apprentice, is freed   7 Jun 1703 G90r surrenders £80 share, disposed of to Martin Boddington   23 Jun 1703 G90v arrangements for annuity from S.C. for his wife and himself   5 Jul 1703 G92r annuity from S.C. for himself and his wife Anne   3 Dec 1705 G125v to be allowed 25 shillings per quarter   22 Dec 1709 G173r deceased

See also BLAGUE, Anne

BLAIR, Elizabeth   6 Oct 1707 G145v widow; to be prosecuted in Chancery for printing and selling counterfeit psalms and almanacks   1 Dec 1707 G147r committee to consider her answer to bill in Chancery

BLAIRE – see BLARE

BLAKE, Emmanuel   11 May 1685 F35r draper of Covent Garden; given bond for the payment of £307 10s by 12 Nov   11 Oct 1686 F65v money for £300 bond raised by entering into another bond with Ann Wells

BLANDFORD, Nicholas   8 Aug 1715 G232r son of Thomas, is bound to William Wilkins, 7 years

BLARE/BLAIRE, Josiah   26 Mar 1683 E166v granted £50 from Tyler bequest   4 Jun 1683 E170v surety for Tyler bequest to be enquired into   2 Jul 1683 F2v surety referred for further enquiry   6 Aug 1683 F2v £50 bond to be taken from him and sureties   1 Sep 1701 G63v cloathed   26 Jan 1703/4 G100v member of S.C. Gave evidence on Robert Woollame's behalf that he had printed S.C.'s almanack

BLINCOE, John, snr – see following entry

BLINCOE, John, jnr   12 Nov 1716 G244v son of John, is bound to Samuel Clarke, 7 years

BLISSE, [ ]   1 Mar 1713/14 G216v of Exeter; Bill in Chancery to be brought against him for printing sham almanacks

BLOUNT, Charles   16 Jun 1684 F17v of Charing Cross and ex-apprentice to William Gilbert, a late member of S.C.; freed   7 Dec 1702 G83v summoned to take cloathing at next Court

BLOUNT, Richard   6 Jun 1698 G8v bound to Daniel Brogden, 7 years

BLUNDELL, Anne   19 Dec 1698 G17v pensioner, deceased; Richard Fairbank to be given her pension

BLYTH, Francis   3 Jun 1689 F119v excused cloathing

BLYTH, Henry   6 Oct 1701 G65r bound to William Pearson, 7 years

BLYTH, William   9 Sep 1706 G134v bound to William Hensman, 7 years

BLYZARD, John   5 Jul 1708 G155r bound to Edmund Richardson, 7 years

BOAT, James   1 Sep 1701 G64r bound to Edward Jones, 7 years

BOATE/BOTE, John   4 Oct 1686 F64v elected waterman in place of Robert Friend, discharged for abusive language; recommended by Thomas Newcomb   8 Nov 1686 F67r competes unsuccessfully to be Bargemaster's Mate   4 Apr 1687 F81v elected waterman

BOATE, Martha   4 Oct 1682 E159r admitted to John Major's 5s pension   20 Dec 1682 E162v given a 7s 6d pension instead of a 5s one   26 Mar 1686 F54v deceased; her 30s pension is voted to Richard Man

BOATE, Mary   21 Jun 1700 G40v deceased; Jane Bandbridge to be given her pension

BODDILY, Anne   7 Apr 1701 G58v freed by Jeremiah Wilkins

BODDINGTON/BODINGTON, Martin   2 Mar 1701/2 G67v freed by patrimony; cloathed   27 Mar 1703 G87r fined for First Renter Warden   7 Jun 1703 G90r elected to Daniel Blague's £80 share   7 Feb 1714/15 G224v elected to Anne Lowndes's £160 share. His £80 share disposed of to Thomas Norris   1 Mar 1715/16 G236v elected Stock-keeper for Livery   1 Mar 1716/17 G247r elected Stock-keeper for Livery

BODDINGTON/BODINGTON, Nicholas   17 Feb 1684/5 F30v elected to the late Stephen Dagnall's £40 share   29 May 1689 F118v cloathed   4 Jul 1692 F173v competes unsuccessfully for Richard Chiswell's £80 share   3 Oct 1692 F180r competes unsuccessfully for the late Widow Crooke's £80 share   26 Mar 1694 F201v elected Stock-keeper at special meeting   8 Apr 1695 F220r elected to Capt. Samuel Roycroft's £80 share. Summoned to next Court to be sworn in   3 Jun 1695 F225r takes partner's oath   26 Mar 1697 F258v elected and sworn in as Renter Warden   7 Apr 1701 G58v Henry Porton is bound to him   1 Sep 1707 G145r elected to the late William Shrewsbury's £160 share. His £80 share disposed of to John Lawrence   25 Mar 1708 G150r elected Assistant   2 Aug 1708 G156v his apprentice Henry Porton is freed   1 Mar 1710/11 G187r elected Stock-keeper for Assistants and takes oath   4 Jul 1713 G211r fined for first and second year of Under Warden. Elected Upper Warden   3 Jul 1714 G220r elected Upper Warden. No other person eligible to stand   1 Mar 1715/16 G236v elected Stock-keeper for Assistants   30 Jun 1716 G241r elected Master   4 Feb 1716/17 G246v to be new trustee of S.C.'s property

BODDINGTON, Phillippa   22 Jun 1699 G25v pensioner, deceased; Anne Harper to be given her pension

BODINGHAM, Walter   6 Sep 1703 G94v bound to John Mayo, 8 years   1 Oct 1711 G195r freed by John Mayo

BODINGTON – see BODDINGTON

BOILEAU, John   1 Sep 1684 F23r reported for dealing in scandalous books (W) 'Argiles Case [i.e. material pertaining to the trial of Archibald Campbell, Marquis of Argyll] and [Henri?] Arnauld'

BOLEWORTH, [   ]   2 Jul 1709 G166v Clerk to request rent arrears

BOLTER, Friswid   26 Mar 1700 G38r deceased; Mary Wailes to be given her pension
See also BOULTER

BOLTON, Richard – see following entry

BOLTON, Samuel   4 Feb 1694/5 F217r son of Richard Bolton of Newcastle-under-Lyme, yeoman; bound to Gilham Hills   9 Feb 1701/2 G67r freed by Gilham Hills

BONDS   11 Apr 1681 E110v monies due to S.C. on bond to be speedily called in   1 Mar 1682/3 E164r to be 'carefully and duly entered' in bond book by the Clerk, the Warden assisting. Loan money due to S.C. to be called in   4 Aug 1684 F22r new clause on loan bonds ordered re. borrowers and sureties not having dealings in seditious literature or illegally in Stock   11 May 1685 F35r Emmanuel Blake, draper of Covent Garden, given bond for payment of £307 10s by 12 Nov and James Kniveton, haberdasher of London, given bond for payment of £205 by 12 Nov   1 Jun 1685 F38r all moneys owing from S.C. @ 6% p.a. to be paid in or parties to take 5% p.a.   9 Feb 1690/1 F148v legal action to be taken to ensure payment of bonds already due   3 Aug 1691 F158r general release from S.C. to Gilbert Wharton to be entered in bond book   7 Dec 1691 F163r Henry Hills jnr pays off a £100 bond by printing done for Stock   2 Nov 1696 F252r bills and bonds delivered to Warden and debts due to Corporation and English Stock to be entered in a book

BOND, George   5 Jul 1697 F264v bound to Tace Sowle   2 Apr 1705 G118v freed by Tace Sowle

BOND, Thomas   4 Jul 1709 G167v bound to Joseph Hazard, 7 years

BONET, Théophile   7 Dec 1685 F48r 'Guide to a Physician' [i.e. *A Guide to the Practical Physician*] by 'Dr Theophilus Bonnett' [i.e. Théophile Bonet], assigned by Thomas Flesher to Edward Jones

BONNER, Claudius   12 Nov 1711 G195r son of William; bound to Elinor Everingham, 7 years

BONNER, William – see previous entry

BONNET – see BONET

BONNICK – see BONWICK

BONNY, William   6 Oct 1690 F143v married a freeman's widow so printing for S.C.; discharged from doing so further on information that he has abused S.C.   3 Nov 1690 F146r to be summoned to explain why he has slandered S.C.   9 Feb 1690/1 F149r summoned to next Court for failing to enter a pamphlet

BONWICK, [   ]   5 Jun 1710 G180r unable to dispose of copy of 'Justin with notes' without consent of Walthoe

BONWICK, Henry   24 Jun 1682 E154r cloathed   1 Mar 1687/8 F97v expelled from Livery by order of Lord Mayor   11 Oct 1688 F108v restored to Livery   6 Apr 1691 F151v fined for Assistant Renter Warden. Oxford committee asked to investigate the charge that Bonwick has printed an 'Exposition of the Church Catechism', which he denies   1 Aug 1692 F177r summoned with Joseph Watts to explain why they have printed Thomas Jekyll's catechism illegally   5 Sep 1692 F178r to be summoned for printing the Church Catechism without licence   6 Dec 1697 G2r Lancelot Walton is bound to him   4 Jul 1698 G11r his apprentice James Bonwick is freed   5 Jun 1699 G25v William Carter is bound to him   3 Nov 1701 G65r elected to William Hunt's £40 share   2 Mar 1701/2 G67v elected Stock-keeper for Yeomanry   18 Dec 1702 G84r elected to Samuel Sprint's £80 share. His £40 share disposed of to William Sussex   1 Mar 1702/3 elected Stock-keeper for Livery   6 Nov 1704 G113r William Martin is bound to him   4 Jun 1705 G120r elected Assistant

BONWICK, James (I)   4 Jul 1698 G11r freed by Henry Bonwick   2 Oct 1710 G184v cloathed   4 Jun 1711 G191r bookseller of Paul's Churchyard; James Bonwick is bound to him

BONWICK, James (II)   4 Jun 1711 G191r bound to James Bonwick, 7 years

BONWICK/BONNICK, John (I)   26 Mar 1686 F54r elected waterman   4 Apr 1687 F81v elected waterman

BONWICK, John (II)   6 May 1706 G131v bound to Rebecca Bonwick, 7 years

BONWICK, Rebecca   6 May 1706 G131v John Bonwick is bound to her   9 Sep 1706 G134v her apprentice William Carter is freed

BOOK OF MARTYRS [i.e. *Acts and Monuments* by John Foxe]   6 Mar 1681/2 E147v licences to print this to be granted at the next Court to highest bidder   3 Apr 1682 E151v Capt. Samuel Roycroft granted licence to print   8 May 1682 E153r articles and amendments between Roycroft and S.C. re. Book of Martyrs sealed; Roycroft ordered to pay £25 to S.C.   7 Dec 1685 F48r articles between S.C. and Roycroft referred to Treasurer   4 May 1702 G70v 'Epitome or Abridgement of the Book of Martyrs' printed illegally by Daniel Browne

See also BROWNE, Daniel

BOOKBINDERS   4 Mar 1694/5 F218v committee appointed re. bookbinders' petition that they are poverty-stricken since prices are low and leather expensive

BOOKER, John – see DUTCH FORTUNE TELLER

BOOKSELLERS   6 Oct 1690 F143v renew petition against hawkers in detail; committee appointed to join with committee of petitioners

See also STALL BOOKSELLERS

BOONE, John   3 Jun 1695 F226r son of Stephen Boone, turner of London; bound to John Marsh

BOONE, Stephen – see preceding entry

BOORMAN, Thomas, snr – see following entry

BOORMAN, Thomas, jnr   8 Aug 1715 G232r son of Thomas; bound to Mary Spicer, 7 years

BOOTH, Edward   22 Jun 1697 F266v Charles Combes is bound to him

BOOTH, Francis   5 Aug 1695 F231r fails to appear in response to summons; elected to Livery and resummoned

BOOTH, Henry   7 Jun 1708 G153v bound to Henry Rhodes, 7 years

BOOTH, John   5 Oct 1713 G214r freed by the executor of Edward Evetts

BOOTH, Samuel – see following entry

BOOTH, Thomas   3 Dec 1694 F216r son of Samuel Booth, haberdasher of London; bound to William Lindsey

BOSTOCK, [ ]   9 Jun 1707 G142r has recently married Henry Hills's widow

BOSTOCK, James   6 Aug 1694 F211v son of Samuel Bostock, St Martin-in-the-Fields, tailor; bound to Mary Thompson, 7 years

BOSTOCK, Samuel – see preceding entry

BOSVILE, Alexander   11 Nov 1695 F235v servant to Samuel Keeble; freed   6 Dec 1697 G2r summoned to take cloathing   4 Jul 1698 G11r Charles Pittard is bound to him   7 Apr 1701 G58v George North is bound to him   12 Jun 1704 G107v Hammond Banks is bound to him   5 Mar 1704/5 G117r his apprentice Anthony Barber is freed   1 Oct 1711 G195r his apprentice Hammond Banks is freed

BOTE – see BOATE

BOTHAM, William   1 Jun 1702 G71v William Addison is bound to him   8 May 1704 G106v Francis Perkins turned over to him   6 May 1706 G131v William Burton is bound to him   3 Jul 1710 G182r of Lambeth Hill, printer; John Long is bound to him   6 Jul 1713 G212r cloathed. His apprentice William Burton is freed. Whiteborne Wells is bound to him   12 Nov 1716 G244v his apprentice William Addison is freed

BOUCHER, John – see following entry

BOUCHER, Thomas   3 Dec 1694 F216r son of John Boucher, Yately, Southampton, gentleman; bound to John Sparkes

BOUGHEN/BOUGHON, Dr Edward   1 Oct 1683 F4r his Catechism in Latin and English is assigned to Henry Mortlock by Mary Garret

BOUGHON – see BOUGHEN

BOULTER, [   ]   7 Dec 1685 F47v in Benjamin Harris's partnership for printing the proceedings of the Westminster Parliament

BOULTER, Margaret   22 Dec 1685 F49v Ann Haddock admitted into quarterly charity in her place

BOULTER/BOLTER, Robert   6 Feb 1681/2 E144r is assigned [John Rea's] 'Flora de seu [i.e. seu de] Florum Cultura' by Richard Marriott   4 Sep 1682 E157v assignment to him to be entered   5 Feb 1683 E163v surrenders £40 share; granted request that Thomas Lacy be admitted to it, 'he having received a valuable consideration from him'

BOULTER, Whattoffe   2 Aug 1703 G94r freed by John Lawrence

BOUND, Benjamin   5 Aug 1689 F122r excused cloathing on plea of 'juniorship and inability'   4 Jun 1694 F208r cloathed   6 Dec 1697 G2r Elizabeth Chamberlain is bound to him   27 Mar 1699 G23r elected Assistant Renter Warden   8 Apr 1700 G38v elected to Mrs East's share   8 Nov 1703 G97r Charles Stephens is bound to him   4 Dec 1710 G186r his apprentice Charles Stephens is freed   19 Jan 1710/11 G186v of Forster Lane, ironmonger; Walter Grevill is bound to him

BOURCHIER, John   3 Feb 1706/7 G138r bound to Bryan Mills, 7 years

BOURN, Edward   7 Oct 1706 G135r freed by Robert Steele

BOURNE, Edmund   5 Oct 1702 G81v bound to Tace Sowle, 7 years

BOURNE, Edne   3 Apr 1699 G24r bound to William Baker

BOURNE, George   6 Dec 1708 G159v bound to Henry Parsons, 7 years   8 Jan 1716/17 G246r freed by Henry Parsons; Benjamin Cotton is bound to him

BOURNE, Joseph   26 Mar 1696 F241r servant to James Dowley; freed

BOWDEN, Jerman   6 Jun 1698 G8v bound to Edward Poole, 7 years

BOWEN, Widow   7 Feb 1703/4 G101v her apprentice Peter Moreton is freed

BOWES, Jasper – see following entry

BOWES, John (I)   10 Sep 1694 F212v son of Jasper Bowes, St Clement Danes, tailor; bound to David Edwards for eight years

BOWES, John (II)   7 Feb 1698/9 G20v bound to Mary Bennett, 7 years

BOWLES, Oliver   6 Sep 1680 E103v his widow to be paid 25s for her 'enlargement out of Prison'

BOWYER, [   ]   6 Dec 1708 G159r responsible for settlement of Mrs Mill's rent arrears

BOWYER, Jonah   8 Nov 1703 G97r freed by Thomas Bennett   3 Nov 1707 G146v cloathed   5 Jul 1708 G155r bookseller; Edward Forster is bound to him   4 May 1713 G209v receives charge as Assistant Renter Warden   5 Jul 1714 G220v John Shuckburgh is bound to him

BOWYER, Katherine 18 Dec 1702 G84r deceased; Adam Winch is given her pension

BOWYER, William 7 Aug 1699 G29r Thomas Jones is bound to him 6 May 1700 G39v cloathed, James Bettenham is bound to him 7 Jun 1703 G90r appointed accountant to Stock-keepers 4 Sep 1704 G111v to be paid salary 5 Aug 1706 G134r and Beckley. To ensure that each tenant of the Corporation produces a receipt for rent paid and that a rental be made 2 Dec 1706 G136v excused cloathing for twelve months 3 Mar 1706/7 G139r his apprentice Thomas Jones is freed 9 Jun 1707 G142v printer; Charles Chaldecote is bound to him. His apprentice James Bettenham is freed 3 Nov 1707 G146v permitted to print Partridge's Almanack in French 26 Mar 1709 G162v fined for First Renter Warden 3 Oct 1709 G171r printer; James Watson is bound to him 23 Mar 1710/11 G188v granted permission to print 'Collections out of Tully's Offices' [i.e. Cicero, *De Officiis*] 5 Jul 1714 G220v his apprentice Charles Chaldecote is freed 6 Dec 1714 G224r Robert Jollyman is bound to him 7 Nov 1715 G234v Richard Spackman turned over to him from Samuel Keimer

BOYER, Monsieur 16 Jun 1684 F17v of Dukes Court, St Martin's Lane; forbidden to trade any longer because 'no Denizen'

BRABURNE, [ ] 3 Nov 1684 F26r attorney; summoned to next Court to explain why John Starkey's £80 share cannot be disposed of, he 'being under outlawry'

BRABURNE, [ ] 20 Dec 1684 F27v brother to Braburne the attorney, who is ill; alleges that the £80 share was settled upon Mrs Starkey; Court defers decision. (W) Committee to consult Lord Chief Justice re. stock of John Starkey and Nathaniel Thompson, both being outlawed

BRADILL – see BRADYLL

BRADFORD, John 5 Dec 1698 G16v to be proceeded against for printing counterfeits of S.C.'s almanacks 7 Oct 1700 G46r and Dennis; Clerk's bill for prosecuting them at S.C.'s suit 5 May 1701 G59v printer; to be proceeded against for printing sham sheet almanack and Ephemeris 2 Jun 1701 G60r to be prosecuted for printing and publishing sheet almanack 15 Nov 1703 of London, printer; Bill in Chancery to be brought against him for printing sham almanacks 26 Jan 1703/4 G100v party to Bill in Chancery. To be prosecuted 2 Mar 1703/4 G103r Counsel's advice to be taken on plea 5 Feb 1704/5 G114v to be proceeded against with all expedition 2 Apr 1705 G118v his apprentice Richard Griffin is freed

BRADLEY, John, snr – see following entry

BRADLEY, John, jnr 2 Jun 1712 G200v son of John, is bound to George Harris, then turned over to Luke Stoker

BRADLEY, Joshua 6 May 1717 G250v son of William, is bound to Philip Barrett, 7 years

BRADLEY, Roger 17 Oct 1696 F251r framemaker in Distaff Lane; illegal press printing almanacks is discovered at his house

BRADLEY, William 6 May 1717 G250v his son Joshua is bound to Philip Barrett, 7 years

BRADSHAW, James 7 Oct 1706 G135r bound to John Mayo, 7 years 2 Nov 1713 G214v freed by Mrs Mayo

BRADSHAW, John 10 Sep 1694 F212v freed by Strangways Mude 6 May 1695 F223v Richard Streete is bound to him 7 Sep 1702 G80v John Marriott is bound to him 5 Jul 1708 G154v of Leadenhall Street, milliner; elected to cloathing 6 Sep 1708 G157r Clerk to call on him to request payment of Livery fine 3 Oct 1709 G171r of

Leadenhall Street, glover; his apprentice John Marriott is freed; Edward Norris is bound to him   6 Mar 1709/10 G176v to be cloathed   1 May 1710 G179r cloathed   5 May 1712 G199v Thomas Parker is bound to him

BRADY, Dr Nicholas   6 May 1698 G7v articles of agreement between Nahum Tate, Nicholas Brady and the Master and Wardens relating to the 'New Version of David's Psalms' read and sealed   4 Sep 1704 G111v requesting S.C. to buy shares from him in the new version of the Psalms   4 Dec 1704 G113v to be paid for share of profit of an impression of Tate and Brady's Psalms   28 May 1706 G131v printed an impression of the new version of the Psalms, contrary to articles made between him and Tate and S.C. Brady claimed it was by way of reprisal against Tate who had done him wrong. On bond of £100 penalty not to do so again. Interest in impression mortgaged to S.C. for £50   7 Mar 1708/9 G161r letter of Thomas Harrison to him concerning printing of the New Version of the Psalms referred to Court   2 May 1709 G164v and Tate. Payments to S.C. to be reduced   23 Jun 1709 G166r request of Thomas Harrison in letter to him concerning printing of 1000 of the new version of the Psalms granted by Court

See also TATE, Nahum; PSALMS: Tate & Brady

BRADYLL/BRADILL, [   ]   6 Jun 1681 E112r committee to investigate his breach of the byelaw concerning a 'Press in a hole'   4 Oct 1682 E159r accused by Richard Janeway of having printed the 'Letter about Abhorrers'   4 Dec 1682 E161r release from prosecution to be delivered to him as soon as he himself delivers a release to S.C.

BRADYLL/BRADILL, Thomas   29 Oct 1679 E94r cloathed   4 Sep 1688 F106v fails to appear to answer the charge of printing Virgil with [John] Minellius's notes, a Stock book   6 Apr 1691 F152v granted leave to sue Peter Parker and Thomas Guy for printing Dyer's works, owned by him   20 Apr 1691 F152v elected Assistant Renter Warden and ordered to be summoned   4 May 1691 F153v fined for Assistant Renter Warden   5 Feb 1693/4 F198v summoned to next Stock-keepers' meeting re. printing several impressions of the [Westminster] Assembly's Catechism   7 May 1694 F203r legal action to be taken to compel him to declare number and size of impressions printed of the Assembly's Catechism   3 Apr 1699 G24r his apprentice Henry Lloyd is freed   4 Aug 1701 G63v Thomas Smith is bound to him   2 Nov 1702 G83r his apprentice Edward Midwinter is turned over to John Matthews   5 Apr 1703 G88r William Maynard is bound to him   5 Feb 1704/5 G115r elected to John Harding's £80 share   4 Jun 1705 G120v Samuel Bickerton is bound to him   2 Jul 1705 G121v S.C. to buy from him the remaining part of the impression of Virgil with Minellius's notes   6 Aug 1705 G122r to mortgage his English Stock share to John Taylor   10 Sep 1705 G123r mortgages share in English Stock to John Taylor   9 Jun 1707 G142v Samuel Bickerton turned over from him to Thomas Bickerton   1 Sep 1707 G145r his apprentice John Letts is freed   12 Apr 1708 G152r printer; John Rawlins is bound to him   5 Jun 1710 G180r Bryan Symonds is bound to him   10 Sep 1711 G194r printer; John Griffith is bound to him

BRAGG, Benjamin   4 Nov 1706 G135v seller of sham almanack, 'The City and Country Remembrancer'   22 Dec 1708 G159v to be made party to S.C.'s bill in Chancery for printing of almanacks   7 Feb 1708/9 G160v sheet almanack printed for him by George Croome

BRAMSTON/BRAMSTONE, Ann   21 Jun 1707 G143r elected to Ann Cox's pension   20 Dec 1710 G186v deceased; Elizabeth Yate is given her pension

BRAMSTON, Fish   6 Nov 1699 G32r Edmund Scofeild is bound to him

BRAND, Edward   7 Aug 1710 G183r freed

BRAND, James   8 Nov 1697 G1v bound to Samuel Lowndes

BRANSON, Thomas   4 Feb 1705/6 G127v bound to Margaret Wild, 8 years

BRAY, [   ]   5 Jun 1710 G180v memorandum to enquire whether he will take his freedom

BREUER, [   ]   5 Oct 1696 (W) to be summoned to take cloathing

BREWER, John   7 Mar 1697/8 G5r gentleman; bond from S.C. to him of £200 penalty to pay £102 10s on 8 September   7 Apr 1712 G199r bond for £100 cancelled

BREWER/BROWER, Ralph – see following entry

BREWER/BROWER, Thomas   12 Nov 1694 F215r son of Ralph Brewer, late girdler of London; bound to Edward Darrell from   1 October   4 May 1702 G71r freed by Edward Darrell   7 May 1705 G119v cloathed   9 Jun 1707 G142v stationer; Henry Sidney is bound to him   5 May 1712 G199v fined for office of Renter Warden   1 Feb 1713/14 G216r elected to Whitledge's £40 share

BREWSTER, [   ]   1 Dec 1679 E95v assignment from Mrs Thrale entered   5 Dec 1681 E140r requests that Samson Evans, a bookseller in Worcester, may have John, son of Thomas Mountford of Kidderminster, bound to him

BREWSTER, Edward   1 Mar 1679/80 E97r elected Stock-keeper for Assistants   2 Aug 1680 E102v authorised to audit Warden's accounts   1 Mar 1680/1 E107v elected Stock-keeper for Assistants with Roger Norton   4 Jul 1681 E115v to assist Roger Norton and John Towse in obtaining amelioration money   5 Dec 1681 E140v tells Court that Leybourne's account with Mrs Hannah Sawbridge is not completed; respite granted until next Court   20 Mar 1681/2 E148v gives evidence on behalf of the relict at the committee re. George Sawbridge's accounts   3 Apr 1682 E150v plea to the administratrix to be reimbursed for paper which George Sawbridge allegedly bought for S.C. is dismissed   8 May 1682 E153r among sureties for the payment of Sir Joseph Seamour's annuity; indemnified by S.C.   3 Jul 1682 E155v among those indemnified from liability to Sir Joseph Seamour in the demise of the hall and tenements. Assigned half of [Eusebius] Pagitt's 'History of the Bible' by Simon Miller   26 Mar 1683 E166v appointed to audit Renter Wardens' accounts with Roger Norton   2 Jul 1683 F2v returns the late Widow Enderby's 10s pension   1 Mar 1683/4 F9v elected Stock-keeper for Assistants with John Bellinger   26 Mar 1686 F53v Widow Thrale transfers the mortgage of her £320 share from the executors of Hannah Sawbridge to him for £100 and interest   19 Nov 1686 F67v administrator of Thomas Sawbridge fails to turn up to the George and Vulture tavern for a meeting about S.C. buying Thomas Sawbridge's interest in Cambridge privilege   23 Mar 1686/7 F80r Henry Hills snr is allowed to mortgage his £320 share to Brewster for £300   1 Aug 1687 F87r is unable to lend Hills the required money so Hills mortgages his Assistant's share to Katherine Sawbridge   12 Oct 1687 F90v fined for 2 years' Under Warden, then elected Upper Warden   5 Dec 1687 F94v together with Nathaniel Ranew, complains about Thomas Bassett and Henry Harefinch   9 Jan 1687/8 F96v ties with John Clarke in competition for the late Mrs Latham's £320 share, and the Master gives him his casting vote. Bassett to be summoned to answer Brewster's and Ranew's complaint   5 Mar 1687/8 F99r he and Ranew allowed to sue Bassett for an alleged moiety of the 'Turkish History' which Bassett has recently reprinted   30 Jun 1688 F103r Court asks him to serve as Upper Warden for another year but he is allowed to fine instead   27 Nov 1688 F110v among those chosen to audit Renter Wardens' accounts   4 Feb 1688/9 F112v committee appointed to treat with him about Cambridge business   6 Jul 1689 F121r elected Master   3 Feb 1689/90 F128v further members added to committee to treat with him about Cambridge business   1 Mar 1689/90 F129v administrator of Thomas and Hannah Sawbridge; has an interest in Cambridge privilege for 3½ years which he offers to sell to S.C. for £100   11 Apr 1690 F134r willing to have his interest in Cambridge business bought for 100 guineas, S.C. also buying materials and school books and Brewster paying all charges to last Lady Day   5 May 1690 F134v Court agrees to committee's conclusions about the Cambridge privilege, altering the date of commencement to next Midsummer Day   2 Jun 1690 F135r elected Master for rest of year   5 Jul 1690 F138r competes unsuccessfully for Master   8 Jul 1690 F139v some of the £1500 borrowed for Stock to go towards paying him for the Cambridge stock and printing privilege   1 Feb 1691/2 F164v his part in concluding Oxford agreement is detailed. Keeble and Vincent summoned to next Court to answer Brewster's complaint against them   7 Mar 1691/2 F166v Keeble and Vincent promise to submit to arbitration over his complaint that they have printed King's Printers' books. With other S.C. feoffees executes transfer of mortgage of Stock estates to indemnify S.C. members re. Oxford   2 Jul 1692 F172v elected Master   5 Feb 1693/4 F198v is desired to purchase for Court the abridgement of Dr [Simon] Ford's comments or annotations upon the church catechism   10 Sep 1694 F212v James Richardson jnr is bound to him   8 Apr 1695 F220r appointed auditor for Renter Wardens' accounts with William Rawlins   6 Jul 1695 F229v among those chosen to audit Warden's accounts   2 Mar 1695/6 F240r elected Stock-keeper for Assistants with Henry Mortlock   4 May 1696 F242v takes Stock-keeper's oath   6 Jul 1696 F246v among those chosen to audit Warden's accounts   5 Oct 1696 F252r prevented from serving on Cambridge committee because of illness   7 Dec 1696 F255r produces abstract of Christopher Meredith's will re. his bequest   3 May 1697 F261v chosen to audit Renter Wardens' accounts with Roger Norton   3 Jul 1697 F263v competes unsuccessfully for Master   6 Oct 1701 G65r his apprentice James Richardson is freed   6 Jul 1702 G78r Henry Lovell turned over to him   16 Oct 1705 G124v to attend Lord Mayor re. Renter Wardens' refusal to provide dinner   9 Sep 1706 G134v informs Court that Christopher Wilkinson wishes to fine for Renter Warden   21 Feb 1716/17 G246v old trustee; conveyance of trusteeship of S.C.'s Hall &c. from him. Lease from City assigned by him to Robert Knaplock and Daniel Midwinter   1 Apr 1717 G249v deceased; his £360 share disposed of to Israel Harrison

BREWSTER, Elinor (W)   5 Dec 1687 F95v deceased; her £160 share voted to Thomas Passenger

BREWSTER, Thomas   7 Jun 1680 E100v freed by Langley Curtis

BRICKLAYER   2 Oct 1699 G31r bills to be paid   4 Mar 1699/1700 G36r bill of £7 for tiling part of the Hall to be paid by Warden Charles Harper   4 Dec 1704 G114r bill to be paid   7 Jul 1707 G143v bill of £18 13s 3d to be paid   4 Oct 1708 G158r bill referred to Master and Wardens for payment   2 Jul 1711 G192v bill to be paid by Master and Wardens   7 Dec 1713 G215r bill for work done on Carter's house and about Hall to be paid

See also HALL

BRICKWELL, William   1 Aug 1681 E117r John Harding to retain £50 loan for a further 3 years, Brickwell and Edward Hill standing surety

BRICKWOOD/BRYCKWOOD, Henry   4 Dec 1699 G34r bound to Thomas Hodgkins, 7 years   3 Feb 1706/7 G138r freed by Thomas Hodgkins   5 Jun 1710 G180r of Malden, Essex; to be summoned to take cloathing   9 Apr 1716 G239r of Malden, Essex; considered a fit person to be brought onto Livery. To be written to by Warden Richard Mount   7 May 1716 G239v to be informed of his election to cloathing   6 Aug 1716 G242r of Malden, Essex; to be summoned to accept cloathing next Court day   6 May 1717 G250v of Malden; Clerk to write again

BRIDGE, [   ]   23 Mar 1703/4 G104v to be summoned to next Court for printing the Ephemeris without S.C.'s permission   3 Apr 1704 G105r admits to printing the Double Ephemeris for George Parker

BRIDGE, Daniel 5 Mar 1704/5 G117r freed by patrimony 2 Jul 1705 G121v Robert Dennet is bound to him 5 May 1707 G142r Samuel Aris turned over to him from William Sayes 2 Aug 1708 G156v Robert Dennet turned over from him to Mathew Jenour 6 Sep 1708 G157v Samuel Aris turned over from him to Richard Janeway 8 Aug 1715 G232r John Bright is bound to him

BRIDGE, Samuel 8 Apr 1700 G39r John Fisher is bound to him 2 Aug 1703 G94r cloathed, Samuel Andrews is bound to him 5 Feb 1704/5 G115r his apprentice William Osborne is freed 3 Feb 1706/7 G138r Samuel Andrews turned over from him to Benjamin Beardwell

BRIDGEMAN, [ ] 6 Sep 1686 F62r letters from him to Sir Roger L'Estrange read recommending Crown approval of Richard Sare as the new Treasurer 11 Oct 1686 F65r reference to Bridgeman's recommendation being contrary to partners' wishes

BRIDGES, Henry 1 Sep 1684 F23v summoned to next Court for printing and selling some of Jonah Deacon's books without permission

BRIGGS, Alice 20 Jun 1713 G210v deceased; William Thackery is given her pension

BRIGGS, John 6 Aug 1694 F211v son of William Briggs of Horsham, carpenter; bound to Joseph Raven

BRIGGS, Philip 26 Mar 1683 E166v elected Under-Beadle 4 Feb 1683/4 F8v given 12s 6d charity 'considering the exceeding hardness of the season' 26 Mar 1684 F11v re-elected porter 26 Mar 1685 F32r given 10s charity. Re-elected porter 26 Mar 1686 F54r re-elected porter 2 Aug 1686 F61v porter; given £7 to complete the sum necessary to apprentice his son to a saddlemaker 4 Apr 1687 F81r re-elected porter 26 Mar 1688 F100r re-elected porter 26 Mar 1689 F116r re-elected porter 26 Mar 1690 F131v re-elected porter or 'under beadle' 9 Feb 1690/1 F148v 20s given to his wife; news of his death is brought to Court immediately afterwards; choice of another porter is adjourned

BRIGGS, William 6 Aug 1694 F211v of Horsham, carpenter; his son John is bound to Joseph Raven

BRIGHT, Thomas – see following entry

BRIGHT, John 8 Aug 1715 G232r son of Thomas; bound to Daniel Bridge, 7 years

BRIMLICOMBE, Samuel 1 Dec 1707 G147r paid 40s to Poor Box to be freed as he was bound by a foreign indenture. Freed by John Grantum

BRIMSMEAD, Rebecca 2 Jun 1701 G60v bound to Elizabeth Astley

BRINCKWORTH, Edward – see following entry

BRINCKWORTH, John 5 Apr 1714 G218r son of Edward; bound to John Baskett, 7 years

BRIND, John 2 Jun 1712 G200v son of Thomas; bound to John Paten, 7 years

BRINGHURST, [ ] 7 Jul 1684 F20r committee appointed to deal with printers who are not members of S.C., including him

BRISCOE, Samuel 6 Aug 1694 F211v servant to Richard Baldwin; freed. John Willis jnr is bound to him 10 Sep 1694 F212r cloathed 5 Jun 1699 G25r petition desiring remittance of £10 of his Livery fine. Order relating to William Onley, his surety for the payment of the £10, to be suspended 7 Apr 1701 G58v Jacob Foden is bound to him 26 Mar 1714 G217v excused serving as Assistant Renter Warden for a year

BRITISH ANNALIST – see ANNALIST

BRITT, John – see following entry

BRITT, Thomas 5 Oct 1713 G214r son of John, is bound to Elinor Everingham, 7 years

BROADHURST, John 2 Jul 1694 F210v son of Thomas Broadhurst of Chester, gentleman; bound to Stephen Keyes

BROADHURST, Thomas – see preceding entry

BROCK, John 2 Nov 1702 G83r bound to Stephen Keyes, 7 years

BROCKETT, [ ] 6 Mar 1681/2 E146v refuses cloathing: given until first Court day in May to reconsider

BROCKETT, Mary 19 Dec 1698 G17v elected to Richard Fairbank's pension 22 Jun 1699 G25v elected to Nathaniel Ponder's pension 22 Mar 1714 G226v deceased; Ursula Dykes is given her pension

BROCKET, Thomas 7 Dec 1685 F48r to be summoned re. failing to free his apprentice, William Burroughs 22 Dec 1685 F49v fails to answer summons; his apprentice is freed and he is again summoned 12 Nov 1694 F214v deceased; his apprentice, Dowsett Sunky, is freed

BROGDEN/BROGDON, Daniel 4 Jun 1694 F208v John Caucking is bound to him 6 Jun 1698 G8v Richard Blount is bound to him 5 Mar 1710/11 G188r his son Samuel is bound to him for 7 years

BROGDEN/BROGDON, Samuel – see preceding entry

BROGDON – see BROGDEN

BROKERS 14 Mar 1686/7 F78v legal advice to be taken as to whether brokers and others not free of S.C. should be allowed to sell books

BROME – see BROOME

BROOK/BROOKES, Elizabeth 7 Mar 1697/8 G4v surrenders her £80 share 21 Jun 1706 G132v elected to Mary Izard's pension 20 Dec 1710 G186v deceased; Anne Mynds is given her pension

See also BROOKES, Widow

BROOK, James 7 Jul 1701 G62r bound to James Crayle, 7 years

See also BROOKE, BROOKES, BROOKS

BROOKE, Abel 5 Sep 1715 G232v son of Ralph, is bound to Richard Mount, 7 years

BROOKE, James 6 Dec 1708 G159v freed by Thomas Ilive

BROOKE/BROOKS, John 5 Jun 1699 G25v Charles Walkden is bound to him 6 Mar 1703/4 G103v Lawrence Dutton is bound to him

BROOKE, Ralph 5 Sep 1715 G232v his son Abel is bound to Richard Mount, 7 years

See also BROOK, BROOKES, BROOKS

BROOKELAND, Joseph 7 Jun 1697 F263r bound to Humphrey Pooler

BROOKES, Christopher 3 Jun 1695 F226v deceased; his widow to retain his pension

BROOKES, James 6 May 1700 G39v James Burden is bound to him 3 Jun 1700 G40r cloathed 6 Dec 1703 G99v Brooke Lawrence is bound to him 1 Sep 1707 G145r stationer; Richard Rose is bound to him 2 Aug 1708 G156v his apprentice James Burden is freed 4 Jul 1709 G167v of London Bridge; William Herbert is bound to him 2 Jun 1712 G200r elected to John Leake's £40 share 7 Jul 1712 G201v elected to William Thackery's £80 share. His £40 share disposed of to Roger Clavell 4 Mar 1716/17 G247v his apprentice William Herbert is freed. Benjamin Oliver is bound to him

BROOKES/BROOKS, John 6 May 1695 F223r cloathed. George Toft is bound to him 12 Jun 1704 G107v William Payton is bound to him 26 Mar 1706 G130r of the

Strand; to be sent for on next choosing of Renter Wardens   21 Jun 1706 G132v his apprentice Charles Walkden is freed   26 Mar 1707 G139v fined for First Renter Warden   1 Sep 1707 G145r elected to one £40 share of Richard Mount's £80 share. Takes oath of partner   4 Dec 1710 G186r stationer in the Strand; Thomas Ridge is bound to him   2 Jun 1712 G200v his apprentice William Paten is freed   1 Mar 1713/14 G216v request that he may be admitted to half of William Leybourne's £80 share in exchange for loan   5 Apr 1714 G218r half of Leybourne's £80 share passed to him   6 Sep 1714 G221v Robert Smith is bound to him

BROOKES, Major – see BROOKES, Widow

BROOKES, Nathan   24 Mar 1709/10 G176v elected to Elizabeth Burrows's pension   23 Jun 1711 G191v deceased; Rebecca Fowler is given his pension

BROOKES, Widow   26 Mar 1696 F241r relict of Major Brookes; allowed to mortgage a £80 share

See also BROOK, Elizabeth

See also BROOK, BROOKE, BROOKS

BROOKESBANKE, John   2 Oct 1699 G31v bound to Benjamin Browne

BROOKESBY/BROOKSBY, Philip   7 Feb 1698/9 G20v his apprentice John Fosterby is freed   5 Feb 1704/5 G115r his apprentice John Walter is freed

BROOKS, James   26 Mar 1705 G117v fined for first Renter Warden

See also BROOK, BROOKE, BROOKES

BROOKSBY – see BROOKESBY

BROOME/BROME, Charles   16 Jun 1684 F17v son of Henry Broome, a late member of S.C.; freed   7 Sep 1685 F44r pays 5 guineas to print 5000 catechisms to annex to [Thomas Ken] the Bishop of Bath and Wells's exposition of the Catechism   7 Dec 1685 F48r confesses to printing more catechisms than he had leave to; promises full account at next Court   1 Mar 1685/6 F51v cloathed   6 Jun 1687 F84v admits to printing 1000 catechisms with exposition 'in a larger letter than heretofore' and promises to see Master and Wardens and make compensation   1 Aug 1687 F86v to pay 1 guinea fine to Stock for printing church catechism   1 Mar 1687/8 F97v expelled from Livery by order of Lord Mayor   11 Oct 1688 F108v restored to Livery   7 Oct 1689 F125r Roger Norton assigns to him 'Urn Burial or the Garden of Cyrus' [i.e. Sir Thomas Browne's *Hydriotaphia*] and [Hamon L'Estrange's] 'Alliance of Divine Offices'   3 Apr 1693 F186r elected First Renter Warden   10 Apr 1693 F186v fined for first Renter Warden   4 Jun 1694 F208v his apprentice Samuel Bunchley is freed   3 Dec 1694 F215v elected to Capt. Edward Darrell's £40 share   20 Dec 1694 F216r refuses £40 share   7 Feb 1697/8 G3r elected to Thomas Hodgkins's £80 share   2 May 1698 G7r and his partners to have the use of the Hall for drawing their lottery of books on payment of 40s to the Warden   1 Aug 1698 G13r the several assignments from Broome to Benjamin Motte and from Motte to Capt. Samuel Roycroft of a moiety of Dr Thomas Comber's 'Companion to the Temple', parts 1–2, read and ordered to be entered   26 Mar 1700 G38r William Cherrett is bound to him

BROOME, Henry   16 Jun 1684 F17v deceased; his son Charles is freed

BROOMER, [ ]   12 Nov 1716 G244v of Uxbridge; to be summoned to cloathing next Court day

BROUGHTON, Francis   1 Dec 1701 G66r bound to Henry Mortlock, 7 years

BROWER – see BREWER

BROWNE, [ ]   1 Dec 1701 G66r to have copies of orders of Court relating to Mrs Susanna Miller's mortgaging the equity of redemption of her stock to Wilcox

BROWNE, Benjamin (I)   7 Oct 1695 F234r servant to James Crayle; freed   11 Nov 1695 F235r cloathed   7 Jun 1697 F263r Joshua Fulford is bound to him   2 Oct 1699 G31v John Brookesbanke is bound to him   4 Aug 1701 G63v Randall Nicholl is bound to him   1 Feb 1702/3 G85r elected to Thomas Spicer, alias Helder's £80 share   9 Sep 1706 G134v Randall Nicholl turned over from him to Samuel Hoole   6 Jun 1709 G165v his apprentice Randall Nicholl is freed

BROWNE, Benjamin (II)   2 Mar 1701/2 G67v bound to John Overton, 7 years

BROWNE, Charles   16 Oct 1697 F269r bookbinder; to be prosecuted for binding counterfeit books and almanacks and refusing Master entry   22 Jun 1698 G9v general release from S.C. read and sealed   6 Oct 1707 G145v stationer; to be prosecuted in Chancery for printing and selling counterfeit psalms and almanacks   1 Dec 1707 G147r committee set up to consider his answer to a Bill in Chancery

BROWNE, Christopher   5 Aug 1689 F122r cloathed   2 Dec 1700 G54r his apprentice John Dennis is freed   7 Apr 1707 G141r elected First Renter Warden   26 Sep 1712 G203v Anne Padbury is bound to him

BROWNE, Daniel, snr   21 Feb 1686/7 F72r to have priority over William Hensman on the Livery list, though freed on the same day, since he was cloathed before Hensman   12 Apr 1692 F168v fined for First Renter Warden   4 Jul 1692 F173v elected to Robert Roberts's £40 share   1 Mar 1692/3 F184r elected Stock-keeper for Yeomanry with Israel Harrison   1 Mar 1693/4 F199v elected Stock-keeper for Yeomanry with William Rogers   2 Jul 1694 F210r competes unsuccessfully for Mrs Newcomb's £80 share   10 Sep 1694 F212v Francis Coggan, the apprentice of William Miller, deceased, is turned over to him   3 Dec 1694 F215v competes unsuccessfully for Bennett Griffin's £80 share   8 Apr 1695 F220r competes unsuccessfully for Capt. Samuel Roycroft's £80 share. Elected to John Penn's £80 share   6 May 1695 F222v takes partner's oath   1 Apr 1697 F260v to ask booksellers, printers and paper manufacturers of Westminster and Temple Bar without for money towards Paper Act test case   1 Mar 1697/8 G4r elected Stock-keeper for Livery   8 Apr 1700 G39r Thomas Browne is bound to him   7 Oct 1700 G46r his apprentice Amos Coppleton is freed by himself and Benjamin Webster   4 May 1702 G70r illegal printing of 'The Epitome or Abridgement of the Book of Martyrs'   7 Dec 1702 G83v to pay an 'acknowledgement' for printing the abridgement of the Book of Martyrs   1 Feb 1702/3 G84v he and John Walthoe would only pay one guinea as 'acknowledgement'. Master to determine the matter   5 Feb 1704/5 G114v complaint against him and others for printing 'Observations on Time Sacred and Profane' [i.e. N.B., Philomath, *Observations*] containing S.C.'s calendar   5 Mar 1704/5 G116v to deliver books and plate relating to 'Observations on Time' to Warehousekeeper   5 May 1707 G141v elected to Richard Chiswell's £160 share. His £80 share disposed of to Robert Knaplock   25 Mar 1708 G150r elected Assistant   7 Jun 1708 G153v Francis Clay is bound to him   4 Dec 1710 G186r of Temple Bar, bookseller; John Pele is bound to him   30 Jun 1711 G192r elected Under Warden. Takes oath and his place   3 Mar 1711/12 G197r to pay remainder of £5 to Abel Swale   13 Apr 1713 G208v John Norcock turned over to him from Egbert Sangar   4 Jul 1713 G211r allowed to fine for second year of Under Warden, first and second year as Upper Warden. Elected Master   3 May 1714 G218v Francis Ranshaw is bound to him   4 Jun 1716 G240v Daniel his son is bound to him   10 Sep 1716 G243r his apprentice Francis Clay is freed   12 Nov 1716 G244r Ralph Weaver Bickerton is bound to him

BROWNE, Daniel, jnr   4 Jun 1716 G240v bound to his father, Daniel

BROWNE, David   1 Mar 1685/6 F51r cloathed

BROWNE, Edward   1 Dec 1701 G66r turned over from William Baker to Robert Steel

BROWNE, Elizabeth   4 Sep 1699 G30v bound to Benjamin Johnson, 7 years

BROWNE, Francis   16 Oct 1697 F269r to act as counsel when Charles Browne and William Onley are prosecuted in the Court of Exchequer for illegal printing

BROWNE, John (I)   8 Apr 1695 F221r Benjamin Mynd, his apprentice, is freed

BROWNE, John (II)   8 Apr 1700 G39r bound to Robert Limpany, 7 years   4 May 1702 G71r freed by patrimony

BROWNE, Jonas   6 Nov 1704 G113r bound to Thomas Benskin, 7 years

BROWNE, Mary   21 Mar 1694/5 F219r takes over Mary Bateson's pension

BROWNE, Philip   2 Apr 1705 G118v bound to William Hawes, 7 years

BROWNE, Rachel   25 Jun 1690 F136v elected to Alice Williams's 40s pension   26 Mar 1694 F201v deceased; Susan Brudenell elected to her pension

BROWNE, Richard, snr – see following entry

BROWNE, Richard, jnr   5 Feb 1693/4 F199r son of Richard Browne of Milbourne Wick, Somerset; bound to Peter Buck for 7 years   14 Mar 1714/15 G226r Robert Hatersly is bound to him

BROWNE, Richard, author   7 Dec 1685 F48r 'Read's Works: Or a Treatise of Chirurgery to be Improved by Dr Richard Browne' [i.e. Alexander Read, *Chirurgorum Comes: Or the Whole Practice of Chirurgery*?], assigned by Thomas Flesher to Edward Jones

BROWNE, Robert   6 Aug 1705 G122v bound to Joseph Downing   3 Nov 1712 G205r freed by Joseph Downing

BROWNE, Samuel   3 Jul 1699 G26v to receive money due on assignment of John Simms's Assistant's share, formerly assigned to George Saunders, deceased, whose executrix is now married to Browne

BROWNE, Susan   2 Aug 1697 F265v given 20s to discharge her from the Compter, where she is in prison for debt

BROWNE, Sir Thomas – see URN-BURIAL

BROWNE, Thomas (I)   8 Apr 1700 G39r bound to Daniel Browne, 7 years

BROWNE, Thomas (II)   2 Mar 1712/13 G207r son of Joseph, is bound to John Humphreys, 7 years

BRUCE, Miss/Mrs   24 Oct 1695 (W) Master to call on Mr Taylor and demand the £10 a year left to one Bruce, and after her decease to the S.C. to buy Bibles to be given to the hospital   11 Nov 1695 (W) Master reported that he had spoken to Mr Taylor who said deceased did not order payment for Bibles until Michaelmas next. Master to demand the money

BRUCE, Jesse   21 Jun 1707 G143r elected to Mary Neale's pension   22 Mar 1715/16 G238r deceased; Isaac Lane is given his pension

BRUDENELL/BRUDENILL/BRUDNELL, John   4 Sep 1699 G30r his son Moses Brudenell is freed by patrimony   1 Feb 1702/3 G85r Samuel Negus turned over to him from Susan Brudenell (repeated under 1 Mar 1702)   7 Aug 1704 G111r Francis Perkins turned over to him

BRUDENELL/BRUDENILL, Moses   4 Sep 1699 G30r freed by John Brudenell, patrimony

BRUDENELL/BRUDNELL, Susan   26 Mar 1694 F201v elected to the late Rachel Browne's pension   22 Jun 1705 G120v deceased; Jane Curtis is given her pension

BRUDENELL/BRUDNALL/BRUDNEL/BRUDNELL, Susanna/Susan   4 May 1702 G71r Samuel Negus is bound to her   1 Feb 1702/3 G85r her apprentice Samuel Negus is turned over to John Brudenell (repeated under 1 Mar 1702)   12 Jun 1704 G107v her apprentice Joshua Fulford is freed

BRUDENILL – see BRUDENELL

BRUDGES – see BRUGES

BRUDNALL, BRUDNEL, BRUDNELL – see BRUDENELL

BRUGES/BRUDGES/BRUGIS, Richard   3 Jul 1704 G110r John Grigg is bound to him   4 Aug 1707 G144v printer; Thomas Reeve is bound to him   3 Nov 1707 G146v cloathed   1 Dec 1707 G147v printer; John Kelly is bound to him   6 Sep 1714 G221v his apprentice Thomas Reeve is freed   4 Jul 1715 G231r Thomas Taunton is bound to him

BRUGIS – see BRUGES

BRUNT, [   ]   4 Jul 1709 G167r £10 rent received from him by Benjamin Tooke snr not accounted for

BRUNTS, Samuel   3 Nov 1707 G146v lease of five houses from S.C. sealed

BRYAN, Benjamin   14 Mar 1714/15 G226r his son Thomas is bound to Robert Staples, 7 years

BRYAN, John William   6 May 1706 G131v bound to Oliver Elliston, 7 years   3 Feb 1706/7 G138r apprentice of Oliver Elliston, turned over to Thomas Simpson

BRYAN, Stephen   3 Jun 1706 G132v freed by Lewis Thomas

BRYAN, Thomas   14 Mar 1714/15 G226r son of Benjamin, is bound to Robert Staples, 7 years

BRYANT, George   5 Apr 1703 G88r John West turned over to him

BUCANARI'S OPERA [i.e. the collected works of Gulielmus Bucanus?]   18 Mar 1686/7 F79v among books in catalogue annexed to Oxford agreement

BUCHANAN, James – see following entry

BUCHANAN/BUCHANON, John   7 May 1694 F204r son of the late James Buchanan of Appleby, Westmorland, clerk; bound to Thomas Dalton   4 Oct 1703 G96r freed by Thomas Dalton   8 Nov 1703 G97r John Grieve is bound to him   6 Nov 1704 G113r Thomas Tate is bound to him   4 Mar 1705/6 G129r Christopher Emerson is bound to him   2 Oct 1710 G184v cloathed   2 Jun 1712 G200v William Cooke is bound to him, his apprentice Thomas Tate is freed   7 Jul 1712 G201v William Gower is bound to him   18 Nov 1715 G234v Christopher Thomas is bound to him   5 Mar 1715/16 G237v his apprentice Abraham Pinchorne is freed   20 Dec 1716 G246r Christopher Thomas turned over from him to Rebecca Somerscales   26 Mar 1717 G248v elected Assistant Renter Warden   1 Apr 1717 G249r excused office of Assistant Renter Warden for a year

BUCHANON – see BUCHANAN

BUCK, Peter   5 Feb 1693/4 F199r Richard Browne is bound to him   9 Sep 1700 G45r excused from cloathing for six months   4 May 1702 G71r Robert Hurst is bound to him   1 Jun 1702 G71v cloathed

BUCK, William   1 Jun 1702 G71v freed by Charles Spicer alias Helder

BUCKERIDGE, Henry   6 Sep 1697 F270r freed by Benjamin Motte

BUCKINGHAM, George Villiers, 2nd Duke of 26 Jun 1684 (W) letter to Master requesting S.C. to grant freedom to James Seguin, brother of Buckingham's chemist

See also REHEARSAL

BUCKLEY, Isaac 6 Dec 1714 G224r son of Samuel, is bound to William Pearson, 7 years

BUCKLEY, Samuel (I) 17 Apr 1701 G59r bookseller; to be employed in disposing of Oxford books overseas 5 May 1701 G59v draft articles between himself and S.C. concerning Oxford books approved 19 May 1701 G60r Articles between S.C. and himself sealed; paid £30 by the Treasurer 1 Dec 1701 G66r excused cloathing until next Court day 9 Feb 1701/2 G67r elected to cloathing 6 Jul 1702 G78r Henry Cartwright turned over to him 22 Apr 1703 G88v accounts between S.C. and himself for visiting France and Holland on the Company's behalf 7 Aug 1704 G110v to be requested to pay debt due to S.C. 4 Sep 1704 G111v to pay £10 of his debt forthwith and the rest to be referred to arbitration 6 Nov 1704 G113r committee to settle matters in difference between S.C. and himself 5 Feb 1704/5 G114v matters in dispute between S.C. and himself to be referred to [Thomas?] Bennett 2 Jul 1705 G121v Master to make agreement with him concerning matters in difference between S.C. and himself 6 Aug 1705 G122r agreement reached concerning differences with S.C. 6 Dec 1714 G224r his son Isaac is bound to William Pearson, 7 years

BUCKLEY, Samuel (II) 1 Dec 1701 G66r freed by Samuel Smith

BUCKTROUT, Mary 1 Sep 1712 G203r daughter of Thomas, is bound to Maurice Atkins, 7 years 3 Nov 1712 G205r turned over to Christian Davis

BUCKTROUT, Thomas – see previous entry

BUILDING 30 Sep 1680 E104v articles between S.C. and Knowles and Warren concerning building to be sealed

See also HALL

BULL, John 5 Jul 1708 G155r bound to Lewis Thomas, 7 years

BULLARD, John 19 Nov 1695 F236r servant to Daniel Blague; freed and cloathed 5 May 1701 G59v Thomas Parry is bound to him 7 Sep 1702 G80v Thomas Parry is turned over from him to Francis Leach

BULLOCK, Nathaniel (I) 22 Jun 1698 G9v general release from S.C. read and sealed

BULLOCK, Nathaniel (II) 7 Apr 1707 G141r bound to Abel Rockall, 7 years 7 Jun 1714 G219v freed by Abel Rockall

BULLOCK, Thomas 1 Sep 1701 G64r bound to William Marshall, 7 years 6 Sep 1708 G157v freed by William Marshall 4 Oct 1708 G158r of Holborn Bridge, stationer; Richard Perry is bound to him

BULLORD – see BULLARD

BUNCE, George 4 Oct 1708 G158r bound to Thomas his father, 7 years 7 Dec 1713 G215r freed by patrimony 4 Oct 1714 G222v James Campbell is bound to him

BUNCE, Thomas 4 Oct 1708 G158r arrears of quarterage to be suspended. Of Old Change; George Bunce, his son, is bound to him

BUNCHER, Edward 6 Mar 1703/4 G103v bound to Jasper Harmer, 7 years

BUNCHLEY, Samuel 4 Jun 1694 F208r servant to Charles Brome; freed

BURCH, Thomas 5 Aug 1700 G44r bound to George Mortimer, 7 years

BURCHAL, Ambrose 4 Oct 1703 G96r bound to George Butter, 7 years

BURDEN, James   6 May 1700 G39v bound to James Brookes, 7 years   2 Aug 1708 G156v freed by James Brookes

BURDETT, Charles   26 Mar 1702 G68v elected Assistant Renter Warden. To be summoned to next Court   13 Apr 1702 G70r fined for Renter Warden

BURDIKIN, [   ]   4 Feb 1711/12 G196r mortgage of John Amery's Livery share, held in trust by him, to be repaid   3 Mar 1711/12 G196v requests Court to dispose of Amery's share

BURDIKIN, Thomas   7 Apr 1690 F133r executor of Mary Rookes; assigns Francis Quarles's 'Argalus and Parthenia' to William Freeman on behalf of the late Thomas Rookes

BURDITT, Charles   4 Jun 1694 F208r cloathed

BUREAU/BUROE, [   ]   16 Jun 1684 F17r trading in Salisbury Exchange and one of the 'French persecuted Protestants'; his freedom to be considered at next Court   1 Sep 1684 F23r reported for dealing in scandalous books – (W) 'Arnauld'

BURFORD, Benjamin   6 Sep 1708 G157v bound to Bryan Mills, 7 years   9 Apr 1716 G239r freed by Bryan Mills

BURGES, Francis   4 Dec 1699 G34r freed by Freeman Collins

BURLEY, William, snr – see following entry

BURLEY, William, jnr   9 Apr 1716 G239r son of William, is bound to Thomas Lingard, 7 years

BURNABY, James   5 May 1701 G59r bound to Margaret Bennett, 7 years

BURNELL, John   12 Nov 1705 G125r bound to John Penn, 7 years

BURNETT, William   4 Oct 1708 G158r bound to Priscilla Harris, 7 years

BUROE, [   ] – see BUREAU

BURRIDGE, Adam   3 May 1697 F262r bound to William Hunt   20 Dec 1701 G66v turned over to James Holland   4 Jun 1705 G120v freed by William Hunt

BURROUGH/BURROWES, Richard   7 Jun 1697 F263r bound to Thomas Parkhurst   12 Jun 1704 G107v freed by Thomas Parkhurst

See also BURROUGHS, BURROW, BURROWES, BURROWS, BURROWSE

BURROUGHS, Widow   26 Mar 1690 F131r to have 20s as her usual allowance, which was omitted at Christmas

BURROUGHS, William   7 Dec 1685 F48r Thomas Brocket to be summoned re. failing to free Burroughs   22 Dec 1685 F49v freed, as Brocket fails to answer summons

See also BURROUGH, BURROW, BURROWES, BURROWS, BURROWSE

BURROW, Thomas   18 Jun 1689 F119v Court called at his request; is freed by patrimony, cloathed and his request to fine for Renter Warden deferred   1 Jul 1689 F120r request to fine for Renter Warden granted; to take his place under the present Renter Wardens

See also BURROUGH, BURROUGHS, BURROWES, BURROWS, BURROWSE

BURROWES, Christopher   12 Jun 1704 G107v bound to Thomas Burrows, 7 years

BURROWES, Samuel   3 Dec 1694 F215v servant to Thomas Guy; freed

See also BURROUGH, BURROUGHS, BURROW, BURROWS, BURROWSE

BURROWS, Elizabeth   24 Mar 1709/10 G176v elected to Mary Nuthall's pension. Nathan Brookes given her pension

BURROWS/BURROWES, Mrs 3 Feb 1688/9 F128v some members of S.C. petition on behalf of her and Mrs Eversden for S.C.'s annual payments to them, omitted last year; referred 7 Oct 1698 G15r to have same rooms in S.C.'s house leased by John Nutt as she had in Mrs Whitlock's lifetime. Her affidavit to be drawn up concerning lights of the Goldsmiths' Company

BURROWS, Thomas 12 Jun 1704 G107v Christopher Burrowes is bound to him 9 Jun 1707 G142r elected to Charles Harper's £160 share on condition that he relinquish all his pretences to be called on the Court of Assistants

See also BURROUGH, BURROUGHS, BURROW, BURROWES, BURROWSE

BURROWSE, Magdalen 24 Mar 1713/14 G217r deceased; Martha Barber given her pension

See also BURROUGH, BURROUGHS, BURROW, BURROWES, BURROWS

BURRY, William 3 May 1714 G219r son of Edward; bound to Israel Harrison, 7 years

BURSCOD – see BURSCOE

BURSCOE/BURSCOD, William 7 Nov 1698 G16r bound to Robert Steele, 8 years 5 Oct 1702 G81v turned over from Robert Steele to Samuel Illidge

BURT, Peter – see following entry

BURT, Samuel 12 Nov 1711 G195r son of Peter, is bound to Thomas Crane, 7 years

BURTON, [ ] (I) 7 Apr 1684 F14r (W) letter from Richard Graham and Burton recommending Capt. William Phillipps as an Assistant loyal to the Crown

BURTON, [ ] (II) 7 Feb 1703/4 G101v his answer required to S.C.'s Bill in Chancery

BURTON, Philip 22 Jun 1698 G9v general release from S.C. read and sealed

BURTON, William 6 May 1706 G131v bound to William Botham, 7 years 6 Jul 1713 G212v freed by William Botham

BUSBY, Dr Richard – see GRAMMARS

BUSH, Edmund 1 Jul 1695 F228r elected to Livery and summoned

BUSH, Edward 5 Aug 1695 F231r cloathed; pays £10 of his fine straight away

BUSH, John – see following entry

BUSH, Joseph 1 Oct 1694 F213v son of John Bush of Raneford, Herts, husbandman; bound to William Haddon 2 Mar 1701/2 G67v freed by William Haddon 27 Mar 1703 G87v Samuel Austin is bound to him 7 Jul 1707 G143v William Hornould is bound to him 6 Nov 1710 G185r mathematical instrument maker; George Underhill is bound to him 6 Jul 1713 G212v his apprentice George Underhill is turned over to Marshall 1 Mar 1713/14 G216v his apprentice Samuel Austin is freed

BUSH, Thomas 4 Jun 1705 G120v bound to Heames Pooler

BUTCHER, Stephen 5 Jun 1699 G25v bound to Edmund Rumball, 7 years

BUTLER 5 Mar 1704/5 G117r £3 of his £4 4s bill to be paid by Under Warden

BUTLER, Benjamin 7 Nov 1698 G16r bound to William Wild, 7 years 4 Feb 1705/6 G127v freed by William Wild

BUTLER, George 6 Jul 1713 G212v his son Thomas is bound to Samuel Butler, 7 years

BUTLER, John 4 Oct 1697 F268v bound to Luke Meredith

BUTLER, Richard (I) 7 May 1688 F101v bookbinder (W) printer, and prisoner in Ludgate; petitions (Copy in W). Court gives his wife 40s and asks her to compound her debts for consideration 6 Aug 1688 F106r petitions; Court orders him a further £6 to clear his debts and Warden ordered to see that Turner and Mrs Redmaine discontinue their lawsuits   23 Jun 1692 F172r elected into the 20s pension of Elizabeth Randall, deceased   27 Sep 1695 F232v deceased; Anthony Izod takes over his pension

BUTLER, Richard (II)   1 Mar 1713/14 G216v son of Thomas; is bound to Christopher Coningsby, 7 years

BUTLER, Samuel   7 Feb 1697/8 G3v bound to Charles Osborne   2 Jul 1705 G121v freed by Charles Osborne   7 Apr 1707 G141r stationer; Bryan Heming is bound to him   3 Mar 1711 G197r excused cloathing until next Court   6 Jul 1713 G212v Thomas Butler is bound to him   5 Oct 1713 G214r summoned to cloathing

BUTLER, Thomas (I)   1 Mar 1713/14 G216v his son Richard is bound to Christopher Coningsby, 7 years

BUTLER, Thomas (II)   6 Jul 1713 G212v son of George; bound to Samuel Butler, 7 years

BUTLER, William, snr – see following entry

BUTLER, William, jnr   12 Nov 1694 F215r son of William Butler of St Sepulchre's, tobacconist; bound to John Leake from 1 October 1694   9 Feb 1701/2 G67r freed by John Leake

BUTTER, George   5 May 1701 G59v his son John Butter is freed by patrimony on payment of his quarterage (entry for freedom transposes names)   6 Jul 1702 G78r William Williams is bound to him   4 Oct 1703 G96r Ambrose Burchal is bound to him

BUTTER, John   5 May 1701 G59v son of George; freed by patrimony on payment of father's quarterage (entry for freedom transposes names)

BUTTERFIELD, Richard   6 Aug 1711 G193r servant of Widow Mills; made free and cloathed

BUTTON, [   ]   6 Oct 1707 G145v and his mother to be prosecuted in Chancery for printing and selling counterfeit psalters and almanacks   10 Oct 1707 G146r Bill in Chancery to be brought against him to discover books imported   3 Nov 1707 G146r subpoena against him and his mother will not be served, at request of Churchill. To make full discovery to S.C.   1 Dec 1707 G147r Clerk to give Awnsham Churchill copy of part of S.C.'s Bill in Chancery against him

BUTTON, Mrs – see preceding entry

BYELAWS – see STATIONERS' COMPANY: BYELAWS

BYTHELL, William   3 May 1703 G89v bound to Thomas Hodgkins, 7 years

CADE, Charles   4 Feb 1705/6 G127v bound to James Oades, 7 years

CADMAN/CADEMAN/CADMANS, William   4 Dec 1682 E160v assigns four 1/5 shares in a chronological history of France [i.e. François Eudes de Mézeray, *A General Chronological History of France*] to Thomas Bassett, Samuel Lowndes, Christopher Wilkinson and Jacob Tonson   4 Aug 1684 F22r with Matthew Gilliflower and John Harding, presents the grievances of 129 S.C. members; Master asks for instances   1 Sep 1684 F23r further to grievances, gives proofs that various French booksellers have dealt in scandalous books   1 Dec 1690 F147r Thomas Dring produces in court Cadman's assignment of half of 'The Rehearsal' [by George Villiers, 2nd Duke of Buckingham] to him, and Francis Saunders renounces claim to it

CAESAR, [Gaius Julius]   18 Mar 1686/7 F79v his 'Commentaries' among books in calendar annexed to Oxford agreement

CAIRNS/CAIRNES, John   6 Dec 1703 G99v bound to John Hunter, 7 years   4 Jun 1711 G191r freed by John Hunter

CAISTER, Thomas   6 May 1689 F117v appointed surety for Treasurer with Samuel Jewell; Clerk to draw up their bond to S.C.

CAKES and ALE   4 Oct 1686 F64r Roger Norton objects, as an auditor of the Warden's accounts, to S.C. and not Wardens paying for these; precedents are cited. Ordered that no cakes and ale to be had henceforth on 6 May

CALDECOTT, Thomas   20 Dec 1706 G137r bound to William Rogers, 7 years   3 Nov 1712 G205r turned over to William Freeman

CALENDAR   26 Mar 1700 G36v request to print calendar containing matters relating to trade to the Indias left to Master and Wardens to settle

CALOWE – see CALLOWE

COMPANY'S CALENDAR – see ALMANACKS

CALLOWE/CALOWE, John   4 Oct 1714 G222v son of William, is bound to John Clarke, 7 years   6 May 1717 G250v turned over from John Clarke to George Oldner
See also KELLOW

CALVERLY, Edmund   5 Apr 1703 G88r bound to Thomas Harbin, 7 years   5 Feb 1710/11 G187r of Southwark, stationer; freed by Thomas Harbin; Joseph Chilly is bound to him   6 Oct 1712 G204v John Serjeant is bound to him

CALVERT, George   2 Jul 1681 E115r fined for Upper Warden   6 Feb 1681/2 E142r competes unsuccessfully for Upper Warden on the death of the previous one, Thomas Newcomb; to forfeit next dividend for selling about 300 copies of Psalms in metre without S.C.'s permission   6 Mar 1681/2 E146v Court order of 6 Feb re. stoppage of his dividend confirmed   5 Feb 1682/3 E163r to be paid £10 of last dividend, sequestered by order of Court of 6 Feb 1681/2   30 Jun 1683 F1r to be excused Upper Wardenship 'by reason of several defects and impediments in Nature'   2 Jul 1683 F2r requests all of sequestered dividend; Court confirms previous ruling and defers to next Court his request to dispose of share   12 Nov 1683 F5r competes unsuccessfully for Mrs Stephens's £320 share   7 Jan 1684 F7v competes unsuccessfully for the late Mrs Roper's £320 share   3 Jul 1686 F58r his £10 dividend, sequestered by courts of 6 Feb 1681/2 and 5 Feb 1682/3, to be disposed of to the poor   2 Aug 1686 F61v Philip Briggs given £7 out of Calvert's sequestered dividend   1 Mar 1687/8 F97v displaced as Assistant by order of Crown and expelled from Livery by order of Lord Mayor   6 Aug 1688 F105r surviving signatory of the original deed of conveyance of St Martin's Ludgate   1 Jul 1689 F120v to re-execute conveyance to present Court members   4 May 1691 F153v voted that he should not be allowed to surrender his £160 share to Thomas Bennett   3 Aug 1691 F158v deceased; his £160 share voted to Nathaniel Ranew

CAMDEN'S GRAMMAR – see CAMDEN, William

CAMBRIDGE UNIVERSITY   8 Nov 1686 F67r committee to treat with administrators of Thomas Sawbridge jnr for interest in Cambridge printing   19 Nov 1686 F67r committee re. buying Sawbridge's interest could not take place because Edward Brewster failed to turn up at the tavern   4 Feb 1687/8 F112v committee to treat with Edward Brewster about Cambridge business   3 Feb 1689/90 F128v Thomas Bassett and Henry Mortlock added to committee appointed on 4th Feb 1687/8 to negotiate with Master about Cambridge   1 Mar 1689/90 F129v at committee meeting, Master offers to sell to S.C. for £100 p.a. his interest in Cambridge printing gained as executor of Hannah and Thomas Sawbridge   11 Apr 1690 F134r Master willing to have his interest bought for 100 guineas, S.C. buying materials and school books and Master paying all charges to last Lady Day   5 May 1690 F134v Court agrees to committee's conclusion, though it alters the date of the commencement to next Midsummer day   8 Jul 1690 F139v some of the £1500 borrowed for Stock to go towards paying Brewster for the Cambridge stock and printing privilege   4 Dec 1690 F147v James Hayes and Benjamin Tooke become obliged to Cambridge on behalf of S.C. for payment of £100 p.a. for University privileges   7 Sep 1691 F159r committee to manage the printing of Stock books at Cambridge to render English Stock more profitable. Court agrees to Hayes appointing Warehousekeeper for printing house. Committee asked to negotiate with Roger Norton re. number of grammars printed at Cambridge   25 Nov 1692 F182v Treasurer to pay the £100 due last March to Cambridge for rent   7 Aug 1693 F190r new Stock to pay rent of £100 p.a. No more than 500 reams p.a. of almanacks and school books, to be sold to S.C. at 20s. per ream, to be printed there   18 Sep 1693 F191v S.C. to print only 3000 of Lilly's Grammar, the same as the University printer who is limited by a 1635 Order of the Council Board   7 Sep 1696 F248v Vice-Chancellor gives details of the printing house the university intends to set up and their wish to rent the S.C.'s printing house; committee appointed   5 Oct 1696 F250r committee gives details of its negotiations with Vice-Chancellor   5 Jun 1699 G25r consideration of printing Greek Testament there   5 May 1701 G59v new sheet almanack to be printed there by S.C.'s printer   2 Mar 1701/2 G67v renewal of agreement with John Hayes, S.C.'s printer there   26 Mar 1702 G69r articles of agreement between S.C. and Hayes sealed   12 Jul 1703 F92v Master and Wardens to attend Head of Queen's College concerning lease of printing house from University   22 Jul 1703 G93r Court decides that privilege of printing there should be secured   2 Aug 1703 G93v committee has attended Vice-Chancellor re. securing the privilege of printing at Cambridge and has resolved not to let the privilege of printing to any person holding Hayes' house   21 Oct 1703 G96r Court has met to discuss letters concerning. Capt. William Phillipps to answer letter from the Vice-Chancellor, and Henry Mortlock to answer letter from Hayes. Feild's lease from to be delivered to Joseph Collyer the Warehousekeeper   6 Dec 1703 G99r Collyer to be indemnified for bond made with Cambridge on S.C.'s behalf   7 Feb 1703/4 G101r committee to consider Hayes' account relating to Cambridge affairs   3 Apr 1704 G105v letter from Hayes relating to printing there to be referred to Stock-keepers   3 Dec 1705 G125v Hayes, S.C.'s printer at Cambridge, has died. Committee to treat with Vice-Chancellor about printing there   8 Dec 1705 G126v Articles between University and S.C.   13 Dec 1705 G126v Articles between S.C. and University, granting S.C. privilege of printing for 21 years, signed on 8 December 1705   11 Mar 1705/6 G129v Articles between S.C. and University sealed   5 Aug 1706 G133v committee to settle Cambridge affairs   9 Sep 1706 G134v Robert Stephens to visit concerning matters relating to S.C.'s printing house there   6 Oct 1707 G145v Robert Stephens to prepare an account of printing letters and materials for   1 Sep 1712 G203r S.C. not to let or make use of Cambridge privilege for 7 years as part of terms of Oxford agreement

See also OXFORD AND CAMBRIDGE UNIVERSITIES, all entries for HAYES and SAWBRIDGE, KING'S PRINTERS, ENGLISH STOCK

CAMBRIDGE PRIMER   7 Jun 1680 E100v printing of stock Cambridge primer assigned to John Macock and Mrs Maxwell

CAMDEN, [William]   18 Sep 1693 F191v S.C. and agents will not comprint on Camden's grammar at Oxford

CAMP, John   2 Oct 1704 G112v bound to John Marshall, 8 years   6 Feb 1709/10 G175v turned over from John Marshall to William Marshall   6 Oct 1712 G204v freed by William Marshall

CAMPBELL, Archibald, Marquis of Argyll – see ARGYLL

CAMPBELL, James   4 Oct 1714 G222v son of John, is bound to George Bunce, 7 years

CAMPBELL, John – see previous entry

CANTERBURY, ARCHBISHOP OF (William Sancroft, consecrated 29 Jan 1678, deprived 1 Feb 1690; John Tillotson, consecrated 31 May 1691, d. 22 Nov 1694)   1 Mar 1683/4 F9r orders that the feast of St Matthias be celebrated on February 24, not 25; almanacks therefore to be rectified by Treasurer   22 Aug 1685 F43r Master tells Court that the Archbishop refuses to license prognostications; Court asks him to head a deputation. Grants Robert Midgely the power to license books in his stead under the revived Printing Act   7 Sep 1685 F43v ordered that all almanacks are to be licensed by him   5 Mar 1685/6 F52v committee meeting resolves that the Wardens shall entreat him not to license stall booksellers   4 Feb 1688/9 F112v dispute with Oxford re. almanacks to be discussed with him   28 Sep 1693 F191v requests that Robert Stephens be allowed access to registers

CAPELL, George – see following entry

CAPELL, Nathaniel   1 Oct 1711 G194v son of George, is bound to Samuel Welchman, 7 years

CAPP, William   1 Dec 1707 G147v bound to John Chantry, 7 years

CAPPELL, Lewis   7 Apr 1712 G199r son of Francis, is bound to Ralph Snow, 7 years

CARDMAKERS   1 Apr 1697 F260v to be approached about giving donations towards a Paper Act test case

CARE, Henry   2 Oct 1682 E158r Richard Janeway confesses to printing 'A Letter to His Royal Highness the D— Y—' [i.e. *A Letter to his Royal Highness the Duke of York* (1681)?] and 'A Letter from the Old Common Council to the New' [i.e. D.N., Old Common-Council-man, *A Letter from an Old Common-Council-Man to One of the New Common-Council* (1682)?] for him

See also ENGLISH LIBERTIES

CARELESSE, Ebenezer   5 Aug 1695 F232r son of John Carelesse of Gloucester, gentleman; bound to John Marshall

CARELESSE, John – see preceding entry

CAREY/CARY, George   6 Nov 1710 G185r son of Henry, is bound to Dorman Newman, 7 years   7 Nov 1715 G234v turned over from Dorman Newman to John Dutton

CAREY, Henry – see preceding entry

See also CARY

CARLTON/CARLETON – see CHARLETON

CARPENTERS   12 Jun 1693 F188v bills of £13 14s paid for work on Hall   10 Jan 1697/8 G18r to take care to prevent damage to Hall from scaffolding used for the Mine Adventure Lottery   15 Jun 1704 G107v bill to be paid   2 Apr 1705 G118r bills paid   4 Feb 1705/6 G127r bill for stands for S.C. during the Queen's visit to St Paul's to be referred to the Master and Wardens   5 Aug 1706 G134r bill for stands for S.C. when Queen visited St Paul's to be settled by Master and Wardens   3 Feb 1706/7 G137v bill to be paid   1 Dec 1707 G147r bill for making S.C.'s stand last Thanksgiving Day to be adjusted by Master and Wardens   4 Oct 1708 G158r bill referred to Master and Wardens for payment   7 Dec 1713 G215r bill for work done about Hall to be paid by Warden   4 Oct 1714 G222r bill of £4 8s for work done for English Stock to be paid by Joseph Collyer

See also HALL

CARPENTER, [ ]   1 Sep 1712 G203r to be paid £150 due on his bond in three months

CARPENTER, Daniel – see following entry

CARPENTER, Peter   7 Apr 1712 G199r son of Daniel; bound to John Clarke, 7 years

CARPENTER, Thomas   1 Mar 1698/9 G21r surety for Benjamin Tooke   1 Mar 1699/1700 G36r surety for Benjamin Tooke   1 Mar 1700/01 G56r surety for Benjamin Tooke   20 Jul 1704 G110r arbitrator on behalf of Benjamin Tooke

CARR, [ ]   25 Jun 1684 F18v free of the Skinners' Company; declares himself willing to be translated to S.C.

CARR, Mrs   7 Feb 1714/15 G224v daughter of Mrs Mary Cooper; Clerk to give her notice that if she does not pay money due to Benjamin Poole before next Court day her share will be disposed of

CARR, Nicholas, snr – see following entry

CARR, Nicholas, jnr   3 Mar 1711/12 G197r son of Nicholas; bound to Nathaniel Cliff, 7 years

CARR, [Samuel]   4 Oct 1686 F64v Keeper of His Majesty's Library; demands a copy of every book printed in and about London under the Printing Act

CARTER, [ ]   6 Sep 1697 F266v asks to renew lease on S.C. house, of which Mrs Mills has head lease. Court tells him that, whatever happens, he will be given plenty of notice   7 Aug 1699 G29r request for new lease deferred   4 Sep 1699 G29v lease to be renewed but does not accept S.C.'s terms   8 Nov 1708 G158v house to be viewed by workmen   23 Jun 1709 G166r S.C.'s tenant in Ave Maria Lane; complaint that foundations of house are in danger due to flooding   4 Jul 1709 G167r Court has considered matter of his house. Capt. William Phillipps to meet Jackson, an officer of the Commissioner of Sewers, to consider how a drain may be made into the common sewer   7 Jul 1709 G168r Ford, bricklayer, to examine pipes and see if water can be prevented from coming into the cellar of his house   1 Sep 1712 G203r his house to be viewed by workmen again   6 Oct 1712 G203v report by Master on repairs needed to his house before he can lease it from the S.C.   1 Dec 1712 G205v workmen's bills for repairing his house to be settled by Master and Wardens   4 May 1713 G209v enquiry as to whether house is worth more rent than he paid   1 Jun 1713 G210r committee of the opinion that his house would not produce more rent

CARTER, [ ]   2 Jul 1709 G166v smith; to undertake repairs to Morphew's house

CARTER, Hannah   3 Mar 1700/1 G57r Elizabeth James is bound to her

CARTER, Henry   2 Apr 1694 F202v Thomas Franklin is bound to him for seven years   7 Nov 1698 G16r his apprentice William Smith is freed   7 Aug 1699 G29r mathematical instrument maker; his apprentice William Watson is freed   5 Feb 1699/1700 G35r William Hunt is bound to him   2 Jun 1701 G60v Thomas Jacques is bound to him   9 Feb 1701/2 G67r his apprentice Thomas Franklin is freed   5 Jul 1703 G92r James Andrews is bound to him   5 Aug 1706 G134r his apprentice William Chapman is freed   7 Nov 1709 G172r mathematical instrument maker; William Hill is bound to him   6 Mar 1709/10 G176v of Witch Street, mathematical instrument maker; Edward Skinner is bound to him   4 Jul 1715 G231r William Jackson is bound to him   10 Sep 1716 G243r Christopher Harrison is bound to him

CARTER, John   5 Apr 1703 G88r bound to John Ford, 7 years

CARTER, Moses   7 Mar 1708/9 G162r bound to Jane Sowle, 7 years

CARTER, Mrs   2 Jun 1712 G200r granted new lease on one of S.C.'s houses in Ave Maria Lane   6 Jul 1713 G212r complaint that vault has broken into the well. Master

113

and Wardens to settle   3 Aug 1713 G212v repairs to be done to her house   2 Aug 1714 G221r house to be whitewashed

CARTER, William   5 Jun 1699 G25v bound to Henry Bonwick, 7 years   9 Sep 1706 G134v freed by Rebecca Bonwick

CARTWRIGHT, Henry   7 Jul 1701 G62r bound to Jasper Roberts, 7 years   6 Jul 1702 G78r turned over to Samuel Buckley from Jasper Roberts

CARTWRIGHT, William   2 May 1698 G7v surety of a person who borrowed money from S.C. Clerk to enquire about him

CARVER   26 Mar 1683 E167v bill to be inspected

CARY, Edward   9 Feb 1690/1 F148r late tenant by lease of Pellipar; copy of letter from him to Skinners' Company re. dividends is read   6 Jul 1691 F157r letter from him setting forth his Irish losses is sent by Clerk of Skinners' Company to S.C.

CARY, Henry   4 Feb 1705/6 G127v bound to Jeremiah Milner, 7 years

CARY, Robert   7 Apr 1712 G198v bond from S.C. of £200 penalty for payment of £103 on 8 October sealed

See also CAREY

CASTLE, [ ]   5 Apr 1703 G88r summoned to next Court to take cloathing

CASTLE, Edward   4 Mar 1694/5 F218v is freed by Henry Mortlock   3 Apr 1704 G105v elected to cloathing   8 May 1704 G106v to be summoned to next Court to take cloathing   7 Aug 1704 G110v to be proceeded against for not accepting cloathing   12 Nov 1705 G125r required to attend next Court to accept cloathing. To be summoned before Lord Mayor if he refuses   27 Mar 1710 G177v to be summoned to take cloathing   3 Apr 1710 G178r to be attended by Clerk requesting his appearance to explain non-acceptance of cloathing   1 May 1710 G179r Court to proceed against him if he does not accept cloathing

CASTLE, George   1 Mar 1685/6 F51v cloathed   1 Mar 1687/8 F97v expelled from Livery by order of Lord Mayor   11 Oct 1688 F108v restored to Livery   26 Mar 1694 F201v elected Renter Warden and summoned   2 Apr 1694 F202r Thomas Dring requests on Castle's behalf that he may fine for Assistant Renter Warden

CATECHISMS   3 Jan 1680/1 E106r Dorman Newman to be questioned re. his complaint against Warden Vere for seizing [Westminster] Assembly's Catechism   7 Feb 1680/1 E107r Mearne and Vere to search for Bishop of London's order for damasking Assembly's Catechism   7 Mar 1680/1 E107v Vere and Mearne to bring the Bishop of London's order for damasking Assembly's Catechism to the next Court   1 Oct 1683 F4r Dr Edward Boughen's 'Catechism in Latin and English' is assigned to Henry Mortlock by Mary Garret   7 Sep 1685 F44r Charles Broome pays 5 guineas to print 5000 catechisms to annex to [Thomas Ken] the Bishop of Bath and Wells's 'Exposition of the Catechism'   7 Dec 1685 F48r Charles Broome confesses to printing more catechisms than he had leave to   6 Jun 1687 F84v Charles Broome admits to printing these, with exposition by the Bishop of Bath and Wells, 'in a larger letter than heretofore'   7 Jul 1690 F138v Watts is given a licence to print an impression of 750 of the Church Catechism for 30s   6 Apr 1691 F152r Oxford committee asked to enquire into the charge that Henry Bonwick has printed an exposition of the Church Catechism   8 Jun 1691 F154r controversy over Dorman Newman's 'uttering and selling' Dr [John] Williams's Catechism, all catechisms and paraphrases being Stock books; Williams is said to be willing to make S.C. an allowance   7 Dec 1691 F163r Luke Meredith fined 30s for printing an impression of 1000 of Dr Sherlock's Catechism [i.e.

Richard Sherlock, *The Principles of Holy Christian Religion*]. Dorman Newman not allowed abatement of £9 fine for printing Dr Williams's Catechism   12 Apr 1692 F168v Luke Meredith pays 30s fine for printing Dr Sherlock's Catechism   1 Aug 1692 F177r Henry Bonwick and Joseph Watts summoned to explain why they have printed [Thomas] Jekyll's Catechism illegally   5 Sep 1692 F178r Henry Bonwick to be summoned for printing the Church Catechism without a licence   3 Oct 1692 F180r Joseph Watts pays 30s for permission to print and sell Church Catechisms and 30s fine for having printed 750 already   4 Sep 1693 F191r Master, Wardens and others to wait upon Dr Williams concerning his catechism   5 Feb 1693/4 F198v Thomas Bradyll summoned to Stock-keepers' meeting re. printing several impressions of the [Westminster] Assembly's Catechism. [Edward] Brewster is desired to purchase Dr [Simon] Ford's 'Comment or Annotations upon the Church Catechism' for S.C.   7 May 1694 F203r both the long and the shorter versions of the [Westminster] Assembly's Catechism and Confession of Faith to be sold for £100 or more. Thomas Bradyll to be compelled to set forth how many of the Assembly's Catechism he has printed   3 Dec 1694 F215v Robert Clavell allowed to print as many of 'Dr Cumber's' [i.e. Thomas Comber's] catechisms as he likes, paying S.C. 4d per quire. Fined £10 for printing 750 Church Catechisms with proofs   6 Jul 1696 F246r Robert Clavell allowed to print a third impression of Dr [Zaccheus] Isham's Catechism, at same price as before   30 Sep 1696 F249v Thomas Parkhurst allowed to print Richard Mayo's Catechism, paying S.C. the same rate as Robert Clavell does for Dr Isham's   7 Feb 1703/4 G101v William Hawes granted permission to print 'Church Catechism with prayers, graces and texts of scripture annexed thereto'   27 Mar 1704 G105r Church Catechism printed with a mistake by Benjamin Motte   3 Apr 1704 G105v Benjamin Motte to rectify mistake in printing of 'Church Catechism with Scripture Proofs' but printing of it to be taken from him   4 Apr 1709 G164r 'Exposition of the Church Catechism' [i.e. *The Church Catechism Explain'd* by John Lewis], printed by William Hawes without leave of S.C.   5 Apr 1714 G218r Church Catechism printed by Henry Hoare. Hawes, who printed it formerly, has paid an acknowledgement to S.C.   3 May 1714 G218v 'Exposition of Mrs Lewis [*sic*] of the Catechism' printed by Downing for Hoare. Wilkins, who printed it formerly, has paid an acknowledgement to S.C.

CATEN, Mrs   3 Mar 1700/1 G57r widow, granted remittance of arrears in quarterage

CATER, Elizabeth   5 Mar 1704 G117r freed by patrimony

CATER, Joseph   5 Dec 1698 G17r his apprentice Thomas Martyn is freed

CATER, Thomas   8 Jun 1696 F243r servant to John Place; freed   1 Aug 1698 G11v cloathed   8 May 1699 G24v Clerk to obtain Livery fine from him

CATHOLICS   3 Apr 1682 E149v Gabriel Cox pleads inability to serve as Renter Warden since he is a convicted Catholic and all his goods have been seized   2 Mar 1690/1 F150r some Assistants suggest that Widow Hills, by being convicted a recusant, has forfeited her share

CAUCKING, John   4 Jun 1694 F208v son of Ralph Caucking of Donum on the Hill, Chester, weaver; bound to Daniel Brogden

CAUCKING, Ralph – see preceding entry

CAUSSIN, Nicholas   3 Feb 1695/6 F238v assignment of his 'Holy Court' to Bennett Griffin entered

CAVE, Edward   6 Feb 1709/10 G175v bound to Freeman Collins, 7 years   4 Mar 1716/17 G247v freed by Susanna Collins

CAVE, Mary   24 Dec 1708 G160r bond from S.C. for payment of £153 15s on 25 June and for payment of £51 5s on 25 September sealed   9 Feb 1712/13 G206r two bonds from S.C. for £200 cancelled

See also following entry

CAVELL, Mary   5 Feb 1699/1700 G35r bond from S.C. of £200 penalty to pay £100 and interest at 5% p.a.

See also preceding entry

CECIL, [ ]   7 Sep 1702 G80r MP for Stamford, Lincs; his request that Pepper's Almanack be printed, made in conjunction with his fellow MP Charles Bertie, is granted

CELLARS   4 Aug 1690 F141r John Baker to pay rent due for storing books in S.C. cellar before he removes them   1 Sep 1690 F142r John Williams summoned to next Court re. rent for S.C. cellars

CHALDECOTE/CHALDECOTTE, Charles   9 Jun 1707 G142v bound to William Bowyer, 7 years   5 Jul 1714 G220v freed by William Bowyer

CHALENER, John   5 Dec 1698 G17r bound to Gerard Dennet, 7 years   2 Dec 1706 G136v freed by Gerard Dennet

CHAMBER OF LONDON – see LONDON, CITY OF

CHAMBERLAIN OF LONDON – see LONDON, CITY OF

CHAMBERLAIN, Elizabeth   6 Dec 1697 G2r bound to Benjamin Bound

CHAMBERLAINE/CHAMBERLAYNE, John   2 May 1709 G165r bound to Matthew Jenour, 7 years   4 Jun 1716 G240v freed by Matthew Jenour

CHAMBERS, Ephraim   1 Feb 1713/14 G216r son of Richard, is bound to John Senex, 7 years

CHAMBERS, Richard – see preceding entry

CHAMBERS, Zachary   2 Oct 1710 G184v bound to Ralph Snow, 7 years

CHANDLER, [ ]   3 Oct 1715 G233v freed by patrimony

CHANDLER, Mary   27 Sep 1710 G184r elected pensioner in place of Mary Snowden

CHANDLER, William   6 Nov 1704 G113r Joseph Crosier is bound to him

CHANDLEY, Thomas   29 May 1689 F118v cloathed

CHANTRY, John, snr – see following entry

CHANTRY/CHAUNTRY, John, jnr   3 Jun 1695 F226r son of the late John Chantry of Canterbury; bound to Edward Morey   6 Jul 1702 G78r freed by Edward Morey   1 Dec 1707 G147v bookseller; William Capp is bound to him

See also CHAUNTRY

CHAPLIN, Jasper   6 Oct 1712 G204r freed by James Adamson

CHAPMAN, [ ]   6 Jun 1709 G165v Clerk to meet commissioners of bankruptcy proceedings against him, concerning letter sent to Court   3 Oct 1709 G171r Clerk to enquire of commissioners of bankruptcy the value of books he held in co-partnership with John Sprint, with a view to purchasing them for S.C.

CHAPMAN, Christopher   7 Feb 1703/4 G101v bound to William Sparkes, 7 years

CHAPMAN, Hannah   22 Jun 1705 G120v deceased; Thomas Spicer alias Helder is given her pension

CHAPMAN, Sir John   4 Mar 1688/9 F114r Lord Mayor of London; commends William Smith for a position as S.C. butler

CHAPMAN, John   7 Jul 1701 G62r bound to Edward Davis, 7 years

CHAPMAN, Richard   5 Aug 1706 G134r Samuel Fairman is bound to him

CHAPMAN, Thomas   8 Nov 1703 G97r his apprentice George Harris is freed

CHAPMAN, William   5 Aug 1706 G134r freed by Henry Carter   4 Oct 1708 G158r
of Bishopgate Street; John Watson is bound to him   5 Oct 1713 G214r Richard
Trantum is bound to him   4 Apr 1715 G227v Henry Trent is bound to him

CHAPMEN   28 Oct 1697 F270r letter signed by the Treasurer to be sent to chapmen
and dealers in almanacks warning them against counterfeit ones

CHAPPELL, Richard   5 Mar 1710/11 G188r bound to David Edwards, 7 years

CHARITY   22 Jun 1687 F85r William Hammond leaves £10 to S.C. poor   7 Nov
1687 F94v John Crosse's charity payment of 20s is made on condition that it should be
one-off, since he is not a freeman of the Company   20 Dec 1688 F112r the late Thomas
Passenger's legacy of 40s to the S.C. poor is paid into the Poor Box   13 Mar 1691/2
F184v committee to inspect S.C.'s charity money and see what fines have been levied for
binding apprentices by foreign indenture

CHARITY SCHOOLS   5 Jul 1708 G155r proposal of Downing concerning printing a
collection of prayers for

CHARLES, William   22 Jun 1705 G120v elected to Margaret Duncomb's pension   21
Mar 1705/6 G129v deceased; Jane Marsh is given his pension

CHARLETON/CHARLTON/CARLTON, [ ]   26 Mar 1701 G57v jnr, elected
Bargemaster's Mate   26 Mar 1702 G68v elected Bargemaster's Mate   26 Mar 1712
G198r elected Bargemaster's Mate

CHARLETON/CHARLTON/CARLTON, Francis   26 Mar 1686 F54r elected waterman   1687–1699 and 1704, 1709, 1716, 1717 Bargemaster's Mate   5 Aug 1689 (W)
request to be made free deferred   10 Jan 1698/9 G18v Bargemaster's Mate; complaint
against him that he had damaged the Barge   7 Feb 1698/9 G20r debate on complaint
against him to be adjourned

CHARLETON/CHARLTON, Henry   7 Mar 1691/2 F167r admitted to an oar in the
barge in place of George Ellis, deceased

CHARLETON/CHARLTON, John   26 Mar 1686 F54r elected waterman   8 Nov
1686 F67r elected Bargemaster's Mate   4 Apr 1687 F81v elected waterman

CHARLETON/CHARLTON, Robert   27 Mar 1710 G177v elected Bargemaster's
Mate   26 Mar 1711 G189r elected Bargemaster's Mate

CHARLETON/CHARLTON/CARLTON, Thomas   1700, 1703, 1705–1708, 1713–
1715 Bargemaster's Mate   26 Mar 1705 G117v in unsuccessful competition for Bargemaster

CHARLTON – see CHARLETON

CHARNLEY, John   1 Oct 1694 F213r excused cloathing until next Court

CHARNOCK, William   5 Aug 1700 G44r bound to John Ford, 7 years

CHARTER   27 May 1684 F14v new one read   10 Jun 1684 F16v John Lilly awarded
50 guineas for his 'great care and pains' in passing the new charter   4 Aug 1684 F22r
committee to consider how to redress grievances presented by William Cadman,
Mathew Gilliflower, John Harding and 126 other S.C. members by means of
charter   27 Nov 1688 F109v surrender of old charter and granting of new one by late
Majesty declared void   3 Dec 1688 F111r committee to take legal advice about
renewing it   28 Jul 1692 F176r charter lost in Great Fire but S.C. is able to send sealed
exemplification of charter to Lord Mayor over Giles Sussex affair

CHARTERHOUSE   2 May 1681 E111v George Tokefeild claims he is in here as a pensioner

CHASE, James   1 Jul 1695 F228v Thomas Chessell is bound to him

CHAUNTRY, [   ]   3 Mar 1706/7 G139r matter of his 20 shares in the 'New Version of the Psalms' deferred to next Court   26 Mar 1707 G140r his proposal for S.C to buy 20 shares in Tate and Brady's Psalms rejected

See also CHANTRY

CHAWBLIN, Henry   7 Oct 1695 F234r servant to Richard Simpson; freed

CHEESE, Tace   4 Jun 1694 F208v Edward Saunders is bound to her   4 Feb 1694/5 F217r deceased; William Hill elected to her £40 share   3 Nov 1701 G65r and Tace Sowle. Their apprentice Edward Saunders is freed

CHEQUE BOOK   5 Oct 1696 F250v neglected since December 1693; to be brought up to date and continued by Upper Warden

CHERRETT, William   26 Mar 1700 G38r bound to Charles Brome, 8 years

CHESHIRE STEWARDS   15 Mar 1693/4 F201r hall to be let to them for their feast at 3 guineas if they wish it

CHESSELL, Samuel – see following entry

CHESSELL, Thomas   1 Jul 1695 F228v son of Samuel Chessell of St Giles-in-the-Fields, cordwainer; bound to James Chase from last Michaelmas

CHESTER   7 Dec 1685 F47v workmen printers complain of illegal printing house there   3 Dec 1694 F215v Ichabod Dawkes petitions against a press at Chester, suggesting that recent seditious pamphlets may come from there   22 Jun 1697 F263r Chester printer to be prosecuted for unlicensed printing of almanacks   5 Feb 1710/11 G186v Bill in Chancery to be brought against Chester carrier for bringing almanacks imported from Ireland to Chester

CHIFFINS, Thomas   2 Jun 1701 G60v bound to Thomas James, 8 years

CHILD/CHILDE, Timothy   4 Oct 1697 F268v William Kempster is bound to him   3 Jul 1699 G27r and Nicholson present paper concerning copyright of 'Satires of Juvenal and Persius'; reference before the Treasurer to be expedited   6 Feb 1709/10 G175r elected to Matthew Wootton's £40 share. Takes oath of partner   1 Mar 1709/10 G176r elected Stock-keeper for Yeomanry   7 May 1711 G190v St Paul's Churchyard, bookseller; Jonathan Nicks is bound to him   1 Mar 1711/12 G197v elected Stock-keeper for Yeomanry   2 Mar 1712/13 G207r elected Stock-keeper for Yeomanry   1 Mar 1713/14 G216v elected Stock-keeper for Yeomanry   1 Mar 1714/15 G225v elected Stock-keeper for Yeomanry   1 Mar 1715/16 G236v elected Stock-keeper for Yeomanry   1 Mar 1716/17 G247r elected Stock-keeper for Yeomanry

CHILD, Humphrey   6 Dec 1703 G99v bound to Christopher Meggs, 7 years   5 Mar 1710/11 G188r freed by Christopher Meggs   7 Apr 1712 G199r Cuthbert Walker is bound to him   4 Apr 1715 G227v John Meggs is bound to him   2 May 1715 G228v John Meggs turned over from him to William Lefosse

CHILD, Richard   2 Nov 1702 G83r bound to James Walker, 7 years

CHILDE – see CHILD

CHILD'S GUIDE   7 Jun 1680 E100v different signatures of stock 'Child's Guide' assigned to various people

CHILLY, Joseph   5 Feb 1710/11 G187r bound to Edmund Calverly, 7 years

CHINERY, Richard, snr – see following entry

CHINERY, Richard, jnr   1 Oct 1694 F213v son of the late Richard Chinery of Kennett, Cambridgeshire, gentleman; bound to William Freeman, 7 years

CHISWELL, Richard   11 Apr 1681 E109v fined for Renter Warden   2 Apr 1683 E168r Mrs White asks to make over her £160 share to Chiswell, who has agreed to buy it for £180; Court advises mortgaging it for £150   2 Jul 1683 F2r competes unsuccessfully for Ann Godbidd's £80 share   7 Sep 1685 F44r to be summoned with Benjamin Tooke and Waterson re. printing a Stock book, 'Daniel and Thursfeild's History' [i.e. Samuel Daniel & John Trussell, *History of England*?]   7 Dec 1685 F47v in Benjamin Harris's partnership for printing the proceedings of the Westminster Parliament   11 Oct 1688 F108v restored to Livery   4 Feb 1688/9 F112v re-elected Assistant   4 Mar 1688/9 F114r elected to the late Rebecca Beadle's £80 share   6 May 1689 F117r to be placed according to his seniority in the Haberdashers' Company, from which he was translated. Takes Assistants' oath and is also sworn into his £80 share   5 Aug 1689 F122v Mrs Beadle's executors complain he has not paid for the share and he explains his dissatisfaction with S.C.'s electing shareholders who do not understand the trade   4 Nov 1689 F126r to have his share voted to someone else if he does not pay for it by next Court   2 Dec 1689 F127v pays for his Yeomanry share   3 Feb 1689/90 F129r to pay £5 in lieu of a dinner on his election as an Assistant   5 Jun 1690 F135v re-elected Assistant   7 Jul 1690 F139r competes unsuccessfully for Thomas Bassett's £160 share   9 Feb 1690/1 F149r competes unsuccessfully for the late Susanna Leigh's £160 share   12 Apr 1692 F169r seen by examination of S.C.'s and Haberdashers' records to be junior to Richard Simpson, and summoned re. his complaint. Voted that he should not have the £160 share fallen vacant on the death of Mrs Passenger   4 Jul 1692 F173v elected to John Simms's £160 share   13 Mar 1692/3 F184v augments committee of 1 March 1692 considering ways to raise money for dividends and carry on Oxford printing   3 Apr 1693 F185v as a co-proprietor of the English Josephus, complains that Roger L'Estrange's new translation will affect his sales   3 Jul 1693 F189v among those chosen to audit Warden's accounts   5 Feb 1693/4 F198r added to committee advising on drain to be shared with St Martin's Ludgate   2 Jul 1694 F210r elected Stock-keeper for Assistants to replace Samuel Lowndes, now Under Warden. Among those chosen to audit Warden's accounts   10 Sep 1694 F212r out of town for some time; Richard Simpson takes over as auditor of Warden's accounts   12 Nov 1694 F214v involved in Matthew Wootton's complaint over Horace   6 Jul 1695 F229v among those chosen to audit Warden's accounts   6 Jul 1696 F246v among those chosen to audit Warden's accounts   30 Sep 1696 F249v on Mrs Royston's behalf demands compensation for boards, &c., left when she moved out of the warehouse   1 Apr 1697 F260v moves that the printer in a test case against Her Majesty's Commissioners for Paper Act should be indemnified   3 Jul 1697 F263v competes unsuccessfully for Under Warden   5 Jul 1697 F264r competes unsuccessfully for Under Warden; subsequently elected and allowed to fine   7 Feb 1697/8 G3v his apprentice Daniel Midwinter is freed   13 Apr 1698 G6v complaint that Henry Mortlock, Robert Clavell and Samuel Smith are comprinting copy of Horace as well as himself and partners, in contravention of byelaws   10 Jan 1698/9 G18v request by Bennett Griffin that he should have Mrs Royston's £40 dividend, he 'maintaining and providing for her'. To be considered at next Court day   7 Feb 1698/9 G20v granted Mrs Royston's £40 dividend   6 Mar 1698/9 G22r proposes that usual allowance of the double quartern books is too great; debate deferred   1 Jul 1699 G26r fined for second year of Under Warden   3 Jul 1699 G27r interest in the copyright of the 'Satires of Juvenal and Persius'   7 Aug 1699 G29r referral of matter of Juvenal and Persius to Treasurer to be enlarged as to time   3 Feb 1700/1 G55v his apprentice Benjamin Cowse is freed   4 Jul 1702 G76v fined for first year of Upper Warden   3 Jul 1703 G91r fined

for Upper Warden   3 Mar 1706/7 G139r fined to preserve seniority to present
Master   5 May 1707 G141v elected to William Rawlins' Assistant's share   7 May
1711 G190r deceased; Assistant's share disposed of to Capt. Samuel Roycroft

CHOLMLEY, John   2 Nov 1691 (W) to pay 4s 5d out of pension towards quarterage
due when his apprentice Morton Peale is freed   6 Nov 1693 F194v pensioner; allowed
to have his son Philip freed by patrimony and to have all quarterage remitted

CHOLMLEY/CHOLMLY, Philip   6 Nov 1693 F194v to be freed by his father John
by patrimony   4 Dec 1693 F196v petitions for £50 from Norton bequest; deferred as
Court does not approve of surety

CHOLMLY – see CHOLMLEY

CHOWNE/CHOWN, Robert   19 Jun 1701 G61r elected to Mary Feild's pension   18
Dec 1702 G84r to have 5 shillings added to pension   23 Mar 1704 G117r elected to
Elizabeth Wright's pension. Dorothy Long is given his pension   20 Jun 1713 G210v
deceased; Mrs Yates is given his pension

CHRISTMAS, Henry   2 Apr 1705 G118v bound to Edward Jones, 7 years

CHRISTOPHER, Edward/Edmund   3 Dec 1705 G126r bound to Jane Marsh, 7
years   6 Oct 1712 G204v turned over to Ralph Holt   2 Nov 1713 G214v freed by
Ralph Holt

CHROSKILL, Richard   8 Apr 1700 G39r bound to Joseph Raven, 7 years

CHURCH, Francis (I)   26 Mar 1685 F32r deceased; his 40s pension voted to Robert
Wright

CHURCH, Francis (II)   9 Jun 1707 G142v bound to Gilham Hills, 7 years

CHURCHILL, Awnsham   28 Mar 1680 E98v promises to keep Dr Bladon's psalters
at the Customs House until agreement is reached   30 Sep 1684 F24r well and pump to
be installed near his back door in Stationers' Court at the expense of the inhabitants of
Ave Maria Lane   3 Jun 1689 F119v refuses cloathing unless he can negotiate to obtain
a greater seniority than he would otherwise have   6 Jul 1691 F157v elected to cloathing
and summoned to next Court re. fine   2 Nov 1691 F162r refuses cloathing, entreating
time to speak with his brother   7 Dec 1691 F163r pays his brother's Livery fine   5
Mar 1693/4 F200v Court to negotiate with him re. Livery fee and damasked paper of
'Doleman [i.e. Robert Persons et al., pseud.] about the English succession'   11 Jun
1694 F209r sends his brother John to Court re. Earl of Pembroke's desire to have an
interlineary Latin-English Aesop printed   10 Sep 1694 F212r summoned re. cloathing   20 Apr 1695 F221v John Churchill, on behalf of his brother Awnsham, requests
that several copies for which he has an assignment be entered; granted   1 Jul 1695
F227v Awnsham Churchill's request to print a beginners' Aesop in English and Latin
referred to committee   2 Dec 1695 F236v agreement with S.C. over Aesop read and
consideration of it deferred   12 Dec 1695 F238r permitted to print 1000 Aesops
without having to pay S.C. anything, providing he sticks to specifications and informs
them of printers   2 Aug 1697 F265r he and his brother John wish to print a new
edition of the interlineary Aesop; Court wishes to see previous agreement   6 Sep 1697
F267r Clerk to deliver him a copy of Court order for 12 Dec 1695 after his brother
renews requests re. Aesop   4 Oct 1697 F268r committee to negotiate with him re. Aesop;
a volume stipulated to be worth 4s or above 'in Quires in money to Booksellers'   28
Oct 1697 F270r stipulations for Aesop altered; now to be of a quality to justify a price
of 3s or over in quires to booksellers   8 Nov 1697 G1r to print Aesop's Fables in
English and Latin. Elected to John North's £80 share   22 Dec 1697 G2v agreement re.
Aesop's Fables confirmed   5 Dec 1698 G16v complaint that the warehouse he rents
from S.C. is out of repair   5 Jun 1699 G25r printing a Greek Testament   7 Aug 1699

G28v committee to view repairs required to S.C. warehouse let to Churchill 6 Nov 1699 G32v Master to discuss with him the joiner's bill for repairing a S.C. warehouse let to him 26 Mar 1700 G38r chosen First Renter Warden. Committee to settle matters in difference between S.C. and him 8 Apr 1700 G38v fined for First Renter Warden. Agreed he should be elected Assistant 6 May 1700 G39r takes oath of Assistant. Cloathed 5 Aug 1700 G44r agrees that payment to workmen for repairs to warehouse should be deducted from his rent 3 Feb 1700/1 G55v recommends that Joseph Ray be elected to an £80 share. Undertakes to ensure that he will pay Livery fine 2 Jun 1701 G60v committee set up to give him satisfaction for S.C. printing 'Poetae Minores' by mistake 7 Jul 1701 G62r Philip Yeo is bound to him 4 May 1702 G70v elected to Elizabeth Thomas's £80 share 5 Oct 1702 G81r elected to Mrs Gilliflower's £160 share 15 Nov 1703 G97v letter from his chapman at Norwich concerning printing and publishing of a sham sheet almanack 22 Nov 1703 G98v dealing with John Gellebrand concerning printing of the Royal Almanack 6 Jul 1706 G133v competes unsuccessfully for Under Warden. Fines to preserve his seniority to Israel Harrison 5 Jul 1707 G143r elected Under Warden 4 Aug 1707 G144r fined for Under Warden 6 Oct 1707 G145v Charles Rivington turned over to him from Emmanuel Matthews 3 Nov 1707 G146r request that Button not be subpoenaed is granted 1 Dec 1707 G147r to be given the prayer of the S.C.'s Bill in Chancery against Button 7 Jun 1708 G153r account of his arrears of rent to S.C. to be drawn up 5 Jul 1708 G155r to be charged rent for his warehouse 6 Sep 1708 G157r paid money by Warden Deputy Collins to pass on to Abel Swale 7 Mar 1708/9 G162r arrears of rent for his warehouse to be settled with Master, Wardens and Stock-keepers 24 Jul 1709 G168v John Partridge writes to Churchill concerning his almanack; Churchill forms part of committee to consider letter 1 Jul 1710 G181r asked to fine for Master 3 Jul 1710 G181v fined for Master 4 Dec 1710 G185v to be asked to write to his correspondent in Ireland concerning Whaley's [i.e. John Whalley's] almanacks to be printed by S.C. 7 Jun 1714 G219v enquiry to be made re. what was paid by him for printing [John] Patrick's Psalms 4 Oct 1714 G222r elected to John Simms's £320 share 2 May 1715 G228r letter from Richard Sare to him read 5 Mar 1715/16 G237v produces a letter from the executors of Dr John Partridge concerning the allowance to him for his almanack. Referred to Stock-keepers

See also following entry

CHURCHILL, Capt. John 11 Jun 1694 F209r is sent to Court by his brother Awnsham re. Earl of Pembroke's desire for a Latin-English interlineary Aesop 20 Apr 1695 F221v on behalf of his brother Awnsham, requests that several copies for which he has an assignment be entered; granted 2 Aug 1697 F265r he and his brother wish to print a new edition of the interlineary Aesop; Court wishes to see previous agreement 6 Sep 1697 F267r produces a 'writing which he called an Agreement' between his brother Awnsham and S.C.; order of Court of 12 Dec 1695 read; Clerk to deliver Awnsham Churchill a copy

CHURCHILL, William 6 Jul 1691 F157v summoned to next Court to be cloathed 8 May 1704 G106v to be summoned to take cloathing

CICERO, Marcus Tullius ('Tully's Offices' (*De Officiis*), 'Tully's Works') 1 Aug 1687 F87r 'Tully's Offices' in three volumes assigned by Sir Roger L'Estrange to Richard Bentley, Jacob Tonson and Joseph Hindmarsh 5 Sep 1692 F177v Thomas Dring complains that Samuel Smith has imported 'Tully's Works' which Dring has the licence to print; referred to committee 23 Mar 1710/11 G188v William Bowyer granted permission to print 'Collections out of Tully's Offices'

CITY OF LONDON – see LONDON, CITY OF

THE CITY AND COUNTRY REMEMBRANCER   4 Nov 1706 G135v sham almanack printed by G. Croome and sold by B. Bragg

CLARE, Francis   6 May 1700 G39v bound to John Wild, 7 years   3 Nov 1707
G146v freed by John Wild

CLARENDON, Edward Hyde, Earl of, author of *The History of the Rebellion and Civil
Wars in England* ('Clarendon's History')   2 Apr 1705 G118r Lewis Thomas of
Oxford to be presented with a copy of the 'History' for good service to S.C. relating to
buying it   9 Sep 1706 G134v John Baskett's agreement with Oxford University for
printing   1 Dec 1707 G147r committee to decide whether to take Baskett's edition in
folio   3 Dec 1707 G148r committee of Stock-keepers decides not to take any part of
Baskett's impression   9 Feb 1707/8 G148v report of committee re. taking Baskett's
version of it in folio agreed to. Baskett's proposals re. impression in octavo debated and
referred to Master, Wardens and Stock-keepers   30 Mar 1708 G151r committee
decided not to take Baskett's octavo impression   12 Apr 1708 G151v Court agrees
with decision of committee not to take Baskett's octavo impression   6 Sep 1708 G157r
Master, Wardens and Stock-keepers to dispose of remaining books upon the best terms
they can, first offering them to Baskett

CLARK – see CLARKE

CLARKE/CLARK, Mrs   7 Jun 1680 E100v assigned signature D of stock 12mo
psalms and signatures G and H of stock primer

CLARKE, Blaze   3 Mar 1706/7 G139r bound to Thomas Mew, 7 years

CLARKE, Deputy – see CLARKE, Henry

CLARKE/CLERKE, Edmund   3 Dec 1683 F6v copy of the Warden's accounts drawn
up by the late Richard Clarke to be delivered to him

CLARKE, Frances (Widow Clarke)   2 Mar 1690/1 F150r petitions as widow of Henry
Clarke; Court remits her a moiety of his Livery fine and allows her to continue printing
almanacks   12 Nov 1694 F214v at request of Jones, her agent, allowed to benefit from
the late Henry Clarke's £160 share provided she indemnifies S.C. from Clarke's
creditors   3 May 1697 F261v mortgage of her £160 share to be transferred by request
of Jones, her agent, if she brings the name of the transferee to next Court   7 Jun 1697
F262v surrenders £160 share; Court promises to try and find someone who will pay
her ready money for it   5 Jul 1697 F264v £160 share disposed of to Stephen Bateman

CLARKE/CLERKE, Hannah   11 Nov 1695 F236r Peter Clarke is bound to her   9
Sep 1700 G45r James Davis is bound to her   7 Dec 1702 G83v Joseph Hunt is bound
to her   5 Jul 1703 G92r her apprentice Luke Weaden is freed   6 May 1706 G131v
Richard Wilder is bound to her   7 Jul 1707 G143v Gwin Needham turned over from
George Shell to her   12 Apr 1708 G152r her apprentice James Davis is freed   4 Jun
1711 G191r John Woodward is bound to her   5 Jul 1714 G220v her apprentices Peter
Clarke and Richard Wilder are freed   6 Sep 1714 G221v John Harwood is bound to her

CLARKE/CLERKE, Henry (I), alias 'Deputy'   20 Jun 1681 E113v elected Assistant   22
Dec 1681 E141r competes unsuccessfully for Richard Clarke's £160 share   21 Feb
1681/2 E145r altercation between him and Robert Scott as to whose right is greater for
Francis Tyton's £160 share; Scott voted into it   20 Apr 1683 E169r competes unsuccessfully for Mrs White's £160 share, surrendered in return for ready money   7 May
1683 E169v to examine lease of warehouse to Thomas Allen   4 Jun 1683 E170v
together with Ambrose Isted, reports that Thomas Allen's lease ought to be
engrossed   1 Oct 1683 F3v elected to the late Mrs Husbands's £160 share   3 Mar
1683/4 F10r Robert Stephens mortgages his £80 share to Clarke for £70 plus
interest   7 Apr 1684 F13v on the list of loyal Assistants presented to the Crown   5 Jul

1684 F19v chosen to audit Warden's accounts with John Macock and Henry Herringman   11 Oct 1684 F25r appointed spokesman for Parker and Guy committee; informs them that S.C. will prosecute   7 May 1685 (W) confirmed member of new Livery   4 Jul 1685 F39v competes unsuccessfully for Under Warden   3 Jul 1686 F59r fined for 2 years' Under Warden   11 Oct 1688 (W) restored to Assistants   6 Jul 1689 F121v competes unsuccessfully for Upper Warden   3 Mar 1690 F130v to approve draft lease to Walter Davis for a house in Amen Corner   2 Jun 1690 F135r elected Under Warden for remainder of the year   5 Jun 1690 F136r before he stands for election to the late Dorothy Thrale's £320 share, Court elect him to committee re. entitlement to shares of those not in trade   5 Jul 1690 F138r elected Upper Warden   7 Jul 1690 F139r competes unsuccessfully for the late Dorothy Thrale's £320 share   4 Jul 1691 F156v competes unsuccessfully for Upper Warden   6 Aug 1694 F211r James Oades is awarded Clarke's £160 share in a commission of bankruptcy but his petition to be admitted to share is deferred

See also CLARKE, Peter

CLARKE/CLERKE, Henry (II)   4 Aug 1684 F21v to be granted £50 from Tyler Bequest (had requested £100) if his sureties are approved   1 Sep 1684 F23r sureties approved   6 Sep 1686 F62v has to find a new surety for his £50 loan from Tyler Bequest, Peter Stone being dead   6 Jun 1687 F84v reprimanded for not giving due notice that a surety, Peter Stone, is dead; the widow will have to be bound in her own right   1 Aug 1687 F87v allowed to bind John Fearne, a refiner in Whitecross Street, as a surety, Peter Stone's widow not wishing to do so   4 Sep 1688 F107r to repay his £50 loan money   1 Oct 1688 F107v Court agrees that his loan should be continued for six months longer; has discharged Widow Stone and given a bond for Peter Fearne   6 May 1689 F117v ordered to repay his £50 loan next Lady Day   5 May 1690 F135r allowed to continue loan until 24 Feb 1690/1   4 Aug 1690 F141v printer; cloathed and promises payment of fine

See also CLARKE, Peter

CLARKE, James   6 Jun 1698 G8v bound to Henry Gellebrand, 7 years

CLARKE, Jane   1 Mar 1691/2 F165v deceased; her £80 share voted to Brabazon Aylmer

CLARKE/CLARK/CLERKE, John (I)   3 Jul 1680 E101r stands unsuccessfully for Upper Warden   2 Jul 1681 E115r fined for Upper Warden   1 Aug 1681 E117v assigns 'Imitation of Christ or the Christian's Pattern' to John Redmaine   5 Sep 1681 E129v of Little St Bartholomew's; 1/3 of 'The Dutch Fortune Teller', 1/2 of [Emmanuel Ford's] 'Ornatus and Artecia' and other books assigned to him by Thomas Vere   21 Feb 1681/2 E144v competes unsuccessfully for the £320 share of Thomas Vere, deceased   30 Jun 1683 F1r competes unsuccessfully for Master   12 Nov 1683 F5r competes unsuccessfully for Mrs Stephens's £320 share   7 Jan 1684 F7v competes unsuccessfully for the late Mrs Roper's £320 share   12 Oct 1687 F90v competes unsuccessfully for Master. Among those chosen to audit Warden's accounts   9 Jan 1687/8 F96v ties with Edward Brewster in competition for the late Mrs Latham's £320 share; Brewster is given the Master's casting vote   6 Aug 1688 F105r surviving signatory of the original deed of conveyance of St Martin's Ludgate   27 Nov 1688 F110v competes unsuccessfully for Master   1 Jul 1689 F120v to re-execute conveyance to present Court members   6 Jul 1689 F121r competes unsuccessfully for Master   3 Dec 1694 F215v John Dutton, his apprentice, is freed   8 Apr 1695 F220r deceased; Samuel Roycroft elected to his £160 share

CLARKE/CLERKE, John (II)   29 May 1689 F118v cloathed   2 Dec 1700 G54r James Howard is bound to him

CLARKE, John (III) 3 May 1697 F262r bound to Ralph Snow 2 Apr 1705 G118v freed by Ralph Snow. Nathan Frith is bound to him 7 May 1705 G120r Thomas Sharpey is bound to him 12 Apr 1708 G151v elected Assistant Renter Warden 3 Oct 1709 G171r within Cripplegate, writing-master; Thomas Mosse is bound to him 6 Nov 1710 G185r bookbinder; Edward Hampson is bound to him 7 Apr 1712 G199r Peter Carpenter is bound to him 6 Jan 1712/13 G206r Samuel Crooke is bound to him 2 Mar 1712/13 G206v to be summoned to next Court to explain why he refuses to make Thomas Sharpey free 7 Sep 1713 G213r writing master; to be excused cloathing for one year. Robert Dymond is bound to him 5 Oct 1713 G214r George Everden is bound to him 7 Dec 1713 G214v his apprentice Thomas Sharpey is freed 5 Apr 1714 G217v excused cloathing for six months 4 Oct 1714 G222r cloathed. John Callowe is bound to him 4 Apr 1715 G227v Samuel Kellow (cf. 'Callowe' in previous entry) is bound to him 12 Nov 1716 G244v his apprentice Nathan Firth is freed 6 May 1717 G250v Richard Hett is bound to him. John Callowe turned over from him to George Oldner

CLARKE, John (IV) 1 May 1710 G179v bound to Richard Janeway

CLARKE/CLERKE, John (V) 4 Sep 1710 G183v bound to Charles Bates

CLARKE, John (VI) 4 Jun 1711 G191r bound to Samuel, his father, 7 years

CLARKE, John (probably to be identified with one of the above individuals) – see following entry

CLARKE, John (VIII) 2 Nov 1713 G214v son of John, is bound to William Innys, 7 years

CLARKE, Mary 5 Feb 1704/5 G115r deceased; her £160 share disposed of to John Harding

CLARKE, Peter 11 Nov 1695 F236r son of Henry Clarke, late of the parish of St Benet's, Paul's Wharf, printer; bound to Hannah Clarke 5 Jul 1714 G220v freed by Hannah Clarke

CLARKE/CLARK/CLERKE, Richard (I) 3 Jul 1680 E101r elected Upper Warden 22 Dec 1681 E141r deceased; his £160 share voted to John Playford. Francis Tyton to be paid £4 6s 8d out of Clarke's stock, money laid out for deceased in the year they were Wardens together 4 Jun 1683 E170r deceased; his son and executor Thomas is paid off for the £80 share mortgaged to Richard by George Eversden by Eversden's remortgaging it to Sarah Martin 3 Dec 1683 F6v deceased; his Warden's accounts to be examined and a copy to be delivered to Edmund Clarke

CLARKE/CLERKE, Richard (II) 2 Jul 1716 G242r son of Henry, is bound to Thomas Cope, 7 years

CLARKE/CLARK/CLERKE, Samuel 6 Apr 1696 F242r freed by redemption 1 Sep 1701 G64r Henry Syms is bound to him 1 Feb 1702/3 G85r Samuel Sims (cf. 'Syms' in previous entry) turned over from him to Joseph Hind 7 Apr 1707 G141r bookseller; Aaron Stoughton is bound to him 3 Oct 1709 G170v bookseller of Birchin Lane; accepts cloathing. Henry Smith is bound to him 4 Jun 1711 G191r bookseller of Birchin Lane; his son John Clarke is bound to him 5 Apr 1714 G218r Henry Smith turned over from him to Arthur Bettesworth 3 May 1714 G219r his apprentice Aaron Stoughton is freed 4 Jun 1716 G240v elected Assistant Renter Warden. Beadle to give him notice thereof 12 Nov 1716 G244v John Blincoe is bound to him

CLARKE/CLERKE, Thomas 4 Jun 1683 E170r George Eversden given leave to mortgage his share to pay him off, as son and executor of Richard Clarke to whom it was mortgaged 16 Mar 1686/7 F79r to be summoned on 4 April for the election of Renter Wardens 2 May 1687 F82v elected First Renter Warden; summoned 22 Jun

1687 F85r fined for First Renter Warden 1 Mar 1687/8 F97v expelled from Livery by order of Lord Mayor 11 Oct 1688 F108v restored to Livery 8 Apr 1700 G38v elected Assistant 3 Feb 1700/1 G55r elected to Capt. William Phillipps's £160 share 1 Jul 1704 G109v elected Under Warden 3 Jul 1704 G109v fined for Under Warden 2 Jul 1705 G121v fined for second year of Under Warden to preserve seniority 1 Jul 1710 G181v elected Upper Warden 3 Jul 1710 G181v fined for first year of Upper Warden 7 Aug 1710 G182v fined for second year of Upper Warden and Master to preserve seniority to Awnsham Churchill 5 Jul 1712 G201r elected Master 15 Jul 1712 G202r has received notice from Beadle that he has been elected Master. Permitted to be excused 22 Dec 1713 G215r elected to Charles Harper's £320 share

CLARKE/CLERKE, William 2 Apr 1688 (W) foreigner, freed 6 Mar 1703/4 G103v George Medden is bound to him

CLAUDIAN 18 Mar 1686/7 F79v among books in catalogue annexed to Oxford agreement

CLAVELL, Katherine 7 May 1711 G190v to be paid £15 p.a. under bond from her father to S.C.

CLAVELL, Robert 1 Mar 1680/1 E107v elected Stock-keeper for Livery 21 Feb 1681/2 E145r voted to the late Mrs Harward's £80 share 1 Mar 1681/2 E145v elected Stock-keeper for Livery 3 Mar 1683/4 F9v elected Assistant in response to Crown's request as a reward for stamping out seditious printing 7 Apr 1684 F14r on the list of loyal Assistants presented to the Crown 2 Jun 1684 F16r competes unsuccessfully for Thomas Cotterell's £160 share 7 May 1685 (W) confirmed member of new Livery 6 Jul 1685 F40v elected Stock-keeper in place of John Bellinger. Elected to the £160 share of Mrs Martin, who has remarried 3 May 1686 F55v among those chosen to audit Renter Wardens' accounts 3 Jul 1686 F59v among those chosen to audit Renter Wardens' accounts 5 Jul 1686 F60v elected and sworn in as Under Warden 6 Sep 1686 F62r Samuel Lowndes replaces him to audit Warden's accounts now he is a Warden 2 Jul 1687 F85v competes unsuccessfully for Under Warden 11 Oct 1688 F108v restored to Livery 27 Nov 1688 F110v elected Under Warden 4 Nov 1689 F126v to be added to the Corporation Act committee 5 Jun 1690 F135v re-appointed Assistant 4 Jul 1692 F173v competes unsuccessfully for the £320 share of John Macock, deceased. To augment Oxford committee 3 Oct 1692 F180r elected to the late Widow Tyton's £320 share 1 Jul 1693 F189r competes unsuccessfully for Upper Warden 3 Jul 1693 F189v among those chosen to audit Warden's accounts 9 May 1694 F204v ties for Upper Warden with Henry Mortlock; Mortlock beats him in second vote, allowed to fine for 1 year's Upper Wardenship to preserve his seniority 30 Jun 1694 F209v fined for second year's Upper Warden 2 Jul 1694 F210r among those chosen to audit Warden's accounts 12 Nov 1694 F214v involved in dispute over printing Horace 3 Dec 1694 F215v fined £10 for printing 750 Church Catechisms with proofs. Leave given him to print as many of 'Dr. Cumber's' [i.e. Thomas Comber's] Catechisms as he likes, paying S.C. 4d per quire 1 Jul 1695 F229r competes unsuccessfully for Master 5 Aug 1695 F232r John Senex jnr is bound to him from 1 July 1695 4 Jul 1696 F245r competes unsuccessfully for Master 6 Jul 1696 F246r allowed to print a third impression of 2000 of Dr [Zachaeus] Isham's Catechism, paying the same price to the Treasurer 30 Sep 1696 F249v Thomas Parkhurst allowed to print [Richard] Mayo's Catechism, paying S.C. the same rate as Clavell does for Dr Isham's 26 Mar 1697 F258v he and Thomas Parkhurst success-fully request that Jonathan Robinson should be excused the Renter Wardenship next year 3 Jul 1697 F263v comes second in competition for Master 13 Apr 1698 G6v complaint that he printed copy of Horace in contravention of byelaws 6 Jun 1698 G8v his apprentice William Hawes is freed 2 Jul 1698 G10r elected Master 3 Jul

1699 G27r interest in the copyright of printing the Satires of Juvenal and Persius 7 Aug 1699 G29r referral of the matter of Juvenal and Persius to Treasurer deferred 6 May 1700 G39v Thomas Baker is bound to him 1 Mar 1702/3 G85v elected Stock-keeper for Assistants and takes oath 2 Mar 1703/4 G102v elected Stock-keeper for Assistants and takes oath 6 Aug 1705 G122r to assist with Election Dinner 4 Mar 1705/6 G129r his apprentice John Senex is freed 9 Sep 1706 G134v Thomas Baker, apprentice to John Jones, freed by him 7 May 1711 G190v bond from S.C. for £150 to pay his daughter Katherine £15 p.a. during her lifetime

CLAVELL, Roger 24 Oct 1693 F193v at request of Robert Clavell, he is freed and cloathed on paying 2 guineas to the Poor Box 25 Mar 1706 G130r of Dorset; to be sent for on next occasion for choosing Renter Wardens 26 Mar 1711 G189r elected Assistant Renter Warden. Clerk to write to him and request speedy answer 7 May 1711 G190r Clerk to reply that his proposition concerning the manner of paying Renter Warden's fine is unacceptable 23 Jun 1711 G191v fined for Renter Warden 7 Jul 1712 G201v elected to James Brookes' £40 share. Clerk to inform him that he is to return £5 for a dinner

CLAY, Francis 7 Jun 1708 G153v bound to Daniel Browne, 7 years 10 Sep 1716 G243r freed by Daniel Browne. Samuel Mills is bound to him

CLEAVE/CLEEVE, Isaac 1 Mar 1685/6 F51r cloathed 1 Mar 1687/8 F97v expelled from Livery by order of Lord Mayor 11 Oct 1688 F108v restored to Livery 15 Apr 1692 F169v fined for Assistant Renter Warden 3 Oct 1692 F180r ties with Benjamin Motte in election to John Hancock's £40 share, and Master gives casting vote to him 4 Mar 1694/5 F219r James Lawrence is bound to him 2 Nov 1696 F252r competes unsuccessfully for Matthew Gilliflower's £80 share 7 Dec 1696 F252v elected to John Hancock's £80 share 1 Mar 1696/7 F255v elected Stock-keeper for Yeomanry with William Rogers 1 Mar 1697/8 G4r elected Stock-keeper for Yeomanry and takes oath 7 Oct 1698 G15r John Baily is bound to him 1 Mar 1699/1700 G36r elected Stock-keeper for Livery and takes oath 1 Mar 1700/1 G56r elected Stock-keeper for Livery and takes oath 5 Apr 1703 G88r Richard Talbott is bound to him 1 Dec 1707 G147v his apprentices John Baily and Elizabeth Rugg are freed 1 Mar 1707/8 G149v William Phelps, servant to Francis Leach, turned over to him. Bookseller; Lewes Sweeting is bound to him

CLEAVE, Mrs 4 Mar 1716/17 G247v deceased; her £80 share disposed of to Wyatt

CLEAVER, Foulke, snr – see following entry

CLEAVER, Foulke, jnr 2 Jul 1694 F210v son of Foulke Cleaver of Ipswich, gentleman; bound to James Rawlins

CLEERE, Rose 7 Jun 1686 (W) bond to her of £400 penalty to pay £205 on 8 December. Note that this entry to be left out of Court book by order of 5 Jul as bond cancelled

CLEEVE, Isaac – see CLEAVE, Isaac

CLEEVE, John 3 Mar 1700/1 G57r bound to Robert Roberts, 7 years

CLEMENT, Richard 12 Sep 1692 F179r summoned to show why he should not be cloathed 3 Oct 1692 F180v to be summoned to cloathing 7 Nov 1692 F181v excused cloathing upon application to Court

CLEMENT, Thomas, snr – see following entry

CLEMENT, Thomas, jnr 1 Jul 1695 F228v son of Thomas Clement snr, St James Clerkenwell, haberdasher; bound to John Wyatt

CLEMENTS, Henry 5 Apr 1703 G88r bound to Thomas Bennett, 7 years 7 Apr

1707 G141r order from Lord Mayor admitting him to freedom of S.C. Freed as servant to Thomas Bennett, deceased   6 Dec 1708 G159v of St Paul's Churchyard; Thomas Allett is bound to him   27 Mar 1710 G177v bookseller in St Paul's Churchyard; to be summoned to take cloathing next Court day   5 Jun 1710 G180r accepts cloathing   4 Dec 1710 G186r west end of St Paul's, bookseller; Richard King is bound to him   7 Jun 1714 G219v Thomas Gibbon is bound to him

CLEMSON, William, snr – see following entry

CLEMSON, William, jnr   5 Dec 1715 G235v son of William; bound to Samuel Negus, 7 years

CLERK   1679–1681 John Lilly   1 Dec 1679 E95r assignments to be drawn up by him   3 May 1680 E99v to pay charges for new byelaw to Lord Chief Justice; money to be raised by Under Warden   5 Jul 1680 E101v to be paid 50s for his salary from the Renter Warden   2 Aug 1680 E102v to be paid 10s for engrossing and copying new byelaw   7 Feb 1680/1 E106v to copy out all portions of Martin's Calendar Book relating to S.C., for a remittance. To demand money from securities of James Collins and Jonathan Edwin   7 Mar 1680/1 E107v to answer Beverly's demands re. rent in arrears of Bishop's bequest   30 Mar 1681 E108v signs for list of Clerk's books   1681–1692 John Garrett   2 May 1681 E111r to advise with John Lilly re. demands from St Faith's churchwardens for Lamb's bequest of 2s per week in arrears 'and one from this Company [sic]'   1 Aug 1681 E117r to inquire at Wagstaff's office re. City order for not building near City wall. To join committee pursuing amelioration money for Ave Maria Lane   7 Nov 1681 E138r to bring Poor Register up to date from 7 Oct 1673 to remedy John Lilly's neglect and to keep it up to date in accordance with oath on admission as Clerk   7 Aug 1682 E156v committee considering relative demerits of current Clerk and John Lilly in performing their duties re. byelaws and pension notes to report at next Court   4 Sep 1682 E157v new funnel of lead to be installed from his garret, separate from that of Richardson. Robert Scott and Ambrose Isted to be added to committee re. Lilly and Clerk's duties   2 Oct 1682 E158v defect in partition wall between his and Robert Everingham's house to be referred to committee   7 Mar 1682/3 E166r to draw up two tables of S.C. benefactors with their gifts and legacies, one for the hall and one for the Court room   26 Mar 1684 F12r John Garrett surrenders his position as Clerk to Master and Wardens in connection with *quo warranto* proceedings   24 Apr 1684 F14r John Garrett, who submitted to Crown on 7 April, is nominated   27 May 1684 F15r John Garrett confirmed in position   7 Jul 1684 F20v committee considering Lilly's and Clerk's work in drawing up byelaws and Clerk's registering pension revived and augmented, to report at next Court   6 May 1685 F33v ordered to carry list of bookdealers outside S.C. to Town Clerk   22 May 1685 F37r not to enter any books except according to James II's commission re. licensing   6 Jul 1685 F40v Warden to pay the arrears of his salary due from Renter Warden   12 Sep 1685 F44v to have the letting of the Hall for feasts and funerals. To minute business of uncompleted committees   2 Nov 1685 F46r list of several committees to be revived, read to Table by Clerk; consideration deferred   22 Dec 1685 F49v to remind them at next Court to 'take his pains in several things done for the company into consideration'   1 Feb 1685/6 F51r committee revived to consider his passing byelaws, entering pension notes, &c., and his remuneration   23 Apr 1686 (W) committee's report on amounts to be paid to him on Corporation and English Stock accounts   3 May 1686 F54v to have £6 paid to him on the Corporation account and £6 on the English Stock account   23 Mar 1686/7 F80r to take schedule of all wainscots, partitions, shelves, dressers and moveables in Warehousekeeper's house. Dividend book always to remain with him so he or his servant can witness all discharges   4 Apr 1687 F81v to enter assignments and makings-over in margin of Entry Book of Copies and to keep a waste register to be read

at Court before being entered, and to be recompensed for this   30 May 1687 F83v
Susan Leigh gives the Clerk the right to sue for recovery of the debts recorded in notes to
her late husband   12 Oct 1687 F91r to enter names of restored and remaining Livery
in Livery Book folio. To give account of elections after membership revision, and names
of restored and remaining Livery, to Town Clerk   7 Nov 1687 F94r to enter in a special
book all fines for Master, Warden, Renter Warden, Livery, &c.   5 Mar 1687/8 F99r to
produce list of particular offenders over binding apprentices at every Court day
apprentices are bound   4 Feb 1688/9 F112v absent; deputy stands in   1 Sep 1690
F142r to make a rental for the Corporation estate. To make an alphabetical list of all
Stock books to make checking on comprinting easier   8 Jun 1691 F154v salary to be
paid by Wardens instead of Renter Wardens   5 Oct 1691 F161r his man to place
Livery in order of seniority on festival days   6 Jul 1692 F174r to copy free workmen
printers' petition for the Treasurer   5 Sep 1692 F177v to write and direct John Hewitt
of Reading to pay Livery fine   7 Nov 1692 F181v after John Garrett's resignation,
committee appointed to oversee selection of next Clerk   1692–1696 Christopher
Grandorge   5 Dec 1692 F183r committee to see that all the Clerk's books in the custody
of John Garrett are delivered to the present Clerk or the Master and Wardens   3 Apr
1693 F186r books to be kept in the room behind the Court room   8 May 1693 F188r
to sue Stephen Keyes for not answering summons to be cloathed and William Downing
for printing Stock books   3 Jul 1693 F190r to note time and place of assignments
opposite original entry in the margin of Register Book   28 Sep 1693 F191v Robert
Stephens allowed access to registers without paying fees, but only on Clerk's presence.
Clerk to draw up a table of his fees, perquisites, profits and duties for Court to confirm
and regulate   2 Oct 1693 F192v to bring Register book into every Court in future   24
Oct 1693 F193v co-partnership articles for sale of Oxford and Cambridge stock to
remain with him until all partners have signed   2 Apr 1694 F202r henceforth to be
paid out of quarterage   6 Aug 1694 F211v ordered to make a copy of the assignment
to James Oades in a commission of bankruptcy of Henry Clarke's £160 share   11 Apr
1695 F221v House of Commons orders him to produce registers re. revival of Printing
Act   1 Jul 1695 F227r to inquire whether any decree was ever made re. Meredith
bequest in the Courts of Judicature   2 Dec 1695 F236v reads out new Printing
Act   12 Dec 1695 F238r to prepare dividend book. To sign and give a copy to
Awnsham Churchill of the agreement between him and S.C. over Aesop   8 Jun 1696
F243r Warden to receive rents of Corporation houses but Clerk still to retain salary; to
attend Warden in rent collecting   6 Jul 1696 F245v George Jones's offer to officiate
during the Clerk's incapacity is rejected as there is no occasion. Benjamin Tooke to
officiate instead   5 Oct 1696 (W) Simms, Rawlins and Lowndes asked to ensure
minutes which the Clerk had neglected to enter are entered by next Court day   2 Nov
1696 (W) minutes not yet entered as Simms said Rawlins, Lowndes and himself had
received no summons to do so   9 Mar 1696/7 F255v committee considers the Clerk's
fees and duties   1697–1717 Simon Beckley   26 Mar 1697 F258v table of fees   3 May
1697 F261v to write out several fair copies of the paper drawn up by John Lilly re.
collecting money for Paper Act, and send them out   7 Jun 1697 F262v to call on
Thomas Moore re. new surety for £50 loan from Tyler Bequest   2 Aug 1697 F265v to
list the names of the committees chosen by the Court within the past year and still
existing. £10 owed to the present Clerk by Christopher Grandorge to be paid off,
together with debts to other S.C. officials   6 Sep 1697 F266v to inform S.C. tenants of
repairs needed   16 Oct 1697 F269r to act as solicitor when Charles Browne and
William Onley are prosecuted in the Court of Exchequer for illegal printing   2 May
1698 G7r to receive counterparts of leases and all other writings belonging to S.C. from
Garrett. To enquire after William Cartwright and report to the Court   1 Aug 1698
G11v to send John Amery a copy of the Order to dispose of his Livery share if not paid

for by the next Court. To deliver to Anthony Nelme the counterpart of the lease of his house   7 Oct 1698 G15r to attend Mrs Burrows and draw up her affidavit concerning lights of the Goldsmiths' Company   5 Dec 1698 G17r to give Mrs Elizabeth Eversden notice of Court's decision to make her leave S.C.'s house unless she pays her rent arrears   7 Feb 1698/9 G20r to make an account of the goods &c. in the house where Nicholas Hooper, the Beadle, lately dwelt   6 Mar 1698/9 G21v to take out a subpoena in Chancery against Peter Parker and Thomas Guy. To attend Mrs Isted about delivering the writings belonging to S.C. To attend Court members going with her 'to her Counsel'. To give Jevon notice to quit possession of S.C.'s house   3 Apr 1699 G23v to recover rent arrears due from Jevon   8 May 1699 G24v to be responsible for suing Wellington for the remaining £10 of his Livery fine. To call on Thomas Cater for his Livery fine. To attend Mrs Isted and take an abstract of the writings in her custody relating to S.C.   5 Jun 1699 G25r to write to Robert Sollars requesting payment of the remaining £10 of his Livery fine   3 Jul 1699 G27r to inform S.C.'s tenants whose leases have expired that they are expected to renew them. To have 2 guineas paid to him by the late Warden Richard Simpson for use of Hall for 'Mine Adventure' and for getting the money for the use of the Hall for drawing the lottery 'The Lady's Invention'   7 Aug 1699 G28r to write to Robert Sollars concerning the remaining part of his Livery fine   2 Oct 1699 G31v to be given names of John Williams's surety for a loan   5 Feb 1699/1700 G35r to write to Richard Randall of Newcastle to inform him of election to the Livery   8 Apr 1700 G38v to write to Randall to acquaint him that the Court does not accept his excuse for not being cloathed. To send to every person chosen to a committee a copy of the order relating thereto and a particular summons in writing   6 May 1700 G39r to write to Randall again with Court's decision   3 Jun 1700 G40r to write to Randall again. To make out note of arrears of quarterage   21 Jun 1700 G41r has delivered into Court three old patents and one new one belonging to S.C. and last byelaws of S.C., and put them in the chest   19 Jul 1700 G43r to write to Mrs Puller concerning payment of S.C.'s debt to her   9 Sep 1700 G44v to write to Randall requesting his appearance at S.C.'s suit   7 Apr 1701 G58r to send Nahum Tate copy of orders   1 Dec 1701 G66r to give Browne copies of Court orders relating to Susanna Miller's mortgage   6 Jul 1702 G77r lawsuit to be entered in Court Book by the former Clerk, John Lilly; G77v to make out copies of orders of Court concerning printers of English Stock   9 Oct 1702 G82r to give notice to tenants of English Stock not to pay any more rent to Benjamin Tooke   27 Mar 1703 G87r to provide an office for himself. To attend committee due to meet Samuel Farly of Exeter   3 May 1703 G89v to write to John Hartley and James Bissell to inform them of election to cloathing   7 Jun 1703 G90r to inform Hartley that Court is not satisfied with his excuse for not accepting the cloathing   2 Aug 1703 G93v to summon John Franks to take cloathing next Court day. To take copy of order of Court of Aldermen or Act of Common Council relating to qualifications of Livery of London   4 Oct 1703 G96r to enquire whether John Franks of Brentford is free of the City of London. To prepare executions in connection with Bill in Chancery against Minshall   21 Oct 1703 G96v to deliver draft document to Benjamin Tooke. To deliver to Joseph Collyer the lease from University of Cambridge to Feild   8 Nov 1703 G96v document for Tooke to sign is approved, and Clerk is ordered to deliver it to him   6 Dec 1703 G99r to send Minshall copy of exceptions taken to his last answer. To write to friend in Norwich re. publishing of sham almanacks. To accompany John Franks of Brentford when taking his oath to discharge him from the cloathing   26 Jan 1703/4 G100v to take advice of Cooper concerning answers of Benjamin Harris to executions of S.C.   3 Apr 1704 G105v to search Chamberlain's Office to see whether William Powle is free of the City   8 May 1704 G106v to write to Franks to request him to take oath before Court of Aldermen   12 Jun 1704 G107r to draw up assignment of William Spiller's house to the S.C. To be attended by Higinson concerning bonds relating to Henry Coley. To call on John Taylor, late Renter Warden, for names of those with quarterage arrears 7 Aug 1704 G110v to call on Samuel Buckley to request payment of debt; rejects Spiller's proposed surety; to write to him and request payment 4 Sep 1704 G111v report concerning Buckley's debt 6 Nov 1704 G113r to prepare bond from S.C. to Thomas Parkhurst 5 Feb 1704/5 G114v to proceed against John Bradford 2 Apr 1705 G118v to inspect tenants' receipts and demand rent arrears 20 Apr 1705 G119r has visited Joshua Phillips in attempt to recover quarterage book 7 May 1705 G119v to request Benjamin Tooke snr to attend Thomas Bennett concerning accounts of Tate and Brady's Psalms 12 Nov 1705 G124v to write to Spiller concerning his debt to S.C. To give Edward Castle notice to attend Court to be cloathed 4 Feb 1705/6 G127v to proceed at law against Spiller for money due to S.C. 6 May 1706 G131r to deliver bond from Joseph Collyer and his sureties to Warden Thomas Hodgkins 21 Jun 1706 G133r to be paid by Collyer for his advance of monies to Thomas Richardson 3 Mar 1706/7 G139r to demand arrears of rent 26 Mar 1707 G139v to write to Obadiah Smith acquainting him of being elected Renter Warden 7 Jul 1707 G143v to call on Edward Head and James Bissell for Livery fines and George Littlebury for not paying balance of his accounts 3 Nov 1707 G146v to call on Pooler and others in arrears with Livery fines. To ensure that Wapshott's lease is cancelled before Samuel Brunts's lease is delivered 1 Dec 1707 G147r to give Awnsham Churchill the prayer of the Bill in Chancery against Button 1 Mar 1707/8 G149r to send all Members of Court a list of those who have held office of Renter Warden or fined for it in preparation for election of Assistants 3 May 1708 G152v to make enquiries of Benjamin Tooke concerning agreement between S.C. and Thomas Jones about printing Welsh Almanacks 7 Jun 1708 G153r to attend next meeting of Stock-keepers concerning Norton's printing of the Grammar. Has delivered to Joseph Collyer account and state of arrears due to the English Stock 22 Jun 1708 G153v to tell Thomas Jones that the S.C. have granted the privilege of printing the Welsh Almanacks to John Rogers 5 Jul 1708 G154v to acquaint Joseph Wilford of election to cloathing. To demand Mrs Petty's rent arrears. To send John Rogers copies of the orders concerning printing of Welsh Almanacks. To write another letter to Jones to the same effect as that sent a fortnight since 2 Aug 1708 G156v to acquaint Nathaniel Nowell jnr that he has been elected to cloathing 6 Sep 1708 G157r to call on Nowell and John Bradshaw and require them to appear to pay Livery fine. To attend John Baskett for answers of Medriach Mead and others 6 Dec 1708 G159r to settle Mrs Mill's rent arrears 4 Apr 1709 G164r to have £40 advance from Joseph Collyer towards paying Randall Tooke's bond. To give Daniel Crayle notice of summons to cloathing 6 Jun 1709 G165v to settle matter in difference between S.C. and Dr Harrison. To meet Commissioners of Bankruptcy against Chapman 2 Jul 1709 G166v to write to Boleworth and Wicks requesting rent arrears 4 Jul 1709 G167r letter to him from Daniel Crayle. To request Richard Harris and Thomas Norris to accept cloathing 5 Sep 1709 G170r to answer letter from Crayle. To prepare list of fees for binding and making free 3 Oct 1709 G171r to enquire of Commissioners of Bankruptcy against Chapman the value of his share of books in co-partnership with Sprint, in order to obtain them for S.C. 22 Dec 1709 G173r to draw up order over-ruling demur put in by John Partridge and John Darby 27 Mar 1710 G177r to inform James Taylor he has been elected Renter Warden 3 Apr 1710 G178r to give Thomas Newman notice of being elected to cloathing. To require appearance from Edward Castle for non-acceptance of cloathing. £150 to be borrowed from a friend of the Clerk's 1 May 1710 G179r reports that Edward Castle has refused to take cloathing 3 Jul 1710 G181v acquaints Court that Awnsham Churchill wishes to fine for Master 6 Nov 1710 G185r to make an endorsement on Charles Gretton's bond to allow him 6% p.a. 4 Dec 1710 G185v Court to indemnify him against suits and costs sustained by refusing to enter the Merlinus Liberatus of Benjamin Harris and the Ephemeris of George Parker   26 Mar 1711 G189r to inform Roger Clavell that he has been elected Assistant Renter Warden   7 May 1711 G190r to inform Roger Clavell that the manner of payment of the Renter Warden's fine which he suggests is not acceptable   13 Mar 1711/12 G198r to write to Norris demanding payment of Livery fine   26 Mar 1712 G198r to inform John Francks that he has been elected as Assistant Renter Warden   5 May 1712 G199v written to by John Francks to say he is unable to serve as Renter Warden   2 Jul 1712 G200r to be paid gratuity of 20 guineas   7 Jul 1712 G201v to inform Roger Clavell that he has been elected to £40 share   13 Apr 1713 G208v to inform Thomas Lewis that he has been elected Renter Warden   4 May 1713 G209v to take a copy of the Bill to be brought in the House of Commons relating to printing   7 Dec 1713 G215r with Warden, to call on Messrs Philip Overton, John Lenthall, James Pulleyne, James Bissell and Christopher Coningsby for sums due   2 Aug 1714 G221r to oversee whitewashing of Mrs Carter's house   7 Feb 1714/15 G224v to give notice to Mrs Carr that Mrs Mary Cooper's share will be disposed of if she does not make payment to Benjamin Poole   26 Mar 1715 G227r to inform Richard Randall that he has been elected Assistant Renter Warden   4 Apr 1715 G227v to write to Randall again   13 Jun 1715 G229r to take out writ against John England for non-payment of Livery fine   4 Jul 1715 G231r to give notice to Matthew Allam that he will be sued if he does not accept cloathing   3 Oct 1715 G233r to attend and advise with Serjeant Pengelly on the declaration against John England in the S.C.'s suit   7 Nov 1715 G234r John England required to pay Clerk's fees for suing him for non-payment of livery fine   5 Dec 1715 G235r delivered to Warden John Sprint a bond from John England to pay his Livery fine. To give notice to Mrs Cooper's son that her share is to be disposed of at February Court   6 Feb 1715/16 G236r to attend Poole re. selling of Mrs Cooper's stock   5 Mar 1715/16 G237r reported that Poole had authorised S.C. to dispose of Mrs Cooper's share in English Stock   26 Mar 1716 G238v to inform Thomas Norman that he has been elected Assistant Renter Warden   7 May 1716 G239v to inform Henry Brickwood that he has been elected to cloathing. To inform James Bissell that he has been elected Assistant Renter Warden   4 Jun 1716 G240r his report on Bissell   6 Aug 1716 G242r to inform Allam that he will be proceeded against if he does not take cloathing. To summon Brickwood to take cloathing   1 Oct 1716 G244r to prosecute Allam for not accepting cloathing   3 Dec 1716 G245r to prosecute Hind. To notify William Ward that he has been elected to cloathing   4 Feb 1716/17 G246v to prepare conveyances of feoffees and trustees of S.C.'s property to the current Master, Wardens and Table   6 May 1717 G250r has delivered Joseph Collyer's bond and sureties to Warden John Sprint. Letter from Thomas Norman read. To write to Norman refusing to allow him to fine for Renter Warden. To write again to Henry Brickwood of Malden

— CLERK'S BILLS   4 Jul 1698 G11r bill for charges in Chancery, Exchequer and elsewhere to be referred to Master, Wardens and Stock-keepers   5 Sep 1698 G14r bill for soliciting in Chancery and otherwise for S.C. deferred until next Court day. Committee appointed to settle   7 Oct 1698 G15r bill for soliciting in Chancery to be paid; to have two guineas in addition for his extraordinary attention in the S.C.'s affairs   7 Aug 1699 G28v bill for charges in Chancery and other business done upon account of S.C. Committee to settle   4 Sep 1699 G30r bill for charges in Chancery and for attending Parliament paid   7 Oct 1700 G46r bill for prosecuting John Bradford and Dennis to be paid   7 Dec 1702 G83v bill for proceedings in Chancery to be paid   7 Feb 1703/4 G101r committee to consider Clerk's bill   5 Feb 1704/5 G114v bill for proceedings in Chancery to be referred to committee for payment   4 Feb 1705/6 G127v bills referred to Master, Wardens and Capt. William Phillipps for payment   20 Dec 1706 G137r bill to be referred to Master and Wardens for payment   1 Mar 1707/8 G149v bill for charges relating to Copyright Bill to be paid. Bill for law charges and Counsels' fees to be referred to Master, Wardens, Robert Andrews and Capt. Phillipps   12 Apr 1708 G152r bill of £15 2s to be settled on payment of subscriptions in support of Copyright Act   7 Jun 1708 G153r bill relating to Copyright Bill to be settled by committee   7 Feb 1708/9 G160v bill for law charges referred to committee   3 Apr 1710 G178r bill of law charges to be referred to Master and Wardens for payment   9 Apr 1711 G189v bill to be referred to Master and Wardens   7 Apr 1712 G199r committee to consider Clerk's bills   2 Jun 1712 G200r to be paid   13 Apr 1713 G208v to be referred to committee considering matters relating to printers   5 Jul 1714 G220v of law charges, committee to consider   4 Jul 1715 G231r for law charges to be referred to Master and Wardens and accounts committee   7 Nov 1715 G234v John England to pay   26 Mar 1716 G238v fees to be paid in advance   4 Mar 1716/17 G247v for law charges and in Chancery to be paid

CLERK'S MAN   6 Aug 1705 G122v complaint that he has taken undue fees for binding apprentices

CLERK (as surname), CLERKE – see CLARKE

CLIFF/CLIFFE, Nathaniel   7 Feb 1703/4 G101v freed by Thomas Parkhurst   3 Oct 1709 G171r of Cheapside, bookseller; Henry Allen is bound to him   5 Jun 1710 G180r cloathed   3 Mar 1711/12 G197r Nicholas Carr is bound to him. Henry Allen turned over from him to Henry Allen

CLIFF, Sarah   13 Jun 1715 G229v George Wright is bound to her

CLIFFORD, Clare   14 Mar 1714/15 G226r elected to Mary Reynolds' pension

CLIFFORD, John   22 Jun 1698 G9v deceased; Anne Alloway given his pension

CLIFFORD, Mrs   5 Feb 1699/1700 G35r £200 loan to S.C. repaid

CLOCK   6 Feb 1709/10 G175v presented to S.C. by Richard Mount and set up in the Court room

CLOCKMAKERS, Company of   6 Oct 1712 G204r to have use of Hall   1 Dec 1712 G205v order of 6 October discharged, as they required use of Hall several more times than S.C. had been informed

CLOTHWORKERS, Company of   6 Aug 1688 F104v Foreman, a stall-bookseller, claims he is free of the Clothworkers' Company

CLUER, Henry – see following entry

CLUER, John   6 May 1695 F223v son of the late Henry Cluer of Basingstoke, cordwainer; bound to Thomas Snowden   4 May 1702 G71r freed by William Snowden   10 Sep 1711 G194r printer; Harrington Dabbs is bound to him

COAKE – see COOKE

COCKERELL, [   ]   1 Mar 1679/80 E97r his apprentice Jonathan Greenwood is freed

COCKERELL/COCKERILL, Thomas (I)   1 Mar 1687/8 F98r summoned to next Court to be nominated for Assistant   5 Mar 1687/8 F99r elected Assistant   7 May 1688 F101v money for his Livery dinner to be added to money for collation on 29 May   7 Oct 1689 F125r elected to John Overton's £40 share   7 Jul 1690 F139r competes unsuccessfully for Benjamin Tooke's £80 share   9 Feb 1690/1 F149r competes unsuccessfully for John Richardson's £80 share   2 Mar 1690/1 F150v elected Stock-keeper for Yeomanry with Brabazon Aylmer   3 Aug 1691 F158v elected to Nathaniel Ranew's £80 share   1 Mar 1691/2 F165v elected Stock-keeper for Livery with Samuel Sprint   26 Mar 1694 F201v elected Stock-keeper at special meeting   6 May 1695

F222v elected to Henry Mortlock's £160 share   3 Jun 1695 F225r takes partner's oath. Thomas Cockerell jnr, his apprentice, is freed   2 Nov 1696 F252r deceased; Matthew Gilliflower elected to his £160 share   6 Jun 1698 G8v his apprentice Herbert Walwyn is freed

COCKERELL/COCKERILL, Thomas (II)   3 Jun 1695 F225v servant to Thomas Cockerell snr; freed   1 Jul 1695 F227v cloathed   4 May 1696 F242v elected as Assistant and summoned   8 Jun 1696 F243r sworn in as Assistant   6 May 1700 G39v Thomas Glenister is bound to him   26 Mar 1701 G57v fined for Renter Warden   9 Feb 1701/2 G67r moiety of his 'Gradus ad Parnassum' purchased by S.C. Elected to Mrs Baker's £80 share   2 Mar 1701/2 G67r elected Stock-keeper for Yeomanry   7 Dec 1702 G83v Simon Le Bow and Uriah Nicholson are bound to him   15 Nov 1703 G97v surrenders £80 share and requests that John Nicholson be admitted to it   10 Sep 1711 G194r his apprentice Simon Le Bow is freed

COFFEE HOUSE JESTS   1 Sep 1684 F23r assigned by Benjamin Thrale to Henry Rhodes

COGGAN, Francis   10 Sep 1694 F212v servant to William Miller, deceased; turned over to Daniel Browne

COGSWELL, John   6 Jul 1691 F157v citizen and currier of London; proposed as surety for £50 loan from Tyler Bequest by Benjamin Johnson

COLE, Francis   3 Feb 1684/5 F30r his widow Mary is allowed to mortgage her £80 share to William Thackery

COLE, Henry, snr – see following entry

COLE, Henry, jnr   7 May 1716 G240r son of Henry, is bound to John Pemberton, 7 years

COLE, James   3 Dec 1684 F26v is allowed to be translated to the Weavers' Company on a contribution to the poorbox and promise of further charity

COLE/COLES, Joseph   13 Apr 1702 G70r citizen and spectacle-maker of London. Bond from S.C. for £100   7 Aug 1704 G110v S.C.'s debt to him paid off   3 Mar 1706/7 G139r citizen and spectacle-maker of London; bond from S.C. of £100 at £200 penalty at 5% p.a. sealed   2 May 1709 G164v bond of £100 to be repaid within next three months   27 Mar 1710 G177v bond of £100 taken from Gilbert Heron to pay off his bond from S.C.

COLE, Mary   3 Feb 1684/5 F30r widow of Francis Cole; is allowed to mortgage her £80 share to William Thackery

COLE, Richard – see following entry

COLE, Robert   10 Sep 1716 G243r son of Richard, is bound to Peter Bettesworth, 7 years

COLE, William   3 Mar 1706/7 G139r bound to John Nutt, 7 years
See also COLES

COLEMAN, John, snr – see following entry

COLEMAN, John, jnr   4 Jul 1715 G231r son of John, is bound to William Etheridge, 7 years

COLEMAN, Richard – see following entry

COLEMAN, William   6 Sep 1714 G221v son of Richard, is bound to William Holland, 7 years

COLES, [ ]   3 Jan 1680/1 E106r his name to be struck off S.C. plate

COLES, Henry   1 Mar 1679/80 E97v £100 bond to him sealed

COLES, John   3 Apr 1710 G178v bound to Philip Barrett, 7 years

COLES, Mrs   3 Jan 1680/1 E106r to receive £20 Christmas dividend, and to be remitted £7 from stock, despite 'controversy'

COLES, Widow   4 Oct 1686 F64r deceased; Samuel Lowndes elected to her £160 share
See also COLE

COLEY/COLY/COOLEY, Henry   6 Feb 1681/2 E144r bond for £300 with £600 penalty to pay £307 in August next sealed   5 Aug 1700 G44r bond for £300 with £600 penalty to pay 5% p.a. sealed   12 Jun 1704 G107r deceased; bonds relating to him to be renewed   3 Jul 1704 G110r deceased; further sum taken up from administrators on bond from S.C.   5 Mar 1704/5 G116v deceased; bonds cancelled

COLLEGE, Stephen – see RAREE-SHOW; HARRIS, Benjamin

COLLIER, Joseph   29 May 1689 F118v pleads inability to be cloathed; Master and Wardens desired to warn him before Lord Mayor and force him to be
See also COLLYER

COLLINS, Arthur   7 Aug 1699 G29r bound to Matthew Wootton, 7 years   6 Oct 1707 G145v freed by Matthew Wootton

COLLINS, Deputy   2 Nov 1702 G82v heard by Court about advertisement in Exeter for bibles &c.   1 Mar 1704/5 G116r elected Stock-keeper for Livery   4 Jun 1705 G120r elected Assistant   2 Jul 1705 G121v auditor of late Master and Wardens' accounts   4 Feb 1705/6 G127r elected to Susan Miller's £160 share   1 Jul 1706 G133r Benjamin Lyon is bound to him   5 Aug 1706 G134r auditor of late Master and Wardens' accounts   5 Jul 1707 G143r candidate for Under Warden   7 Jul 1707 G143v auditor of late Master and Wardens' accounts. Freeman Collins is bound to him   4 Aug 1707 G144r elected Under Warden and takes oath   6 Oct 1707 G145v his apprentice William Eyres is freed   12 Apr 1708 G152r John Roberts is bound to him   3 Jul 1708 G154r elected Under Warden and takes oath   6 Feb 1709/10 G175v Edward Cave is bound to him   1 Jul 1710 G181r competes unsuccessfully for Upper Warden   3 Jul 1710 G182r elected Upper Warden   30 Jun 1711 G192r competes unsuccessfully for Upper Warden   13 Aug 1711 G193v to assist Master, Wardens and Stock-keepers in management of Stock affairs   5 Jul 1712 G201r elected Upper Warden

COLLINS, Freeman, snr   8 May 1682 E152r cloathed   2 Nov 1685 F46r elected to Bennett Griffin's £40 share in consideration of being James Cotterell's son-in-law (Cotterell's death has precipitated the elections)   4 Sep 1688 F106v owns to printing the Metamorphoses (with details of sheets and impression) for Thomas Dring and Abel Swale; referred   6 Apr 1691 F151v elected First Renter Warden   3 Aug 1691 F158v competes unsuccessfully for Nathaniel Ranew's £160 share   1 Aug 1692 F177r he and William Baker to pay balance of Renter Wardens' accounts   1 Mar 1693/4 F199v elected Stock-keeper for Livery with William Crooke   2 Jul 1694 F210r elected to the £80 share of Mrs Newcombe, now remarried   6 Aug 1694 F211r sworn into £80 share. Lawrence Vere, his servant, is freed   2 Dec 1695 F237r William Walrond is bound to him   4 Sep 1699 G30r Samuel Farlow is bound to him   2 Oct 1699 G31v William Eyres is bound to him   4 Dec 1699 G34r his apprentice Francis Burges is freed   6 May 1700 G39v Thomas Urry is bound to him   11 Nov 1700 G46v his apprentice John Dormer is freed   7 Jul 1707 G143v his son Freeman is bound to him, 7 years   3 May 1708 G152v his apprentice Thomas Dermer is freed   2 Mar 1712/13 G206v deceased   5 Jul 1714 G220v his apprentice Benjamin Lyon is freed

COLLINS, Freeman, jnr   7 Jul 1707 G143v bound to Freeman his father, 7 years   3 Aug 1713 G212v freed by patrimony   5 Oct 1713 G214r enquiry to be made about £5 not paid by him   4 Mar 1716/17 G248r Robert Hardwick is bound to him

COLLINS, Henry   8 Nov 1703 G97r his apprentice John Wind is freed

COLLINS, James   1 Dec 1679 E95v summoned to next pension Court   5 Jul 1680 E102r to be prosecuted if he does not bring the money he owes S.C. to the next Court   2 Aug 1680 E102v to be prosecuted unless he pays off his bond before the next general Court   7 Feb 1680/1 E107r to be prosecuted if his £50 loan money is not paid back before next Court   7 Mar 1680/1 E107v his surety to pay £50 at next Court   3 Oct 1681 E130v disposal of his £40 share deferred until next Court   7 Nov 1681 E137v Collins's £40 share voted to Thomas Passenger; he forfeited it by mortgaging it without permission   5 Dec 1681 E140v assignment to Samuel Lowndes of Joseph Glanvill's 'Saducismus Triumphatus ... and a Letter of Dr Henry Moore'   1 Mar 1687/8 F97v expelled from Livery by order of Lord Mayor

COLLINS, Mary   18 Dec 1707 G148r elected to Mary Spurdance's pension

COLLINS, Mrs   3 Feb 1706/7 G137v deceased; her £80 share disposed of to John Baskett

COLLINS, Susanna   7 May 1716 G240r freed by John Roberts   6 Aug 1716 G242v Richard Parrott is bound to her   4 Mar 1716/17 G247v her apprentice Edward Cave is freed

COLLYER, John   8 Nov 1703 G97r Thomas Whitmore is bound to him   1 Dec 1712 G205v Samuel Hodgkison is bound to him

COLLYER/COLLIER, Joseph   1702–1717 Treasurer/Warehousekeeper   26 Oct 1702 G82v proposes John Guy and Christopher Hussey as securities and bond drawn up

See also TREASURER, WAREHOUSEKEEPER

COLLYER, Thomas   7 Aug 1704 G111r bound to Thomas Willmer, 7 years   1 Oct 1711 G195r freed by Thomas Willmer

COLLYER, William   8 Apr 1700 G39r bound to Peter Richmond, 7 years   5 Feb 1704/5 G115r turned over from William Sayes to James Willshire   1 Sep 1712 G203r freed by James Willshire

See also COLLIER

COLSTON, John   11 Nov 1695 F235v servant to James Marriner; freed

COLY – see COLEY

COMBER/CUMBER, Thomas, Dr   1 Aug 1698 G13r the several assignments from Charles Broome to Benjamin Motte and from Motte to Capt. Samuel Roycroft of a moiety of parts 1–2 of Comber's 'Companion to the Temple' read and ordered to be entered

See also CATECHISMS

COMBES, Charles (I)   22 Jun 1697 F266v bound to Edward Booth

COMBES, Charles (II)   5 Feb 1704/5 G115r bound to Lewis Thomas, 7 years

COMBES, Henry – see following entry

COMBES, Thomas   7 Dec 1713 G215r son of Henry, is bound to James Knapton, 7 years

COMBS/COMBESBY, Richard   6 Mar 1703/4 G103v bound to William Harvey, 7 years   6 Aug 1711 G193r freed by William Harvey

COMBESBY – see COMBS

COMMITTEES   12 Sep 1685 F44v Clerk to minute business of uncompleted committees   2 Nov 1685 F46r list of several committees to be revived read to Table by Clerk; consideration deferred   2 Aug 1697 F265v Clerk to list the names of the committees chosen by the Court within the past year and still existing   3 Jul 1699 G27r all committees that have matters depending to be revived   8 Apr 1700 G39r members of committees to be sent a copy of the order relating thereto and to receive a summons in writing to each meeting of the committee   5 Aug 1700 G44r those in existence before the election of the present Master and Wardens to be continued

COMMON COUNCIL   2 Oct 1682 E158r Richard Janeway confesses to having printed 'A Letter from the Old Common Council to the New' for Henry Care

COMMON SERJEANT   6 Sep 1703 G94v his opinion sought on whether any freeman of the S.C. who is not free of the City of London can be cloathed   6 Jul 1713 G211v Duncan Dee; his opinion that Henry Million the Beadle is a good witness for S.C.

COMMON PRAYER – see PRAYER BOOK

COMPANION TO THE TEMPLE – see COMBER, Thomas

COMPENDIUM OF DEVOTION (by Benjamin Whichcote) – see TREATISE OF PRAYER AND THANKSGIVING

THE COMPLETE SCHOOL-MISTRESS   4 Mar 1705/6 G129r counterfeit copies sold by Gwillam   26 Mar 1706 G130v committee to consider sale to Gilbert Beauchamp at Bristol fair

COMPRINTING – see ILLEGAL PRINTING

COMPTON, [   ]   4 Aug 1707 G144v committee to meet him, Topham and other MPs in order to get an Act of Parliament for securing copyright

COMPTON, Henry, Bishop of London – see LONDON, BISHOP OF

CONDUIT, Edward   2 May 1698 G7v freed by Henry Playford

CONIERS/CONYERS, Joshua   3 May 1686 F55v complains that Dennison has printed his ballad 'Virtue and Constancy Rewarded' under another title; summoned to next Court   6 Apr 1691 F152v summoned to next Court re. John Back and Thomas James printing a copy of his   8 Jun 1691 F154v he and John Back accuse each other of comprinting on them; afterwards he is shown to have printed Partridge, a stock book [i.e. Partridge's Almanack?]

CONINGSBY/CONNINGSBY, Christopher   5 May 1690 F135r summoned for cloathing but asks for time to consider   4 May 1691 F153v cloathed and promises fine   11 Nov 1695 F235v Samuel Bartlett, his apprentice, is freed   6 Jun 1698 G8v his apprentice Philip Barrett is freed. James Merrest is bound to him   1 Feb 1702/3 G85r John Thurloe is bound to him   7 Jul 1707 G143v John Norcott is bound to him   26 Mar 1712 G198r fined for Assistant Renter Warden   7 Dec 1713 G215r owing part of Renter Warden's fine   1 Mar 1713/14 G216v Richard Butler is bound to him

CONLY, Jane   5 Aug 1700 G44r bound to Robert Jole, 7 years

CONNINGSBY – see CONINGSBY

CONSTRUING BOOK – see LILLY, William

CONYERS, George   7 Dec 1696 F253r request to be excused cloathing for a year deferred   1 Feb 1696/7 F255r excused cloathing   4 Oct 1697 F268v Thomas Ballard is freed by him

See also following entry

CONYERS, John   9 Feb 1701/2 G67r John King is bound to him (however, 'John' is crossed out and 'George' substituted)   4 Jul 1709 G167v his apprentice John King is freed

See also CONIERS

COOK, Samuel   2 Mar 1701/2 G67v his apprentice Samuel Drury is freed

COOK (Thomas Walker 1698–1699; John Pether 1699–1704; thereafter none elected)   20 Oct 1699 G32r Court decides that the S.C.'s cook, Walker, rather than a cook which the S.C. has not chosen, should prepare dinner for S.C. on Lord Mayor's Day   26 Mar 1705 G117v Court decides not to choose a cook for the year   10 Sep 1705 G123v cook's bill of fare to be used for Lord Mayor's Day   1 Oct 1705 G124r his bill of fare to be used for Lord Mayor's Day

COOKE, [   ]   6 Nov 1682 E160r former glazier of S.C.; deceased

COOKE, Daniel   5 Feb 1704/5 G115r his son Thomas Cooke is freed by patrimony

COOKE, Edmund   2 Jun 1712 G200v his son William is bound to John Buchanan, 7 years

COOKE, James   3 Oct 1692 F180v Cooke's 'Mellificium Chirurgae or the Marrow of Chirurgery' assigned by Benjamin Shirley to William Marshall

COOKE/COOKES, Richard   9 Sep 1706 G134v bound to Henry Kift, 7 years   1 Nov 1714 G223r freed by Henry Kift

COOKE, Samuel   9 Sep 1700 G45r his apprentice George Marshall is freed   1 Sep 1701 G64r John Randoll is bound to him

COOKE, Simon   5 Feb 1693/4 F199r Jonas Malsbery is bound to him, 7 years

COOKE, Thomas   5 Feb 1704/5 G115r son of Daniel Cooke; freed by patrimony

COOKE/COAKE, William (I)   6 May 1700 G39v bound to Henry Morris, 7 years   3 Jul 1704 G110r turned over from Henry Morris to John Royden   3 Dec 1705 G126r turned over from Royden to Benjamin Beardwell

COOKE, William (II)   2 Jun 1712 G200v son of Edmund; bound to John Buchanan, 7 years

COOKES – see COOKE

COOLEY, Ephraim   7 Aug 1682 E156v Thomas Vere's executor; makes an assignment to Jonah Deacon

See also COLEY

COOPER, [   ]   2 Jun 1701 G60r Counsellor at Law; opinion concerning unauthorised printing and publishing of sheet almanack and Ephemeris by John Bradford   26 Jan 1703/4 G100v to give advice to Clerk concerning answers of Benjamin Harris   2 Mar 1703/4 G103r advice to be taken concerning John Bradford

COOPER, Edward   1 Mar 1713/14 G216v son of Edward; bound to Emmanuel Matthews, 7 years

COOPER, James   5 Apr 1703 G88r bound to Thomas Leigh, 7 years   5 Mar 1704/5 G117r turned over from Thomas Leigh to William Smith   1 Oct 1705 G124r turned over from William Williams (sic) to Francis Leach   6 Sep 1708 G157v turned over from Francis Leach to Dryden Leach   5 Jun 1710 G180v freed by Dryden Leach

COOPER, Mary   13 Mar 1711/12 G198r S.C.'s answer to Benjamin Poole and John Stowe's bill in Chancery concerning her £160 share   19 Dec 1712 G206r her dividend to be stopped because of suit in Chancery against S.C. relating to her stock   7 Feb 1714/15 G224v share to be disposed of if money not paid to Poole by her daughter Mrs

Carr   14 Mar 1714/15 G226r grants request that her stock might not be disposed of until next Court day   4 Apr 1715 G227v disposal of share to be postponed until next Court day   2 May 1715 G228v son's request that her stock should not be disposed of until end of Michaelmas term granted   5 Dec 1715 G235r £160 share to be disposed of at next Court. Clerk to give notice of this to her son   6 Feb 1715/16 G236r Clerk to settle disposal of her stock   5 Mar 1715/16 G237r her £160 share disposed of to Dryden Leach. To receive the overplus of the dividends until her death

COOPER, William (I)   7 Jan 1683/4 F8r elected to John Leigh's £80 share   3 Mar 1683/4 F9v elected Assistant in accordance with Crown's request as a reward for stamping out seditious printing. Fined for Renter Warden so he is eligible for Court   7 Apr 1684 F14r on the list of loyal Assistants presented to the Crown   7 May 1685 (W) confirmed as member of new Livery   5 Jul 1686 F60v elected Stock-keeper in place of Warden John Baker   7 Feb 1686/7 F70v elected to the late John Playford's £160 share   1 Mar 1686/7 F77r elected Stock-keeper for Assistants with John Towse   12 Oct 1687 F90v query as to why he was displaced from the Assistants but not the Livery; asks Master to find out from the Secretary of State   13 Oct 1687 F92r acknowledged to be displaced from both Assistants and Livery and from post of Stock-keeper   7 Nov 1687 F94r restored to places as Assistant, as Stock-keeper and as member of the Livery pursuant to the Town Clerk's approval of him   1 Mar 1687/8 F97v displaced as Assistant by order of Crown and expelled from Livery by order of Lord Mayor   11 Oct 1688 F108v restored to Livery   27 Nov 1688 F110v among those chosen to audit Renter Wardens' accounts. Competes unsuccessfully for Under Warden

COOPER, William (II)   5 Aug 1700 G44r bound to John Harding, 7 years   6 Oct 1707 G145v freed by William Harding

COOTE, Edmund – see ENGLISH SCHOOLMASTER

COPE, John (I)   1 Dec 1707 G147v bound to Gerrard Dennet, 7 years

COPE, John (II)   14 Mar 1714/15 G226r son of Thomas; bound to Joseph Hazard, 7 years

See also following entry

COPE, Thomas   2 Mar 1701/2 G67v John Smith is bound to him   4 Oct 1703 G96r his apprentice William Kitchiner is freed   6 Dec 1708 G159v Christopher Wellbank is bound to him   6 Oct 1712 G204v John Hooper is bound to him   2 Jul 1716 G242r Richard Clarke is bound to him

COPELAND, John   7 Nov 1692 F181v of St John Street; summoned to be cloathed   6 Feb 1692/3 F184r excused cloathing

COPPING, George   11 Apr 1681 E109v fined for Renter Warden   4 Feb 1688/9 F112v re-elected Assistant   4 Mar 1688/9 F114r sworn in as new Assistant. Competes unsuccessfully for the late Rebecca Beadle's £80 share   6 May 1689 F117r ranked third of Assistants never elected as Master or Warden. Elected to the late John Baker's £160 share   6 Jul 1689 F121v competes unsuccessfully for Under Warden   5 Jun 1690 F135v re-elected Assistant   5 Jul 1690 F138v competes unsuccessfully for Under Warden   6 Apr 1691 F152r among those chosen to audit Renter Wardens' accounts   2 Jul 1692 F172v fined for first year of Under Warden   5 Feb 1693/4 F198r added to committee advising on drain to be shared with St Martin's Ludgate   3 Jul 1697 F263v elected Under Warden   5 Jul 1697 F264r fined for Under Warden   10 Jan 1698/9 G18v added to committee to consider Printing Act   4 Jul 1702 G76v fined for Upper Warden to preserve seniority   3 Jul 1703 G91v fined for Upper Warden   9 Sep 1706 G134r deceased; Livery share disposed of to William Hensman

COPPLETON, Amos   7 Oct 1700 G46r freed by Benjamin Webster and Daniel Browne

COPSON, Samuel   5 Jun 1699 G25v bound to William Redmaine, 8 years

COPYRIGHT   17 Aug 1681 E127v byelaw   4 Mar 1694/5 F218v salvo to be fixed to all entries made in past or future where copyright belongs to S.C. or a private person
See also ACTS OF PARLIAMENT

CORBIN, Leonard, snr – see following entry

CORBIN, Leonard, jnr   6 Jul 1713 G212v son of Leonard; bound to John Walthoe, 7 years

CORDERIUS [i.e. works of Mathurin Cordier]   6 Sep 1714 G221v letter from William Willymott to Benjamin Tooke concerning printing of

CORDIER, Mathurin – see CORDERIUS

CORNELIUS TACITUS – see TACITUS

CORPORATION   13 Apr 1698 G6v committee to enquire into estate of   7 Feb 1703/4 G101r committee to consider affairs of corporation and English Stock   5 Aug 1706 G134r rental to be made of rents due to   5 Apr 1714 G218r committee to inspect and report on state and affairs of corporation   6 Feb 1715/16 G236r committee to inspect and report on affairs of corporation
See also ACTS OF PARLIAMENT

COTTERELL, [   ]   7 Jun 1680 E100v assigned signature D of Stock Child's Guide   7 May 1683 (W) paid 12d to Poor Box for 'coming after Court was sat'

COTTERELL, Abraham   3 Apr 1704 G106r bound to Thomas Bevor, 7 years

COTTERELL, James   2 Jul 1681 E115v competes unsuccessfully for Under Warden   1 Jul 1682 E155r competes unsuccessfully for Under Warden   12 Nov 1683 F5r competes unsuccessfully for Mrs Stephens's £320 share   7 Jan 1683/4 F8r competes unsuccessfully for the late Mrs Roper's £320 share   26 Mar 1684 F11v chosen to audit Warden's accounts with John Macock   2 Jun 1684 F16r elected to Widow Pakeman's £320 share   5 Jul 1684 F19v elected as Under Warden   11 May 1685 F34v his name on the Livery list is vetoed by Lord Mayor. Committee to tell Lord Mayor that the Secretaries of State's accusations against him have been disproved   20 May 1685 F35v approved as Liveryman by Lord Mayor   4 Jul 1685 F39r fined for second year of Under Warden and for two years' Upper Warden   2 Nov 1685 F45v deceased; his £320 share voted to John Bellinger   4 Oct 1686 F64r precedent for S.C. paying for cakes and ale is cited from his and Henry Hills' Warden's accounts

COTTERELL, Thomas   7 Apr 1684 F13v on the list of loyal Assistants presented to the Crown   8 Apr 1695 F220v competes unsuccessfully for the late Mary Kirton's £160 share

COTTON, Benjamin, snr – see following entry

COTTON, Benjamin, jnr   8 Jan 1716/17 G246r son of Benjamin; bound to George Bourne, 7 years

COTTON, George   6 Aug 1711 G193r son of Hugh; bound to John Barber, 7 years

COTTON, Hugh – see preceding entry

COTTON, Jonathan   1 Jul 1700 G41r to be made free despite his master's arrears in quarterage. Freed by John Redmaine

COULTER, John   3 Apr 1704 G106r bound to Ralph Snow, 7 years

COUNSEL   3 Jul 1710 G182r Sir Simon Harcourt to be retained as by S.C.

COUNTRY CHAPMEN   8 Nov 1697 G1r letter sent to them to prevent printing and publishing of counterfeit almanacks

COUNTY FEAST   3 Dec 1711 G195v Hall not to be let for it without permission of Court   1 Dec 1712 G205v Hall not to be let for it without permission of Court

COURT – see STATIONERS' COMPANY: COURT

COURT BOOK   23 Jul 1702 G72r–G75r proceedings and judgement in suit against Richard Randall of Newcastle entered in

COURT OF ALDERMEN   20 May 1685 F35v translation committee to appear before them to accept dealers of books who are freemen of other companies into S.C.   1 Jun 1685 F38v translation committee to appear there next day   5 May 1690 F134v Master, Wardens and certain Assistants to attend on 6 May   8 May 1704 G106v Franks requested to take oath before

See also LORD MAYOR

COURT OF CONSCIENCE   21 Jun 1700 G40v members who refuse to pay their quarterage arrears to be summoned before   1 Jul 1700 G41r Macock summoned before for arrears of quarterage. Gilbertson summoned before   12 Jun 1704 G107r members with arrears of quarterage to be summoned before   5 May 1707 G141v Newboult summoned before, Beadle to attend

COURTHORPE/COURTHORP, Bryan   6 Feb 1681/2 E142v made free by redemption by order of Lord Mayor's Court and cloathed   11 Oct 1688 F108v restored to Livery   4 Jul 1692 (W) his apprentice William Holland of Aldermanbury is turned over. F173v competes unsuccessfully for Nathaniel Ponder's £40 share   12 Sep 1692 F179r master of the newly made freeman William Holland of Aldermanbury, whose name is sent to Lord Chamberlain

COURTHORPE/COURTHOPE, Thomas   1 Dec 1707 G147v bound to William Holland, 8 years

COWELL, John – see following entry

COWELL, Thomas Smith   5 Aug 1695 F232r son of John Cowell of Tewkesbury, Gloucestershire, yeoman; bound to Richard Everingham from   1 Jul 1695   1 Mar 1702/3 G86r freed by Robert Everingham

COWSE, Benjamin   3 Feb 1700/1 G55v freed by Richard Chiswell

COX, Ann   21 Mar 1705/6 G129v elected to her husband Robert's pension   21 Jun 1707 G143r deceased; Ann Bramston is given her pension

COX, Gabriel   11 Apr 1681 E110v excused from becoming Renter Warden for a year   27 Mar 1682 E149r elected First Renter Warden   3 Apr 1682 E149v pleads inability to serve as Renter Warden since as a convicted Catholic all his goods have been seized; Court excuses him   12 Oct 1687 F91v elected Assistant Renter Warden instead of George Wells, now displaced from the Livery   13 Oct 1687 F92r asks to be excused Renter Wardenship for this year; granted   1 Mar 1687/8 F97v expelled from Livery by order of Lord Mayor   11 Oct 1688 F108v restored to Livery

COX, John (I)   6 Nov 1704 G113r bound to George Read, 7 years   4 Feb 1711/12 G196v freed by George Read

COX, John (II)   6 Oct 1712 G204v son of Thomas; bound to Richard Sare, 7 years

COX, Mrs   23 Jun 1710 G180v deceased; Bridget Thomas is given her pension

COX, Nicholas   4 Jun 1705 G120r indebted to English Stock. Letter of licence read but consideration thereof left until next Court day   4 Aug 1707 G144r letter of licence and composition signed by his creditors to be accepted by S.C.

COX, Robert   19 Dec 1692 F183r elected into the pension of Teles, deceased   12 Dec 1695 F238r elected to the late Alice Moore's pension   22 Jun 1697 F263v elected to the late Mary Harris's pension   22 Jun 1699 G25v elected to Mary Brockett's pension   21 Mar 1705/6 G129v deceased; his wife Ann given his pension

COX, Thomas (I)   5 May 1707 G142r bound to Ebenezer Tracy, 7 years

COX, Thomas (II)   6 Oct 1712 G204v his son John is bound to Richard Sare, 7 years

CRABTREE, Henry   30 Sep 1684 F24r has written a new almanack called Merlinus Rusticus

CRABTREE, John   7 May 1716 G240r son of Samuel; bound to Daniel Mead, 7 years

CRABTREE, Samuel   2 Apr 1694 F202v freed by Edward Ward;   7 May 1716 G240r his son John is bound to Daniel Mead

CRADDOCK/CRADOCK, Joseph   6 Sep 1703 G94v bound to Daniel Midwinter, 7 years   26 Sep 1712 G203v freed by Daniel Midwinter

CRAILE – see CRAYLE

CRANE, James   3 Apr 1704 G105v and John Keeblebutter. Bond from S.C. of £200 penalty   3 Jul 1704 G109v and John Keeblebutter. Bond re-sealed due to error

CRANE, Richard, snr – see following entry

CRANE, Richard, jnr   6 Nov 1710 G185r son of Richard; bound to Matthew Jenour, 7 years

CRANE, Thomas (I)   4 Sep 1704 G112r paid part of quarterage arrears. William Bembridge is bound to him   12 Nov 1711 G195r Samuel Burt is bound to him   6 Oct 1712 G204v his apprentice William Bembridge is freed

CRANE, Thomas (II)   1 Sep 1707 G145r bound to Alexander Milbourne, 7 years   5 Sep 1715 G232v freed by Elizabeth Milbourne

CRATCH, William   12 Nov 1705 G125r bound to Ann Keyes, 7 years

CRAWFORD, Anne   23 Jun 1710 G180v deceased; Johanna Strainge is given her pension

CRAWFORD, Elizabeth   20 Dec 1700 G54r elected to Joan Jackson's pension

CRAWLEY, Widow   11 Apr 1681 E109v her 10s pension transferred after her death to Widow Dew

CRAYLE, Benjamin   3 Jun 1689 F119r cloathed   7 Oct 1689 F125r he and Joseph Streeter to be prosecuted by Robert Stephens for printing and publishing 'Sodom or the Quintessence of Debauchery'   7 Feb 1698/9 G20v his apprentice William Watts is freed

CRAYLE, Daniel   4 Apr 1709 G164r of Newark; elected to cloathing   4 Jul 1709 G167r Court finds his excuse for not accepting cloathing inadequate   5 Sep 1709 G170r of Newark; Court still of opinion that he should not be excused cloathing. To be proceeded against if he refuses

CRAYLE/CRAILE, James   4 Oct 1686 F64v elected to livery   8 Nov 1686 F67r cloathed on last Lord Mayor's Day and summoned to appear at this Court   1 Mar 1687/8 F97v expelled from Livery by order of Lord Mayor   11 Oct 1688 F108v restored to Livery   3 Apr 1693 F185v fined for First Renter Warden   7 Oct 1695 F234r Benjamin Browne, his apprentice, is freed   11 Nov 1695 F234v competes unsuccessfully for the late James Adamson's £40 share (W) Taylor, formerly Crayle's man, cloathed   4 Oct 1697 F268v elected to Marshall's £40 share   7 Aug 1699 G28r assignment of copies to Samuel Sprint and J[ohn?] Nicholson read and deferred to next Court day   7 Jul 1701 G62r James Brook is bound to him   1 Feb 1702/3 G85r his apprentice Thomas Hall is freed

CREAK/CREEK, Bazaleel   3 May 1703 G89v bound to Edward Hawkins, 7 years   12 Nov 1705 G125r turned over from Edward Hawkins to Benjamin Yarnes

CREED – see PEARSON, John, Bishop of Chester

CRISPE, Henry   6 Dec 1697 G2r his apprentice Samuel White is freed

CROFT/CROFTS, John   8 May 1682 E152r goldsmith of Foster Lane; substitutes for Hatley as surety for John Penn's continuation of £100 loan from S.C.   3 Dec 1683 F6v goldsmith; Penn asked to propose an alternative surety to him on the grounds that he has 'gone aside'

See also CROFTS

CROFTS, Henry, snr – see following entry

CROFTS, Henry, jnr   3 Oct 1715 G233v son of Henry; bound to Thomas Bickerton, 7 years

CROFTS, John   5 Feb 1699/1700 G35r bound to Robert Vincent, 7 years   3 Mar 1706/7 G139r freed by Robert Vincent   1 Sep 1707 G145r stationer; George Webb is bound to him   6 Feb 1709/10 G175v of Fleet Street, stationer; Richard Eaton is bound to him   12 Nov 1716 G244v Zachariah Mackature is bound to him

See also CROFT

CROKATT, Gilbert – see following entry

CROKATT, James   5 Dec 1715 G235v son of Gilbert; bound to John Walthoe, 7 years

CROMPTON, William   6 Mar 1703/4 G103v bound to Jeffrey Wale, 7 years

CROOK, Andrew   28 Mar 1680 E98v his apprentice Thomas Grover is freed

CROOK, William   3 Apr 1710 G178v bound to John Lilly, 7 years
See also CROOKE

CROOKE, John   9 Jun 1707 G142v bound to John Heptingstall, 7 years   2 Aug 1714 G221r freed by John Heptingstall

CROOKE, Mary   2 Dec 1689 F127r allowed to mortgage her £80 share to John Towse for £70 plus interest   5 Sep 1692 (W) widow; her apprentice George Thompson is freed   12 Sep 1692 F179r master of newly made freeman George Thompson of Addle Hill, whose name is sent to Lord Chamberlain   3 Oct 1692 F180r deceased; her £80 share voted to Israel Harrison

CROOKE, Samuel   6 Jan 1712/13 G206r son of Thomas; bound to John Clarke, 7 years

CROOKE, Thomas – see preceding entry

CROOKE, Widow   5 Sep 1681 E129r her £320 share voted to Thomas Vere as his Master's prerogative

CROOKE/CROOK, William   1 Mar 1682/3 E164v elected Stock-keeper for Yeomanry with Thomas Sawbridge   7 May 1685 (W) confirmed as member of new Livery   3 Aug 1685 F42v John How confesses to printing a book in which Crooke owns part of the right   26 Mar 1686 F53v fined for First Renter Warden   1 Mar 1686/7 F77r elected Stock-keeper for Livery with George Wells   11 Oct 1688 F108v restored to Livery   13 Mar 1692/3 F184v sworn in as Stock-keeper   1 Mar 1692/3 F184r elected Stock-keeper for Livery with Samuel Sprint   1 Mar 1693/4 F199v elected Stock-keeper for Livery with Freeman Collins   3 May 1697 F262r his apprentice Richard Bassett is freed

See also CROOK

CROOME, Anne   19 Dec 1698 G17v elected to Anne Crouch's pension   21 Jun 1700 G40v William Birch to be given her pension

CROOME, George   25 Jun 1684 F18v freeman of the Leathersellers' Company; declares himself willing to be translated to S.C.   7 Jul 1684 F20r committee appointed to deal with printers who are not members of S.C., including him   2 Apr 1688 (W) freeman of Leathersellers' Company, is freed by S.C.   1 Oct 1688 F107v confesses to printing ABC with additions and distributing all but c.200; penalty remitted if he resigns right and rest of impression   9 Feb 1690/1 F149r summoned to next Court for failing to enter a pamphlet   7 Feb 1697/8 G3r excused cloathing   4 Nov 1706 G135v printer of sham almanack, The City and Country Remembrancer; to submit himself to Court and give it satisfaction   5 Jul 1708 G155r printer. Richard Smith is bound to him   7 Feb 1708/9 G160v confesses to printing S.C.'s almanack illegally; bond of £100 penalty not to print any more of S.C.'s almanacks or copies

CROOME, John   2 Apr 1688 F100r journeyman printer and prisoner in Ludgate; petitions for £6 for fees, chamber rent and discharge; Court to see to his release

CROSGROVE, Henry   5 Aug 1700 G44r bound to Thomas Milbourne, 7 years

CROSIER, Joseph   6 Nov 1704 G113r bound to William Chandler, 7 years

CROSKILL – see CROSSKILL

CROSLEY, Nathan   7 Jul 1701 G62r bound to Ralph Simpson, 7 years

CROSS, Nathaniel, snr – see following entry

CROSS, Nathaniel, jnr   7 May 1716 G240r son of Nathaniel; bound to Joseph Harper, 7 years

CROSSE/CROSS, John   7 Sep 1685 F44r formerly a graver; given 10s charity at John Baker's request   7 Nov 1687 F94v John Gadbury commends him to John Baker and Thomas Bassett as their old servant; Baker secures for him a one-off payment of 20s

CROSSE, Philip   5 Dec 1698 G17r bound to John Heptingstall, 7 years

CROSSE, Richard   2 Jul 1716 G242r son of William; bound to George Sawbridge, 7 years

CROSSE, William (I)   7 Oct 1698 G15r his apprentice Isaac Gunn is freed   6 Mar 1698/9 G22r John Saltmarsh is bound to him   5 Aug 1706 G134r John Abbut is bound to him. His apprentice Isum Bennett is freed   3 Feb 1706/7 G138r his apprentice John Saltmarsh is freed

CROSSE, William (II)   7 Aug 1710 G183r freed by John Darby

CROSSE, William (III – perhaps to be identified with I)   2 Jul 1716 G242r his son Richard is bound to George Sawbridge, 7 years

CROSSKILL/CROSKILL, Richard   7 Aug 1704 G111r freed by patrimony   4 Sep 1704 G112r John Sackfeild is bound to him   10 Sep 1711 G194r his apprentice John Sackfeild is freed

CROUCH, Anne   27 Sep 1698 G13v elected to Mary Rix's pension   19 Dec 1698 G17v deceased; Anne Croome is given her pension

CROUCH, Nathaniel (I)   5 Aug 1689 F122r given until next Court to decide about cloathing   12 Sep 1692 F179r summoned to show why he should not be cloathed

CROUCH, Nathaniel (II)   12 Nov 1711 G195r freed by patrimony   5 Apr 1714 G217v excused cloathing

CROUCH, Samuel   2 Aug 1680 E102v cloathing deferred until after consultation with Master and Wardens; declares submission to Court's decision   11 Apr 1681

E109v is assigned [Herbert Palmer's] 'The Memorials of Godliness and Christianity' by Mrs Underhill   4 Oct 1686 F64v elected to cloathing   8 Nov 1686 F67r excused Livery   2 May 1692 F171r cloathed and promises fine   3 Apr 1710 G178r elected First Renter Warden

CROUCH, Thomas   12 Nov 1711 G195r freed by patrimony

CROW, Jacob   1 Dec 1707 G147v bound to Thomas White, 7 years

CROWDER, William   5 Feb 1704/5 G115r bound to Sarah Holt, 7 years   2 Jun 1712 G200v freed by Sarah Holt

CROWN (Charles II, 29 May 1660–6 Feb 1684/5; James II, 6 Feb 1684/5–11 Dec 1688; William III & Mary Stuart, 13 Feb 1689–8 Mar 1702; Anne, 8 Mar 1702–1 Aug 1714; George I, 1 Aug 1714–11 Jun 1727)   20 Jun 1681 E113r mandate re. Crown control of press read   3 Mar 1683/4 F9v King Charles II's letter (copy in W) re. electing certain S.C. members to Court of Assistants for stamping out seditious printing. Court agrees to letter and six new Assistants are elected   26 Mar 1684 F11v subpoena served on S.C. directing it to appear at the Court of Kings Bench to answer to a *quo warranto*   27 Mar 1684 F12v S.C.'s response to *quo warranto* cites graciousness of Crown in granting charter; submits to Crown's choice of Assistants. (W) Master urges S.C. to be mindful of Crown's generosity   7 Apr 1684 F13v Master supervises the drawing-up of a list of Assistants loyal to the government, to be presented to the Crown   27 May 1684 F14v address to King thanking him for new charter is read to Court   20 Dec 1684 F27v communicates desire to suppress libels via Roger L'Estrange; committee formed to negotiate with him   30 Dec 1684 F28r S.C.'s petition to Crown concerning suppression of libels, drafted by Roger L'Estrange, to be presented on 2 January   29 Jan 1684/5 F29r order referring the suppression of seditious books to Roger L'Estrange, signed by the Earl of Sunderland, is read   17 Feb 1684/5 F30v L'Estrange asks Court to list all dealers in books not among their freemen, so Crown through Lord Mayor can coerce them to become free of S.C.   6 Apr 1685 F33v letter from the Earl of Sunderland requesting that dealers in books who are free of other companies be translated to the S.C. Lord Mayor conveys Crown's wishes to S.C. to nominate a new Livery. (W) Letter from Lord Mayor setting out Crown's wishes in respect of City companies   21 May 1685 (W) royal command to Roger L'Estrange, signed by Lord Sunderland, renewing regulations concerning licensing and restriction of number of presses   22 May 1685 F36r Roger L'Estrange produces James II's commission re. licensing   22 Dec 1685 F49r committee consulting with Sir Roger L'Estrange on free workmen printers' petition decides to send Crown an abbreviated version   3 Oct 1687 F89r order displacing Master, Wardens and Assistants, restoring former Assistants, and another from the Lord Mayor displacing certain liverymen and restoring others   12 Oct 1687 F89v re-elections   13 Oct 1687 F92r committee appointed to draw up an address of thanks to the Crown   17 Oct 1687 F93r address of thanks to Crown signed by Court   5 Dec 1687 F95r commission approving the several choices of officers for the companies of London and dispensing with oaths of allegiance read   1 Mar 1687/8 F97v order via Town Clerk to displace various Assistants and liverymen   7 May 1688 F101r Peter Parker and Thomas Guy complain about complaints made about them by S.C. to Crown   1 Oct 1688 F107r S.C. submits to the order of King and Counsel re. S.C. and King's printers encroaching on Oxford privileges   11 Oct 1688 F108r restoration of livery and Assistants   27 Nov 1688 F109v declares that S.C. made no surrender of its new charter; new officials elected   2 Dec 1689 F127v Lord Mayor solicits subscriptions for a loan to the Crown from S.C. 'upon the act of subsidy of 12d in the pound'   2 Jun 1690 F135r Act for restoring the City of London to its ancient rights and privileges   12 Jul 1690 F139v Court to subscribe money towards army in service of Crown   15 Jul 1690 F140r subscriptions collected   18 Jul 1690 F141r account of subscriptions to be delivered to the Committee of the City of London   2 Mar 1690/1 F149v loan of £200,000 sought for fitting out the navy   25 Jun 1691 F156r Court declares Stock unable to contribute to loan to Crown to cover expenses in Ireland, because of debt, but individual subscriptions to be collected   23 Sep 1691 F160v request for loan of £200,000 for additional excise for navy   23 Mar 1691/2 F167r Court replies in negative to mayoral precept desiring it to lend money to Crown   12 Apr 1692 F168v Crown sends Henry Million into Ireland re. linen manufacture, so he is unable to take up Renter Wardenship   1 Aug 1692 F176v Court moves its feast day to 18 August as Crown has appointed 10 August for a public feast   12 Sep 1692 F178v Court agrees to soliciting subscriptions for loan to Crown from members outside City, but says the Stock is too much in debt to contribute   7 Nov 1692 F181v Court agrees to soliciting subscriptions for loan to Crown from members outside City, but refuses to loan from Stock   8 May 1693 F187r attempting to raise £1m for war against France. City asked for contribution to pay navy. S.C. to solicit subscriptions from members outside City but unable to contribute anything from Stock. Henry Hills given certificate to claim reward for discovering an illegal press   4 Sep 1693 F190v Court agrees to Lord Mayor's precept to extort subscriptions from members outside City towards Crown loan, but refuses to loan from Stock   15 Mar 1693/4 F201r Court agrees to soliciting subscriptions for loan to Crown, but refuses to loan from Stock   10 Dec 1696 F253r Court agrees to soliciting subscriptions for loan to Crown, but refuses to loan from Stock   24 Apr 1697 F261r Court agrees to soliciting subscriptions for loan to Crown, but refuses to loan from Stock   16 Oct 1697 F269r Court agrees to soliciting subscriptions for loan to Crown, but refuses to loan from Stock   8 Nov 1697 G1v provision for Livery attending on day of His Majesty (William III) passing through the City to be left to Master and Wardens   4 Feb 1705/6 G127r stands for S.C. when the Queen came to St Paul's   5 Aug 1706 G134r carpenter's bill for stands for S.C. when the Queen came to St Paul's

See also ENGLISH STOCK, LETTERS PATENT, LORD MAYOR, PRINTING ACT

CROWNEFEILD, Adrian   7 Dec 1713 G215r son of Cornelius; bound to Robert Ponder, 7 years

CROWNEFEILD, Cornelius – see preceding entry

CROWTHER, Margaret   20 Dec 1693 F197r deceased; her pension voted to Mary Reynolds

CRUMP, John   26 Mar 1683 E166v agreed that he should pay £10 of his £50 loan from S.C. by them retaining his next two dividends from his £40 share; his share used as surety for remainder   11 Oct 1688 F108v restored to Livery

CRUMP, Mary   13 Apr 1702 G70r has surrendered £40 share in English Stock. Disposed of to Samuel Keeble   24 Mar 1713/14 G217r elected to Elizabeth Thrailes's pension   24 Sep 1714 G222r elected to Adam Winch's pension. Jane Mawson is given her pension   27 Sep 1715 G233r deceased; Jane Mawson is given her pension

CRUMP, Thomas   6 Jun 1709 G165v bound to Abraham Parkins, 7 years

CULLIN, John   4 Feb 1694/5 F217r son of Thomas Cullin, baker, of London; bound to Henry Playford   2 Mar 1701/2 G67v freed by Henry Playford

CULLIN, Thomas – see preceding entry

CUMBER – see COMBER

CUMBERLAND, Richard   6 Aug 1694 F211v Edmund Holloway is bound to him   2 Nov 1702 G83r his apprentice Edmund Holloway is freed

145

CUPPER, Thomasine   5 Oct 1685 F45r given 5s charity in response to petition   3 Oct 1687 F89r elected to Joan Jackson's 30s pension

CURDELL, Alexander   3 Nov 1707 G146v bound to James Holland, 7 years

CURGHEY, John, snr – see following entry

CURGHEY, John, jnr   6 Jan 1712/13 G206r son of John; bound to Bartholomew Gale, 7 years   2 Aug 1714 G221r turned over to Peter Wallis

CURLL, Edmund   5 Jun 1710 G180r summoned to take cloathing next Court day. Thomas Dryer turned over to him from Andrew Bell

CURSON, John   5 Jul 1703 G92r bound to Thomas Osborne   2 Oct 1710 G184v freed by Thomas Osborne   2 Jun 1712 G200v Samuel Lever is bound to him

CURTICE, Edward   23 Mar 1679/80 E98r freed by Sarah Griffin

CURTIS, Jane   22 Jun 1705 G120v elected to Susan Brudnell's pension   23 Mar 1707/8 G150r deceased; Adam Turner is given her pension

See also CURTIS, Mrs

CURTIS, John   9 Feb 1690/1 F149r summoned to next Court for failing to enter a pamphlet

CURTIS, Langley   7 Jun 1680 E100v his apprentice Thomas Brewster is freed   25 Aug 1680 E103r he and John Playford admonished for printing 'The Pacquet of Advice' anonymously in breach of the new byelaw   5 Oct 1681 E130v David Mallett claims that he was given Heraclitus and the Observator to print by Curtis   1 Mar 1682/3 E164r petition for £100 loan money rejected   20 Dec 1687 F96r given £1 charity

CURTIS, Mary   3 Apr 1704 G106r William Wood is bound to her   20 Dec 1710 G186v struck out of list of pensioners as not in so poor a condition   4 Jun 1711 G191r her apprentice William Wood is freed

CURTIS, Mrs [Jane?]   6 Mar 1688/9 F114v accused by Robert Stephens of printing unlicensed pamphlets. Claims Sir William Waller and Sir Robert Payton ordered them. Dismissed with a warning

See also CURTIS, Jane

CURTIS, William   7 Feb 1686/7 F71v 18s taken out of Poor Box for the discharge of William Curtis from Ludgate Prison   26 Mar 1698 G5v elected to Thomas Egglesfeild's pension

CUSTOMS HOUSE   28 Mar 1680 E98v Dr Bladon's psalters kept there by Awnsham Churchill until agreement is reached   3 Apr 1682 E151r committee to negotiate with Roger Norton and Henry Hills re. charge for Customs House seizure of books   5 Sep 1687 F88r Master and Wardens seize psalms printed overseas there   4 Aug 1690 F141v Hutchins, merchant, fined £5 for importing Bibles, psalters and singing psalms, seized at Customs House   12 Apr 1692 F168v Robert Stephens given salary for waiting on Wardens weekly at Customs House   1 Jul 1695 F227v Master and Wardens to negotiate with Commissioners of Customs House for leave to view books about to be imported. Catalogue to be made of all books formerly seized by Master and Wardens now lying in S.C. warehouse   5 Aug 1695 F230r Master informed by commissioners that he needs leave from one of the Secretaries of State to view books; Court ask him to obtain this. Order of 1 July to be observed for catalogue of books seized at the Customs House

CUTHBERT, William   7 May 1711 G190v bound to George Sawbridge, 7 years

CUTLERS' COMPANY   22 May 1685 F37v agrees to turn book-dealing members over to S.C.   18 Jun 1689 F120r William Wild, formerly free of Cutlers', to take his place in the S.C. Livery according to the date of his City freedom

CUXON, Hugh – see following entry

CUXON, John   7 Feb 1714/15 G225r son of Hugh; bound to David Richmond, 7 years   1 Apr 1717 G249v turned over from David Richmond to Henry Parker

DABBS, Harrington, snr – see following entry

DABBS, Harrington, jnr   10 Sep 1711 G194r son of Harrington; bound to John Cluer, 7 years

DACON, William   13 Apr 1713 G208v freed by patrimony

DAGNALL/DAGNAL, Stephen   17 Feb 1684/5 F30v deceased; his £40 share voted to Nicholas Boddington

DALTON/DOLTON, Isaac   3 Jun 1700 G40v bound to Elizabeth Holt, 7 years   9 Jun 1707 G142v freed by Elizabeth Holt

DALTON, Thomas   3 Jun 1689 F119r cloathed   7 May 1694 F204r John Buchanan is bound to him   26 Mar 1697 F258v elected Renter Warden   27 Mar 1697 F260r excused Renter Wardenship for a year on account of being out of town   27 Mar 1699 G22v fined for Renter Warden   7 Aug 1699 G29r John Pratt is bound to him   4 Oct 1703 G96r his apprentice John Buchanan is freed   8 Nov 1703 G97r Nicholas Wood is bound to him   5 Feb 1704/5 G115r his apprentice John Pratt turned over to Anne Morris

DANBY, John   3 Dec 1694 F215v competes unsuccessfully for Capt. Edward Darrell's £40 share

DANCER, Nathaniel   6 Nov 1704 G113r John Randoll is turned over to him   3 Nov 1712 G205r his apprentice John Randoll is freed

DANCING   27 Mar 1699 G23r letting of Hall for dance

DANIEL, Samuel (author of *History of England* with John Trussell)   7 Sep 1685 F44r Benjamin Tooke, Richard Chiswell and Waterson are summoned re. printing 'Daniel and Thursfeild's History' (*sic*), a Stock book   5 Oct 1685 F44v Clerk to search for the entry of the 'History'   2 Nov 1685 F45v found to be entered for 5 March 1619; Waterson to be summoned   7 Dec 1685 F47v Waterson asked to prove prior title to avert legal proceedings   3 May 1686 F55r Mrs Waterson and sons disobey summons to explain their title to the book and the Court threatens to sequester their dividends   7 Feb 1686/7 F71r Mills declares that the book was entered to Mr Waterson on 27 Jun 1612 and the Clerk is ordered to check for prior entries   1 Mar 1687/8 F77v Court satisfied that Mrs Waterson has title to the 'History' and orders that her dividend should be paid

DANVERS, Henry   7 Aug 1699 G29r freed

DANVERS, Mary   1 Dec 1707 G147v leatherseller; Theophilus Thurogood is bound to her

DANVERSE, Henry   1 Feb 1702/3 G85r Thomas Stafford is bound to him

DAPWELL, Walter   4 Mar 1705/6 G129r freed by Francis Leach

DARBEY, John   3 Jun 1689 F119r cloathed

DARBY, John, snr   2 Apr 1694 F202r elected Assistant Renter Warden   7 May 1694 F203r sworn in as Assistant Renter Warden   12 Nov 1694 F215r David Gray, his apprentice, is freed   4 Mar 1694/5 F219r his son John is freed by patrimony   3 Jun 1695 F225v John Humphreys, his apprentice, is freed   11 Nov 1695 F235v Master tells Court that he has been unable to bring Darby and Capt. John Williams, late Renter Wardens, to account   3 May 1697 F261v will be repaid £4 10s owed by his fellow ex-Renter Warden Capt. John Williams from Mrs Williams's dividend and hence he can pay John Pether's debt   2 Dec 1700 G54r and James Astwood. Their apprentice William Smith is freed   2 Jun 1701 G60v Henry Woodfall is bound to him   2 Nov 1702 G83r complaint by his apprentice George Royden that he refused to make him free. To attend next Court to answer charge   7 Dec 1702 G83v examined concerning his refusal to make his apprentice free, but it is decided that the matter lies properly before the Chamberlain   1 Mar 1702/3 G86r his apprentice George Royden is freed   6 Dec 1703 G99v Joshua Nottage is bound to him   4 Feb 1705/6 G127v his apprentice Thomas Gibbs is freed. John Rhodes is bound to him   5 Jul 1708 G155r his apprentice Henry Woodfall is freed   24 Jul 1709 G168v and James Roberts summoned to attend next Court   1 Aug 1709 G169r and Roberts heard by Court   7 Dec 1709 G172v S.C.'s Bill in Chancery against him and John Partridge   17 Dec 1709 G173r printer of 'Letter to a Member of Parliament from John Partridge touching the Almanack for 1710'. Answer to be prepared to this   22 Dec 1709 G173r and Partridge. Order upon the over-ruling of their demur to be drawn up and subpoena taken out by S.C. for costs and further answer   6 Feb 1709/10 G175v printer; Jarvis Downs is bound to him   6 Aug 1711 G193r his apprentice Joshua Nottage is freed   10 Sep 1711 G194r printer; David Griffith is bound to him   5 May 1712 G199v John Andrew Holloway turned over to him from Charles Walkden   2 Mar 1712/13 G206v competes unsuccessfully for Mrs Mills's £80 share   13 Apr 1713 G208v competes unsuccessfully for John Overton's £80 share   14 May 1713 G210r committee to settle differences between him and John Partridge and S.C.   1 Jun 1713 G210r agent for John Partridge; meeting held with him about allowance payable to Partridge for his almanack   7 Sep 1713 G213r with Richard Mount to adjust time and manner of payment of £100 to Partridge   22 Dec 1713 G215r successful candidate for Matthew Wootton's £80 share   13 Jun 1715 G229v John Wilson is bound to him

DARBY, John, jnr   4 Mar 1694/5 F219r son of John Darby; freed by patrimony   3 Jun 1695 F225r cloathed   2 Oct 1699 G31v Samuel Humphreys is bound to him   11 Nov 1700 G46v John Money is bound to him   5 May 1701 G59v Thomas Heyt is bound to him   27 Mar 1703 G86v fined for First Renter Warden   1 Dec 1707 G147v his apprentice John Money is freed   7 Aug 1710 G183r his apprentice William Crosse is freed

DARBY, Samuel   4 Feb 1705/6 G127v freed by Thomas Milbourne

DARBY, Thomas   4 Oct 1697 F268v freed by patrimony

DARKER, John   5 May 1701 G59v bound to Sarah Darker, 7 years   3 Oct 1709 G171r freed by John Grantham   20 Dec 1710 G186v of Bartholomew Close, printer; James Mechell is bound to him

DARKER, Samuel   7 Oct 1698 G15r Thomas Moyce is bound to him   5 Aug 1700 G44r his apprentice John Smith is freed

DARKER, Sarah   5 May 1701 G59v John Darker is bound to her

DARRACK/DARROAK, Thomas   1 Jun 1702 G71v bound to Robert Tookey, 7 years   6 Jun 1709 G165v freed by Robert Tookey

DARRELL/DORREL/DORRELL, Edward, snr, Capt.   5 Jul 1686 F60v Stock-keepers to pay him £100   11 Oct 1688 F108v restored to Livery   8 Jul 1690 F139r Stock borrows £1500 to meet among other commitments paper bills from Capt. Darrell and others   6 Apr 1691 F151v fined for Assistant Renter Warden   12 Nov 1694 F215r Thomas Brewer bound to him from   1 October   3 Dec 1694 F215v elected to Bennett Griffin's £80 share   4 Feb 1694/5 F216v sworn into his £80 share   7 Jun 1697 F263r his son Edward is bound to him   4 May 1702 G71r his apprentice Thomas Brewer is freed   2 Dec 1706 G136v has fined for Sheriff of London. Elected Assistant   3 Feb

1706/7 G137v takes oath of Assistant. To be included in S.C.'s books as John Baskett's senior   7 Apr 1707 G140v elected to Judith Raw's £160 share. His £80 share disposed of to Benjamin Tooke   5 Jul 1707 G143r agrees to pay fines for two years Under Warden and two years Upper Warden if he is elected Master. Elected Master   3 Dec 1707 G148r signs re. not taking Clarendon   3 Jul 1708 G154r competes unsuccessfully for Master   2 Aug 1708 G156r to provide better paper for Apollonius   8 Nov 1708 G158v elected to Mrs Towse's Assistant's share. His £160 share disposed of to Jacob Tonson snr   30 Jun 1716 G241r competes unsuccessfully for Master

DARRELL, Edward, jnr   7 Jun 1697 F263r bound to Edward Darrell snr

DARROAK – see DARRACK

DAVENPORT, Edward   23 Dec 1714 G224r elected to Clement Williams's pension   27 Sep 1716 G243v elected to Clement Williams's pension. Benjamin Hicks given his pension

DAVENPORT, James   7 Feb 1708/9 G160v bound to Ralph Simpson, 7 years

DAVIES, Henry   5 Dec 1714 G224v bound to John Baskett, 7 years

DAVIES, Joseph   2 Oct 1699 G31v bound to William Harvey

DAVIES/DAVIS, Mrs   8 Apr 1700 G38v committee to view S.C.'s house occupied by her   6 May 1700 G39r to have a lease of her house for 7 years at £10 p.a.   21 Jun 1700 G41r lease read and sealed in Court   4 Jul 1715 G231r house to be viewed by committee re. repairs   8 Aug 1715 G231v committee found her house in indifferent repair. Court orders house to be let

DAVIS, Charles   8 Nov 1708 G158v bound to Nathaniel Nowell, 7 years

DAVIS, Christian   3 Nov 1712 G205r Mary Bucktrout turned over to him

DAVIS, Daniel   2 Dec 1706 G136v bound to John Wynd, 8 years

DAVIS, David   2 Jun 1712 G200v his son John is bound to Philip Gwillim, 7 years

DAVIS, Edward   7 Jul 1701 G62r John Chapman is bound to him   2 Aug 1703 G94r George Wingrave is bound to him   12 Apr 1708 G152r gunsmith; Richard Jones is bound to him   12 Nov 1716 G244v Richard Bayley is bound to him

DAVIS, James   9 Sep 1700 G45r bound to Hannah Clarke, 7 years   12 Apr 1708 G152r freed by Hannah Clarke   4 Feb 1711/12 G196v Thomas Davis turned over to him from Dryden Leach   3 Oct 1715 G233v his apprentice Thomas Davis is freed

DAVIS, John   2 Jun 1712 G200v son of David; bound to Philip Gwillim, 7 years

DAVIS, Mainwaring, snr – see following entry

DAVIS, Mainwaring, jnr   4 Mar 1716/17 G248r son of Mainwaring; bound to Andrew Parker, 7 years

DAVIS, Richard   1 Sep 1712 G203r Benjamin Barrett turned over from him to William Shaw

DAVIS/DAVYES, Sir Thomas   5 Sep 1687 F88r George Rodes refers to when, under Sir Thomas as Master, he paid his Livery fine   4 Nov 1706 G136r precedents to be searched to see what was done by Court upon his being elected Sheriff of London   2 Dec 1706 G136v precedents for his being elected Master of S.C. when elected Sheriff of London reported on

DAVIS, Thomas (I)   7 May 1705 G120r bound to Anne Snowden, 7 years

DAVIS, Thomas (II)   3 Oct 1709 G171r bound to George Sawbridge, 7 years

DAVIS, Thomas (III)   4 Feb 1711/12 G196v turned over from Dryden Leach to James Davis   3 Oct 1715 G233v freed by James Davis

DAVIS, Walter   26 Mar 1683 E166v competes unsuccessfully for Beadle   5 Sep 1687 F88r asks for his rent to be lowered and repairs carried out before he takes out a new lease; Master and Wardens to report   3 Oct 1687 F89r Court reduces his rent to £10 p.a. provided he carries out certain repairs   7 Nov 1687 F94v to carry out his part of the agreement re. putting his house in order before S.C. gives him the lease   3 Mar 1689/90 F130v Clerk to prepare draft lease now that Davis has repaired house   5 May 1690 F135r lease sealed; trustees desired to execute it, with S.C. indemnifying them

DAVIS, William (I)   7 Mar 1697/8 G5r freed by Samuel Manship   5 Feb 1704/5 G114v complaint against him and others for printing 'Observations on Time Sacred and Profane' [by N.B., Philomath], containing S.C.'s calendar   5 Mar 1704/5 G116v with Daniel Browne and Thomas Slater, liable for prosecution under S.C.'s Bill in Chancery if books and plates of 'Observations on Time' are not delivered to Warehousekeeper   7 May 1705 G119v cloathed

DAVIS, William (II)   7 Feb 1698/9 G20v bound to Edward Jones, 7 years   4 Mar 1705/6 G129r freed by Mary Jones

See also DAVIES

DAVISON, Sarah   4 Oct 1686 F64v deceased; Widow Dow admitted to her 40s pension

DAVY, William   8 Apr 1700 G39r bound to Margaret Wild, 7 years   3 Nov 1707 G146v freed by Margaret Wild

DAVYES – see DAVIS

DAWES, George   11 Apr 1681 E110v elected Renter Warden   2 May 1681 E110v fined for Renter Warden   26 Mar 1683 E167v Benjamin Sherley assigns him 'A View of Admiral Jurisdiction' [i.e. John Goodwin, *Synegoros Thalassios*] and 'The Life, Trial and Arraignment of Sir Walter Raleigh'   16 Jun 1684 F17v John Walthoe, an ex-apprentice of his, is freed   7 May 1685 (W) confirmed as member of new Livery   1 Mar 1687/8 F97v expelled from Livery by order of Lord Mayor   11 Oct 1688 F108v restored to Livery

DAWGS, Edward   8 Apr 1700 G39r bound to James Oades, 7 years

DAWKES/DAWKS, Ichabod   2 Oct 1693 F193r fined 30s for binding an apprentice by foreign indenture   3 Dec 1694 F215v petitions against a press at Chester, suggesting that recent seditious pamphlets may come from there; Court refers it to Crown   7 Oct 1698 G15r Richard Peacock is bound to him   5 Aug 1700 G44r cloathed; Joseph Haynes is bound to him   2 Aug 1703 G94r his apprentice Hugh Meere is freed   6 Dec 1703 G99v to be given more work from S.C.   6 Nov 1704 G113r John Norman turned over to him   6 Aug 1705 G122v James Abree is bound to him   1 Oct 1705 G124r his apprentice Richard Pocock is freed   3 Nov 1707 G146v his apprentice Joseph Haynes is freed   2 May 1709 G165r Rowland Stephens is bound to him   6 Oct 1712 G204v his apprentice James Abree is freed   26 Mar 1713 G207v excused office of Renter Warden for one year   2 Aug 1714 G221r Thomas Bell is bound to him   2 May 1715 G228v William Bird is bound to him

DAWKES, Thomas   4 Jun 1683 E170v fined 10s for having bound his apprentice, William Spire, at a scrivener's by foreign indenture when he brings him in to be freed

DAWSON, John   4 Oct 1708 G158r bound to Christopher Meggs, 7 years

DAWSON, Richard   6 May 1689 F117v deceased; Ralph Simpson is ordered to find a new surety for his £50 loan

DE LUDIS ORIENTALIBUS – see HYDE, Thomas

DEACON, Bridget   8 May 1704 G106v Samuel Deacon is bound to her   2 Jul 1711 G192v her apprentice Samuel Deacon, her son, is freed

DEACON, Jonah   7 Aug 1682 E156v made an assignment by Ephraim Cooley, Thomas Vere's executor   1 Sep 1684 F23v complains that Henry Bridges is printing and selling books of his without permission; latter summoned to next Court   3 Dec 1684 F27r William Whitwood assigns him 'No Jest Like a True Jest, Being ... the Merry Life ... of Capt. James Hind'   13 Apr 1698 G6v assignment of books to himself and John Wilde from William Thackery to be entered

DEACON, Samuel   8 May 1704 G106v bound to Bridget Deacon, 7 years   2 Jul 1711 G192v freed by his mother Bridget   1 Feb 1713/14 G216r Henry Lingard is bound to him   7 Feb 1714/15 G225r Henry Lingard turned over from him to Edward Midwinter

DEALERS IN BOOKS   6 May 1685 F33v to be translated from other companies to S.C. by order of crown. (W) List prepared by Master   20 May 1685 (W) those free of other companies to be translated to S.C. on 21 May

DEAN, [ ]   26 Mar 1707 G140r to have use of Hall on 4 April for a music entertainment, on paying three guineas to Warden

DEANE, James   3 Aug 1685 F42r Widow Mallett confesses to printing the unlicensed ballad 'Monmouth Routed' for James Deane, who informed Roger L'Estrange

DEE, Duncan   6 Jul 1713 G212r Common Serjeant; gives opinion that although Henry Million voted when disenfranchised he was still a good witness for S.C.

DELANDER, John   5 Feb 1699/1700 G35r bound to Thomas Penford, 7 years

DELAPORTE, Gabriel – see following entry

DELAPORTE, Nathaniel   5 Aug 1695 F231v son of the late Gabriel Delaporte of London, merchant; bound to Thomas Harrison

DELL, [ ]   20 Jul 1700 G43v Commissioner of Norton's bankruptcy, to be applied to concerning the patents printing house and other things late of Norton to be disposed of

DELL, John   9 Feb 1701/2 G67r bound to William Whitehead, 7 years

DENNET/DENETT/DENNITT, Gerard   5 Dec 1698 G17r John Chalener is bound to him   2 Dec 1706 G136v his apprentice John Chalener is freed   1 Dec 1707 G147v John Cope is bound to him

DENNETT/DENNET, Robert   2 Jul 1705 G121v bound to Daniel Bridge, 7 years   2 Aug 1708 G156v turned over from Daniel Bridge to Matthew Jenour   4 Jun 1716 G240v freed by Matthew Jenour

DENNIS, [ ]   7 Oct 1700 G46r and John Bradford. Clerk's bill for prosecution at S.C.'s suit

DENNIS, John   2 Dec 1700 G54r freed by Christopher Browne

DENNIS, Millicent   22 Dec 1681 E141v removed from a 5s pension to a 7s 6d one in place of Humphrey Toy, deceased   4 Oct 1682 E159r deceased; John Major admitted to her pension

DENNISON, [ ]   3 May 1686 F55v Joshua Coniers complains that Dennison has printed his ballad 'Virtue and Constancy Rewarded' under another title; summoned to next Court

DENNITT – see DENNET

DERBY, William   20 Nov 1703 G98r pewterer; to be made a party to S.C.'s bill in Chancery

DERMER, John   2 Oct 1693 F193r 10s paid to Renter Wardens at this Court to discharge his arrears of quarterage, 'he being a poor man'   3 Mar 1700/1 G57r Thomas Dermer is bound to him

DERMER, Thomas   3 Mar 1700/1 G57r bound to John Dermer, 7 years   3 May 1708 G152v freed by Freeman Collins

DESBOROUGH, Ann   23 Mar 1687/8 F80r elected into the 30s pension of her deceased husband Christopher   22 Jun 1702 G76r elected to Daniel Barber's pension

DESBOROUGH, Christopher   23 Mar 1687/8 F80r deceased; his wife Ann elected to his pension

DEVOUT COMMUNICANT [Anon.]   4 Dec 1699 G33v assigned by Richard Hargrave to William Freeman

DESPREZ, Ludovicus – see HORACE

DEW, Anne   11 Apr 1681 E109v to be paid the 10s pension formerly paid to the late Widow Crawley   26 Mar 1698 G5v deceased; Richard Fairbank is given her pension

DEW, William   5 Jul 1714 G220v John Rouse is bound to him

DEWELL, Ann   26 Mar 1684 F11r remarried; Mary Greene elected to her 5s pension

DICKINS, Ambrose   26 Mar 1707 G139v bond from S.C. of £200 penalty at 5% sealed

DICKINS, Sarah   24 Mar 1701/2 G68r elected to Ann Harper's pension and Patience Ghent given her pension   22 Dec 1708 G159v her pension to be made up to 20 shillings a quarter   21 Mar 1716/17 G248r deceased; Millicent Shell is given her pension

DICKINSON, Edward   4 Apr 1687 F81v elected waterman

DICKON – see DICKSON

DICKSON, [ ]   1 Dec 1707 G147v bond from S.C. of £100 to be paid off

DICKSON/DICKON/DIXON, Abraham   2 Oct 1699 G31v bound to James Walker   7 Jun 1708 G153v freed by James Walker   5 Jun 1710 G180v William Lutford is bound to him   6 Aug 1711 G193r Daniel Harding is bound to him

DIGHTON, John   5 Dec 1709 G172r bound to Bernard Lintott, 7 years

DIKES – see DYKES

DIM, Samuel   6 May 1695 F223r John Johnson, his apprentice, is freed

DIMOCK, [ ]   1 Sep 1690 F142r asked to give a written account of his purchase from Gaines of a press seized by S.C. for illegally printing Stock books

DINERS   3 Jul 1686 F59v persons dined at S.C.'s table uninvited. In future only officers of S.C. and those invited by them to dine

DINNERS – see FEASTS

DISCOURSE ABOUT ... NOVELTY   6 Apr 1685 F32v a moiety of 'A Discourse About the Charge of Novelty' [by Gregory Hascard] is assigned by Robert Horne to Abel Swale

DISCOURSE ABOUT TRADITION [by Symon Patrick]   6 Apr 1685 F32v a moiety of 'A Discourse About Tradition, &c.' is assigned by Robert Horne to Abel Swale

DIVIDENDS – see ENGLISH STOCK

DIXON – see DICKSON

DOCTOR FAUSTUS   1 Sep 1690 F142r Court agrees to buy the 'History of the Life and Death of Dr. Faustus' from Henry Mortlock and Benjamin Tooke   6 Oct 1690 F143r to be entered in trust for S.C.

DODD, Nathaniel   9 Feb 1707/8 G148v freed by redemption and paid 40 shillings to Poor Box   5 Jul 1708 G155r freed by Benjamin Harris snr

DODD/DOD, Robert   2 Oct 1710 G184v bound to Thomas Baker, 7 years   1 Oct 1711 G195r turned over from Thomas Baker to Maurice Atkins

DODSON, John   4 May 1713 G209v son of Thomas; bound to Thomas Franklin, 7 years

DODSON, Thomas – see preceding entry

DOLEMAN, John   3 May 1697 F265r freed by Thomas Bassett   7 Aug 1699 G29r Richard Hatchman is bound to him   5 Jul 1703 G92r Daniel Stephens is bound to him   7 Feb 1708/9 G160v of Butcher Row; Phillip Phillips is bound to him   3 Nov 1712 G205r his apprentice Richard Hatchman is freed   5 Jul 1714 G220v his apprentice Daniel Stephens is freed

DOLEMAN, R. (pseud.) – see PERSONS, Robert, *et al.*

DOLEMAN, William   2 Oct 1699 G31v bound to Robert Williamson

DOLPHIN, William   12 Jun 1704 G107v bound to Samuel Keble, 7 years

DOLTON – see DALTON

DON QUEVEDO   3 Jul 1693 F190r 'Don Quevedo's Visions Made English', by Roger L'Estrange, is assigned by Henry Herringman to John Hindmarsh and Richard Sare

DONATIONS   6 Feb 1709/10 G175r committee to consider donations to S.C. and report to Court

DOOLEY/DOOLY, John   22 Jun 1699 G25v elected to Mary Orme's pension   20 Dec 1701 G66r deceased; Elizabeth Wells is given his pension

DORREL/DORRELL – see DARRELL

DOREY, Philip   6 Sep 1708 G157v bound to Ralph Snow, 7 years

DORMER, John   11 Nov 1700 G46v freed by Freeman Collins

See also DERMER

DOUBLE QUARTERN BOOKS   6 Mar 1698/9 G22r motion from Richard Chiswell that usual allowance too great; decision adjourned

DOVER, James   7 Feb 1697/8 G3v his ex-apprentice William Garrett, turned over to Job Killington, is freed   5 Aug 1700 G44r John Goodchild is bound to him   6 Sep 1703 G94v George Fellowes is bound to him   7 Aug 1704 G111r Daniel Rogers turned over to him   9 Sep 1706 G134v Henry Morley turned over to him from Ann Milbourne. His apprentices Edward Beale and Daniel Rogers are freed   7 Feb 1708/9 G160v of Liberty Tower; Thomas Round is bound to him and his apprentice Jeremiah Smith is freed   3 Jul 1710 G182r of Tower Hill, printer; Moyse Edwards is bound to him   5 Oct 1713 G214r his apprentice Henry Morley is freed

DOW, Widow   4 Oct 1686 F64v elected to the late Sarah Davison's 40s pension   3 Oct 1687 F89r deceased; her 40s pension is voted to Joan Jackson

DOWING, Thomas   6 Oct 1712 G204v son of Francis; bound to John Wilde, 8 years

DOWLEY, James   26 Mar 1696 F241v his apprentice, Joseph Bourne, is freed

DOWLEY, John   4 Mar 1694/5 F218v fishmonger of London; given a bond for payment of £507 10s on 5 June 1695   7 Oct 1695 F233v to be paid £500 and bond cancelled; £300 offered at this Court at 5% p.a. to be taken up towards payment of debt   24 Oct 1695 F234v bond due on English Stock to be continued, notwithstanding notice   11 Nov 1695 F235r citizen and fishmonger; given a bond of £1000 penalty for payment of £506 5s by 12 February 1695/6; earlier bond to be cancelled   2 Dec 1695 F237r earlier bond of £1000 penalty at 6% p.a. cancelled   7 Jun 1714 G219v deceased; money taken in to pay off £500 bond to Alice Aynge his executrix

DOWNEING – see DOWNING

DOWNES, Dudley   26 Mar 1697 F258v competes unsuccessfully to replace Christopher Grandorge as Clerk

DOWNES, George   7 May 1685 (W) confirmed member of new Livery   1 Jun 1685 F38v elected to Godfrey Head's £40 share   1 Mar 1687/8 F97v expelled from Livery by order of Lord Mayor   11 Oct 1688 F108v restored to Livery   3 Jun 1689 F119r allowed to mortgage his £40 share to Samuel Sprint for £40   4 May 1691 F153r request that Thomas Yates should have his £40 share is granted   26 Mar 1692 F167v set aside for a year from serving or fining for Renter Warden   3 Mar 1706/7 G138v Margaret Downes is freed by him by patrimony

DOWNES, Margaret   3 Mar 1706/7 G138v freed by George Downes, by patrimony

DOWNHAM, [   ]   16 Jun 1684 F17v of Moorfields; affirms his father was free of the Haberdashers' Company and submits to S.C. for further consideration. (W) pleaded great poverty

DOWNHAM, John – see following entry

DOWNHAM, Thomas   7 May 1716 G240r son of John; bound to Henry Porton, 7 years

DOWNHAM, William   8 May 1704 G106v John Moore is bound to him

DOWNING, [   ]   7 Jul 1684 F21r Francis Smith is allowed to sue him for having dealings in a book belonging to him since 7 Oct 1681   5 Jul 1708 G155r letters about printing a collection of prayers for the charity schools to be considered by Master, Wardens and Stock-keepers   3 May 1714 G218v printed 'Exposition of Mrs Lewis of the Catechism' [i.e. John Lewis, *The Church Catechism Explain'd*?] for Henry Hoare

DOWNING, Ann   1 Dec 1707 G147v her apprentice Lawrence Thompson is freed   6 Dec 1708 G159v widow; William Roberts is bound to her

DOWNING, Joseph   6 Sep 1703 G94v freed by patrimony   5 Mar 1704/5 G117r Joshua Money is bound to him   6 Aug 1705 G122v Robert Browne is bound to him   12 Nov 1705 G124v excused from cloathing for three months   2 Dec 1706 G136v cloathed   1 Dec 1707 G147v Henry Greep turned over to him   6 Oct 1712 G204v his apprentice Joshua Money is freed   3 Nov 1712 G205r his apprentice Robert Browne is freed   26 Mar 1713 G208r elected Assistant Renter Warden   13 Apr 1713 G208r not permitted to be excused office of Assistant Renter Warden and charge read to him   4 Jun 1716 G240v John Hart is bound to him   12 Nov 1716 G244v John Lewis is bound to him

DOWNING/DOWNEING, William, snr   8 May 1693 F188r to be sued by Clerk for printing Stock books   7 May 1694 F203v his son and servant William is freed   24 Oct 1695 F234v his nut and spindle, taken from him for printing the Oxford primer, to be returned on his promising good behaviour (W) and to be a witness against Norris, who set him on work   9 Sep 1700 G45r Lawrence Thompson is bound to him   5 Mar 1704/5 G117r Thomas Spencer turned over to him   5 May 1707 G142r his apprentice Thomas Spencer is freed   9 Apr 1711 G189v of St John's Lane, printer; John Greenhalgh is bound to him   4 Jul 1715 G231r Robert Greenhalgh is bound to him

DOWNING, William, jnr   7 May 1694 F203v son and servant of William Downing; freed

DOWNS, Jarvis   6 Feb 1709/10 G175v bound to John Darby, 7 years

DOWTHWAITE, Bernard – see following entry

DOWTHWAITE, William   5 Oct 1713 G214r son of Bernard; bound to Emmanuel Matthews, 7 years

DOYLY, Charles   5 Mar 1679/80 E97v bond to him of £600 penalty cancelled

DR FAUSTUS – see DOCTOR FAUSTUS

DRAKE, Nathan, snr – see following entry

DRAKE, Nathan, jnr   10 Sep 1711 G194r son of Nathan; bound to Matthew Wootton, 7 years

DRAPER, Mrs   5 Dec 1692 F183r lives in part of S.C. tenement let to Nicholas Hooper; her petition and a letter from Dr Sherlock read; referred   7 Feb 1697/8 G3r £5 paid on her behalf for hire of the Hall for a ball

DRAPER, William   16 Jun 1691 F155v joiner, deceased; his house in Amen Corner now to be tenanted by Nicholas Hooper

DREWETT, William   5 Mar 1710/11 G188r John Miflin turned over to him from John Bennett

DRING, Daniel   4 Feb 1694/5 F217r servant to Thomas Dring; freed

DRING, Dorothy   8 Apr 1695 F220r given bond of £1000 penalty for payment of £512 10s by 9 October 1695   3 Feb 1695/6 F239r remarries; her £160 share is voted to John Place   5 Jul 1703 G92r bond of £500 cancelled

DRING, Joshua   7 Sep 1691 F160r of Churchover, Warwickshire; given bond of £2000 penalty for payment of £1025 by 7 March 1691/2   7 Jul 1701 G62r to be paid £1000 owed to him by S.C.   4 Aug 1701 G62v bond repaid

DRING, Peter   7 Feb 1686/7 F71r summoned and promises to pay an old debt of about £9 due to S.C. when he is able   6 Oct 1690 F143v to be summoned re. not paying his debt by bond to S.C.   2 Mar 1690/1 F150r petition for post of porter not read because of the many times he has failed to pay money due on bond   1 Mar 1694/5 F218r competes unsuccessfully for Treasurer   2 Mar 1695/6 F240r competes unsuccessfully for Treasurer   1 Mar 1696/7 F255v competes unsuccessfully for Treasurer   2 Mar 1703/4 G102v competes unsuccessfully for Warehousekeeper   1 Mar 1704/5 G116r competes unsuccessfully for Warehousekeeper   1 Mar 1705/6 G128v competes unsuccessfully for Warehousekeeper

DRING, Thomas   1 Mar 1679/80 E97r has William Jacob's £40 share surrendered to him; he indemnifies S.C. Elected Stock-keeper for Yeomanry   1 Mar 1681/2 E145v elected Stock-keeper for Livery with Robert Clavell   7 Jan 1683/4 F8r competes unsuccessfully for Henry Herringman's £160 share   7 Apr 1684 F14r on the list of loyal Assistants presented to the Crown   2 Jun 1684 F15v promises to fine for Renter Warden   2 Jun 1684 F16r given £500 bond for payment of £515 on 3 Dec next   7 May 1685 (W) confirmed as member of new Livery   2 Nov 1685 (W) memo that he was not in Court but came to dinner   26 Mar 1686 F53r to take in £200 of the £500 at 6% p.a. in S.C.'s hands, or continue at 5% p.a. Agreed to continue at 5% for six months   26 Mar 1686 F54v pays 12d charity for being absent from Court without leave of Master   7 Feb 1686/7 F70r specified that he should have a copy of orders concerning Treasurer and make all complaints within a week   21 Feb 1686/7 F71v misunderstanding over procedure to give in complaints; to negotiate with committee   2 Jul 1687 F85v among those chosen to audit Warden's accounts   4 Sep 1688 F106v Freeman Collins claims he was printing [Ovid's] Metamorphoses, a Stock book, for Dring and Abel Swale; told to negotiate with them   11 Oct 1688 F108v restored to Livery   4 Feb 1688/9 F112v re-elected Assistant   1 Mar 1688/9 F113v elected Stock-keeper for Asssistants with John Bellinger   6 May 1689 F117r ranked tenth of Assistants never elected as Master or Warden   7 Oct 1689 F125r elected to the late John Hancock snr's £160 share   7 Apr 1690 F133r accused by Abel Swale of printing his Juvenal and Persius; dispute referred to committee. To compensate English Stock for printing Virgil   5 Jun 1690 F135v re-elected Assistant   5 Jul 1690 F138r among those chosen to audit Warden's accounts   18 Jul 1690 F140v S.C. gives him a bond to pay £205 on 18 Jan 1691 with a £400 penalty   1 Dec 1690 F147r produces in Court William Cadman's assignment of half of [Buckingham's] 'The Rehearsal' to him, and Francis Saunders renounces claim to it   7 Sep 1691 F160r £500 bond cancelled; money raised by entering into another bond with Joshua Dring   2 Nov 1691 F162r he, Robert Scott and Abel Swale to pay 2d per book for printing 3000 Virgils without a licence   7 Dec 1691 F162v reopens question of Virgil; Court votes for fine to be reduced to 1d per book, to be deducted from dividends if not paid by then   22 Dec 1691 F163v Robert Scott asks for relief from last Court order on his behalf; not granted   12 Apr 1692 F169r to pay into Poor Box a £5 legacy from will of George Pawlitt   2 May 1692 F170v bond taken out to Thomas Marriott to discharge bond to Dring for £205 to be paid on 18 June 1690, which is cancelled   4 Jul 1692 F173v chosen to audit Renter Wardens' accounts   5 Sep 1692 F177v complains that Samuel Smith has imported Ciceros although Dring has the S.C. licence to print them; referred to committee   3 Oct 1692 F180r re. difference with Samuel Smith. Committee presents its award and order; approved and entered; reference to Liber A   3 Apr 1693 F185v requests that William Freeman be allowed to fine for First Renter Warden; granted   26 Mar 1694 F201v elected Stock-keeper at special meeting   2 Apr 1694 F202r requests on George Castle's behalf that he may fine for Assistant Renter Warden   4 Feb 1694/5 F217r his apprentice, Daniel Dring, freed   6 Mar 1698 G21v deceased; declaration from Peter Parker and Thomas Guy against Henry Mortlock and himself debated   20 Oct 1699 G32r articles between Parker and Guy, Mortlock and Dring, Master, Wardens and Assistants of S.C. read and settlement of problem debated   4 Dec 1699 G33v deceased; discharge executed by Parker and Guy to and for Mortlock and Dring's administrator, and the Master and Wardens   7 Jun 1703 G90r deceased; Hargrave requests £500 due to him from S.C., as the new husband of Dring's widow

DRINKELL, James   19 Feb 1705/6 G128r haberdasher; complaint that he has sold sham psalters and psalms without S.C.'s permission   4 Mar 1705/6 G128v haberdasher in Cannon Street; evidence of his selling counterfeit psalters at Bristol fair given by Gilbert Beauchamp   1 Apr 1706 G130v committee to consider matter of counterfeit psalters sold by him

DRIVER, John   6 Mar 1703/4 G103v bound to Margaret Bennett, 8 years   4 Jul 1709 G167v turned over from Margaret Bennett to Thomas Howlatt

DRIVER, Margaret   28 Sep 1709 G170v deceased; William Barlow is given her pension   22 Dec 1709 G173r deceased; William Redmaine is given her pension

DRIVER, Rachel   22 Jun 1694 F209v deceased; Mary Lambourne is given her pension

DRIVER, Samuel   12 Dec 1695 F238r elected to the late John Harwood's pension

DRURY, Samuel   2 Mar 1701/2 G67v freed by Samuel Cook. John Read is bound to him

DRYER, Joseph   3 Jul 1710 G182r bound to Thomas Osborne, 7 years

DRYER/DYER, Thomas   4 Mar 1705/6 G129r bound to Andrew Bell, 7 years   5 Mar 1710/11 G188r turned over from Andrew Bell to Edmund Curll   13 Apr 1713 G208v freed by Andrew Bell

See also DYER

DRYNG, Sarah   22 Mar 1714/15 G226v elected to Mary Redmaine's pension

DUBLIN'S CALENDAR – see ALMANACKS

DUCKETT, Matthew   20 Dec 1694 F216r elected to the late Thomas Pattenden's pension   25 Mar 1703 G86v deceased; Katharine Hall is given his pension

DUFFE, Henry – see DUSTE, Henry

DUKE OF YORK [James]   2 Oct 1682 E158r Richard Janeway confesses to printing 'A Letter to His Royal Highness the D — Y —' for Henry Care

DUNCOMBE, Eleazar   7 Sep 1702 G80v bound to Charles Spicer, alias Helder, 7 years   26 Sep 1712 G203v freed by Mary Spicer, alias Helder

DUNCOMBE, John, Esq   4 Oct 1703 G95v bond from S.C. of £600 sealed. Money used to discharge bonds to Capt. William Phillipps

DUNCOMB, Margaret   22 Jun 1705 G120v deceased; William Charles is given her pension

DUNSCOMBE, Widow   20 Dec 1687 F96r given £1 charity

DUNSTALL, John   3 Feb 1700/1 G55v bound to John Fowell, 7 years   8 Nov 1703 G97r turned over to James Ellis

DUNTON, John   9 Feb 1690/1 F148v fined 50 shillings for not entering 'The Magpie' and printing it under the names of B. Griffits and W. Griffits, offending Bennett Griffin   12 Sep 1692 F179r summoned to show why he should not be cloathed   3 Oct 1692 F180v summoned to take cloathing   7 Nov 1692 F181v cloathed and promises payment of fine

DURAN, Thomas   9 Feb 1707/8 G149r bound to Adam Hampton, 7 years

DUSTE/DUFFE, Henry   2 Dec 1695 F237v son of John Malcolm Duste, St Giles-in-the-Fields, gentleman; bound to Alexander Milbourne   7 Dec 1702 G83v freed by Alexander Milbourne

DUSTE, John Malcolm – see preceding entry

DUTCH FORTUNE TELLER [by John Booker]   5 Sep 1681 E129v assigned by Thomas Vere to John Clarke snr

DUTTON, Baptist   1 Mar 1683/4 F9r son of Richard Dutton and apprentice of Benjamin Tooke; discharged from apprenticeship

DUTTON, John (I)   3 Dec 1694 F215v freed by John Clarke

DUTTON, John (II)   1 Sep 1707 G145r bound to James Read, 8 years   5 Sep 1715 G232v freed by James Read   7 Nov 1715 G234v George Carey turned over to him from Newman

DUTTON, Lawrence   6 Mar 1703/4 G103v bound to John Brooke, 7 years

DUTTON, Richard   1 Mar 1683/4 F9r his son Baptist is discharged from his apprenticeship to Benjamin Tooke

DUTY OF A COMMUNICANT – see WHOLE DUTY OF A COMMUNICANT

DYER, Elizabeth   7 Jun 1714 G219v widow; bond from S.C. of £400 penalty to pay £206 on 8 December sealed

DYER, Richard, snr – see following entry

DYER, Richard, jnr   9 Apr 1716 G239r son of Richard; bound to Stephen Lee, 7 years

DYER, [William]   6 Apr 1691 F152v His 'Works' [i.e. *Christ's Famous Titles*, &c.] the property of Thomas Bradyll; Court allow him to sue Peter Parker and Thomas Guy for printing them   13 Mar 1692/3 F184v Ralph Simpson complains that Peter Parker has printed Dyer's works and reads assignment; committee to inspect register

See also DRYER

DYKES, Edward   16 Oct 1697 F269r freed by William Wild

DYKES/DIKES, Ursula   27 Mar 1699 G23r elected to Lucy Ford's pension   28 Sep 1702 G80v elected to Anne Alloway's pension   22 Mar 1714/15 G226v elected to Mary Brockett's pension. Mary Redmaine given her pension

DYMOND, Charles – see following entry

DYMOND, Robert   7 Sep 1713 G213v son of Charles; bound to John Clarke, 7 years

EARESON, Charles   1 Oct 1711 G194v son of Henry; bound to Joseph Pomfrett, 7 years

EARESON, Henry – see preceding entry

EARNEST INVITATION – see GLANVILL, Joseph

EAST, [   ]   2 Aug 1680 E103r elected to Jonathan Edwin's £40 share

EAST, Mrs   8 Apr 1700 G38v deceased; her share to be disposed of to Benjamin Bound

EAST, Richard   15 Jul 1690 F140r refuses to subscribe towards raising horse and dragoons for the Crown   2 Mar 1690/1 F150r £4 deducted for his dividend as a fine for having combined with John Starkey, Lawson and others to force admission on to Court   1 Feb 1691/2 F165r deceased; widow granted his dividend of £5 detained by Treasurer because of his contempt of Master and Court

EASTERN GAMES – see HYDE, Thomas

EATON, Richard   6 Feb 1709/10 G175r bound to John Crofts, 7 years

EATON, Thomas   7 Aug 1710 G183r bound to Mary Redmaine, 7 years

ECCLESTON, [   ]   17 Dec 1709 G173r Court refuses to buy copies of the several school books offered by him to them

EDWARDS, [   ]   2 Aug 1680 E102v bond to S.C. discharged   5 May 1701 G61v bill in Chancery against him and Peter Parker for illegally printing and publishing S.C. calendar   7 Jul 1701 G61v bill in Chancery concerning printing of S.C. calendar. Not to be proceeded against further, on payment of charges of prosecution and bond not to print any more of S.C.'s copies

EDWARDS, David   10 Sep 1694 F212v John Bowes is bound to him for eight years   4 Jul 1698 G11r Thomas Bayley is bound to him   20 Dec 1701 G66v has paid quarterage to Warden Sprint. His apprentice John Law is freed   7 Dec 1702 G83v John Law turned over from him to George Strahan   6 Sep 1703 G94v Tryolus Excell is bound to him   4 Mar 1705/6 G129r William Wyse, apprentice to Mary Tonson, is freed by him   5 Mar 1710/11 G188r of Fetter Lane, printer; Richard Chappell is bound to him

EDWARDS, Ezra   7 May 1705 G120r bound to his father, 7 years   9 Feb 1712/13 G206v freed by patrimony

EDWARDS, James   5 Feb 1699/1700 G35r bound to Benjamin Beardwell, 7 years

EDWARDS, Moyse   3 Jul 1710 G182r bound to James Dover, 7 years   4 Jun 1716 G240v turned over to Benjamin Harris

EDWARDS, Peter   1 Oct 1705 G124r bound to Abel Roper, 7 years

EDWIN, Jonathan   1 Dec 1679 E95v £50 due by him to S.C. to be called in; summoned to next general Court   5 Jul 1680 E102r to be prosecuted if he does not bring money due to S.C. to next Court   2 Aug 1680 E102v to be prosecuted unless he pays off his bond before the next general Court. East elected to his £40 share   8 Nov 1680 E105r his £40 to be paid to Robert Scott   7 Feb 1680/1 E107r to be prosecuted if his £50 loan money is not paid back before next Court   7 Mar 1680/1 E107v his surety to pay £50 at the next Court   11 Apr 1681 E110r his surety to bring money to next Court   2 May 1681 E111v money to be called in from his surety   6 Jun 1681 E113r bond to be delivered up to his sureties, John Low and Baker, on payment of £40   5 Sep 1681 E129v sureties pay £40; Court makes over the bond to John Low as they request

EDWYN, Jonathan   5 Sep 1698 G14v freed by Gilham Hills

EGERTON, Thomas   6 Dec 1714 G224r freed by Samuel Keeble

EGGELLTON, Richard – see following entry

EGGELLTON, Robert   5 Sep 1715 G232v son of Richard; bound to Samuel Osborne, 7 years

EGGLEFEILD – see EGGLESFEILD

EGGLESFEILD/EGLESFFEILD, [   ]   7 Oct 1695 F233v given 20s to defray some of his rent, his landlord having seized all his possessions

EGGLESFEILD/EGLESFEILD/EGLESFIELD, Francis   11 Apr 1681 E109v assigns Aesop's Fables and a moiety of Quarles's Emblems to Samuel Mearne   3 Apr 1682 E150r account between him and Stock settled and entered in full   1 Mar 1682/3 E164v his bond not to be called in with others as it is secured by the Stock   3 Dec 1683 F6v to appear at next Court with Robert Stephens to answer Charles Mearne's complaint   19 Dec 1683 F7r dividend to go to Under Warden in part-payment of his debt to S.C.   1 Mar 1687/8 F97v expelled from Livery by order of Lord Mayor   18 Jul 1690 F141r allowed to mortgage his £160 share for £100 plus interest to Ambrose Isted

EGGLESFEILD, Frances   7 Feb 1697/8 G3r deceased; her £160 share disposed of to Thomas Hodgkins

EGGLESFEILD/EGLESFEILD/EGLESFIELD, John   26 Mar 1683 E166v granted £50 from Tyler bequest   2 Apr 1683 E168r surety for £50 loan from Tyler bequest not approved   2 Aug 1714 G221r sued for arrears of quarterage; petition postponed until next Court

EGGLESFEILD/EGGLEFIELD/EGGLESFIELD, Thomas   26 Mar 1698 G5r deceased; William Curtis to be given his pension   27 Sep 1698 G13r deceased; Diana Battersby to be given his pension in exchange for providing for him. To be replaced in Pension Book by Mary Rix

EGLESFIELD, EGLESFFEILD – see EGGLESFEILD

ELECTIONS   3 Jul 1686 F58v motion for ballot-box defeated   7 Mar 1686/7 F78r election day for officers adjourned to first Monday in April to prevent it falling on Easter Eve (26 March)   2 Jul 1687 F85v voted that officers should be elected by ballot   6 Jul 1689 F121r voted that the voting should be by a show of hands   5 Jul 1690 F137v voting for Master and Wardens to take place by means of the ballot-box (W) copy of voting sheet   7 Jul 1690 F139r agreed that in future two persons, rather than three, should be scored for to go to ballot-box for election of Master, Wardens and partners of English Stock   9 Feb 1690/1 F149r voted that ballot-box should not be burnt, despite objections to using it   8 Apr 1700 G39r notice of any election to office to be set down in summons to next Court

ELECTION DINNER – see FEASTS

ELLIOTT, Elizabeth   7 Mar 1697/8 G4r widow; consideration of petition praying for relief deferred until next Pension Court

ELLIOTT, Robert   4 Jul 1692 F174r workmen printers petition against his being received into S.C.'s service at Oxford; referred to Oxford committee

ELLIOTT, Thomas   3 May 1703 G89v bound to Robert Fleet, 7 years   1 Sep 1712 G203r freed by Jane Steele

ELLIS, Cadwallader   13 Apr 1694 F202v of Poole in Merioneth, schoolmaster; his son Joseph is bound to Andrew Sowle

ELLIS, Evan   7 Aug 1704 G111r freed by patrimony

ELLIS, Francis   8 May 1704 G106v William Marsh is bound to him

ELLIS, George   26 Mar 1686 F54r elected waterman   4 Apr 1687 F81v elected waterman   7 Mar 1691/2 F167r deceased; Henry Charleton admitted to his oar in the barge

ELLIS, James   8 Nov 1703 G97r John Dunstall turned over to him   4 Feb 1711/12 G196v John Milner turned over to him from William Stephens

ELLIS, John, snr – see following entry

ELLIS, John, jnr   1 Oct 1716 G244r son of John; bound to Nathaniel Moody, 7 years

ELLIS, Joseph   13 Apr 1694 F202v son of Cadwallader; bound to Andrew Sowle

ELLISTON, Mrs   13 Apr 1713 G208v deceased; her £40 share disposed of to Samuel Ashurst

ELLISTON, Oliver   3 Jun 1689 F119r cloathed   4 Dec 1693 F196r competes unsuccessfully for share declined by Abel Swale   4 Feb 1694/5 F217r Philip Guidee is bound to him   26 Mar 1696 F241r elected Renter Warden with John Baskett   3 Aug 1696 F246v elected to William Baker's £40 share   5 May 1701 G59v Samuel Ashurst is bound to him   6 May 1706 G131v John William Bryan is bound to him   3 Feb 1706/7 G138r John William Bryan turned over from him to Thomas Simpson

ELMES, Robert   1 Feb 1691/2 (W) freed by Humphrey Pooler   6 Aug 1694 F211v John Wright is bound to him   1 Jul 1695 F227v cloathed. Verey Hastlefoote is bound to him   5 Dec 1698 G17r Agar Warren is bound to him   13 Apr 1702 G70r Henry Andrews is bound to him   26 Mar 1706 G130r excused from office of Renter Warden for one year   3 Jun 1706 G132v his apprentice Agar Warren is freed   9 Sep 1706 G134v Dean Peacock is bound to him   7 Feb 1708/9 G160v of Cheapside; Thomas Rutter is bound to him   1 Feb 1713/14 G216r his apprentice Dean Peacock is freed   26 Mar 1714 G217r fined for First Renter Warden   3 May 1714 G218v elected to Elizabeth Miller's £40 share   2 Aug 1714 G221r Samuel Parker is bound to him   6 Feb 1715/16 G236r Samuel Tomkins is bound to him

ELPHICK, Edmund – see following entry

ELPHICK, George   2 Jul 1711 G192v son of Edmund; bound to William Holland, 7 years

ELPHICK, John   7 Jun 1708 G153v bound to John Lenthall, 7 years

ELY, Mary   21 Jun 1700 G40v Elizabeth Lightfoot is given her pension

EMERSON, Christopher   4 Mar 1705/6 G129r bound to John Buchanan, 7 years

ENDERBY, Widow   2 Jul 1683 F2v deceased; Edward Brewster returns her 10s pension   1 Oct 1683 F3r Ursula Barker admitted to her pension

ENGLAND, John   1 Mar 1702/3 G86r freed by Joseph Tutle   5 Apr 1703 G88r Robert Stephens is bound to him   4 Oct 1703 G96r Samuel Saunders turned over to him   3 May 1708 G152v Thomas Baker is bound to him   3 Mar 1711/12 G197r his apprentice Robert Stephenson is freed   22 Dec 1713 G215v cloathed   13 Jun 1715 G229r Clerk to take out a writ against him for non-payment of Livery fine   3 Oct 1715 G233v Clerk advising Serjeant Pengelly on suit against him   7 Nov 1715 G234r sued for non-payment of Livery fine. To be tried if he does not pay charges at law, fees of

Clerk and Beadle and give bond to S.C. for payment of Livery fine in instalments   5 Dec 1715 G235r bond for payment of Livery fine in instalments delivered by Clerk

ENGLISH GARDENER   4 Sep 1682 E157v assigned by Thomas Pierrepont to Peter Parker

ENGLISH LIBERTIES [by Henry Care]   7 Dec 1685 F47v Benjamin Harris petitions re. the damasking of this book, found at his house, which he claims is waste paper; Court promises to ask Secretaries of State

ENGLISH SCHOOLMASTER   18 Mar 1686/7 F79v to be altered; among books in catalogue annexed to the Oxford agreement

ENGLISH STOCK   19 Dec 1683 F7r Robert Stephens, in response to petition, is granted £8 for services rendered to the English Stock. Committee to consult with Sergeant Pemberton or other counsel re. application of byelaw concerning disobedient Stock partners   13 Nov 1689 F126v Court called to discuss the 'promoting and advancing' of the Stock interest 'there never being more need'   13 Apr 1693 F186v members summoned to subscribe to the amended proposal; ordered that Treasurer should allow remaining members to subscribe to it   4 Sep 1693 F190v draft articles of new Stock approved and ordered to be printed   24 Oct 1693 F193v new partners authorised to buy paper, agree on type, direct books and prices and give limited credit to shareholders. 26 Mar 1694 F201v Stock-keepers elected at special meeting   7 Jun 1703 G90v meeting of partners of English Stock, but insufficient number to transact any business according to the constitution of the Agreement and Articles   7 Feb 1703/4 G101r committee to consider affairs of Corporation and English Stock   13 Aug 1711 G193v committee to assist Stock-keepers in management of Stock affairs

— ACCOUNTS   3 Apr 1682 E151r no account books to be removed from the Common Hall or Treasurer's house without permission of Court except in emergencies   2 Jun 1684 F15v £300 raised by entering into a bond with Thomas Dring is to go towards paper bills, &c., incurred by Stock   16 Jun 1684 F18r Robert Stephens petitions for a salary as recompense for his services in preventing piracy upon the English Stock; referred to next Court   1 Feb 1685/6 F50v Stock-keepers to call for money due to printers and paper suppliers and committee set up to help with concluding Corporation account   1 Mar 1685/6 F51v committee reports that some printers have not been paid for three years; resolved to give quarterly accounts and regulate Treasurer   3 May 1686 F55v Richard Royston makes difficulties about forfeiting his £320 share because he printed Stock books without permission. Adiel Mill and Procter both to be paid £60 due to them from Stock   5 Jul 1686 F60v to pay John Macock £50, Thomas Newcomb and partner £100, and Capt. Edward Darrell £100   6 Sep 1686 F62v Margaret Haly is advised to apply to Stock-keepers for money due to her from English Stock   11 Oct 1686 F66r Stock-keepers to give warrant to Treasurer to pay £37 18s 6d to Bennett Griffin   6 Dec 1686 F68r paper stationers to be paid £300, or as much of that as possible, of the money due to them. Printers to be paid for work done for Stock in 1683 and 1684   7 Feb 1686/7 F71r committee set up re. Stock books   23 Mar 1686/7 F80v warrants to be made out to pay the most necessitous of the Stock creditors   5 Sep 1687 F88v Henry Hills requests that money due to him should not be stopped to pay off his loan; granted if the account comes to nearly £100   19 Dec 1688 F111v Treasurer explains why ca. £500 of the dividend money is lacking and it is ordered that £500 should be borrowed for 3 months   20 Dec 1688 F111v bond to Thomas Felham, vintner, to borrow £500   7 Oct 1689 F124r in view of S.C.'s debts, dinners paid for by share owners to cease but Master, Wardens, Assistants and Stock-keepers to be paid   4 Nov 1689 F126r orders relating to the retrenching of expenses again voted upon and confirmed   5 Jul 1690 F138r committee to consider how to raise money for Stock paper and discharge some of the Stock debts   8 Jul 1690 F139r committee to borrow £1500 at 5% p.a. to pay for 3000 reams of paper, Cambridge stock and bills for paper   18 Jul 1690 F140v committee for raising money report that they have raised £1000 and 4 bonds are approved; penalties dated 18 Jul and payments 18 Jan   7 Dec 1691 F162v Henry Hills jnr pays off a £100 bond by printing work done for Stock   22 Dec 1691 F163v on Court days, Upper Warden to enter receipts and payments made by Corporation and English Stock as a check on Under Warden and Treasurer   7 Nov 1692 F182r committee chosen to consider whether an accountant should be appointed to regularise English Stock accounts   6 Nov 1693 F194v 2 'bills of parcels' to be taken when paper is bought, one kept by Treasurer, the other by Stock-keepers, and regular entries made   24 Oct 1695 F234v £500 due from S.C. on Stock to John Dowley to be continued, notwithstanding the notice given him to take it in   26 Mar 1697 F259r list of Clerk's fees for   1 Aug 1698 G11v £100 due from English Stock to Corporation to be paid   4 May 1702 G70v money borrowed for English Stock for which Common Seal of the S.C. was used to be charged in future to the Wardens' accounts   7 Sep 1702 G80r £500 to be borrowed for it as it was indebted to the Oxford Stock and more money was needed for the better management of it   3 May 1703 G89r accountant to be employed to assist Stock-keepers   3 Apr 1704 G105v bond of £100 to John Keeblebutter and James Crane taken up on behalf of Stock   24 Apr 1713 G209r profits to be used first to repay Thomas Guy money advanced to pay English Stock printers and only then to pay dividends   7 Sep 1713 G213r amounts in Master and Wardens' accounts concerning English Stock to be paid in future to Warden by Joseph Collyer   5 Oct 1713 G213v money disbursed by William Freeman for Stock; not to be paid by Collyer as he had paid several sums on account of corporation. Accounts to be kept distinct in future   7 Dec 1713 G214v Collyer to get in all money due to it for almanacks or otherwise from persons mentioned in a list delivered to him

— BYELAWS   1 Aug 1681 E117v rules and ordinances implementing Letters Patent   5 Oct 1681 E131r byelaws

— DIVIDENDS   1 Dec 1679 E95v money due to English Stock to be stopped out of dividends (this order is regularly repeated on dividend payment days)   5 Dec 1681 E139v greater control over payment of dividends in respect of stockholders not present in person   19 Dec 1683 F7v dividends to be £40 for £320 share, £20 for £160 share, £10 for £80 share   22 Dec 1685 F49v dividends to be £40 for £320 share, £20 for £160 share, £10 for £80 share   7 Jun 1686 F56v anyone pleading on Randall Taylor's behalf to pay £20 to the poor from dividends   23 Mar 1686/7 F80v dividend book always to remain with Clerk so he or his servant may witness all discharges   19 Dec 1688 F111r dividends to be £40 for Assistant's share, £20 for Livery share, £10 for Yeomanry share and £5 for half-Yeomanry share   20 Dec 1689 F128r dividends of £40, £20, £10 and £5 to be paid on Christmas Eve and detained if their possessor is in debt to Stock or Corporation   1 Dec 1690 F147r dividends to be £40, £20, £10 and £5; to be paid on Christmas Eve   7 Dec 1691 F162v to be paid on Christmas Eve   25 Nov 1692 F182v dividends deferred until first Monday in February on account of Oxford charges   6 Oct 1693 F193r 1692 dividends to go to subscribers of new stock, the amount to be discharged from the first instalment of their subscription   20 Dec 1693 F197v 1692 dividends to be made out for partners not subscribing to new Stock; all new Stock partners to subscribe to dividend book   7 May 1694 F203r new dividend book to be prepared, the old one being full, to begin with the 1693 dividends   3 Dec 1694 F215v dividends to be made out this Christmas for the year 1693 at the usual rate   8 Apr 1695 F220r no dividend for 1694 because of price of paper, Oxford's comprinting on Stock books and the charges of obtaining Oxford privilege   6 May 1695 F222r committee to settle dispute over sinking 1694 dividend 12 Dec 1695 F238r dividend to be made among partners on 14 December; Clerk to prepare dividend book 2 Nov 1696 F252r Treasurer to give credit for 1697 almanacks to partners desiring to print; up to amount of dividends, to come out of next dividends 22 Dec 1696 F254r dividend to be paid next Thursday at usual rates; all money due to Stock to be subtracted 22 Dec 1697 G2v to be paid on 24 December. All money owing to English Stock to be first deducted 19 Dec 1698 G17v full dividend to be paid on 24 December 19 Dec 1699 G34v full dividend to be paid on 23 December 20 Dec 1700 G54r to be paid in same manner as last year 1 Dec 1701 G65v payment ordered 18 Dec 1702 G84r to be paid on Christmas Eve 20 Dec 1703 G100r full dividend to be paid next Friday 4 Dec 1704 G113v full dividend to be paid on 23 December 3 Dec 1705 G125v to be paid on 24 December 2 Dec 1706 G136v full dividend to be paid on 24 December 1 Dec 1707 G147v full dividend to be paid on 24 December 6 Dec 1708 G159r full dividend to be paid on 24 December 5 Dec 1709 G172r full dividend to be paid on 24 December 4 Dec 1710 G186r full dividend to be paid 3 Dec 1711 G195v half dividend to be paid next Friday 19 Dec 1712 G205v full dividend to be paid on 24 December 7 Dec 1713 G214v three-quarters dividend to be paid on 24 December 6 Dec 1714 G223v three-quarters dividend to be paid on 24 December. Standing order for the future that all members be summoned to the morning of the dividend day and the oath of partner read to them before they receive the dividend 7 Feb 1714/15 G224v standing order for the future that if any partner dies after the December Court, the dividend of that person shall be applied for the benefit of the English Stock 5 Dec 1715 G235r three-quarters dividend to be paid on 24 December 3 Dec 1716 G245v three-quarters dividend to be paid on 24 December

— OXFORD STOCK, relations with 10 Apr 1693 F186r Oxford proposals to be engrossed again before Stock partners subscribe to them 6 May 1695 F222r committee to settle dispute about the conditions and amounts between English and Oxford Stock 7 Mar 1708/9 G161v accounts between it and Oxford Stock to be settled 4 Apr 1709 G163v state of account between it and Oxford Stock discussed and adjusted 10 Sep 1711 G194r committee to meet John Baskett and Williams to ensure its protection despite granting of Oxford Stock privileges to another 1 Oct 1711 G194v no agreement reached with Williams

— PRINTING 6 Dec 1686 F68r paper stationers to be paid £300, or as much of that as possible, of the money due to them. Printers to be paid for work done for Stock in 1683 and 1684 25 Jul 1701 G62v committee reports that byelaws require any partner illegally printing books mentioned in the letters patent granted to the partners to forfeit his stock, which will then be distributed by the Master and Wardens to the poor 1 Sep 1701 G64r paper for it to be kept in Royston's warehouse 3 Nov 1701 G65r any Master, Warden or Stock-keeper who is a printer not to have more Stock work during office than before holding office 1 Jun 1702 G71v no printer to deliver his part of an impression of any English Stock work for the S.C. until the other printers are ready to deliver their parts 6 Oct 1712 G204r bill to be paid by Under Warden 13 Apr 1713 G208r lack of money to pay. Committee to consider how to pay 24 Apr 1713 G209r those working on behalf of English Stock to be paid with £800 advanced by Thomas Guy against bonds from S.C. 3 May 1714 G218v S.C. unable to repay Guy's loan so bonds renewed

— PROPERTY 6 Aug 1688 F105r deed of conveyance of Stock estate, St Martin within Ludgate; surviving signatories convey it to the present Assistants 4 Sep 1688 F107r Widow Eversden's house to be repaired at cost to the Stock 1 Oct 1688 F107v conveyance of ground and houses in St Martin's Ludgate to new feoffees sealed 1 Sep 1690 F142r Treasurer to make a rental of the Stock estate for every Court day to track down arrears; Clerk to do this for Corporation   6 Oct 1690 F144r rental of Stock and Corporation estate, with arrears of S.C. tenants, to be renewed by Treasurer and Clerk at monthly courts following quarter days   3 Aug 1691 F158r arrears of rent due to English Stock and Corporation read out; ordered to be re-read at the next general Court when the Master is present   7 Sep 1691 F159v tenants of English Stock to take out leases for houses and warehouses from Michaelmas Day for agreed periods. Tenants in arrears to pay up or be sued; quarterly payments and immediate warnings to be maintained; Treasurer to have copies of these orders   22 Dec 1691 F164r letter of attorney to be made from feoffees of Stock estate to Robert Stephens to possess the goods of tenants in arrears   7 Mar 1691/2 F166v assignment of mortgage of Stock estate to Master and Wardens, Henry Mortlock, Roger Norton and John Bellinger. Former feoffees indemnified. Feoffees of Stock estate not present to be summoned   4 Sep 1693 F191r Randall Taylor is to have the rent of his Stock tenement increased if he does not comply with the Printing Act   1 Oct 1694 F213r Master appoints committee to inspect English Stock and Corporation houses for repairs   12 Nov 1694 F214v housing committee authorises several repairs to English Stock and Corporation houses   3 Dec 1694 F215v Master, Wardens and Stock-keepers asked to consider John Whitlock's request to lease the Stock property he lives in   7 Oct 1695 F233r committee formed to decide whether to renew John Garrett's lease of one of the Stationers' Court houses   8 Jun 1696 F243r Warden to receive rents for Wood Street and other houses instead of Clerk, who will attend Warden; S.C. arms to be fixed on houses   5 Aug 1706 G134r rental to be made of the rents of   7 Jun 1708 G153v Clerk has delivered to Joseph Collyer account of arrears of rent due to English Stock   4 Oct 1708 G158r Collyer to prepare state of rents due to English Stock   21 Feb 1716/17 G246v trust of houses and lands belonging to English Stock situated near Hall transferred to new trustees

— SHARES   5 Feb 1682/3 E163r persons elected into shares to pay the Treasurer ready money; shares to be disposed of 'by hands only'   26 Mar 1683 E167r 1 person voted to a £160 share or 2 voted to £80 shares to provide a dinner for Court on 29 May on barge to commemorate Evan Tyler   2 Jul 1683 F2v order for all those elected into shares to pay ready money henceforth to be considered at next Court   3 May 1686 F55v Richard Royston makes difficulties about forfeiting his £320 share because he printed Stock books without permission   7 Feb 1687/8 (W) partner's oath not to be administered until money for share paid to Treasurer   7 Oct 1689 F124r all those elected to a £160 share to pay £15 and to a £80 share £10, to be paid to the Warden for the use of the S.C.   5 Jun 1690 F136r committee set up re. entitlement to shares of those not printers, booksellers or bookbinders   7 Jul 1690 F139r Court orders that only two persons shall be in the running for Stock shares   6 Feb 1692/3 F183v legal advice to be taken over possibility of increasing number of shares; dividend not paid because money is tied up in Oxford affairs   4 Dec 1693 F195r Thomas Parkhurst forfeits share for comprinting, under byelaw. Abel Swale declines to accept his £40 share; Jacob Tonson is elected and ordered to pay when those elected in July do   2 Jul 1694 F210v Sedgwick demands £80 for a share assigned him in the statute of bankruptcy awarded against Adiel Mill, a Stock partner   12 Nov 1694 F214v Court resolves to consider how to secure S.C. in the event of the clandestine mortgage of Dorman Newman's share   4 Mar 1694/5 F218v shares recently fallen vacant to be disposed of at the next general Court in April   3 Jul 1699 G26v consideration of motion that Court should dispose of the share of any partner who mortgaged his share without leave of the Court to be adjourned to next Court day   6 Mar 1703/4 G103r standing order that anyone elected into a stock shall pay usual money in lieu of a dinner within a month of accepting and pay money for the stock within '4:3 months' (sic) after his admittance   4 Feb 1705/6 G127r resolution to stand by former order that no member of a confederacy be elected into any share or put in the list of candidates   6 May 1706 G131r ordered that an instrument be executed by all persons elected into English Stock shares in future, providing that no mortgages of stock may be made without permission of Court. Stock mortgaged without permission to be sold by Court   3 Mar 1706/7 G139r disposal of shares deferred until next Court   7 Apr 1707 G140v part of order of 4 February 1705 discharged

— STOCK BOOKS   3 May 1680 E99v £47 worth of Stock books to be delivered to Hartley, and credit given him for £100 worth   7 Jun 1680 E100v list of printers for different signatures of Stock books   26 Mar 1681 E108r William Bateman to have £320 credited in English Stock books   5 Jul 1681 E116v committee set up to consider whether the prices of any Stock books should be lowered   3 May 1686 F55r table to be hung up in Court room or council chamber of all S.C. books. Richard Royston makes difficulties about forfeiting his £320 share because he printed Stock books without permission   8 Nov 1686 F66v 'Menelius's' [i.e. John Minellius's] 'Notes on Ovid' and all other foreign and domestic notes on S.C. books to be entered to Master in trust for S.C.   7 Feb 1686/7 F71r committee to peruse catalogue of Stock books to see if any private members' books overlap and which need alteration or reprinting   18 Mar 1686/7 F79v committee meeting decides that Court should consider whether certain books in the Oxford catalogue are to be printed   7 Apr 1690 F133r Thomas Dring to compensate English Stock for printing Virgil   1 Sep 1690 F142r Clerk to make an alphabetical list of all Stock books to make checking on comprinting easier. Gaines's press, recently sold to Dimock, is seized by S.C. when Gaines prints Stock books illegally   2 Mar 1690/1 F150v importation of Stock books: Richard Wild confesses to importing 'Menelius' [i.e. John Minellius] upon Terence, and [Thomas] Farnaby upon Ovid and Juvenal; he and Samuel Smith to appear at next Court   7 Sep 1691 F159r Cambridge presses to be used to print Stock books to render Stock more profitable   6 Nov 1693 F194v committee to inquire into precedents for punishing those who comprint on Stock books   4 Dec 1693 F195r Thomas Parkhurst forfeits share for comprinting, under byelaw   20 Apr 1695 F221v all Stock books to be registered before imminent expiry of Printing Act, Clerk executing deed to this effect   1 Feb 1696/7 F254v committee appointed to decide what rights S.C. has to copies, and what rates they were purchased at   7 Jul 1701 G62r committee to consider S.C.'s copies   2 Dec 1706 G136v Baxter and Andrew Toake to examine and correct all classical authors belonging to G146r 10 Oct 1707 importation of Stock books

— SUBSCRIPTIONS   12 Jul 1690 F139v Lord Mayor suggests subscribing money from Stock towards horse and dragoons for the Crown but this is not done   2 Mar 1690/1 F149v judged too much in debt to lend money to Crown on the late land tax for building up the navy   25 Jun 1691 F156r judged too much in debt to allow of lending money to Crown   23 Sep 1691 F160v judged too much in debt to lend Crown money for navy on Additional Excise   23 Mar 1691/2 F167r judged incapable of lending money to Crown   12 Sep 1692 F178v deemed impossible to lend any money from Joint Stock to the Crown   7 Nov 1692 F181v Court refuses to advance money from it for Crown loan   4 Sep 1693 F191r Court refuses mayoral precept to lend money from Stock to Crown   15 Mar 1693/4 F201r judged unfit to lend money to Crown on surety of Land Tax Act

— TOOKE AFFAIR   1 Jun 1702 G71r on examining accounts the Stock-keepers have discovered that the Stock has received a great prejudice. Committee to re-examine. Ordered that it be a standing rule for the future that no printer shall deliver his part of any work for S.C. until all the other printers are ready to do so. Note of monies and charges entered by the Treasurer in the cheque book to be taken by Warden after every

Court and delivered to the Stock-keepers   6 Jul 1702 G77v Master reports from committee examining accounts of English Stock that the Stock has been wronged. Clerk to make out copies of Orders of Court concerning printers. Benjamin Tooke given copy of charge against him concerning accounts of English Stock   14 Jul 1702 G78r meeting of partners called to discuss activities of Tooke   16 Jul 1702 G78v meeting of partners to discuss activities of Tooke. He has paid English Stock printers more than he has accounted for   23 Jul 1702 G79r Master reports that Tooke refused to deliver warehouse, books &c. to Stock-keepers and refused to pay Oxford rent   5 Oct 1702 G81v judgement of Attorney General that it was mismanaged by Tooke   9 Oct 1702 G82r Clerk to give notice to tenants not to pay any more rent to Tooke

See also ABC, CATECHISMS, CICERO, CUSTOMS HOUSE, GRAMMARS, OVID, OXFORD UNIVERSITY, PSALMS, STOCK-KEEPERS, TREASURER/WAREHOUSE-KEEPER, TOOKE, Benjamin

ENGLISH, William   3 Nov 1679 E95r freed by Nathaniel Ponder

ENTRY BOOK OF COPIES – see REGISTER BOOK

EPHEMERIS/EPHEMERIDES   5 May 1701 G59v Ephemeris published by Bradford in breach of S.C.'s copyright   2 Jun 1701 G60r opinion of Cooper concerning printing and publishing of Double Ephemeris. Hunt and George Parker to be prosecuted for selling   4 May 1702 G70v complaint that Thomas Hodgkins has printed the 'Ephemerides of the Celestial Motions for Six Years, Calculated by John Wing' for John Taylor   1 Jun 1702 G71r debate about illegal printing of Ephemerides adjourned   8 Nov 1703 G96v Stock-keepers to consider Dr John Gadbury's request to print Ephemerides   15 Nov 1703 G97v letter from Gadbury to Joseph Collyer concerning printing of Ephemerides; Gadbury to be attended by Collyer   20 Dec 1703 G100r Gadbury's letters concerning Ephemerides   14 Mar 1703/4 G104r George Parker examined for printing Ephemerides   23 Mar 1703/4 G104v Ephemeris printed by Bridge without S.C.'s permission   3 Apr 1704 G105r Bridge admits to printing Double Ephemeris for George Parker   5 Dec 1709 G172r Parker to be sued on his bond for publishing a calendar in the Ephemeris   8 Dec 1709 G172v Sir Edward Northey to decided whether Parker's Ephemeris constitutes a calendar or not   4 Dec 1710 G185v Clerk refused to enter Parker's Ephemeris

See also ALMANACKS

EPITOME OR ABRIDGEMENT – see BOOK OF MARTYRS

ERASMUS, Desiderius   15 Apr 1692 F170r his 'Colloquies' assigned to William Freeman by Elizabeth Flesher

ERICK, Edward   1 May 1709 G179v bound to William Holland, 7 years

ESCUTCHEONS   7 Feb 1697/8 G3v bills of Spycer and Wright, herald painters, for making these for S.C.

ESNEAD, Charles   2 Apr 1688 (W) foreigner, is freed

ETHERIDGE, William   4 Dec 1704 G114r bound to William Gunby, 7 years   5 May 1712 G199v freed by Elizabeth Gunby   4 Jul 1715 G231r John Coleman is bound to him

ETTMÜLLER, Michael – see THEORY ... OF PHYSIC

EUCLID   5 Jul 1703 G92r committee to sell books of, lately come from Oxford

EUDES DE MÉZERAY, François – see MÉZERAY

EVANCE, Jane   19 Dec 1692 F183r deceased; her pension voted to Francis Oliver

EVANS, [ ]   16 Jun 1684 F17r his former apprentice Roger Neild is freed

EVANS, Edward   7 Nov 1698 G16r bound to Benjamin Harris, 7 years

EVANS, Elizabeth   26 Mar 1684 F11r remarried; Thomas Seale elected to her 7s 6d share

EVANS, John   6 Jun 1698 G8v bound to William Horton, 8 years   7 Aug 1704 G111r turned over to Sarah Holt   6 Aug 1705 G122v freed by Sarah Holt

EVANS, Samson   5 Dec 1681 E140r Brewster requests successfully that Evans may be permitted to have John, son of William Mountford of Kidderminster, bound to him in Worcester

EVE, Benjamin   7 Mar 1708/9 G162r bound to Edmund Powell, 7 years

EVENS, Joan   2 Apr 1688 F100v bookbinder's widow; receives 10s charity and is ordered to apply to the next pension Court for further relief

EVENS, William   26 Mar 1686 F54r elected waterman   4 Apr 1687 F81v elected waterman

EVERDEN, George, snr – see following entry

EVERDEN, George, jnr   5 Oct 1713 G214r son of George; bound to John Clarke, 7 years

EVERINGHAM, [ ]   11 Nov 1700 G46v house to be viewed by Master, Wardens and workmen re. lease   3 Feb 1700/1 G54v report from committee to view his house   2 Mar 1701/2 G67v offered a new lease if repairs undertaken. Survey ordered   24 Mar 1701/2 G68r committee to survey his house   26 Mar 1702 G69r report from committee which surveyed his house. To have lease for 21 years in return for payment for repairs   13 Apr 1702 G69v does not accept committee's decision that he should carry out own repairs. S.C. to repair his house and he will retain it at former rent   1 Feb 1702/3 G85r to return draft of his lease. To pay cost of painting dining room. S.C. to pay for palisado pales before door

EVERINGHAM, Elinor   6 Oct 1707 G145v her apprentice Henry Reeve is freed   6 Jun 1709 G165v stone cutting in passage between her house and that of Whitledge to be viewed by Morphew committee and repairs ordered   2 Jul 1709 G166v masonry work on the passage between her house and that of Whitledge to be carried out by Harbin   12 Nov 1711 G195r Claudius Bonner is bound to her   5 Oct 1713 G214r Thomas Britt is bound to her   2 Aug 1714 G221r her apprentice John Shilton is freed   14 Mar 1714/15 G226r to leave her house by midsummer, in exchange for which Court will be kind concerning arrears of rent   4 Jul 1715 G231r house to be viewed by committee to see what repairs needed   8 Aug 1715 G231v house in indifferent repair. Proposal for settling arrears of rent referred to Master, Wardens and Stock-keepers   5 Sep 1715 G232v her apprentice Israel Simpson is freed   7 May 1716 G239v £80 share passed to William Taylor at her request

EVERINGHAM, John   5 Sep 1698 G14v his apprentice John Hunt is freed

EVERINGHAM, Richard   3 Jun 1695 F226v David Kyte is bound to him   5 Aug 1695 F232r Thomas Smith Cowell is bound to him

EVERINGHAM, Robert   29 Oct 1679 E94r cloathed   6 Mar 1681/2 E147v recovers £5 of £10 forfeited through breaking a S.C. byelaw   2 Oct 1682 E158v defect in partition wall between his and the Clerk's house to be referred to committee   1 Sep 1684 F23v petition for £50 loan rejected   12 Sep 1685 F44v committee to assess repairs for vault and passage, representing part of his property   7 May 1688 F101v to be summoned to answer a complaint that he has employed foreign journeyman printers   11 Oct 1688 F108v restored to Livery   11 Apr 1690 F133v fined for Assistant Renter Warden   7 Jul 1690 F139r printer to Thomas Mathew; Court advises that he should get his Singing Psalms subscribed for Mathew   13 Mar 1692/3 F185r appears to free his apprentice Thomas Smith; fined for binding him by foreign indentures   1 Apr 1697 F260v volunteers as printer bringing test case under Paper Act re. whether paper to be printed on is liable for duty   6 Dec 1697 G2r William Sudworth is bound to him   2 May 1698 G7v his apprentice Andrew Meires is freed   7 Oct 1698 G15r John Watts is bound to him   7 Feb 1698/9 G20v his apprentice Richard Joseph is freed   3 Jun 1700 G40r John Lilly to pay costs of suit against him in respect of Act of Parliament for duty upon paper, in which he acted on behalf of S.C.   2 Mar 1701/2 G67v John Stilton is bound to him   1 Mar 1702/3 G86r his apprentice Thomas Smith Cowell is freed   3 May 1703 G89r lease from S.C. of house in Ave Maria Lane for 21 years sealed   6 Mar 1703/4 G103v elected to Thomas Bennett's £80 share   3 Apr 1704 G105v takes oath of Partner   5 Feb 1704/5 G115r his apprentice William Sudworth is freed   2 Apr 1705 G118v Israel Simpson is bound to him

EVERINGHAM, William   2 Oct 1699 G31v his apprentice Marmaduke Norfolke is freed

See also EVERINGTON

EVERINGTON, John   6 Mar 1698/9 G22r Henry Reeve is bound to him

See also EVERINGHAM

EVERSDEN, Ann   6 Mar 1681/2 E148r daughter of George Eversden; £20 bond to be paid to her husband Zachary Grant on her marriage, which has now taken place

EVERSDEN, Elizabeth   4 Feb 1683/4 F8v widow of George Eversden; given 7s 6d from Poor Box   3 Mar 1683/4 F10v S.C. trustees to seize her late husband George's goods to the value of £22 16s for rent arrears, she giving a bill of sale and bond for payment of arrears on 25 June. (W) Report of trustees investigating accounts   20 Dec 1684 F27r and daughter (W) paid 40s charity   20 Dec 1687 F96r given £2 charity   4 Sep 1688 F107r her house to be repaired at cost to the English Stock   5 Aug 1689 F122v produces a bond for £20 plus interest to be paid to Sarah Eversden on her marriage, shortly to take place with Thomas Bawden; to be paid   3 Feb 1689/90 F128v some members petition on behalf of her and Mrs Burrows for S.C.'s annual payments to them, omitted last year; referred   26 Mar 1690 F131r to have 40s as her usual allowance which was omitted at Christmas   9 Feb 1690/1 F148r is refused her dividend, previously stopped for arrears of rent   12 Dec 1695 F238r 20s to be abated from the rent due to S.C. by her   5 Sep 1698 G14r accounts with S.C. to be made up by Treasurer for next Court day   7 Nov 1698 G15v state of accounts between her and S.C.; she owes £36 10s plus £20 due from her husband on bond   5 Dec 1698 G17r to be given notice by Clerk to leave S.C.'s house unless she discharges her arrears of rent   3 Apr 1699 G23r permitted to stay in her house until next quarter-day, on payment of last quarter's rent   27 Mar 1703 G87r office for Clerk to be provided in her house. In arrears of rent. To renounce possession of her house and an account of her debts to be drawn up   20 Sep 1703 G95r desiring her house to be repaired. Master and Wardens to view with workmen   7 Jun 1708 G153r account of her rent arrears to S.C. to be prepared by Joseph Collyer   5 Jul 1708 G154v Collyer to settle account with her. S.C. to get what money they can from her and take a bond for the rest   2 Aug 1708 G156r her dividend to be allowed against rent arrears, but still owes S.C. £35 10s   5 Mar 1710/11 G188r Thomas Marlar to be granted lease of her house near the Hall after her death   7 May 1711 G190r deceased; her £80 share disposed of to Robert Vincent

EVERSDEN, George   6 Mar 1681/2 E148r £20 bond to be paid to Zachary Grant on day of his marriage to Eversden's daughter Ann; this is called in, and another similar bond is drawn up for Eversden's other daughter Sarah   4 Jun 1683 E170r allowed to mortgage £80 share to Sarah Martin for £80 to pay off mortgage to Thomas Clarke, son of Richard Clarke, deceased   19 Dec 1683 F7r sent 40s charity at the request of several members of the Table   3 Mar 1683/4 F10v deceased; S.C. trustees to seize goods as payment for rent owed by his widow

See also EVERSDEN, Elizabeth

EVERSDEN, Sarah   6 Mar 1681/2 E148r daughter of George Eversden; £20 bond to be paid to her on her marriage

See also EVERSDEN, Elizabeth

EVETT/EVETTS, Edward   5 Feb 1682/3 E163v granted £100 loan from Norton's bequest on good surety   2 May 1687 F82v allowed to repay half of his £100 loan from Norton's bequest on Midsummer Day and the rest at Michaelmas   29 May 1689 F118v cloathed   6 Sep 1697 F267r Robert Thoroson is freed by him   5 Oct 1713 G214r John Booth is freed by his executor

EVITT, John   5 Feb 1699/1700 G35r freed by William Warter

EXCELL, Tryolus   6 Sep 1703 G94v bound to David Edwards, 8 years

EXCHEQUER   4 Jul 1698 G11r Clerk's bill for charges in

EXCOMMUNICATIONS OF MUGGLETON   5 Mar 1679/80 E97v Exton's bill of £3 6s 6d for this [one of the pamphlets relating to Lodowick Muggleton] to be paid

EXETER   2 Nov 1702 G82v investigation of advertisement there for Bibles, psalms and Common Prayer books

EXPOSITION OF THE CATECHISM – see LEWIS, John

EXPOSITION OF THE CREED – see PEARSON, John

EXPOSITION ON THE CHURCH-CATECHISM [by Thomas Ken, Bishop of Bath and Wells]   7 Sep 1685 F44r Charles Broome pays 5 guineas to print 5000 catechisms to annex to the Bishop's 'Exposition of [i.e. on] the Catechism'   6 Jun 1687 F84v Charles Broome admits printing the Bishop of Bath and Wells's 'Exposition on the Catechism' in larger type than before

EXTON, [   ]   5 Mar 1679/80 E97v his bill of £3 6s 6d for 'Excommunications of Muggleton' [i.e. one of the pamphlets relating to Lodowick Muggleton] to be paid

EYRE, Anthony   6 Jun 1698 G8v bound to George Littlebury, 7 years

EYRES, Henry   5 Feb 1704/5 G114v of Warrington; to be party to S.C.'s bill in Chancery for printing sham almanack, 'The Annalist', for 1705

EYRES, William   2 Oct 1699 G31v bound to Freeman Collins   6 Oct 1707 G145v freed by Freeman Collins

FABIAN, [   ]   29 May 1689 F118v pleads inability to be cloathed; Master and Wardens desired to warn him before the Lord Mayor and force him to be

FABIAN, George   4 Feb 1705/6 G127v bound to William Pearson, 7 years   13 Apr 1713 G208v freed by William Pearson

FAIRBANK/FAIREBANK/FAIRBANKE/FAIREBANKE, Richard   26 Mar 1694 F201v elected to the pension of the late Ann Baskervile   27 Mar 1697 F260r elected to the pension of Rachel Arton, deceased   26 Mar 1698 G5v elected to Anne Dew's pension   19 Dec 1698 G17v elected to Anne Blundell's pension. Mary Brockett given his pension   20 Dec 1705 G126r deceased; Mary Neale given his pension

FAIRMAN, Samuel   5 Aug 1706 G134v bound to Richard Chapman, 7 years

FAITHORNE, Henry   26 Mar 1686 F54r to be granted £50 from Norton bequest if his sureties are approved   6 May 1689 F117v ordered to repay his £50 loan by 30

April next 9 Feb 1690/1 F148v has 'failed in the world'; his father is allowed as his son's surety for £50 loan. Given a month to sell his son's stock in repayment

FARAM, Francis 2 Apr 1705 G118v apprentice of William Richardson, first turned over to Edmund Richardson and then to Thomas Horne, is freed by William Richardson

FARLOW, Samuel 4 Sep 1699 G30r freed by Freeman Collins

FARLY/FARLEY, Samuel 27 Mar 1703 G87r of Exeter; committee to take a bond from him not to print the Exeter Almanack illegally any longer 1 Sep 1707 G145r of Exeter; his letter to be considered by Master, Wardens and Stock-keepers 22 Dec 1708 G159v to be made party to S.C.'s Bill in Chancery for printing almanacks

FARMER, Daniel 1 Oct 1711 G194v son of William; bound to Emmanuel Matthews, 7 years

FARNABY, Thomas – see OVID

FARRINGDON WITHIN 5 Sep 1681 E129v committee to attend its Alderman, Deputy and Council re. minister's tithes

FAUSTUS, DR 1 Sep 1690 F142r Court agrees to buy the 'History of the Life and Death of Dr Faustus' from Henry Mortlock and Benjamin Tooke 6 Oct 1690 F143r to be entered in trust for S.C.

FEARNE, John 1 Aug 1687 F87v refiner in White Cross Street; to stand surety for Henry Clarke's £50 loan 1 Oct 1688 F107v enters into bond with Clarke re. his loan so Clarke is enabled to continue it for 6 months

FEASTS 4 Aug 1684 F21v decided to adjourn Sweeting's feast from 10 August to 13 August, and that Company members should not be obliged to appear in gowns at it (W) 'considering the heat of the season'. Sweeting's will to be searched for in the Prerogative Office and a copy entered in the S.C.'s Register 6 Jul 1689 F121v feast to be held on 8 August rather than 10 August 18 Jul 1690 F140v Master's feast to be moved to 5 August because 10 August falls on a Sunday 3 Aug 1691 F158v Master's feast to be held on 20 August rather than 10 August because of wainscotting taking place in Court Room 1 Aug 1692 F176v Master's and Sweeting's feast to be held on 18 August, as 10 August is the day appointed by the Crown for a public feast 7 Aug 1693 F190v Sweeting's feast to be held on the usual day of 10 August 5 Aug 1695 F230r move not to hold feast on 10 August is rejected, when it is pointed out that this might endanger bequests. Assistants to have only one guest. Voted to have printed tickets but no music; no-one to remove victuals from Hall until after feast with appropriate permission 12 Aug 1695 F232v ordered to have music after all 3 Aug 1696 F246v 10 August election dinner to be held on 11 August 1 Aug 1698 G11v to be held on Thursday 11 August. No women to be invited. Master and Wardens to take charge of it 27 Jul 1699 G27r to be held on 10 August 19 Jul 1700 G43r to be held on 13 August. Music to be provided 4 Aug 1701 G63v to be held on 12 August 6 Jul 1702 G77v musicians to be hired 3 Aug 1702 G79v to be held on 13 August 2 Aug 1703 G94r to be held on 19 August 3 Jul 1704 G110r to be held on 10 August 6 Aug 1705 G122r to be held on 16 August. Provisions and musicians for 5 Aug 1706 G133v to be held on 13 August 4 Aug 1707 G144r to be held on 14 August 2 Aug 1708 G156r to be held on 10 August 1 Aug 1709 G169v to be held on 16 August 7 Aug 1710 G183r to be held on 17 August 6 Aug 1711 G193r to be held on 14 August 4 Aug 1712 G202r to be held on 12 August 3 Aug 1713 G212v to be held on 11 August 2 Aug 1714 G221r to be held on 17 August 8 Aug 1715 G232r to be held on 16 August 6 Aug 1716 G242r to be held on 14 August

FEES AND FINES 7 Nov 1687 F94r for office, &c., to be entered into a book for the purpose provided by Clerk 6 Aug 1705 G122v table of fees for bindings and freedoms to be drawn up   5 Sep 1709 G170r list of fees of Clerk and Beadle for binding and making free to be prepared by Clerk   1 Nov 1714 G223r for binding and making free to be set up in the lobby   6 Dec 1714 G223v table to be printed and set up in lobby

FEILD, [   ]   20 Oct 1703 G96v his lease from University of Cambridge to be delivered to Joseph Collyer

FEILD, Mary   19 Jun 1701 G61r Robert Chowne given her pension

FEILD, Simon   2 May 1698 G7v freed by Thomas Hodgkins

FEILDER, Thomas   6 Sep 1703 G95r Churchwarden of St Martin's Ludgate; party to agreement with S.C. over a drain passing through S.C.'s land

FELL, John – see LIFE OF DR HAMMOND

FELLOW, Robert   6 Sep 1697 F267r bound to Robert James

FELLOWES, George   6 Sep 1703 G94v bound to James Dover, 7 years

FELTHAM, Thomas   20 Dec 1688 F111v vintner; bond for £507 10s to him sealed   9 Feb 1690/1 F149r deceased; his executors are asked to accept 5% p.a. in settlement of £500 he lent to S.C. 2 years ago for 3 months at 6% p.a.; not accepted so loan to be repaid

FELTON, [   ]   5 Apr 1703 G88r his apprentice Peter Tanner, who had been turned over to George Grafton, is freed

FELTON, Adam   26 Mar 1683 E166r elected Renter Warden   1 Oct 1683 F3r elected to Thomas Spicer alias Helder's £40 share   25 Oct 1683 F4r to be elected First Renter Warden because of Samuel Hoyle's having 'gone aside'. Samuel Hoyle to be sent a letter ordering him to settle accounts with Felton and Samuel Lowndes and deliver the Renter Warden's book to him   12 Nov 1683 F5v elected to John Bassett's £80 share   7 Apr 1684 F14r on the list of loyal Assistants presented to the Crown   7 May 1685 (W) confirmed as member of new Livery   2 Nov 1685 F45v competes unsuccessfully for John Bellinger's £160 share   1 Feb 1685/6 F50r elected to Ambrose Isted's £160 share

FELTON, Mary   7 Dec 1696 F252v deceased; John Hancock elected to her £160 share

FENN, [   ]   21 Oct 1686 (W) acts as surety for a bond entered into by Obadiah Blagrave

FENN, Elizabeth   2 Oct 1699 G31v John Lahunt bound to her

FENN, John   26 Mar 1680 E98r freed by Thomas Rhodes

FENTHAM, [   ]   6 Apr 1691 F152r bond of £1000 penalty entered into with Ursula Fitzer to pay his executors

FENWICK, Edward   8 May 1693 F187v merchant taylor; given a bond of £1000 penalty for payment of £512 10s by 9 November 1693

FERROUR, Thomas   20 Dec 1706 G137r bound to Richard Simpson, 7 years

FERRY, Anne   24 Mar 1711/12 G198r elected to Hannah Smith's pension

FERRYS, Hester   23 Jun 1710 G180v elected to Johanna Strainge's pension   27 Sep 1710 G184r deceased; Martha Widows given her pension

FFOSTER/FFORSTER – see FORSTER

FFRANCK – see FRANK

FIELDING, Richard   6 Aug 1688 F106r freed even though discovered to have been bound at a scrivener's to John Grantham

FIFTEEN COMFORTS   3 Aug 1685 F42v Samuel Heyrick refuses to sue John How for printing a copy of his, 'The Fifteen Comforts of Rash and Inconsiderate Marriage'

FIGURA – see GRAMMAR

FILLIMORE, Jonathan – see following entry

FILLIMORE, Robert 3 Dec 1716 G245v son of Jonathan; bound to Benjamin Simpson, 8 years

FINCH, John 6 Jun 1698 G8v bound to John Flinston, 7 years

FIRBANK, Richard 25 Jun 1684 F18r his former apprentice Henry Rogers is freed

FIREBRASSE, Sir Basil 7 Oct 1689 F124r Warden's accounts reveal that £50 was paid to him for wine for the Lord Chancellor in the middle of the Oxford dispute

FIRST BOOK FOR CHILDREN – see COMPLETE SCHOOL-MISTRESS

FIRTH, John 2 May 1709 G165r freed by John Leake

FIRTH, Nathan 12 Nov 1716 G244v freed by John Clarke. Thomas Pickard bound to him. Cloathed

FISH/FISHE/FISHER, Thomasine 5 Jul 1686 F60v given bond for payment of £512 10s on 4 January 1687; money used to pay £500 due on bond to Hannah Sawbridge's executors 10 Apr 1693 F186v is paid £512 10s and bond cancelled; money raised by entering into another bond with Robert Hesilrige and George Mackreth 4 Mar 1694/5 F218r Treasurer to inform her that the £500 plus interest due to her will be paid in the first week of next term 3 Jun 1695 F225r bond originally to Hesilrige and Mackreth for Mrs Fish's use; '£500 odd' is paid and bond cancelled 3 Mar 1700/1 G57r bond from S.C. to her of £200 penalty to pay £112 10s (£102 10s in margin) on 4 August sealed 7 May 1705 G119v bond from S.C. to her of £200 sealed 9 Feb 1707/8 G148v £50 taken in from churchwardens of St Thomas the Apostle towards payment of her £100 bond from S.C.

FISHER, [ ] 5 Oct 1685 F45r complains that Mrs Sawbridge has printed his copy

FISHER, Bardsey 13 Dec 1705 G126v Vice-Chancellor of Cambridge University; signatory to articles between S.C. and university

FISHER, Charles 20 Dec 1710 G186v bound to Thomas Hall, 7 years

FISHER, John 8 Apr 1700 G39r bound to Samuel Bridge, 7 years 1 Sep 1707 G145r freed by Bryan Mills

FISHER, Sir Richard 7 May 1682/3 E169v bond for £200 entered into, to pay off a bond for the same amount to John Godden 2 Jun 1684 F15v is paid £200 and bond cancelled; money raised by entering into another bond with Thomas Dring

FISHER, William 5 Sep 1687 F88r surrenders his £40 share; (W) letter surrendering his share 13 Oct 1687 F91v elected Assistant but does not appear to take oath 17 Oct 1687 F93r discharged from attendance as Assistant since he lives far away, is infirm and has lately parted with his Stock share 1 Mar 1687/8 F97v displaced as Assistant by order of Crown and expelled from Livery by order of Lord Mayor

See also FISH

FISHWICK, James 9 Feb 1707/8 G149r bound to Richard Wellington, 7 years

FITCH, Widow 5 Oct 1681 E131r paid 10s charity

FITTER, Abraham 2 Oct 1704 G112v bound to Ralph Snow, 7 years

FITZER, Ursula 6 Apr 1691 F152r given a bond of £1000 penalty dated 11 March for payment of £508 6s 8d by 11 Jul 7 Sep 1691 F160r £500 bond cancelled

FLEET, Robert 3 May 1703 G89v Thomas Elliott bound to him

FLEMING, William 7 Oct 1706 G135r bound to Hugh Meere, 7 years 2 Nov 1713 G214v freed by Hugh Meere

FLESHER, Elizabeth (Widow Flesher) 6 Aug 1688 F104v ordered to stop printing but asks Court not to withdraw its favour until stock sold; allowed sheet and half of Galen's Almanack, not psalter or primer 15 Apr 1692 F170r widow of James Flesher; assigns Erasmus's 'Colloquies', [Robert] Record's 'Arithmetic' and 'Wit's Commonwealth' [i.e. Nicholas Ling, *Politeuphueia*] to William Freeman 6 Sep 1697 F267r disposal of her £160 share to be deferred until next Court day 4 Oct 1697 F268v deceased; John Amery elected to her £160 share

FLESHER, James 15 Apr 1692 F170r deceased; his widow and executrix Elizabeth assigns three books to William Freeman

FLESHER, Miles 21 Feb 1681/2 E145r elected to Robert Clavell's £40 share 7 May 1685 (W) confirmed as member of new Livery 1 Mar 1686/7 F77r elected Stock-keeper for Yeomanry with Robert Andrews 1 Mar 1687/8 F98v elected Stock-keeper for Livery with Charles Harper 2 Jul 1688 F104r deceased; John Hancock jnr voted to his share 8 Apr 1695 F221r Thomas Parker, his apprentice, is freed

FLESHER, Thomas 1 Aug 1681 E117v assigned Dr [Alexander] Read's 'Manual of Anatomy or Dissection of the Body' by Benjamin Thrale 24 Jun 1682 E154r cloathed 7 Dec 1685 F48r assigns four medical books to Edward Jones 11 Oct 1688 F108v restored to Livery 26 Mar 1692 F167v set aside for a year from serving or fining for Renter Warden 19 Nov 1695 F236r his apprentice John Nicholson is freed

FLETCHER, John 4 Sep 1699 G30v bound to William Gunby, 7 years 7 Aug 1704 G111r turned over to Edward Terrill 2 Jun 1712 G200v Miles Townsend bound to him 2 May 1715 G228v his apprentice Miles Townsend turned over to John Randoll

FLINSTON/FLINSTONE, John 2 Dec 1695 F237r is freed by Thomas Yates 6 Jun 1698 G8v John Finch is bound to him

FLOOD, [ ] 6 Dec 1703 G99v and Baker of Norwich; Clerk to enquire whether involved in selling and publishing sham almanacks

FLORY, John 3 May 1697 F262r freed by Elizabeth Redmaine

FLORUS, Lucius Annaeus 25 Sep 1690 F143r committee to treat with Thomas Parkhurst, [S.] Smith and Benjamin Motte re. printing an impression of 'Lucius Florus' [i.e. *Rerum Romanarum Epitome?*] 6 Oct 1690 F143v committee required to reach agreement re. this and report

FLOWER, Hector Thomas 3 Dec 1716 G245v freed by patrimony

FLOWER, John 3 Jul 1710 G182r freed by patrimony

FLOWREY, James 23 Jun 1710 G180v elected to William Redmaine's pension 27 Sep 1710 G184r elected to Beatrice Turner's pension; Joan Jennour given his pension

FODEN, Jacob 7 Apr 1701 G58v bound to Samuel Briscoe, 7 years 6 Mar 1703/4 G103v turned over to William Pearson 5 Jul 1708 G154v freed by William Pearson

FOORD, John 5 Jul 1708 G155r stationer; Joseph Morgan bound to him

FORD, [ ] 6 Jun 1709 G165v bricklayer; bill of £3 to be paid by Joseph Collyer 7 Jul 1709 G168r bricklayer; to examine the Thames water pipes in front of Carter's house to see if water can be prevented from coursing into the cellar thereof

FORD, Allyn 4 Aug 1707 G144v his son John is freed by patrimony

FORD, Simon, Dr – see CATECHISMS

FORD, Emmanuel – see ORNATUS AND ARTESIA; PARISMUS

FORD, James 6 Sep 1714 G221v his apprentice John Jackson turned over to John Moore

FORD, John, snr (I) – see following entry

FORD, John, jnr (II)   24 Oct 1694 F214r son of John Ford of Christ Church, Surrey, mariner; bound to Richard Mawson from 8 October

FORD, John (III)   6 Dec 1697 G2r Charles Grist bound to him   5 Aug 1700 G44r William Charnock bound to him   5 Apr 1703 G88r John Carter bound to him   4 Apr 1709 G164r of London Wall; John Jackson bound to him   7 Feb 1714/15 G225r John Nicholson bound to him   6 Feb 1715/16 G236r his apprentice Charles Whitcraft is freed

FORD, John (IV)   4 Dec 1699 G34r bound to John Penn, 8 years

FORD, John (V)   4 Aug 1707 G144v son of Allyn, freed by patrimony

FORD, Lucy   27 Mar 1699 G23r did not appear to collect her pension, having some monies left her by a friend. Ursula Dykes given her pension

FORD, Richard   2 Apr 1705 G118v bound to John Lawrence, 7 years   6 Oct 1712 G204v freed by John Lawrence

FORD, Thomas   26 Mar 1686 F54r elected waterman   4 Apr 1687 F81v elected waterman

FOREIGN BOOKS   6 Nov 1704 G113r committee to dispose of S.C.'s foreign books

FOREIGN INDENTURES   7 Feb 1698/9 G20r James Smallshaw fined 30s for being bound by   2 Apr 1705 G118v fine paid for Andrew Hind being bound by   7 Nov 1709 G171v fine paid by William King for binding an apprentice by

FOREMAN, [   ]   6 Aug 1688 F104v stall bookseller of Moorfields; claims that he was bred to the trade and is free of the Clothworkers'; to be sued for contempt

FORSTER, Edward   5 Jul 1708 G155r bound to Jonah Bowyer, 7 years

FORSTER/FFORSTER/FOSTER/FFOSTER, Mark   5 Oct 1702 G81v Robert Willoughby turned over from Edward Hawkins to him   4 Mar 1705/6 G129r his apprentice Robert Willoughby is freed   6 Sep 1714 G221v John Stephens turned over to him   14 Mar 1714/15 G226r his apprentice John Stephens is freed

FORSTER, Richard   6 Feb 1709/10 G175v bound to William Littleboy

FORSTER, Thomas   6 Jun 1709 G165v freed by patrimony

FOSTER, Elinor   18 Dec 1702 G84r to have 5 shillings added to her pension

FOSTER – see FORSTER

FOSTERBY, John   7 Feb 1698/9 G20v freed by Philip Brookesby

FOULKES, David – see following entry

FOULKES, John   4 Oct 1714 G222v son of David; bound to Robert Podmore, 7 years See also FOWKES

FOWELL, Anne   24 Sep 1714 G222r elected to Daniel Ryley's pension   27 Sep 1715 G233r deceased; Elizabeth Slade given her pension

FOWELL, John   3 Feb 1700/1 G55v John Dunstall bound to him   4 Feb 1705/6 G127v William Rogers bound to him

FOWKES, David – see following entry

FOWKES, Edward   1 Oct 1711 G194v son of David; bound to John Barber, 7 years See also FOULKES

FOWLE, Daniel   5 Jul 1703 G92r trustee of bond from S.C. to Daniel and Anne Blague

FOWLER, John   6 Jul 1702 G78r bound to Robert Vincent, 7 years   1 Aug 1709 G169v freed by Robert Vincent   6 Aug 1716 G242v Edward Allen bound to him

FOWLER, Rebecca   23 Jun 1711 G191v elected to Nathan Brookes' pension   21 Mar 1712/13 G207v deceased; Valentine Acton given her pension

FOWLES, Nicholas   26 Mar 1686 F54r elected waterman   4 Apr 1687 F81v elected waterman

FOX, Charles   5 Sep 1715 G232v son of Thomas; bound to Jane Steele, 7 years

FOX, Joseph   5 Jul 1708 G154v cloathed   5 Sep 1709 G170r bookseller, of Westminster Hall; Timothy Fox bound to him

FOX, Richard   5 Dec 1681 E140r request granted to lend £100 to S.C. at 5% p.a., at next Court   22 Dec 1681 E141v bond between him and S.C. for £100 for 6 months at £200 penalty sealed   13 Apr 1698 G6v bond from S.C. to him repaid

FOX, Thomas (I)   29 May 1689 F118v cloathed

FOX, Thomas (II)   3 Feb 1695/6 F239r solicitor; committee appointed to inspect his bill   3 May 1697 F262r committee appointed to discuss his letter in which he desires payment for 'soliciting matters of the ... S.C.'   6 Sep 1697 F267r Samuel Heyrick to be added to the committee concerning Fox's bill of 3 May 1697   4 Jul 1698 G11r report from committee to consider his bill. £12 to be paid to him in full discharge thereof

FOX, Thomas (III – possibly to be identified with I)   5 Sep 1715 G232v his son Charles is bound to Jane Steele, 7 years

FOX, Thomas (IV)   12 Nov 1716 G244v son of Nathaniel; bound to William Smith, 7 years

FOX, Timothy   5 Sep 1709 G170r bound to Joseph Fox, 7 years

FOX, Widow   8 Nov 1697 G1v now married to Whittingham, who requests £100 due to her on bond from S.C.

FOX, William   23 Jun 1709 G166r deceased; his widow given his pension

FOXE, John – see BOOK OF MARTYRS

FRAMEWELL, William   6 Jul 1700 G43r freed by Robert Stephens

FRANCIS, Jacob   3 May 1708 G152v bound to Thomas Wilmer, 7 years

FRANCIS, Thomas   26 Mar 1709 G163r elected Bargemaster's Mate

FRANCKLYN – see FRANKLIN

FRANCKNELL, John   6 May 1700 G39v John Shaw bound to him

FRANCKS, John   26 Mar 1712 G198v elected Assistant Renter Warden   5 May 1712 G199v to be excused from office of Assistant Renter Warden for a year because he is afflicted with the palsy

See also FRANK, FRANKE, FRANKES, FRANKS

FRANK/FFRANCK, John (I)   7 May 1711 G190v of Brentford, mason; his nephew John Frank is bound to him   5 Jul 1714 G220v his apprentice John Frank is turned over to Robert Kidwell

FRANK/FFRANCK, John (II)   7 May 1711 G190v bound to his uncle John Frank, 7 years   5 Jul 1714 G220v apprentice of John Frank, turned over to Robert Kidwell

See also FRANCKS, FRANKE, FRANKES, FRANKS

FRANKE, John   7 Apr 1701 G58v William Mosse bound to him

See also FRANCKS, FRANK, FRANKES, FRANKS

FRANKES, John   1 Oct 1694 F213r allowed to defer acceptance of cloathing until next Court. Thomas Spencer is bound to him

See also FRANCKS, FRANK, FRANKE, FRANKS

FRANKLIN/FRANKLYN, Richard – see following entry

FRANKLIN/FRANCKLYN/FRANKLYN, Thomas (I)   2 Apr 1694 F202v son of Richard Franklin of Willesden, husbandman; bound to Henry Carter for seven years   9 Feb 1701/2 G67r freed by Henry Carter   5 Oct 1702 G81r John Wheeler bound to him   6 Aug 1705 G122v George Baxter bound to him   9 Jun 1707 G142v Peter Bettesworth bound to him   7 Jul 1712 G201v his apprentice Roger Whittyate is freed   4 May 1713 G209v John Dodson bound to him   22 Dec 1713 G215v William Risdell bound to him   5 Mar 1715/16 G237v Joseph Ladley bound to him   6 Aug 1716 G242v his apprentice Peter Bettesworth is freed

FRANKLIN, Thomas (II)   1 Feb 1702 G85r bound to Ralph Snow, 7 years

FRANKLYN – see FRANKLIN

FRANKLYNE, Thomas   3 Jul 1710 G182r of London Bridge, mathematical instrument maker; George Adams bound to him

See also FRANKLIN

FRANKNELL, John   5 Oct 1702 G81v turns over his apprentice Henry Peach to [blank]

FRANKS, John   3 Feb 1695/6 F239r John Locker, his apprentice, is freed   5 Sep 1698 G14r stonecutter of Brentford; elected to cloathing   7 Jun 1703 G90r stonecutter of Brentford; member of the S.C., to be summoned to cloathing next Court day   5 Jul 1703 G92r John Fry bound to him. Refuses to accept cloathing   2 Aug 1703 G93v of Brentford; required to accept cloathing next Court day unless he discharges himself by oath to the Lord Mayor   4 Oct 1703 G96r of Brentford; Clerk to enquire whether free of the City of London   8 Nov 1703 G97r of Brentford; to be proceeded against for refusal of cloathing   6 Dec 1703 G99v of Brentford; to take oath before Lord Mayor and Court of Aldermen to discharge himself from cloathing   8 May 1704 G106v of Brentford; Clerk to request him to take oath before Court of Alderman as he offered to do   3 Jun 1706 G132v William Sutton bound to him

See also FRANCKS, FRANK, FRANKE, FRANKES

FREE WORKMEN PRINTERS – see PRINTERS

FREEDOM   10 Jun 1684 F16v printers, booksellers, bookbinders and dealers in books operating outside S.C. to be summoned to next Court to show cause why they exercise the said trades without taking their freedom

FREEMAN, Daniel   2 Aug 1697 F265v he and Samuel Freeman are freed by Robert Stephens

FREEMAN, Samuel   2 Aug 1697 F265v he and Daniel Freeman are freed by Robert Stephens

FREEMAN, William   1 Mar 1682/3 E164r granted £50 of Tyler's bequest   1 Mar 1685/6 F51r summoned to be cloathed but does not appear   26 Mar 1686 F54r cloathed   2 May 1687 F82r pays in £50 loan from Tyler's bequest   1 Mar 1687/8 F97v expelled from Livery by order of Lord Mayor   11 Oct 1688 F108v restored to Livery   7 Apr 1690 F133r Thomas Burdikin, executor for the late Thomas Rookes, assigns him Francis Quarles's 'Argulus and Parthenia'   15 Apr 1692 F170r assigned Erasmus's 'Colloquies', [Robert] Record's 'Arithmetic' and 'Wit's Commonwealth' [i.e. Nicholas Ling, *Politeuphueia*] by Elizabeth Flesher   27 Mar 1693 F185v elected First Renter Warden and summoned   3 Apr 1693 F185v Thomas Dring requests on Freeman's behalf that he be allowed to fine for First Renter Warden; granted   1 Oct 1694 F213v Richard Chinery jnr bound to him   8 Apr 1695 F220r competes unsuccessfully for Nicholas Boddington's £40 share. Elected to Daniel Browne's £40 share   11

Nov 1695 F235v his apprentice Richard Standfast is freed   1 Mar 1698/9 G21r elected Stock-keeper for Yeomanry   4 Dec 1699 G33v assignment from Richard Hargrave of 'Systema Horticultura', 'The Devout Communicant' and 'An Infallible Way to Content-ment' to be registered   1 Mar 1700/1 G56r elected Stock-keeper for Yeomanry   5 Oct 1702 G81v James Leak is bound to him   5 Mar 1704/5 G117r elected to Judith Webb's £80 share   1 Mar 1705/6 G128v elected Stock-keeper for Livery   1 Mar 1706/7 G138v elected Stock-keeper for Livery   1 Mar 1707/8 G149v elected Stock-keeper for Livery   3 May 1708 G152r elected Assistant   7 Jun 1708 G153r takes oath of Assistant; to be added to committee considering Benjamin Harris's arrears   1 Aug 1709 G169v Edward Nutt is bound to him   7 Nov 1709 G172r his apprentice James Leak is freed   6 Feb 1709/10 G175r elected to Mrs Bennett's £160 share. His £80 share disposed of to Matthew Wootton   3 Jul 1710 G182r auditor of late Master and Wardens' accounts   2 Jul 1711 G192v auditor of late Master and Wardens' accounts   5 Jul 1712 G201r elected Under Warden and takes oath   3 Nov 1712 G205r Thomas Caldecott turned over to him   2 Mar 1712/13 G207r Jacob Tonson fined for Under Warden to preserve seniority to Freeman   24 Apr 1713 G209r signatory to S.C.'s notes   4 Jul 1713 G211r fined for second year of Under Warden and first and second year of Upper Warden   7 Sep 1713 G213r John Leake's £80 share given to him as surety   5 Oct 1713 G213v money disbursed by him as Warden for English Stock not to be paid by Joseph Collyer who has already paid several sums on this account   5 Apr 1714 G218r auditor of late Renter Wardens' accounts   3 May 1714 G218v signs note to Thomas Guy   2 Aug 1714 G221r auditor of late Master and Wardens' accounts   2 Jul 1715 G230r competes unsuccessfully for Master   4 Jul 1715 G231r auditor of late Master and Wardens' accounts and late Renter Wardens' accounts. To view houses of Mrs Everingham and Mrs Davies   30 Jun 1716 G241r competes unsuccessfully for Master   2 Jul 1716 G241v fined for Master to preserve seniority to Nicholas Boddington   4 Feb 1716/17 G246v to be a new trustee of S.C.'s property   21 Feb 1716/17 G246v one of the new trustees of S.C.'s property

FREEMEN   4 Jul 1692 F173v list of newly made freemen to be sent to Lord Chamberlain   12 Sep 1692 F179r list of newly made freemen to be sent to Lord Chamberlain   5 Oct 1696 F251r two unspecified   2 Nov 1696 F252r six unspeci-fied   7 Dec 1696 F253r two unspecified   1 Feb 1696/7 F260r eight unspecified   24 Apr 1697 F261r two freemen by patrimony

FREER, John   4 Aug 1701 G63v John Taylor bound to him   7 Apr 1707 G141r bookbinder; John Maystetter bound to him   7 Feb 1714/15 G225r Edward Ketelby bound to him

FREIND, Robert   26 Mar 1686 F54r elected waterman   4 Oct 1686 F64v waterman; discharged for 'scurrilous and abusive words and reflecting on S.C.'

FRENCH, Nathaniel   3 May 1708 G152v freed by patrimony

FRERE, John   5 Sep 1698 G14v Jonathan Maughan bound to him

FRITH, [   ]   1 Mar 1681/2 E146r mentioned in connection with Richard Janeway's illegally anonymous pamphlet

FRITH, Isaac, snr   1 Jul 1695 F228r Joseph Oakes, his apprentice, is freed   6 Jun 1698 G8v Charles Gilbert bound to him   2 Mar 1701/2 G67v his apprentice John Randall is freed   1 Jun 1702 G71v Isaac Frith is bound to him   6 Aug 1705 G122v his apprentice Charles Gilbert is freed   6 Oct 1712 G204v his son Isaac is freed

FRITH, Isaac, jnr   1 Jun 1702 G71v bound to Isaac Frith snr, 7 years   6 Oct 1712 G204v freed by his father

FRITH, John   13 Apr 1702 G70r bound to John Leake, 7 years

FRITH, Nathan 2 Apr 1705 G118v bound to John Clarke, 7 years

FROST, James 1 Mar 1702/3 G86r bound to Ann Lowndes, 7 years

FRY, John 5 Jul 1703 G92r bound to John Franks, 7 years

FRYER, William 6 Apr 1696 F242r his apprentice John Bennett is freed 2 Oct 1699 G31v his apprentice William Bennett is freed

FULFORD, Joshua 7 Jun 1697 F263r bound to Benjamin Browne 12 Jun 1704 G107v freed by Susanna Brudnel

FULL AND JUST ACCOUNT OF THE PRESENT STATE OF THE OTTOMAN EMPIRE – see PRESENT STATE OF ETHIOPIA

FULLER, John, snr – see following entry

FULLER, John, jnr 7 Sep 1713 G213v son of John; bound to Medrick Mead, 7 years

FURNES, John – see following entry

FURNES, Reginald 6 Jul 1713 G212v son of John; bound to William Holland, 7 years

GADBURY & TRIGG 6 Dec 1680 E105v Benjamin Harris complains he is abused in these almanacks; Maxwell (?) the printer ordered to omit abuses in next impression

GADBURY, Dr John 7 Nov 1687 F94v sends letter, (W) dated 4 October, re. his agreement with John Baker and Thomas Bassett over both 1688 almanack and Raven's; commends John Crosse to S.C. for charity 4 Oct 1703 G95v met by Master, Wardens and Capt. William Phillipps, but no agreement reached

See also ALMANACKS, EPHEMERIS/EPHEMERIDES

GADBURY, William 16 Jun 1684 F17v of Whitechapel and former apprentice to a bookseller in Wickham, Berks; submits himself to S.C. re. freedom

GAINES, [ ] 4 Dec 1682 E161r release from prosecution to be delivered to him as soon as he himself delivers a release to S.C. 1 Sep 1690 F142r his press, which he has previously sold to Dimock, is seized by S.C. because he printed Stock books illegally 5 Sep 1690 F142v Robert Stephens is paid £5 for discovering Gaines's press

GALE, Bartholomew 20 Dec 1704 G115v bound to Christopher Meggs, 7 years 3 Mar 1711/12 G197r freed by Christopher Meggs 6 Jan 1712/13 G206r John Curghey bound to him

GALEN/GALLEN, Thomas, GALEN'S/GALLEN'S ALMANACK – see ALMANACKS

GALLEY, Gammer 6 Nov 1682 E160r to clean the Hall 'as formerly' until next Christmas 5 Feb 1682/3 E163v to be paid 20s a quarter for cleaning 3 Jul 1686 F58r bedridden; her daughter is allowed to clean the hall

GARDEN 5 Sep 1681 E128v committee to negotiate with the committee for City lands re. rent arrears for ground in Hall garden adjoining City wall 3 Apr 1682 E151r 'House of Easement' to be built in Hall garden 8 May 1682 E152v committee to renew lease of a piece of ground called the Mount in S.C. garden from the City of London for as long as possible 2 Nov 1691 F161v to be kept free of boys playing 22 Dec 1691 F164r moved that the lease from City of walled ground in S.C. garden expires at Christmas 1695 and the lease is in the Warden's chest 20 Dec 1693 F197v great gates leading into garden to be repaired 4 May 1696 F242r palisadoes of enclosure lately made in garden to be painted 8 Jun 1696 F243r committee to consider lights made into garden 6 Jul 1696 F245v committee to negotiate with Oliver re. lights 3 Aug 1696 F246r Master tells Court he has been 'at pains' over lights in garden 7 Sep 1696 F248r Lord Mayor to resolve the difference between S.C., Oliver and Mills the surveyor on lights 5 Oct 1696 F250r waiting on Lord Mayor about lights into garden deferred   8 Apr 1700 G39r Nicholas Hooper, Robert Stephens and Benjamin Tooke to ensure that no boys play there nor pigeons be kept there   6 Sep 1703 G95r S.C.'s agreement with parish of St Martin's Ludgate for making a drain in   22 Jun 1705 G120v pales to be painted   26 Mar 1709 G163r proposal of churchwardens of St Martin's Ludgate to make a vault under   4 Apr 1709 G163v S.C. would agree to this proposal for 50 guineas   1 Oct 1711 G194v further consideration of proposal to make a vault under   12 Nov 1711 G195r grant for making vault sealed   5 Dec 1715 G235v request by churchwardens of St Martin's Ludgate to lay river water into pipe in

See also CITY OF LONDON, HALL

GARDEN OF CYRUS – see URN BURIAL

GARDNER, [   ]   1 Feb 1702/3 G85r denied permission to print a French almanack in English

GARRET, Mary   1 Oct 1683 F4r assigns Dr Edward Boughen's Catechism in Latin and English to Henry Mortlock

GARRETT – see GARRETT, John

GARRETT, Charles   12 Jun 1704 G107v freed by James Thomas

GARRETT/GARRET, John   3 Jan 1680/1 E106r to assist John Lilly, the Clerk, until 26 March   1681–1692 Clerk   26 Mar 1681 E108r elected Clerk. To take delivery of S.C. books from John Lilly in the afternoon of next Wednesday   30 Mar 1681 E108v takes delivery of and signs for S.C. books from John Lilly   1 Aug 1681 E117v to take delivery of all S.C. writings and papers from John Lilly   7 Apr 1684 F14r his continuing as Clerk submitted to Crown   12 Sep 1685 F44v committee to assess repairs for vault and passage, representing part of his property   7 Nov 1692 F181v thanks Court and asks leave to resign; Court appoints committee to oversee selection of next Clerk   21 Nov 1692 F182r renews request to resign on account of other commitments; granted   5 Dec 1692 F183r S.C.'s books held by him while Clerk to be returned   7 Oct 1695 F233r committee formed to consider whether his lease of a Stock house in Stationers' Court should be renewed   11 Nov 1695 F235r lease to be renewed for 21 years at £25 p.a. from expiration of present lease but without liberty to encroach on ground further than is already pallisaded (W) to repair tiling of house as a condition of renewal   3 Feb 1695/6 F238v to be abated a quarter's rent towards the charge of repairing his house upon his executing counterpart of lease   6 Apr 1696 F241v lease to him commencing at Midsummer 1698 is sealed   2 May 1698 G7r to deliver to Clerk the counterparts of leases and other writings in his custody belonging to S.C.   27 Mar 1699 G23r in nomination for Clerk   3 May 1708 G152v house where he dwelt to be leased to Whitledge

GARRETT, [   ] – see following entry

GARRETT, John   1 Jul 1700 G41v son of ? Garrett of Oxford, to be bound to Thomas Lewis   6 Jul 1700 G43r bound to Thomas Lewis, 7 years

GARRETT, William   7 Feb 1697/8 G3v turned over by James Dover; freed by Job Killington

GARTHWAITE, Mrs   3 May 1708 G152v deceased; her £80 share disposed of to John Walthoe

GATFEILD, John   7 May 1694 F203v servant of Giles Sussex; freed

GATHAM, William   7 Apr 1701 G58v William Henwood bound to him

GATHERNE, William   3 Feb 1706/7 G138r his apprentice Michael Lucas is freed

GAUDEN, Bishop John   3 Dec 1684 F27r late Bishop of Exeter; his 'Whole Duty of a Communicant' is assigned to Henry Rodes by Simon Neale

GAUTRUCHE, Pierre – see POETICAL HISTORIES

GAZETTE, THE   3 Apr 1693 F185v Roger L'Estrange's new translation of Josephus is advertised here   28 Oct 1697 F270r S.C. to advertise in the Gazette to warn people about counterfeit almanacks   8 Nov 1697 G1r advertisement put in for preventing the publishing and printing of counterfeit almanacks   6 Dec 1697 G2r advertisement to be put in to encourage detection of counterfeit stitched almanacks   29 Jul 1700 G43v advertisement in concerning sale of Norton's patents   8 Dec 1709 G172v advertisement to be placed in concerning Benjamin Harris's illegally publishing Partridge's almanack   4 Dec 1710 G185v advertisement to be placed in Gazette, Post-man and Post Boy concerning Benjamin Harris's illegal publishing of almanack

GEARY, [   ]   16 Oct 1705 G124v music-master; to provide a good trumpet and four other musicians   7 Nov 1709 G171v music-master; 20 shillings deducted from payment to him for music on Lord Mayor's Day on account of its poor quality

GELLEBRAND, [   ]   6 Mar 1681/2 E146v in the course of Samuel Mearne's and Robert Scott's disagreement over a warehouse, it is discovered that Gellebrand sublet it to Martin   2 May 1683 E169r S.C. warehouse formerly let to Gellebrand is let to Robert Scott

GELLEBRAND/GILLIBRAND/GELLIBRAND, [   ]   3 Feb 1700/1 G55r executor for his mother. Letter ordering whoever is elected to her Livery share to pay the money by Lady Day   4 Aug 1707 G144r committee to meet him to decide what to do concerning importing of S.C.'s books and copies   10 Oct 1707 G146r to have gratuity of 10 guineas for discovery of Bibles, psalters and psalms lately imported from Rotterdam

GELLEBRAND, Edward   24 Jun 1682 E154r cloathed

GELLEBRAND/GELLYBRAND, Henry   6 Jun 1698 G8v James Clarke bound to him

GELLEBRAND/GELLIBRAND/GELLYBRAND/GILLYBRAND, John   2 May 1681 E111r cloathed   7 Dec 1685 F47v prisoner; to be prosecuted for unlawfully printing a sheet almanack   1 Mar 1687/8 F97v expelled from Livery by order of Lord Mayor   4 Sep 1693 F191r wishes to assign Bishop [John] Wilkins's '[Mercury: or the] Swift and Secret Messenger' to Richard Baldwyn; Court question Gellebrand's title to it so assignment deferred   5 May 1701 G59v his son Samuel Gellebrand is freed by patrimony   20 Nov 1703 G98r examined concerning advertisement from the Royal Almanack. To be made party to bill in Chancery   22 Nov 1703 G98v no subpoena to be taken out against him for the present   6 Dec 1703 G99v subpoena in Chancery to be served against him to answer S.C.'s Bill   7 Feb 1703/4 G101v his answer to Bill in Chancery   10 Feb 1703/4 G102r his answer to Bill in Chancery read

GELLEBRAND/GILLIBRAND, Mrs   3 Feb 1700/1 G55r deceased; Robert Roberts elected to her Livery share

GELLEBRAND/GELLIBRAND, Obedience   2 Dec 1700 G54r Thomas Hall bound to her

GELLEBRAND/GELLIBRAND, Samuel   5 May 1701 G59v freed by John Gellebrand by patrimony

GELLIFLOWER – see GILLIFLOWER

GELLIBRAND, GELLYBRAND – see GELLEBRAND

GENERAL ASSEMBLY   27 Mar 1684 F12v of S.C. held to decide response to *quo warranto* proceedings

GENT, Thomas   2 Oct 1710 G184v bound to Edward Midwinter, 7 years

GENT – see GHENT

GEORGE, Richard   2 Aug 1697 F265v elected to William Hill's £40 share; being a Quaker he is not sworn in, but promises to keep the contents of the oath   6 Oct 1701 G65r Francis Pattison bound to him   12 Nov 1705 G125r Francis Pattison turned over from him to William Sheffield   3 Mar 1706/7 G139r his apprentice Francis Pattison turned over to Richard Smith

GEORGE, Thomas   4 Dec 1704 G113v deceased; his £40 share disposed of to Robert Whitledge

GERMA, Henrietta Maria   7 May 1716 G240r daughter of Suckling; bound to Thomas Parry, 7 years

GERMIN, Benjamin   8 May 1704 G106v bound to Samuel Heyrick, 7 years

GERRARD, John   6 Feb 1692/3 F184r cloathed   3 Feb 1695/6 F239r Court refuses to discharge him, John Sparkes and Thomas Penford from S.C. so they can take up freedoms of Ironmongers' Company   6 Nov 1699 G33r Charles Noy bound to him   26 Mar 1706 G130v elected First Renter Warden

GHENT/GENT, Patience   24 Mar 1701/2 G68r elected to Sarah Dickins' pension   22 Jun 1702 G76r elected to Sarah Dickins' pension   22 Mar 1715/16 G238r elected to Isaac Lane's pension. Millicent Shell is given her pension

GIBBON, Anthony – see following entry

GIBBON, Thomas   7 Jun 1714 G219v son of Anthony; bound to Henry Clements

GIBBONS, John – see following entry

GIBBONS, Samuel   3 Aug 1713 G213r son of John; bound to Owen Lloyd, 7 years

GIBBS, Robert   13 Apr 1698 G6v freed by patrimony

GIBBS, Thomas   4 Feb 1705/6 G127v freed by John Darby snr

GIBSON, [Edmund]   17 May 1695 F224r 450 of his 'Portus Julus' [i.e. William Somner, *Julii Caesaris Portus Iccius*, ed. & intro. Gibson] at 10d per book sent from Oxford; committee to take advice about selling them   7 Oct 1695 (W) committee seeking a reduction from Oxford in cost of books on last cargo from Ireland, including Gibson's

GIBSON, William   2 Aug 1708 G156v bound to Mary Spicer, alias Helder, 7 years   7 May 1716 G240r freed by Mary Spicer, alias Helder

GIFFORD, James   3 Aug 1696 F246v to be given a bond of £400 penalty for payment of £205 by 4 February 1697

GIFFORD, Robert   3 Mar 1706/7 G139r Felix Habberley is bound to him   4 Aug 1712 G202v Charles Beesley is bound to him

GILBERT, Charles   6 Jun 1698 G8v bound to Isaac Frith, 7 years   6 Aug 1705 G122v freed by Isaac Frith

GILBERT, James   1 Sep 1701 G64r bound to George Littlebury, 7 years   3 Feb 1706/7 G138r apprentice to George Littlebury, turned over to John Hartley

GILBERT, Joshua   3 Apr 1699 G24r bound to Thomas Teonge   6 May 1706 G131v freed by Thomas Teonge   7 Apr 1707 G141r barber; William Smith is bound to him   7 Feb 1708/9 G160v of Wapping; William Heall is bound to him   2 Oct 1710 G184v of Wapping, barber. Cloathed. Henry Hidutch is bound to him   16 Oct 1716 G244r his apprentice William Smith is freed

GILBERT, Stephen, snr – see following entry

GILBERT/GILBURT, Stephen, jnr   5 Feb 1693/4 F199r younger son of Stephen Gilbert, merchant-taylor of London; bound to Mary Head, widow, for 7 years   5 May

1701 G59v freed by Mary Head   5 Mar 1710/11 G188r printer of Bull and Mouth Street; David Walkwoods bound to him

GILBERT, William (I)   16 Jun 1684 F17v his former apprentice Charles Blount is freed

GILBERT, William (II)   6 Aug 1705 G122v bound to John Williams

GILBERTSON, [ ]   1 Jul 1700 G41v summoned to Court of Conscience. Pays quarterage arrears but is remitted 6 shillings in respect of S.C.'s debt to him

GILBERTSON, James   1 Mar 1679/80 E97r freed by John Williamson   29 May 1689 F118v pleads inability to be cloathed; Master and Wardens desired to inquire into this   10 Sep 1694 F212r excused cloathing

GILBURT – see GILBERT

GILES, Fletcher   26 Mar 1700 G38r bound to John Hartley, 7 years

GILES, William   2 Oct 1710 G184v bound to Robert Steele, 7 years

GILLIBRAND, GILLYBRAND – see GELLEBRAND

GILLIFLOWER/GELLIFLOWER, Matthew   6 Nov 1682 E16or request to be remitted legal costs incurred through being sued for his Livery fine, now paid, deferred until next Court   4 Dec 1682 E161r presents legal costs of 43s to Court; Court returns him 23s   4 Aug 1684 F22r with William Cadman and Thomas Harding, presents the grievances of 129 S.C. members; Master asks for instances   1 Sep 1684 F23r further to grievances, gives proof of various French booksellers dealing in scandalous books   7 May 1685 (W) confirmed as member of new Livery   3 Aug 1685 F42v John How confesses to printing a book in which he has part of the right   1 Feb 1685/6 F5or elected to John Amery's £40 share   6 Dec 1686 F68v complains of hawkers; committee appointed   1 Mar 1687/8 F97v expelled from Livery by order of Lord Mayor   11 Oct 1688 F108v restored to Livery   6 May 1689 F117v elected Assistant Renter Warden and summoned to next Court   29 May 1689 F118v fined for Assistant Renter Warden   7 Jul 1690 F139r elected to Benjamin Tooke's £80 share   2 Nov 1696 F252r elected to the late Thomas Cockerell's £160 share   1 Apr 1697 F26ov to ask booksellers, printers and paper manufacturers of Westminster and Temple Bar without for money towards Paper Act test case

GILLIFLOWER, Mrs   5 Oct 1702 G81r deceased; Awnsham Churchill elected to her £160 share in English Stock

GILLISON, William   3 Mar 1706/7 G139r bound to Ann Williams, 7 years

GILLYBRAND – see GELLEBRAND

GILPIN, John   5 Mar 1704/5 G117r bound to Job How, 7 years   1 Mar 1713/14 G216v freed by Job How

GILPIN, Richard   4 Mar 1705/6 G129r bound to William Haddon, 7 years

GLADMAN, Haworth   7 Aug 1710 G183r bound to John Hawkins   5 Jul 1714 G22ov apprentice to John Hawkins, turned over to Joseph Hazard

GLANVILL, Joseph   5 Dec 1681 E140v his 'Saducismus Triumphatus' is assigned to Samuel Lowndes by James Collins   7 May 1688 F101r his 'An Earnest Invitation to the ... Lord's Supper', 7th edn, assigned by John Baker to Joshua Phillipps and Joseph Watts

GLAZIER'S BILLS   4 Dec 1704 G113v to be paid by Joseph Collyer and Under Warden   3 Dec 1705 G125v to be paid by Under Warden   23 Jun 1709 G166r to be paid by Under Warden 'as cheap as he can'   6 Sep 1714 G221r to be paid by Master and Wardens   7 Feb 1714/15 G225r to be paid

GLENISTER, Thomas   6 May 1700 G39v bound to Thomas Cockerell, 7 years   3 Nov 1712 G205r freed by John Wyatt

GLOVER, [ ] 7 Nov 1698 G16r vintner; requests use of Hall on behalf of stewards of St Cecilia's Feast, offering £5 for the same. Permitted if they make good all spoil and damage 11 Nov 1700 G46v vintner; requests use of Hall on behalf of stewards of St Cecilia's Feast. 6 guineas to be paid and damages to be made good

GODBID/GODBIDD, Ann 7 May 1683 E169v surrenders her £80 share to Court requesting them to elect John Playford, her partner who has agreed to pay her; deferred 4 Jun 1683 E170v disposal of her yeomanry share deferred 2 Jul 1683 F2r deceased; her £80 share disposed of to John Playford jnr

GODBID, William 1 Mar 1679/80 E97r frees John Johnson

GODDEN, John 26 Jun 1682 E154v bond to S.C. for £400 penalty to pay £200 at 5% sealed; to repay a bond for the same amount due to Trench 7 May 1683 E169v £200 bond to him cancelled; bond for same amount entered into with Sir Richard Fisher to pay him off

GODMAN, Deborah 22 Mar 1715/16 G238r elected to Martha Widows' pension. Replaced by Elizabeth Norton

GODOLPHIN, John – see VIEW OF THE ADMIRAL JURISDICTION

GODWIN, Mary 22 Jun 1697 F263v elected to the pension of Andrew Rothwell, deceased 22 Jun 1702 G76r elected to Daniel Barber's pension. Replaced by Priscilla Mosse

GOFFE, Thomas 7 Feb 1708/9 G160v bound to Alice Mayos, 7 years 5 Mar 1715/16 G237v freed by Alice Mayos

GOLDING, Ann 22 Dec 1681 E141v deceased; Eleanor Golding given her 10s pension

GOLDING, Eleanor 22 Dec 1681 E141v given a 10s pension instead of a 5s one in place of Ann Golding, deceased 21 Mar 1694/5 F219r deceased; Elizabeth Wright elected to her pension

GOLDSMITHS' COMPANY 7 Mar 1697/8 G4v committee to deal with them concerning lights 4 Jul 1698 G10v committee revived to consider lights of houses belonging to Goldsmiths 7 Oct 1698 G15r committee to meet Master and Wardens of the Goldsmiths' Company re. their lights looking into S.C.'s ground and adjoining the Hall

GOODCHILD, John 5 Aug 1700 G44r bound to James Dover, 7 years

GOODDEN, [ ] 5 Mar 1687/8 F99r counsellor at law; appears on behalf of Samuel Hoyle, who claims right to an £80 share which was disposed of to Richard Simpson on 7 June 1686

GOODMAN, John 26 Mar 1696 F241r takes over the pension of Francis Herne

GOODWIN, James 3 Feb 1695/6 F239r servant to William Rayment; freed

GOODWIN/GOODWYN, Timothy 1 Mar 1685/6 F51r elected to cloathing 3 May 1686 F55r has refused to pay Livery fine of £20 and disobeyed summons; resolved that he should be prosecuted (W) letter from him saying he does not wish to be a member of Livery 7 Jun 1686 F57r Court refuse his request to be discharged from the Livery 27 Mar 1693 F185v elected Assistant Renter Warden and summoned 3 Apr 1693 F185v fined for Assistant Renter Warden 8 Apr 1695 F220v competes unsuccessfully for Daniel Browne's £40 share; elected to James Taylor's £40 share 6 May 1695 F222v takes partner's oath 2 Mar 1695/6 F240r elected Stock-keeper for Yeomanry with Benjamin Motte 4 May 1696 F242v takes Stock-keeper's oath 1 Mar 1698/9 G21r elected Stock-keeper for Yeomanry 3 Feb 1700/1 G55r elected to Robert Roberts'

£80 share. His £40 share disposed of to Benjamin Tooke jnr   8 Nov 1703 G97r his apprentice Edward Valentine is freed   1 Mar 1706/7 G138v and John Walthoe to be paid £30 towards fees and charges of the copyright bill due to Jodrell   1 Sep 1707 G145r in unsuccessful competition for Ann Williams' £160 share   1 Mar 1707/8 G149v and John Walthoe to bring to next Court an account of the subscriptions relating to the copyright act   25 Mar 1708 G150r elected Assistant   12 Apr 1708 G151v takes oath of Assistant   7 Jun 1708 G153r added to committee concerning Benjamin Harris's arrears   6 Feb 1709/10 G175r candidate for Mrs Bennett's £160 share but resigns his pretensions   3 Jul 1710 G182r auditor of late Master and Wardens' accounts   7 May 1711 G190r elected to Capt. Samuel Roycroft's £160 share. His £80 share disposed of to Daniel Midwinter   5 Jul 1712 G201r competes unsuccessfully for Under Warden   7 Jul 1712 G201v auditor of late Master and Wardens' accounts   24 Apr 1713 G209r signatory to S.C.'s notes to Thomas Guy   4 Jul 1713 G211r fined for two years for Under Warden and two years for Upper Warden   3 May 1714 G218v signed note to Guy   2 Jul 1716 G241v fined for Master. Pays fine to Warden

GOREING, Elizabeth   20 Dec 1700 G54r deceased; Jane Bandbridge given her pension

GOREING, Thomas   26 Mar 1680 E98r elected Renter Warden

GORING, [ ]   27 Mar 1697 F260r voted to the pension of Dorothy Lambert, deceased

GORING, Lovet   26 Mar 1697 F258v competes unsuccessfully to replace Christopher Grandorge as Clerk

GORSUCH, Myles   12 Jun 1704 G107v bound to Edward Head, 7 years

GOSLING – see GOSTLING

GOSLYN, Robert   5 Jun 1710 G180r of Fleet Street; summoned to take cloathing

GOSTLIN, Robert   3 Aug 1713 G213r Thomas Worrall bound to him

GOSLING/GOSTLING, Robert   7 Aug 1699 G29r bound to Samuel Keeble, 7 years   4 Nov 1706 G136r freed by Samuel Keeble   3 Jul 1710 G182r cloathed

GOULSTON, Richard   13 Jun 1715 G229v son of Robert; bound to William Reason, 7 years

GOULSTON, Robert – see preceding entry

GOWER, William, snr – see following entry

GOWER, William, jnr   7 Jul 1712 G201v son of William; bound to John Buchanan, 7 years

GRADUS AD PARNASSUM   1 Dec 1701 G65v Benjamin Tooke's moiety in this to be purchased by S.C. and assigned in trust for the English Stock   9 Feb 1701/2 G66v debate about whether Tooke should have more money for his moiety. Thomas Cockerell's moiety also purchased by S.C.   26 Mar 1702 G69v copy of Tooke's instrument for assigning to S.C. his interest in the moiety

GRAFTON, George   5 Aug 1689 F122r excused cloathing on plea of 'juniorship and inability'   4 Nov 1689 F126v cloathed   5 Apr 1703 G88r his apprentice Peter Tanner is freed   26 Mar 1709 G163r elected First Renter Warden   6 Jun 1709 G165v Renter Warden, receives charge from Warden   4 Oct 1714 G222v competes unsuccessfully for John Heptingstall's £80 share   7 Feb 1714/15 G224v competes unsuccessfully for Martin Boddington's £80 share. Elected to the late Mary Jones's £80 share. His £40 share disposed of to James Holland

GRAFTON, William   5 Sep 1687 F88r elected to William Fisher's £40 share

GRAHAM, Richard   7 Apr 1684 F14r (W) letter from Richard Graham and Burton recommending Capt. William Phillipps as an Assistant loyal to the Crown

GRAINGER, John, snr – see following entry

GRAINGER, John, jnr   1 Dec 1712 G205v son of John; bound to William Pearson, 7 years

GRAMMARS   7 Sep 1691 F159v committee to agree with Roger Norton on number of grammars to be printed at Cambridge   1 Feb 1691/2 F164v Norton agrees to pay S.C. £30 p.a. for not printing his grammar at Oxford, as he did to Peter Parker and Thomas Guy   7 Mar 1691/2 F166v Mrs Harris promises to give Norton a full account of her printing his Accidence and Grammar   18 Sep 1693 F191v S.C. and agents not to comprint on [William] Camden's Greek Grammar, [William] Lilly's Grammar, Accidence, construing book and other items at Oxford. S.C. to print only 3000 p.a. of Lilly's Grammar at Cambridge, the number to which the University printer is limited   12 Nov 1694 F214v Bennett and Mrs Redmaine dispute title to Dr Richard Busby's 'Rudimentum Grammatica' [i.e. *Rudimentum Grammaticae Graeco-Latinae Metricum* or *Rudimentum Grammaticae Latinae Metricum*?] and 'Rudimentum Anglo-Latinum' [i.e. *Rudimentum Anglo-Latinum Grammaticae*]; consideration deferred   3 Dec 1694 F215v Busby's works to be entered to Bennett with a salvo   4 Nov 1706 G136r matter of Norton's printing to be left to Master, Wardens and Stock-keepers   6 Oct 1707 G145v Master, Wardens and Stock-keepers to dispose of impression of   7 Jun 1708 G153r Master, Wardens and Stock-keepers to settle matter of Norton's printing grammar at Oxford and Cambridge

GRANDORGE, Christopher   1692–1696 Clerk   21 Nov 1692 F182r chosen to be Clerk until 26 March 1692/3; George Tokefeild also in competition   5 Dec 1692 F183r sworn in as Clerk   27 Mar 1693 F185v re-elected Clerk   6 Jul 1696 F245v Nicholas Hooper to draw up Court minutes which Grandorge has failed to enter. Benjamin Tooke officiates as Clerk during Grandorge's illness and receives fees for Grandorge   5 Oct 1696 F250v Nicholas Hooper to enter all apprentices and Court orders that Grandorge has neglected   1 Mar 1696/7 F255r orders of Court not entered by him are passed and ordered to be entered   9 Mar 1696/7 F257r Clerk succeeding Grandorge to pay him £24 p.a.   26 Mar 1697 F258v uncle tells Court that Grandorge is still ill, recommends Oliver Martin to take over and asks for maintenance. Court say that their answer was given on 9 Mar   7 Jun 1697 F262v committee to inspect and settle his accounts   5 Jul 1697 F264v £10 due to Hooper to be deducted from S.C.'s annual salary to him   2 Aug 1697 F265v draws £30 from the Under Warden to which he is not entitled; ordered that two other debts be first paid out of his salary   4 Oct 1697 F268r money he owes Nicholas Hooper to be deducted from his salary. Writes to S.C.; ordered that his accounts should be made up and any money still due to him should be paid   26 Mar 1698 G5r competes unsuccessfully for Clerk   6 Jun 1698 G8r desires a sum of money from S.C. Required first to deliver to Master any writings in his custody belonging to S.C.   4 Sep 1699 G30r letter to Tooke read in Court. Warden Samuel Heyrick to demand writings in his custody belonging to S.C. in return for what money he thinks proper   2 Oct 1699 G31r 12s 6d given to him. Writings belonging to S.C. brought from him into Court and put into the chest. Committee appointed to inspect his accounts   26 Mar 1702 G68v competes unsuccessfully for Clerk   27 Mar 1704 G105r competes unsuccessfully for Clerk

GRANT, Zachary   6 Mar 1681/2 E148r husband of Ann Eversden; his wife's bond of £20 inherited from her father plus interest is repaid to him

GRANTHAM, Gater   9 Feb 1712/13 G206v freed by patrimony

GRANTHAM, John   6 Aug 1688 F106r discovered when he brings his apprentice Richard Fielding to be freed that he was bound at a scriveners'; fine of £5 remitted   6 Jul 1702 G78r Francis Woolly bound to him   8 May 1704 G106v Benjamin Shelley turned over to him from William Horton   9 Feb 1707/8 G149r printer, of Bartholomew Close; William Wells is bound to him   3 Oct 1709 G171r his apprentice John Darker is freed   2 Nov 1713 G214v his apprentice William Wells is turned over to Thomas Hodgkins   7 Feb 1714/15 G225r Marmaduke Smith is bound to him

GRANTUM, John   1 Dec 1707 G147v his apprentice Samuel Brimlicombe is freed

GRAVES, Widow   5 Sep 1681 E131r paid 10s charity

GRAVES, William   9 Feb 1712/13 G206v son of John; bound to William Taylor, 7 years

GRAY, David   12 Nov 1694 F215r freed by John Darby

GRAY, James (I)   3 Dec 1694 F216r elected to the late Elizabeth Peirson's pension   26 Mar 1701 G57v deceased; Thomas Hodgkinson given his pension

GRAY, James (II)   1 Aug 1709 G169v freed by patrimony

GRAY, John   4 Dec 1693 F197r butcher of Leigh Hall, Bucks; his son William is bound to Abel Rockall

GRAY, William   4 Dec 1693 F197r son of John Gray; bound to Abel Rockall for 7 years   7 Jul 1701 G62r freed by Abel Rockall and Robert Whitlidge   13 Apr 1702 G70r Robert Mawson is bound to him   6 Oct 1707 G145v bookseller; Thomas Ashfield is bound to him   2 May 1709 G165r his apprentice Robert Mawson is freed   6 Feb 1715/16 G236r Robert Viney is bound to him

GREAVES, Thomas   6 Mar 1709/10 G176v bound to John Bennett, 7 years

GREEK TESTAMENT   18 Mar 1686/7 F79v among books in catalogue annexed to Oxford agreement   5 Jun 1699 G25r Court considers whether to print at Cambridge; Awnsham Churchill is also printing a Greek testament

GREEN, Elizabeth   3 Dec 1716 G245r bond from S.C. of £600 for payment of £307 10s to her sealed

GREEN, George   4 Apr 1709 G164r bound to Christopher Norris, 7 years

GREEN, John   9 Feb 1701/2 G67r freed by Samuel Wallsall   2 May 1709 G165r of Butchers' Row; Samuel Beaver bound to him

GREEN, Mary   3 Dec 1716 G245r bond from S.C. of £600 for payment of £307 10s to her sealed

GREEN, Richard   6 May 1700 G39v bound to John Penn, 7 years

GREEN, Sarah   3 Dec 1716 G245r bond from S.C. of £800 for payment of £410 to her sealed

GREEN, Thomas   7 Apr 1712 G199r his son William is bound to Eliza Milbourne, 7 years

GREEN, William (I), snr – see following entry

GREEN, William (II), jnr   6 Nov 1710 G185r son of William; bound to John Beresford

GREEN, William (III)   7 Apr 1712 G199r son of Thomas; bound to Eliza Milbourne, 7 years

See also GREENE

GREENAWAY, Richard   3 Apr 1699 G24r freed by Matthew Wootton

GREENE, Henry   7 Aug 1704 G111r freed

GREENE, Mary   26 Mar 1684 F11r elected into the 5s pension of Ann Dewell, she having lately married

GREENE, Widow   7 Aug 1682 E156r deceased; Benjamin Tooke elected to her £40 share

See also GREEN

GREENHALGH, Jonathan   9 Apr 1711 G189v bound to William Downing, 7 years

GREENHALGH, Robert   4 Jul 1715 G231r son of William; bound to William Downing, 7 years

GREENHALGH, William – see preceding entry

GREENHILL, Richard   7 Dec 1702 G83v bound to Humphrey Jackson, 7 years   2 Oct 1710 G184v freed by Humphrey Jackson

GREENUP, Richard   2 May 1681 E111v paid 40s charity

GREENWOOD, Jonathan   1 Mar 1679/80 E97r freed by Cockerell

GREEP, Henry   7 May 1705 G120r bound to Richard Janeway, 7 years   1 Dec 1707 G147v apprentice of Richard Janeway, turned over to Joseph Downing

GREGORY, Ambrose   6 May 1695 F223v of Southwark, gentleman, deceased; his son Moses is bound to Thomas Norris

GREGORY, Daniel   5 Aug 1689 F122r excused cloathing on plea of 'juniorship and inability'   3 Oct 1692 F180v petition for £100 loan, proposing surety, referred to next Court   5 Dec 1692 F183r petition for £100 loan from Norton's bequest referred to committee   13 Mar 1692/3 F185r petition rejected

GREGORY, Moses   6 May 1695 F223v son of the late Ambrose Gregory; bound to Thomas Norris   6 Jul 1702 G78r freed by Thomas Norris

GRENEWELL, Lewis   26 Mar 1697 F258v competes unsuccessfully to replace Christopher Grandorge as Clerk

GRETTON, Charles   28 Sep 1702 G80v citizen and clockmaker of London; bond from S.C. to him of £600 sealed   6 Nov 1710 G185r to be allowed 6% p.a. on his bond from S.C. of £200

GRETTON, Dorothy   5 Oct 1713 G213v bond to her from S.C. for £200 penalty to pay £103 on 6 April sealed   7 Jun 1714 G219v bond to her from S.C. of £400 penalty to pay £205 on 8 December sealed

GREVILL, Walter   19 Jan 1710/11 G186v bound to Benjamin Bound, 7 years

GREY, James   27 Sep 1695 F232v elected to the late Johanna Lee's pension

GREY, Samuel   5 Aug 1706 G134r freed by patrimony

GRIEVE, James   8 Nov 1703 G97r bound to John Buchanan, 7 years

GRIFFEN, Benjamin   3 Feb 1679/80 E96v to be paid his mother's dividend of £10

GRIFFEN, Mrs   19 Dec 1679 E96r on account of her death, her English Stock dividend to remain in Treasurer's hands   3 Feb 1679/80 E96v Capt. William Phillipps elected to her £80 share

See also GRIFFIN

GRIFFIN, Bennett/Benedict (also GRIFFIN, Garden)   11 Oct 1680 E104v elected to a £40 share, a moiety of Henry Twyford's £80 share   7 May 1685 (W) confirmed as member of new Livery   6 Jul 1685 F40v elected Assistant Renter Warden in place of John Richardson   3 Aug 1685 F42v elected First Renter Warden in place of John Overton   2 Nov 1685 F45v elected to Capt. William Phillipps's £80 share   11 Oct

1686 F66r to be paid £37 18s 6d from English Stock 4 Sep 1688 F107r to be summoned to answer complaints of free workmen printers that he has taken supernumerary apprentices 11 Oct 1688 F108v restored to Livery 1 Mar 1688/9 F113v elected Stock-keeper for Livery with Richard Tonson 6 May 1689 F117r desires to become an Assistant and is told that the Table is full at present 2 Dec 1689 F127v his renewed claim to a place on the Court by right of seniority is rejected 9 Feb 1690/1 F148v complains that John Dunton has printed 'The Magpie' in the name of B. Griffits 7 May 1694 F203v elected Assistant 4 Jun 1694 F208r sworn in as Assistant 3 Dec 1694 F215v elected to Dorman Newman's £160 share, fallen vacant because of Newman's bankruptcy 20 Dec 1694 F216r sworn into his £160 share 4 Mar 1694/5 F218r is added to drain committee 3 Feb 1695/6 F238v has two assignments to him registered: 'Peirson upon the Holy Creed' [i.e. Bishop John Pearson, *An Exposition of the Creed*] and [Nicholas] Caussin, 'Holy Court' 3 Jul 1697 F263v competes unsuccessfully for Under Warden 5 Jul 1697 F264v elected Under Warden 13 Apr 1698 G6r added to Oxford committee. Request that a committee be set up for auditing Master and Wardens' accounts granted 2 May 1698 G7v Thomas Wood is bound to him 4 Jul 1698 G10v to be added to committee concerning Goldsmiths' Company lights 10 Jan 1698/9 G18v requests that Richard Chiswell should have £40 dividend due to Mrs Royston as he has provided for her 3 Jul 1699 G26v auditor of Master and Wardens' accounts 4 Dec 1699 G34r complaint about price and rate of printing [Charles] Hoole's 'Sententiae'. Allowed 36 shillings by Treasurer 6 May 1700 G39v reports from committee who viewed Mrs Davis' house 3 Jun 1700 G40v Henry Lovell is bound to him 6 Jul 1700 G43r fined for second year of Under Warden to preserve seniority

GRIFFIN, Christian 9 Feb 1707/8 G149r widow; her apprentice Thomas Wood is freed 7 Apr 1712 G199r deceased; her £160 share disposed of to John Lawrence

GRIFFIN, Garden: alternative to GRIFFIN, Bennett

GRIFFIN, John 6 May 1695 F223v son of William; bound to Robert Williams

GRIFFIN, Philip 6 Jul 1695 F229v among those chosen to audit Warden's accounts

GRIFFIN, Richard 2 Apr 1705 G118v his apprentice John Bradford freed

GRIFFIN, Sarah 23 Mar 1679/80 E98r frees Edward Curtice 9 Feb 1712/13 G206r widow; bond from S.C. of £400 penalty to pay £206 on 10 August 6 Sep 1714 G221v to be notified that S.C. will only pay 5% on her £200 bond instead of 6% as a consequence of the Act of Parliament

GRIFFIN, William 6 May 1695 F223v victualler of St Sepulchre's; his son John is bound to Robert Williams

See also GRIFFEN

GRIFFITH, David 8 Nov 1703 G97r bound to Edmund Powell, 7 years 10 Sep 1711 G194r son of Isaac; bound to John Darby, 7 years

GRIFFITH, Isaac – see preceding entry

GRIFFITH, John 10 Sep 1711 G194r son of Thomas; bound to Thomas Bradyll, 7 years

GRIFFITH, Thomas – see preceding entry

GRIFFITS, B. & W. (pseud.) – see DUNTON, John

GRIGG, John 3 Jul 1704 G110r bound to Richard Bruges, 7 years

GRIMSTON, John 1 Apr 1717 G249v son of William; bound to Samuel Palmer, 7 years

GRIMSTON, William – see preceding entry

GRIST, Charles   6 Dec 1697 G2r bound to John Ford

GROUND – see LAND, GARDEN

GROVE, Kingsmill   4 Sep 1699 G30v bound to John Walthoe, 7 years

GROVER, Elizabeth   4 Dec 1710 G186r widow of Aldersgate Street, letter-founder; William Todd bound to her   5 May 1712 G199v Francis Atkinson and William Grover bound to her   12 Nov 1716 G244v John Owen bound to her

GROVER, John   8 Jun 1696 F243r Edward Bell, his apprentice, is freed

GROVER, Thomas   28 Mar 1679/80 E98v freed by Andrew Crook   6 Sep 1697 F267r Robert Michell is bound to him   9 Sep 1700 G45r pays quarterage for 3 years to Renter Warden. His apprentice John Philpot is freed   7 Jul 1701 G62r his apprentice Robert Middlewright is freed   4 Oct 1703 G96r Edward Warboyse is bound to him   6 May 1706 G131v Thomas Ashfield is bound to him   3 Feb 1706/7 G138r his apprentice Robert Michell is freed   7 Feb 1708/9 G160v William Walldrom is bound to him   5 May 1712 G199v his son William is bound to Elizabeth Grover, 7 years

GROVER, William   5 May 1712 G199v son of Thomas; bound to Elizabeth Grover, 7 years

GRUBB, Edward   5 Sep 1698 G14v bound to Charles Spicer alias Helder

GRUMBELL, John   6 Apr 1696 F242r servant to John Hayes; freed

GRYMES, Robert   22 Jun 1698 G9v and his wife. General release from the S.C. read and sealed

GUIDE TO A PHYSICIAN – see BONET, Théophile

GUIDE TO ETERNITY [by Giovanni Bona, trans. Roger L'Estrange]   1 Aug 1687 F87r assigned by Roger L'Estrange to Richard Bentley, Jacob Tonson and Joseph Hindmarsh

GUIDEE, Philip, snr – see following entry

GUIDEE, Philip, jnr   4 Feb 1694/5 F217r son of Philip Guidee, doctor in physic of London; bound to Oliver Elliston

GUILDHALL   22 May 1685 F37v book-dealing members of other companies to be received into S.C. there next Tuesday

GUILLAM, [   ] – see GWILLAM

GUINEAS   11 Nov 1695 F235v Benjamin Tooke concerned that rate may fall from 30 shillings per guinea

GULIVER, Josiah   6 Aug 1705 G122v bound to John Harding

GUMBLEY – see GUNBY

GUNBY/GUMBLEY, Elizabeth   5 May 1712 G199v her apprentice William Etheridge is freed

GUNBY, William   4 Sep 1699 G30v John Fletcher is bound to him   4 Dec 1704 G114r William Etheridge is bound to him

GUNN, Isaac   7 Oct 1698 G15r freed by William Crosse   2 Dec 1700 G54r Thomas Sanders is bound to him   5 Jul 1703 G92r Hugh Roberts is bound to him

GUNNEY, Richard   5 Oct 1702 G81v freed by William Richardson

GUNNING, Richard   5 Sep 1715 G232v William Harper is bound to him

GUY, John (I)   26 Oct 1702 G82v bookseller. Surety for Joseph Collyer

GUY, John (II – possibly to be identified with I) – see following entry

GUY, John Hudson   5 Sep 1715 G232v son of John; bound to Richard Harris, 7 years

GUY, Thomas   5 Jul 1686 F60v Moses Pitt assigns 'Poetical Histories' to Thomas Guy   17 Oct 1687 F92v fined for Assistant Renter Warden   1 Mar 1687/8 F97v expelled from Livery by order of Lord Mayor   11 Oct 1688 F108v restored to Livery   7 May 1694 F203v his apprentice Thomas Varnam is freed   3 Dec 1694 F215v his apprentice Samuel Burrowes is freed   7 Oct 1695 F233v elected an Assistant   20 Oct 1699 G32r committee to deal with him and Peter Parker   6 Sep 1703 G94v John Osborne is bound to him   7 Feb 1703/4 G101v his apprentice Edmund Parker is freed   12 Apr 1708 G151v takes oath of Assistant   3 Jul 1708 G154r voted that he should stand as a candidate for Master   4 Jul 1709 G167v Jeremiah Batley is bound to him   1 Oct 1711 G194v to lend S.C. £100 at 6%   3 Mar 1711/12 G197r Jeremiah Batley turned over from him to Thomas Varnam   1 Sep 1712 G203r his apprentice John Osburn is freed   3 Nov 1712 G205r bond from S.C. to him of £2000 penalty to pay £1120 is sealed and delivered to Joseph Collyer who is to receive the money from Guy   1 Dec 1712 G205r bond to him from S.C. of £1200 penalty to pay £636 sealed and delivered to Collyer who is to receive the money from Guy. Money taken up to deliver the like sum due to Mrs Mason on bond   24 Apr 1713 G209r willing to advance £800 to pay printers, having notes of £50 each drawn on Collyer signed by 16 members of the Table   3 May 1714 G218v S.C. not able to repay £800 advanced by him to pay printers so he accepts new notes in exchange. Ten notes signed (there being no more members of the Table present)   5 Mar 1715/16 G237v 6 notes drawn on Collyer for payment of £50 each to Thomas Guy dated 7 February, signed by members of the Table   6 May 1717 G250r intention of being a charitable benefactor to the S.C. and its poor. Thomas Varnam, his heir at law, therefore elected Assistant

See also PARKER (Peter) and GUY (Thomas)

GWILLAM, GUILLAM – see GWILLIM

GWILLIM/GWILLAM/GUILLAM/GWILLIUM, [ ] 4 Mar 1705/6 G129r bookseller of Bishopsgate Street; evidence that he sold counterfeit copies of '[First Book for Children, or] The Complete Schoolmistress' at Bristol Fair   26 Mar 1706 G130v committee to consider matter of counterfeit 'Complete Schoolmistress' sold by him

See also GWILLIM, John

GWILLIM/GWILLYM, John   6 Oct 1707 G145v to be proceeded against in Chancery for printing and selling counterfeit psalms and almanacks   1 Dec 1707 G147r committee to consider his answer to the S.C.'s Bill in Chancery   4 Dec 1710 G185v to be served with a copy of the writ of execution against Benjamin Harris

GWILLIM, Philip   2 Jun 1712 G200v John Davis bound to him

GWILLIUM, GWILLYM – see GWILLIM

HABBERLEY, Felix   3 Mar 1706/7 G139r bound to Robert Gifford, 7 years

HABERDASHERS   14 Mar 1686/7 F78v Archbishop of Canterbury and Bishop of London to be entreated for leave to enter caveats against licensing haberdashers and foreigners to sell books

HABERDASHERS' COMPANY   16 Jun 1684 F17v Parteridge of the Haberdashers' declares himself willing to be translated to S.C.   12 Apr 1692 F169r Capt. John Mould, their Clerk, certifies that Richard Chiswell was freed by them on 3 Oct 1662 and cloathed in 1672   2 Mar 1695/6 F239v William Baker, translated from the Haberdashers', retains his seniority in S.C. livery

HACKETT, Gustavus, snr – see following entry

HACKETT, Gustavus, jnr   7 Apr 1712 G199r son of Gustavus; bound to St John Baker, 7 years

HADDOCK, Anne   22 Dec 1685 F49v admitted into quarterly charity instead of Margaret Boulter   4 Oct 1686 F64v elected to the late Elizabeth Wildgoose's 40s pension   22 Jun 1698 G9r deceased; Nathaniel Ponder elected to her pension

HADDOCK, Mary   25 Mar 1703 G86v elected to Beatrice Turner's pension

HADDOCKS, Edward – see MADDOC, Edward

HADDON, [ ]   3 Nov 1707 G146v mathematical instrument maker. Excused cloathing for 12 months. Edmund Male is bound to him

HADDON, John   2 May 1715 G228v son of William, is bound to his father, 7 years

HADDON, William   1 Oct 1694 F213v Joseph Bush is bound to him   6 Nov 1699 G33r Thomas White is bound to him   8 Apr 1700 G39r John Morgan is bound to him   2 Mar 1701/2 G67v his apprentice Joseph Bush is freed   4 Mar 1705/6 G129r Richard Gilpin is bound to him   7 Jul 1707 G143v his apprentice Thomas White is freed   6 Sep 1714 G221v Richard Bates is bound to him   2 May 1715 G228v his son John is bound to him

HADDUCK, Thomas   5 Dec 1709 G172r bound to Andrew Parker, 7 years

HADSON, Samuel   6 Oct 1701 G65r freed by William Parsons (turnover)

HALE, Robert   3 May 1708 G152v freed by William Yorke

HALES, George   12 Nov 1711 G195r son of Thomas, is bound to Ralph Arnold, 7 years

HALES, Thomas – see preceding entry

HALEY, Thomas   22 Sep 1680 E104r cloathed

HALFORD, John, snr – see following entry

HALFORD, John, jnr   6 Aug 1716 G242v son of John, is bound to John Leake, 7 years

HALL   25 Aug 1680 E103v committee set up re. building on 'Void Ground between the Hall and Mrs Maxwells' and to negotiate with workmen, at charge of Stock   26 May 1681 E112r committee decide on enlargement of parlour in new building on east side of Hall; staircase for first and second storeys removed to north-east corner   5 Sep 1681 E129r Francis Tyton, Thomas Vere, Thomas Newcomb and Henry Herringman seal an indenture of demise of Hall and tenements for Sir Joseph Seamour   7 Nov 1681 E137r pavier to be paid for paving courtyard before Hall and Treasurer's house   4 Sep 1682 E157r Hall facade and doorway leading into passage to be repaired   7 Sep 1685 F44r no Warden henceforth to lay out more than 40s on Hall repairs without leave or Court order   12 Sep 1685 F44v Clerk to have the letting of the Hall for feasts and funerals   5 Oct 1685 F45r irons to be fixed in roof 'in apt places for the hanging branches of candlesticks'   4 Jul 1687 F86r Warden to buy 2 dozen turkey-work chairs for the 'Common Dining Parlour'   1 Aug 1687 F86v Clerk to draft conveyance from surviving feoffees to Court for Hall, ground, and houses in Stationers' Court, Ave Maria Lane and Amen Corner   5 Sep 1687 F88r committee to peruse draft conveyance of   6 Aug 1688 F105r a nonconformist minister is refused permission to rent the Hall as a meeting-place for his congregation   1 Jul 1689 F120v former conveyance to be cancelled and new one drawn up covering all current Assistants. Surviving feoffees of old agreement to execute the same and be indemnified   5 Aug 1689 F122v conveyance from surviving feoffees to present Assistants is sealed   3 Feb 1689/90 F129r motion for a 'Projection pediment or shell' made over the Hall entrance and alteration of stone steps deferred   3 Mar 1689/90 F130v benefactors' list to be written in gold in wainscot panelling towards upper end of Hall   11 Apr 1690 F134r workmen to give estimate for the projected stone steps and penthouse on the front of the Hall   1 Dec 1690 F146v proposal to convert existing kitchen into warehouses bringing in ca. £30 p.a. and to build new kitchen in void ground and bring in twice the current 40s fee for feasts. Committee appointed   9 Feb 1690/1 F148r Samuel Heyrick allowed to print in kitchen. Kitchen business adjourned until next Court   2 Mar 1690/1 F149v kitchen committee asked to negotiate cost with workmen and to consider alterations to Court rooms and provision of butteries   6 Jul 1691 F158r brick wall to be erected dividing back-yard from fore-yard to prevent boys coming in and breaking the windows   3 Aug 1691 F158v Master's feast postponed because of wainscoting taking place in Court Room   2 Nov 1691 F161v new keys to be made for doors going into kitchen entry   7 Dec 1691 F162r John Shorter has paid 15s for 'the types and figures of Christ in a lackered [i.e. lacquered] frame', a present to be hung in the Court room. Door leading from Treasurer's house into S.C. dining room to be filled up   2 May 1692 F170v Capt. John Williams allowed to continue using buttery under Hall as a warehouse on payment of 50s per year   3 Apr 1693 F186r Clerk's books to be kept in room behind the Court room   12 Jun 1693 F188v Smith's bill for £2 1s 1d and two carpenters' bills amounting to £13 14s for work done on the Hall to be paid   6 Nov 1693 F194r Hall not to be let for St Cecilia's Day for under £5; scaffolding, tables, couches and wainscot all considered   15 Mar 1693/4 F201r to be let to Cheshire stewards and garden. Piece of wood with spikes to be fastened on wall coving on left of steps going up to Hall   20 Dec 1694 F216r door between Hall and Treasurer's house to be temporarily opened for the more convenient carrying of dividends out of the Hall   3 Jun 1695 F224v committee to investigate preventing of S.C.'s right by stopping up lights looking into ground behind Hall and elsewhere   4 May 1696 F242r roof on west side to be repaired and covered with Dutch tile. Palisadoes to be painted   3 Aug 1696 F246v Warden to pay for the pantiler   5 Oct 1696 F251r carpenter's bill of £7 18s 7d and bricklayer's bill of £7 11s to be paid after adjustment by Warden and John Simms   7 Feb 1697/8 G3r recently hired for a ball at a cost of £5; Master and Wardens to consider necessary repairs, following damage caused by scaffolding. Agreed that henceforth not to be let when scaffolding required   2 May 1698 G7r Charles Broome and his partners to have the use of it for drawing their lottery of books   7 Nov 1698 G16r to be used for the St Cecilia's Day Feast on payment of £5   19 Jan 1698/9 G18r to be used for lottery for the Mine Adventure   27 Mar 1699 G23r to be let for dancing   3 Apr 1699 G24r Master and Wardens to be responsible for tiling of side of   3 Jul 1699 G27r used for the Mine Adventure and drawing a lottery   7 Aug 1699 G28v bill for wainscotting in the back room behind the Court room   27 Sep 1699 G30v to be let to Governors of Greenwich Hospital   8 Nov 1699 G33r to be let to stewards of the St Cecilia's Day Feast   4 Mar 1699/1700 G36v to be repaired and bricklayer's bill for tiling to be paid   3 Jun 1700 G40r committee to consider bills for glazing, whitewashing and painting   11 Nov 1700 G46v to be let for the St Cecilia Feast   20 Dec 1701 G66v Cavendish Weeden granted use of twice a week for a year for performance of divine music   26 Mar 1702 G68v to be let to Edward Stracy for 2 months for the sale of household goods   1 Jun 1702 G71v to be used for a funeral   2 Nov 1702 G83r let for annual feast of Warwickshire gentlemen   29 Jan 1702/3 G84v Court decides not to let for only 5 guineas for an entertainment of music when scaffolding would be used   5 Apr 1703 G88r smith's bill for work on   27 Mar 1703 G87r S.C.'s books to be kept in the room behind the Court room of the Hall   10 Sep 1705 G123r Robert Stephens has made an unauthorised wicket through a door on the south side which is ordered to be nailed up   26 Mar 1707 G140r Dean to have use of for a music entertainment   7 Aug 1710 G183r wooden pipes about it to be replaced with lead ones   3 Dec 1711 G195v not to be let for any county feast without leave of the Court   6 Oct 1712 G204r Company of Clockmakers to have use of   1 Dec 1712 G205v not to be let for any county feast without leave of the Court. Order of Court of 6 October concerning Clockmakers to be discharged   1 Mar 1713/14 G216v Margaret Webster replaces Mrs Battersby as cleaner of the Hall   2 Aug 1714 G221r not to be let for less than two guineas except for a funeral. Master and Wardens to be responsible for painting, whitewashing and glazing it   1 Nov 1714 G223r proprietors of the Office of Insurance to have for one guinea as before   3 Oct 1715 G233v not to be let for the Oxfordshire Feast for under 5 guineas   26 Mar 1716 G238v money for use of to be paid in advance   21 Feb 1716/17 G246v trust of transferred to new trustees

See also GARDEN

HALL, [   ]   5 May 1690 F135r summoned to be cloathed but excused on plea of insufficiency

HALL, John – see SELECT OBSERVATIONS

HALL, Katherine   25 Mar 1703 G86v elected to Matthew Duckett's pension   18 Dec 1707 G148v deceased; Mary Snowdon given her pension

HALL, Samuel   3 Jul 1704 G110r bound to John Usborne, 7 years

HALL, Thomas   2 Dec 1700 G54r bound to Obedience Gellebrand, 7 years   1 Feb 1702/3 G85r freed by James Crayle   5 Jul 1708 G154v cloathed   20 Dec 1710 G186v of Paternoster Row, stationer; Charles Fisher is bound to him

HALL, William   20 Nov 1703 G98r to be made party to S.C.'s Bill in Chancery when his Christian name is known   26 Jan 1703/4 G100v of Lincoln; defendant to S.C.'s Bill in Chancery against Robert Woollame

HALSEY, Robert   7 Mar 1697/8 G5r freed by Thomas Parkhurst

HALY, [   ]   7 Jun 1680 E100v assigned signature B of stock Child's Guide

HALY, Margaret   6 Sep 1686 F62v advised to apply to Stock-keepers for money due to her from English Stock

HAMMER, Giles   30 Dec 1684 (W) witnesses John Marlow's bond

HAMMOND, William   22 Jun 1687 F85r of Shipton-in-Craven, Yorkshire, deceased; leaves £10 to the S.C. poor

HAMPSON, Edward   6 Nov 1710 G185r bound to John Clarke

HAMPTON, Adam   4 Jul 1698 G11r William Watts is bound to him   1 Feb 1702/3 G85r Thomas Baiten is bound to him   9 Feb 1707/8 G149r of Church Lane, joiner; Thomas Duran is bound to him

HANCH, Robert   3 Nov 1679 E95r freed by William Whitwood

HANCOCK, John (I)   22 Sep 1680 E104r in competition for John Macock's £160 share   5 Sep 1681 E129r elected to Thomas Vere's £160 share   27 Nov 1688 F110v fined for 2 years' Under Warden to preserve his seniority at Table, being incapable of serving through age and infirmity   7 Oct 1689 F125r deceased; his £160 share disposed of to Thomas Dring

HANCOCK, John (II)   17 Oct 1687 F93r fined for Assistant Renter Warden on his father's request   1 Mar 1687/8 F98r summoned to next Court to be nominated for Assistant   5 Mar 1687/8 F99r elected Assistant   2 Jul 1688 F104r elected to the late Miles Flesher's £40 share   3 Oct 1692 F180r elected to Walter Kettleby's £80 share   2 Nov 1696 F252r competes unsuccessfully for the late Thomas Cockerell's £160 share   7 Dec 1696 F252v elected to the late Mary Felton's £160 share

HARBIN, [ ] 1 Feb 1696/7 F255r excused cloathing 6 Oct 1701 G64v excused cloathing for some time

HARBIN, [ ] 2 Jul 1709 G166v mason; to carry out masonry work in passage between houses of Whitledge and Mrs Everingham

HARBIN, Richard 4 Sep 1699 G30v bound to Edward Jones, 7 years 6 Feb 1715/16 G236r freed by John Nutt 1 Apr 1717 G249v Thomas Allestree turned over to him from Sarah Holt 6 May 1717 G250v cloathed

HARBIN, Thomas 5 Jun 1699 G25v Bryant Hartgill is bound to him 5 Apr 1703 G88r Edmund Calverly is bound to him 5 Feb 1710/11 G187r his apprentice Edmund Calverly is freed 3 Oct 1715 G233v Philip Warne is bound to him

HARBOTTLE, R[ ] 2 Oct 1682 E158r Richard Janeway confesses to printing 'Strange News from Hick's Hall' for him

HARCOURT, Sir Simon 3 Jul 1710 G182r to be retained as Counsel for S.C.

HARCOURT, Stephen 3 Aug 1702 G79v apprentice to Jasper Roberts, deceased; turned over to Benjamin Tooke jnr

HARDEN, William 7 Jul 1701 G62r bound to Richard Hunt, 7 years

HARDIE, Christopher 4 Dec 1699 G34r bound to George Read, 7 years

HARDIN, John 3 Jul 1710 G182r of St Martin's Lane; John Murdock is bound to him

HARDING, Daniel, snr – see following entry

HARDING, Daniel, jnr 6 Aug 1711 G193r son of Daniel, is bound to Abraham Dickson, 7 years

HARDING, David 3 Aug 1713 G213r son of Daniel, is bound to John Heptingstall, 7 years

HARDING, John 2 May 1681 E111r allowed to continue his £50 loan three years longer if he can find another surety to replace one deceased 6 Jun 1681 E112v to repay £50 loan at next Court or give better surety 4 Jul 1681 E116r business referred to next Court 1 Aug 1681 E117r to retain £50 loan for a further 3 years on the presentation of a new bond by Edward Hill and William Bickwell 4 Aug 1684 F22r with William Cadman and Matthew Gilliflower, presents grievances of 129 S.C. members; Master asks for instances 1 Sep 1684 F23r further to grievances, gives proof that various French booksellers are dealing in scandalous books 3 Dec 1684 F26v required to repay £50 loan; he asks for further time on the grounds that one of his sureties is dead, and is given until Christmas 3 Feb 1684/5 F30r to be sued for non-repayment of £50 loan 2 Mar 1684/5 F31r allowed to give two more sereties and to defer payment of £50 loan for six months on condition that they are adequate 6 Apr 1685 F32v sureties approved, and loan continued for 6 months 6 Dec 1686 F68v complains of hawkers; committee appointed 1 Mar 1687/8 F97v expelled from Livery by order of Lord Mayor 11 Oct 1688 F108v restored to Livery 26 Mar 1689 F115v elected First Renter Warden but pleads inability to serve; Court is ordered to look into this 6 May 1689 F117r excused First Renter Wardenship for a year 26 Mar 1690 F131v elected First Renter Warden 7 Apr 1690 F132v petitions with Brabazon Aylmer and Samuel Keeble to increase number of Renter Wardens and cut down individual cost; rejected. Sworn in as First Renter Warden 5 May 1690 F134v refuses Renter Warden's book and office; byelaws re. forfeiture read and ordered to be put in suit if he persists in refusal 15 Jul 1690 F140r Renter Warden. To go round to houses of members soliciting money for troops for Crown 22 Oct 1690 F144v not allowed to fine for office of Renter Warden, but made to pay for Lord Mayor's dinner he had not provided as Renter Warden 9 Feb 1690/1 F149r elected to Thomas Hodgkins's £40 share 25 Jun 1691 F155v to appear at next Court with James Oades to pay the balance of their Renter Wardens' accounts 7 Nov 1692 F181v elected to William Shrewsbury's £80 share 8 Nov 1697 G1v John Parker is bound to him 5 Aug 1700 G44r William Cooper is bound to him 5 Oct 1702 G81r competes unsuccessfully for Mrs Gilliflower's £160 share 6 Mar 1703/4 G103v competes unsuccessfully for Richard Simpson's £160 share and John Place's £160 share 5 Feb 1704/5 G115r elected to Mary Clarke's £160 share. His £80 share disposed of to Thomas Bradyll 6 Aug 1705 G122r Bradyll is allowed to mortgage Harding's ex-share to John Taylor. Josiah Guliver is bound to Harding 4 Aug 1712 G202v John Williams is bound to him

HARDING, Thomas 3 Feb 1695/6 F239r freed by Elizabeth Randall

HARDING, William 6 Oct 1707 G145v his apprentice William Cooper is freed

HARDWICK, Robert 4 Mar 1716/17 G248r son of John, is bound to Freeman Collins, 7 years

HAREFINCH, Henry 5 Dec 1687 F94v to be summoned with Thomas Bassett to answer the complaint of Edward Brewster and Nathaniel Ranew

HAREFINCH, Widow 2 Mar 1690/1 F150v now Mrs Sharplesse; her husband to be prosecuted since she continued to print despite Sharplesse not being free of S.C.

HARFINCH, [ ] 7 Jul 1684 F20r committee appointed to deal with printers who are not members of S.C., including him

HARFORD, Benjamin, snr – see following entry

HARFORD, Benjamin, jnr 1 Jun 1713 G210v son of Benjamin, is bound to Thomas James, 7 years

HARFORD, Heritage 6 Oct 1701 G65r bound to John Howe, 7 years

HARGRAVE, [ ] 7 Jun 1703 G90r requesting £500 due to him from S.C. as husband of the widow of Thomas Dring. To deliver Dring's bond to be cancelled

HARGRAVE, Richard 6 Mar 1698/9 G22r assignment from him read and ordered to be entered in the Register book 4 Dec 1699 G33v assignment to William Freeman of three books, 'Systema Horticultura' [by John Worlidge], 'The Devout Communicant' [anon.] and 'An Infallible Way to Contentment' [by Abednego Seller] to be entered into register book

HARGRAVE, Thomas 3 Oct 1692 F180v to be summoned to cloathing 7 Nov 1692 F181v cloathed and promises payment of fine

HARGREAVES, Christopher 7 Aug 1704 G111r freed by John Leake

HARLE, Richard 4 May 1702 G71r bound to John Sparks, 7 years

HARMAN, Robert 2 Nov 1702 G83r bound to Richard Bassill, 7 years 5 May 1712 G199v freed by Richard Bassill 2 Nov 1713 G214v Richard Weedon is bound to him 31 Aug 1716 G242v Richard Weedon turned over from him to Thomas Atkins

HARMER, Jasper 3 Jul 1682 E155r cloathed 1 Mar 1687/8 F97v expelled from Livery by order of Lord Mayor 11 Oct 1688 F108v restored to Livery 4 Apr 1691 F151r elected First Renter Warden and ordered to be summoned 6 Apr 1691 F151v fined for First Renter Warden 2 Jul 1694 F210r competes unsuccessfully for Freeman Collins's £40 share 4 Feb 1694/5 F217r competes unsuccessfully for the late Tace Cheese's £40 share 5 Oct 1702 G81r elected to Thomas Bennett's £40 share 6 Mar 1703/4 G103v Edward Buncher is bound to him. Competes unsuccessfully for Brabazon

Aylmer's £80 share 5 Feb 1704/5 G115r competes unsuccessfully for John Harding's £80 share 7 Apr 1707 G140v Competes unsuccessfully for Capt. Edward Darrell's £80 share. Elected to John Baskett's £80 share. His £40 share disposed of to Christopher Bateman

HARMONY OF SCRIPTURES [i.e. *Scripture Harmonies*] 8 May 1682 E152v by Dr [John] Lightfoot; assigned to Thomas Parkhurst by Simon Miller

HARPER, Anne 26 Mar 1696 F241r elected into the pension of Anne Barrett, deceased(?) 22 Jun 1699 G25v elected to Phillippa Boddington's pension 24 Mar 1701 G68r (repeated under 22 Jun 1702) lately married. To be replaced in pension book by Sarah Dickins

HARPER, Charles 1 Mar 1680/1 E107v elected Stock-keeper for Yeomanry with Benjamin Tooke 21 Feb 1681/2 E145r competes unsuccessfully for the £80 share of Mrs Harward, deceased 3 Feb 1684/5 F30r elected to John Starkey's £80 share 7 May 1685 (W) confirmed member of new Livery 3 Aug 1685 F42r fined for Assistant Renter Warden 1 Mar 1687/8 F97v expelled from Livery by order of Lord Mayor. Elected Stock-keeper for Livery with Miles Flesher 11 Oct 1688 F108v restored to Livery 2 Mar 1690/1 F150v elected Stock-keeper for Livery with Samuel Sprint 3 Oct 1692 (W) his apprentice Samuel Rickards is freed 3 Jul 1693 F189v elected to the late Henry Twyford's £160 share 7 May 1694 F203v elected Assistant and summoned 4 Jun 1694 F208r sworn in as Assistant 1 Mar 1694/5 F217v elected Stock-keeper for Assistants with William Rawlins 30 Sep 1696 F249v occupies warehouse once used by Mrs Royston; she demands satisfaction for boards, &c., left behind 3 Jul 1697 F263v competes unsuccessfully for Under Warden 5 Jul 1697 F264r competes unsuccessfully for Under Warden 13 Apr 1698 G6v Charles Smith is bound to him 6 Jun 1698 G8v his apprentice Thomas Leigh freed 10 Jan 1698/9 G18v added to committee to consider Printing Act 1 Jul 1699 G26r elected Under Warden and not permitted to fine 4 Mar 1699/1700 G36r to pay bricklayer's bill 6 Jul 1700 G41v fined £5 for second year of Under Warden 5 Aug 1700 G44r to be added to all committees in place before election of present Master and Wardens 1 Mar 1702/3 G85v elected Stock-keeper for Assistants 8 May 1704 G106v John Hooke is bound to him 1 Jul 1704 G109r fined for Upper Warden 5 Feb 1704/5 G114v Clerk's bill for proceedings in Chancery referred to him 4 Jun 1705 G120v his apprentice Charles Smith is freed 30 Jun 1705 G121r fined for Upper Warden to preserve his seniority 6 Jul 1706 G133r competes unsuccessfully for Master 5 Aug 1706 G133v assists William Rawlins in paying his fine for Master 5 May 1707 G141v competes unsuccessfully for Mrs Leake's £320 share 9 Jun 1707 G142r elected to £320 share of Henry Hills's widow. His £160 share disposed of to Thomas Burrows 5 Jul 1707 G143r competes unsuccessfully for Master 4 Aug 1707 G144v brings silver flagon (gift of William Rawlins, deceased) into Court 3 Dec 1707 G148r signs re. not taking Clarendon 26 Mar 1708 G150v informs Court that James Rawlins wishes to fine for First Renter Warden. To be added to committee re. Clarendon in octavo 3 Jul 1708 G154r elected Master 2 Jul 1709 G166v competes unsuccessfully for Master 7 Jul 1709 G168r informs Court that they were called to swear in new Master, and to consider matter in dispute between S.C. and Dr Partridge 1 Aug 1709 G169r competes unsuccessfully for Master 7 Jul 1712 G201v his apprentice John Hooke is freed 24 Apr 1713 G209r signatory to S.C.'s notes to Guy 3 Aug 1713 G212v auditor of Master and Wardens' accounts 22 Dec 1713 G215r deceased; his £320 share disposed of to Thomas Clarke

HARPER, Humphrey 5 Sep 1715 G232v his son William is bound to Richard Gunning, 7 years

HARPER, Joseph   5 Feb 1704/5 G115r freed by John Beresford   10 Sep 1711 G194r bookbinder; John Roddam is bound to him   7 May 1716 G240r Nathaniel Cross is bound to him

HARPER, William   5 Sep 1715 G232v son of Humphrey, is bound to Richard Gunning, 7 years

HARRINDIND – see HARRINDINE

HARRINDINE, Abraham   3 Mar 1711/12 G197r his son John is bound to Egbard Sangar, 7 years   3 Aug 1713 G213r his son John is bound to William Wyatt, 7 years [i.e. turnover?]

HARRINDINE/HARRINDIND, John   3 Mar 1711/12 G197r son of Abraham, is bound to Egbard Sangar, 7 years   3 Aug 1713 G213r son of Abraham, is bound to William Wyatt, 7 years [i.e. turnover?]

HARRIS, [   ]   1 Apr 1697 F260v to ask booksellers, printers and paper manufacturers of Little Britain and Duck Lane for money towards Paper Act test case

HARRIS, Benjamin, snr (I)   1 Dec 1679 E95v cloathed (but put out of Court on 1 March 1679/80 and entry scored out)   1 Mar 1679/80 E97r dropped from Livery because of 'having undergone the punishment of Law'   6 Dec 1680 E105v complains he has been abused in Gadbury and Trigg's almanacks; Mrs Maxwell the printer ordered to omit abuses in next impression   11 Apr 1681 E110r Astwood clears him of asking for 'A Raree-Show' [attr. Stephen College] to be printed   7 Sep 1685 F44r to be summoned re. printing 'The Protestant's [i.e. Protestant] Tutor'   5 Oct 1685 F45r assures Court he has printed no copies of 'The Protestant Tutor' since 1682; apologises and offers to swear he never will again   7 Dec 1685 F47r petition (copy in W) read re. damasking of copies of 'English Liberties' found at his house; Court promises to ask Secretaries of State. Suggests he has printed similar things in partnership with Court members; lists those he comprinted 'Westminster Parliament' with (copy in W)   22 Dec 1685 F49v informed that S.C. has managed to defer but possibly not to rescind action against him by Secretary of State   1 Mar 1685/6 F52r in view of his poverty the Court allows him the profit from the damasked paper after charges are deducted   7 Nov 1698 G16r owing 24s quarterage arrears. 12s quarterage arrears abated, his circumstances being low. Edward Evans is bound to him. His apprentices Benjamin and Vavasor Harris are freed by patrimony   20 Nov 1703 G98r and his son. Agrees to pay S.C.'s costs in case against them for printing S.C.'s almanacks. Master and Wardens to have permission to search their warehouses   26 Jan 1703/4 G100v advice to be taken concerning S.C.'s exceptions to his answers   2 Oct 1704 G112v Thomas Turner is bound to him   1 Dec 1707 G147v bookseller; Ralph Humble is bound to him   1 Mar 1707/8 G149r answer of himself and his two sons read. No exceptions to be taken against these answers until the answers of John Atkin and Medrick Mead received   7 Jun 1708 G153r members added to committee for considering his arrears   5 Jul 1708 G155r his apprentice Nathaniel Dodd is freed   4 Oct 1708 G157v debate relating to his answers resumed. Committee to advise with Counsel and move the Court for an injunction 'next seal or the second seal'   5 Dec 1709 G172r suspected to be printer and publisher of false Partridge's Almanack with a calendar. Master and Wardens to enquire into this   8 Dec 1709 G172v advertisement concerning his printing of Partridge's Almanack to be placed in the Gazette and several other public newspapers. Counsel to give advice on whether prognostications printed with S.C.'s calendar is a breach of the injunction against him   1 May 1710 G179v of Gracechurch Street, printer; Benjamin Maddam is bound to him   4 Dec 1710 G185v Clerk has refused to enter his almanack called 'Merlinus Liberatus'. Letter concerning almanack published by him for the year VIII debated. Committee to draw up an advertisement to be put in the Gazette, Post-man and Post Boy concerning the publishing of the almanacks   4 Jun 1716 G240v Moyse Edwards turned over to him

HARRIS, Benjamin, jnr (II)   7 Nov 1698 G16r freed by patrimony   1 Mar 1702/3 G86r Richard Howard is bound to him   4 Feb 1716/17 G246v his apprentice Richard Howard is freed

HARRIS, Benjamin (III)   12 Nov 1705 G125r freed by William Harris, his father

HARRIS, Christopher   7 Feb 1703/4 G101v bound to William Yorke, 7 years

HARRIS, Eliza   7 Dec 1702 G83v John King is bound to her

HARRIS, George   8 Nov 1703 G97r freed by Thomas Chapman   2 Jun 1712 G200v John Bradley is bound to him, then turned over from him to Luke Stoker

HARRIS, John   6 Jun 1692 F172r freeman 'of some other company'; admitted to freedom on payment of £1 to the Poor Box   1 Aug 1692 F177r cloathed and promises fine; (W) his apprentice Henry Barnard is freed   12 Sep 1692 F179r master of newly made freeman Henry Barnard in the Poultry, whose name is sent to Lord Chamberlain   6 Aug 1694 F211v Daniel Mead is bound to him   2 Mar 1701/2 G67v his apprentice Daniel Mead is freed

HARRIS, Mary   22 Jun 1697 F263v deceased; her pension voted to Robert Cox

HARRIS, Mrs   7 Mar 1691/2 F166v promises to meet with Roger Norton and discuss her printing his Accidence and Grammar

HARRIS, Priscilla   4 Oct 1708 G158r of Petty France; William Burnett is bound to her

HARRIS, Richard   26 Mar 1709 G162v of Tower Hill; question concerning his being made free on 5 Oct 1691   4 Apr 1709 G164r to be summoned to attend next Court day to accept cloathing   2 May 1709 G165r elected to cloathing. Beadle to give notice to attend next Court day   4 Jul 1709 G167v to attend next Court to accept cloathing under threat of prosecution   7 Nov 1709 G172r cloathed   5 Sep 1715 G232v John Hudson Guy is bound to him   26 Mar 1717 G248v elected First Renter Warden   1 Apr 1717 G249r fined for first Renter Warden

HARRIS, Sarah   7 Dec 1685 F47r petition re. selling counterfeit books to Jencks the haberdasher is read; she delivers up the counterfeits and recants

HARRIS, Thomas   6 Sep 1714 G221v his son William is bound to Richard Sare, 7 years

HARRIS, Vavasor   7 Nov 1698 G16r freed by patrimony

HARRIS, William   3 Jul 1699 G27v his apprentice John Titchborne is freed   12 Nov 1705 G125r his son Benjamin Harris is freed   6 Sep 1714 G221v son of Thomas, is bound to Richard Sare, 7 years

HARRISON, Abraham   6 Nov 1682 E160r of Blossom's Inn in St Lawrence Lane; to be glazier to S.C. in place of Cooke, deceased

HARRISON, Christopher   10 Sep 1716 G243r son of Thomas, is bound to Henry Carter, 7 years

HARRISON, Thomas – see preceding entry

HARRISON, Dr   9 Jun 1707 G142v and his wife to be proceeded against at law according to opinion of Sir Edward Northey   9 Feb 1707/8 G148v trial to take place the sitting after this term   6 Jun 1709 G165v matter in difference between S.C. and himself to be left to Clerk to settle

HARRISON, Israel (I)   8 May 1682 E152r cloathed   7 Jul 1690 F139r competes unsuccessfully for Matthew Gilliflower's £40 share   4 Apr 1691 F151r fined for first Renter Warden   3 Aug 1691 F158v elected to Thomas Cockerell's £40 share   3 Oct

1692 F180r elected to the late Widow Crooke's £80 share   1 Mar 1692/3 F184r elected Stock-keeper for Yeomanry with Daniel Browne   1 Mar 1698/9 G20r elected Stock-keeper for Livery   5 Aug 1700 G44r Israel Harrison is freed by him   9 Sep 1700 G45r William Meers is bound to him   1 Jun 1702 G71v David Shilfox is bound to him   4 Jun 1705 G120r elected Assistant   2 Jul 1705 G121v auditor of late Master and Wardens' accounts   4 Feb 1705/6 G127r elected to Mary Horne's £160 share. His £80 share disposed of to Thomas Horne   6 Jul 1706 G133v elected Under Warden   5 Aug 1706 G134r Nathaniel Moody is bound to him   2 Dec 1706 G136v Francis Morse is bound to him   5 Jul 1707 G143r competes unsuccessfully for Under Warden   4 Aug 1707 G144r elected Under Warden and fined for second year   6 Oct 1707 G145v his apprentice William Mears is freed   1 Mar 1707/8 G149v elected Stock-keeper for Assistants   7 Aug 1710 G182v fined for first year of Upper Warden to preserve his seniority to Deputy Collins   30 Jun 1711 G192r elected Upper Warden   6 Aug 1711 G193r William March is bound to him   2 Mar 1712/13 G206v to be acting Upper Warden in place of Freeman Collins, deceased   24 Apr 1713 G209r signatory to S.C.'s notes   4 Jul 1713 G211r fined for Master   5 Oct 1713 G214r his apprentice Nathan Moody is freed   3 May 1714 G218v signs note to Thomas Guy. William Bury is bound to him   4 Oct 1714 G222r competes unsuccessfully for the late John Simms's £320 share   2 Jul 1716 G241v auditor of Master and Wardens' accounts   1 Apr 1717 G249v elected to Edward Brewster's £320 share. His £160 share disposed of to Daniel Midwinter

HARRISON, Israel (II)   5 Aug 1700 G44r freed by Israel Harrison and cloathed

HARRISON, James   4 Mar 1716/17 G248r son of John, is bound to James Holland, 7 years

HARRISON, John (I) – see preceding entry

HARRISON, John (II)   8 Nov 1697 G1v freed   1 Feb 1713/14 G216r Abraham Rue turned over to him from Thomas Harrison

HARRISON, Robert   27 Sep 1705 G123v elected to Mary Wailes's pension   22 Dec 1708 G159v elected to Susanna Walthus's pension. Grace Middlewright given his pension   28 Sep 1709 G170v his pension augmented by 20s   22 Mar 1714/15 G226v deceased; Isaiah Ward given his pension

HARRISON, Thomas (I)   5 Aug 1695 F231v Nathaniel Delaporte is bound to him   6 Nov 1710 G185r bookseller; Abraham Rues is bound to him   1 Feb 1713/14 G216r Abraham Rues turned over from him to John Harrison

HARRISON, Thomas (II)   7 Mar 1708/9 G161v of Sidney College, Cambridge; letter from him to Dr Nicholas Brady requesting permission to print the 'New Version of Psalms' at Cambridge and for S.C. to give a number of Psalms towards the charity school. Court not willing to grant this   23 Jun 1709 G166r to be permitted to print 1000 of the 'New Version of Psalms'

HARROTT, Stephen   7 Apr 1701 G58v bound to Jasper Roberts, 7 years

HART, John   4 Jun 1716 G240v son of William, is bound to Joseph Downing, 7 years

HART, William (I)   1 Sep 1701 G64r freed by Francis Leach (turnover)

HART, William (II)   1 Dec 1701 G66r bound to Peter Wallis, 7 years

HART, William (III – perhaps to be identified with I)   4 Jun 1716 G240v his son John is bound to Joseph Downing, 7 years

HARTGILL, Bryant   5 Jun 1699 G25v bound to Thomas Harbin, 7 years

HARTLEY, [   ]   3 May 1680 E99v to be given £47 worth of stock books, and credit for £100 worth

HARTLEY/HARTLY, John   1 Aug 1692 (W) is freed by Christopher Bateman   12 Sep 1692 F179r of Gray's Inn and newly made free of Christopher Bateman; name sent to Lord Chamberlain   1 Feb 1696/7 F255r re-summoned re. cloathing   26 Mar 1700 G38r Fletcher Giles is bound to him   5 Apr 1703 G88r to be summoned to next Court to take cloathing   3 May 1703 G89v elected to cloathing again. To receive personal notice from Clerk   7 Jun 1703 G90r Court unwilling to accept his excuse for not accepting cloathing. A further definite answer required   1 Jul 1706 G133r of Fleet Street; to be summoned to next Court day to take cloathing   1 Sep 1707 G145r bookseller; Thomas Sharpe is bound to him   12 Apr 1708 G152r stationer; John Atkinson is bound to him   1 Mar 1713/14 G216v Thomas Sharpe turned over from him to John Matthews   4 Oct 1714 G222v Liveryman; paid a guinea from Poor Box   13 Jun 1715 G229r bankrupt; to be given 40s by Warden Richard Mount towards paying his fees and being discharged from prison

HARVEY, John   20 Nov 1703 G98r bodice-maker of Lincoln; to be made party to S.C.'s Bill in Chancery

HARVEY/HARVY, William   7 Aug 1699 F29r freed by John Penn   2 Oct 1699 G31v Joseph Davies is bound to him   6 Mar 1703/4 G103v Richard Combs is bound to him   4 Sep 1710 G183v of the Temple, stationer; John King is bound to him   6 Aug 1711 G193r his apprentice Richard Combes (referred to as Combesby) is freed   1 Feb 1713/14 G216r John Hootton is bound to him   7 Feb 1714/15 G225r John King turned over from him to Peter Tanner   13 Jun 1715 G229v Jonathan Skinner is bound to him

HARWARD, Mrs   21 Feb 1681/2 E145r deceased; her £80 share voted to Robert Clavell

HARWELL, Isaac – see following entry

HARWELL, John   1 Sep 1712 G203r son of Isaac; bound to Edmund Powell, 7 years

HARWOOD, John (I)   27 Sep 1695 F232v elected to James Grey's pension   12 Dec 1695 F238r deceased; his pension goes to Samuel Driver

HARWOOD, John, snr (II) – see following entry

HARWOOD, John, jnr (III)   6 Sep 1714 G221v son of John, is bound to Hannah Clarke, 7 years

HARWOOD, Stephen, snr – see following entry

HARWOOD, Stephen, jnr   3 Mar 1706/7 G139r son of Stephen, is freed by patrimony

HASCARD, Gregory – see DISCOURSE

HASTINGS, John, snr – see following entry

HASTINGS, John, jnr   4 Dec 1693 F196v son of John Hastings of Charlbury, Oxfordshire; is bound to John Bennett for 7 years from 6 November

HASTINGS, Theophilus   2 Aug 1697 F265v bound to John Mayo

HASTLEFOOTE, Thomas – see following entry

HASTLEFOOTE, Verey   1 Jul 1695 F228r son of Thomas Hastlefoote of Messing, Essex; is bound to Robert Elmes

HATCH, Henry   2 Oct 1710 G184v bound to William Hatch, 7 years

HATCH, William   7 Nov 1698 G16r bound to Thomas Hodgkins, 7 years   12 Nov 1705 G125r freed by Thomas Hodgkins   2 Oct 1710 G184v of St John's Lane, printer; Henry Hatch is bound to him

HATCHMAN, Richard   7 Aug 1699 G29r bound to John Doleman, 7 years   3 Nov 1712 G205r freed by John Doleman

HATERSLY – see HATTERSLEY

HATHAM, Matthew   6 Sep 1697 F267r bound to John Back

HATLEY, [   ]   8 May 1682 E152r John Croft substitutes for him as surety for John Pen's continuation of £100 loan to S.C.   6 Jul 1702 G77r desires a remittance of part of the costs of a law suit on behalf of Richard Randall of Newcastle

HATLEY, John   3 Feb 1706/7 G138r cloathed. James Gilbert, apprentice of George Littlebury, is turned over to him

HATSELL/HATTELL, Lawrence   8 May 1682 E152r cloathed   4 May 1691 F153v fined for Assistant Renter Warden   7 Nov 1698 G16r Timothy Bedford is bound to him

HATTERSLEY/HATERSLY, Robert, snr – see following 2 entries

HATTERSLEY/HATERSLY, Robert, jnr   14 Mar 1714/15 G226r son of Robert, is bound to Richard Brown, 7 years

HATTERSLEY, Timothy   12 Nov 1716 G244v son of Robert, is bound to Elizabeth Nutt, 7 years

HATTON, David   30 Dec 1684 (W) witnesses John Marlow's bond

HAWES, Lary   13 Apr 1713 G208v son of William, is bound to John Usborne, 7 years

HAWES, William (I) – see preceding entry

HAWES, William (II)   6 Jun 1698 G8v freed by Robert Clavell and cloathed   2 Oct 1699 G31v Emmanuel Read is bound to him   7 Feb 1703/4 G101v granted permission to print a number of Church Catechisms with added prayers, graces and texts   2 Apr 1705 G118v Philip Browne is bound to him   4 Apr 1709 G164r summoned for printing a catechism under the title of the 'Exposition of the Church Catechism' by [John] Lewis, without S.C.'s leave. To give explanations next Court day   5 Apr 1714 G218r bookseller; paid an acknowledgement to the S.C. for printing the Church Catechism

HAWKERS   10 Jun 1684 F16v application to be made to Lord Chief Justice re. suppression of hawkers   5 Mar 1685/6 F52v committee resolves to employ someone to arrest all hawkers   6 Dec 1686 F68v Matthew Gilliflower, Joseph Knight and John Harding complain of them; committee appointed   14 Mar 1686/7 F78v committee recommends that Court employ someone to apprehend hawkers   4 Apr 1687 F81v person to be chosen to apprehend hawkers   7 May 1688 F101v several freed; ordered, as a 'disencouragement', that this will not happen henceforth   3 Jun 1689 F119r Brabazon Aylmer, William Rogers, Jonathan Robinson and others petition against hawkers and are admitted to the committee   1 Aug 1689 F121v committee meeting; agreed that Lilly should organise the facts and take legal advice. Petitioners to pay half the cost and S.C. half   6 Oct 1690 F143v booksellers renew petition against hawkers in detail; committee appointed to join with a committee of petitioners   8 Oct 1690 F144r committee asks Master and Wardens to ask the Bishop of London to withdraw and discontinue licences granted to hawkers   15 Oct 1690 F145r committee appoints subcommittee to draw up heads and clauses for a possible supplementary Printing Act   1 Dec 1690 F146v draft of Act re. suppressing pedlars, hawkers and petty chapmen approved and half charges paid; Court to use its influence

HAWKINS, Charles   3 Mar 1700/1 G57r bound to William Hawkins, 7 years   2 Aug 1708 G155v freed by Robert Whitledge   6 Mar 1709/10 G176v of Creed Lane, bookbinder; Isaac Wainhouse is bound to him   5 Apr 1714 G218r Isaac Wainhouse turned over from him to Robert Whitledge

HAWKINS, Edward   5 Sep 1698 G14v Robert Willoughby is bound to him   5 Oct 1702 G81v Robert Willoughby turned over from him to Mark Forster   3 May 1703 G89v Bazaleel Creak is bound to him   2 Aug 1703 G94r William Sheffield turned over to him (also under 6 Sep 1703 G94v)   6 Aug 1705 G122v his apprentice William Sheffield is freed   12 Nov 1705 G125r Bazaleel Creak turned over from him to Benjamin Yarnes

HAWKINS, John   13 Apr 1698 G6v bound to Richard Janeway, 7 years   7 May 1705 G120r freed by Richard Janeway   7 Aug 1710 G183r of Creed Lane, printer; Haworth Gladman is bound to him   5 Jul 1714 G220v Haworth Gladman turned over from him to Joseph Hazard

HAWKINS, Matthew   9 Feb 1701/2 G67r bound to James Knapton, 7 years   4 Jul 1709 G167v freed by James Knapton

HAWKINS, William   2 Mar 1690/1 F150r competes unsuccessfully for porter   3 Mar 1700/1 G57r Charles Hawkins is bound to him   21 Mar 1716/17 G248r elected to Millicent Shell's pension

HAXBY, Martha   7 Sep 1702 G80v bound to William Prickett, 7 years

HAY, William   1 Sep 1712 G203r freed by Emmanuel Matthews

HAYES, Elizabeth   20 Dec 1682 E162v deceased; Martha Boate is given her 7s 6d pension

HAYES, [ ] – see HAYES, John

HAYES, James   4 Dec 1690 F147v he and Benjamin Tooke become obliged to Cambridge University on behalf of S.C. for the payment of £100 p.a. for university privileges   7 Sep 1691 F159r Court regularises his appointing a Warehousekeeper for the Cambridge printing-house, not in the original agreement. (W) He requested payment over and above £60 p.a. which was judged not to be a competent subsistence for him and his family

HAYES, John, snr   1 Mar 1687/8 F97v expelled from Livery by order of Lord Mayor   6 Apr 1696 F242r John Grumbell, his apprentice, is freed   2 Nov 1696 F252r elected to Matthew Gilliflower's £80 share   7 Sep 1696 F248v writes to S.C. re. Cambridge setting up a printing-press   2 Mar 1701/2 G67v S.C.'s printer at Cambridge. Agreement between S.C. and him for privilege of printing there to be renewed for 11 years   26 Mar 1702 G69r articles of agreement between S.C. and himself sealed   3 May 1703 G89r letter from him concerning repairs to S.C.'s house in Cambridge read and debated   2 Aug 1703 G93v S.C. committee will not let the privilege of printing to anyone holding Hayes's house   21 Oct 1703 G96r Henry Mortlock to reply to his letter   7 Feb 1703/4 G101r committee considering his account relating to Cambridge affairs   3 Apr 1704 G105v letter relating to printing at Cambridge to be referred to Stock-keepers   3 Dec 1705 G125v S.C.'s printer at Cambridge, deceased; his £80 share disposed of to John Sprint

HAYES, John, jnr   3 Jun 1706 G132r of Cambridge; letter from him referred to Master, Wardens and Stock-keepers so that Joseph Collyer may return an answer to it   1 Sep 1707 G144v administrator to his father, John Hayes of Cambridge; general release sealed

HAYES, Richard   2 Dec 1695 F237v yeoman of Evesham; his son Silvanus is bound to Samuel Heyrick

HAYES, Robert   7 Sep 1702 G80v bound to John Baskett, 7 years   7 Nov 1709 G172r freed by John Baskett   24 May 1710 G179v of Change Alley, stationer; Robert Baxter is bound to him   4 Feb 1711/12 G196r summoned to take cloathing at next Court   7 Apr 1712 G198v cloathed

HAYES, Silvanus   2 Dec 1695 F237v son of Richard Hayes of Evesham, yeoman; is bound to Samuel Heyrick

HAYES, William   4 Jun 1705 G120v bound to Emmanuel Mathews

HAYHURST, Robert   9 Feb 1690/1 F149r summoned to next Court for failing to enter a pamphlet

HAYLEY, [ ]   7 Feb 1686/7 F71v 20s taken from Poor Box for his relief

HAYNES, Joseph   5 Aug 1700 G44r bound to Ichabod Dawkes, 7 years   3 Nov 1707 G146v freed by Ichabod Dawkes

HAYNES, Richard   4 Oct 1703 G96r freed by patrimony

HAZARD, [ ]   7 May 1711 G190v elected to Robert Vincent's £40 share

HAZARD, James   4 Sep 1704 G112r Thomas Walker turned over to him from Richard Humphreys

HAZARD, Jasper   7 Jul 1701 G62r freed by Thomas Norman and Robert Whitledge

HAZARD, Joseph   1 Feb 1702/3 G85r Francis Jeffreys is bound to him   4 Sep 1704 G112r his apprentice Henry Peach is freed   4 Jul 1709 G167v Thomas Bond is bound to him   1 Aug 1709 G169v cloathed   5 Feb 1710/11 G187r of Stationers' Court, bookbinder; his apprentice Francis Jeffreys is freed. Philip Hurst is bound to him   4 Aug 1712 G202v his apprentice Thomas Walker is freed   5 Jul 1714 G220v Haworth Gladman turned over to him from John Hawkins   14 Mar 1714/15 G226r John Cope is bound to him   4 Apr 1715 G227v house formerly occupied by Mrs Mills to be let to him for 21 years from midsummer at £18 p.a.   4 Jul 1715 G230v lease from S.C. of Mills' house for 21 years at £18 annual rent sealed   20 Dec 1716 G246r Philip Hurst turned over from him to Francis Jeffreys   1 Apr 1717 G249v elected First Renter Warden

HEAD, Edward   12 Jun 1704 G107v Myles Gorsuch is bound to him   1 Oct 1705 G124r cloathed   7 Apr 1707 G141r letter-founder; John Arnat is bound to him   7 Jul 1707 G143v Clerk to call on him for Livery fine   3 Oct 1709 G171r letter-founder; Steward Spicer is bound to him

HEAD, Godfrey   26 Mar 1680 E98r elected Assistant Renter Warden   2 May 1681 E110v Roger Norton and John Towse are chosen to audit his Renter Warden's accounts   5 Feb 1682/3 E163r elected to Thomas Sawbridge's £40 share   2 Jul 1683 F1v to pay ready money for share before next Court on pain of forfeiting it, under the terms of Evan Tyler's will   6 Aug 1683 F2v he and Thomas Sawbridge appeal to Table re. order of last Court, which is consequently respited until next Court   6 Nov 1683 F4v disposal of his and Thomas Sawbridge's shares to be deferred until next Court   7 May 1685 (W) confirmed as member of new Livery   1 Jun 1685 F38v elected to John Simms's £80 share   21 Jul 1685 F41r to be summoned re. order from Peter Parker and Thomas Guy to cast letters for almanack printing   3 Aug 1685 F42r tells Court that Parker and Guy's order re. type for psalms has been revoked, and a Quaker has ordered type for Pennsylvania   22 Dec 1685 F49r fined his dividend for sending a press and letters for printing to Pennsylvania   1 Feb 1685/6 F50r apologises; his withheld dividend is refunded on his giving 20s to the Poor Box   7 Mar 1686/7 F78r allowed to mortgage his £80 share to John Towse for £60   11 Oct 1688 F108v restored to Livery

HEAD, Mary   5 Feb 1693/4 F199r widow; Stephen Gilbert jnr is bound to her for seven years   5 May 1701 G59v her apprentice Stephen Gilbert is freed   6 Oct 1712 G204v John Arnat turned over to her. Steward Spicer turned over to her   14 Mar 1714/15 G226r John Astbury is turned over to her

HEAD, Richard – see ART OF WHEEDLING

HEALL, William   7 Feb 1708/9 G160v bound to Joshua Gilbert, 7 years

HEARNE, Francis   22 Jun 1694 F209v takes over the pension of Mrs Jacob

HEATHCOTT, William   2 Mar 1712/13 G207r John Benson is bound to him   4 Jul 1715 G231r John Benson turned over from him to James Read

HEDGES – see HODGES

HELDER – see SPICER

HELLAM, John   2 Mar 1701/2 G67v bound to Philip Wood, 7 years

HELLER, [   ]   6 Jun 1692 F172r excused cloathing on grounds of inability

HELMES, John   1 Jul 1706 G133r freed by William Hensman. William Helmes is bound to him   7 Sep 1713 G213v William Helmes is freed by him

HELMES, William   1 Jul 1706 G133r bound to John Helmes, 7 years   7 Sep 1713 G213v freed by John Helmes

HEMING, Bryan   7 Apr 1707 G141r bound to Samuel Butler, 7 years

HEMINGWAY, Abraham   4 Oct 1708 G158r bound to Benjamin Baker, 7 years   7 Nov 1715 G234v freed by Bartholomew Baker

HENNING, Henry – see following entry

HENNING, Robert   3 Dec 1694 F216r son of Henry Henning, founder, of London; bound to Robert Vincent

HENSMAN, William   4 Oct 1686 F64v elected to livery   8 Nov 1686 F67r cloathed on last Lord Mayor's Day   21 Feb 1686/7 F72r Daniel Browne to have priority over him on the Livery list, though they were freed together, as he was cloathed before Hensman   4 Jul 1687 F86r elected to Bernard White's £80 share   12 Apr 1692 F168v fined for First Renter Warden   2 Aug 1697 F265v John Holmes is bound to him   5 Sep 1698 G14v William Beale is bound to him   1 Jul 1706 G133r his apprentice John Helmes is freed   9 Sep 1706 G134r elected to George Copping's £160 share. His £80 share disposed of to Christopher Wilkinson. William Blyth is bound to him   7 Jun 1708 G153v his apprentice William Beal is freed

HENSON, John   8 May 1704 G106v bound to James Rawlins, 7 years   1 Sep 1712 G203r freed by James Rawlins

HENWOOD, William   7 Apr 1701 G58v bound to William Gatham, 7 years

HEPINSTALL – see HEPTINGSTALL

HEPTINGSTALL/HEPINSTALL/HEPTINSTALL, John   1 Mar 1682/3 E164r granted £50 of Tyler's bequest   2 May 1687 F82r to repay his £50 loan from Tyler bequest by   1 August   29 May 1689 F118v cloathed   26 Mar 1695 F219v elected Renter Warden with William Horton   8 Apr 1695 F221r name in margin   7 Oct 1695 F233v elected to Benjamin Motte's £40 share   11 Nov 1695 F236r Robert Powell is bound to him   1 Mar 1697/8 G4r elected Stock-keeper for the Yeomanry   5 Dec 1698 G17r Philip Crosse is bound to him   3 Jul 1699 G27v printer; his apprentice David Oakes is freed   11 Nov 1700 G46v Howard Kettlewell is bound to him   5 Oct 1702 G81r to be summoned to Court to answer charges   2 Nov 1702 G82v charged with printing two impressions of Psalms for Henry Playford without permission of Court. S.C. paid by Playford, and Heptingstall discharged   3 Jul 1704 G110r his apprentice Robert Powell is freed   2 Apr 1705 G118v John Tilly is bound to him   9 Jun 1707 G142v printer; John Crooke is bound to him   7 Mar 1708/9 G162r to answer charges of printing 'Select Psalms for the Use of the Parish Church and Chapels of St James' Westminster', without S.C.'s leave, next Court day   4 Apr 1709 G164r to be summoned to next Court day to give answer re. printing 'Select Psalms' without S.C.'s leave   4 Jul 1709 G167r to attend Master, Wardens and Stock-keepers who are settling the matter of Mrs Baldwin   7 Nov 1709 G171v competes unsuccessfully for Mrs Blagrave's £80 share   6 Feb 1709/10 G175r elected to William Rogers' £80 share. His £40 share disposed of to Richard Parker   7 Apr 1712 G199r his apprentice John Tilly is freed. Isaiah Ward is turned over to him   3 Aug 1713 G213r David Harding is bound to him   2 Aug 1714 G221r his apprentice John Crooke is freed   4 Oct 1714 G222r elected to Awnsham Churchill's £160 share   5 Sep 1715 G232v his apprentice Isaiah Ward is freed

HEPTINSTALL – see HEPTINGSTALL

HERACLITUS   3 Oct 1681 E130r David Mallett to be prosecuted for not printing his name on 'Several Weighty Queries concerning Heraclitus and The Observator'   5 Oct 1681 E130v David Mallett defends himself for printing it, saying that he was given it by Langley Curtis

HERALD PAINTERS   2 Aug 1680 E102v to repair and amend trophies   8 Nov 1680 E105r Jeremiah Wright, the herald painter, to be paid for trophies   7 Mar 1697/8 G4v to be paid by Treasurer for making banners and escutcheons

HERBERT, Thomas, 8th Earl of Pembroke – see PEMBROKE, Earl of

HERBERT, William   4 Jul 1709 G167v bound to James Brookes, 7 years   4 Mar 1716/17 G247v freed by James Brookes

HERNE, Francis   22 Jun 1694 F209v given Mrs Jacob's pension   26 Mar 1696 F241r to take over the pension of Robert Wright, turned out for not being free of S.C.   22 Jun 1698 G9v deceased; his widow Rachel elected to his pension

HERNE, Rachel   22 Jun 1698 G9v elected to her husband Francis Herne's pension   28 Sep 1702 G80v deceased; Anne Alloway is given her pension

HERNE, Thomas   5 Aug 1695 F231r elected to Livery and summoned   7 Oct 1695 F233v excused Livery when a letter from him is read

HERON, Gilbert   27 Mar 1710 G177v of London, chapman; bond from S.C. of £200 penalty to pay £103 on 26 Sep 1710 sealed   5 Oct 1713 G213v £100 owed to him on bond by S.C. paid

HERRICK – see HEYRICK

HERRINGMAN, Edmund, snr – see following entry

HERRINGMAN, Edmund, jnr   5 Mar 1693/4 F200v son of Edmund Herringman, hosier of London, deceased; bound to William Rogers for seven years

HERRINGMAN, Henry   2 Aug 1680 E102v authorised to audit Warden's accounts   7 Feb 1680/1 E106v promises to bring Martin's Calendar Book to next Court   2 May 1681 E111r asked to stand as surety for S.C. to Sir Joseph Seamour, with Francis Tyton   5 Sep 1681 E129r seals an indenture of demise of the Hall and tenements to Sir Joseph Seamour   7 Nov 1681 E137v to be present with Samuel Mearne while Robert Scott enters a number of books cheaply   1 Mar 1681/2 E145v elected Stock-keeper for Assistants with Roger Norton   3 Apr 1682 E150v dispute between him and Samuel Mearne re. books and parts of books assigned to Mearne by Mrs Kinton; referred to committee. As Thomas Newcomb's executor, awards S.C. a silver bowl in discharge of Newcomb's legacy of £20   1 Jul 1682 E155r competes unsuccessfully for Under Warden   3 Jul 1682 E155v difference with Samuel Mearne involving Robert Scott re. books entered to Mearne in 1673; to be resolved before next Court   7 Aug 1682 E156r with Robert Scott, granted leave to prosecute persons printing or selling books not in register. As no meeting has been held re. difference over copies, agreed that entry of copies by Mearne was null and void   4 Jun 1683 E170v asked together with Ambrose Isted to take legal advice re. [John] Playford's 'Vade Mecum'   6 Nov 1683 F4r list of books bought from Robinson to be entered for

40s 12 Nov 1683 F5r competes unsuccessfully for Mrs Stephens's £320 share 7 Jan 1683/4 F8r elected to the late Mrs Roper's £320 share 7 Apr 1684 F13v on the list of loyal Assistants presented to the Crown 5 Jul 1684 F19v chosen to audit Warden's accounts with John Macock, John Bellinger and Henry Clarke. Competes unsuccessfully for Under Warden 7 May 1685 (W) confirmed member of new Livery 4 Jul 1685 F39r fined for two years' Under Warden because of want of choice for Upper Warden, then fined for two years' Upper Warden. His request that Robert Horne be allowed to fine for Under Warden is granted. Elected Master 3 Jul 1686 F58v re-elected Master, but excused on request to the Table 1 Aug 1687 F87v debate concerning precedency between Herringman, John Towse and John Bellinger referred to next Court 5 Sep 1687 F88v Towse to pay a £5 fine and then take precedence of both Herringman and Bellinger 11 Oct 1688 F108v restored to Assistants 7 Oct 1689 F124r John Towse claims precedence over Herringman and John Bellinger; confusion discovered re. order of 5 Sep 1687. Deferred 4 Nov 1689 F126v to be added to the Corporation Act committee 25 Jun 1691 F156r Clerk ordered to write to him re. Lord Mayor's precept for S.C. members out of town to lend money to Crown 23 Sep 1691 F160v Master orders that he be written to about loaning money to Crown for navy on surety of Additional Excise 1 Feb 1691/2 F164v his part in concluding Oxford agreement is detailed 7 Mar 1691/2 F166v mentioned on indenture transferring Stock estate to those being indemnified against engagements with Oxford 1 Jul 1693 F189r elected Master; out of Court so ordered that he should be told 3 Jul 1693 F189v allowed to be excused Mastership because of ill-health. Assigns to John Hindmarsh and Richard Sare 'Don Quevedo's [i.e. Francisco de Quevedo's] Visions made English', translated by Roger L'Estrange 3 Jul 1697 F263v competes unsuccessfully for Master 2 Jun 1698 G10r competes unsuccessfully for Master 1 Jul 1699 G26r competes unsuccessfully for Master 6 Jul 1700 G41v competes unsuccessfully for Master 5 Jul 1701 G61r competes unsuccessfully for Master 4 Jul 1702 G76v competes unsuccessfully for Master 15 Jul 1703 G93r competes unsuccessfully for Master 10 Feb 1703/4 G102r his gift of £20 to be spent on a silver flagon 6 Mar 1703/4 G103v deceased; his £320 share voted to Richard Simpson 14 Mar 1703/4 G104r his gift of silver flagon to be put with rest of S.C.'s plate and to be inscribed

HERRINGMAN, John 4 May 1702 G71r bound to Brabazon Aylmer, 7 years

HERRINGMAN, Mrs 6 Mar 1703/4 G103v deceased; her £320 share disposed of to Richard Simpson

HESILRIGE/HESILRIGG, Robert 10 Apr 1693 F186v bond to him and George Mackreth of £1000 penalty for payment of £512 10s on 4 Oct 1693 sealed 3 Jun 1695 F225r bond for the use of Mrs Fish of '£500 and odd pounds' cancelled

HESILRIGG – see HESILRIGE

HESIOD 18 Mar 1686/7 F79v in Greek and Latin; among books in catalogue annexed to Oxford agreement

HETT, John – see following entry

HETT, Richard 6 May 1717 G250v son of John, is bound to John Clarke, 7 years

HEWITT/HEWETT, John 1 Feb 1691/2 F165v of Reading; cloathed 5 Sep 1692 F177v of Reading; elected into Livery

HEYRICK/HERRICK, Samuel 3 Apr 1682 E149v elected Assistant Renter Warden 8 May 1682 E152r accepts post of Renter Warden 1 Mar 1683/4 F9r elected Stock-keeper for Livery with Samuel Lowndes 7 Apr 1684 F14r on the list of loyal Assistants presented to the Crown 2 Jun 1684 F16r to hold position of Stock-keeper for Livery until next election despite having been made an Assistant 7 May

1685 (W) confirmed member of new Livery   6 Jul 1685 F40v he and others complain
that John How has printed their copies; How summoned to next Court   3 Aug 1685
F42v refuses to sue John How for printing a copy of 'The Fifteen Comforts of Rash and
Inconsiderate Marriage'   7 Dec 1685 F47v in Benjamin Harris's partnership for printing
the proceedings of the Westminster Parliament   11 Oct 1688 F108v restored to
Livery   4 Feb 1688/9 F112v re-elected Assistant   6 May 1689 F117r ranked eighth of
Assistants never selected as Master or Warden   4 Nov 1689 F126v to be added to the
Corporation Act committee   5 Jun 1690 F135v re-elected Assistant   9 Feb 1690/1
F148r given leave to use S.C. kitchen to publish 'The Trials of the Lord Preston and the
late Mr [John] Ashton' if he augments Poor Box   2 May 1692 F170v chosen to audit
Renter Wardens' accounts with Samuel Lowndes   30 Jun 1694 F209v competes
unsuccessfully for Under Warden; allowed to fine for 1 year to preserve his seniority   6
Jul 1695 F229v competes unsuccessfully for Under Warden   5 Aug 1695 F230r
allowed to fine for second year's service as Under Warden to preserve his seniority   2
Dec 1695 F237v Silvanus Hayes is bound to him   2 Mar 1695/6 F239v tells Court that
Abel Swale is illegally printing the Metamorphoses   4 Jul 1696 F245r competes
unsuccessfully for Upper Warden, but subsequently elected Upper Warden when Capt.
William Phillipps fines   3 Jul 1697 F263v competes unsuccessfully for Upper
Warden   2 Jul 1698 G1or auditor of Master and Wardens' accounts   3 Jul 1699
G26r chosen Upper Warden   3 Feb 1700/1 G54v ordered that he should not be
summoned to Court of Assistants in future because of his circumstances   5 May 1701
G59v arrested for a considerable debt on 1 August and suntil (sic) in Fleet prison.
Ordered that he should be discharged from being an Assistant of the S.C.   3 Aug 1702
G79v Richard Moland is bound to him   2 Aug 1703 G94r his apprentice Samuel
Walker is freed   7 Feb 1703/4 G101v Edward Wade is bound to him   8 May 1704
G106v Benjamin Germin is bound to him

HEYT, Thomas   5 May 1701 G59v bound to John Darby jnr, 7 years

HICKERINGALE – see HICKERINGILL

HICKERINGILL, Edmund   7 Oct 1689 F125r Robert Stephens to be paid 30s for
seizing Hickeringale's [i.e. Hickeringill's?] pamphlet

HICKMAN, Henry   20 Dec 1701 G66v his apprentice William Hickman is freed

HICKMAN, James   6 Oct 1707 G145v waterman; Joseph Makepeace is bound to him

HICKMAN, Obadiah   3 Jul 1704 G11or bound to James Marriner, 7 years   12 Nov
1711 G195r freed by James Marriner

HICKMAN, William   20 Dec 1701 G66v freed by Henry Hickman, patrimony

HICKS, Benjamin   27 Sep 1716 G243v elected to Edward Davenport's pension

HIDUTCH, Henry   2 Oct 1710 G184v bound to Joshua Gilbert, 7 years

HIGGINS, Roger   2 Oct 1710 G184v to be paid 6% p.a. for £400 due to him on S.C.'s
bond

HIGGINSON, [ ]   1 Oct 1711 G194v granted request for £100 of his £200 bond
from S.C. to be repaid

HIGGINSON, Roger   5 Mar 1704/5 G116v bond from S.C. of £800 penalty to pay
£410 on 5 Sep 1705 sealed, in exchange for bonds of deceased father-in-law Henry Coley

HIGINSON, [ ]   12 Jun 1704 G107r to attend Clerk on behalf of Jane Higinson and
have bonds relating to Henry Coley, deceased, renewed

HIGINSON, Jane   12 Jun 1704 G107r Higinson to attend Clerk on her behalf

HILL, [ ]   22 Sep 1680 E104r to have 40s salary paid quarterly   2 Dec 1695 F237r
his bond to be cancelled at next Court

HILL, Edward   1 Aug 1681 E117r John Harding to retain his £50 loan for a further 3 years, Hill and William Brickwell standing surety

HILL, James   7 Mar 1708/9 G162r freed by patrimony

HILL, John (I)   1 Oct 1694 F213r offers to 'discover' several malpractices; referred to Master and Wardens

HILL, John (II)   3 Apr 1704 G106r bound to Robert Stephens, 7 years

HILL, John, snr (III) – see following entry

HILL, John, jnr (IV)   1 Feb 1713/14 G216v son of John, is bound to Lewis Thomas, 7 years

HILL, Warren   26 Mar 1686 F54r elected waterman   4 Apr 1687 F81v elected waterman

HILL, William (I)   27 Mar 1682–1686 Bargemaster's Mate   8 Nov 1686 F67r resigns as Bargemaster's Mate; John Charlton is elected in his place

HILL/HILLS, William (II)   5 Sep 1692 F177v bond for £500 penalty to pay £256 5s on 6 March 1692/3 sealed   4 Feb 1694/5 F217r cloathed. Elected to the late Tace Cheese's £40 share   5 Jul 1697 F264v competes unsuccessfully for Stephen Bateman's £80 share   2 Aug 1697 F265v elected to (the late?) Mrs Argent's £80 share and sworn in   1 Mar 1699/1700 G36r competes unsuccessfully for Treasurer   1 Mar 1700/1 G56r competes unsuccessfully for Treasurer   1 Mar 1708/9 G161r competes unsuccessfully for Warehousekeeper   5 Apr 1714 G217v excused office of Renter Warden for one year   26 Mar 1715 G227r excused office of Renter Warden for one year

HILL, William (III)   7 Nov 1709 G172r bound to Henry Cater, 7 years
See also HILLS

HILLER/HILLIER, Nathaniel   5 May 1701 G59v Samuel Osborne is bound to him   7 Jun 1708 G153v his apprentice Samuel Osborne is freed

HILLER, Richard   6 Jul 1691 F157v promises to accept cloathing on next Lord Mayor's Day

HILLIARD, [   ]   7 Feb 1697/8 G3r excused cloathing

HILLIER, [   ]   5 Feb 1699/1700 G35r desire not to accept cloathing granted
See also HILLER

HILLS/HILL, Aaron   7 Mar 1708/9 G162r gentleman; Crown grants him sole rights to 'The History of Ethiopia, Egypt, the Three Arabias, Palestine and the Whole Ottoman Empire' [i.e. *The Present State of Ethiopia*], apparently compiled by him, for 14 years. To be entered in Register book

HILLS/HILL, Gilham   1 Mar 1679/80 E97r son of Henry Hills, freed by patrimony   4 Feb 1694/5 F216v son and administrator of Henry Hills; petitions re. his father's dividend; consideration deferred and widow summoned. Samuel Bolton is bound to him   6 Apr 1696 F241v cloathed   5 Sep 1698 G14v his apprentice Jonathan Edwyn is freed   4 Aug 1701 G63v William Scott is bound to him   9 Feb 1701/2 G67r his apprentice Samuel Bolton is freed   26 Mar 1702 G68v chosen Renter Warden. To be summoned to next Court   13 Apr 1702 G70r to be excused from office of Renter Warden for one year   2 Jul 1705 G121v James Jones is bound to him   12 Nov 1705 G125r his apprentice Thomas Rowse is freed   9 Jun 1707 G142v stationer; Francis Church is bound to him. His apprentice Henry Lovell is freed   4 Apr 1709 G164r his apprentice James Jones is freed   1 Aug 1709 G169v his apprentice William Scott is freed   7 Aug 1710 G183r Henry Lebrand is turned over to him

HILLS, Henry (I)   1 Mar 1679/80 E97r his son Gilham freed by patrimony   3 Jul

1680 E101v competes unsuccessfully for Under Warden   2 Jul 1681 E115v competes unsuccessfully for Under Warden   3 Apr 1682 E151r committee to negotiate with him and Roger Norton re. charges for seizure of books at Customs House   1 Jul 1682 E155r elected Under Warden   30 Jun 1683 F1v re-elected Under Warden for second year   12 Nov 1683 F5r elected to Mrs Stephens's £320 share   5 Jul 1684 F19v elected Upper Warden with no opponents   7 Apr 1685 (W) confirmed as member of new Livery   4 Jul 1685 F39r fined for second year of Upper Warden   4 Oct 1686 F64r precedent for S.C. paying for cakes and ale is cited from his and James Cotterell's Wardens' accounts   11 Oct 1686 F65v forfeits share to S.C. poor for printing illegal almanacks; summoned   8 Nov 1686 F66v committee to consider his printing of the Catholic Almanack   20 Dec 1686 F69r difference re. Catholic Almanack to be referred to John Lilly and then to Henry Trinder of the Middle Temple. Treasurer to make out two bonds to him that S.C. will stand by either John Lilly's or Henry Trinder's decision   7 Mar 1686/7 F78r 20s paid to him out of Poor Box for burial of Ursula Barker   23 Mar 1686/7 F80r allowed to mortgage his £320 share to Edward Brewster for £300   22 Jun 1687 F85r tells Court that Thomas Newcomb desires to fine for Assistant Renter Warden   2 Jul 1687 F85v among those chosen to audit Warden's accounts   1 Aug 1687 F87r allowed to mortgage his £320 share to Katherine Sawbridge since Edward Brewster is unable to lend him the money   12 Oct 1687 F90v elected Master   5 Mar 1687/8 F99r William Rawlins to lend him £300 on transfer of his Assistant's share to pay off mortgage to Katherine Sawbridge   30 Jun 1688 F102v re-elected Master, with a specific brief to continue the regulation of printing   27 Nov 1688 F110v restored as Assistant. Competes unsuccessfully for Master   4 Aug 1690 F141v deceased; when he was Master fined Hutchins, merchant, 50 guineas plus £5 for importing Stock books seized at Customs, instead of prosecuting him   7 Dec 1691 F162v deceased; his £320 share was mortgaged to Widow Sawbridge for £300 and Hoyle demands the interest from it   4 Feb 1694/5 F216v Gilham Hills, his son and administrator, petitions re. his father's dividend; consideration deferred   9 Jun 1707 G142r deceased; his £320 share had been mortgaged to Sawbridge and assigned to Mrs Mearne. His widow has recently married Bostock so share disposed of

See also HILLS, Gilham

HILLS, Henry (II)   6 Nov 1682 E159v request for £100 loan for 3 years granted   4 Dec 1682 E160v bond for £100 loan to him accepted   3 Dec 1683 F6v to propose an alternative surety to the late Mainstone for £100 loan money   7 Dec 1685 F47r asks for his £100 loan to be extended; his sereties to be inquired into   3 May 1686 F55v presses formerly owned by John Mayo and Simon Hinch are sold to him   7 Jun 1686 F56r presses delivered to him; valued at £9   11 Oct 1686 F65v to repay £100 loan from S.C.   5 Sep 1687 F88v asks S.C. not to stop money due to him for Stock work for repayment of his £100 loan; account to be inspected and paid in full if nearly £100   6 Aug 1688 F105r messenger of the press for S.C.; petitions for a salary and is given the usual salary of £10 p.a.   6 May 1689 F117v ordered to propose a new surety for the remaining term of his £100 loan in place of Arthur Watson, deceased   7 Dec 1691 F163r has repaid the £100 bond by means of printing done for the English Stock   8 May 1693 F188r demands certificate for discovering William Downing's press in order to claim government's £20 reward; granted this plus £5 and expenses

HILLS, Mrs   4 Feb 1694/5 F216v summoned re. her late husband's dividend

HILLS, Widow   2 Mar 1690/1 F150r Court declines to take official notice of her conviction for recusancy and the fact that she might have forfeited her share   9 Jun 1707 G142r has recently married Bostock, so her husband's £320 share is disposed of
See also HILL

HILLYARD, Francis – see following entry

HILLYARD, Thomas   4 Jun 1716 G240v son of Francis, is bound to William Taylor, 7 years

HINCH/HINCE, Simon   22 Dec 1685 F48v petition of John Mayo, Baldwin, Hinch and John Palmer   1 Feb 1685/6 F50v his petition with Mayo and Palmer rejected as being 'the direct contrary to their former confession'   3 May 1686 F55v Under Warden sells two presses of Mayo, Hinch and others to Henry Hills

HINCHCLIFFE/HINCHLIFFE, William   9 Jun 1707 G142v bound to Arthur Bettesworth, 7 years   5 Jul 1714 G220v freed by Arthur Bettesworth

HINCHLIFFE – see HINCHCLIFFE

HINCHMAN, William   2 May 1681 E111v calling in of loan money suspended until next Court on account of his lameness   6 Jun 1681 E113r to continue £50 loan until next Michaelmas on same surety

HINCKLEY, Richard – see following entry

HINCKLEY, William   4 Jun 1716 G240v son of Richard, is bound to William Stephens, 7 years

HINCKLY, William   5 Aug 1706 G134r bound to William Warter, 7 years

HIND, [   ]   3 Dec 1716 G245r to be prosecuted by Clerk

HIND, Andrew   2 Apr 1705 G118v bound by foreign indenture. Freed by Tace Sowle   7 Feb 1708/9 G160v of Salisbury Court; John Bagnall is bound to him   3 Jul 1710 G182r John Bagnall turned over from him to William Wise   6 Oct 1712 G204v Henry Lebrand turned over to him

HIND, Capt. James   3 Dec 1684 F27r William Whitwood assigns Hind's life-story 'No Jest like a True Jest' to Jonah Deacon

HIND, Joseph   1 Feb 1702/3 G85r Samuel Sims turned over to him from Samuel Clark

HIND, Thomas   1 Nov 1714 G223r son of William, is bound to William Maynard, 7 years

HIND, William – see preceding entry

HINDLEY, George   5 Feb 1693/4 F198v servant to Thomas Lacy; freed

HINDMARSH, John   3 Jul 1693 F190r Henry Herringman assigns to him and Richard Sare 'Don Quevedo's [i.e. Francisco de Quevedo's] Visions made English', by Roger L'Estrange

HINDMARSH, Joseph   3 Apr 1682 E150v cloathed   1 Aug 1687 F87r assigned part of 'three translations or books' (itemised) by Sir Roger L'Estrange   5 Sep 1687 F88r elected to Robert Andrews's £40 share   11 Oct 1688 F108v restored to Livery   15 Jul 1690 F140r refuses to subscribe towards raising horse and dragoons for the Crown   9 Feb 1690/1 F149r summoned to next Court for failing to enter a pamphlet   6 Apr 1691 F152r elected Assistant Renter Warden   20 Apr 1691 F152v Court summoned at his request; wishes to fine for Assistant Renter Warden   4 Dec 1693 F196r Richard Sare asks to have 'Letters Writ by a Turkish Spy' entered to himself and Hindmarsh   6 May 1694/5 F223v John Stokes jnr is bound to him   7 Sep 1702 G80v his apprentice George Strahan is freed

HINDMARSH, Mrs   6 May 1700 G39v married; her £40 share disposed of to Robert Vincent

HINTON, Thomas, snr   2 Nov 1702 G83r freed by James Rawlins   1 Sep 1712 G203r his son Thomas is bound to him

HINTON, Thomas, jnr   1 Sep 1712 G203r bound to Thomas, his father, 7 years

HIPPINSTALL, John   8 May 1693 F188r comes in to free William Peirson and is fined 30s for binding him by a foreign indenture

HISTORY OF ETHIOPIA – see PRESENT STATE OF ETHIOPIA

HISTORY OF THE BIBLE   3 Jul 1682 E155v by [Eusebius] Pagitt; assigned by Simon Miller to Edward Brewster

HISTORY OF FRANCE   4 Dec 1682 E160v William Cadman assigns four 1/5 shares in 'A Chronological Abridgement or Extract of the History of France' [i.e. of François Eudes de Mézeray, *A General Chronological History of France*?] in 4 vols.

HISTORY OF PARISMUS   4 Feb 1694/5 F217r together with five other books, assigned to William Wilde by William Thackery

HITCHCOCK, Augustus   7 Jun 1708 G153v bound to James Searle, 7 years

HITCHCOCK, John   4 Aug 1707 G144v bound to William Redmayne, 7 years

HITCHES, Christopher   7 Jun 1708 G153v bound to James Knapton, 7 years

HOARE, Henry   5 Apr 1714 G218r Clerk to attend him in order to give him satisfaction of S.C.'s right to the printing of the Church Catechism and inform him that William Hawes, who printed the same catechism, paid an acknowledgement to S.C.   3 May 1714 G218v Clerk to acquaint him that Wilkins who printed the same 'Exposition of Mrs Lewis of the Catechism' [i.e. John Lewis, *The Church Catechism Explain'd*] as that printed by Downing for Hoare, paid an acknowledgement for doing so to S.C.

HOBBS, Thomas   8 Nov 1697 G1v bound to Thomas Tebb   4 Dec 1704 G114r freed by Thomas Tebb   2 Aug 1708 G156v bookbinder; John Meddhopp is bound to him

HODGES, John   5 Feb 1693/4 F199r butcher of Cripplegate; his son Josiah is bound to Benjamin Beardwell for seven years   4 Feb 1705 G127v Edward Poulter turned over to him from Abel Roper

HODGES/HEDGES, Josiah   5 Feb 1693/4 F199r son of John Hodges of Cripplegate, butcher; bound to Benjamin Beardwell, 7 years   3 Mar 1700/1 G57r freed by Benjamin Beardwell, under name of Hedges

HODGES, Robert   3 Apr 1699 G24r bound to James Oades

HODGES, Roger   2 Jul 1701 G60v bound to John Williams, 8 years   1 Aug 1709 G169v freed by John Williams

HODGKIN – see HODGKINS

HODGKINS/HODGKIN/HODGSKINS, Thomas   3 Jul 1682 E155r cloathed   7 May 1685 (W) confirmed member of new Livery   2 Nov 1685 F46r competes unsuccessfully for Bennett Griffin's £40 share   6 Sep 1686 F62v elected to Adiel Mill's £40 share   26 Mar 1688 F99v elected First Renter Warden   1 Mar 1689/90 F129v elected Stock-keeper for Yeomanry with Samuel Sprint   9 Feb 1690/1 F149r elected to John Richardson's £80 share   4 Sep 1693 F191r refused leave to bind an apprentice as he has two already, despite his alleging that one is sick and useless   1 Mar 1696/7 F255r elected Stock-keeper for Livery with Brabazon Aylmer   5 Jul 1697 F264v competes unsuccessfully for Frances Clarke's £160 share   4 Oct 1697 F268v competes unsuccessfully for the late Mrs Flesher's £160 share   7 Feb 1697/8 G3r elected to Frances Egglesfeild's £160 share   2 May 1698 G7v his apprentice Simon Feild is freed   7 Nov 1698 G16r William Hatch is bound to him   2 Oct 1699 G31v Abraham Parkins is bound to him   4 Dec 1699 G34r Henry Brickwood is bound to him   6 May 1700 G39r takes oath of Assistant   4 May 1702 G70v complaint that he has printed for John Taylor 'An Ephemerides of the Celeshall [i.e. 'coelestial'] Motions for Six Years'

which contained S.C.'s calendar. Not permitted to print any more of the said books   3
May 1703 G89v William Bythell is bound to him   8 May 1704 G106v Thomas
Thorncomb is turned over to him   3 Jul 1704 G109v elected Under Warden   7 Aug
1704 G110v ABC permitted to be printed in his spelling book for Thomas Ballard on
payment of 10s per 1000   2 Apr 1705 G118r to ensure Meredith bequest is sent to
Kempsey school   30 Jun 1705 G121r elected Under Warden   12 Nov 1705 G125r
his apprentice William Hatch is freed   4 Feb 1705/6 G127v Samuel Hughes is bound to
him   4 Nov 1706 G136r Abraham Parkins is bound to him   3 Feb 1706/7 G138r his
apprentice Henry Brickwood is freed   5 Jul 1707 G143r competes unsuccessfully for
Upper Warden   7 Jul 1707 G143v auditor of Master and Wardens' accounts. William
Richardson bound to him   2 Jul 1709 G166v elected Upper Warden   1 Aug 1709
G169v John Turner, apprentice to William Keeble, turned over to him   3 Jul 1710
G181v competes unsuccessfully for Upper Warden   7 Aug 1710 G182v fined for second
year of Upper Warden and for Master to preserve seniority to Awnsham Churchill   2
Jun 1712 G200r elected to Mrs Bassett's Assistant's share. His £160 share disposed of
to John Sprint   24 Apr 1713 G209r signatory to S.C.'s notes to Thomas Guy   1 Jun
1713 G210v his apprentice John Turner is freed   2 Nov 1713 G214v William Wells
turned over to him from John Grantham   3 May 1714 G218v signs note to Guy   22
Dec 1715 G235v bond from S.C. to him for payment of £100 plus interest to be
prepared for next Court day   6 Feb 1715/16 G236r bond from S.C. to him read and
sealed   1 Apr 1717 G249v proposal for an annuity for himself and his wife agreed to
by Court. Hodgkins to consider terms proposed by Court

HODGKINSON, Thomas   26 Mar 1701 G57v elected to James Gray's pension   28
Sep 1702 G80v pensioner, deceased; his pension given to Mary Swaile

HODGKISON, Richard – see following entry

HODGKISON, Samuel   1 Dec 1712 G205v son of Richard; bound to John Collyer, 7
years

HODGSKINS – see HODGKINS

HODGSON, Samuel   10 Sep 1694 F212v son of Thomas Hodgson, patten-maker of
London; bound to Thomas Shepherd

HODGSON, Thomas – see preceding entry

HODSON, Thomas   3 May 1703 G89v freed by Christopher Bateman

HOLDEN, [   ]   4 Oct 1714 G222r executor of Thomas Parkhurst; requests that John
Simms's Assistant's share mortgaged to Parkhurst be disposed of

HOLDEN, Francis   6 Sep 1697 F267r freed by Thomas Lewis

HOLDEN, Thomas   3 Mar 1706/7 G139r Jeremiah Lammas turned over from Henry
Perris to him

HOLFORD, Samuel   16 Jun 1684 F17v of Pall Mall and free of the Saddlers'
Company; declares himself willing to be translated to S.C.   12 Sep 1692 F179r
summoned to show why he should not be cloathed   5 Feb 1693/4 F198v elected to
Livery and summoned   7 May 1694 F203v elected to Livery; allowed to defer
acceptance until next monthly Court in order to sever ties with the Saddlers'
Company   4 Jun 1694 F208r refuses cloathing as he is liable to be called on the Livery
of the Saddlers' Company

HOLLAND, James   4 Feb 1694/5 F217r servant to Robert Whitledge; is freed   20
Dec 1701 G66v Adam Burridge turned over to him. Pays quarterage of 10s to Warden
Samuel Sprint   5 Jul 1702 G92r William Yorke is bound to him   3 Nov 1707 G146v
bookseller; cloathed. Alexander Curdell is bound to him   16 Jan 1710/11 G186v of St

Paul's Churchyard, bookseller; Samuel Powell is bound to him 1 Sep 1712 G203r
William Loefeild is bound to him 4 May 1713 G209v excused office of Renter Warden
for one year 5 Apr 1714 G217v elected Assistant Renter Warden 7 Feb 1714/15
G225r elected to George Grafton's £40 share 9 Apr 1716 G239r James Smith turned
over to him from Daniel Mead 4 Mar 1716/17 G248r James Harrison is bound to him

HOLLAND, William 4 Jul 1692 (W) of Aldermanbury, apprentice of Bryan Courthorpe; is turned over 12 Sep 1692 F179r of Aldermanbury and newly made free of
Bryan Courthorpe; name sent to Lord Chamberlain 2 Nov 1702 G83r Thomas
Beardsworth is bound to him 3 Jul 1704 G110r George Sharpe is bound to him 1
Apr 1706 G131r Robert Hughes is bound to him 6 Oct 1707 G145v cloathed. His
apprentice Richard Wyatt is freed 1 Dec 1707 G147v japanner; Thomas Courthorpe
is bound to him 1 May 1710 G179v of Aldermanbury, japanner; Edward Erick is
bound to him 2 Jul 1711 G192v George Elphick is bound to him 6 Jul 1713 G212v
Reginald Furnes is bound to him 1 Feb 1713/14 G216r his apprentice George Sharpe
is freed 5 Apr 1714 G217v excused office of Renter Warden for one year 6 Sep 1714
G221v William Coleman is bound to him 26 Mar 1715 G227r excused from office of
Renter Warden until next Court day 4 Apr 1715 G227v ordered to attend next Court
day and take office of Renter Warden or pay his fine 26 Mar 1716 G238v elected First
Renter Warden 9 Apr 1716 G239r excused office of First Renter Warden for one year

HOLLINGHURST, Robert 8 May 1682 E152r continues as surety for John Penn's
£100 loan from S.C.

HOLLIS, William 3 Jul 1704 G110r bound to Edward Terrill, 7 years

HOLLOWAY, Edmund 6 Aug 1694 F211v son of John Holloway of Larington,
Wiltshire, innholder; bound to Richard Cumberland 2 Nov 1702 G83r freed by
Richard Cumberland

HOLLOWAY, John – see preceding entry

HOLLOWAY, John 7 Nov 1709 G172r bound to Mary Veazy, 7 years 1 Apr 1717
G249v freed by Mary Veazy

HOLLOWAY, John Andrew 7 Jun 1708 G153v bound to Charles Walkden, 7
years 5 May 1712 G199v turned over from Charles Walkden to John Darby

HOLMES, Benjamin 7 Oct 1706 G135r bound to Samuel Hoyle, 7 years

HOLMES, Christopher 3 Oct 1709 G171r bound to Edward Lewis, 7 years

HOLMES, John 2 Aug 1697 F265v bound to William Hensman

HOLMES, John 5 Mar 1710/11 G188r bound to John Wilde, 8 years

HOLMES, Philip 3 Feb 1679/80 E96v summoned to next General Court

HOLMES, Samuel 1 Oct 1705 G124r bound to Samuel Welshman, 7 years 1 Jun
1713 G210v freed by Samuel Welshman 1 Oct 1716 G244r Francis Midford is bound
to him

HOLT, Elizabeth 3 Jun 1700 G40v Isaac Dalton is bound to her 9 Jun 1707 G142v
her apprentice Isaac Dalton is freed

HOLT, Sir John – see LORD CHIEF JUSTICE

HOLT, Mrs 1 Mar 1702/3 G85v deceased; her £80 share disposed of to Samuel Keeble

HOLT, Ralph (I) 2 Jul 1683 F2r complains that his type for Sheet B of Saunders's
Almanack has been given to Samuel Roycroft; decision deferred until end of year 7 Jan
1683/4 F8r competes unsuccessfully for Henry Herringman's £160 share 7 Jul 1684
F20v reminds Court of his dispute with Samuel Roycroft re. Sheet B of Saunders's
Almanack; allowed to print it for the year ensuing 7 May 1685 (W) confirmed as

member of new Livery 3 Jul 1686 F59v to be summoned re. his complaint against Roycroft 5 Jul 1686 F60v appears before Court; the quarrel is referred to Master, Wardens and Stock-keepers 13 Oct 1687 F91v sworn in as Assistant

HOLT, Ralph (II) 1 Sep 1712 G203r freed by patrimony 6 Oct 1712 G204v Edward Christopher turned over to him 2 Nov 1713 G214v his apprentice Edward Christopher is freed

HOLT, Sarah 6 Mar 1703/4 G103v freed by patrimony. Her apprentice Joseph Tough is freed; Francis Stephens is bound to her 7 Aug 1704 G111r John Evans is turned over to her 5 Feb 1704/5 G115r William Crowder is bound to her 6 Aug 1705 G122v her apprentice John Evans is freed 6 Aug 1711 G193r Richard Ward is bound to her. Her apprentice Francis Stephens is freed 2 Jun 1712 G200v Thomas Allestree is bound to her. Her apprentice William Crowder is freed 1 Apr 1717 G249v Thomas Allestree turned over from her to Richard Harbin

HOLT, Widow 6 Aug 1688 F104v ordered to stop printing, but on giving her assurance to obtain a licence, allowed to continue printing almanacks which her late husband had printed

HOLT, William 18 Jul 1690 F140v bond from S.C. of £1000 penalty to pay £512 10s on 18 Jan 1691 4 Feb 1694/5 F216v his £500 loan at 5% p.a. to S.C. to be continued at 6% p.a. at his request

HOLY COURT – see CAUSSIN, Nicolas

HOLY CREED – see PEARSON, John, Bishop of Chester

HOMER 18 Mar 1686/7 F79v in Greek and Latin; among books in catalogue annexed to Oxford agreement

HOMER, William 8 Nov 1703 G97r bound to Henry Parsons, 7 years

HOOD, Robert – see following entry

HOOD, Thomas 6 Oct 1712 G204v son of Robert; bound to Anne Motte, 7 years 4 Oct 1714 G222v turned over from Anne Motte to William Wilkins

HOOKE, John 8 May 1704 G106v bound to Charles Harper, 8 years 7 Jul 1712 G201v freed by Charles Harper 1 Mar 1713/14 G216v Edward Stiles is bound to him

HOOKE, Richard 7 Jun 1697 F263r bound to Humphrey Pooler

HOOKER, [ ] 1 Oct 1694 F213r demands the £160 share assigned to him by S.C. in a statute of bankruptcy against Dorman Newman; deferred 12 Nov 1694 F214v paid the £160 from Newman's share; Court resolves to consider how to secure themselves from future clandestine mortgages

HOOKES, James, snr – see following entry

HOOKES, James, jnr 3 Dec 1711 G195v son of James; bound to William Sparkes, 7 years

HOOLE, Charles 4 Dec 1699 G34r complaint by Bennett Griffin of cost of printing Hoole's 'Sententiae'

HOOLE, Samuel 9 Sep 1706 G134v Randall Nicoll turned over to him from Benjamin Brown 4 Jul 1709 G167v Jonathan Taylor turned over to him from William Taylor

HOOPER, John, snr – see following entry

HOOPER, John, jnr 6 Oct 1712 G204v son of John; bound to Thomas Cope, 7 years

HOOPER, Nicholas 2 Mar 1690/1 F150r petitions successfully to be elected Under Beadle or Porter. To be disenfranchised 4 Apr 1691 F151v re-elected Under Beadle 16 Jun 1691 F155v to be let a house in Amen Corner to Midsummer Day next at £16 p.a.

and from the end of that year as tenant at will   26 Mar 1692 F168r presents petition complaining about Randall Taylor and Jonathan Whitlock, and is elected to Taylor's position as Beadle   1692–1702 Beadle   5 Dec 1692 F183r one of his tenants, Mrs Draper, petitions Court   4 Jun 1694 F208r petitions for favour regarding rent comparable to that shown to his predecessors; deferred   3 Jun 1695 F225v petition for rent abatement deferred; ordered that he should in the meantime make up with Treasurer the amount depending for rent   11 Nov 1695 F234v his bill for Acts, &c., written when S.C. was trying to continue the Printing Act, is referred to Master and Wardens   6 Jul 1696 F245v to draw up Court minutes that Christopher Grandorge has omitted to enter   5 Oct 1696 F250v to enter all apprentices and Court orders that Grandorge has neglected   4 Oct 1697 F268r bill to Upper Warden for £5 6s 3d allowed and ordered to be paid by Under Warden. Committee considering his bills decide that Benjamin Tooke should pay him 15s 8d and Grandorge's debt should be paid out of his salary   7 Nov 1698 G15v owes S.C. £47 1s 6d. To pay £10 yearly, to be deducted from his salary   5 Dec 1698 G17r petition read out concerning his misfortunes and losses. Rent due from him to last Michaelmas to be remitted. Hearing that he has recently let his house for £16 p.a., this sum to be deducted from his salary   7 Feb 1698/9 G20r Clerk to make out an account of all the fixed goods in the house where he lately dwelt   8 Apr 1700 G39r to help ensure that no boys play in S.C. garden or pigeons be kept there   7 Oct 1700 G45v house to be let to Charles Lewis. Hooper to have the use of a room in the house rent free   2 Dec 1700 G47v inconvenience caused to Charles Lewis by his residence   5 Oct 1702 G81r deceased; his eldest son to officiate until new Beadle chosen at Christmas   5 Apr 1703 G88r deceased; house to be leased by John Nutt   3 May 1703 G89r died very much in debt

HOOPER, Thomas (I)   6 Oct 1701 G65r freed by patrimony   5 Apr 1703 G88r bill for acting as Beadle to be paid. To deliver up books and papers belonging to S.C., and Beadle's gown and staff   3 May 1703 G89r son of Nicholas Hooper; requesting money to put his younger brother out as an apprentice. Given £5 from Poor Box, 10s from Master and 5s from each member of table

HOOPER, Thomas (II)   3 Apr 1699 G24r bound to Edward Jones   6 May 1706 G131v freed by Mrs Jones, widow of Edward

HOOTTON, John, snr – see following entry

HOOTTON, John, jnr   1 Dec 1713 G216v son of John; bound to William Harvey, 7 years

HOPE, Elizabeth   23 Mar 1707/8 G150r elected to Jane Bambridge's pension

HOPKINS, James, snr – see following entry

HOPKINS, James   5 Sep 1715 G232v son of James; bound to John Sackfield, 7 years

HOPKINS, John   7 Feb 1708/9 G160v bound to Elizabeth Smith, 7 years

HOPKINS, William   4 Feb 1705/6 G127v bound to William Kitchener, 7 years

HOPPER, George   12 Apr 1692 F169r excused cloathing for the present   3 Aug 1696 F246v deceased; his £80 share is disposed of to Jacob Tonson

HORACE   12 Nov 1694 F214v dispute involving several people over printing of 'Quinti Horatii Flacci ... Interpretatione ... Ludovici Deprezar [i.e. Desprez] in Usum ... Delphini'   13 Apr 1698 G6v complaint of Richard Chiswell that Henry Mortlock, Robert Clavell and Samuel Smith are printing his copy of Horace

HORN BOOK   7 Jun 1680 E100v John Macock assigned printing of stock horn book

HORNE, [   ] (I)   19 Dec 1690 F147v bricklayer; gives Court a model of new kitchen and Court members given until next monthly Court to consider

HORNE, [ ] (II)   4 Mar 1694/5 F218r allowed to have entered to him 'several Copies or parts of Copies' which he shows in Court

HORNE, George   8 Apr 1695 F220r cloathed and elected to Nicholas Boddington's £40 share   6 Nov 1699 G32r disposes of his £40 share to William Hunt

HORNE, Mary   4 Feb 1705/6 G127r deceased; her £160 share disposed of to Israel Harrison

HORNE, Robert   20 Jun 1681 E113r Crown mandate that he should become an Assistant   5 Sep 1681 E129r competes unsuccessfully for Thomas Vere's £160 share   22 Dec 1681 E141r competes unsuccessfully for Richard Clarke's £160 share   6 Feb 1681/2 E143v competes unsuccessfully for Thomas Newcomb's £160 share   5 Feb 1682/s E163r elected to John Towse's £160 share   1 Mar 1682/3 E164v elected Stock-keeper for Assistants with Roger Norton   7 May 1683 E170r desired to consult with John Playford committee about disposal of Mrs Godbid's share   7 Apr 1684 F13v on the list of loyal Assistants presented to the Crown   6 Apr 1685 F32v assigns various theological books, itemised, to Abel Swale   7 May 1685 (W) confirmed as member of new Livery   4 Jul 1685 F39v Henry Herringman's request that Horne be allowed to fine for two years' Under Warden is granted. Among those chosen to audit Renter Wardens' accounts   6 Jul 1685 F40r promises to fine for two years' Under Warden

HORNE, Thomas   4 Oct 1686 (W) on original list of new liverymen, though not chosen in the end   20 Dec 1694 F216r nominated to take over the £40 share that Charles Brome has refused; summoned   4 Feb 1694/5 F216v sworn into his £40 share   26 Mar 1702 G68v fined for Renter Warden   2 Apr 1705 G118v his former apprentice Francis Faram is freed   4 Feb 1705/6 G127r elected to Israel Harrison's £80 share; his £40 share disposed of to Thomas Benskin. John Richardson is bound to him   3 May 1714 G219r his apprentice John Richardson is freed

HORNER, William   8 Nov 1703 G97r bound to Henry Parsons   7 May 1711 G190v freed by Henry Parsons

HORNOULD, William   7 Jul 1707 G143v bound to Joseph Bush, 7 years

HORTON, Edward   22 Dec 1681 E141r elected to George Wells's £40 share   6 May 1685 F34r elected to the late John Playford's £80 share   7 May 1685 (W) confirmed as member of new Livery   2 May 1687 F83r deceased; his £80 share voted to John Penn

HORTON, James   3 Feb 1706/7 G138r bound to William Pearson, 7 years

HORTON, William   29 May 1689 F118v cloathed   26 Mar 1695 F219v elected Renter Warden with John Heptingstall   6 May 1695 F222v elected to Samuel Smith's £40 share and takes partner's oath   6 Jun 1698 G8v John Evans is bound to him   5 Sep 1698 G14v his apprentice Alexander Ashburne is freed   7 Nov 1698 G16r Thomas Spencer is bound to him   3 Mar 1700/1 G57r (repeated under 26 Mar 1701 G58r) Benjamin Shelley is bound to him   6 Oct 1701 G64v disposes of his £40 share to John Arden   8 May 1704 G106v Benjamin Shelley turned over from him to John Grantham   5 Mar 1704/5 G117r Thomas Spencer turned over from him to Edmund Powell and then to Willliam Downing

HOTHAM, Matthew   2 Oct 1704 G112v freed by John Bark   4 Dec 1710 G185v to be served with a copy of the writ of execution against Benjamin Harris

HOUGHAM, [ ]   28 Oct 1697 F269v herald-painter; to make S.C.'s banner and the City's banner at the cost of £12 and to deliver it by 3 November   7 Mar 1697/8 G4v escutcheon painter; to bring back S.C.'s and City's banners and a pole before being paid

HOUGHTON, George   4 Mar 1716/17 G248r son of Robert; bound to Joseph Pomfrett, 8 years

HOUGHTON, Robert – see preceding entry

HOUSE OF COMMONS   4 Jun 1694 F207v Court tell it that they cannot as a corporation supply all England with stamped paper but will impose parcel rate for members   24 Mar 1695/6 F240v Lord Mayor sends precept that all S.C. members should subscribe to the Association the House of Commons has entered into   1 Mar 1706/7 G138v Joddrell, the clerk of the House of Commons, to have fees and charges for Bill in Parliament paid to him

See also ACTS OF PARLIAMENT

HOUSE OF LORDS   9 Mar 1695/6 F240r orders S.C. to search for a Jacobite pamphlet of March 1695 and report on 14 March; Court leaves it to Master and Wardens   7 Aug 1699 G28r payment to doorkeepers there, for attendance in relation to Act of Parliament for laying duty on paper

HOUSE OF OFFICE   4 Sep 1682 E157r pipe and funnel to be provided from Clerk's garret, separate from Richardson's funnel

HOUSES   8 Jun 1696 F243r S.C.'s arms to be fixed to all houses belonging to Corporation or English Stock   6 Sep 1697 F269v houses of some of S.C.'s tenants to be surveyed by a carpenter and a bricklayer; Clerk to inform tenants of repairs needed

See also ENGLISH STOCK

HOUSETOWNE, Alexander – see following entry

HOUSETOWNE, John   1 Dec 1712 G205v son of Alexander; bound to William Newbolt, 7 years

HOW, Job   5 Mar 1704/5 G117r John Gilpin is bound to him   1 Mar 1713/14 G216v his apprentice John Gilpin is freed

HOW, John   8 May 1682 E153r submits suit between him and S.C. re. counterfeit almanacks to Court; fined 20 nobles and legal fees   6 Jul 1685 F40v summoned to next Court re. complaints of Samuel Heyrick and others that he has printed their copies   3 Aug 1685 F42v confesses to printing 'The Fifteen Comforts of Rash and Inconsiderate Marriage', to which three others owned the right, but Heyrick waives right to prosecute   5 May 1690 F134v summoned to explain a letter containing scandalous reflections on Ambrose Isted   7 Feb 1708/9 G160v William Yates is bound to him   6 Aug 1716 G242v his apprentice William Yates is freed

HOW, Josiah   7 Jul 1712 G201v son of Philip; bound to John Marriott, 7 years

HOW, Philip – see preceding entry

HOWARD, James   2 Dec 1700 G54r bound to John Clarke, 7 years

HOWARD, John   1 Feb 1713/14 G216r his son Stephen is bound to Thomas Howlatt, 7 years

HOWARD, Richard   1 Mar 1702/3 G86r bound to Benjamin Harris jnr, 7 years   4 Feb 1716/17 G246v freed by Benjamin Harris

HOWARD, Stephen   1 Feb 1713/14 G216r son of John; bound to Thomas Howlatt, 7 years

HOWE, John   6 Oct 1701 G65r Heritage Harford is bound to him

HOWELL, Mordecai – see following entry

HOWELL, John   7 Dec 1713 G215r son of Mordecai; bound to Joseph Marshall, 7 years

HOWKINS, John   15 Apr 1692 F170r his appendix to [Robert] Record's 'Arithmetic', assigned to William Freeman by Elizabeth Flesher at the same time the book itself is assigned

HOWLATT, Thomas, snr – see following entry

HOWLATT, Thomas, jnr   2 Apr 1694 F202v son of Thomas Howlatt of St Giles in the Fields, tailor; bound to Margaret Bennett, widow, 7 years   6 Jun 1709 G165v freed by the administratrix of Margaret Bennett   4 Jul 1709 G167v John Driver and Francis Reading turned over to him from Margaret Bennett   1 Feb 1713/14 G216r Stephen Howard is bound to him

HOYLE, [ ]   7 Dec 1691 F162v scrivener; asks for interest on the late Henry Hills's share mortgaged to Widow Sawbridge for £300; Master agrees when debts are paid

HOYLE, Samuel, snr   26 Mar 1683 E166r elected Renter Warden   6 Aug 1683 F3r his proposal to take up Mrs Kendon's £80 share deferred until next Court   1 Oct 1683 F3v elected to Mrs Kendon's £80 share   25 Oct 1683 F4r because of Hoyle's having 'gone aside' and not likely to make the usual provision for Lord Mayor's Day, Second Renter Warden Adam Felton is elected First Renter Warden for the remainder of the year. Hoyle to be sent a letter ordering him to settle accounts with Samuel Lowndes and Adam Felton and deliver the Renter Warden's books to them. (W) letter from Master and Wardens to Hoyle mentioning 'trouble fallen upon you'   3 Mar 1683/4 F10v request to mortgage his £80 share to Rands, not a S.C. member, rejected; share to be disposed of at next Court if money due to Rands' wife, Widow Kendon, is not repaid by then. (W) letter from Hoyle   2 Jun 1684 F15v disposal of his £80 share postponed until next Court   3 Feb 1684/5 F30r petition to Court to dispose of John Starkey's stock and pay the money to his wife is granted   7 Jun 1686 F57r Court to dispose of his £80 share to Richard Simpson after frequent admonishments and a complaint from Rands that he had failed to pay for it. His servant appears with a Counsel's opinion stating that S.C. is acting illegally; Master suspends swearing-in of partners   5 Mar 1687/8 F99r pretends claim to an £80 share disposed of to Richard Simpson in 1686; Court leaves it to him whether to sue or not   15 Jun 1688 F102r files bill of complaint re. Widow Kendon's share   7 Sep 1702 G80v Samuel Hoyle is bound to him   7 Oct 1706 G135r Benjamin Holmes is bound to him   9 Jun 1707 G142r scrivener; produces in Court mortgage of Henry Hills's £320 share to Sawbridge and assignment thereof to Mrs Mearne

HOYLE, Samuel, jnr   7 Sep 1702 G80v bound to Samuel Hoyle, patrimony

HUBBARD, [ ]   3 Jun 1689 F119v excused cloathing

HUBBARD, Peter   1 Dec 1701 G66r bound to Robert Jole, 7 years

HUBBARD, Robert   1 Oct 1711 G194v son of Thomas; bound to Thomas Warren, 7 years

HUBBARD, Thomas – see preceding entry

HUBBART, [ ]   5 Aug 1695 F231r does not appear on summons; elected into Livery and resummoned

HUBBERT, Francis   4 Dec 1699 G34r John Kindon is bound to him

HUDDLESTONE, George   4 Oct 1697 F268v freed by Samuel Lowndes

HUDSON, Green   7 Aug 1704 G111r bound to William Onley, 7 years   1 Oct 1711 G195r freed by administratrix of William Onley

HUDSON, Thomas   6 Jun 1698 G8v bound to Joseph Oake, 7 years

HUGGONSON, John   4 Sep 1716 G242v son of William; bound to Edward Saunders, 7 years

HUGGONSON, William – see preceding entry

HUGHES, Howell – see following entry

HUGHES, John   6 Jul 1713 G212v son of Howell; bound to John Sackfeild, 7 years

HUGHES, Robert   1 Apr 1706 G131r bound to William Holland, 7 years

HUGHES, Samuel   4 Feb 1705/6 G127v bound to Thomas Hodgkins, 7 years

HUGHES, Thomas   6 Nov 1710 G185r bookbinder; John Royden is bound to him

HULL, Rebecca   22 Mar 1715/16 G238r elected to Elizabeth Seale's pension

HUMBLE, Ralph   1 Dec 1707 G147v bound to Benjamin Harris, 7 years

HUMFRY, HUMFRYES, HUMFRYS – see HUMPHREYS

HUMPHREY – see HUMPHREYS

HUMPHREYS/HUMFRY/HUMFRYES/HUMFRYS/HUMPHRYES, John (I)   3 Jun 1695 F225v servant to John Darby; freed   5 Sep 1698 G14v Richard Humphreys is bound to him   4 Jun 1705 G120v James Ogston is bound to him   5 Aug 1706 G134r his apprentice Richard Humphreys is freed   4 Nov 1706 G136r cloathed. Printer; Thomas Aubrey is bound to him   4 Aug 1707 G144v William Wilkins turned over from James Rawlins to him   4 Jun 1711 G191r printer; William Lane is bound to him   2 Mar 1712/13 G207r Thomas Browne is bound to him

HUMPHREYS, John (II)   3 Dec 1716 G245v freed by patrimony

HUMPHREYS, Mrs   7 May 1688 F100v tells Court she has sold her press to Andrew Sowle; bond to this effect given up to be cancelled

HUMPHREYS/HUMPHREY, Richard (I)   6 Oct 1690 F144r freed; his master, Richard Baldwin, fined 20s for accepting turnover of him from Joseph Hutchinson, a foreigner   6 Mar 1703/4 G103v Thomas Walker is bound to him   4 Sep 1704 G112r his apprentice Thomas Walker is turned over to James Hazard

HUMPHREYS/HUMPHRYES, Richard (II)   5 Sep 1698 G14v bound to John Humphreys   5 Aug 1706 G134r freed by John Humphreys   5 Sep 1709 G170r bookbinder of Blackfriars; John Stagg is bound to him

See also HUMPHREYS, Richard (I)

HUMPHREYS/HUMPHRYES, Samuel   2 Oct 1699 G31v bound to John Darby jnr

HUMPHREYS/HUMFRYES/HUMPHRYES, William   2 Mar 1712/13 G207r Joshua Powell is bound to him   28 Sep 1713 G213v Joshua Powell turned over from him to William Scott   1 Feb 1713/14 G216r his apprentice William Wilkins is freed

HUMPHRYES – see HUMPHREYS

HUNT, [ ]   2 Jun 1701 G60r bookbinder; to be prosecuted for selling a double Ephemeris

HUNT, Amy   24 Mar 1711/12 G198r deceased; Hannah Smith given her pension

HUNT, John (I)   12 Nov 1694 F214v excused cloathing for the present   5 Aug 1695 F231v does not appear on summons; elected into Livery and re-summoned   7 Oct 1695 F233r refuses cloathing; Court defers prosecution and orders enquiry into his circumstances   11 Nov 1695 F235r to be prosecuted for refusing cloathing (W) reputed to be worth near £5000   3 Feb 1695/6 F239r accepts cloathing, paying £20 down and 40s towards the legal charges that his refusal cost S.C.   26 Mar 1708 G150v elected Assistant Renter Warden   12 Apr 1708 G151v fined for First Renter Warden

HUNT, John (II)   5 Sep 1698 G14v freed by John Everingham

HUNT, Joseph   7 Dec 1702 G83v bound to Hannah Clark

HUNT, Philip   8 Apr 1700 G39r bound to Thomas Huse, 7 years

HUNT, Richard   12 Dec 1695 F238r his apprentice John Shortharell is freed   7 Jul 1701 G62r William Harden is bound to him

HUNT, William   3 May 1697 F262r Adam Burridge is bound to him   7 Mar 1697/8 G5r his apprentice Thomas Richardson is freed   1 Aug 1698 G13r given until next Court day to decide whether to take cloathing   5 Sep 1698 G14v cloathed   6 Nov 1699 G32v elected to George Horne's £40 share   5 Feb 1699/1700 G35r bound to Henry Carter, 7 years   3 Nov 1701 G65r deceased; his £40 share disposed of to Henry Bonwick   4 Jun 1705 G120v his apprentice Adam Burridge is freed

HUNTER, John   2 Aug 1703 G94r admitted freeman by redemption in accordance with order of Lord Mayor of 29.Jul 1703   6 Dec 1703 G99v John Cairns is bound to him   5 Mar 1704/5 G117r James Barnes is bound to him   7 Jun 1708 G153v tailor; Percival Hutchinson is bound to him   4 Jun 1711 G191r his apprentice John Cairns is freed

HUNTER, William   6 Oct 1707 G145v bound to John Nutt, 7 years   6 Feb 1715/16 G236r freed by John Nutt   2 Jul 1716 G242r Robert Ryley turned over to him from John Nutt   10 Sep 1716 G243r cloathed

HUNTLEY, Edward – see following entry

HUNTLEY, John   1 Jul 1695 F228r son of Edward Huntley of Middlesex, pewterer; bound to Thomas Snowden

HURST, Philip   5 Feb 1710/11 G187r bound to Joseph Hazard, 7 years   20 Dec 1716 G246r turned over from Joseph Hazard to Francis Jeffreys

HURST, Robert   4 May 1702 G71r bound to Peter Buck, 7 years

HURST, Robert   2 Nov 1702 G83r bound to Philip Barrett, 7 years

HURT, Christopher, snr (I) – see following entry

HURT, Christopher, jnr (II)   1 Oct 1694 F213v son of Christopher Hurt snr, Whitechapel, gentleman; bound to John Marsh

HURT, Christopher (III) – see following entry

HURT, William   2 Apr 1694 F202v son of Christopher Hurt of London, glazier; bound to George Powell, 7 years   4 Sep 1710 G183v cloathed. John Philmott is turned over to him from Ann Snowden

HUSBANDS/HUSBONDS, Mrs/Widow   5 Jul 1680 E101v mortgages her Livery share to George Sawbridge for £30   1 Oct 1683 F3v deceased; Henry Clarke admitted to her £160 share

HUSE, Joseph   9 Feb 1712/13 G206v son of Thomas; bound to his father, 7 years

HUSE, Thomas   13 Apr 1698 G6v Elizabeth Ketcheyman is bound to him   8 Apr 1700 G39r Philip Hunt is bound to him   5 May 1707 G142r bookbinder; Richard Steel is bound to him   9 Feb 1712/13 G206v his son Joseph is bound to him

HUSSEY, Anne   9 Feb 1712/13 G206v bond from S.C. of £200 penalty to pay £103 on 10 August sealed

HUSSEY, Christopher   3 Jun 1689 F119v excused cloathing   1 Feb 1691/2 (W) John Pere is freed by him   7 Nov 1692 F181v of Little Britain; summoned to be cloathed   5 Dec 1692 F183r excused cloathing   11 Nov 1695 F235r excused cloathing on Court's receipt of his letter pleading inability   20 Oct 1702 G82v bookseller; surety for Joseph Collyer as Treasurer

HUSSEY, Elizabeth   6 Sep 1714 G221v notice to be given to her that S.C. will not pay more than 5% interest on her £100 bond in accordance with Act of Parliament for lowering of interest rates

HUSSEY, Mary   1 Dec 1707 G147v bond from S.C. of £400 penalty to pay £205 in six months sealed   24 Dec 1708 G160r bond from S.C. to pay £102 10s on 25 Jun 1709

sealed   4 Apr 1709 G164r bond from S.C. of £400 penalty to pay £205 on 5 Oct 1709
sealed   9 Feb 1712/13 G206r bond from S.C. of £200 penalty to pay £103 on 10
August sealed. Former bond of £200 to her cancelled   6 Sep 1714 G221r notice to be
given to her that from Michaelmas S.C. will not pay more than 5% interest on her £100
bond in accordance with Act of Parliament for lowering interest rates

HUTCHINS, [   ]   4 Aug 1690 F141v merchant; paid Henry Hills when Master 50
guineas and £5 for a dinner for importing Stock books seized at the Customs House

HUTCHINSON, Joseph   6 Oct 1690 F144r Richard Baldwin fined 20s for having
Richard Humphrey turned over to him from Hutchinson, a foreigner

HUTCHINSON, Percival   7 Jun 1708 G153v bound to John Hunter, 7 years

HUTCHINSON, Thomas   5 Oct 1713 G214r bound to Edmund Parker, 7 years

HYATT, [   ]   7 Sep 1713 G213r desires to be excused cloathing

HYETT/HYATT, Richard   3 Oct 1709 G171r of Bartholomew Close, japanner;
William Neck is bound to him   9 Apr 1711 G189v of Bartholomew Close, japanner;
William Betty is bound to him

HYDE, Edward, Earl of Clarendon – see CLARENDON

HYDE, [Thomas], Dr   17 May 1695 F224r 470 of his 'Eastern Games' [i.e. *De Ludis
Orientalibus*] at 3s 6d per book sent from Oxford; committee to take advice about
selling them   7 Oct 1695 (W) committee seeking a reduction from Oxford in cost of
books on the last cargo that came from Ireland, including Dr Hyde's

HYDRIOTAPHIA – see URN-BURIAL

IBBOTTSON, Mrs   4 Jun 1694 F208r deceased; her £40 share disposed of to James
Adamson

IBBUTT, John   7 May 1716 G240r son of Matthew; bound to Samuel Messer, 7 years

IBBUTT, Matthew – see preceding entry

IGNORAMUS JUSTICO [i.e. Edmund Whitaker, *Ignoramus Justices*, or the anonymous *Ignoramus Justice*?]   2 Oct 1682 E158r Richard Janeway confesses to printing
this for Francis Smith's wife

ILES, Widow   20 Dec 1687 F96r given £1 charity

ILIVE, Jane   3 Jun 1706 G132v her apprentice John Philpott is freed

ILIVE, Thomas   7 Feb 1698/9 G20v his apprentice James Philpott is freed   7 Apr
1701 G58v James Jones is bound to him   6 Oct 1701 G64v cloathed   1 Mar 1707/8
G150r printer; Thomas Thompson is bound to him   4 Oct 1708 G158r of Aldersgate
Street, printer; Thomas Nightingall is bound to him   6 Dec 1708 G159v his apprentice
James Brooke is freed   1 Aug 1709 G169v Thomas Thompson turned over from him
to William Redmaine   3 Oct 1715 G233v his apprentice Thomas Nightingall is freed

ILLEGAL PRINTING – see PRINTING, ILLEGAL

ILLIDGE, George – see following entry

ILLIDGE, Samuel   4 Jun 1694 F208v son of George Illidge of Nantwich, Chester,
joiner; bound to Robert Steele   1 Jun 1702 G71v freed by Robert Steele   5 Oct 1702
G81v William Burscoe turned over from Robert Steele to him   7 Feb 1703/4 G101v
James Steward turned over to him

IMITATION OF CHRIST (attr. Thomas à Kempis)   1 Aug 1681 E117v John Clarke
assigns this to John Redmaine

IMPORTING, ILLEGAL   3 Nov 1701 G65r Wellington to be prosecuted for importing
S.C.'s books contrary to byelaws; committee to consider this   4 Aug 1707 G144r

committee to meet Gellebrand to decide what to do about importing of S.C.'s books and copies   10 Oct 1707 G146r Bibles, psalters and psalms imported from Rotterdam discovered by Gellebrand. Bill in Chancery to be prepared against Button to discover all books imported in this manner   5 Feb 1710/11 G186v Bill in Chancery against Chester carrier for bringing almanacks imported from Ireland into Chester

INCE, Edward   1 Sep 1701 G64r bound by Thomas Warren, 7 years   7 Feb 1708/9 G160v freed by Thomas Warren

INETT, [John], Dr   4 Sep 1710 G183v tenants of Oxford to try and prevail with the delegates for S.C. to take only 100 of his 'Origines Anglicanis' [i.e. 'Anglicanae']

INFALLIBLE WAY TO CONTENTMENT, AN (by Abednego Seller)   4 Dec 1699 G33v assigned by Richard Hargrave to William Freeman

INNETT – see INETT

INNYS, John   3 Jul 1710 G182r bound to his brother, William Innys

INNYS, William   1 Jun 1702 G71v bound to Benjamin Walford, 7 years   6 Jun 1709 G165v freed by Benjamin Walford   27 Mar 1710 G177v of St Paul's Churchyard, bookseller; to be summoned by Beadle to attend next Court day to accept cloathing   3 Apr 1710 G178r cloathed   3 Jul 1710 G182r of St Paul's Churchyard, bookseller; William Noble turned over from Benjamin Walford to him. His brother John Innys is bound to him   2 Nov 1713 G214v John Clarke is bound to him   1 Feb 1713/14 G215v elected to John Nutt's £40 share   1 Mar 1713/14 G216v takes oath of partner   1 Apr 1717 G249r fined for First Renter Warden

INSURANCE, OFFICE OF   1 Nov 1714 G223r its proprietors to have use of Hall for one guinea as before

IRELAND   25 Jun 1691 F156r Lord Mayor requires S.C. to lend Crown money upon two Acts towards service in Ireland   12 Apr 1692 F168v Henry Million excused Renter Wardenship on grounds that he is commanded into Ireland by Crown re. linen manufacture   10 Oct 1692 F181r committee to meet other Companies concerned in the Irish plantation at Skinners' Hall to hear tenants' proposals   7 Oct 1695 (W) committee seeking a reduction from Oxford University in cost of books on the last cargo from Ireland   2 May 1698 G7r state of S.C.'s lands and estates in Ireland read. To be entered in a register of the S.C.'s writings

See also PELLIPAR

IRONMONGERS' COMPANY   3 Feb 1695/6 F239r Court refuses to discharge John Sparkes, John Gerrard and Thomas Penford from S.C. so they can take up freedom of Ironmongers' Company

IRONSIDE, Dr Gilbert   1 Oct 1688 F107r Vice-Chancellor of Oxford University; petitions Crown re. S.C. and King's Printers allegedly encroaching on Oxford privileges. (W) Petition cites Henry Hills and defends Peter Parker and Thomas Guy, the Oxford printers   20 Dec 1688 F112r letter to him re. differences between S.C. and Oxford about almanacks is read and approved   4 Feb 1688/9 F112r refers dispute re. almanacks to Parker and Guy

ISHAM, Zaccheus – see CATECHISMS

ISTEAD – see ISTED

ISTED/ISTEAD, Ambrose   20 Jun 1681 E113r Crown mandate that he should become an Assistant   2 Jul 1681 E115r ordered that his Renter Warden's fine be paid   27 Mar 1682 E149r elected to audit Renter Wardens' accounts   4 Sep 1682 E157v to be added, with Robert Scott, to committee re. John Lilly and Clerk's duties as to byelaws and pension notes   7 May 1683 E169v to examine lease of warehouse to

Thomas Allen   4 Jun 1683 E170v asked together with Henry Herringman to take legal advice as to John Playford's 'Vade Mecum'. With Henry Clarke, reports that Thomas Allen's lease should be engrossed   7 Apr 1684 F13v on the list of loyal Assistants presented to the Crown   7 May 1685 (W) confirmed as member of new Livery   1 Jun 1685 F38r appointed to audit Renter Wardens' accounts instead of Robert Scott, who was out of England. Appointed to inquire whether the City of London can grant a longer time in lease for the Mount   4 Jul 1685 F39v elected Under Warden; Henry Clarke also in competition. His request to fine for two years of Under Warden is turned down because sufficient candidates for Upper Warden are available   1 Feb 1685/6 F50r elected to Widow Sawbridge's Assistant's share   3 Jul 1686 F58v fined for second year of Upper Warden   4 Oct 1686 F64r alleges precedents for charging cakes and ale to S.C. rather than Wardens   2 Jul 1687 F85v ties with John Baker in vote for Upper Warden and is beaten on second vote   11 Oct 1688 F108v restored to Assistants   27 Nov 1688 F110v competes unsuccessfully for Upper Warden   26 Mar 1689 F116r elected Upper Warden in place of John Baker, deceased   6 Jul 1689 F121r elected Upper Warden for second year running   5 May 1690 F134v John How summoned to explain a letter containing scandalous reflections on Isted   2 Jun 1690 F135r on reversal of *quo warranto*, elected Upper Warden for remainder of year   5 Jul 1690 F138r elected Master   18 Jul 1690 F141r Francis Egglesfeild mortgages Livery share to him for £100   4 Jul 1691 F156v re-elected Master; John Bellinger also in competition

See also ISTED, Mrs

ISTED, John   8 Nov 1703 G97r freed by Abel Roper

ISTED/ISTEAD, Mrs   4 Jul 1698 G10v requested to deliver up writings relating to S.C. and counter-security entered into by S.C. to her husband, Ambrose Isted and others concerning comprinting at the University of Oxford; on so doing to be indemnified by S.C. from any costs or claims   6 Mar 1698/9 G22r members of Court to go with her to her own counsel re. delivering up of writings belonging to S.C.   8 May 1699 G24v Clerk to take an abstract of the writings in her custody relating to S.C.   4 Sep 1699 G29v Susanna Miller's £160 share mortgaged to her for £120. Equity of redemption of the said share to be remortgaged   6 Dec 1703 G99v interest on mortgage on Mrs Miller's stock to be paid from dividend   20 Dec 1703 G100r her interest in Mrs Miller's dividend   6 May 1706 G131r money arising from Mrs Miller's share to be paid to her as she has a mortgage on it   3 Feb 1706/7 G137r the deceased Mrs Miller's mortgage to her is exempt from being paid to Thomas Parkhurst   3 Nov 1707 G146v her dividend to be stopped because she refuses to deliver up writings belonging to S.C.

IZARD, [   ]   2 Apr 1688 F100v keeper of Ludgate; S.C. to negotiate with him about discharging the journeyman printer John Croome from prison

IZARD, Mary   21 Jun 1706 G132v deceased; Elizabeth Brook is given her pension

IZOD, Anthony   27 Sep 1695 F232v elected to the late Richard Butler's pension

JACKMAN, Leake   7 Sep 1713 G213v son of Nicholas; bound to Thomas Osborne, 7 years

JACKMAN, Nicholas – see preceding entry

JACKSON, [   ] (I)   6 May 1706 G131v affidavit declaring that neither he nor any other person in trust for him had any of the counterfeit psalters or other books when served with the subpoena at the S.C.'s suit

JACKSON, [   ] (II)   4 Jul 1709 G167r officer of the Commissioners of the Sewers. Capt. William Phillipps to consult with him concerning Carter's house

JACKSON, Charles   6 Jul 1713 G212v his son Francis is bound to John Nicholson, 7 years

JACKSON, Daniel   7 Mar 1708/9 G162r freed by Thomas Parkhurst

JACKSON, Francis   6 Jul 1713 G212v son of Charles; bound to John Nicholson, 7 years

JACKSON, Humphrey   1 Oct 1694 F213v son of John Jackson of Reading, cordwainer; bound to John Meakes   3 Nov 1701 G65r freed by John Meakes and John Berrisford   7 Dec 1702 G83v Richard Greenhill is bound to him   2 Oct 1710 G184v his apprentice Richard Greenhill is freed

JACKSON, Joan   3 Oct 1687 F89r elected to the late Widow Dow's 40s pension   20 Dec 1700 G54r Elizabeth Crawford given her pension

JACKSON, John (I)   1 Oct 1694 F213v cordwainer of Reading; his son Humphrey is bound to John Meakes

JACKSON, John (II)   4 Apr 1709 G164r bound to John Ford, 7 years   6 Sep 1714 G221v turned over from James Ford to John Moore

JACKSON, Leonard   4 Feb 1711/12 G196r John Amery's £160 share mortgaged to him 12 years previously. Burdikin, for whom mortgage was held in trust, requesting payment

JACKSON, Richard   4 Jul 1715 G231r his son William is bound to Henry Carter, 7 years

JACKSON, William (I)   8 Apr 1700 G39r bound to Daniel Midwinter, 7 years   5 May 1707 G142r freed by Daniel Midwinter

JACKSON, William (II)   4 Jul 1715 G231r son of Richard; bound to Henry Carter, 7 years

JACKSON, William, snr (III) – see following entry

JACKSON, William, jnr (IV)   5 Sep 1715 G232v son of William; bound to William Scott, 7 years   10 Sep 1716 G243r turned over from William Scott to John Watts

JACOB, Mrs   22 Jun 1694 F209v elected to the late Alice Williams's pension

JACOB, William   1 Mar 1679/80 E97r surrenders his £40 share to Thomas Dring in writing   2 Jul 1688 F103v asks for his Livery fine of 18 years ago back on account of poverty; Christopher Wilkinson is given £10 from the Poor Box for his relief   27 Mar 1693 F185r elected into the pension of John Major, deceased

JAMES, [   ]   7 Oct 1700 G46r cloathed

JAMES, Andrew   7 Feb 1708/9 G160v bound to George James, 7 years

JAMES, Henry, Dr   12 Jul 1703 G92v Head of Queen's College, Cambridge; to be attended by Master and Wardens concerning lease of printing house from University   22 Jul 1703 G93r report from Master and Wardens who had attended him

JAMES, Elinor   6 Jul 1713 G212v her apprentice Jonathan Baldwin is freed

JAMES, Elizabeth   3 Mar 1700/1 G57r bound to Hannah Carter

JAMES, George   6 Aug 1705 G122v freed by Benjamin Motte   7 Feb 1708/9 G160v of Paternoster Row; Andrew James is bound to him   4 Apr 1709 G164r John Vasey turned over to him from John Matthews   5 Jun 1710 G180r cloathed   6 Oct 1712 G204v his apprentice Joseph Veasey [i.e. John Vasey?] is freed   2 Mar 1712/13 G207r Benjamin Jones is bound to him   1 Mar 1713/14 G216v Samuel Neville is bound to him

JAMES, John   2 Dec 1695 F237v Charles Paine jnr is bound to him

JAMES, Mrs   4 Aug 1701 G63r consents to William Wade's request for freedom

JAMES, Robert   6 Sep 1697 F267r Robert Fellow is bound to him   5 Dec 1698 G17r a request that he be excused cloathing for some time. Cyprian Thompson is bound to him   5 Jun 1699 G25v cloathed

JAMES, Thomas (I)   6 Apr 1691 F152v summoned to next Court with John Back re. their printing a copy belonging to Joshua Coniers   10 Sep 1694 F212r excused cloathing   7 Oct 1700 G46r Joseph Stockley is bound to him   2 Jun 1701 G60v Thomas Chiffins is bound to him   4 Aug 1701 G63r letter from him to Clerk opposing the making free of William Wade   1 Sep 1701 G64r his apprentice William Wade is freed   2 Mar 1701/2 G67v Jonathan Billing is bound to him   4 Aug 1712 G202v John Astbury is bound to him   1 Jun 1713 G210v Benjamin Harford is bound to him   4 Jul 1715 G231r William Matkins is bound to him   8 Aug 1715 G231v letter-founder; to attend next Court to take cloathing   5 Sep 1715 G232r cloathed

JAMES/JENES, Thomas (II)   3 Jun 1700 G40v bound to Jane Rayment, 7 years   4 Feb 1705/6 G127v turned over from Jane Rayment to Owen Lloyd   9 Jun 1707 G142v freed by Owen Lloyd

JAMES, Thomas (III)   3 Jun 1700 G40v bound to Robert Andrews, 7 years   9 Feb 1707/8 G149r freed by Robert Andrews

JAMES, William   8 Nov 1703 G97r bound to John Beresford, 7 years

JANEWAY/JANNAWAY/JANNEWAY/JENEWAY, Richard   1 Mar 1681/2 E146r after lengthy questioning about an anonymous pamphlet, 'A Letter from a Person of Quality ... About Abhorrers and Addressers', prosecuted with forfeiture of £20 under byelaw   3 Apr 1682 E150r submits to Court concerning almanacks found at his house; they order him to reimburse legal fees to S.C. and pay £5 to English Stock as a fine for damage done by almanacks   2 Oct 1682 E158r confesses to printing various itemised pamphlets, including the 'Letter ... About Abhorrers', and accuses Edward Powell of failing to indemnify him; summoned to next Court   4 Oct 1682 E159r signs petition and statement of names; produces Edward Powell's receipt; suggests Bradyll printed the 'Letter ... about Abhorrers'   13 Apr 1698 G6v John Hawkins is bound to him   6 May 1700 G39v not permitted to bind a second apprentice unless he first takes cloathing. Cloathed. John Norman is bound to him   5 Oct 1702 G81v Henry Peach, an ex-apprentice of Janeway's, is turned over for a second time   5 Jul 1703 G92r Nicholas Smith is turned over to him   4 Sep 1704 G112r his apprentice Henry Peach is freed by Joseph Hazard   7 May 1705 G120r Henry Greep is bound to him. His apprentice John Hawkins is freed   3 Mar 1706/7 G139r Joseph Robinson turned over to him from Edward Midwinter   6 Oct 1707 G145v his apprentices Nicholas Smith and William Littleboy are freed   1 Dec 1707 G147v his apprentice Henry Greep turned over to Joseph Downing   6 Sep 1708 G157v Samuel Aris turned over to him from Daniel Bridge   3 Oct 1709 G171r Henry Mawson turned over to him from Mrs Mawson   6 Mar 1709/10 G176v his apprentice Joseph Robinson is freed   1 May 1710 G179v of Whitefriars, printer; John Clarke is bound to him   5 Jun 1710 G180v Richard Jones is bound to him   5 Feb 1710/11 G188r his apprentice Samuel Aris is freed

JANNY, Thomas   3 Jul 1710 G182r bound to William Taylor, 7 years

JANSEN, Nathaniel   6 Nov 1704 G113r John Randoll is turned over to him

JANSENN, Sir Theodore   13 Apr 1699 G24r Master and Wardens to attend him with their case relating to the further duty to be laid on paper

JAQUES, Thomas   2 Jun 1701 G60v bound to Henry Carter

JARVIS, John   26 Mar 1686 F54r elected waterman   4 Apr 1687 F81v elected waterman

JAY, Elyphall   4 Dec 1693 F197r Philip Payne is bound to him

JEFFERIES, Sir Robert – see LORD MAYOR

JEFFREYS, Lord George   27 Nov 1688 F110r Lord Chancellor; delivers S.C. back the surrender of its charter

JEFFREYS/JEFFRIS, Francis   1 Feb 1702/3 G85r bound to Joseph Hazard, 7 years   5 Feb 1710/11 G187r freed by Joseph Hazard   6 Aug 1716 G242v John Rivington is bound to him   20 Dec 1716 G246r Philip Hurst is turned over to him from Joseph Hazard

JEFFREYS/JEFFRYES, Joseph   7 Feb 1714/15 G225r son of William; bound to Cornelius Rainsford, 7 years

JEFFREYS, William – see preceding entry

JEKYLL'S CATECHISM (by Thomas Jekyll) – see CATECHISMS

JENCKS, [ ]   7 Dec 1685 F47r haberdasher; pleads ignorance that the books that Sarah Harris sold him were counterfeits of Stock books

JENES – see JAMES

JENEWAY – see JANEWAY

JENKINS, Leoline, Sir   20 Jun 1681 E113r signatory of Crown mandate to S.C.   3 Mar 1683/4 F10r signatory of Crown letter to S.C.

JENKINSON, Matthew   5 Jul 1703 G92r bound to John Vasey, 7 years

JENNER, Sir Thomas   3 Mar 1683/4 F11r Recorder of the City of London; Master and Wardens to tell him personally that a door from Amen Court to S.C. garden is impossible as the site is for warehouses

JENNINGS, John   7 Jul 1712 G201v son of John; bound to Richard Simpson, 7 years

JENNOR, JENNOUR – see JENOUR

JENOUR, [ ]   8 Aug 1715 G231v cloathed and so able to bind a third apprentice. David Kinneir is bound to him

JENOUR/JENNOUR, Joan   27 Sep 1710 G184r elected to James Flowrey's pension

JENOUR, John   7 Aug 1699 G29r freed by patrimony

JENOUR/JENNOR, Lancelot   7 Apr 1701 G58v bound to Matthew Jenour, 7 years

JENOUR/JENNOUR, Matthew   7 Apr 1701 G58v Lancelot Jenour is bound to him   9 Sep 1706 G134v Edward Leadbeter turned over to him from Thomas Mead   2 Dec 1706 G136v Nicholas Powell turned over to him from Thomas Mead   2 Aug 1708 G156v Robert Dennett turned over to him from Daniel Bridge   2 May 1709 G165r of Giltspur Street; John Chamberlaine is bound to him   6 Nov 1710 G185r printer; Richard Crane is bound to him   6 Oct 1712 G204v his apprentice Nathaniel Parsell is freed   4 Jun 1716 G240v his apprentices John Chamberlaine and Robert Dennett are freed

JEVON, [ ]   6 Mar 1698/9 G22r to be given notice to quit one of S.C.'s houses   3 Apr 1699 G23v rent arrears and key to be collected from him as soon as possible

JEWELL, Samuel   6 May 1689 F117v appointed surety for Treasurer with Thomas Caister; Clerk to draw up their bond to S.C.

JODDRELL, [ ]   1 Mar 1706/7 G138v the clerk of the House of Commons; fees and charges for Bill in Parliament to be paid to him

JOELL, Robert   29 May 1689 F118v cloathed   8 Jun 1691 F154v allowed 3 more months to pay off last £10 of Livery fine on account of financial losses, and his prosecution called off

JOHNSON, [ ]   28 Oct 1697 F267r herald-painter; to make the S.C.'s streamer at the cost of £7 (W) £6 and to deliver it by 3 November

JOHNSON, Benjamin   6 Jul 1691 F157v to be granted £50 loan from Tyler Bequest if his securities are approved; unusually full addresses given   7 Sep 1691 F160r securities approved   23 Sep 1691 F161r allowed to substitute John Marshall, a spectacle-maker in Fleet Street, for Joseph Weildy as surety   4 Jun 1694 F208r his apprentice John Randall is freed   8 Jun 1696 F243r loan money due from him to be called in   2 May 1698 G7v Richard Taylor is bound to him   4 Sep 1699 G30v Elizabeth Browne is bound to him   7 Sep 1702 G80v Joseph Pomfrett is bound to him   1 Oct 1711 G195r his apprentice Joseph Pomfrett is freed

JOHNSON, Cassandra   22 Dec 1681 E141v admitted to a 5s pension   26 Jun 1682 E154r married; Susanna Prichard admitted to her pension

JOHNSON, Hester   7 Jun 1708 G153r widow; her apprentice Richard Taylor is freed

JOHNSON, James   3 May 1703 G89r bound to George Sawbridge, 7 years

JOHNSON, John (I)   1 Mar 1679/80 E97r freed by William Godbid   4 Oct 1708 G158r party to S.C.'s bond of £200 for payment of £5 p.a. to poor of the Liberty of Great and Little Tower-hill

JOHNSON, John (II)   6 May 1695 F223r freed by Samuel Dim

JOHNSON, John (III)   8 Apr 1700 G39r bound to Stephen Keyes, 7 years

JOHNSON, John (IV)   3 Dec 1711 G195v his son Thomas is bound to Robert Knaplock, 7 years

JOHNSON, John (V)   1 Dec 1712 G205v freed by Charles Lea's widow

JOHNSON, Mrs   6 May 1695 F222r executrix of John Bellinger; tells Court that Mrs Bellinger has remarried; Court promises payment of £320 share under terms of will

JOHNSON, Thomas (I)   7 Aug 1704 G111r bound to John Nutt, 8 years

JOHNSON, Thomas (II)   3 Dec 1711 G195v son of John; bound to Robert Knaplock, 7 years

JOHNSON, William (I)   1 Mar 1687/8 F97v expelled from Livery by order of Lord Mayor

JOHNSON, William (II)   5 Dec 1698 G17r bound to William Pearson, 7 years   3 Dec 1705 G126r freed by William Pearson

JOHNSON, William (III)   4 Dec 1699 G34r bound to Robert Roberts, 7 years

JOINERS   14 Mar 1686/7 F78v legal advice to be taken as to whether joiners and others not free of S.C. should be allowed to sell books   2 Apr 1705 G118r joiner's bill to be paid by Joseph Collyer

JOINT STOCK – see ENGLISH STOCK: Subscriptions

JOLE, John   5 Feb 1699/1700 G35r freed by patrimony

JOLE, Robert, snr – see following entry

JOLE, Robert, jnr   4 Dec 1693 F196v son of Robert, freed by patrimony   11 Nov 1695 F236r William Tegg is bound to him   5 Aug 1700 G44r Jane Conly is bound to him   1 Dec 1701 G66r Peter Hubbard is bound to him   7 Aug 1704 G111r Roger Whiteyate is bound to him

JOLLYMAN, Robert   6 Dec 1714 G224r son of William; bound to William Bowyer, 7 years

JOLLYMAN, William – see previous entry

JONES, [   ]   12 Nov 1694 F214v asks that Henry Clarke's widow be allowed to benefit from his £160 share during her widowhood   3 May 1697 F261v agent of Mrs Frances Clarke who requests permission to transfer the mortgage of her £160 share   2 Mar 1701/2 G67v elected Stock-keeper for Livery   4 Oct 1708 G157v his letter to Andrews to be referred to committee considering case of Benjamin Harris

JONES, Anne   1 Feb 1713/14 G216r Thomas Turner is bound to her

JONES, Arthur   3 Mar 1683/4 F11r to be granted £50 from Tyler Bequest if his securities are approved   26 Mar 1684 F11v securities approved   4 Jul 1687 (W) memo re. Jones' loan   6 May 1689 F117v he and securities ordered to pay his £50 loan by next Michaelmas   3 Mar 1689/90 F130v having often failed to pay a bond for £50 due to S.C. it is to be delivered to John Lilly for legal action

JONES, Benjamin   2 Mar 1712/13 G207r son of Isaac; bound to George James, 7 years

JONES, Edward (I)   1 Mar 1679/80 E97r freed by Thomas Newcomb snr   7 Dec 1685 F48r Thomas Flesher assigns him four medical books   1 Mar 1685/6 F51r cloathed   1 Mar 1687/8 F97v expelled from Livery by order of Lord Mayor   11 Oct 1688 F108v restored to Livery   15 Apr 1692 F169v elected Assistant Renter Warden   4 Jul 1692 F173v Renter Warden; competes unsuccessfully for Robert Roberts's £40 share   3 Oct 1692 F180v competes unsuccessfully for Israel Harrison's £40 share   7 Nov 1692 F181v elected to John Harding's £40 share   3 Jul 1693 F189v the auditors of the Renter Wardens' accounts drawn up by Jones and John Miller report that the balance is £19 2s 2d   2 Dec 1695 F237r John Morphew is bound to him   6 Apr 1696 F242r John Bales, his apprentice, is freed   7 Feb 1698/9 G20v William Davis is bound to him   3 Apr 1699 G24r Thomas Hooper is bound to him   4 Sep 1699 G30v Richard Harbin is bound to him   1 Sep 1701 G64r James Boat is bound to him   1 Feb 1702/3 G85r his apprentice John Morphew is freed   6 Mar 1703/4 G103v elected to Brabazon Aylmer's £80 share. His £40 share disposed of to Robert Knaplock   3 Apr 1704 G106r Thomas Walthoe is bound to him   2 Apr 1705 G118v Henry Christmas is bound to him

JONES, Edward (II)   2 Apr 1705 G118v freed by John Penn

JONES, Frances   26 Mar 1685 F32r given 2s 6d charity

JONES, Francis   6 Oct 1712 G204v freed by patrimony

JONES, George   6 Jul 1696 F245v thanked for his offer to officiate during the Clerk's incapacity but told that at present there is no occasion

JONES, Hugh   3 Mar 1689/90 F130v the bond in which he is involved for £50 due to S.C. is to be delivered into legal hands because of Arthur Jones not paying

JONES, Isaac   2 Mar 1712/13 G207r his son Benjamin is bound to George James, 7 years

JONES, James (I)   7 Apr 1701 G58v bound to Thomas Ilive, 7 years

JONES, James (II)   2 Jul 1705 G121v bound to Gilham Hills, 7 years   4 Apr 1709 G164r freed by Gilham Hills

JONES, John (I)   1 Aug 1692 (W) freed by executrix of Thomas Newcomb   12 Sep 1692 F179r in 'R. Colledge rents' in St Andrew-by-the-Wardrobe and newly made free of Thomas Newcomb's executors; name sent to Lord Chamberlain   4 Sep 1699 G30v Thomas Baker is bound to him   9 Sep 1706 G134v his apprentice Thomas Baker is freed by Robert Clavell   4 Oct 1708 G157v and Thomas Jones to be made party to S.C.'s Bill in Chancery against John Atkin and others   5 Dec 1709 G172r of Blackfriars, printer; Richard King is bound to him

JONES, John (II)   1 Feb 1696/7 F254v freed by redemption on giving 2 guineas to the Poor Box; also cloathed, promising fine at two six-monthly intervals

JONES, Mary   4 Mar 1705/6 G129r her apprentice William Davis is freed   7 Feb 1714/15 G225r deceased; her £80 share disposed of to George Grafton

JONES, Mrs   6 May 1706 G131v widow of Edward; her apprentice Thomas Hooper is freed

JONES, Richard (I)   12 Apr 1708 G152r bound to Edward Davis, 7 years

JONES, Richard (II)   5 Jun 1710 G180v bound to Richard Janeway, 7 years

JONES, Robert   3 May 1697 F262r freed by Samuel Nash

JONES, Sarah   3 Nov 1712 G205r freed by patrimony

JONES, Thomas (I)   1 Mar 1679/80 E97r agreement re. his printing Welsh Almanack to be officially sealed   7 Apr 1701 G58r elected to cloathing on 7 May 1700, accepted   3 May 1708 G152v books of S.C. to be searched for an order of Court between S.C. and himself about printing the Welsh Almanack   22 Jun 1708 G153v Clerk to acquaint him that as he had not paid money, according to the agreement, for printing Welsh Almanack, S.C. have granted privilege to John Rogers   5 Jul 1708 G155r Clerk to send him another letter, the same as that of a fortnight since   4 Oct 1708 G157v and John Jones to be made party to S.C.'s Bill in Chancery against John Atkin and others

JONES, Thomas (II)   7 Aug 1699 G29r bound to William Bowyer, 7 years   3 Mar 1706/7 G139r freed by William Bowyer

JONES, Sir William   1 Feb 1680/1 E106v deputation to attend him in drafting Act of Parliament; also to consult Robert Atkins and Sir George Treby

JOSEPH, Richard   7 Feb 1698/9 G20v freed by Robert Everingham

JOSEPHUS, Flavius   3 Apr 1693 F185v Thomas Bassett, Nathaniel Ranew and Richard Chiswell complain that Roger L'Estrange's new translation will affect their sales

JOYNER, John   3 Feb 1706/7 G138r freed by patrimony

JOYNER, Lancelot   3 Feb 1706/7 G138r his son John is freed by patrimony

JOYNER, Richard   5 Aug 1706 G134r bound to James Walker, 7 years

JULII CAESARIS PORTUS ICCIUS (by William Somner) – see GIBSON, Edmund

JULIUS CAESAR, Gaius – see CAESAR, Gaius Julius

JUSTINUS, Marcus Junianus ('Justin')   1 Sep 1690 F142r Court agrees to buy Justin's History [i.e. *Historiae Philippicae*] from Henry Mortlock and Benjamin Tooke   6 Oct 1690 F143r Justin's History to be entered in trust for S.C.   5 Jun 1710 G180r Stock-keepers to deal with John Walthoe about how to dispose of Justin with notes

JUVENAL (Decius Junius Juvenalis)   7 Apr 1690 F133r Abel Swale accuses Thomas Dring of printing the Satires of Juvenal and Persius, his copy; dispute referred to committee   2 Mar 1690/1 F150v Richard Wild accused of importing Juvenal, a Stock book   5 Jun 1699 G25r B. Walford's request that a caveat be entered against re-entering copies in the register granted   3 Jul 1699 G27r paper from Nicholson and Timothy Child concerning copyright for printing. Richard Chiswell, Robert Clavell and Samuel Sprint have an interest in the Satires. Reference before Treasurer to be expedited   7 Aug 1699 G29r extension of period of reference before Treasurer

KARY, [ ]   6 Aug 1705 G122v of Broad Street, musician; to provide a trumpet and five musicians for Election Dinner

KATER, Elizabeth   20 Dec 1705 G126r Elizabeth Lowther is bound to her

KAYCKWICK, [ ] 7 Jun 1680 E100v his apprentice John Littleton is freed

KEBLE, Carey 6 Aug 1705 G122v bound to Samuel Manship

KEBLE – see KEEBLE

KEEBLE, [ ] 1 Feb 1691/2 F165r he and Vincent summoned to next Court to answer Edward Brewster's complaint against them 7 Mar 1691/2 F166v he and Vincent promise to submit to arbitration on Edward Brewster's complaint about them printing King's Printers' books

KEEBLE/KEBLE, Samuel, snr 7 May 1685 (W) confirmed member of new Livery 4 Oct 1686 F64r elected to Obadiah Blagrave's £40 share 11 Oct 1688 F108v restored to Livery 1 Mar 1688/9 F113v elected Stock-keeper for Yeomanry with William Rogers 7 Apr 1690 F132v petitions with John Harding and Brabazon Aylmer to increase number of Renter Wardens and cut down individual cost; rejected 4 Apr 1691 F151r fined for Assistant Renter Warden 3 Oct 1692 F180r competes unsuccessfully for Walter Kettleby's £80 share 7 May 1694 F203v requests to surrender his £40 share; Richard Bentley elected to it 5 Aug 1695 F232r William Keeble bound to his father Samuel from 8 April 1695 11 Nov 1695 F235v his apprentice Alexander Bosvile is freed 7 Dec 1696 F252v competes unsuccessfully for John Hancock's £80 share 1 Apr 1697 F260v to ask booksellers, printers and paper manufacturers in Fleet Street and Temple Bar within for money towards Paper Act test case 4 Oct 1697 F268v competes unsuccessfully for John Amery's £80 share 7 Feb 1697/8 G3r competes unsuccessfully for Thomas Hodgkins' £80 share 7 Mar 1697/8 G4v competes unsuccessfully for Daniel Peacock's £80 share and Elizabeth Brookes's £80 share 7 Oct 1698 G15r competes unsuccessfully for Mrs Whitlock's £80 share 7 Aug 1699 G29r Robert Gosling is bound to him 13 Apr 1702 G70r elected to Mary Crump's £40 share 1 Mar 1702/3 G85v elected to Mrs Holt's £80 share. His £40 share disposed of to James Roberts 5 Jul 1703 G92r takes oath of partner 12 Jun 1704 G107v William Dolphin is bound to him 4 Dec 1704 G114r his son William Keeble is freed and cloathed 4 Nov 1706 G136r his apprentice Robert Gostling is freed 7 Jun 1707 G142v his son Samuel Keeble is bound to him 7 Aug 1710 G183r his son Samuel Keeble is freed 7 Dec 1713 G215r Edward Blackburne is bound to him 6 Dec 1714 G224v his apprentice Thomas Egerton is freed

KEEBLE/KEBLE, Samuel, jnr 7 Jun 1707 G142v bound to his father Samuel, 7 years 7 Aug 1710 G183r freed by patrimony

KEEBLE/KEBLE, William 5 Aug 1695 F232r bound to his father Samuel from 8 April 1695 4 Dec 1704 G114r freed by his father by service and cloathed 6 May 1706 G131v John Turner is bound to him 1 Aug 1709 G169v John Turner turned over from him to Thomas Hodgkins

KEEBLEBUTTER, John 3 Apr 1704 G105v and James Crane, bond from S.C. of £200 penalty to pay £105 sealed 3 Jul 1704 G109r and James Crane, bond resealed due to error 4 Oct 1708 G158r party to S.C.'s bond for payment of £5 p.a. to poor of the liberty of Great and Little Tower-hill

KEENE, William 22 Jun 1698 G9v general release from S.C. sealed

KEIMER/KEYMER, Samuel 6 Dec 1703 G99v bound to Bryan Mills, 7 years 4 Feb 1711/12 G196v freed by Bryan Mills 3 Mar 1711/12 G197r Elias Moreton is bound to him 5 Apr 1714 G218r cloathed. Richard Spackman is bound to him 3 May 1714 G219r John Phillmott turned over to him 7 Nov 1715 G234v Richard Spackman turned over from him to William Bowyer 6 May 1717 G250v his apprentice John Philmott is freed

KELLINGTON, Richard 6 Jul 1702 G78r freed by patrimony

KELLOW, Samuel 4 Apr 1715 G227v son of William; bound to John Clarke, 7 years

KELLOW, William – see previous entry

See also CALLOWE

KELLY, John 1 Dec 1707 G147v bound to Richard Brugis

KEMP, Robert 4 May 1702 G71r freed by Robert Vincent

KEMPIS, Thomas à – see IMITATION OF CHRIST

KEMPSEY/KEMSEY/KELMSLEY MANOR 4 May 1702 G70v in Worcestershire; Christopher Meredith's gift to poor of the district 1 Mar 1702/3 G86r Meredith's bequest of books to 2 Apr 1705 G118r Under Warden to ensure that Meredith's gift is sent to the school there 4 Mar 1705/6 G128v Master and Wardens to arrange for the sending of Bibles to the poor of the district, according to the will of the donor 6 Mar 1709/10 G176v arrears of money due to the poor of the district for Bibles and schoolbooks. Henry Mortlock to deal with this 4 Aug 1712 G202v care to be taken to provide books for the school belonging to the Manor

KEMPSTER, William 4 Oct 1697 F268v bound to Timothy Child

KEMPTON, Rex 8 Nov 1703 G97r bound to William Norton, 7 years

KEMSEY MANOR – see KEMPSEY MANOR

KEN, Thomas, Bishop of Bath and Wells – see EXPOSITION ON THE CHURCH-CATECHISM

KENDALL – see KENDON, Alice

KENDON, [ ] 26 Mar 1680 E98v bond for £500 at 5% to him to be sealed and former bond cancelled

KENDON/KENDALL, Alice 6 Aug 1683 F3r her application to sell £80 share, and Samuel Hoyle's proposal to take it up, deferred until next Court 1 Oct 1683 F3v her £80 share disposed of to Samuel Hoyle 3 Mar 1683/4 F10v involved in Samuel Hoyle's negotiations with her husband Rands over mortgaging Hoyle's £80 share 11 May 1685 F35r now Mrs Rands; 2 bonds to Emmanuel Blake and James Kniveton taken out to discharge her bond of £500 1 Jun 1685 F38r is paid £512 10s and bond cancelled 7 Jun 1686 F57r Rands complains that his wife has not been paid by Samuel Hoyle for her £80 share; Court was to have disposed of it for cash but disposal deferred on receipt of counsel's opinion 1 Mar 1687/8 F98r her husband demands refund and interest for his wife's £80 share which the Court pays, deducting 6 months' interest 15 Jun 1688 F102r Samuel Hoyle files a bill of complaint re. her share forfeited when she married Rands

KENNETT, White 24 Oct 1695 F234r order for printers to return 30 'Oxford Antiquities' [i.e. Kennett's *Parochial Antiquities … in … Oxford*?] to Oxford

KENT, Samuel 5 Sep 1709 G170r bound to Robert Tooke, 7 years

KEPPEY, Thomas 1 Jun 1702 G71v bound to Thomas Knell, 7 years

KETCHEYMAN, Elizabeth 13 Apr 1698 G6v bound to Thomas Huse, 7 years

KETELBY, Edward 7 Feb 1714/15 G225r son of Ralph; bound to John Freer, 7 years

KETELBY, Ralph – see preceding entry

KETTILBY – see KETTLEBY

KETTLEBY/KETTILBY, Walter 2 May 1681 E111v loan of £50 called in; his request for continuance postponed 5 Sep 1681 E129r summoned to next Court because of non-appearance at this 3 Oct 1681 E130v non-appearance re. £50 loan money noted 26 Mar 1683 E166v granted permission to pay off his loan at next Midsummer day   1 Mar 1683/4 F9r elected Stock-keeper for Yeomanry with William Shrewsbury   7 Apr 1684 F14r on the list of loyal Assistants presented to the Crown   2 Jun 1684 F15v promises to fine for Renter Warden. Elected to Christopher Wilkinson's £40 share to make up his £40 share to £80. To hold position of Stock-keeper for the Yeomanry until next election despite having been made an Assistant   7 May 1685 (W) confirmed member of new Livery   2 May 1687 F82v he and Benjamin Tooke to pay £25 each to defray a £50 loan to John Wallis   6 Jun 1687 F84r he and Tooke given until Michaelmas to pay Wallis's loan   11 Oct 1688 F108v restored to Livery   4 Feb 1688/9 F112v re-elected Assistant   6 May 1689 F117r ranked fourteenth of Assistants never elected as Master or Warden   5 Jun 1690 F135v re-elected Assistant (sic)   1 Feb 1691/2 F165r Samuel Smith is summoned to next Court to answer Kettleby's complaint   4 Jul 1692 F173v competes unsuccessfully for John Simms's £160 share   3 Oct 1692 F180r elected to Robert Clavell's £160 share   3 Jul 1693 F189v among those chosen to audit Warden's accounts   4 Jun 1694 F208r among those chosen to audit Renter Wardens' accounts   3 Jul 1697 F263v competes unsuccessfully for Under Warden   5 Jul 1697 F264v competes unsuccessfully for Under Warden twice; admitted to a £5 fine for a year to preserve his seniority. Among those chosen to audit Warden's accounts   6 Sep 1697 F266v ordered to tell Anthony Nelme, occupant of one of S.C.'s houses, that he will be informed about his lease in ample time   3 Jul 1699 G26v auditor of Master and Wardens' accounts   6 Jul 1700 G43r fined for second year of Under Warden to preserve seniority   1 Mar 1700/1 G56r elected Stock-keeper for Assistants   2 Mar 1701/2 G67v elected Stock-keeper for Assistants   4 Jul 1702 G77r elected Upper Warden and takes oath   3 Jul 1703 G91v elected Upper Warden and takes oath   6 Dec 1703 G99v accounts as Warden signed off   6 Jul 1706 G133r elected Master and takes oath   5 May 1707 G141v competes unsuccessfully for William Rawlins' Assistant's share. Elected to Mrs Leake's £320 share. His £160 share disposed of to Marshall   5 Jul 1707 G143r competes unsuccessfully for Master   21 Feb 1716/17 G246v conveyance of trusteeship of Hall from him and others to new trustees

KETTLEWELL, Howard   11 Nov 1700 G46v bound to John Heptingstall, 7 years

KETTLEWELL, Robert   1 Mar 1685/6 F51r cloathed   3 May 1686 F55r has refused to pay Livery fine and disobeyed summons; resolved that he should be prosecuted for Livery fine of £20   1 Mar 1687/8 F97v expelled from Livery by order of Lord Mayor   11 Oct 1688 F108v restored to Livery

KEYES, Ann   12 Nov 1705 G125r William Cratch is bound to her

KEYES/KEYS, Stephen   7 Mar 1691/2 F166v periwig-maker and freeman of S.C.; appears to bind an apprentice. Is tendered cloathing and is given time to consider   12 Apr 1692 F169r summoned to next Court to be cloathed   5 Sep 1692 F177v elected to Livery and summoned   5 Dec 1692 F183r Clerk to warn him that unless he answers his next summons and accepts cloathing he will be prosecuted   8 May 1693 F188r Clerk to sue him for not answering his summons to be cloathed   12 Jun 1693 F188v cloathed   2 Jul 1694 F210v John Broadhurst is bound to him   4 Mar 1694/5 F218r excused a moiety of the £1 5s legal costs of the suit commenced against him by S.C. on his refusing to be cloathed   1 Jul 1695 F228r John Ballett jnr is bound to him   8 Apr 1700 G39r John Johnson is bound to him   2 Nov 1702 G83r John Brock is bound to him   1 Mar 1702/3 G86r Thomas Warrett is bound to him

KEYMER – see KEIMER

KEYS – see KEYES

KIDGELL, John   7 Jun 1680 E100v freed by Neville Simons

KIDWELL, Robert   5 Jul 1714 G220v John Franck turned over to him

KIFFT/KIFFTE/KIFT, Henry   2 Oct 1693 F192v excused cloathing until next Lady
Day   2 Jul 1694 F210v David Arnold, his apprentice, is freed   2 Nov 1696 F251v
cloathed   26 Mar 1701 G57v summoned to attend Court. Fined for Renter Warden   2
Mar 1701/2 G67v his apprentice Thomas Turner is freed   1 Feb 1702/3 G85r James
Watt is bound to him 6 Mar 1703/4 G103v his apprentice Robert Kifft is freed   9 Sep
1706 G134v Richard Cooke is bound to him   4 Apr 1709 G164r of Little Tower Hill;
Henry Sedgeley is bound to him   1 Nov 1714 G223r his apprentice Richard Cookes is
freed

KIFFT/KIFFTE, Robert   6 Mar 1703/4 G103v freed by Henry Kifft

KIFFT/KIFT, Mrs   7 May 1716 G240r deceased; her executor grants Henry Sedgeley
his freedom

KILLINGTON, Job   7 Feb 1697/8 G3v his apprentice William Garrett is freed

KINDON, John   4 Dec 1699 G34r bound to Francis Hubbert, 7 years   3 Dec 1711
G195v freed by John Nicholson

KING – see CROWN

KING'S ARMS   6 May 1700 G39v committee to oversee placement in Hall

KING'S LIBRARY   4 Oct 1686 F64v [Samuel] Carr, the keeper of the King's Library,
requests a copy of every book printed in and about London, under the Printing Act   7
Nov 1687 F94r [Henry Frederick or James] Thynne requests a copy of every book
printed for the King's Library, under the Printing Act, including those printed before the
last Act expired   7 Feb 1687/8 (W) letter from King's librarian reminding S.C. to
comply with the Act of Parliament and send a copy of each book printed to the King's
Library   1 Feb 1692 F165r order requiring all members to send Master three copies of
books for the Crown and universities to be revived, printed and distributed

KING'S BANNER   7 Mar 1697/8 G4v to be returned to the Hall by Wright

KING'S PRINTERS   28 Mar 1680 E99r contract agreed with them for printing Pearl
Psalms   7 Aug 1682 E156r George Sawbridge committee to draw up account between
S.C., King's Printers and Sawbridge estate before next Court   7 Mar 1682/3 E165r
Sawbridge committee report that the £417 17s 2d owing to the King's Printers is found
to have been discharged   11 Oct 1684 F25r Peter Parker and Thomas Guy request at
committee meeting to make the same agreement with S.C. as S.C. have with King's
Printers   21 Jul 1685 F41r S.C. vote to negotiate with Oxford without King's
Printers   7 Oct 1689 F124r those with shares in Stock to have dividends stopped
towards payment for wine given to Lord Chancellor during Oxford dispute   7 Mar
1691/2 F166v Keeble and Vincent to answer complaint by Edward Brewster that they
had printed books belonging to the King's Printers   2 May 1692 F171r Oxford
committee to consider drawing up a treaty with   6 Feb 1692/3 F184r Oxford
committee granted powers to buy 1500 Books of Common Prayer from them   12 Jun
1693 F188v Oxford committee to have power to negotiate with them re. Oxford
printing

KING'S SPEECH   21 Mar 1716/17 G248r printed clandestinely. Master, Wardens
and Stock-keepers to consider

KING, [   ]   7 Nov 1709 G171v paviour; his bill of £3 paid by Joseph Collyer

KING, Edward   6 Dec 1708 G159v bound to Abel Roper, 7 years

KING, Gregory   6 Jul 1691 F157v of the Heralds' Office; proposed as surety for loan
from Tyler Bequest by Benjamin Johnson

KING, Humphrey   13 Jun 1715 G229v son of Richard; bound to Thomas Willmer, 7 years

KING, Job   2 Mar 1701/2 G67v his apprentice Thomas Adams is freed   6 Mar 1709/10 G176v of Little Britain, bookbinder; Isaac Stelby is bound to him

KING, John (I)   5 Jun 1699 G25r freed by Jonathan Robinson

KING, John (II)   9 Feb 1701/2 G67r bound to John (crossed out, and 'George' substituted) Conyers, 7 years   4 Jul 1709 G167v freed by John Conyers

KING, John (III)   7 Dec 1702 G83v bound to Eliza Harris, 7 years

KING, John (IV)   4 Sep 1710 G183v bound to William Harvey, 7 years   7 Feb 1714/15 G225r turned over from William Harvey to Peter Tanner

KING, John (V)   7 Apr 1712 G199r son of Thomas; bound to George Marshall, 7 years

KING, Sir Peter   6 Jun 1709 G165r to be attended by Master, Wardens and Capt. William Phillipps and to be retained as S.C.'s Counsel for 5 guineas' fee

KING, Richard (I)   5 Dec 1709 G172r bound to John Jones, 7 years

KING, Richard (II)   4 Dec 1710 G186r bound to Henry Clements, 7 years

KING, Richard (III)   13 Jun 1715 G229v his son Humphrey is bound to Thomas Willmer, 7 years

KING, Robert   3 May 1703 G89r John Thomas Yates is bound to him

KING, Thomas (I)   3 Oct 1709 G171r freed by patrimony   2 Oct 1710 G184v of Little Britain, bookseller; Edward Twin is bound to him

KING, Thomas (II)   7 Apr 1712 G199r his son John is bound to George Marshall, 7 years

KING, William   7 Nov 1709 G171v fined £5 for binding an apprentice by foreign indenture. His apprentice turned over to Robert Stephens

KINGMAN, John   6 Oct 1712 G204v son of Robert; bound to Abel Rockall, 7 years

KINGMAN, Robert – see preceding entry

KINGSLEY, John   4 Feb 1694/5 F217r servant to William Warter; freed

KINNEIR, David, snr – see following entry

KINNEIR, David, jnr   8 Aug 1715 G232r son of David; bound to Matthew Jenour, 7 years

KIRBY, Widow   5 Dec 1681 E140v her £40 share voted to George Wells

KIRTON, Mary   8 Apr 1695 F220v deceased; John Penn elected to her £160 share

KIRTON, Mrs   3 Apr 1682 E150v dispute between Samuel Mearne and Henry Herringman re. books and parts of books assigned to Mearne by her

KITCHENER, William   4 Feb 1705/6 G127v William Hopkins is bound to him   5 Dec 1709 G172r of Hatton Garden, joiner; John Moor is bound to him   4 Oct 1714 G222v Henry Margo is bound to him   6 Dec 1714 G224v his apprentice John Starr is freed

KITCHINER, William   4 Oct 1703 G96r freed by Thomas Cope

KNAPLOCK, Robert   7 Oct 1700 G45v to be excused (from cloathing?) entry subsequently struck out   11 Nov 1700 G46v cloathed   6 Mar 1703 G103v elected to Edward Jones' £40 share   12 Nov 1705 G125r Robert Smith is bound to him   1 Mar 1705/6 G128v elected Stock-keeper for Yeomanry   1 Mar 1706/7 G138v elected Stock-keeper for Yeomanry   26 Mar 1707 G139r fined for Renter Warden   5 May 1707 G141v elected to Daniel Browne's £80 share   7 Jul 1707 G143v takes oath of

Partner   3 Dec 1707 G148r signs re. not taking Clarendon   1 Mar 1707/8 G149v
elected Stock-keeper for Yeomanry and takes oath   25 Mar 1708 G150v elected
Assistant in second ballot   7 Jun 1708 G153r added to committee of 1 Dec 1707 re.
Benjamin Harris arrears   2 Aug 1708 G156r to provide a better paper for Apol-
lonius   6 Nov 1710 G185r acquaints Court that a gentlewoman of 80 wishes to pay
S.C. £200 in exchange for £40 a year for her life. Court decides on £30 p.a.   13 Aug
1711 G193v to assist Master, Wardens and Stock-keepers in management of English
Stock affairs   10 Sep 1711 G194r to meet John Baskett and Williams re. granting of
Oxford English Stock privileges   1 Oct 1711 G194v Master reports that his and
Mortlock's meeting with Baskett and Williams did not reach an agreement   3 Dec 1711
G195v Thomas Johnson, son of John, is bound to him   1 Mar 1711/12 G197r elected
Stock-keeper for Assistants   2 Jun 1712 G200r resigns claim to Thomas Hodgkins's
£160 share   6 Oct 1712 G204r signs report of Baskett committee. Elected to the late
William Rogers's £160 share. His £80 share disposed of to John Taylor   1 Dec 1712
G205v his apprentice Robert Lowden Smith is freed. William Power, son of John, is
bound to him   2 Mar 1712/13 G207r elected Stock-keeper for Assistants   24 Apr
1713 G209r signatory to S.C.'s note to Thomas Guy   3 Aug 1713 G212v auditor of
late Master and Wardens' accounts   1 Mar 1713/14 G216v elected Stock-keeper for
Assistants   2 Aug 1714 G221r auditor of late Master and Wardens' accounts   6 Dec
1714 G224r William Moore bound to him   1 Mar 1714/15 G225v elected Stock-
keeper for Assistants   2 May 1715 G228r acquaints Court that James Round desires
to fine for First Renter Warden   2 Jul 1715 G230r competes unsuccessfully for Under
Warden   4 Jul 1715 G231r auditor of Master and Wardens' accounts. Clerk's bill
referred to him   4 Jun 1716 G240v auditor of late Renter Wardens' accounts   4 Feb
1716/17 G246v to be new trustee of S.C.'s property   21 Feb 1716/17 G246v trust of
S.C.'s property conveyed to him as new trustee. Lease from City assigned to him   4 Mar
1716/17 G247v to pay Clerk's bill   6 May 1717 G250v auditor of Renter Wardens'
accounts

KNAPTON, James   3 Jun 1689 F119v given until next Court to consider cloathing   5
Aug 1689 F122r excused cloathing on plea of 'juniorship and inability'   12 Nov 1694
F214v cloathed   9 Feb 1701/2 G67r Matthew Hawkins is bound to him   5 Apr 1703
G88r his apprentice Robert Billing is freed   7 Jun 1708 G153v Christopher Hitches is
bound to him   4 Jul 1709 G167v his apprentice Matthew Hawkins is freed   3 Apr
1710 G178r elected Assistant Renter Warden   5 Mar 1710/11 G187v elected to
Nathaniel Nowell's £40 share   4 Feb 1711/12 G196v his son John is bound to him   1
Mar 1711/12 G197v (minute copied after that of 3 Mar 1711/12) Stock-keeper for
Yeomanry   3 Mar 1711/12 G197r competes unsuccessfully for John Walthoe's £80
share   7 Apr 1712 G199r elected to John Lawrence's £80 share. His £40 share disposed
of to John Matthews   6 Oct 1712 G204r signatory of report of committee concerning
printing of psalms in Oxford   2 Mar 1712/13 G207r elected Stock-keeper for Yeomanry   7 Dec 1713 G215r Thomas Combes is bound to him   1 Mar 1713/14 G216v
elected Stock-keeper for Yeomanry   1 Mar 1714/15 G225v elected Stock-keeper for
Yeomanry   2 May 1715 G228v elected Assistant   5 Mar 1715/16 G237v signs note
for payment to Thomas Guy. To be indemnified by S.C.   4 Feb 1716/17 G246v to be a
new trustee of S.C.'s property   21 Feb 1716/17 G246v trust of S.C.'s property
conveyed to him as new trustee   1 Apr 1717 G249v competes unsuccessfully for Israel
Harrison's £160 share

KNAPTON, John   4 Feb 1711/12 G196v bound to James his father, 7 years

KNELL, Clement   7 Feb 1697/8 G3v freed by patrimony

KNELL, Mary   6 Nov 1710 G185r Thomas Malleott is bound to her   9 Apr 1711
G189v of Turnboll Street, butcher; Jarvis Adams is bound to her

KNELL, Robert 5 Apr 1703 G88r freed by James Orme

KNELL, Thomas 1 Jun 1702 G71v Thomas Keppey is bound to him

KNIGHT, Elizabeth 27 Sep 1715 G233r elected to Mary Lambourne's pension

KNIGHT, Joseph 7 Mar 1681/2 E108r cloathed 7 May 1685 (W) confirmed as member of new Livery 6 Dec 1686 F68v complains of hawkers; committee appointed 7 Feb 1686/7 F70v competes unsuccessfully for Daniel Peacock's £40 share. Elected to William Whitwood's £40 share 11 Oct 1688 F108v restored to Livery 4 Apr 1691 F151r fined for Assistant Renter Warden 6 Apr 1696 F241v deceased; Francis Saunders elected to his £40 share 7 Sep 1696 F249r deceased; his sister's husband asks for the payment of £40 not given when Knight's share was disposed of to Francis Saunders because awaiting payment of debt to S.C. Case referred to John Lilly 5 Oct 1696 F252v administrators submit his debt of £24 to the Court; Court pay £40 to them; £5 charity given to Poor Box in thanks 26 Mar 1698 G5v deceased; executors give £5 for poor of S.C.

KNIGHT, Thomas 9 Sep 1700 G45r bound to Alexander Milbourne, 7 years 1 Sep 1712 G203r freed by Alexander Milbourne

KNIVETON, James 11 May 1685 F35r haberdasher of London; given bond for the payment of £205 by 12 November 20 Dec 1694 F216r payment of £200 plus interest due to him from S.C. deferred with his consent until next May 3 Jun 1695 F225r is paid £205 and bond cancelled; money raised by entering into another bond with Samuel Mansell

KNOCK, Charles 4 Sep 1704 G112r bound to James Willshire, 8 years

KNOLLS – see KNOWLES

KNOWLES/KNOLLS, [ ] 30 Sep 1680 E104v articles between S.C., Knowles and Warren for building to be sealed 26 Mar 1681 E108v to be paid £5 for laying floor of 'New Parlour' with deal boards, over and above articles 26 Mar 1683 E167v his carpenter's bill to be inspected 6 Oct 1684 F24v carpenter; reports that arches over and vaults under Ave Maria Lane passage are dangerous; committee appointed to oversee repairs 6 Apr 1696 F241v carpenter; committee appointed to assess and pay his bill 7 Feb 1697/8 G3v carpenter; debate about his bill for setting up stands in St Paul's Churchyard deferred 7 Mar 1697/8 G4v carpenter; bill referred to Master and Wardens

KNOWLES, Christopher – see following entry

KNOWLES, James 3 Jun 1715 G229v son of Christopher; bound to Samuel Austin, 7 years

KUNHOLT, Gabriel 1 Aug 1681 E117v cloathed

KYTE, David 3 Jun 1695 F226v son of Nicholas Kyte of Honnyborne, Gloucestershire, yeoman; bound to Richard Everingham jnr

KYTE, Nicholas – see preceding entry

LACOCK, [ ] 20 Dec 1703 G100r speaking on Susanna Miller's behalf concerning her dividend

LACY, James, snr – see following entry

LACY, James, jnr 10 Nov 1713 G214v son of James; bound to William Taylor, 7 years

LACY, Thomas 5 Feb 1682/3 E163v elected to Robert Boulter's £40 share, 'he having received a valuable consideration from him for the same' 8 Apr 1690 F133v elected Assistant Renter Warden 11 Apr 1690 F133v fined for Assistant Renter Warden 7 Nov 1692 F181v competes unsuccessfully for William Shrewsbury's £80 share 3 Jul

1693 F189v elected to Charles Harper's £80 share 5 Feb 1693/4 F198v his apprentice, George Hindley, is freed 3 Feb 1700/1 G55r competes unsuccessfully for Robert Roberts's £80 share 19 Dec 1712 G206r deceased; his £80 share disposed of to Ebenezer Tracey

LADLEY, Joseph 5 Mar 1715/16 G237v son of Robert; bound to Thomas Franklin, 7 years

LADLEY, Robert – see preceding entry

LAHUNT, John 2 Oct 1699 G31v bound to Elizabeth Fenn

LAMAS, Martha 22 Jun 1708 G153v deceased; Susannah Malthus given her pension

LAMB/LAMBE, William – see LAMB'S CHARITY

LAMB'S CHARITY 2 May 1681 E111r Lamb's bequest of 2s per week to St Faith's in arrears 1 Mar 1683/4 F9r continued in the parish of St Austin's after St Faith's burnt down; reference given to Liber A, 11a, b, 12a. Twelve pensioners of S.C. to say Lord's Prayer there weekly and receive charity. (W) Pensioners listed 2 May 1687 F82v deed of gift and covenant consulted (Liber A, ff. 11–12); determined that the Court was not obliged to hear the sermon of 6 May 7 May 1688 F101r Court determines to use the money not laid out in sermon or charity to augment the Tyler Bequest for a collation on 29 May 7 Apr 1690 F132v £8 6s 8d to be spent on a dinner for the Court on 6th May in commemoration of Lamb and Evan Tyler 6 Aug 1694 F211r churchwarden complains that the charity money given by Lamb and Paine was not distributed 10 Sep 1694 F212r St Faith's committee reports that all Lamb's money has been distributed 8 Apr 1700 G38v benefactor of S.C. Committee to investigate fact that charity of one penny per week in bread to six poor persons of parish of St Faith's has not been fully supplied for some time 4 Aug 1701 G63r churchwardens of St Faith's parish desiring benefit of Lamb's gift. S.C.'s books to be inspected relating thereto 1 Sep 1701 G64r gift to poor of St Faith's parish to be paid once a year from Michaelmas next 6 Oct 1701 G64v weekly payment of gift to poor of St Faith's parish to continue as before

See also ST AUSTIN'S, ST FAITH'S

LAMBERT, Dorothy 26 Mar 1684 F11r elected into the 10s pension of Ann Norton, deceased 27 Mar 1697 F260r deceased; Goring given her pension

LAMBOURNE, Mary 22 Jun 1694 F209v elected to the late Rachel Driver's pension 27 Sep 1715 G233r deceased; Elizabeth Knight given her pension

LAMMAS, Jeremiah 3 Feb 1706/7 G138r bound to Henry Perris 3 Mar 1706/7 G139r turned over from Henry Perris to Thomas Holden

LAND 6 Feb 1692/3 F183v Master and Wardens to treat with committee for letting of City land re. renewing lease of ground adjoining City wall 8 May 1693 F187r report from committee which has dealt with City lands committee that new lease for grounds behind Hall could be taken for 41 years at £20 4s p.a. if built upon; for 31 years if not. Committee to negotiate with surveyors re. building warehouse on S.C. land behind the Hall, and building on land leased from City 6 Jul 1696 F246r receipt for fine, order for lease, Warden's accounts and other papers re. ground behind Hall to be brought to Court, and lease taken 3 Aug 1696 F246r Master tells Court that the lease from the City of the ground behind the garden will soon be ready 7 Sep 1696 F248v lease to be sealed at the next sitting of the Court of Aldermen 5 Oct 1696 F250r City Comptroller has not yet seen to the lease but will do so at committee's next meeting

See also MOUND, ST MARTIN'S LUDGATE, WAREHOUSES

LANE, Isaac 9 Sep 1700 G45r excused 20s of father's quarterage arrears and paid 20s. Freed by patrimony 20 Jun 1713 G210v elected to Margaret Webster's pension   24 Mar 1713/14 G217r elected to Martha Barber's pension. John Twynne given his pension   24 Sep 1714 G222r elected to Mary Leake's pension   22 Mar 1715/16 G238r elected to Jesse Bruce's pension. Patience Ghent given his pension

LANE, Thomas   3 Feb 1700/1 G55v bound to Edward Moore, 7 years

LANE, William   4 Jun 1711 G191r bound to John Humphreys, 7 years

LAPLEY, William   2 Jun 1712 G200v freed by patrimony

LARDNER, John   5 May 1707 G142r bound to John Beresford, 8 years

LARKIN, George   4 Feb 1683/4 F8v Under Warden and Treasurer ordered to curtail his printing of unlicensed almanacks and report at next Court   3 Mar 1706/7 G139r Peter Leman is bound to him

LARKIN, John   5 Apr 1714 G218r his apprentice Peter Leman is freed

LATHBURY, Edward   7 Mar 1708/9 G162r bound to Jacob Tonson, 7 years

LATHBURY, William   6 May 1706 G131v bound to John Senex, 8 years

LATHAM, Susan   9 Jan 1687/8 F96v deceased; her Assistant's share is disposed of to Edward Brewster   6 Jul 1689 F121v deceased; her executors present a silver trencher to S.C.

LATIN TESTAMENT   5 Sep 1698 G13v Henry Nelme's administrator to be paid for printing

LAURENCE – see LAWRENCE

LAW/LAWS, John   20 Dec 1701 G66v bound to David Edwards, 7 years   7 Dec 1702 G83v apprentice to David Edwards, turned over to George Strahan

LAWRANCE – see LAWRENCE

LAWRENCE, [   ]   3 Feb 1700/1 G55r asking for committee of Court to meet those who had entered into an agreement concerning the holding of the office of Renter Warden

LAWRENCE, Brooke   6 Dec 1703 G99v bound to James Brookes, 7 years

LAWRENCE, Henry – see following entry

LAWRENCE, James   4 Mar 1694/5 F219r son of Henry Lawrence of Long Ashton, Somerset, gentleman; bound to Isaac Cleave

LAWRENCE/LAURENCE/LAWRANCE, John (I)   29 May 1689 F118v allowed to defer his decision of whether to come on the Livery until next Court   3 Jun 1689 F119r cloathed   9 Feb 1690/1 F149r summoned to next Court for failing to enter a pamphlet   26 Mar 1701 G57v elected First Renter Warden   2 Aug 1703 G94r his apprentice Whattoffe Boulter is freed   2 Apr 1705 G118v Richard Ford is bound to him   16 Oct 1705 G124v bill of fare for Lord Mayor's Day when he was Renter Warden   1 Sep 1707 G145r elected to Nicholas Boddington's £80 share   25 Mar 1708 G150v elected Assistant in second ballot   17 Jul 1708 G155v member of Oxford committee   1 May 1710 G179v his son John Lawrence freed by patrimony   7 Apr 1712 G199r elected to Mrs Griffin's £160 share. His £80 share disposed of to James Knapton   6 Oct 1712 G204v his apprentice Richard Ford is freed   24 Apr 1713 G209r signatory to S.C.'s notes to Thomas Guy   4 Jul 1713 G211r fined for first year as Under Warden. Elected Under Warden (second year)

LAWRENCE/LAWRANCE, John (II)   1 May 1710 G179v freed by John his father, by patrimony. Cloathed. Elected to George Mortlock's £40 share   1 Feb 1713/14 G215v deceased; his £40 share disposed of to Samuel Manship

LAWSON, [   ]   2 Mar 1690/1 F150r Richard East has £4 deducted from his dividend for having colluded with him

LAWSON, Anthony   15 Jul 1690 F140r refuses to subscribe towards raising horse and dragoons for the Crown

LAWTON, William   5 May 1707 G142r deceased; his apprentice William Lucas is freed

LEA, Charles   1 Dec 1712 G205v John Johnson is freed by his widow

LEA, Widow – see previous entry

LEABORNE, John   4 Feb 1705/6 G127v freed by patrimony

LEACH, [   ]   6 Mar 1688/9 F114v owns to printing an unlicensed pamphlet but pleads that it was begun in his absence and that the person responsible had promised to license it

LEACH, Dryden   1 Oct 1705 G124r son of Francis; freed by patrimony   12 Nov 1705 G125r Nathaniel Mist is bound to him   5 Jul 1708 G155r his apprentice Thomas Perry is freed   6 Sep 1708 G157r James Cooper turned over to him from Francis Leach   22 Dec 1708 G159v cloathed   3 Oct 1709 G171r printer; John Parrey is bound to him   5 Jun 1710 G180v his apprentice James Cooper is freed   9 Apr 1711 G189v John Rush is turned over to him from Edward 'Haddocks' [i.e. Maddoc]   1 Oct 1711 G194v Samuel Wickell is bound to him   4 Feb 1711/12 G196v Thomas Davis is turned over from him to James Davis   4 Aug 1712 G202v Bagnall is turned over to him   1 Sep 1712 G203r his apprentice Alexander Bell is freed   3 Nov 1712 G205r George Reddropp is bound to him   7 Nov 1715 G234v William Leonard is bound to him   5 Mar 1715/16 G237r agrees to fine for Renter Warden. Ordered to attend next meeting of Stock-keepers to make up accounts with them and pay money due to Corporation or English Stock from him upon that account. Elected to Mrs Cooper's £160 share; agreement whereby she gets overplus of dividend and he has only the interest at 5%   26 Mar 1716 G238v fined for First Renter Warden   2 Jul 1716 G242r John Parry turned over from him to Thomas Parry

LEACH/LEECH/LEIGH, Francis   16 Jun 1684 F18r to be granted £50 from Tyler Bequest if his sureties are approved   25 Jun 1684 F18v sureties approved   1 Oct 1688 F107v given 6 months longer to repay his loan from Tyler Bequest   6 May 1689 F117v ordered to repay his £50 loan next 6 November   1 Aug 1692 (W) frees Mary Travers, bound by foreign indenture   12 Sep 1692 F179r master of newly made freeman Mary Travers, whose name is sent to Lord Chamberlain   4 Sep 1699 G30r cloathed   7 Oct 1700 G46r Benjamin Metcalfe is bound to him   1 Sep 1701 G64r his apprentice William Hart is freed   7 Sep 1702 G80v Thomas Parry turned over to him from John Bullord   7 Feb 1703/4 G101v William Phelps turned over to him from Edmund Powell   1 Oct 1705 G124r his son Dryden freed by patrimony. James Cooper turned over to him from William Williams   3 Dec 1705 G126r his apprentice James Nott is freed   4 Feb 1705/6 G127v his apprentice Francis Watson is freed   4 Mar 1705/6 G129r William Thompson is bound to him. His apprentice Walter Dapwell is freed   1 Mar 1707/8 G150r William Phelps is turned over from him to Isaac Cleave   6 Sep 1708 G157v deceased; James Cooper is turned over from him to Dryden Leach   1 Aug 1709 G169v his apprentice Benjamin Metcalfe is freed

LEADBETER/LEDBETER, Edward   3 Dec 1705 G126r bound to Thomas Mead, 8 years   9 Sep 1706 G134v turned over from Thomas Mead to Matthew Jenour

LEAK, Francis   1 Mar 1702/3 G86r Edward Shawler turned over to him from Joseph Tokey and freed

LEAK/LEAKE, James   5 Oct 1702 G81v bound to William Freeman, 7 years   7 Nov 1709 G172r freed by William Freeman

LEAKE, John (I)   29 May 1689 F118v cloathed   4 Dec 1693 F196r assigns to Richard Sare and Joseph Hindmarsh 'Letters Writ by a Turkish Spy'   12 Nov 1694

F215r William Butler jnr is bound to him   6 Sep 1697 F267r comes in to free an apprentice and is fined a guinea for binding him by a foreign indenture. Charles Price is freed by him   6 Dec 1697 G2r elected to Peter Maplesden's £40 share   26 Mar 1698 G5r elected First Renter Warden   7 Oct 1698 G15r John Marsh is bound to him   7 Aug 1699 G28v and Luke Meredith, former Renter Wardens. Fined for not paying £22 balance of Renter Wardens' accounts and for not obeying S.C. byelaws   6 Nov 1699 G32v and Luke Meredith, late Renter Warden. Order of 7 Aug 1699 for fine to be annulled, balance of accounts as Renter Warden having been paid   3 Mar 1700/1 G57r William Wigley is bound to him   9 Feb 1701/2 G67r his apprentice William Butler is freed   13 Apr 1702 G70r John Frith is bound to him   7 Aug 1704 G111r his apprentice Christopher Hargreaves is freed   12 Apr 1708 G152v his apprentice William Wigley is freed   3 May 1708 G152v printer; John Watis is bound to him   2 May 1709 G165r his apprentice John Firth is freed   7 May 1711 G190r competes unsuccessfully for Mrs Eversden's £80 share   2 Jun 1712 G200r elected to John Sprint's £80 share. His £40 share disposed of to James Brookes   6 Oct 1712 G204r takes oath of partner   7 Sep 1713 G213r permitted to make his £80 share a surety to William Freeman   7 Nov 1715 G234v Stephen Anderton is bound to him   6 Aug 1716 G242v John Halford is bound to him

LEAKE, John (II)   12 Nov 1705 G125r freed by patrimony

LEAKE, Mary   24 Sep 1714 G222r deceased; Isaac Lane given her pension

LEAKE, Mrs   5 May 1707 G141v deceased; her £320 share disposed of to Walter Kettleby

LEASES   5 Jun 1699 G25v counterparts of S.C.'s leases of houses in Wood Street to be looked after and entry of all S.C.'s leases to be made more perfect   3 Jul 1699 G27r tenants whose leases are expired to renew them   21 Feb 1716/17 G246v leases from City to S.C. re-assigned to new trustees

LEATHER BUCKETS   3 Apr 1704 G105v more to be provided in Hall

LEATHERSELLERS' COMPANY   22 May 1685 F37v agrees to turn book-dealing members over to S.C.

LE BOW, Simon   7 Dec 1702 G83v bound to Thomas Cockerell, 8 years   10 Sep 1711 G194r freed by Thomas Cockerell

LEBRAND, Henry   4 Nov 1706 G136r bound to Bryan Mills   6 Jun 1709 G165v turned over from Bryan Mills to Anne Snowden   7 Aug 1710 G183r turned over to Gilham Hills   6 Oct 1712 G204v turned over to Andrew Hind

LEDBETER – see LEADBETER

LEE, George   5 Sep 1692 (W) freed by Stephen Lee by patrimony   12 Sep 1692 F179r of Aldermanbury and newly made free of his father Stephen Lee; name sent to Lord Chamberlain   13 Jun 1715 his son Stephen is bound to Thomas Wilmer, 7 years

LEE, Johanna   27 Sep 1695 F232v deceased; James Grey takes over her pension

LEE, Richard   2 Apr 1688 (W) freeman of the City of London, freed by S.C.

LEE, Stephen (I)   5 Sep 1692 (W) frees his son George   12 Sep 1692 F179r master and father of newly made freeman George Lee of Aldermanbury, whose name is sent to Lord Chamberlain   4 Sep 1699 G30r his son Thomas Lee freed by patrimony   9 Apr 1716 G239r Richard Dyer is bound to him

LEE, Stephen (II)   13 Jun 1715 G229v son of George; bound to Thomas Wilmer, 7 years

LEE, Thomas   4 Sep 1699 G30r freed by Stephen Lee, by patrimony

LEECH, [ ]   26 Jun 1682 E154v allowed further time to consider his call to the Livery
See also LEACH

LEETE, Thomas   7 Aug 1682 E156r petition granted for 40s to obtain a Habeas
Corpus to remove him from Cambridge gaol to the King's Bench

LEETE, Widow   3 Apr 1682 E151v given 12s 6d charity

LEFOSSE, William   2 May 1715 G228v John Meggs turned over to him from
Humphrey Child

LEGATT, Mrs   22 Sep 1680 E104r her £320 share disposed of

LEGG, John   8 Nov 1697 G1v bound to John Baker

LEIGH, Edward   1 May 1710 G179r bond from S.C. to him for payment of £154 10s
on 4 October sealed

LEIGH, Francis – see LEACH, Francis

LEIGH, John   1679–1686 Treasurer   1 Mar 1679/80 E97r elected as Treasurer   6
Dec 1680 E105v elected to a moiety of Henry Twyford's £80 share   1 Mar 1682/3
E164v elected Treasurer; to renew sureties in accordance with the orders of 1 March
1678   12 Nov 1683 F5r competes unsuccessfully for Henry Hills's £160 share   7 Jan
1683/4 F8r elected to Henry Herringman's £160 share   7 May 1685 (W) confirmed
member of new Livery   3 Aug 1685 F42r fines as Assistant Renter Warden   6 Sep
1686 F62r deceased

LEIGH, Joseph   3 Nov 1679 E94v refunded £11 10s and paid £5 in recognition of
good services to English Stock   4 Sep 1682 E157v deceased; his £80 share voted to
Charles Mearne

LEIGH, Mrs Susan/Susanna   8 Nov 1686 F66v committee appointed to negotiate with
Stock-keepers on her behalf   26 Nov 1686 F67v owes a balance of £151 18s 10d to
S.C.; decision over bonds and bills taken by John Leigh in trust for S.C. is deferred   6
Dec 1686 F68r allowed £18 as interest on £100 loan made by Leigh to S.C. To pay debt
of £151 18s 10d to S.C.   16 Mar 1686/7 F79r to prepare for a final account and
discharge of husband's commitments to S.C. by next pension Court   23 Mar 1686/7
F80r Adiel Mill produces accounts; rent arrears to be forgiven, bonds to be made over,
balance (W) £81 4s to be paid and books delivered to S.C.   4 Apr 1687 F81v general
release from S.C. sealed; to be delivered on payment of the balance on the account, and
on receiving her general release   30 May 1687 F83v has sealed a general release and
made over all her husband's bonds and notes for debts to S.C.; indemnified by S.C.   1
Mar 1687/8 F97r presents two mortgages of shares to her late husband, one from
Henry Twyford and one from Nathaniel Thompson; Court allows them   9 Feb 1690/1
F149r deceased; her £160 share voted to John Richardson

LEIGH, Thomas   6 Jun 1698 G8v freed by Charles Harper and cloathed   3 Jul 1699
G27v John Midwinter is bound to him   5 Apr 1703 G88r James Cooper is bound to
him   5 Mar 1704/5 G117r his apprentice James Cooper turned over to William
Smith   1 Oct 1705 G124r his former apprentice James Cooper turned over to Francis
Leach

LEMAN, Peter   3 Mar 1706/7 G139r bound to George Larkin, 7 years   5 Apr 1714
G218r freed by John Larkin

LENTHALL/LENTALL, John   4 Sep 1699 G30v bound to William Warter, 7 years   9
Sep 1706 G134v freed by William Warter   7 Jun 1708 G153v stationer; John Elphick
is bound to him   6 Jun 1709 G165v of Fleet Street; Bartholomew Rawlins is bound to
him   7 Apr 1712 G198v cloathed   7 Dec 1713 G215r owing £10 for his Livery

fine 7 Nov 1715 G234r elected into £40 share of his mother-in-law Mrs Warter 4 Jun 1716 G240v William Williams is bound to him

LEONARD, Michael – see following entry

LEONARD, William 7 Nov 1715 G234v son of Michael; bound to Dryden Leach, 7 years

LESSONS OF THE PIPE 4 Apr 1687 F80v Salter owns to possessing ca.100 of 'The Lessons of the Pipe called the Flageolet' and ca. 50 of 'The Lessons of the ... Recorder' [i.e. the anonymous *Lessons for the Recorder*]

LESSONS OF THE RECORDER – see preceding entry

L'ESTRANGE, Hamon 7 Oct 1689 F125r Roger Norton assigns L'Estrange's 'Alliance of Divine Offices' to Charles Brome

L'ESTRANGE, Robert – see following entry

L'ESTRANGE/LESTRANGE, Sir Roger (occasionally 'Robert') 26 Mar 1681 E108v John Lilly's bill for business between S.C. and L'Estrange to be paid 27 Oct 1684 (W) letter of complaint that libels had been printed against him, which had not been registered. Requesting S.C. to take action on these grounds 3 Nov 1684 F26r committee to tell him that S.C. has no power under the byelaws to discipline John Southby for printing a libel against him 20 Dec 1684 F27v Surveyor of the Press; Crown communicates desire to suppress libels through him, and a committee is formed for negotiation 23 Dec 1684 (W) letter apologising for delay in preparing petition 27 Dec 1684 F27v committee meeting; his petition re. suppressing libels approved 'with adding 3 words in the margent [i.e. margin] only' 30 Dec 1684 F28r Surveyor of the Press; petition re. suppressing of libels read 29 Jan 1684/5 F29r Crown order referring the suppression of seditious books to L'Estrange, signed by Lord Sunderland, is read 17 Feb 1684/5 F30v desires S.C. to compile a list of dealers in books who are freemen of other companies, so Crown and Lord Mayor can coerce them to become freemen of S.C. 6 May 1685 F33v letter from Lord Sunderland orders a complete list of booksellers outside S.C. and a report for L'Estrange 21 May 1685 (W) royal command to L'Estrange, signed by Lord Sunderland, renewing regulations concerning licensing and restriction of number of presses 22 May 1685 F36r produces James II's commission re. licensing 3 Aug 1685 F42r Widow Mallett confesses to printing the ballad 'Monmouth Routed' for James Deane, who informed L'Estrange; Court decides to remit her prosecution if L'Estrange agrees 7 Dec 1685 F47v committee to discuss free workmen printers' petition with him 22 Dec 1685 F49r committee consulting with him on free workmen printers' petition decide to send an abbreviated version to the Crown 6 Sep 1686 F62r letters from him and from Bridgeman to him read, recommending Crown approval of Richard Sare as the new Treasurer 8 Sep 1686 F63r his letter re. election of Treasurer 28 Feb 1686/7 F72r Richard Sare's Livery fine is remitted 'as a respect from this Court' to L'Estrange 1 Aug 1687 F87r assigns to Richard Bentley, Jacob Tonson and Joseph Hindmarsh his translation of 'A Guide to Eternity', Cicero's Offices (3 vols) and Seneca's Morals (W) letter requesting entry of assignment 26 Mar 1688 F99v writes asking S.C. to excuse Joseph Bennet from the Renter Wardenship for this year 3 Apr 1693 F185v three proprietors of the English Josephus complain that L'Estrange's new translation will affect their sales 3 Jul 1693 F190r his translation of Don [Francisco de] Quevedo's 'Visions' is assigned by Henry Herringman to John Hindmarsh and Richard Sare

LETI, Gregorio 1 Sep 1684 F23r Bernard is reported for dealing in scandalous books (W) 'Gregorio Leti and Arnauld'

LETTER ... ABOUT ABHORRERS   6 Mar 1681/2 E146r complaint against Richard Janeway that he sold an anonymous pamphlet, 'A Letter from a Person of Quality ... About Abhorrers and Addressers'   2 Oct 1682 E158r Richard Janeway confesses to printing 'The Letter About Abhorrers and Addressers' for Edward Powell

LETTER FROM A PERSON OF QUALITY – see preceding entry

LETTER FROM AN OLD COMMON-COUNCIL-MAN [by D.N.] – see CARE, Henry, & JANEWAY, Richard

LETTER TO A MEMBER OF PARLIAMENT – see PARTRIDGE, John

LETTERS WRIT BY A TURKISH SPY – see TURKISH SPY

LETOUR, Randoll   7 May 1711 G190v bound to Edmund Powell, 8 years

LETTERS PATENT   24 Apr 1684 F14r draft read and approved   27 May 1684 F14v Crown continues old privileges in Letters Patent and grants some new ones

LETTS, John   1 Sep 1707 G145r freed by Thomas Bradyll

LEVENS, Thomas   2 Aug 1697 F265v freed by Richard Sare

LEVER, Edward – see following entry

LEVER, Samuel   2 Jun 1712 G200v son of Edward; bound to John Curson, 7 years

LEWES, Thomas   7 Jun 1697 F262v excused cloathing for 810 days

LEWIS, Charles   7 Oct 1700 G46r to take a lease of Nicholas Hooper's house for 7 years   2 Dec 1700 G47v granted request for further allowance of 40s p.a. against rent on account of inconvenience of Hooper's residence   3 May 1703 G89r joiner; lease to John Nutt of house formerly occupied by Lewis

LEWIS, Edward (I)   6 Sep 1697 G264r bound to Benjamin Motte   6 Nov 1704 G113r freed by Benjamin Motte   3 Oct 1709 G171r of Fetter Lane, bookbinder; Christopher Holmes is bound to him

LEWIS, Edward (II)   2 May 1698 G7v bound to William Sparkes, 7 years   7 May 1705 G120r freed by William Sparkes

LEWIS, George   22 Jun 1698 G9v general release from S.C. sealed

LEWIS, John, snr – see following entry

LEWIS, John, jnr   12 Nov 1716 G244v son of John; bound to Joseph Downing, 7 years

LEWIS, John, author of catechism – see CATECHISMS

LEWIS, Thomas   6 Sep 1697 F267r Francis Holden is freed by him   1 Jul 1700 G41r of Oxford, permitted to bind John Garrett   6 Oct 1701 G65r elected to cloathing   1 Dec 1701 G65v cloathed   26 Mar 1713 G208r elected First Renter Warden   4 May 1713 G209r fined for Renter Warden

LEYBOURNE, [   ]   7 Nov 1681 E137r ordered to negotiate with Mrs Sawbridge before next Court to disprove allegations of mortgaging his £80 share to Sawbridge   5 Dec 1681 E140v Edward Brewster tells Court that Leybourne's account with Mrs Sawbridge is not finished; given respite until next Court   5 Jun 1710 G180r Court rejects his proposal of having the house and ground belonging to him and his son conveyed to S.C. in return for providing for his lunatic son

LEYBOURNE/LEYBOURN, William   1 Mar 1687/8 F97v expelled from Livery by order of Lord Mayor   13 Aug 1711 G193v permitted to mortgage his £80 share   1 Mar 1713/14 G216v request that John Brookes have half his £80 share in exchange for loan is adjourned to next Court meeting   5 Apr 1714 G218r requests that £40 of his share might pass to John Brookes and the remainder might remain his; granted   1 Oct 1716 G244r deceased; his £40 share disposed of to Ranew Robinson

LEYBURN, [   ]   3 Oct 1681 E130v disposal of his £80 share deferred until next Court

LIBELS   27 Dec 1684 F27v meeting of committee concerning   30 Dec 1684 F28r L'Estrange's petition re. suppressing of libels (W) 'for regulation of the Press' read

LIBER A   6 May 1685 F30r reference to f.157   11 May 1685 F34v reference in margin to f.158 re. livery list   20 May 1685 F35v reference as before   3 Aug 1685 F41v reference to f.159   22 Aug 1685 F43r f.159 reference in margin   5 Oct 1685 F45r Bishop of Oxford's letters to be written out at ff.160–165   1 Mar 1685/6 F51v reference to f.165   2 May 1687 F82v reference to ff.11–12   5 Dec 1687 F95r reference to ff.168, 171   1 Mar 1687/8 F97v reference to f.173   11 Oct 1688 F108v reference to f.173   25 Jun 1690 F136v f.177 referred to in margin   12 Jul 1690 F139v f.16 referred to in margin   15 Jul 1690 ff.140r & 141r referred to re. Lord Mayor's directions to raise troops for the Crown   3 Oct 1692 F180r referred to over dispute between Thomas Dring and Samuel Smith   4 Dec 1693 F195r reference to it in deciding Thomas Parkhurst's penalty for comprinting

LIBER C   4 Dec 1693 F195r reference to it in deciding Thomas Parkhurst's penalty for comprinting

LICENSING   22 May 1685 F37r order that members of S.C. should obey James II's commissions and public notice should be made of them. Four additions to James II's commission re. licensing   22 Aug 1685 F43r Robert Midgeley presents ecclesiastically authorised deputation empowering him to license books under the revived Printing Act   14 Mar 1686/7 F78v Master and Wardens to attend Archbishop of Canterbury and Bishop of London to entreat leave to enter caveats against licensing haberdashers and foreigners

See also ACTS OF PARLIAMENT

LIFE OF DR HAMMOND [by John Fell]   2 Nov 1685 F46r Robert Scott, George Wells and Richard Bentley complain that Richard Royston has printed their 'Life of Dr. Hammond'   7 Dec 1685 F47v Wells and Bentley accuse Royston of printing their 'Life of Dr. Hammond'; deferred   1 Feb 1685/6 F50v Royston is allowed further time to discuss with Wells and Bentley

LIFE OF RALEIGH [by John Shirley]   26 Mar 1683 E167v assigned to Dawes by Benjamin Sherley

LIGHTFOOT, Dr John   8 May 1682 E152v his 'Harmony of the Scriptures' [i.e. *Scripture Harmonies*] assigned to Thomas Parkhurst by Simon Miller

LIGHTFOOT/LIGHTFOOTE, Elizabeth   21 Jun 1700 G40v elected to Mary Ely's pension   14 Mar 1703/4 G104r her burial costs of 20s to be paid from pension   23 Mar 1703/4 G104r deceased; Elinor Whipp is given her pension

LILLEY, Richard   8 Apr 1695 F221r Ralph Snow, his apprentice, is freed

LILLINGSTON/LILLINGTON, William   2 Jul 1694 F210v servant to Richard Younge; freed. Younge is fined 2s 6d for not turning over Lillingston at the Hall   6 Jun 1698 G8v John Barnard is bound to him

LILLY, John (I)   1680–1681 Clerk   3 Jan 1680/1 E106r to continue Clerk until 26 March, assisted by John Garrett   26 Mar 1681 E108r resigns as Clerk. To deliver S.C. books in his possession to John Garrett on the afternoon of Wednesday next. To have 2 bills paid: one of 14 February last, one of £5 for business between S.C. and Roger L'Estrange, plus £2 3s for Smart and 10s for going to Whitehall   30 Mar 1681 E108v delivers S.C. Court and register books, &c., to John Garrett   2 May 1681 E111r Clerk to advise with him re. demands from St Faith's churchwardens for Lamb's bequest of 2s per week in arrears and 1s from S.C.   1 Aug 1681 E117r asked to inform Court further of the contents of the wills of William and John Norton, beyond what is be found in S.C. records. To deliver all S.C. writings and papers to the present Clerk, John Garrett   7 Nov 1681 E138r former Clerk. Discovered that he neglected to keep up the 'Poor's Register' from 7 Oct 1673; John Garrett ordered to remedy this   20 Mar 1681/2 E148v gives evidence to committee re. George Sawbridge's accounts   7 Aug 1682 E156v committee considering his and current Clerk's demerits for certain duties of a clerk to report at next Court   4 Sep 1682 E157v Robert Scott and Ambrose Isted to be added to the committee considering respective duties of Clerk and Lilly   3 Dec 1683 F6r to consider demands of Evan Tyler's executors for the interest on his money in S.C. hands due up to the day of his death   10 Jun 1684 F16v awarded 50 guineas for his 'great care and pains' in passing the new Charter   7 Jul 1684 F20v committee considering his contribution to the byelaws revived and augmented, to report at next Court   29 Apr 1685 F33r S.C.'s attorney at law. At committee meeting when lawsuit is commenced against Peter Parker and Thomas Guy, requests that committee treats with Bishop of Oxford   18 Aug 1685 F42v with Under Warden, to answer Bishop of Oxford's letter, confirming draft agreement though altering expressions as suggested   6 Dec 1686 F68r bill of £28 3s 10d to be examined and paid   20 Dec 1686 F69r difference between S.C. and Henry Hills to be referred to Lilly or Henry Trinder if he does not arbitrate by 15 Jan   15 Jun 1688 F102r has drawn up an answer to Samuel Hoyle's bill of complaint re. Widow Kendon's £80 share, forfeited when she married Rands   4 Feb 1688/9 F112v his advice to be taken re. dispute with Oxford University   1 Aug 1689 F121v to organise the facts about hawkers and take legal advice   5 Aug 1689 F122v to advise with Sir Francis Pemberton and Sergeant Trinder re. Richard Chiswell's complaint about unqualified shareholders   8 Oct 1690 F144r to draw up S.C.'s case re. hawkers to present to the Bishop of London   8 Jun 1691 F154r gives Gilbert Wharton a note discharging him from an obligation for law charges to S.C.   1 Feb 1691/2 F165r ordered at John Towse's request to postpone legal proceedings against Anthony Baskervile for six months re. non-payment of Livery fine   26 Mar 1692 F167v Warden to pay his legal charges for sueing Thomas Wall re. non-payment of Livery fine   12 Apr 1692 F168v desired to stay legal proceedings against Richard Randall re. non-payment of Livery fine   6 Jun 1692 F171v ordered to postpone legal proceedings against William Redman re. non-payment of Livery fine   4 Jun 1694 F208r to be paid £8 5s 10d for his service in discovering offenders against the Printing Act   7 Sep 1696 F249r case of Joseph Knight's share referred to him   2 Nov 1696 F252r asks that Mrs Mills be paid some money to enable her to pursue a lawsuit nearly resolved; paid £5   17 Mar 1696/7 F257r called in to draw up the breviate on the new Paper Act   1 Apr 1697 F260r produces bond re. test case under Printing Act; agreed that he should be paid ten guineas   3 May 1697 F261v draws up a paper about collecting moneys for Paper Act test case   7 Feb 1697/8 G3v bill for charges at law to be paid. S.C.'s papers in his possession to be delivered up   4 Jul 1698 G11r bill for law charges to be paid   7 Aug 1699 G28r bill of 40s 8d to be paid by Treasurer   8 Apr 1700 G38v Master has taken his advice re. case of Herbert Walwyn   3 Jun 1700 G40r to be paid cost of suit taxed against Robert Everingham concerning Act for laying Duty on Paper   7 Jul 1701 G62r index to Court Books, which he began, to be continued   26 Jun 1702 G77r Court Book to be delivered to him to enter proceedings and judgment of suit against Richard Randall of Newcastle   3 Aug 1702 G79v to attend committee seeking Attorney General's opinion on Benjamin Tooke case

LILLY, John (II)   26 Jan 1703/4 G100r brazier of Louth, Lincolnshire; defendant in S.C.'s Bill in Chancery against Woollame, &c.

LILLY, John (III) 3 Apr 1710 G178v of Gracechurch Street, cook; William Crooke is bound to him 7 Feb 1714/15 G225r James Shepherd is bound to him

LILLY, John (IV) 5 Sep 1709 G170r freed by patrimony

LILLY, Joseph 5 Sep 1709 G170r petition that his son may be made free without payment of quarterage arrears. Paid 10s to Renter Warden and excused the rest. His son John is freed

LILLY, Mrs 6 Mar 1681/2 E146v to be paid £20 via Ashbole for the copy of her husband's almanack

LILLY, Richard 22 Jun 1699 G25v elected to Mary Rix's pension 28 Sep 1709 G170v pension augmented by 20s 23 Jun 1710 G180v deceased; William Redmaine is given his pension

LILLY, William – see GRAMMARS

LIMPANY, Edward 27 Mar 1699 G23r elected Renter Warden and receives charge from Upper Warden

LIMPANY/LYMPANY, Robert 20 Dec 1689 F128v cloathed, promising payment of fine 4 Feb 1694/5 F217r Abraham Odell is bound to him 7 Dec 1696 (W) resolved he has a right to have a share in the Stock as his father and grandfather were members of the S.C. and 'always dealing in books' 4 Sep 1699 G30r elected to Francis Saunders' £40 share. John Beauchamp is bound to him 8 Apr 1700 G39r John Browne is bound to him 3 Mar 1706/7 G139r Theophilus Stoaks is bound to him 10 Sep 1711 G194r his apprentice George Medwyn is freed

LINDSEY, William 4 Sep 1693 F191r cloathed 3 Dec 1694 F216r Thomas Booth is bound to him

LINEN 12 Apr 1692 F168v Henry Million excused Renter Wardenship on being sent into Ireland by Crown re. linen manufacture

LING, Nicholas 15 Apr 1692 F170r 'Wit's Commonwealth' [i.e. Ling's *Politeuphuia*] assigned to William Freeman by Elizabeth Flesher

LINGARD, Christopher 2 Jul 1694 F210v fined 2s 6d when his apprentice Robert Wilson is freed for not turning him over at the Hall

LINGARD, Henry 1 Feb 1713/14 G216r son of William; bound to Samuel Deacon, 7 years 7 Feb 1714/15 G225r turned over from Samuel Deacon to Edward Midwinter

LINGARD, Thomas, snr 3 Feb 1700/1 G55v Thomas Lingard is bound to him 4 Dec 1704 G114r Samuel Messer is bound to him 9 Feb 1707/8 G149r his apprentice Thomas Lingard is freed 4 Jul 1709 G167v Old Bailey. George Abbott is bound to him 7 Aug 1710 G182v cloathed 3 Dec 1711 G195v his apprentice Samuel Messar is freed 9 Apr 1716 G239r William Burley is bound to him

LINGARD, Thomas, jnr 3 Feb 1700/1 G55v bound to Thomas Lingard, 7 years 9 Feb 1707/8 G149r freed by Thomas his father 7 Nov 1715 G234v Edward Simms is bound to him

LINGARD, William 1 Feb 1713/14 G216r his son Henry is bound to Samuel Deacon, 7 years

LINTOTT, Bernard 4 May 1702 G70v Thomas Smith is turned over to him 5 Jul 1708 G154v cloathed 5 Dec 1709 G172r bookseller; John Dighton is bound to him 2 May 1715 G228r elected Assistant Renter Warden 13 Jun 1715 G229r charge of Assistant Renter Warden read to him by Upper Warden 9 Apr 1716 G239r elected to Richard Parker's £40 share 7 May 1716 G240r takes oath of partner 4 Mar 1716/17

G247v competes unsuccessfully for Mrs Cleave's £80 share   1 Apr 1717 G249v competes unsuccessfully for Daniel Midwinter's £80 share

LITCHFEILD, Henry   8 May 1704 G106v bound to John Penn, 7 years

LITTLEBERRY – see LITTLEBURY

LITTLEBOY, Benjamin   6 Feb 1709/10 G175v bound to William Rockall, 7 years

LITTLEBOY, William   9 Sep 1700 G45r bound to Marmaduke Norfolke, 7 years   6 Oct 1707 G145v freed by Richard Janeway   6 Feb 1709/10 G175v Richard Forster is bound to him

LITTLEBURY/LITTLEBERRY, George   5 Oct 1691 F161r summoned to next Court re. his present unwillingness to accept cloathing   2 Nov 1691 F162r cloathed and promises fine   6 Aug 1694 F211v John Stannard is bound to him   6 Jun 1698 G8v Anthony Eyre is bound to him   7 Aug 1699 G29r Lovett Saunders is bound to him   1 Sep 1701 G64r James Gilbert is bound to him   26 Mar 1706 G130v elected Assistant Renter Warden   3 Feb 1706/7 G138r James Gilbert turned over from him to John Hatley   7 Jul 1707 G143v Clerk to call on him for balance of accounts

LITTLER, John   3 Oct 1709 G171r bound to John Wild, 8 years

LITTLETON, Edward   15 Nov 1700 G47r of the City of Westminster; bond from S.C. of £200 penalty to pay £102 10s   6 Nov 1704 G113r deceased; £100 and interest due from S.C. to be paid

LITTLETON, John   7 Jun 1680 E100v freed by Kayckwick

LIVERY   17 Aug 1681 E128r byelaw   6 May 1685 F34r precept from Lord Mayor requiring Court to nominate new Livery. List of Table and 30 liverymen agreed, to be presented to Lord Mayor the following day. (W) Copy of this and order from Lord Mayor, and list of those nominated by S.C.   7 May 1685 (W) list of those approved by Lord Mayor as members of new Livery   11 May 1685 F34v order of Lord Mayor of 7 May requiring liverymen to swear oath read. Committee to inform Lord Mayor and Court of Aldermen that S.C. has not hitherto administered such an oath   30 Jul 1685 (W) letter listing names of liverymen   3 Aug 1685 F41v confirmation of Livery members is obtained from Lord Mayor   1 Feb 1685/6 F50r committee set up to draw up list of members willing to be cloathed if the Lord Mayor allows additions to the Livery   4 Oct 1686 F64v eleven new liverymen elected. (W) original list also includes Samuel Tidmarsh, Henry Rogers, Thomas Northcott and Thomas Horne, who did not get chosen   8 Nov 1686 F67r Lord Mayor approves new additions   21 Feb 1686/7 F72r Daniel Browne to have priority over William Hensman on the Livery list as he was cloathed first, though they were freed together   4 Jul 1687 F86r new call on the Livery to be closed   12 Oct 1687 F90r pursuant to His Majesty's letters patent and Lord Mayor's order, most of the current Livery dismissed. Those removed from Livery at time of late surrender of Charter restored   13 Oct 1687 F92r all remaining Livery members restored to those places and precedencies which they held before the S.C. Charter was surrendered   7 Nov 1687 F94r all fines for the office to be recorded by the Clerk   11 Oct 1688 F108r Court members, assembled to elect Lord Mayor, are read an order restoring all liverymen removed at the time of the *quo warranto*   3 Dec 1688 F111r all Livery members to be restored to it according to seniority   6 May 1689 F117v 30 senior freemen to be summoned to next Court and called on to the Livery   3 Feb 1689/90 F129r present call to the Livery to be closed   15 Jul 1690 F140r Livery and Yeomanry, with some abstentions, subscribe towards raising horse and dragoons for the Crown   1 Sep 1690 F142r members summoned for cloathing to come to next monthly Court   5 Oct 1691 F161r Renter Wardens complain of their behaviour on festival days   12 Sep 1692 F178v voted that no new members should be cloathed but that various members should be summoned to explain reasons for not being cloathed   7 Jun 1694 F208v Arthur Otway and John Salusbury are summoned under the new Livery byelaw; they fail to appear but are still elected to Livery   19 Nov 1695 F236r John Nicholson, Richard Parker and John Bullard are freed and cloathed simultaneously   4 May 1696 F242v present call to be shut up   5 Oct 1696 F251r byelaws to be put in execution against members refusing to pay Livery fines   6 Sep 1697 F266v order from Lord Mayor that no freeman worth less than £1000 shall be cloathed in the big twelve companies and no freeman worth less than £500 shall be cloathed elsewhere   28 Sep 1697 F267v to come in best gowns at Michaelmas next for election of Lord Mayor   3 Apr 1699 G23v members who have held office of Renter Warden or paid their fines to be placed after Court of Assistants in Livery book. Persons who have not paid Livery fines to be sued at decision of Master and Wardens   5 Feb 1699/1700 G35r list of freemen prepared in order to find men proper to take cloathing   11 Nov 1700 G46v call on livery to be shut and no future call to last more than 2 years   6 Sep 1703 G94v opinion of Common Serjeant sought as to whether any freeman who is not of the City of London can be cloathed   4 Sep 1704 G112r Master and Wardens to take care of standing for Livery for Thanksgiving Day   5 Mar 1704/5 G117r call from 3 February 1700 shut up   6 Sep 1708 G157r call to be shut up   1 Mar 1714/15 G225v call to be shut up

LIVERY BOOK   6 Nov 1682 E159v lists of those who polled at Lord Mayor's election to be entered in Livery register   11 May 1685 F34v reference in margin to f.45 re. Livery list   20 May 1685 F35v reference as before   3 Aug 1685 F41v reference to f.49   12 Oct 1687 F91r Clerk to enter restored and remaining Livery in this

LIVERY COMPANIES – see LONDON, CITY OF: LIVERY COMPANIES

LIVERY LIST   3 Oct 1692 F180v committee appointed to regulate and settle Livery list before entering it in Livery book   3 Jul 1699 G27r altered according to order of 7 February 1698, read and approved after some amendments   3 Jun 1700 G40v Committee to produce

LIVERY OF LONDON – see LONDON

LIVY [Titus Livius]   18 Mar 1686/7 F79v among books in catalogue annexed to Oxford agreement

LLOYD, George   5 Dec 1681 E140v son of Samuel Lloyd, late Stationer; to be apprenticed to Robert Stephens with the intent of being turned over to Thomas Snowden

LLOYD, Henry   3 Apr 1699 G24r freed by Thomas Bradyll   11 Nov 1700 G46v John Price is bound to him   18 Dec 1702 G84r his apprentice John Price turned over to Thomas Arne

LLOYD, Owen   3 May 1703 G89v freed by John Penn   4 Feb 1705/6 G127v Thomas James turned over to him from Jane Rayment   7 Oct 1706 G135r John Blackburn is bound to him   9 Jun 1707 G142v his apprentice Thomas Jenes is freed   3 Nov 1707 G146v cloathed   1 Dec 1707 G147v stationer; William Sells is bound to him   3 Aug 1713 G213r Samuel Gibbons is bound to him   26 Mar 1714 G217v excused from office of First Renter Warden for a year   26 Mar 1715 G227r fined for First Renter Warden   8 Aug 1715 G232r Thomas Nutt is bound to him   1 Apr 1717 G249v elected to Samuel Ashurst's £40 share

LLOYD, Samuel   5 Dec 1681 E140v late Stationer; his son John to be apprenticed to Robert Stephens with the intent of being turned over to Thomas Snowden

LLOYD, Simon, snr – see following entry

LLOYD, Simon, jnr   5 Mar 1715/16 G237v son of Simon; bound to Warden Richard Mount, 7 years

LLOYD, William – see OXFORD, Bishop of

LOADER, Richard   8 Nov 1708 G158v turned over from Elizabeth Thomas to John Bennett

LOANS   11 Apr 1681 E110v all loan moneys called in   1 Aug 1681 E117r loan moneys called in   1 Mar 1682/3 E164r to be called in, except for Mrs Stephens's and Francis Egglesfeild's which are secured by their Stock   2 Nov 1685 F46r loan moneys to be called in

See also BONDS, CROWN, ENGLISH STOCK

LOCKER, John   3 Feb 1695/6 F239r servant to John Franks; freed

LOEFEILD, William, snr – see following entry

LOEFEILD, William, jnr   1 Sep 1712 G203r son of William; bound to James Holland, 7 years

LOFTUS, [   ]   7 Dec 1696 (W) to be paid £4 of £6 bill as Wardens had told him when they went to view barge   6 Dec 1697 G2r shipwright; bill for blocking and cleaning barge   2 Oct 1699 G31r bargemaster; his bill for mending barge to be left to Master and Wardens for payment   6 Oct 1701 G65r to attend bargemaster next spring tide to trim and launch barge   4 Nov 1706 G135v to be paid by the Warden for fitting up S.C.'s barge

LONDON, BISHOP OF [i.e. Henry Compton]   22 Aug 1685 F43r authorises Robert Midgely to license books on his behalf under the revived Printing Act   5 Mar 1685/6 F52v committee meeting resolves that the Wardens shall entreat him not to give licences to stall booksellers   4 Feb 1688/9 F112v dispute with Oxford re. almanacks to be discussed with him

LONDON, CITY OF   1 Aug 1681 E117r Clerk to make inquiries at Wagstaff's office re. City order for not building near City Wall   6 May 1685 F33v no dealers in books to be made free of the City of London unless they are first turned over to S.C.   22 May 1685 F37v dispute over who should pay translation fees due to City of London, Town Clerk and City Officers when book-dealing members of other companies are translated to S.C.   27 Nov 1688 F110r the Lord Chancellor, Lord George Jeffreys, has delivered the surrenders of charters back to all the City companies   18 Jul 1690 F141r Master and Wardens to deliver to the Committee of the City of London, by 4 pm, an itemised account of the money to be advanced by S.C. and its members inside and outside City for horse and dragoons

See also AVE MARIA LANE, LAND, TOWN CLERK

— CHAMBER OF LONDON   6 Jun 1681 E112v committee considering arrears due to this body for St Paul's preachers to give directions for payment   7 Nov 1681 E138r City Solicitor sends letter re. S.C.'s £115 arrears to preachers of St Paul's Cross; Court decide to borrow £100 and pay the amount to the City Chamber   1 Jun 1685 F38r demands 3½ years' rent for mount; deferred while Ambrose Isted inquires whether the City can grant a longer lease   2 Dec 1689 F127v Lord Mayor, soliciting for subscriptions for a loan to the Crown, asks for them to be paid in there

— CHAMBERLAIN OF LONDON   4 Jul 1692 F173r to be informed of the names and addresses of newly made freemen in future   12 Sep 1692 F179r list of newly made freemen, given in full, to be sent to Chamberlain of London   2 Dec 1695 F236v to be paid £20 demanded by the City for a preaching bill   7 Dec 1702 G83v John Darby examined concerning his refusal to make his apprentice free; decided that this is the Chamberlain's responsibility   3 Apr 1704 G105v Clerk to search at his office to see whether William Powle is free of the City

— CITY LANDS COMMITTEE   5 Sep 1681 E128v committee to negotiate with City Lands committee re. rent arrears for ground in Hall garden adjoining City wall and re. amelioration money for Ave Maria Lane   8 May 1682 E152v committee to renew lease from City of a piece of ground called the Mount in S.C. garden for as long as possible   2 Jun 1683 (W) meeting of committee about the City ground by the wall   3 May 1686 F55v lease of mount in garden to be renewed from City of London   2 Aug 1686 F61r lease for mount in S.C.'s garden applied for to the committee for City Lands; Sir Peter Ritch and others will report to this committee   1 Aug 1687 F86v committee to negotiate with committee for City Lands re. renewing lease for mount in garden by London Wall   7 Dec 1696 (W) Master brought in a lease from City to S.C.

See also LAND

— COURT OF ALDERMEN   6 Dec 1703 G99v John Franks to take oath before them to discharge himself from cloathing   8 May 1704 G106v Clerk to ask John Franks of Brentford to take oath before

— LIVERY COMPANIES   22 May 1685 F37v Barber Chirurgeons' Company agrees to turn book-dealing members over to S.C.

See also SADDLERS' COMPANY, SCRIVENERS' COMPANY

— LIVERY OF LONDON   2 Aug 1703 G93v Clerk to take Copy of Order of Court of Alderman or Act of Common Council relating to qualification of

— LORD MAYOR   6 Feb 1681/2 E142r S.C. to dine as a Corporation with the Lord Mayor   6 Nov 1682 E159v lists of those who polled at Lord Mayor's election to be entered in Livery register   4 Dec 1682 E161r John Baker arrives late at Court because he has been commanded to wait on the Lord Mayor   5 Feb 1682/3 E163r S.C. to dine as a corporation with the present Lord Mayor, Sir William Pritchard   3 Dec 1683 F6v S.C. to dine with Sir Henry Tulce, Lord Mayor   10 Jun 1684 F16v petitioned that all printers, booksellers, bookbinders and dealers in books free of other Livery companies of London should be translated into S.C. under the new charter   17 Feb 1684/5 F30v Roger L'Estrange asks Court to list all dealers in books not among S.C.'s freemen, so Crown through Lord Mayor can coerce them   6 May 1685 F33v letter from Crown requiring Lord Mayor and Court of Aldermen to ensure translation of all dealers in books from other companies to S.C. Precept from him read requiring S.C. to nominate Livery; list drawn up for him   7 May 1685 (W) copy of order of Lord Mayor for turning over those from other companies, with names of individuals. Also S.C.'s own list of individuals   8 May 1685 (W) order for companies to send their new charters to the Town Clerk to be enrolled in the journals of Court [of Aldermen?]   11 May 1685 F34v approves all Livery names except James Cotterell and Thomas Passenger, and requires notice of which liverymen failed to take their oaths. Committee to tell him that there is no precedent for administering oaths to Livery, and that the men he accuses have been cleared   20 May 1685 F35v Master and Wardens required to appear before him on 21 May for book-dealers outside S.C. to be translated   22 May 1685 F37v grants S.C. until 26 May to consider who pays translation fees for book-dealing members of other companies   3 Aug 1685 F41v gives confirmation of Livery members. Upholds the decision of John Overton, left off the Livery for opposing the government, not to serve as Renter Warden   1 Feb 1685/6 F50r Sir Robert Jefferies; committee to draw up list of members willing to be cloathed if he allows additions to the Livery. Assistants to dine with him   26 Mar 1686 (W) memo: the order of the Lord Mayor for the Livery   4 Oct 1686 F64v Master and Wardens to apply to him for approval of additions to Livery   8 Nov 1686 F67r approves new additions to Livery   6 Dec 1686 F68r Court to dine with Lord Mayor   16 Mar 1686/7 F79r Court to apply to him about reinstating S.C. members who committed the offence of mispolling   12 Oct 1687 F89v order, in compliance with orders of Crown, to S.C. to remove Master, Wardens, Assistants and Livery and appoint new ones (those who were Assistants and Livery at the time of the surrender of the late Charter)   1 Mar 1687/8 F97v order to restore Benjamin Tooke as an Assistant, and to restore various people and expel others from the Livery in compliance with orders of Crown; Clerk to bring a list of Master, Wardens, Assistants and Livery to Court of Aldermen   11 Oct 1688 F108r orders all liverymen removed at the time of the late *quo warranto* to be restored (W) copy of order   4 Mar 1688/9 F114r Sir John Chapman; commends William Smith for the position of S.C. butler   2 Dec 1689 F127v Sir Thomas Pilkinton asks S.C. for subscriptions for a loan to Crown 'upon the act of subsidy of 12d in the pound'; some Assistants say they will pay   4 Mar 1689/90 (W) order from Lord Mayor for Clerk to prepare list of Livery   6 Mar 1689/90 (W) S.C. to provide Lord Mayor with list of names of any liverymen who have not taken the oath. S.C. has failed to comply with orders of 4 and 5 March to provide list of Livery   5 May 1690 F134v John Bellinger to stand in for Master at a dinner of Aldermen on 6 May; names of accompanying deputation given   5 Jun 1690 F136r John Starkey, dissatisfied with his place in Court, threatens to seek remedy before the Lord Mayor   25 Jun 1690 F136v sends Order dated 19 June re. petition of John Starkey and others against S.C.'s Court; committee appointed and S.C.'s answer to be sent to Lord Mayor   12 Jul 1690 F139v asks S.C. to subscribe towards raising horse and dragoons for Crown. Court agrees to pay £45 for one of each and summons Livery on 15 July to subscribe. Asks S.C. members living outside town to subscribe separately for raising horse and dragoons for the Crown   15 Jul 1690 F140r Livery and Yeomanry, with some abstentions, subscribe towards horse and dragoons for the Crown according to mayoral request   18 Jul 1690 F141r Master and Wardens to bring, by 3 o'clock, an account of sums subscribed towards horse and dragoons by the Company itself, and by Company members living outside the Lord Mayor's jurisdiction   22 Oct 1690 F144v Renter Wardens fined £50 for not providing Lord Mayor's dinner, Lord Mayor having been sworn in in May rather than October pursuant to the Act of Parliament   2 Mar 1690/1 F149v asks S.C. stock and members to subscribe towards lending Crown £200,000 on late land tax for navy   16 Jun 1691 F155r orders Court of S.C. to be summoned to Court of Aldermen re. petition of Giles Sussex to be elected an Assistant   25 Jun 1691 F155v Master tells Court that the Lord Mayor thinks Giles Sussex should become an Assistant, but the Court votes otherwise. Sends precept requiring S.C. to lend money for Crown service in Ireland upon two Acts; Court volunteers personal subscriptions   23 Sep 1691 F160v orders Court to exact subscriptions from out-of-town members for City's loan to Crown upon additional excise for Navy   23 Mar 1691/2 F167r Court replies to his precept desiring members and Stock to lend money to Crown; Stock is incapable, and members will lend in wards   4 Jul 1692 F173r sends precept requiring Master and Wardens to list the freemen and liverymen of theirs not free of the City   18 Jul 1692 F174v Master and Wardens summoned to Guildhall re. not admitting Giles Sussex to Court   26 Jul 1692 F175r in obedience to mayoral order Master summons Court to elect Giles Sussex; voted down and committee appointed to maintain S.C. rights   28 Jul 1692 F175v reasons for not admitting Sussex to be submitted to him; these are copied out in full   12 Sep 1692 F178v orders subscriptions for Crown on surety of Poll Act from members outside London, and which is voted against from Stock   7 Nov 1692 F181v Court agrees to his order to procure subscriptions to Crown from members living outside City but refuses to lend from Stock   8 May 1693 F187r Court agrees to his order to subscribe money towards Crown paying sailors, but not from Stock   4 Sep 1693 F190v Court agrees to his precept to extort subscriptions from members outside City towards Crown loan, but refuses to lend from Stock   2 Oct 1693 F192v requires all usual S.C. ornaments to be

provided for next Lord Mayor's Day   15 Mar 1693/4 F201r Court agrees to precept
ordering members to lend to Crown on surety of Land Tax Act, but not to lending from
Stock   2 Jul 1694 F210r summons Nelme, a S.C. tenant, for not having a drainpipe   10 Sep 1694 F212r precept read re. Beadle summoning Livery for election of 2
sheriffs at Guildhall on 13 September   1 Oct 1694 F213r John Salusbury is ordered to
be summoned before him, having disobeyed repeated summonses for cloathing   5 Oct
1694 F213v asks S.C. to pay the legal fees re. Salusbury; Court leaves it to Master and
Wardens   3 Dec 1694 F215v sends precept ordering S.C. to send names of all freemen
to the Chamber of London from time to time, so that they may be compelled to take the
freedom of the City   24 Mar 1695/6 F240v sends precept for summoning all S.C.
members to subscribe to the Association the House of Commons has lately entered
into   7 Sep 1696 F248v question of lights in S.C.'s garden referred to   5 Oct 1696
F250r Master to defer waiting on Lord Mayor about lights in garden until new
incumbent arrives   10 Dec 1696 F253r precept requiring members outside City to
subscribe to armed forces; Court agrees but does not lend from Stock   24 Apr 1697
F261r sends precept re. subscriptions to the Exchequer Bill from S.C. members; Court
accepts but subscribes no money from Stock   6 Sep 1697 F266v order from Lord
Mayor that no freeman worth less than £1000 shall be cloathed in the big twelve
companies and no freeman worth less than £500 shall be cloathed elsewhere   28 Sep
1697 F267v precept from Lord Mayor for liverymen to come at Michaelmas next in
best gowns for election of the Lord Mayor and all S.C.'s usual ornaments to be made
ready   16 Oct 1697 F269r Court agrees to precept to raise subscriptions for disbanding
foreign troops, &c., but lends nothing from Stock   28 Oct 1697 F269v in obedience to
a precept, Court members determine how to renovate their panoply for the royal
progress through the City   8 Apr 1700 G38v Herbert Walwyn to be summoned before
for non-acceptance of cloathing   2 Aug 1703 G94r John Franks of Brentford to attend
if he wishes to discharge himself from cloathing. Gave order of 29 Jul 1703 that John
Hunter should be freed by redemption   6 Dec 1703 G99v Franks of Brentford to take
oath before him and Court of Aldermen to discharge himself from cloathing   20 Apr
1705 G119r Renter Wardens to be summoned before him if they do not return
quarterage book   16 Oct 1705 G124v to be attended by Master and Wardens, Edward
Brewster, Henry Mortlock, and Thomas Parkhurst concerning Renter Wardens' refusal
to provide dinner   12 Nov 1705 G125r Edward Castle to be summoned before him if
he refuses to take cloathing   7 Apr 1707 G141r order from him admitting Henry
Clements to freedom of S.C.

— LORD MAYOR'S DAY   6 Oct 1684 F25r Under Warden to provide a new coat for
bargemaster in time for Lord Mayor's Day   22 Dec 1685 F49r shipwright's bill for
barge for last Lord Mayor's Day to be paid   5 Oct 1691 F161r Livery to be seated in
order of seniority on festival days in future   3 Oct 1692 F180r S.C. banners to be
repaired in time for next Lord Mayor's Day   7 Sep 1696 F249r bargemaster to have a
new coat for   4 Oct 1697 F268r Renter Wardens not to invite more than six people
each to dinner next Lord Mayor's Day   20 Oct 1699 G32r Renter Wardens to employ
the S.C.'s cook for and to provide their own provisions if they wish   7 Oct 1700 G45v
no member to be admitted to barge on unless wearing a gown   5 Oct 1702 G81r no-
one to be admitted to barge on without their Livery gowns   4 Oct 1703 G95v no
person to be admitted to barge on without gowns, and no children to be admitted   2
Oct 1704 G112v former order that no person be admitted to barge on without gowns
and no boys to be admitted to be continued   10 Sep 1705 G123r barge to be repaired
for. Renter Wardens to provide dinner for according to late cook's bill of fare   1 Oct
1705 G124r Renter Wardens to provide dinner for according to late cook's bill of
fare   16 Oct 1705 G124v Renter Warden to be compelled to provide bill of fare for

Lord Mayor's dinner like that in time of John Lawrence and Thomas Bennett 7 Oct 1706 G135r Bargemaster to have new Livery for 4 Oct 1708 G158r Master and Wardens to provide music for. No member of S.C. to be admitted to barge except in gowns 7 Nov 1709 G171v music for was very bad 3 Mar 1711/12 G197r charges of dinner for 1 Nov 1714 G223r Renter Wardens thanked for handsome entertainment on. Master thanked for presenting Liverymen with favours on that day 5 Sep 1715 G232v new banners and barge cloth to be provided for 3 Oct 1715 G233v for the future Master and Wardens to have fewer tickets for guests in view of increase in Livery

— SHERIFF OF LONDON 2 Dec 1706 G136v Edward Darrell fined for

See also DAVIS, Sir Thomas

LONG, Dorothy 23 Mar 1704/5 G117r elected to Robert Chowne's pension

LONG, Edward 7 Oct 1706 G135r freed by patrimony

LONG, John 3 Jun 1695 F226r his son William is bound to Matthew Allam

LONG, John 3 Jul 1710 G182r bound to William Botham, 7 years

LONG, William 3 Jun 1695 F226r son of John Long of Claver Scever, Wiltshire; bound to Matthew Allam

LONGBOTHAM, Richard 6 May 1717 G250v son of William; bound to Richard Bassill, 7 years

LONGBOTHAM, William – see preceding entry

LONGMAN, Ezekiel – see following entry

LONGMAN, Thomas 19 Jun 1716 G240v son of Ezekiel; bound to John Osborne, 7 years

LORD CHANCELLOR 7 Oct 1689 F124r Warden's accounts reveal that wine was presented to him in the middle of the Oxford dispute 3 Oct 1709 G171r granted injunction prohibiting printing of Partridge's Almanack

See also JEFFREYS, Lord George

LORD CHIEF JUSTICE 3 May 1680 E99v to be paid charges for new byelaw by clerk 10 Jun 1684 F16v application to be made to him re. suppression of hawkers 4 Aug 1690 F141v Sir John Holt; Andrew Sowle to be taken before him by Robert Stephens for printing an unlicensed pamphlet

LORD MAYOR OF LONDON – see LONDON: LORD MAYOR

LORD PRIVY SEAL – see PEMBROKE, Thomas Herbert, Earl of

LORD TREASURER 13 Aug 1711 G193r applied to by Master and Wardens concerning duty on almanacks

LORIMER, Jasper 4 Dec 1693 F196r competes unsuccessfully for share declined by Abel Swale

LOTTERY 2 May 1698 G7r Charles Broome and his partners to have the use of the Hall for drawing a lottery of books 3 Jul 1699 G27r 'The Lady's Invention' drawn at the Hall

LOUNDS – see LOWNDES

LOVE AND CONSTANCY – see VIRTUE AND CONSTANCY

LOVEDAY, John 6 Aug 1711 G193r son of William; bound to James Taylor, 7 years

LOVEDAY, William – see preceding entry

LOVELL, Henry 3 Jun 1700 G40v bound to Bennett Griffin, 7 years 6 Jul 1702 G78r turned over to Edward Brewster 9 Jun 1707 G142v freed by Gilham Hills

LOVELL, Sara   22 Jun 1699 G25v elected to Douglas Todd's pension

LOW, John   6 Jun 1681 E113r Jonathan Edwin's bond to be delivered up to himself and Baker, Edwin's securities, on payment of £40   5 Sep 1681 E129v Jonathan Edwin's securities have bond made over to him

LOWE, John, snr – see following entry

LOWE, John, jnr   7 Jul 1712 G201v son of John; bound to John Usborne, 7 years

LOWEN, John   5 Feb 1699/1700 G35r freed by William Lowen   6 Jul 1713 G212v William Peacock is bound to him

LOWDEN SMITH, Robert – see SMITH, Robert Lowden

LOWEN/LOWIN, William   5 Mar 1693/4 F200v excused cloathing   5 Feb 1699/1700 G35r his apprentice John Lowen is freed

LOWNDES, [ ]   14 May 1711 G191r account of number of almanacks printed and sold by S.C. for past two years to be put before him re. resolution of committee of House of Commons for laying money on almanacks

LOWNDES/LOWNDS, Ann   1 Mar 1702/3 G86r James Frost is bound to her   7 Feb 1714/15 G224v deceased; her £160 share disposed of to Martin Boddington

LOWNDES/LOWNDS, John   22 Jun 1698 G9v elected to Magdalen Barnes' pension   22 Jun 1705 G120v deceased; Nicholas Pape is given his pension

LOWNDES/LOUNDS, Samuel   5 Dec 1681 E140v assignment to Lowndes from James Collins of Joseph Glanvill's 'Saducismus Triumphatus ... and a Letter of Dr. Henry Moore'   4 Dec 1682 E160v assigned one fifth of [Mézeray's] 'History of France' by William Cadman   1 Mar 1682/3 E164v elected Stock-keeper for Livery with Thomas Passenger   25 Oct 1683 F4r elected Assistant Renter Warden. Samuel Hoyle to be informed and make up his account with Lowndes and Adam Felton   12 Nov 1683 F5v elected to Adam Felton's £40 share to make his share up to £80   1 Mar 1683/4 F9r elected Stock-keeper for Livery with Samuel Heyrick   7 Apr 1684 F14r on the list of loyal Assistants presented to the Crown   2 Jun 1684 F16r to hold position of Stock-keeper for the Livery until next election despite having been made an Assistant   7 May 1685 (W) confirmed as member of new Livery   6 Sep 1686 F62r chosen to audit Renter Wardens' accounts in place of Warden Clavell   4 Oct 1686 F64r elected to the late Widow Coles's £160 share. Reports that the Warden's accounts are correct, contrary to Roger Norton's view   11 Oct 1688 F108v restored to Livery   4 Feb 1688/9 F112v re-elected Assistant   6 May 1689 F117r ranked ninth of Assistants never elected as Master or Warden   5 Jun 1690 F135v re-elected Assistant   6 Oct 1690 F143v given a bond of £200 penalty for £100 plus 5% interest p.a., dated 17 Sep 1690 and to be paid in 6 months' time   4 Dec 1690 F147v given a bond of £200 penalty for the payment of £102 10s by 17 March 1690/1   1 Feb 1691/2 F165r proposes that a friend should lend S.C. £400 at 5% p.a.; agreed to accept it before Lady Day and to use towards paying Universities for stock   2 May 1692 F170v chosen to audit Renter Wardens' accounts with Samuel Heyrick   3 Apr 1693 F186r auditor of Renter Wardens' accounts with Christopher Wilkinson   3 Jul 1693 F189v with Christopher Wilkinson, reports that the balance of the late Renter Wardens' (Miller's and Jones's) accounts is £19 2s 2d   5 Feb 1693/4 F199v elected Stock-keeper for Assistants with John Simms   30 Jun 1694 F209v competes unsuccessfully for Under Warden, but subsequently elected when William Rawlins chooses to fine   2 Jul 1694 F210r Richard Chiswell is elected Stock-keeper in his stead   6 Jul 1695 F229v re-elected Under Warden; his request to be excused is turned down   4 Jul 1696 F245r competes unsuccessfully for Upper Warden   7 Sep 1696 F249r puts the case of Joseph Knight's sister, lately the holder of his £40 share, who was not paid when it was disposed of as money retained until Knight's debt to S.C. is satisfied; legal advice taken 5 Oct 1696 F250r delivers to Court the papers of his first year's Under Wardenship which are ordered to be put in the chest; (W) asked to ensure that minutes which Clerk has neglected to enter are entered by next Court day 3 Jul 1697 F263v elected Upper Warden 4 Oct 1697 F268v George Huddlestone is freed by him 8 Nov 1697 G1v James Brand is bound to him 7 Jun 1698 G9r party to articles with Oxford University 2 Jul 1698 G10r elected Upper Warden

LOWTHER, Elizabeth 20 Dec 1705 G126r bound to Elizabeth Kater

LUCAS, Michael 3 Feb 1706/7 G138r freed by William Gatherne

LUCAS, William, snr (I) – see following entry

LUCAS, William, jnr (II) 5 Aug 1695 F231v son of William Lucas, late of St Mary's Savoy, Middlesex, seedsman; bound to Thomas Whitledge 2 Aug 1703 G94r freed by Thomas Whitledge

LUCAS, William (III) 5 May 1707 G142r freed by William Lawton

LUCIUS FLORUS – see FLORUS, Lucius Annaeus

LUDGATE 4 May 1691 F153v 40s paid from Poor Box towards discharging William Birch from Ludgate

LUKE, John – see following entry

LUKE, Joseph 5 Sep 1715 G232v son of John; bound to Thomas Tate, 7 years

LUPERT, Peter – see following entry

LUPERT, Stiles 6 Jul 1713 G212v son of Peter; bound to Charles Walkden

LUTFORD, William 5 Jun 1710 G180v bound to Abraham Dickson, 7 years

LYLLIE, [ ] 22 Jun 1705 G120v reference to his cousin Mr Allen the attorney
See also LILLY

LYMPANY – see LIMPANY

LYON, Benjamin 1 Jul 1706 G133r bound to Freeman Collins, 8 years 5 Jul 1714 G220v freed by Collins

MABBATT, Samuel 6 May 1695 F223v son of the late Thomas Mabbatt, St Andrew's Holborn, scrivener; bound to Mary Tonson

MABBATT, Thomas – see preceding entry

MACE, Ellen 26 Mar 1707 G139v bond from S.C. of £200 penalty at 5% p.a. sealed

MACHELL, Thomas 20 Dec 1716 G246r elected to Elizabeth Strainge's pension

MACKATURE, Edward – see following entry

MACKATURE, Zachariah Josiah 12 Nov 1716 G244v son of Edward; bound to John Crofts, 7 years

MACKRETH, George 10 Apr 1693 F186v with Robert Hesilrige, given a bond of £1000 penalty for payment of £512 10s on 4 October 1693 3 Jun 1695 F225r bond for use of Mrs Thomasine Fish for 'five hundred and odd pounds' cancelled

MACKWORTH, Sir Humphry 10 Jan 1698/9 G18r trustee of the Mine Adventure, granted request to have use of the Hall for the lottery

MACOCK, [ ] 12 Nov 1694 F214v his apprentice Edmund Powell, turned over to Benjamin Motte, is freed 1 Jul 1700 G41r summoned to Court of Conscience for arrears of quarterage. Not permitted to pay 7 years in lieu of whole

MACOCK, John 1 Mar 1679/80 E97r frees John Mason 18 Apr 1680 E99r to audit barge accounts with Roger Norton 7 Jun 1680 E100r barge accounts audited.

Assigned signature A of Stock 12mo psalms, signatures A and B of psalter, signatures C and D of primer, the printing of the Cambridge primer with Mrs Maxwell and printing of Stock horn book   3 Jul 1680 E101r elected Master   22 Sep 1680 E104r elected to Mrs Legatt's £320 share   30 Jun 1683 F1r competes unsuccessfully for Master   2 Jul 1683 F2r elected Stock-keeper in place of Roger Norton, now the Master   26 Mar 1684 F11v chosen to audit Warden's accounts with James Cotterell   7 Apr 1684 F13v on the list of loyal Assistants presented to the Crown   5 Jul 1684 F19r competes unsuccessfully for Master. Chosen to audit Warden's accounts with Henry Herringman, John Bellinger and Henry Clarke   7 May 1685 (W) confirmed as member of new Livery   3 May 1686 F55v he and Roger Norton to estimate a fair price for the two presses of John Mayo, Simon Hinch, Baldwin and John Palmer, to be sold to Henry Hills jnr   7 Jun 1686 F56r ill, so Robert Roberts substitutes for him to determine value of presses   3 Jul 1686 F59v among those chosen to audit Renter Wardens' accounts   5 Jul 1686 F60v Stock-keepers to pay him £50   4 Oct 1686 F64r reports that the Warden's accounts are correct, contrary to Roger Norton's view   12 Oct 1687 F91r among those auditing Warden's accounts   2 Apr 1688 F100r chosen to audit Renter Wardens' accounts   6 Aug 1688 F105r surviving signatory of the original deed of conveyance of St Martin's Ludgate   27 Nov 1688 F110v competes unsuccessfully for Master   1 Jul 1689 F120v to re-execute conveyance to present Court members   4 Jul 1692 F173v deceased; John Simms is elected to his £320 share   1 Aug 1692 F177r deceased; executors deliver a silver cup designed to pair George Sawbridge's gift to Wardens; 6s paid to Poor Box as it is lighter

MACOCK, Thomas   1 Jul 1695 F227v excused cloathing for 2 months

MADDAM, Benjamin   1 May 1710 G179v bound to Benjamin Harris, 7 years

MADDOC/HADDOCKS, Edward   12 Nov 1705 G125r John Rush is bound to him   9 Apr 1711 G189v John Rush turned over from him to Dryden Leach

MADDOC/MADOC, Katherine   4 Jul 1698 G11r her apprentice William Turner is freed   3 Dec 1705 G126r her apprentice Jeremiah Milner is freed

MAGNUS, [ ]   16 Jun 1684 F17r his apprentice John Smith is freed

MAGPIE [name of pamphlet]   9 Feb 1690/1 F148v John Dunton owns to printing this under the names of B. Griffitts and B. Griffits when Bennett Griffin complains of him

MAHEW – see MAYHEW

MAIDSTONE, Francis   26 Mar 1686 F53v surety for Mrs Starkey   4 Feb 1688/9 F113r John Starkey to be given Maidstone's bond on giving his discharge for share. Bond taken out to indemnify S.C. when Starkey's £80 share was paid to his wife

MAINSTONE, [ ]   3 Dec 1683 F6v deceased; Henry Hills jnr to propose an alternative surety to him for £100 loan money

MAJOR, John   4 Oct 1682 E159r admitted to the 7s 6d pension of Millicent Dennis, deceased   27 Mar 1693 F185r deceased; his pension voted to Jacob

MAKEPEACE, Joseph   6 Oct 1707 G145v bound to James Hickman

MALE, Edward   3 Nov 1707 G146v bound to William Haddon, 7 years

MALLCOTT, Thomas   6 Nov 1710 G185r son of William; bound to Mary Knell, 7 years

MALLCOTT, William – see preceding entry

MALLETT, David   3 Oct 1681 E130r to be prosecuted for not printing his name on 'Several Weighty Queries Concerning Heraclitus and the Observator'   5 Oct 1681 E130v defends himself at length re. 'Heraclitus and the Observator', saying that Langley

Curtis asked him to print it 7 Feb 1686/7 F70r interrogated about his right to print 'contrary to Act of Parliament' and forbidden to continue; refuses to give over trade 2 Apr 1688 F100v free workmen printers complain that he has bound a supernumerary apprentice at a scriveners'; summoned

MALLETT, Widow 3 Aug 1685 F42r confesses to printing the ballad 'Monmouth Routed' for James Deane, who informed Roger L'Estrange; Court decides not to prosecute if Roger L'Estrange agrees to this

MALSBERY, John – see following entry

MALSBERY, Jonas 5 Feb 1693/4 F199r son of John Malsbery of Morton Pinkeney, Northamptonshire, cordwainer; bound to Simon Cooke for seven years

MALTHUS, Susannah 22 Jun 1708 G153v elected to Martha Lamas's pension

MAN, Ann 6 Aug 1688 F105r with her husband, Samuel, the original owner of ground and houses in parish of St Martin's Ludgate who signed a deed of conveyance to a previous Court

MAN, Mrs 7 Nov 1692 F181v deceased; Christopher Wilkinson elected to her £320 share

See also MAN, Ann

MAN, Richard 26 Mar 1686 F54v elected to the late Martha Boate's 30s pension

MAN, Samuel 6 Aug 1688 F105r with his wife, Ann, the original owner of ground and houses in parish of St Martin's Ludgate who signed the deed of conveyance to a previous Court

MANN, Thomasine 20 Dec 1701 G66r deceased; Daniel Barber given her pension

MANNERS, Christopher 4 Mar 1688/9 F114r competes unsuccessfully for position of S.C. butler

MANNEY, Robert 6 Oct 1712 G204v freed by Anne Motte

MANSELL, Richard 2 May 1715 G228v son of William; bound to Roger Whiteheart, 7 years

MANSELL, Samuel 3 Jun 1695 F225r apothecary of London; given a bond of £400 penalty for payment of £205 by 4 December 1695

MANSELL, William 2 May 1715 G228v his son Richard is bound to Roger Whiteheart, 7 years

MANSHIP/MANSHIPP, Samuel 15 Apr 1692 F170r cloathed and promises payment of fine 1 Apr 1697 F260v to ask booksellers, printers and paper manufacturers of Cornhill for money towards Paper Act test case 28 Oct 1697 (W) John West is bound to him 7 Mar 1697/8 G5r his apprentice William Davis is freed 26 Mar 1705 G117v chosen Assistant Renter Warden 2 Apr 1705 G118r receives charge as Assistant Renter Warden from Warden 30 Jun 1705 G121r present at Court 6 Aug 1705 G122v Carey Keble is bound to him 1 Oct 1705 G124r with fellow Renter Warden, to provide dinner for next Lord Mayor's Day 16 Oct 1705 G124v Renter Warden; prepared to provide dinner according to custom 1 Feb 1713/14 G215v elected to John Lawrence's £40 share

MANUAL OF THE ANATOMY – see READ, Alexander

MAPLESDEN, Peter 1 Feb 1691/2 F165r of Newcastle upon Tyne; cloathed 6 Dec 1697 G2r of Newcastle upon Tyne, deceased; his £40 share disposed of to John Leake

MAPLESDEN, Thomas 4 Sep 1704 G112r bound to George Roydon, 7 years

MARANA, Giovanni Paolo – see TURKISH SPY

MARGO, Henry, snr – see following entry

MARGO, Henry, jnr   4 Oct 1714 G222v son of Henry; bound to William Kitchener, 7 years

MARKS, Richard   5 May 1701 G59v bound to James Astwood, 7 years

MARLAR, Thomas   5 Mar 1710/11 G188r freed by redemption and cloathed. To be granted lease of house dwelt in by Mrs Eversden for 21 years after her death   12 Nov 1711 G195r lease of his house at £16 p.a. for 21 years read and sealed   6 Jul 1713 G212v John Millis is bound to him

MARLO – see MARLOW

MARLOW, [ ]   18 Apr 1680 E99r Treasurer to pay sums requested by Master and Wardens for the prosecution of S.C.'s case against Marlow   6 Dec 1680 E105v almanacks to be printed with his type, bought at cost price   2 Jul 1683 F2r Ralph Holt complains that Marlow's type for sheet B of Saunders's almanack [i.e. Richard Saunders, *Apollo Anglicanus*] which S.C. sold him has been given to Samuel Roycroft

MARLOW, John (I)   4 Aug 1684 F21v request granted to retain £50 loan from Norton Bequest for three more years   6 Oct 1684 F24v Clerk to enquire into his sureties for £50 loan   3 Nov 1684 F25v sureties approved, old bond to be cancelled and new one for £50 drawn up   30 Dec 1684 (W) witnesses to his bond dated 4 August 1684 – Giles Hammer, John Nodes, David Hatton   11 Oct 1686 F65v to repay £50 loan or give new surety in place of one deceased   4 Jul 1687 (W) memo: Marlow's loan   1 Aug 1687 F86v deceased; George Quilt's wife to repay £20 of a £50 loan for which her husband had been one of Marlow's securities. Remainder to be paid in instalments

MARLOW/MARLO, John (II)   7 Dec 1702 G83v bound to John Overton, 7 years   5 Dec 1715 G235v freed by the executor of John Overton

MARRINER, James   11 Nov 1695 F235v John Colston, his apprentice, is freed   3 Jul 1704 G110r Obadiah Hickman is bound to him   12 Nov 1711 G195r his apprentice Obadiah Hickman is freed

MARRIOTT/MARRIOT, [ ]   5 Mar 1704/5 G116v desiring his £200 to be repaid by the S.C. in May   7 May 1705 G119v bond of £200 from S.C. cancelled   13 Jun 1715 G229r to be summoned to next Court to take cloathing   5 Sep 1715 G232v to attend again next Court day and in the meantime enquiry to be made into his circumstances to see whether he is able to take cloathing   3 Dec 1716 G245r excused cloathing for one year

MARRIOTT, Augustine   2 May 1692 F170v bond to him of £400 penalty to pay £205 on 3 November 1692, sealed

MARRIOTT/MARRIOT, John   7 Sep 1702 G80v bound to John Bradshaw, 7 years   3 Oct 1709 G171r freed by John Bradshaw   7 Jul 1712 G201v Josiah How is bound to him   3 Oct 1715 G233v elected to cloathing

MARRIOTT, [General] Richard   6 Feb 1681/2 E144r assigns [John Rea's] 'Flora: Seu, de Florum Cultura' to Robert Boulter   2 Mar 1684/5 F31v competes unsuccessfully for Treasurer   1 Mar 1685/6 F52r competes unsuccessfully for Treasurer   1 Mar 1688/9 F113r competes unsuccessfully for Treasurer   1 Mar 1689/90 F129v competes unsuccessfully for Treasurer   2 Mar 1690/1 F150v competes unsuccessfully for Treasurer   1 Mar 1691/2 F165v competes unsuccessfully for Treasurer   1 Mar 1693/4 F199v competes unsuccessfully for Treasurer   1 Mar 1696/7 G4r competes unsuccessfully for Treasurer

MARROW OF CHIRURGERY – see COOKE, James

MARSH, Jane   3 Dec 1705 G126r Edward Christopher is bound to her   21 Mar 1705/6 G129v elected to William Charles' pension

MARSH, John (I)   1 Oct 1694 F213v Christopher Hurt jnr is bound to him   3 Jun 1695 F226r John Boone is bound to him   7 Dec 1696 F253r cloathed   2 Aug 1697 F265v James Twedy is bound to him   5 Dec 1698 G16v to be prosecuted for non-payment of Livery fine   4 Dec 1699 G34r Seth Wild is bound to him   3 Feb 1700/1 G55v James Searle is bound to him   3 Feb 1706/7 G138r deceased; his apprentice Thomas Mew is freed   7 Apr 1707 G141r his apprentice Seth Wild is freed   7 Jun 1708 G153v his apprentice James Searle is freed

MARSH, John (II)   7 Oct 1698 G15r bound to John Leake, 7 years

MARSH, John (III)   6 Jun 1709 G165v bound to Richard Mount, 7 years   2 Jul 1716 G242r freed by Warden Mount

MARSH, John (IV)   6 Aug 1711 G193r his son William is bound to Israel Harrison, 7 years

MARSH, Mrs   6 Nov 1704 G113r her apprentice James Twedy is freed

MARSH, William   8 May 1704 G106v bound to Francis Ellis, 7 years   6 Aug 1711 G193r son of John; bound to Israel Harrison, 7 years

MARSHALL, [   ]   4 Oct 1697 F268v elected to John Amery's £80 share   5 May 1707 G141v competes unsuccessfully for Richard Chiswell's £160 share. Elected to Walter Kettleby's £160 share. His £80 share disposed of to Mount   6 Jul 1713 G212v George Underhill turned over to him from Joseph Bush

MARSHALL, Edward   12 Nov 1694 F215r citizen and cook of London; his daughter Sarah is bound to William Warter

MARSHALL, George   9 Sep 1700 G45r freed by Samuel Cooke   2 Jul 1705 G121v Samuel Shelley is bound to him   7 Apr 1712 G199r John King is bound to him

MARSHALL, John (I)   23 Sep 1691 F161r spectacle-maker; surety of Benjamin Johnson

MARSHALL, John (II)   4 Mar 1694/5 F218v servant of William Marshall; freed   5 Aug 1695 F232r Ebenezer Carelesse is bound to him   4 Dec 1699 G34r cloathed   5 Aug 1700 G44r John Bladen is bound to him   27 Mar 1704 G105r fined for First Renter Warden   2 Oct 1704 G112v John Camp is bound to him   5 Mar 1704/5 G117r elected to William Freeman's £40 share   1 Sep 1707 G145r bookseller; Thomas Pryor is bound to him   6 Feb 1709/10 G175v John Camp turned over from him to his father William Marshall

MARSHALL, Joseph   1 Jun 1702 G71v freed by patrimony. Cloathed   27 Mar 1703 G87r fined for Assistant Renter Warden   8 Nov 1703 G97r elected to Mrs Smith's £40 share   9 Jun 1707 G142v stationer; Theodorus Sanders is bound to him   7 Dec 1713 G215r John Howell is bound to him   2 Aug 1714 G221r his apprentice Theodorus Sanders is freed

MARSHALL, Sarah   12 Nov 1694 F215r daughter of Edward Marshall, citizen and cook of London; bound to William Warter

MARSHALL, William   11 Apr 1690 F133v fined for Assistant Renter Warden   3 Oct 1692 F180v [John Hall's] 'Select Observations' and [James Cooke's] 'Marrow of Chirurgery' assigned to him by Benjamin Shirley   7 Nov 1692 F181v competes unsuccessfully for John Harding's £40 share   3 Jul 1693 F189v competes unsuccessfully for Thomas Lacy's £40 share   4 Dec 1693 F196r competes unsuccessfully for share declined by Abel Swale   4 Jun 1694 F208r competes unsuccessfully for the late Mrs Abbott's £40 share   2 Jul 1694 F210r elected to Freeman Collins's £40 share and summoned to next Court   6 Aug 1694 F211r sworn into £40 share   4 Mar 1694/5 F218v his apprentice John Marshall is freed   1 Sep 1701 G64r Thomas Bullock is bound to him   6 Sep 1708 G157v his apprentice Thomas Bullock is freed   6 Feb 1709/10 G175v John Camp turned over to him from John Marshall, his son   6 Oct 1712 G204v his apprentice John Camp is freed

See also MARSHALL, [   ], WHITE alias MARSHALL, William

MARTIN, [   ]   19 Mar 1696/7 F257v informs Court that printers are waiting for their opinion on paper duty

MARTIN, John (I)   18 Apr 1680 E99r to pay in money left over when barge accounts settled to Under Warden   7 Jun 1680 E100r to pay £18 3s credit on barge account to Under Warden   3 Jul 1680 E101r competes unsuccessfully for Upper Warden   11 Apr 1681 E110r deceased; to be replaced as surety for S.C. to Sir Joseph Seamour   2 May 1681 E111r deceased; substitute found for him as surety to Sir Joseph Seamour   6 Mar 1681/2 E146v in course of Samuel Mearne's and Robert Scott's disagreement over a warehouse, it is discovered that Gellebrand sublet it to him   6 Jul 1685 his widow remarries and her £160 share is voted to Robert Clavell

See also MARTIN, Mrs

MARTIN, John (II)   3 May 1708 G152v freed by Joseph Wilford

MARTIN, Mrs   3 Jan 1680/1 E106r to deliver up her husband's S.C. papers   6 Jun 1681 E112v presents S.C. with silver bowl in discharge of her deceased husband's legacy   4 Jul 1681 E116r request that her late husband's copies go to Robert Scott and George Wells to be considered at next Court   7 Nov 1681 E137v Robert Scott succeeds in negotiating a low assignment fee of 50s for those books 'of little or no value' which she assigned to him   6 Jul 1685 F40v widow of John Martin; remarries and her £160 share is voted to Robert Clavell

See also MARTIN, Sarah

MARTIN, Oliver   26 Mar 1697 F258v recommended by Christopher Grandorge to take over from him as Clerk

MARTIN, Sarah   4 Jun 1683 E170r George Eversden given leave to mortgage his £80 share to her for £80

MARTIN, William   6 Nov 1704 G113r bound to Henry Bonwick, 7 years

MARTYN, Thomas   5 Dec 1698 G17r freed by Joseph Cater and Andrew Sowle

MASEY, Richard   4 Jun 1711 G191r bound to John Morphew, 7 years

MASON   7 Nov 1709 G171v bill to be paid

MASON, John   1 Mar 1679/80 E97r freed by John Macock

MASON, Mary   7 Aug 1704 G110v of London; bond of £600 from S.C. to be transferred to her from Mrs Webb   4 Sep 1704 G111v bond from S.C. of £1200 penalty for payment of £630 on 2 Sep 1705 sealed   1 Dec 1712 G205v her bond to be repaid from bond to Thomas Guy

MASON, Thomas   2 Aug 1714 G221r Joseph Mercer turned over to him

MASTER   5 Jul 1679 E87v Samuel Mearne elected   3 Jul 1680 E101r John Macock elected   2 Jul 1681 E115r Thomas Vere elected   1 Jul 1682 E154v Samuel Mearne elected   2 Apr 1683 E168r 'Our Mr. came late and took the Chair'   30 Jun 1683 F1r Roger Norton elected   5 Jul 1684 F19r Roger Norton elected   4 Jul 1685 F39v Henry Herringman elected   3 Jul 1686 F59r John Bellinger elected   8 Nov 1686 F66v 'Menelius's' [i.e. John Minellius's] 'Notes on Ovid' and all other foreign and domestic notes on S.C. books, to be entered to him in trust for S.C.   2 Jul 1687 F85v Roger

Norton elected   7 Nov 1687 F94r all fines for the office to be recorded by the Clerk   5
Mar 1687/8 F99r William Rawlins to lend him £300 on the transfer of his £320 share,
to pay off Katherine Sawbridge to whom it is mortgaged   30 Jun 1688 F102v Henry
Hills elected   6 Jul 1689 F121r Edward Brewster elected   5 Jul 1690 F138r Ambrose
Isted elected   6 Apr 1691 F152v immediately after Court to supervise Clerk drawing
up a mortgage of Thomas Bassett's £320 share to William Rawlins   8 Jun 1691 F154v
he and other Proprietors of the Lights allowed to meet in S.C.'s Court room twice a
week   4 Jul 1691 F156v Ambrose Isted elected   1 Feb 1691/2 F164v his part in concluding Oxford agreement is detailed   7 Mar 1691/2 F166v indemnified by transfer
of mortgage of Stock estate against engagement with Oxford   2 May 1692 F170r
declaration of trust re. Oxford from him, Henry Mortlock and John Bellinger read and
approved   2 Jul 1692 F172v Edward Brewster elected   12 Sep 1692 F178v tells Court
what is on the agenda   8 May 1693 F187r thanked by Court for keeping them up to
date with Oxford situation   1 Jul 1693 F189r John Bellinger voted Master   3 Jul
1693 F189v John Bellinger elected Master; late Master thanked   30 Jun 1694 F209v
John Simms elected   6 Jul 1695 F229r John Simms elected   4 Jul 1696 F245r Henry
Mortlock elected   3 Jul 1697 F263v Henry Mortlock elected   26 Mar 1698 G5v letter
to Vice-Chancellor of Oxford University concerning treaty between University and S.C.
read   13 Apr 1698 G6r reports that University of Oxford will not abate part of the
payment of £200 formerly made by the S.C. to the University   18 Apr 1698 G7r report
from Oxford committee that amendments have been made to the Articles   6 Jun 1698
G8r writings belonging to the S.C. in Christopher Grandorge's possession to be delivered
to him   27 Jun 1698 G9r suggests that members of S.C. should have same surety as
was given to parties to former Articles with University of Oxford   2 Jul 1698 G10r
Robert Clavell elected   5 Sep 1698 G13v proposes that settlement of Clerk's bill should
be deferred. To examine repairs required to barge   10 Jan 1698/9 G18v added to
committee to consider Printing Act   27 Mar 1699 G23r to arrange letting of Hall for
dancing   5 Jun 1699 G25r seeking Court's advice re. sending paper to Cambridge for
printing an impression of the Greek Testament there   1 Jul 1699 G26r Robert Clavell
elected   6 Nov 1699 G32v to discuss with Awnsham Churchill the joiner's bill for
mending S.C.'s warehouse let to him   5 Feb 1699/1700 G35r informs Court that he
has caused a list of freemen to be drawn up in order to find men proper to take cloathing.
Proposes that Richard Randall of Newcastle should come onto the cloathing   4 Mar
1699/1700 G36v informs Court that Hall needs to be repaired. Ordered that this should
be done   8 Apr 1700 G38v reports that he has taken advice of Lilly in respect of
Herbert Walwyn's refusal to accept cloathing   1 Jul 1700 G41r reports that committee
for disposal of Oxford books has met. To meet again to conclude the matter. Reports
that barge needs to be new bottomed   6 Jul 1700 G41v Capt William Phillipps elected   3
Feb 1700/1 G54v reports from committee to view houses of Robert Roberts and
Everingham   7 Apr 1701 G58v rule for the future that he should have only one vote in
any election or making of any order of the Court   5 Jul 1701 G61v Capt. William
Phillipps elected   6 Oct 1701 G64v appointed to go to Oxford about S.C.'s affairs   26
Mar 1702 G69r reports from committee to view Everingham's house   4 Jul 1702 G76v
Capt. William Phillipps elected   7 Sep 1702 G80r reports from committee which
attended Attorney General re. opinion on Tooke   28 Sep 1702 G80v bond from S.C.
to Charles Gretton to borrow £300 delivered to him   9 Oct 1702 G82r bond from S.C.
to Mrs Elizabeth Wilson to borrow £500 delivered to him   1 Feb 1702/3 G84v reported
that Daniel Browne and John Walthoe have attended him to make acknowledgement to
S.C. for printing the 'Abridgment of the Book of Martyrs' and would only give 1 guinea.
Left to Master to settle the matter   25 Mar 1703 G86v chosen to go to Oxford to
renew contract between S.C. and University   5 Apr 1703 G87v gives account of

proceedings at Oxford 22 Apr 1703 G88v to write to Lewis Thomas of Oxford by way of an answer to the Vice-Chancellor's letter, saying Court cannot agree to the Vice-Chancellor's proposal 3 May 1703 G89r informs Court that he has written to the Vice-Chancellor of Oxford 7 Jun 1703 G90r bond from S.C. to a friend of his of £1000 3 Jul 1703 G91r William Rawlins elected 5 Jul 1703 G92r Court to be called on Thursday seven-night to settle the election of Master 12 Jul 1703 G92v informs Court that he has received opinion of Attorney General on Tooke 15 Jul 1703 G93r Rawlins desires to be excused. Thomas Parkhurst elected 6 Sep 1703 G94v to meet John Gadbury the almanack maker 21 Oct 1703 G96v reports from committee re. Tooke's affairs 8 Nov 1703 G96v letter to him from Gadbury read. Reprimands Robert Stephens for giving out names of persons to be summoned to be made Assistants. Letter to him from Tate read 6 Dec 1703 G99v letter to him from Ichabod Dawkes, desiring more work; Capt. William Phillipps's accounts as Master signed off 20 Dec 1703 G100r two letters to him from Gadbury read 14 Mar 1703/4 G104r informs Court that Thomas Wilmer wishes to be made free 1 Jul 1704 G109r Richard Simpson elected 22 Jun 1705 G120v to oversee painting of pales in garden 30 Jun 1705 G121r Richard Simpson elected 2 Jul 1705 G121v to make agreement with Buckley 6 Aug 1705 G122r reports that an agreement has been reached with Buckley 8 Dec 1705 G126v signatory to Articles agreed with University of Cambridge 6 Jul 1706 G133r Walter Kettleby elected and takes oath 4 Nov 1706 G135v precedents to be searched to see what was done by Court on Sir Thomas Davis and Sawbridge being elected Masters of the S.C. when elected Sheriffs of London 2 Dec 1706 G136v report on these precedents 3 Feb 1706/7 G137v to order payment of carpenter's and smith's bills 5 Jul 1707 G143r Edward Darrell elected 4 Aug 1707 G144r to be indemnified for signing letter of licence and composition relating to Nicholas Cox. Note to him concerning meeting of the creditors of Jeffrey Wale read 1 Dec 1707 G147r to adjust carpenter's bill 1 Mar 1707/8 G149r to adjust Clerk's bill 3 Jul 1708 G154r Charles Harper elected 7 Feb 1708/9 G160v to adjust and order payment of Clerk's bill for law charges 6 Jun 1709 G165r reports from committee to view Morphew's house. To attend Sir Peter King and retain him as S.C.'s Counsel 23 Jun 1709 G166r to answer letter to Dr Nicholas Brady from Thomas Harrison concerning the printing of the new version of the Psalms 2 Jul 1709 G166v Robert Andrews elected 24 Jul 1709 G168v Robert Andrews asks to be excused office of Master 1 Aug 1709 G169v Robert Andrews excused from office on payment of usual fine of £10. Capt. William Phillipps elected 1 May 1710 G179r auditor of late Renter Wardens' accounts 3 Jul 1710 G181v Capt. William Phillipps elected. Awnsham Churchill to fine 7 Aug 1710 G182v Thomas Hodgkins and Thomas Clarke fine to preserve seniority 30 Jun 1711 G192r Capt. William Phillipps elected 13 Aug 1711 G193v to treat with persons in order to deal with the duties laid on almanacks in accordance with the Act of Parliament 10 Sep 1711 G193v acquaints Court that he has prevailed with Commissioners of Stamp Office to take a bond from the S.C. for paying the duties on stamping of almanacks. To meet John Baskett and Williams to consider whether English Stock is effectively protected in the granting of Oxford privileges 1 Oct 1711 G194v reports that no agreement has been reached in his meeting with Baskett and Williams 2 Jun 1712 G200r reports from committee to consider Clerk's bills 5 Jul 1712 G201r Thomas Clarke elected 15 Jul 1712 G202r Thomas Clarke excused. Capt. William Phillipps elected 1 Sep 1712 G203r reports from committee to meet Baskett and Williams. Orders another view of Carter's house by the workmen 6 Oct 1712 G203v report on repairs needed to Carter's house. Signs report of Baskett committee 21 Mar 1712/13 G207v Henry Mortlock acting in place of Capt. William Phillipps, deceased 24 Apr 1713 G209r acquaints Court of opinion of committee re. printers 4 May 1713

G209v to consider rent on Carter's house   1 Jun 1713 G210r reports that committee are of the opinion that Carter's house would not produce more rent   4 Jul 1713 G211r Israel Harrison fines, Daniel Browne elected   3 Aug 1713 G212v reports that a view of Mrs Carter's house had been made   2 Nov 1713 G214r reports that Mills will not be granted a new lease   22 Dec 1713 G215v John Baskett fined to preserve seniority   3 Jul 1714 G220r John Baskett elected   1 Nov 1714 G223r given thanks of the Court for presenting all the Liverymen with favours on Lord Mayor's Day   7 Feb 1714/15 G224v report in Chancery concerning Mrs Cooper's debt to Poole   26 Mar 1715 G227r undertakes that Samuel Ashurst will pay the usual fine for Renter Warden   2 May 1715 G228v letter to him from Nahum Tate re. borrowing on his share of the New Version of the Psalms   2 Jul 1715 G230r John Baskett elected on Upper Warden's casting vote   3 Oct 1715 G232v to have only two tickets for Lord Mayor's Day and 10th of August in future   9 Apr 1716 G239r moves Court that William Taylor might be elected Renter Warden   4 Jun 1716 G240v auditor of Renter Wardens' accounts   30 Jun 1716 G241r John Baskett excused. Jacob Tonson elected and fined. Nicholas Boddington elected   2 Jul 1716 G241v William Freeman and Timothy Goodwin fine to preserve seniority to Boddington   21 Feb 1716/17 G246v tells Court that it has been called for sealing writings for transferring trusteeship of S.C.'s Hall, houses and ground from old surviving trustees to new ones   4 Mar 1716/17 G247v to adjust and order payment of Clerk's bill for law charges in Chancery

MASTER AND WARDENS   7 Nov 1681 E137v to be indemnified against costs, losses and damages incurred by transacting S.C. business   3 Jul 1682 E155v demise of Hall and tenements to indemnify Master and Wardens and others from engagement to Sir Joseph Seamour   27 May 1684 F15r thanked by Common Hall for their care, integrity and prudent management in obtaining new letters patent   5 Jul 1684 F19r voted that the old custom for the choice of Master and Wardens should be observed   4 Jul 1685 F39v elected by hands and not by balloting box   2 Jul 1687 F85v swear oaths of allegiance and supremacy and the oath prescribed in the Act for Well Governing and Regulation of Corporations   12 Oct 1687 F91r late ones to deliver plate, keys, papers, &c. to present ones, and prepare their accounts to be audited. New ones among those auditing the accounts of late ones   3 Dec 1688 F111r committee to investigate transactions of Master and Wardens and other officers since   3 October 1687   7 Oct 1689 F124v to be paid 5s for attendance at Court since dinners have been stopped in view of S.C. debts   4 Nov 1689 F126r voluntarily reduce their attendance fees to 2s 6d   8 Apr 1690 F133v and Assistants to have usual allowance for attendance although a Bye-Court   6 Apr 1691 F152r compile an agreement with Oxford in their own names and those of Roger Norton and John Bellinger, soon to be submitted to Court   2 May 1692 F171r to take advice from Assistants re. printing materials for Oxford and consider heads for proposed treaty with King's Printers   4 Jul 1692 F173r to list S.C. members not free of the City and ensure that in the future the Lord Chamberlain is informed of newly made freemen   18 Jul 1692 F174v summoned to Guildhall re. not admitting Giles Sussex to Court   1 Aug 1692 F176v thanked for maintaining S.C.'s rights over Giles Sussex   6 Feb 1692/3 F183v empowered to treat with committee for letting of City lands, re. renewing their lease of the ground adjoining the City wall   8 Nov 1697 G1v to deal with Livery's attendance on the day of His Majesty's passing through the City and entertainment of the S.C. on that day   7 Feb 1697/8 G3r to consider repairs to the Hall   7 Mar 1697/8 G4v Knowles the carpenter's bills referred to   18 Apr 1698 G7r to go with revised Oxford articles to Counsel and then to Oxford   6 May 1698 G7v articles of agreement read and sealed between Nahum Tate, Nicholas Brady and the Master and Wardens concerning the New Version of David's Psalms   1 Aug 1698 G11v to take charge of Election Dinner   5 Dec 1698

G16v to examine need for repairs to Awnsham Churchill's warehouse   7 Feb 1698/9
G20r to view damage to barge and bargehouse   3 Apr 1699 G24r responsible for tiling
of side of Hall   13 Apr 1699 G24r to attend Sir Theodore Jansenn with their case
relating to the duty to be laid on paper   7 Aug 1699 G28r to take care of repairs to
barge   2 Oct 1699 G31v to pay Loftus's bill for mending barge, bricklayers' bill and a
bill for slating   8 Nov 1699 G33r to come to agreement with stewards of St Cecilia's
Day Feast over cost of renting Hall   4 Dec 1699 G33v discharge from Peter Parker and
Thomas Guy   4 Mar 1699/1700 G36v to advise what course of action should be taken
against Herbert Walwyn who has refused cloathing   26 Mar 1700 G36v to deal with
request to print a calendar containing matters re. trade to the Indias   7 Oct 1700 G46r
to adjust Clerk's bill of charges in Chancery   11 Nov 1700 G46v to view Everingham's
and Robert Roberts's houses with workmen re. repairs   5 May 1701 G59v to be
responsible for overseeing printing of new sheet almanack at Cambridge by S.C.'s
printer   2 Jun 1701 G60r responsible for proceeding against John Bradford for printing
and publishing the S.C.'s almanack, and George Parker and Hunt for selling a double
Ephemeris. To have a place made in the lobby for the better accommodation of the
Renter Wardens for receiving quarterage   1 Sep 1701 G63v to settle bills for work on
Robert Roberts's house   1 Dec 1701/2 G65v have inspected Register book relating to
entry by Benjamin Tooke of 'Gradus ad Parnassum'. It had been registered before he
became Treasurer   2 Mar 1701/2 G67v to view Everingham's house with workmen   4
May 1702 G70v to attend Sir Edward Northey, Attorney General, and pay him a
retainer of 5 guineas   1 Jun 1702 G71r to take Counsel's advice on how to proceed
against printers of 'The Child's Psalter' and 'A Psalter for Children'   3 Aug 1702 G79v
to obtain Attorney General's opinion on Tooke case   7 Sep 1702 G80r letter from
Charles Bertie and Mr Cecil, MPs for Stamford, Lincs, requesting permission to print
Pepper's Almanack   7 Dec 1702 G83v Clerk's bill for proceedings in Chancery to be
referred to; to decide acknowledgement to be paid by Daniel Browne for printing
'Abridgment of the Book of Martyrs'   12 Jul 1703 G92v to attend Dr Henry James,
Head of Queen's College, to discuss renewal of lease for the Printing House from
Cambridge University   22 Jul 1703 G93r report from meeting with Dr James   6 Sep
1703 G95r gallon of claret to be paid to   20 Sep 1703 G95r to view Mrs Eversden's
house with workmen re. repairs   4 Oct 1703 G95v have met John Gadbury but no
agreement reached   5 Nov 1703 G97v have received a letter from Thomas Cockerell
surrendering his £80 share   20 Nov 1703 G98r to have permission to search warehouses of Benjamin Harris and his son to ensure they are not printing illegal almanacks,
books or copies   22 Nov 1703 G98v to meet John Gellebrand if he makes any
application to them   7 Feb 1703/4 G101v to be given notice by William Hawes of name
of printer and size of each intended impression of 'The Church Catechism with Prayers,
Graces and Texts of Scripture Annexed Thereto'   2 Mar 1703/4 G103r to take advice
of Counsel concerning John Bradford's plea   6 Mar 1703/4 G103r to agree how
money due from William Spiller and his brother should be paid   14 Mar 1703/4
G104r to advise with Counsel concerning George Parker's Ephemerides   4 Sep 1704
G112r to take care of standing of the Assistants and the Livery on Thanksgiving
Day   2 Oct 1704 G112v to settle smith's bill   4 Dec 1704 G114r to adjust and order
payment of bricklayer's bill   20 Dec 1704 G115v (minute copied after that of 5 Feb
1704/5) to order payment of painter's bill   5 Feb 1704/5 G114v to order payment of
Clerk's bill for proceedings in Chancery   2 Apr 1705 G118r carpenter's bills and
joiner's bills referred   22 Jun 1705 G120v to take care of painting of pales in the
garden   6 Aug 1705 G122r to take care of provisions for Election Dinner   16 Oct
1705 G124v to attend Lord Mayor re. Renter Wardens' refusal to provide dinner   3
Dec 1705 G125v to settle painter's bill for the palisado pales   4 Feb 1705/6 G127v

Clerk's bills referred to. Carpenter's bill for the standing of the S.C. when the Queen came to St Paul's referred for payment   4 Mar 1705/6 G128v to settle and order sending of Bibles for the poor people of Kempsey Manor   5 Aug 1706 G133v to pay bill of Stevens the cook and carpenter's bill for stands for S.C. when Queen visited St Paul's   9 Sep 1706 G134v to take care about launching barge   20 Dec 1706 G137r Clerk's bill referred to them for payment   7 Jul 1707 G143v to settle plumber's and bricklayer's bills   4 Aug 1707 G144r to deal with Jeffrey Wale, who owes money to the English Stock   1 Mar 1707/8 G149v Clerk's bill for law charges to be referred to them   2 Aug 1708 G156v to provide the dinner and entertainment on 10 August and for Thanksgiving day   4 Oct 1708 G158r carpenter's, bricklayer's and smith's bills referred to them for payment. To provide music for the next Lord Mayor's Day according to custom   7 Feb 1708/9 G160v Clerk's bill referred to them for payment   6 Jun 1709 G165r to attend Sir Peter King   2 Jul 1709 G166v to deal with repairs to Morphew's house and mason's work in the passage between Whitledge and Mrs Everingham's houses   1 Aug 1709 G169v ordered to go into printing houses which they suspect are printing any of the S.C.'s copies or almanacks   7 Nov 1709 G171v bills of workmen for work on Morphew's house, and mason's bill for work done in passage by Whitledge's house, referred to for adjustment   5 Dec 1709 G172r to enquire into suspicion that Benjamin Harris printed and published a false Partridge's Almanack and a calendar   8 Dec 1709 G172v to take advice of Sir Edward Northey as to whether Parker's Ephemeris is a calendar or not. Also to discuss with counsel concerning the prognostications printed by Benjamin Harris   3 Apr 1710 G178r to pay Clerk's bill of law charges   9 Apr 1711 G189v to pay Clerk's bill   4 Jun 1711 G190v thanks of Court to be given to for the service done for the S.C. concerning the Bill for laying a duty upon all almanacks   2 Jul 1711 G192v read charge to Renter Wardens John Mayo and John Matthews. To adjust and order payment of bricklayer's bill   10 Jul 1711 G192v have attended Commissioners of the Stamp Office re. stamping of almanacks, but were told Lord Treasurer was responsible   2 Jun 1712 G200r to view Mrs Carter's house concerning repairs   6 Oct 1712 G203v to employ mason to make repairs to Mrs Carter's house   3 Nov 1712 G205r to order payment of bargemaster's bill   1 Dec 1712 G205v workmen's bills for repairing Mrs Carter's house to be settled by   13 Apr 1713 G208v to be added to committee to consider matters relating to the printers   6 Jul 1713 G212r to consider complaint of Mrs Carter   3 Aug 1713 G212v to oversee repairs to Mrs Carter's house   7 Sep 1713 G213r amounts owing to them in respect of English Stock   5 Oct 1713 G214r to consider Mills's request for new lease   7 Dec 1713 G215r to adjust and order payment of bricklayer's, carpenter's and shipwright's bills   1 Feb 1713/14 G216v their agreement to charge of Thomas Parkhurst's will read and entered in Court book   1 Mar 1713/14 G216v to take measures for the recovery of Joseph Oake's Livery fine   7 Jun 1714 G219r to attend Commissioners of the Stamp Office and request them to summon Thomas Norris before them   5 Jul 1714 G220v to consider Clerk's bill of law charges   2 Aug 1714 G221r to resolve differences between S.C. and Norris. To be responsible for painting, whitewashing and glazing the Hall. To be responsible for whitewashing Mrs Carter's house   6 Sep 1714 G221r to adjust and order payment of glazier's bill   7 Feb 1714/15 G225r to pay bills of painter, plasterer and glazier   4 Jul 1715 G231r Clerk's two bills of law charges referred to them for payment   5 Sep 1715 G232v to view Anthony Nelme's house re. granting a new lease. To provide new banners and a barge cloth for Lord Mayor's Day   3 Oct 1715 G233v to view barge   5 Dec 1715 G235v to consider request of Churchwardens of St Martin's Ludgate to lay river water into pipe belonging to S.C. in the garden   1 Oct 1716 G244r to take care that barge trimmed and launched the next spring tide   4 Mar 1716/17 G247v to pay Clerk's bill for law charges in Chancery

— ACCOUNTS   4 Oct 1697 F268v to be passed and entered   13 Apr 1698 G6v committee set up to audit at Bennett Griffin's request   1698–1716 audited annually   7 Sep 1713 G213r contain small items which in fact belong to English Stock. Joseph Collyer to pay them for English Stock in future

MASTER, WARDENS AND ASSISTANTS   20 Oct 1699 G32r Articles with Thomas Guy and Peter Parker, Henry Mortlock and Thomas Dring

MASTER, WARDENS AND STOCK-KEEPERS   4 Jul 1698 G11r bill of Michell for charges in Chancery, Exchequer, &c. referred to. Clerk's bill for charges in Chancery, Exchequer and elsewhere referred to   5 Oct 1702 G81v house, warehouse, papers and books of Benjamin Tooke to be delivered to them   8 Nov 1703 G97r to consider Nahum Tate's proposal to sell to the S.C. his interest in the New Version of the Psalms   4 Sep 1704 G111v to consider request of Dr Nicholas Brady to buy shares in the New Version of the Psalms   5 Feb 1704/5 G114v to settle affair of Tooke relating to Tate and Brady's Psalms   2 Jul 1705 G121v to agree settlement with Thomas Bradyll for purchase of part of impression of 'Virgil with Menelius [i.e. John Minellius] his notes'   3 Jun 1706 G132r letter from John Hayes of Cambridge referred to   4 Nov 1706 G136r to settle matter of Norton printing the grammar   2 Dec 1706 G136v to arrange for classical authors belonging to the English Stock to be examined and corrected   1 Sep 1707 G145r to consider letter of Samuel Farley of Exeter   6 Oct 1707 G145v to deal with impression of grammars   9 Feb 1707/8 G148v John Baskett's proposals re. impression of Clarendon's History in octavo referred to   30 Mar 1708/9 G151r decide not to take impression of Clarendon in octavo on terms proposed   7 Jun 1708 G153r to settle matter concerning Norton's printing of the grammar at Oxford and Cambridge   5 Jul 1708 G155r to consider letter from Downing about printing a collection of prayers for charity schools   7 Mar 1708/9 G162r to settle rent arrears with Awnsham Churchill   23 Jun 1709 G166r to settle matters concerning printing of the new version of psalms   4 Jul 1709 G167r to settle matters with Mrs Baldwin   13 Aug 1711 G193v to be assisted in management of Stock affairs   1 Sep 1712 G203r to consider the price the Oxford grantees should pay for printing psalms in folio and quarto   7 Jun 1714 G219r to look into the grants to see by what means S.C. have a right to the printing of several copies of schoolbooks   6 Sep 1714 G221v to consider letter from William Willymott concerning the printing of Corderius   4 Oct 1714 G222v to consider what action to take over a sheet almanack called 'Dublin's Calendar'   7 Feb 1714/15 G225r to settle matters with Robert Stephens relating to the warehouses   2 May 1715 G228v letter from Tate referred to them   4 Jul 1715 G230v letter from Tate referred to them   8 Aug 1715 G231r to consider proposal to deal with Mrs Everingham's arrears   10 Sep 1716 G243r to give notice of change in rate of interest paid by the S.C.   21 Mar 1716/17 G248r to consider paper of the King's speech printed clandestinely

MATHARD, Richard   4 Jun 1711 G191r bound to James Read, 7 years

MATHEW, Thomas   1 Aug 1687 F87r licensed to print 2000 metrical psalms with music under certain itemised conditions   3 Mar 1689/90 F131r asks S.C. to relieve him of 1600 of impression of 2000 metrical psalms with musical notes for cost price   7 Jul 1690 F139r request again turned down, but Court advises him to ask Robert Everingham, his printer, to get them subscribed for him

MATHEWS – see MATTHEWS

MATKINS, William, snr – see following entry

MATKINS, William, jnr   4 Jul 1715 G231r son of William; bound to Thomas James, 7 years

MATTHEWS/MATHEWES/MATHEWS/MATTHEWES, Emmanuel 6 May 1700 G39v Thomas Turford is bound to him 19 Jun 1701 G61r his apprentice Gilbert Beauchamp is freed 1 Sep 1701 G63v cloathed 2 Nov 1702 G83r Edmund Paybody is bound to him 4 Jun 1705 G120v William Hayes is bound to him 1 Sep 1707 G145r elected to one £40 share of Richard Mount's £80 share 6 Oct 1707 G145v his apprentice Charles Rivington turned over to Awnsham Churchill 9 Feb 1707/8 G149r bookbinder; Benjamin Baxter is bound to him 26 May 1709 G162v fined for First Renter Warden 4 Sep 1710 G183v his apprentice Charles Rivington is freed 2 Jul 1711 G192v his apprentice Edmund Paybody is freed 1 Oct 1711 G194v Daniel Farmer is bound to him 1 Sep 1712 G203r his apprentice William Hay is freed 5 Oct 1713 G214r William Dowthwaite is bound to him 1 Mar 1713/14 G216v Edward Cooper is bound to him

MATTHEWS, Giles 3 Oct 1681 E130v failure to appear to be cloathed noted 11 Oct 1686 F66r to be cloathed at next Court (note in another hand: 'He never appeared nor was presented to the Court of Aldermen')

MATTHEWS/MATHEWS, John (I) 4 Jul 1698 G11r Thomas Wiggins is bound to him 1 Sep 1701 G63v cloathed 6 Jul 1702 G78r Robert Staples is bound to him 2 Nov 1702 G83r his apprentice Edward Midwinter is freed 7 Aug 1704 G111r John Vasey is bound to him 10 Sep 1705 G123v his apprentice Thomas Wiggins is freed 4 Mar 1705/6 G129r William Antrobus turned over to him from James Orme 4 Apr 1709 G164r his apprentice John Vasey is turned over to George James 23 Jun 1711 G191v elected Second Renter Warden 2 Jul 1711 G192v charge read to him by Master and Wardens 3 Mar 1711/12 G197r Renter Warden; to be allowed £10 towards the dinner on Lord Mayor's Day, being fifth fine of Renter Warden 7 Apr 1712 G199r elected to James Knapton's £40 share 6 Oct 1712 G204v his apprentice William Antrobus is freed. His apprentice Robert Staples is freed 19 Dec 1712 G206r competes unsuccessfully for the late Thomas Lacy's £80 share 7 Dec 1713 G215r Charles Micklewright is bound to him 1 Mar 1713/14 G216v Thomas Sharpe turned over to him from John Hartley 3 Oct 1715 G233v see following entry [which may indicate his decease]

MATTHEWS, John (II) 3 Oct 1715 G233v son of John; bound to Mary, his mother, 7 years

MATTHEWS, Mary 3 Oct 1715 G233v her son John is bound to her 7 Nov 1715 G234v her apprentice Thomas Sharpe is freed

MATTHEWS/MATHEWS/MEADOWS, William 9 Feb 1701/2 G67r bound to Ralph Simpson, 7 years 4 Apr 1709 G164r freed by Ralph Simpson

MAUGHAN, Jonathan 5 Sep 1698 G14v bound to John Frere

MAWSON, Henry 4 Jun 1705 G120v bound to Mrs Mawson, his mother 3 Oct 1709 G171r turned over from his mother to Richard Janeway

MAWSON, Jane 24 Sep 1714 G222r elected to Mary Crump's pension. Elizabeth Strainge given her pension 27 Sep 1715 G233r elected to Mrs Crump's pension. John Beddow given her pension

MAWSON, Mary 20 Dec 1701 G66r elected to Mary Spurdance's pension

MAWSON, Mrs 4 Jun 1705 G120v her son Henry Mawson is bound to her 3 Oct 1709 G171r Henry Mawson turned over from her to Richard Janeway

MAWSON, Richard 1 Oct 1694 F213v servant to Capt. William Phillipps; freed 24 Oct 1694 F214r John Ford jnr is bound to him from 8 October

MAWSON, Robert 13 Apr 1702 G70r bound to William Gray, 7 years 2 May 1709 G165r freed by William Gray

MAXWELL, Mrs   7 Jun 1680 E100v assigned signature A of stock Child's Guide and assigned printing of Cambridge primer with John Macock   6 Dec 1680 E105v as printer of the John Gadbury and Thomas Trigg almanacks, ordered to omit abuse of Benjamin Harris in future impressions   8 May 1682 E152v assignment of Christopher Wase's 'Methodi Practica [i.e. 'Practicae'] Specimen' to Thomas Parkhurst confirmed. Committee set up to investigate whether her house needs repairing

MAY, John, snr – see following entry

MAY, John, jnr   4 Jun 1716 G240v son of John; bound to Robert Stephens, 7 years

MAYDWELL, [ ]   10 Sep 1705 G123r S.C. advertises against the project designed to exhibit his Bill in Parliament

MAYER, William   3 May 1708 G152v bound to George Read, 7 years

MAYHEW/MAHEW, Andrew   8 May 1704 G106v John Beckington is bound to him   1 Jul 1706 G133r his son Thomas is bound to him   2 Jul 1711 G192v his apprentice John Beckington is freed by his widow

MAYHEW, Thomas   1 Jul 1706 G133r bound to his father Andrew, 7 years   4 Apr 1709 G164r turned over from his father to Charles Smith   1 Mar 1713/14 G216v freed by patrimony

MAYNARD, John   7 Jun 1697 F263r Richard Adcock is freed by him   6 Oct 1712 G204v freed by patrimony

MAYNARD, William   5 Apr 1703 G88r bound to Thomas Bradyll, 7 years   6 Oct 1712 G204v freed by patrimony   1 Nov 1714 G223r butcher; Thomas Hind is bound to him

MAYO, Hannah   7 Jul 1712 G201v John Townsend is bound to her

MAYO/MAYOS, John (I)   22 Dec 1685 F48v petition of Mayo, Baldwin, Simon Hinch and John Palmer   1 Feb 1685/6 F50v his petition with Hinch and Palmer rejected as being 'the direct contrary to their former confession'   3 May 1686 F55v Under Warden sells the two presses of Mayo, Hinch and others to Henry Hills; Roger Norton and John Macock to fix fair price   7 Jun 1686 F56r Robert Roberts, substituting for Macock, reports the presses are worth £9   2 Aug 1686 F61v renews appeal for clemency; Court, partly because he is related to Thomas Newcomb, votes him £5 to cover debts for press   2 Aug 1697 F265v Theophilus Hastings is bound to him   3 Jun 1700 G40v David Richmond is bound to him   6 Sep 1703 G94v Walter Bodingham is bound to him   20 Sep 1703 G95r cloathed   7 Oct 1706 G135r James Bradshaw is bound to him   9 Jun 1707 G142v his apprentice David Richmond is freed   7 Feb 1708/9 G160v of Fleet Street; his son John Mayo is bound to him   27 Mar 1710 G177r excused office of Renter Warden for one year   26 Mar 1711 G189r elected First Renter Warden   2 Jul 1711 G192v charge read to him by Master and Wardens   1 Oct 1711 G195r his apprentice Walter Bodingham is freed

MAYO, John (II)   7 Feb 1708/9 G160v bound to John, his father, 7 years

MAYO, Mrs   2 Nov 1713 G214v her apprentice James Bradshaw is freed

MAYO, Richard – see CATECHISMS

MAYOR OF LONDON – see LONDON: LORD MAYOR

MAYOS, Alice   7 Feb 1708/9 G160v of Addle Hill; Thomas Goffe is bound to her   5 Mar 1715/16 G237v her apprentice Thomas Goffe is freed

See also MAYO

MAYSTETTER, John   7 Apr 1707 G141r bound to John Freer, 7 years

MEAD, [ ] 4 Feb 1705/6 G127v printer; to attend next Court to give reasons for printing Terence without S.C.'s permission 19 Feb 1705/6 G128r discussion of his printing William Willymott's edition of Terence 6 Sep 1708 G157r Clerk to attend John Baskett to obtain the answers of Mead and others

MEAD/MEADE, Daniel 6 Aug 1694 F211v son of Richard Mead, late stationer of London; bound to John Harris 2 Mar 1701/2 G67v freed by John Harris 4 Jun 1705 G120v Thomas Wilson is bound to him 3 Mar 1711/12 G197r James Mead is bound to him 9 Apr 1716 G239r James Smith turned over from him to James Holland 7 May 1716 G240r John Crabtree is bound to him

MEAD, James, snr – see following entry

MEAD, James, jnr 3 Mar 1711/12 G197r son of James; bound to Daniel Mead, 7 years

MEAD, John 5 Dec 1709 G172r bound to his father Medriach, 7 years

MEAD/MEADE, Medriach/Medrick/Meredith 5 Jul 1697 F264v Robert Allen is bound to him 6 Dec 1697 G2r William Sheffield is bound to him 24 Mar 1701/2 G68r John Thomas is bound to him 9 Feb 1707/8 G148v bookbinder; bill in Chancery to be brought against him 1 Mar 1707/8 G149r to be proceeded against for an immediate answer to charges 5 Dec 1709 G172r his son John Mead is bound to him 7 Sep 1713 G213v John Fuller is bound to him
See also MEAD, [ ]

MEAD/MEADE, Richard, snr 5 Sep 1692 (W) frees his sons Richard and Thomas 12 Sep 1692 F179r master (and father) of newly made freemen Richard and Thomas Mead of Clerkenwell, whose names are sent to Lord Chamberlain 6 Aug 1694 F211v stationer, deceased; his son Daniel is bound to John Harris

MEAD, Richard, jnr 5 Sep 1692 (W) freed by his father, Richard 12 Sep 1692 F179r of Clerkenwell and newly made free of his father Richard Mead; name sent to Lord Chamberlain

MEAD/MEADE, Thomas 5 Sep 1692 (W) freed by his father, Richard 12 Sep 1692 F179r of Clerkenwell and newly made free of his father Richard Mead; name sent to Lord Chamberlain 3 Jul 1699 G27v Robert Walker is bound to him 2 Aug 1703 G94r cloathed. Nathaniel Parsell is bound to him 3 Dec 1705 G126r Edward Leadbeter is bound to him 9 Sep 1706 G134v his apprentice Edward Leadbeter is turned over to Matthew Jenour 2 Dec 1706 G136v his apprentice Robert Walker is freed. His apprentice Nicholas Powell is turned over to Matthew Jenour 12 Apr 1708 G152r writing master; Daniel Shorter is bound to him

MEADOWS, William – see MATTHEWS, William

MEAGER, Leonard – see ENGLISH GARDENER

MEAKES/MEAKS, John 1 Oct 1694 F213v Humphrey Jackson is bound to him 3 Nov 1701 G65r his apprentice Humphrey Jackson is freed

MEAKINS, John 3 Aug 1702 G79v William Reason is bound to him 7 Nov 1709 G172r his apprentice William Reason is freed

MEAKS – see MEAKES

MEARNE, [ ] 3 Dec 1684 (W) King's bookbinder, to cease supplying King and Council with almanacks

MEARNE, Charles 24 Jun 1682 E154r cloathed; pays fine on spot 4 Sep 1682 E157v voted to the late Joseph Leigh's £80 share 3 Dec 1683 F6v Robert Stephens and Francis Egglesfeild to appear at next Court to answer Mearne's complaint 7 Sep

1685 F43v presents silver salver to S.C. as a gift from his mother, Samuel Mearne's widow   6 Sep 1686 F62v deceased; his £80 share is voted to Adiel Mill

MEARNE, Mrs   1 Sep 1684 F23v William Whitwood transfers the mortgage of his £40 share from her to James Taylor   3 Feb 1700/1 G54v deceased; her £320 share disposed of to Capt. William Phillipps   9 Jun 1707 G142r assignment of mortgage of Henry Hills's £320 share from Sawbridge to her; share disposed of to Charles Harper

MEARNE, Samuel   7 Jun 1680 E100r protests as Master against Court's decision not to answer or bring a crossbill against Robert Scott's bill   3 Jul 1680 E101r competes unsuccessfully for Master   7 Feb 1680/1 E106v promises to bring all S.C. papers in his custody to next Court. He and Thomas Vere desired to search for the Bishop of London's order damasking the [Westminster] Assembly's Catechism   7 Mar 1680/1 E107v with Vere, to bring the Bishop of London's order for damasking the Assembly's Catechism to the next Court. To be reminded of his promise to hand over papers relating to S.C.   11 Apr 1681 E109v [Francis?] Egglesfeild assigns him 'Aesop's Fables' and a moiety of Quarles's 'Emblems'   7 Nov 1681 E137v to be present with Henry Herringman while Robert Scott enters a number of books cheaply. To provide a dinner on the next Court day   5 Dec 1681 E139r Stock dividends suspended because of his failure to provide a dinner or explain why not   6 Feb 1681/2 E142r order re. his share annulled; he promises to give a venison dinner to the Court   21 Feb 1681/2 E144v elected Master in place of Thomas Vere who has died in office   6 Mar 1681/2 E146v lengthy outline of his disagreement with Robert Scott over a warehouse   3 Apr 1682 E150v dispute between him and Henry Herringman re. books and parts of books assigned to Mearne by Mrs Kinton referred to committee   8 May 1682 E153r among sureties for payment of Sir Joseph Seamour's annuity; indemnified by S.C.   1 Jul 1682 E154v elected Master   3 Jul 1682 E155v difference between him and Henry Herringman and Robert Scott re. books entered to Mearne in 1673 to be resolved before next Court   7 Aug 1682 E156v no meeting with Herringman and Scott re. difference over copies; agreed that his entry of copies in 1673 is null and void   4 Jun 1683 E170r deceased   3 Mar 1683/4 F10r deceased; Robert Stephens has discharged the mortgage of his £80 share to Mearne before remortgaging it to Henry Clarke. Capt. John Williams has discharged the mortgage of his £160 share to Mearne before remortgaging it to Judith Webb   7 Sep 1685 F43v his widow gives a silver salver to S.C.

MEARS/MEERES/MEERS, William   9 Sep 1700 G45r bound to Israel Harrison, 7 years   6 Oct 1707 G145v freed by Israel Harrison   2 Aug 1708 G156v stationer; cloathed. Richard Palmer is bound to him   3 Mar 1711/12 G197r elected to James Roberts' £40 share   26 Mar 1717 G248v excused office of First Renter Warden for one year

See also MEERES

MECHAM, John   7 Feb 1697/8 G3v freed by Edward Ward   7 Mar 1697/8 G5r Robert Scott is bound to him

MECHELL, James   20 Dec 1710 G186v bound to John Darker, 7 years

MEDDEN, George   6 Mar 1703/4 G103v bound to William Clerke, 7 years

MEDDHOPP, [   ]   2 Aug 1708 G156v bound to Thomas Hobbs, 7 years

MEDWYN, George   10 Sep 1711 G194r freed by Robert Lympany

MEEKES, John   6 Dec 1697 G2r is bound to Anthony Barker

MEERE, Hugh   2 Aug 1703 G94r freed by Ichabod Dawkes   3 Apr 1704 G106r Thomas Tresare is bound to him   7 Oct 1706 G135r William Fleming is bound to him   2 Nov 1713 G214v his apprentice William Fleming is freed   4 Feb 1716/17 G246v cloathed. Hugh Blackwell is bound to him

MEERES, [ ]   4 Aug 1712 G202v the musician; to provide music for S.C. for dinner on August 12th

MEERES, John   9 Feb 1712/13 G206v son of Thomas; bound to William Stephens, 7 years

MEERES, Thomas – see preceding entry
See also MEARS

MEERS – see MEARS, MEERES

MEGGS, Christopher   6 Dec 1703 G99v Humphrey Child is bound to him   20 Dec 1704 G115v Bartholomew Gale is bound to him   4 Oct 1708 G158r of Forster Lane; John Dawson is bound to him   5 Mar 1710/11 G188r his apprentice Humphrey Child is freed   3 Mar 1711/12 G197r his apprentice Bartholomew Gale is freed   4 Apr 1715 G227v see following entry

MEGGS, John   4 Apr 1715 G227v son of Christopher; bound to Humphrey Child, 7 years   2 May 1715 G228v turned over from Humphrey Child to William Lefosse

MEIRES, Andrew   2 May 1698 G7v freed by Robert Everingham

MELLIFICIUM CHIRURGAE – see MARROW OF CHIRURGERY

MEMBER OF PARLIAMENT   17 Dec 1709 G173r letter from John Partridge to concerning his almanack

MEMORIALS OF GODLINESS AND CHRISTIANITY [by Herbert Palmer]   11 Apr 1681 E109v assigned by Mrs Underhill to Samuel Crouch

MEMORIAL EXTRACTED OUT OF THE MODEST ENQUIRY   4 Aug 1690 F141r Wilkins summoned for printing this without licence, and asks pardon

MEMORIALS   15 Apr 1692 F169v assignment entered from Nathaniel Ponder to Jacob Tonson of [Sir Bulstrode Whitlock's] 'Memorials of the English Affairs (Charles I — Charles II)'

MENDALL, Richard   5 Sep 1698 G14v bound to Abel Roper   3 Dec 1705 G126r freed by Benjamin Beardwell

MENDY, John   3 May 1697 F262r freed by patrimony

MENELIUS [i.e. John Minellius] – see TERENCE, OVID, VIRGIL

MERCER, Joseph   2 Aug 1714 G221r turned over to Thomas Mason

MERCER, Thomas   2 Aug 1697 F265v cloathed, promising payment at two six-monthly intervals   26 Mar 1702 G68v fined for Renter Warden

MERCHANT TAYLORS' COMPANY   16 Jun 1684 F17v Robert Smith of the Merchant Taylors' declares himself willing to be translated to S.C.

MERCHANT'S SPECULUM   5 Dec 1698 G16v or 'The Shopkeeper's Necessary Companion', counterfeit almanack printed by John Bradford

MEREDITH, [ ]   7 Feb 1698/9 G20v opposed to payment of Mrs Royston's £40 dividend to Richard Chiswell in return for his maintaining her

MEREDITH, Christopher   23 Mar 1691/2 F167r Court to consider at next meeting whether the £10 received annually under the terms of his will is employed according to his wishes   3 Jun 1695 F224v committee appointed to inspect Court books re. Meredith bequest   1 Jul 1695 F227r Clerk to inquire whether any decree concerning Meredith bequest was ever made in the courts of judicature   5 Oct 1696 F250r Master and Wardens to inquire into what increase there is in Meredith bequest   7 Dec 1696 F253r Master and Wardens to inquire into books to be given to a free school in the country and re. Meredith's London estate   2 Aug 1697 F265r Bishop of Worcester sends message re. Meredith bequest; ordered that a case be drawn up by the Clerk and legal advice taken   4 May 1702 G70v committee to inspect S.C.'s books concerning his gift to the poor of 'Kelmsley' [i.e. Kempsey] in Worcestershire   1 Mar 1702/3 G86r bequest of books to tenants of Kempsey Manor   2 Apr 1705 G118r Warden Hodgkins to ensure his gift of books sent to Kempsey school   5 Jun 1710 G180v £10 to be lent to any member of the S.C. on surety in accordance with his will

MEREDITH/MERRIDITH, Luke   29 May 1689 F118v cloathed   5 Oct 1691 F161v Court tells Master that he is about to print John Patrick's metrical translation of psalms; referred to Cambridge committee   7 Dec 1691 F163r fined 2d per book for 2 impressions of 1500 and 2000 of Dr Patrick's psalms and 30s for an impression of Dr Sherlock's catechism   7 Mar 1691/2 F166v fined 20s for persistently refusing to appear on summons and summoned to next Court to pay it   12 Apr 1692 F168v pays 20s fine for contempt of Court and 30s for printing Sherlock's catechism but begs to be excused 2d per book for printing 3500 of Patrick's Psalms   4 Oct 1697 F268v John Butler is bound to him   26 Mar 1698 G5r elected Assistant Renter Warden   7 Aug 1699 G28v complaint that £22 is due from him and John Leake, Renter Wardens for last year. Fined for disobedience of byelaws in neglecting summons to last monthly Court   6 Nov 1699 G32v and Leake. Order of 7 Aug 1699 imposing fine to be annulled, balance of accounts as Renter Warden having been paid

MEREDITH, Royston   4 Jun 1705 G120v bound to Thomas Bennett   4 Nov 1706 G136r turned over from Thomas Bennett to Richard Wilkins   4 May 1713 G209v freed by Richard Wilkins

MERLIN REVIVED   2 Oct 1682 E158r Richard Janeway confesses to printing this for Francis Smith's youngest son Samuel

MERLINUS LIBERATUS   4 Dec 1710 G185v Clerk refuses to enter this for Benjamin Harris

MERLINUS RUSTICUS   30 Sep 1684 F24r new almanack of this name, written by Henry Crabtree, to be printed for S.C.
See also ALMANACKS

MERREST, James   6 Jun 1698 G8v bound to Christopher Coningsby, 7 years

MERRIDITH – see MEREDITH

MERRYMAN, Henry   3 May 1708 G152v bound to William Yorke, 7 years

MESSAR, John – see following entry

MESSAR/MESSER, Joseph   4 Feb 1711/12 G196v son of John; bound to Samuel, his brother, 7 years

MESSAR, Samuel   4 Dec 1704 G114r bound to Thomas Lingard, 7 years   3 Dec 1711 G195v freed by Thomas Lingard   4 Feb 1711/12 G196v his brother Joseph is bound to him, 7 years   7 May 1716 G240r John Ibbutt is bound to him

MESSENGER OF THE PRESS – see HILLS, Henry, jnr; STEPHENS, Robert

MESSER – see MESSAR

METAMORPHOSES – see OVID

METCALFE, Benjamin   7 Oct 1700 G46r bound to Francis Leach, 7 years   1 Aug 1709 G169v freed by Francis Leach

METHODI PRACTICAE SPECIMEN   8 May 1682 E152v by Christopher Wase; assignment of it to Thomas Parkhurst by Mrs Maxwell confirmed

MEW, Thomas   3 Feb 1706/7 G138r apprentice to John Marsh; freed, his master and mistress both being dead   3 Mar 1706/7 G139r Blaze Clarke is bound to him   6 Dec 1708 G159v of Loathbury [Lothbury?]. John Perkins is bound to him

MEWES, William   5 May 1701 G59v bound to William Richardson, 7 years   5 Jul 1708 G155r freed by Thomas Wilmer

MÉZERAY, François Eudes de – see HISTORY OF FRANCE

MICHELL, [   ]   5 Oct 1696 F250v solicitor in Chancery; to take out attachments against those who have not answered S.C.'s bill in Chancery about comprinting   4 Jul 1698 G11r bill for charges in Chancery, Exchequer &c. to be referred to Master, Wardens and Stock-keepers

MICHELL, Robert   6 Sep 1697 F267r bound to Thomas Grover   3 Feb 1706/7 G138r freed by Thomas Grover

MICKLEWRIGHT, Charles   7 Dec 1713 G215r son of Robert; bound to John Matthews, 8 years

MICKLEWRIGHT, Robert, snr – see preceding and following entries

MICKLEWRIGHT, Robert, jnr   7 Dec 1713 G215r son of Robert; bound to John Baskett, 7 years

MIDDLETON, Arthur   8 Aug 1715 G232r son of William; bound to Samuel Paul, 7 years

MIDDLETON, Thomas – see following entry

MIDDLETON/MIDLETON, William (I)   4 Feb 1694/5 F217r son of Thomas Middleton of Hampstead, gentleman, deceased; bound to Ralph Simpson from 25 December 1694   4 Oct 1703 G96r freed by Ralph Simpson

MIDDLETON, William (II)   8 Aug 1715 G232r his son Arthur is bound to Samuel Paul, 7 years

MIDDLEWRIGHT, Grace   22 Dec 1708 G159v elected to Robert Harrison's pension   19 Dec 1712 G205v elected to Hannah Smith's pension. Her pension given to Daniel Reyley

MIDDLEWRIGHT, Robert   7 Jul 1701 G62r freed by Thomas Grover

MIDFORD, Francis   1 Oct 1716 G244r son of Robert; bound to Samuel Holmes, 7 years

MIDFORD, Robert – see preceding entry

MIDGELY, Robert   22 Aug 1685 F43r bachelor in physic; presents ecclesiastically authorised deputation empowering him to licence books on behalf of bishops under revived Printing Act (W) copy of the deputation   4 Dec 1693 F196r letter from him read licensing 'Letters Writ by a Turkish Spy' to be printed

MIDLETON – see MIDDLETON

MIDWINTER, Daniel   7 Feb 1697/8 G3v freed by Richard Chiswell   7 Nov 1698 G16r cloathed   8 Apr 1700 G39r William Jackson is bound to him   6 Sep 1703 G94v Joseph Cradock is bound to him   27 Mar 1704 G104r fined for First Renter Warden   9 Sep 1706 G134v elected to Christopher Wilkinson's £40 share   5 May 1707 G142r his apprentice William Jackson is freed   4 Aug 1707 G144v John Bateman is bound to him   1 Mar 1708/9 G161r elected Stock-keeper for Yeomanry   1 Mar 1709/10 G176r elected Stock-keeper for Yeomanry   1 Mar 1710/11 G187v elected Stock-keeper for Yeomanry   7 May 1711 G190r elected to Timothy Goodwin's £80 share. His £40 share disposed of to Thomas Varnam   1 Mar 1711/12 G197v elected Stock-keeper for Livery   26 Sep 1712 G203v his apprentice Joseph Craddock is freed. His apprentice John Midwinter is freed   6 Oct 1712 G204r signatory of committee report concerning printing of psalms in Oxford   2 Mar 1712/13 G207r elected Stock-keeper for Livery   1 Mar 1713/14 G216v elected Stock-keeper for Livery   7 Feb

1714/15 G225r his apprentice John Bateman is freed   1 Mar 1714/15 G225v elected Stock-keeper for Livery   2 May 1715 G228v elected Assistant   4 Jul 1715 G230v takes oath of Assistant   1 Mar 1715/16 G236v elected Stock-keeper for Assistants   5 Mar 1715/16 G237v signs note for payment to Thomas Guy   2 Jul 1716 G241v competes unsuccessfully for Benjamin Tooke's £160 share   4 Feb 1716/17 G246v to be one of the new trustees of the S.C.'s property   21 Feb 1716/17 G246v trust conveyed to him as new trustee. Lease from City assigned to him   1 Mar 1716/17 G247r elected Stock-keeper for Assistants   1 Apr 1717 G249v elected to Israel Harrison's £160 share. His £80 share disposed of to Samuel Ashurst

MIDWINTER, Edward   2 Nov 1702 G83r apprentice to Thomas Bradyll, turned over to John Matthews and freed by him   1 Mar 1702/3 G86r Joseph Robinson is bound to him   3 Mar 1706/7 G139r his apprentice Joseph Robinson is turned over to Richard Janeway   5 Jul 1708 G155r printer; Josiah Ward is bound to him   3 Apr 1710 G178v Benjamin Odell turned over to him from Benjamin Motte   2 Oct 1710 G184v of Pye Corner, printer; Thomas Gent is bound to him   7 Feb 1714/15 G225r Henry Lingard turned over to him from Samuel Deacon

MIDWINTER, Emmanuel   6 Aug 1711 G193r his apprentice Samuel Negus is freed

MIDWINTER, John   3 Jul 1699 G27v bound to Thomas Leigh, 8 years   26 Sep 1712 G203v freed by Daniel Midwinter

MIFLIN, John   2 Aug 1708 G156v bound to John Bennett, 7 years   5 Mar 1710/11 G188r turned over from John Bennett to William Drewett

MILBOURNE/MILBURN, Alexander   2 Dec 1695 F237r Philip Wood, his apprentice, is freed. Henry Duste is bound to him   9 Sep 1700 G45r Thomas Knight is bound to him   7 Dec 1702 G83v his apprentice Henry Duste is freed   2 Dec 1706 G136v Samuel Savage turned over to him from Charles Bates   1 Sep 1707 G145r printer; Thomas Crane is bound to him   1 Sep 1712 G203r his apprentice Thomas Knight is freed   6 Oct 1712 G204r his apprentice Samuel Savage is freed

MILBOURNE, Ann   9 Sep 1706 G134v wife of Thomas; her apprentice Henry Morley turned over to James Dover

MILBOURNE, Eliza   7 Apr 1712 G199r William Green is bound to her

MILBOURNE/MILBOURN/MILLBOURN/MILLBOURNE, Elizabeth   5 Sep 1715 G232v her apprentice Thomas Crane is freed   8 Jan 1716/17 G246r John Snell is bound to her

MILBOURNE, Joseph   9 Feb 1707/8 G148v hawker; bill in Chancery to be brought against him   3 May 1708 G152v not to be proceeded against further for selling sham almanacks

MILBOURNE, Mrs   3 Oct 1709 G171r deceased; her £40 share disposed of to John Nutt

MILBOURNE/MILBORNE/MILBURNE, Thomas   6 May 1685 F34r elected to Edward Horton's £40 share   7 May 1685 (W) confirmed as member of new Livery   11 Oct 1688 F108v restored to Livery   26 Mar 1689 F115v excused Assistant Renter Wardenship for 1 year   26 Mar 1690 F131v elected Assistant Renter Warden   7 Apr 1690 F132v pleads inability to become a Renter Warden this year; accepted   26 Mar 1692 F167v set aside for a year from serving or fining for Renter Warden   27 Mar 1693 F185r excused office of Renter Warden   26 Mar 1694 F201v voted that he should not be chosen Renter Warden   5 Aug 1700 G44r Henry Crosgrove is bound to him   5 Jul 1703 G92r his apprentice William Smythers is freed. Henry Morley is bound to him   4 Feb 1705/6 G127v his apprentice Samuel Darby is freed

See also MILBURN, MILBURNE

MILBURN, [ ] 7 Jun 1680 E100v assigned signature C of Stock Child's Guide
See also MILBOURNE, MILBURNE

MILBURNE, Thomas 7 Feb 1686/7 F70r interrogated about his right to print contrary to Act of Parliament and forbidden to continue; promises to give over trade
See also MILBOURNE, MILBURN

MILL/MILLS, Adiel 7 May 1685 (W) confirmed as member of new Livery 3 Aug 1685 F42r elected Assistant Renter Warden 3 May 1686 F55v to be paid £60 due to him from English Stock 6 Sep 1686 F62v elected to the late Charles Mearne's £80 share 23 Mar 1686/7 F80r produces Mrs Leigh's accounts on her behalf 2 Jul 1694 F210v committee to meet Sedgwick over his claim to a £80 share assigned to him in Adiel Mill's statute of bankruptcy 6 Jun 1698 G8v £80 share demanded by Sedgwick on behalf of his wife, assignee of the Commissioners of Bankruptcy award against Adiel Mill. Request not granted because of bill in Chancery between Sedgwick and S.C. 1 Aug 1698 G13r counterpart of lease made by S.C. to him to be delivered by Clerk to Anthony Nelme

See also MILLS, MILL, Joan

MILL/MILLS, Joan 4 Jul 1692 F174r leads application asking S.C. to renew leases granted to her husband for Ave Maria Lane and Amen Corner properties; Court defer this 3 Feb 1695/6 F239r Treasurer to lend her £10 from S.C. 6 Apr 1696 F241v answer of S.C. to a bill in Chancery at the suit of Joan Mill, executrix to Adiel Mill, is sealed 2 Nov 1696 F252r paid £5 to assist her with a lawsuit nearly solved 6 Sep 1697 F266v widow of Adiel Mill; her request to renew the leases of 2 houses from S.C., her own and Anthony Nelme's, is deferred 8 Nov 1697 G1v request to take a lease on her house to be considered 6 Jun 1698 G8r rent for her house set at £8, she permitting the flue or funnel belonging to Nelme's house to be held and enjoyed by him as hitherto 7 Oct 1698 G15r permitted to have a lease for her present house for 7 years at £8 p.a. 7 Feb 1698/9 G20v lease from S.C. of house in Amen Corner sealed 2 Jun 1701 G60v common yard of her house and that rented by Nelme to be divided 6 Dec 1703 G99r to have a further term of 8 years added to her lease 10 Feb 1703/4 G102r her lease sealed 7 Jun 1708 G153r account of her rent arrears to S.C. to be prepared 5 Jul 1708 G154v Joseph Collyer to make up her account, concerning dividend money and rent due from her and £15 borrowed from S.C. 6 Dec 1708 G159r committee to settle matter of her rent arrears 6 Aug 1711 G193r her apprentice Richard Butterfield is freed 2 Mar 1712/13 G206v deceased; her £80 share disposed of to Arthur Bettesworth 4 May 1713 G209v lease to her to be inspected to see how much time it has left to run 3 Aug 1713 G212v house formerly inhabited by her to be surveyed and repairs assessed 7 Feb 1714/15 G225r house formerly occupied by her to be let by Master and Wardens 4 Apr 1715 G227v house formerly occupied by her to be let to Joseph Hazard
See also MILLS, MILL, Adiel

MILLEN, John 19 Jun 1701 G61r his apprentice Gilbert Beauchamp is freed

MILLER, Elizabeth 2 May 1698 G7v Roger Tuckyer is bound to her 3 May 1714 G218v resigns her £40 share and requests that Robert Elms be voted into it 27 Sep 1715 G233r elected to Martha Barber's pension 22 Mar 1715/16 G238r deceased; Martha Widows is given her pension

MILLER, Isaac, snr – see following entry

MILLER, Isaac, jnr 3 Mar 1711/12 G197r son of Isaac; bound to Jacob Tonson, 7 years

MILLER, John 1 Mar 1685/6 F51r cloathed 7 Feb 1686/7 F70v elected to Daniel Peacock's £40 share 1 Mar 1687/8 F98v elected Stock-keeper for Yeomanry with William Rogers 1 Mar 1689/90 F129v elected Stock-keeper for Livery with Samuel Roycroft 12 Apr 1692 F168v elected First Renter Warden 3 Jul 1693 F189v the auditors of the Renter Wardens' accounts drawn up by himself and Edward Jones report that the balance is £19 2s 2d 7 May 1694 F204r Gilbert Beauchamp bound to him 22 Jun 1698 G9v general release from S.C.

MILLER, Mrs 20 Dec 1700 G54r widow of William Miller; given 20s in relief

See also MILLER, William

MILLER, Simon 4 Jul 1681 E116r voted that time should be taken to consider whether he, Thomas Parkhurst and others should be made Assistants 8 May 1682 E152v assigns Dr [John] Lightfoot's 'Harmony of the Scriptures' [i.e. *Scripture Harmonies*] to Thomas Parkhurst 3 Jul 1682 E155v assigns half of Eusebius Pagitt's 'History of the Bible' to Edward Brewster 3 Mar 1683/4 F9v becomes an Assistant in accordance with Crown's request as a reward for stamping out seditious printing 7 Apr 1684 F14r on the list of loyal Court members presented to the Crown 29 Jan 1684/5 F29v with Thomas Bassett, ordered to give a dinner to Court members or pay a penalty of £10 3 Feb 1684/5 F30r his and Thomas Bassett's £10 penalty discharged on providing dinner 7 May 1685 (W) confirmed as member of new Livery 3 Jul 1686 F59v wishes to be excused from Under Wardenship and to be dismissed from Assistants 2 Aug 1686 F61r Court requests to see him before discharging him from being Assistant; he sends answer that he is unable to come but begs it to discharge him all the same 6 Sep 1686 F62r allowed to be discharged from Court on condition that he testifies to this in the Court Book. (W) Letter making request 11 Oct 1688 F108v restored to Livery

MILLER, Susan/Susanna 7 Aug 1699 G28v paper relating to her share in English Stock referred to next Court 4 Sep 1699 G29r permitted to remortgage her £160 share to John Wilcox 1 Dec 1701 G66r Browne to have copies of orders concerning her mortgaging the equity of redemption of her stock to Wilcox 6 Dec 1703 G99v overplus of her dividend after payment of Mrs Isted's interest to be paid as a surety for Wilcox's mortgage on Miller's stock 20 Dec 1703 G100r petition concerning Wilcox's receipt of overplus of her dividend. Joseph Collyer to pay her £5 for board and lodging 4 Feb 1705/6 G127r deceased; her Livery share disposed of to Deputy Collins 6 May 1706 G131r money from her share in English Stock to be paid to Mrs Isted 3 Feb 1706/7 G137r died intestate; remainder of her money in English Stock, besides mortgage to Mrs Isted and Thomas Parkhurst, to be paid to Parkhurst. Her daughter's debt to Collyer to be paid from remainder

MILLER, William 1 Mar 1679/80 E97v elected Stock-keeper for Livery 1 Mar 1680/1 E107v elected Stock-keeper for Livery with Robert Clavell 13 Oct 1687 F91v elected Assistant but does not appear to take oath 17 Oct 1687 F92v accepts place of Assistant 5 Dec 1687 F95r fine of £8 for trying to force his way on to the Court mitigated to £5 as he has purchased a Livery share. Submits to £5 being retained from his next dividend but asks that his precedence in Court should not be affected 9 Jan 1687/8 F96v to pay the £5 which was not in fact deducted from his last dividend 30 Jun 1688 F103r among those chosen to audit Renter Wardens' accounts; competes unsuccessfully for Under Warden 4 Feb 1688/9 F112v re-appointed Assistant 6 May 1689 F116v ranked fourth of Assistants never elected as Master or Warden 6 Jul 1689 F121v among those chosen to audit Warden's accounts 5 Jun 1690 F135v re-appointed Assistant 4 Jul 1691 F156v among those chosen to audit Renter Wardens' accounts. Competes unsuccessfully for Under Warden 23 Jun 1692 F172v competes unsuccessfully for Under Warden   2 Jul 1692 F172v given leave to fine for first year's service as Under Warden   7 Nov 1692 F182r told to take legal advice over Roger Norton's suing him for allegedly printing a book to which Norton affirms a right   1 Jul 1693 F189r competes unsuccessfully for Under Warden   10 Sep 1694 F212v deceased; his apprentice Francis Coggan is turned over to Daniel Browne

See also MILLER, Mrs

MILLERT, John – see following entry

MILLERT, Roger   4 Feb 1695/6 F217r son of the late John Millert of St Martin in the Fields, gentleman; bound to Charles Osborne

MILLETT, John   29 May 1689 F118v cloathed

MILLIAN – see MILLION

MILLION/MILLIAN, Henry   26 Mar 1692 F167v elected First Renter Warden and summoned   12 Apr 1692 F168v excused Renter Wardenship on writing to say that he has been ordered into Ireland on Crown service for linen manufacture   27 Mar 1693 F185r elected Renter Warden and fines   1703–1717 Beadle   27 Mar 1703 G87v elected Beadle. To be disenfranchised from S.C. in order that he may be a witness in S.C.'s affairs   5 Apr 1703 G88r to have all rooms and cellars in house formerly occupied by Nicholas Hooper (except ground floor leased by John Nutt) while he is Beadle   5 Feb 1704/5 G114v his petition relating to Nutt read   2 Apr 1705 G118v petitions against Nutt who is attempting to turn him out of his room in Nutt's house   12 Apr 1708 G152r to collect money subscribed in support of Copyright Act   6 Mar 1709/10 G176r under terms of new lease, to have rooms in Morphew's house for as long as he remains Beadle   6 Jul 1713 G211v Common Serjeant's opinion that he is a good witness for the S.C. read. Promises not to poll any more as a liveryman of S.C., as he has disenfranchised himself in order to be a good witness

MILLIS, James – see following entry

MILLIS, John   6 Jul 1713 G212v son of James; bound to Thomas Marlar, 7 years

MILLS, [   ] (I)   7 Feb 1686/7 F71r of the Temple; tells Court on behalf of Mrs Waterson that Samuel Daniel's 'History of England' has been entered to Mr Waterson. Clerk ordered to search

MILLS, [   ] (II)   2 Aug 1697 F265r committee to view the houses of William Woolley, Anthony Nelme and 'all other houses which Mills holds of this company'   5 Oct 1713 G214r request for new lease on his house in Amen Corner referred to next Court   2 Nov 1713 G214r not to be granted new lease for less than £14 p.a.   7 Dec 1713 G214v his sisters to hold the house formerly leased to their mother for 1½ years at £14 p.a.

See also GARDEN

MILLS, Bryan   5 Feb 1693/4 F199r son of Nathaniel Mills of St Mary Overies, Southwark, barber and chirurgeon; bound to John Astwood for seven years   7 Jul 1701 G62r freed by John Astwood   6 Dec 1703 G99v Samuel Keimer is bound to him   4 Nov 1706 G136r printer; Henry Lebrand is bound to him   3 Feb 1706/7 G137v printer; cloathed. John Bourchier is bound to him   1 Sep 1707 G145r his apprentice John Fisher is freed   6 Sep 1708 G157v printer; Benjamin Burford is bound to him   6 Jun 1709 G165v Henry Lebrand turned over from him to Anne Snowden   4 Feb 1711/12 G196v his apprentice Samuel Keimer is freed   9 Apr 1716 G239r his apprentice Benjamin Burford is freed

MILLS, John, snr   10 Sep 1716 G243r his son Samuel is bound to Francis Clay, 7 years.

See also following entry

MILLS, John, jnr   1 Jun 1713 G210v son of John; bound to Thomas Shelmerdine, 7 years

MILLS, Nathaniel   5 Feb 1693/4 F199r of St Mary Overies, Southwark, barber and chirurgeon; his son Bryan is bound to John Astwood, 7 years

MILLS, Richard   2 Apr 1683 E168v to take a bond for £5 payable in a year's time   21 Mar 1705/6 G129v petition that his bond of £5 to S.C. be delivered up as he is unable to pay it. Delivered to him by Warden Thomas Hodgkins   23 Jun 1709 G166r elected to Adam Turner's pension

MILLS, Samuel   10 Sep 1716 G243r son of John; bound to Francis Clay, 7 years

MILLS, Thomas   29 Sep 1715 G233r elected to Mary Redmaine's pension

MILLS, William   7 May 1716 G240r freed by patrimony

See also MILL

MILNER, Jeremiah   3 Dec 1705 G126r freed by Katherine Maddoc   4 Feb 1705/6 G127v Henry Cary is bound to him

MILNER, John   4 Nov 1706 G136r bound to William Stephens, 7 years   4 Feb 1711/12 G196v turned over from William Stephens to John Ellis

MILNER, Thomas   5 Sep 1698 G14v freed by patrimony

MILTON, John   10 Jan 1698/9 G18r complaint that Richard Simpson has put his name to his 'Life and Works'

MIND, Benjamin   3 May 1708 G152v bookbinder; Charles Whitecroft is bound to him

MINDS, Anne   29 Sep 1715 G233r deceased; Mary Redmaine is given her pension

MINE ADVENTURE   10 Jan 1698/9 G18r Court agrees that trustees of the Mine Adventure may use the Hall   3 Jul 1699 G27r Hall used for

MINELLIUS, John – see OVID, TERENCE, VIRGIL

MINNIKIN, George   5 Sep 1698 G14r his apprentice, Thomas Moore, is freed

MINORS, Robert   22 Jun 1698 G9v general release from S.C.

MINORS, Thomas   9 Sep 1700 G44v cloathed

MINSHALL/MINSHUL, [ ]   9 Feb 1701/2 G67r S.C.'s bill in Chancery against him   4 Oct 1703 G96r his son to be made a party to S.C.'s bill in Chancery against him   6 Dec 1703 G99r of Chester; Clerk to send him copy of exceptions taken to his last answer   15 Jun 1704 G107v of Chester; to send to S.C.'s warehouse all of S.C.'s books in his possession which are unsold

MINSHALL, Thomas   29 May 1689 F118v elected Assistant Renter Warden   7 Dec 1691 F163r summoned to next Court to explain why he and Thomas Snowden have not made up their Renter Wardens' accounts and paid Warden the balance   7 Apr 1701 G58r his apprentice Peter Wallis is freed

MINTON, Thomas   3 Feb 1695/6 F239r servant to Edward Poole; freed

MIST, Nathaniel   12 Nov 1705 G125r bound to Dryden Leach, 7 years

MITCHELL, John   1 Feb 1713/14 G216r bound to Robert White, 7 years

MOGGS, Daniel   1 Jul 1695 F228v John Baskervile jnr is bound to him

MOLAND, Richard(?)   3 Aug 1702 G79v bound to Samuel Heyrick, 7 years

MONCKTON, Philip   3 May 1714 G218v given 40s from the Poor Box to go to America

MONDAY, Anne   22 Jun 1704 G108r deceased; Hannah Smith is given her pension

MONEY/MONY, John   11 Nov 1700 G46v bound to John Darby, 7 years   1 Dec 1707 G147v freed by John Darby

MONEY, Joshua/Joseph   5 Mar 1704/5 G117r bound to Joseph Downing, 7 years   6 Oct 1712 G204v freed by Joseph Downing

MONEY, Joseph – see preceding entry

MONGAR, John   4 Sep 1704 G112r bound to Tace Sowle, 7 years

MONINS, William   2 Aug 1697 F265v bound to William Pierce

MONMOUTH ROUTED   3 Aug 1685 F42r Widow Mallett confesses to printing this ballad for James Deane

MONTGOMERY/MONNTGOMERY, Hugh   1 Jul 1695 F228v son of William Montgomery of Edinburgh, merchant; bound to Andrew Bell   4 Jul 1702 G77r freed by Andrew Bell

MONTGOMERY, William – see preceding entry

MONY – see MONEY

MOODY, Nathaniel   5 Aug 1706 G134r bound to Israel Harrison, 7 years   5 Oct 1713 G214r freed by Israel Harrison   1 Oct 1716 G244r John Ellis is bound to him

MOOR, John   5 Dec 1709 G172r bound to William Kitchener, 7 years

MOORE, Alice   12 Dec 1695 F238r deceased; Robert Cox elected to her pension

MOORE, Dr   7 May 1688 F101r preached William Lamb's anniversary sermon in St Austin's on 6 May and was paid 6s 8d

MOORE/MOOR, Edward   3 Feb 1700/1 G55v Thomas Lane is bound to him   13 Jun 1715 G229r to be summoned to next Court to take cloathing   4 Jul 1715 G231r stationer, of Snow Hill; excused from cloathing for one year   1 Oct 1716 G244r of Snow Hill; to be summoned next Court day to accept cloathing   4 Mar 1716/17 G247v to be summoned by the Beadle to next Court to accept cloathing

MOORE, John (I)   8 May 1704 G106v bound to William Downham, 7 years

MOORE, John (II)   1 Dec 1712 G205v freed by patrimony   6 Sep 1714 G221v John Jackson is turned over to him from James Ford

MOORE, John (III)   6 Dec 1714 G224r his son William is bound to Robert Knaplock, 7 years

MOORE, Robert   16 Jun 1684 F17r of Lincoln's Inn Fields; submits to a £15 fine and is freed

MOORE, Thomas (I)   4 Aug 1684 F21v to be granted £50 of Tyler Bequest if his sureties are approved   1 Sep 1684 F23r sureties approved   7 Apr 1690 F132v bond for £50 to be put in suit against him following information of his printing the stock book 'The Old Primer'   2 Apr 1694 F202r fined £5 for binding an apprentice by foreign indentures   7 May 1694 F203v his ex-apprentice Henry Pointing is refused freedom on the grounds that he was bound at a scrivener's   3 May 1697 F262r requests more time to pay back £50 loan from Tyler Bequest as one of his sureties is dead; to bring new one to next Court   7 Jun 1697 F262v bond and surety to be delivered to clerk who will call on Moore and ask for new sureties

MOORE, Thomas (II)   5 Sep 1698 G14r freed by George Minnikin. Cloathed

MOORE, William   6 Dec 1714 G224r son of John; bound to Robert Knaplock, 7 years

MOREA, Edward   5 Dec 1698 G16v to be prosecuted for non-payment of Livery fine   3 Jul 1699 G27r struck out of Livery because unable to pay his fine

MORETON, Elias   3 Mar 1711 G197r son of Randolph; bound to Samuel Keimer, 7 years

MORETON, Peter   7 Feb 1703/4 G101v freed by Widow Bowen

MORETON, Randolph   3 Mar 1711 G197r his son Elias is bound to Samuel Keimer, 7 years

MOREY, Edward   3 Jun 1695 F225r cloathed. John Chantry jnr is bound to him   6 Jul 1702 G78r his apprentice John Chantry is freed

MORGAN, John   8 Apr 1700 G39r bound to William Haddon, 7 years

MORGAN, Joseph   5 Jul 1708 G155r bound to John Foord, 7 years

MORLAND, Richard   3 Aug 1702 G79v bound to Samuel Heyrick, 7 years

MORLEY, Henry   5 Jul 1703 G92r bound to Thomas Milbourne, 7 years   9 Sep 1706 G134v turned over from Ann Milbourne to James Dover   5 Oct 1713 G214r freed by James Dover   6 May 1717 G250v Thomas Punchard is bound to him

MORLEY, John   7 Sep 1713 G213v son of William; bound to Arthur Bettesworth, 7 years

MORLEY, William – see preceding entry

MORPHEW, [   ]   2 May 1709 G164v desiring to renew his lease if S.C. will undertake repairs. Committee to view house   6 Jun 1709 G165r report from committee which has viewed his house. Further view to take place with workmen to assess repairs required   2 Jul 1709 G166v Master and Wardens to agree repairs required to his house with workmen   7 Nov 1709 G171v bills of workmen employed on his house left to Master and Wardens for adjustment and Joseph Collyer for payment   6 Mar 1709/ 10 G176r exemption to be included in his lease for Henry Million the Beadle to have rooms in his house   27 Mar 1710 G177v to be summoned to attend next Court to return the draft of the lease of his house   3 Apr 1710 G178r draft of lease returned. Lease to be engrossed   1 May 1710 G179r lease from S.C. to him sealed

MORPHEW, John   2 Dec 1695 F237r son of Stephen Morphew of Case Horton, Surrey, yeoman; bound to Edward Jones   4 Feb 1702/3 G85r freed by Edward Jones   2 Oct 1710 G184v cloathed   4 Jun 1711 G191r of Stationers' Court, bookseller; Richard Masey is bound to him

MORPHEW, Stephen – see preceding entry

MORRACE, Henry   8 Nov 1697 G1v freed

MORRIS, Anne   5 Feb 1704/5 G115r John Pratt turned over to her from Thomas Dalton

MORRIS, Henry   6 May 1700 G39v William Cooke is bound to him   3 Jul 1704 G110r his apprentice William Cooke turned over to John Roydon

MORRIS, Matthew   27 Mar 1682 E149r admitted to 10s pension in place of Mary Rothwell, deceased

MORS, John   3 Apr 1710 G178v bound to George Mortimer, 7 years

MORSE, Francis   2 Dec 1706 G136v bound to Israel Harrison, 7 years

MORTIMER/MORTIMORE, George   6 Oct 1690 F143v refuses cloathing pleading inability; given until next Court to consider and Under Warden ordered to make inquiries   6 Jul 1691 F157v excused cloathing for a year   5 Dec 1692 F183r cloathed   5 Aug 1700 G44r Thomas Burch is bound to him   26 Mar 1705 G117v elected First Renter Warden   2 Apr 1705 G118r receives charge as First Renter Warden from the Warden   16 Oct 1705 G124v Renter Warden. Unwilling to provide dinner for Lord Mayor's Day according to custom   3 Nov 1707 G146v grocer; Samuel Paul is bound to him   3 Apr 1710 G178v of Tuttle Street, grocer; John Mors is bound to him   6 Dec 1714 G224r William Vincent is bound to him   8 Aug 1715 G232r his apprentice Samuel Paul is freed

MORTLACK – see MORTLOCK

MORTLOCK/MORTLACK, Thomas   4 Nov 1689 F126v to be added to the Corporation Act committee

MORTLOCK, George   4 Mar 1705/6 G129r freed by patrimony. Cloathed   5 May 1707 G141v elected to Robert Knaplock's £40 share   1 May 1710 G179v elected to William Mount's £80 share. His share disposed of to John Lawrence   26 Mar 1711 G189r fined for First Renter Warden

MORTLOCK/MORTLACK, Henry   1 Oct 1683 F4r is assigned Dr Edward Boughon's [i.e. Boughen's] Latin/English catechism by Mary Garret   13 Oct 1687 F91v sworn in as Assistant   5 Dec 1687 F95r Court mitigates his £8 fine for trying to force his way on to the Court to £5 as he stands candidate for a £160 share. Submits to his £5 fine being retained out of his next dividend but asks that his precedence in Court will not be affected. Elected to Thomas Passenger's £80 share   9 Jan 1687/8 F96v elected to Edward Brewster's £160 share. To pay the £5 which was not in fact deducted from his last dividend   1 Mar 1687/8 F97v expelled from Livery by order of Lord Mayor. Displaced as Assistant by order of Crown   11 Oct 1688 F108v restored to Livery   4 Feb 1688/9 F112v re-elected Assistant   6 May 1689 F117r ranked second of Assistants never elected as Master or Warden   1 Jul 1689 F120v voted not to restore to him the £5 fine he had incurred through trying to force himself on to the Court   6 Jul 1689 F121v among those chosen to audit Warden's accounts; competes unsuccessfully for Under Warden   3 Feb 1689/90 F128v with Thomas Bassett, added to committee appointed to negotiate with Master re. Cambridge   1 Mar 1689/90 F129v elected Stock-keeper for Assistants with John Bellinger   5 Jun 1690 F135v re-appointed Assistant   5 Jul 1690 F138r elected Under Warden   7 Jul 1690 F138v Christopher Wilkinson elected as Stock-keeper in his place   1 Sep 1690 F142r sells three books to Court for the same price that he and Benjamin Tooke paid William Whitwood for them   4 Jul 1691 F156v elected Under Warden; William Miller also in competition   1 Feb 1691/2 F164v his part in Oxford agreement is detailed   7 Mar 1691/2 F166v indemnified by transfer of mortgage of Stock estate against engagement with Oxford   2 May 1692 F170r declaration of trust re. Oxford from him, Master and John Bellinger read and approved   4 Jul 1692 F174r to augment Oxford committee   1 Aug 1692 F177r tells Court that a friend of his will lend S.C. £250 at 5% p.a. for Oxford; offer accepted   3 Oct 1692 F180r competes unsuccessfully for the late Widow Tyton's £320 share   1 Mar 1692/3 F184r elected Stock-keeper for Assistants with Nathaniel Ranew   3 Jul 1693 F189v among those chosen to audit Warden's accounts   6 Oct 1693 F193r seals and executes deed for new Stock at Oxford and Cambridge with John Bellinger   26 Mar 1694 F201v elected Stock-keeper at special meeting   9 May 1694 F204v ties with Robert Clavell in vote for Upper Warden and beats him in second vote   30 Jun 1694 F209v re-elected Upper Warden   12 Nov 1694 F214v promises to discuss with Matthew Wootton and others their complaint that he and others have printed Horace   4 Mar 1694/5 F218v Edward Castle, his apprentice, freed   8 Apr 1695 F221r Henry Wright is bound to him   6 May 1695 F222r elected to Mrs Bellinger's £320 share on her remarriage; takes partner's oath   2 Mar 1695/6 F240r elected Stock-keeper for Assistants with Edward Brewster   4 Jul 1696 F245r elected

Master   3 Jul 1697 F263v re-elected Master   13 Apr 1698 G6v complaint that he is printing copy of Horace in contravention of the byelaws   2 May 1698 G7r as surviving person mentioned in leases belonging to S.C. held by John Garrett, consents to order that he should deliver them to present Clerk   6 Jun 1698 G8r informs Court that Christopher Grandorge wishes to present a sum of money to S.C.   7 Jun 1698 G9r party to Articles with University of Oxford   4 Jul 1698 G10v to be added to committee re. lights of houses belonging to Goldsmiths' Company. To request Oxford University for a release for himself and Roger Norton from a bond of £2000 for performance agreements between University and S.C. Informs Court that he has requested Mrs Isted to deliver writings belonging to S.C. Reports that committee to consider Thomas Fox's bill have decided £12 is the maximum that should be paid   7 Feb 1698/9 G20r appointed to committee re. Robert Stephens's account for warehouses   6 Mar 1698/9 G21v declaration against him in relation to affairs of S.C. from Thomas Guy and Peter Parker. To accompany Mrs Isted to her meeting with Counsel re. writings belonging to S.C.   20 Oct 1699 G32r party to Articles between Guy and Parker and S.C.   4 Dec 1699 G33v discharged from obligations to Guy and Parker   1 Mar 1700/1 G56r elected Stock-keeper for Assistants   3 Mar 1700/1 G56v reports from committee to meet those who had entered into Renter Wardens' agreement   7 Apr 1701 G58r reports from committee set up to meet representatives of Renter Wardens that they cannot come to agreement on the terms proposed. Auditor of Renter Wardens' accounts   6 Oct 1701 G64v appointed to go to Oxford about S.C.'s affairs   1 Dec 1701 G66r Francis Broughton is bound to him   2 Mar 1701/2 G67v elected Stock-keeper for Assistants   13 Apr 1702 G70r auditor of late Renter Wardens' accounts   6 Jul 1702 G78r auditor of late Renter Wardens' accounts. His apprentice Henry Wright is freed   25 Mar 1703 G86v to go to Oxford re. renewing Articles   5 Apr 1703 G87v report from visit to Oxford   3 May 1703 G89r letter to him from Hayes of Cambridge concerning repairs required to S.C.'s house there   5 Jul 1703 G92r auditor of Master and Wardens' accounts   21 Oct 1703 G96r to reply to letter to him from Hayes of Cambridge   7 Feb 1703/4 G101r added to committee considering Hayes' account re. Cambridge affairs   3 Apr 1704 G105v auditor of late Renter Wardens' accounts   5 Feb 1704/5 G114v Clerk's bill for proceedings in Chancery referred to him   1 Mar 1704/5 G116r elected Stock-keeper and takes oath   16 Oct 1705 G124v to attend Lord Mayor re. Renter Wardens' refusal to provide dinner   8 Dec 1705 G126v signatory to Articles with University of Cambridge   19 Feb 1705/6 G128r letter sent to him by William Willymott, editor of Terence   4 Mar 1705/6 G129r his son George Mortlock is freed by patrimony   3 Jun 1706 G132r £200 to be taken in from his friend to repay £300 to William Richardson   4 Nov 1706 G135v elected Stock-keeper in place of Thomas Bennett   1 Mar 1706/7 G138v elected Stock-keeper for Assistants   5 Jul 1707 G143r competes unsuccessfully for Master   7 Jul 1707 G143v auditor of late Master and Wardens' accounts   4 Aug 1707 G144r to meet Topham, Compton and other members of the House of Commons to get an Act of Parliament for securing of property of books and copies   3 Dec 1707 G148r signs agreement re. not taking Clarendon   1 Mar 1707/8 G149v elected Stock-keeper for Assistants   3 May 1708 G152v auditor of late Renter Wardens' accounts   5 Jul 1708 G154v auditor of late Renter Wardens' accounts   17 Jul 1708 G155v letter to him from Lewis Thomas of Oxford re. S.C.'s agreement with University. Articles of agreement read between University of Oxford and himself, Capt. William Phillipps and Robert Andrews, re. the privilege of printing at Oxford. Ordered to go to Oxford. Member of Oxford committee   2 Aug 1708 G156r reports from Oxford committee that an agreement has been reached with the University concerning printing at Oxford   7 Feb 1708/9 G160v Edward Stillingfleet is bound to him   4 Jul 1709 G167r auditor of late Master and Wardens' accounts   1 Aug 1709 G169v elected

Stock-keeper in place of Capt. William Phillipps   1 Mar 1709/10 G176r elected Stock-keeper for Assistants   6 Mar 1709/10 G176v to be responsible for providing books to Kempsey Manor, payment for which is in arrears   3 Jul 1710 G182r auditor of late Master and Wardens' accounts   1 Mar 1710/11 G187r elected Stock-keeper for Assistants   26 Mar 1711 G189r request that his son George might fine for First Renter Warden granted   10 Sep 1711 G194r to meet John Baskett and Williams re. granting of Oxford University privileges   2 Jun 1712 G200r auditor of late Renter Wardens' accounts   7 Jul 1712 G201v auditor of late Master and Wardens' accounts. Edward Sawtell is bound to him   21 Mar 1712/13 G207v acting Master in place of Capt. William Phillipps   24 Apr 1713 G209r signatory to S.C.'s notes   5 Apr 1714 G218r auditor of late Renter Wardens' accounts   3 Jul 1714 G220r competes unsuccessfully for Master

MOSSE, Priscilla   22 Jun 1702 G76r given Mary Godwin's pension   27 Sep 1710 G184r deceased; Elizabeth Steele is given her pension

MOSSE, Thomas   3 Oct 1709 G171r bound to John Clarke, 7 years

MOSSE, William   7 Apr 1701 G58v bound to John Franke, 7 years

MOSSON, Robert   8 Dec 1709 G172v to be party to S.C.'s Bill in Chancery against John Partridge and John Darby

MOTT – see MOTTE

MOTTE/MOTT, Anne   5 Mar 1710/11 G188r Aldersgate Street, printer; Edward Say is bound to her   6 Oct 1712 G204v her apprentice Robert Manney is freed. Thomas Hood is bound to her   6 Sep 1714 G221v William Reyner is bound to her   4 Oct 1714 G222v her apprentice Thomas Hood is turned over to William Wilkins   8 Aug 1715 G232r her apprentice Samuel Palmer is freed

MOTTE/MOTT, Benjamin, snr   1 Mar 1685/6 F51r cloathed   1 Mar 1687/8 F97v expelled from Livery by order of Lord Mayor   4 Sep 1688 F106r fined 1 guinea for printing Terence, a Stock book   11 Oct 1688 F108v restored to Livery   25 Sep 1690 F143r committee to treat with Thomas Parkhurst, Smith and him re. printing of Lucius [Annaeus] Florus, Justin and Barton's Psalms   6 Oct 1690 F143v committee required to reach agreement with him and report   12 Apr 1692 F169r fined for Assistant Renter Warden   3 Oct 1692 F180r ties with Isaac Cleeve in election to John Hancock's £40 share; Master gives casting vote to Cleeve. Elected to Israel Harrison's £40 share   12 Nov 1694 F214v Edmund Powell, turned over to Motte from Macock, is freed   8 Apr 1695 F220r competes unsuccessfully for John Penn's £80 share   6 May 1695 F222v competes unsuccessfully for Thomas Cockerell's £80 share   7 Oct 1695 F233v elected to the late Mrs Sawbridge's £80 share   2 Mar 1695/6 F240r elected Stock-keeper for Yeomanry with Timothy Goodwin   4 May 1696 F242v takes Stock-keeper's oath   6 Sep 1697 F267r Henry Buckeridge is freed by him. Edward Lewis is bound to him   1 Aug 1698 G13r assignment from Charles Broome to Motte, and from Motte to Capt. Samuel Roycroft, of a moiety of Dr Thomas Comber's 'Companion to the Temple', parts 1–2, read and ordered to be entered   3 Jul 1699 G27v James Slatter is bound to him   5 Aug 1700 G44r Richard Sendall is bound to him   2 Jun 1701 G60v S.C.'s Psalms printed by him without permission   7 Jul 1701 G62r attending Court concerning printing of S.C.'s Psalms. Committee to consider precedents for punishment   4 Aug 1701 G62v to forfeit interest in English Stock for printing S.C.'s Psalms   1 Sep 1701 G63v to be fined 50s for printing S.C.'s Psalms without leave   27 Mar 1704 G105r to be summoned concerning misprint in Church Catechism printed for S.C.   3 Apr 1704 G105v promises to rectify mistake in printing of 'Church Catechism with Scripture Proofs' but it is ordered that the printing of this be taken from him   2 Oct 1704 G112v Robert Nanney is bound to him   6 Nov 1704 G113r his apprentice Edward Lewis is freed   6 Aug 1705 G122v his apprentice George James is freed   3 Feb 1706/7 G138r his apprentice James Slatter is freed   9 Jun 1707 G142v printer; Benjamin Odell is bound to him   7 Jun 1708 G153v printer; Samuel Palmer is bound to him   3 Apr 1710 G178v Benjamin Odell turned over from him to Edward Midwinter   3 Jul 1710 G182r his apprentice Benjamin Benbow is freed   29 Sep 1710 G184r of Aldersgate Street, printer; Edward Say is bound to him   13 Jun 1715 G229v Jonathan Russell is bound to him

MOTTE, Benjamin, jnr   7 Feb 1714/15 G225r freed by patrimony

MOTTE/MOTT, Charles   7 Jul 1712 G201v son of Benjamin; bound to Maurice Atkins, 7 years   2 Aug 1714 G221r turned over to Ranew Robinson

MOULD, John, Capt   12 Apr 1692 F169r Clerk of Haberdashers' Co.; certifies that Richard Chiswell was freed by them on 3 Oct 1662 and cloathed in 1672

MOULD, Nathaniel   3 Jul 1682 E155r prisoner in the King's Bench; given charity payment of £5

MOUNT   8 May 1682 E152v committee to renew lease from City of a piece of ground called the Mount in S.C. garden, for as long as possible   1 Jun 1685 F38r officer of the Chamber of London demands 3½ years' rent for it   3 Aug 1685 (W) Clerk to give Warden Ambrose Isted an account of the loan of the Mount   3 May 1686 F55v lease of Mount in S.C.'s garden from City of London to be renewed   2 Aug 1686 F61r report made to committee for City Lands concerning   1 Aug 1687 F86v committee formed to negotiate with Committee for City Lands re. renewing lease from City to S.C. of the mount in the garden by London Wall

MOUNT, [ ]   5 May 1707 G141v elected to Marshall's £80 share

MOUNT, Fisher   1 Apr 1717 G249r freed by his father Warden Richard Mount, accepts cloathing and fined for First Renter Warden. To have the third £80 share that becomes available

MOUNT, Richard   21 Jun 1693 F188v bookseller of Tower Hill; cloathed   7 Nov 1698 G16r William Mount is bound to him   27 Mar 1703 G87r elected Assistant Renter Warden   5 Apr 1703 G88r Ralph Arnold is bound to him   27 Mar 1704 G104r requests S.C. to take in £100 on bond from poor of the Tower Liberty   5 Feb 1704/5 G115r to pay £10 more to S.C. on bond of poor of Little Tower Hill hamlet   1 Sep 1707 G145r competes unsuccessfully for William Shrewsbury's £160 share. Elected to Anne Williams's £160 share. His £80 share divided into two £40 shares, disposed of to Emmanuel Matthews and John Brookes   1 Mar 1707/8 G149v elected Stock-keeper for Yeomanry   25 Mar 1708 G150r elected Assistant. To be summoned to next Court   26 Mar 1708 G150v his son William Mount is freed   12 Apr 1708 G151v takes oath of Assistant   2 Aug 1708 G156r to provide a better paper for Apollonius   4 Oct 1708 G158r bond from S.C. to him, John Johnson and John Keeblebutter of £220 for payment of £5 yearly for the use of the poor of the liberty of Tower Hill sealed   8 Nov 1708 G158v declines his son William's pretences to Jacob Tonson snr's £80 share   6 Jun 1709 G165v of Tower Hill; John March bound to him   6 Feb 1709/10 G175v thanks of the Court to be given to him for the clock presented by him to the S.C. and set up in the Court room   1 May 1710 G179v assignment of Brabazon Aylmer's £160 share to him and release from Aylmer read. The stock to be disposed of to his son William Mount   12 Nov 1711 G195r his apprentice Ralph Arnold is freed   24 Apr 1713 G209r signatory to S.C.'s notes to Thomas Guy   1 Jun 1713 G210r reports from committee to meet Partridge and Darby   4 Jul 1713 G211r fined for first year as Under Warden. Competes unsuccessfully for second year as Under Warden   3 Aug

1713 G212v auditor of late Master and Wardens' accounts   7 Sep 1713 G213r left to him and Darby to settle times and manner of payment of £100 to Partridge   3 Jul 1714 G220r elected Under Warden   2 Jul 1715 G230v elected Upper Warden (only eligible candidate)   5 Sep 1715 G232v Abel Brooke is bound to him   5 Mar 1715/16 G237v his apprentice Thomas Page is freed. Simon Lloyd is bound to him   9 Apr 1716 G239r to write to Henry Brickwood re. cloathing   4 Jun 1716 G240v auditor of late Renter Wardens' accounts   30 Jun 1716 G241r elected Upper Warden (only eligible candidate)   2 Jul 1716 G242r his apprentice John Marsh is freed   4 Feb 1716/17 G246v to be new trustee of S.C.'s property   21 Feb 1716/17 G246v appointed new trustee   1 Mar 1716/17 G247r elected Stock-keeper for Assistants   1 Apr 1717 G249r his son, Fisher Mount, is freed

MOUNT, William   7 Nov 1698 G16r bound to Richard Mount, 9 years   26 Mar 1708 G150v freed by his father, Richard Mount. Cloathed. Fined for First Renter Warden   8 Nov 1708 G158v candidate for Jacob Tonson's £80 share but his father declines his pretences to this share   7 Nov 1709 G171v elected to Mrs Blagrave's £80 share   1 May 1710 G179v elected to Brabazon Aylmer's £160 share, which had been assigned to his father. His £80 share is disposed of to George Mortlock

MOUNTFORD, John   5 Dec 1681 E140r son of William Mountford of Kidderminster, Worcestershire; allowed to be bound to Samson Evans at Brewster's request

MOUNTFORD, William – see preceding entry

MOYCE, Thomas   7 Oct 1698 G15r bound to Samuel Darker, 7 years

MUDE, Strangways   10 Sep 1694 F212v John Bradshaw, his apprentice, is freed

MUGGLETON, Lodowick   5 Mar 1679/80 E97v Exton's bill of £3 6s 6d for 'Excommunications of Muggleton' [unidentified pamphlet relating to the Muggletonians] to be paid

MUGGS, Mary   20 Dec 1705 G126r deceased; Elizabeth Andrews is given her pension

MUMFORD, [ ]   2 Aug 1697 F265r committee to treat with Mumford re. his printing the psalm-book 'that was this day produced in Court by the Master'   6 Sep 1697 F265r given leave to print a version of the Psalms in name of S.C., paying a small acknowledgement

MURDOCK, John   3 Jul 1710 G182r bound to John Hardin, 7 years

MUSIC   20 Dec 1701 G66v Cavendish Weeden to use Hall twice a week for a year for performance of divine music   29 Jan 1702/3 G84v request for Hall to be used for an entertainment of music   1 Jul 1706 G133r for last Thanksgiving Day to be paid for as it was the year before   26 Mar 1707 G140r Dean to have use of Hall for musical entertainment   4 Oct 1708 G158r for Lord Mayor's Day to be provided by Master and Wardens   7 Nov 1709 G171v on Lord Mayor's Day was very bad

See also ST CECILIA'S DAY

MUSICIANS   6 Jul 1702 G77v to be provided for election dinner   6 Aug 1705 G122v to be provided for election dinner   16 Oct 1705 G124v to be provided by Geary   8 Nov 1708 G158v to be paid half of what they are usually paid by Under Warden and Renter Wardens (30s and 20s respectively)

MYND, Benjamin   8 Apr 1695 F221r servant to John Browne; freed

MYNDS, Anne   20 Dec 1710 G186v elected to Elizabeth Brooke's pension

MYNDS, Benjamin   4 May 1702 G71r John Radford is bound to him

N., D. (author of 'A letter') – see CARE, Henry; JANEWAY, Richard

NANNEY, Robert   2 Oct 1704 G112v bound to Benjamin Motte, 8 years

NAPPER, Ann   25 Jun 1690 F136v deceased; Alice Williams is elected to her 40s pension

NASH, [   ]   1 Mar 1709/10 G176v churchwarden of Kempsey Manor; desiring that two years' arrears of £6 p.a. due to the poor tenants of the manor for Bibles and school books be cleared

NASH, Samuel   4 Nov 1689 F126v cloathed   3 May 1697 F262r Robert Jones, his apprentice, is freed

NEAL, John   1 Dec 1707 G147v bound to Robert Steel, 7 years

NEALE/NEAL, Mary   20 Dec 1705 G126r elected to Richard Fairbank's pension   21 Jun 1707 G143r deceased; Jesse Bruce is given her pension

NEALE, Simon   3 Dec 1684 F27r assigns 'The Whole Duty of a Communicant', by John Gauden, late Bishop of Exeter, to Henry Rodes

NECK, William   3 Oct 1709 G171r bound to Richard Hyatt, 7 years

NEEDHAM, Benjamin   4 Jun 1694 F208v Edward Andrewes is bound to him

NEEDHAM, Gwin   4 Sep 1704 G112r bound to George Shell, 8 years   7 Jul 1707 G143v turned over from George Shell to Hannah Clarke

NEGUS, Samuel   4 May 1702 G71r bound to Susan Brudenell by order of Court, 7 years   1 Feb 1702/3 G85r turned over from Susan Brudenell to John Brudenell   6 Aug 1711 G193r freed by Edward Midwinter   5 Dec 1715 G235v William Clemson is bound to him

NEILD, Roger   16 Jun 1684 F17r of Westminster and ex-apprentice of Evans and Willis, members of S.C.; his freedom to be taken at next Court

NELME/NELMES, Anthony   2 Jul 1694 F210r S.C. tenant; Sedgwick appears on his behalf to ask for money for a drainpipe, as the Act of Parliament for rebuilding the City directs, and Nelme is granted £3 towards it   2 Aug 1697 F265r his house to be viewed with other houses 'which Mills holds of this company'   6 Sep 1697 F266v Mrs Mill's request to renew the lease of his house and her own is deferred. Nelme asks to be granted a lease of his house; Kettleby ordered to tell him that whatever happens, he will be given plenty of time   6 Jun 1698 G8r flue or funnel passing through Mrs Mill's house to be enjoyed by his house as before. Sedgwick refuses request to take down wainscotting in his house   1 Aug 1698 G11v committee to treat with him about affairs between S.C. and his deceased brother (Henry). To be delivered counterpart of his house's lease, made from S.C. to Adiel Mill   6 Mar 1698/9 G22r to take a lease of one of S.C.'s houses in possession of Jevon   8 May 1699 G24v draft of lease from S.C. of two houses in Ave Maria Lane agreed, at rent of £60 p.a. for 20 years   5 Jun 1699 G25r lease of two houses from S.C. sealed   2 Jun 1701 G60v granted request for common yard of one of his houses in Ave Maria Lane and house inhabited by Mrs Mill to be divided   5 Sep 1715 G232v desires to renew lease on two houses, alleging party wall defective. Master and Wardens to view houses and report to next Court

NELME, Henry   2 Apr 1694 F202v servant to Peter Parker; freed   22 Jun 1698 G9v matters in difference between S.C. and himself agreed. Bond sealed from him to Treasurer, penalty £60, to pay £30 within 7 months. Articles between him and S.C. sealed. General release between him and others and S.C. sealed. Cloathed   5 Sep 1698 G13v deceased; his administrator has agreed to pay the £30 agreed for printing the impression of the Latin Testament. Committee empowered to conclude agreement with administrator

NEVILL, John   6 Sep 1697 F267r freed by patrimony by his late father Joseph. To be given freedom gratis as his mother cannot otherwise afford it

NEVILL, Joseph – see preceding and following entries

NEVILL, Mrs   1 Feb 1696/7 F254v widow of Joseph Nevill, complains of poverty and asks S.C. to free her son free of charge; Court remits her quarterage

See also NEVILLE

NEVILLE, John – see following entry

NEVILLE, Samuel   1 Mar 1713/14 G216v son of John; bound to George James, 7 years

See also NEVILL

NEWALL, John   5 Aug 1689 F122r excused cloathing on plea of juniorship and inability

NEWBERRY – see NEWBOROUGH

NEWBOLD – see NEWBOLT

NEWBOLT/NEWBOULT, [ ]   5 May 1707 G141v summoned to Court of Conscience to pay arrears of quarterage   9 Jun 1707 G142r his summoning to Court of Conscience to be put off until next Court day

NEWBOLT, George, snr – see following entry

NEWBOLT/NEWBOLD/NEWBOULT, George, jnr   3 May 1714 G219r son of George; bound to James Rawlins, 7 years   6 Feb 1715/16 G236r turned over from James Rawlins to James Roberts

NEWBOLT, William   7 Feb 1686/7 F71v Nathaniel Thompson to be summoned re. refusing to free him; if he does not appear Newbolt is to be freed   7 Mar 1686/7 F78r freed upon Thompson's failure to appear   1 Dec 1712 G205v John Housetown is bound to him

NEWBOROUGH/NEWBERRY/NEWBURROUGH, Thomas   3 Jun 1689 F119v allowed until next Court to consider cloathing   3 Oct 1692 F180v to be summoned to cloathing   7 Nov 1692 F181v cloathed and promises payment of fine   8 Nov 1703 G97r his apprentice Maurice Atkins is freed

NEWBOULD, William   4 Feb 1705/6 G127v bound to John Barber, 7 years

NEWBOULT – see NEWBOLT

NEWBURROUGH – see NEWBOROUGH

NEWBY, Mrs   10 Sep 1705 G123r petition asking for relief as her grandfather Richard Ockouls made a bequest of £2000 to the company about 100 years ago

NEWCASTLE, MAYOR OF   6 May 1700 G39r Richard Randall required to make an affidavit before the Mayor of Newcastle that he is not worth £500, if he wishes to avoid being proceeded against for not taking cloathing

NEWCOMB, Mrs   8 May 1693 F187v Williams on her behalf complains that Eleanor Smith has not paid £40 debt; Court orders Mrs Smith's £40 share to be disposed of   2 Jul 1694 F210r remarries and her husband's £80 share falls vacant; Freeman Collins is elected to it

See also following entry

NEWCOMB, Thomas (I)   1 Mar 1679/80 E97r frees Edward Jones   7 Jun 1680 E100v assigned signatures A and B of stock primer and signatures E and F of stock psalter   3 Jul 1680 E101r fined for Assistant year of Under Warden   11 Oct 1680 E104v to be paid for the 'Management' of the Printing Act; promises to pay a proportionable part   2 Jul 1681 E115r elected Upper Warden   5 Sep 1681 E129r seals an indenture of demise of the Hall and tenements for Sir Joseph Seamour   7 Nov 1681 E138v to have custody of indentures and other writings relating to S.C.   5 Dec 1681 E140r requests to enter 88 books 'of little value' assigned to him by George Thomason; allowed low rate of 15s to S.C. and 15s to clerk   6 Feb 1681/2 E142r deceased; Francis Tyton is elected to replace him as Upper Warden. John Bellinger is elected to his £160 share   3 Apr 1682 E151r Henry Herringman, his executor, awards S.C. a silver bowl in discharge of Newcomb's legacy of £20   4 Sep 1682 E157r executors to pay John Towse £6 13s 4d for election dinner   30 Jun 1683 F1r Francis Tyton is allowed to count 1 year's normal service and six months' substitution for Newcomb (deceased) as Upper Warden as 2 years   2 Aug 1686 F61v deceased; John Mayo is shown clemency by Court partly because he is a relation of Newcomb's   1 Aug 1692 (W) his executrix frees John Jones   12 Sep 1692 F179r deceased; executrix is master of the newly made freeman John Jones of St Andrew by the Wardrobe, whose name the Chamberlain needs

NEWCOMB/NEWCOMBE, Thomas (II)   7 May 1685 (W) confirmed as member of new Livery   6 Jul 1685 F40v elected to Robert Clavell's £80 share   5 Jul 1686 F60v Stock-keepers to pay him £100   4 Oct 1686 F64v recommends John Boate as new waterman   7 Feb 1686/7 F70v competes unsuccessfully for the late John Playford's £160 share   16 Mar 1686/7 F79r to be summoned on 4 April for the election of Renter Wardens   22 Jun 1687 F85r allowed to fine for Assistant Renter Warden   11 Oct 1688 F108v restored to Livery   8 Apr 1695 F220v his apprentice Richard Newcomb is freed

NEWCOMB/NEWCOMBE, Richard   8 Apr 1695 F220v freed by Thomas Newcomb

NEWLAND, George   7 May 1705 G119v gentleman; bond from S.C., penalty £200, to pay £102 10s is sealed

NEWMAN, Dorman, snr   3 Nov 1679 E95r Jonathan Wilkins, his apprentice, is freed   3 Jan 1680/1 E106r to be questioned by a committee about his complaint against Warden Thomas Vere for seizing the [Westminster] Assembly's Catechism   2 May 1681 E111r elected Renter Warden   5 Dec 1681 E139r stock dividend suspended because of his failure to provide a dinner or explain why not   8 Nov 1686 F66v summoned for illegal printing of the calendar of S.C. almanack   6 Dec 1686 F68v refuses to give satisfaction re. calendar; Master informs him that he is to be summoned between now and next Court   13 Oct 1687 F91v sworn in as Assistant   5 Dec 1687 F96r competes unsuccessfully for the late George Wells's £80 share   9 Jan 1687/8 F97r elected to Henry Mortlock's £80 share   30 Jun 1688 F103r among those chosen to audit Renter Wardens' accounts   4 Mar 1688/9 F114r sworn in as new Assistant   6 May 1689 F116v ranked seventh of Assistants never elected as Master or Warden. He and Nathaniel Ranew ordered to pay the charge of £24 not paid when they were Renter Wardens   1 Jul 1689 F120v to pay Renter Warden's charges before next Court or be fined for disobedience   5 Aug 1689 F122r he and Nathaniel Ranew given until next Court to prepare an account of their charges as Renter Warden   7 Oct 1689 F124r submits with Ranew to Court's decision, 'their Renter Wardens' dinners being insufficient'   2 Dec 1689 F127v competes unsuccessfully for Robert Scott's £160 share and is elected to the late Mrs Paxton's £160 share   5 Jun 1690 F135v re-elected Assistant   4 May 1691 F153v to be summoned to next Court   8 Jun 1691 F154r accused of selling Dr Williams's Catechism but affirms that he sold them for Williams; ordered to pay statutory rate   7 Dec 1691 F163r not allowed abatement of the £9 he was fined on 8 June for selling Dr Williams's Catechism   4 Dec 1693 F195v Court refers to Newman's illegal printing of Scotch psalms with Thomas Parkhurst   1 Oct 1694 F213r Hooker's demand for the £160 share assigned to him by S.C. in a statute of bankruptcy against Newman is deferred   3 Dec 1694 F215v his £160 share is voted to Bennett Griffin

NEWMAN, Dorman, jnr   7 Feb 1708/9 G160v freed by patrimony   6 Nov 1710 G185r bookseller; George Carey is bound to him   7 Nov 1715 G234v George Carey is turned over from him to John Dutton

NEWMAN, Henry   1 Dec 1712 G205v freed by patrimony

NEWMAN, Hugh   1 Sep 1701 G64r Thomas Thorncomb is bound to him

NEWMAN, Thomas   3 Apr 1710 G178r elected to cloathing

NEWSPAPERS – see GAZETTE

NEWTON, Ambrose   7 Mar 1697/8 G5r bound to William Warter

NEWTON, John   4 Dec 1699 G34r cloathed   7 Apr 1701 G58v his apprentice John Ayres is freed   6 Dec 1703 G99v his apprentice William Norwood is freed   20 Dec 1711 G196r elected to Martha Widows's pension

NICHOLL/NICOLL, Randall   4 Aug 1701 G63v bound to Benjamin Browne, 7 years   9 Sep 1706 G134v turned over from Benjamin Browne to Samuel Hoole   6 Jun 1709 G165v freed by Benjamin Browne   2 Jun 1712 G200r cloathed

NICHOLLS, William   4 Oct 1708 G158r bound to William Yorke, 7 years

NICHOLSON, [ ]   3 Jul 1699 G27r and Timothy Child present a paper concerning the copyright of printing the Satires of Juvenal and Persius. Discussion with Benjamin Tooke, the Treasurer, to be expedited   7 Aug 1699 G28r assignment to Samuel Sprint and himself from James Crayle of several copies including 'Shower on Eternity' [i.e. Bartholomew Shower, *Serious Reflections on Time and Eternity*] read but decision on entry deferred until next Court day

NICHOLSON, J. [John?] – see preceding and following entries

NICHOLSON, John, snr   19 Nov 1695 F236r servant to Thomas Flesher; freed and cloathed   3 Mar 1700/1 G57r apprentice of himself and John Salisbury, Samuel Ballard, is freed   15 Nov 1703 G97v elected to Thomas Cockerell's £80 share   2 Mar 1703/4 G102v elected Stock-keeper for Yeomanry   1 Mar 1704/5 G116r elected Stock-keeper for Yeomanry   26 Mar 1706 G130r fined for First Renter Warden   3 Dec 1711 G195v his apprentice John Kindon is freed   6 Jul 1713 G212v Francis Jackson is bound to him   7 Feb 1714/15 G225r his son John is bound to John Ford, 8 years

NICHOLSON, John, jnr   7 Feb 1714/15 G225r son of John; bound to John Ford, 8 years

NICHOLSON, Uriah   7 Dec 1702 G83v bound to Thomas Cockerell, 8 years

NICKS, Jonathan   7 May 1711 G190v bound to Timothy Child, 7 years

NICOLL – see NICHOLL

NIGHTINGALL, Thomas   4 Oct 1708 G158r bound to Thomas Ilive, 7 years   3 Oct 1715 G233v freed by Thomas Ilive

NO JEST – see HIND, James

NOBLE, William   5 Feb 1708/9 G160v bound to Benjamin Walford, 7 years   3 Jul 1710 G180r turned over from Benjamin Walford to William Innys

NODES, John   30 Dec 1684 (W) witnesses John Marlow's bond

NOEL, NOELL – see NOWELL

NOONE, John   6 Oct 1712 G204v John Stephens turned over to him

NORBURY, Christopher   7 Feb 1698/9 G20v bound to Robert Roberts, 7 years   4 Mar 1705/6 G129r freed by Robert Roberts

NORCOCK, James – see following entry

NORCOCK, John   1 Sep 1712 G203r son of James; bound to Egbard Sangar, 7 years   13 Apr 1713 G208v turned over from Egbard Sangar to Daniel Browne

NORCOTT, John   7 Jul 1707 G143v bound to Christopher Coningsby, 7 years

NORFOLKE, Marmaduke   2 Oct 1699 G31v freed by William Everingham   9 Sep 1700 G45r William Littleboy is bound to him

NORMAN, Andrew   6 Jul 1700 G43r bound to Margaret Bennett, 7 years

NORMAN, John   6 May 1700 G39v bound to Richard Janeway, 7 years   6 Nov 1704 G113r turned over to Ichabod Dawkes

NORMAN, Thomas   7 Jul 1701 G62r an apprentice of Robert Whitledge and himself, Jasper Hazard, is freed   6 Mar 1709/10 G176v of Greenwich, brewer; to be summoned to take cloathing   26 Mar 1716 G238v elected Assistant Renter Warden   7 May 1716 G239v excused office of Assistant Renter Warden   1 Apr 1717 G249v elected Assistant Renter Warden   6 May 1717 G250r not permitted to fine for Renter Warden

NORRIS, [   ]   4 Aug 1690 F141v solicitor in Chancery; tells Court that Hutchins paid Henry Hills a fine for importing Stock books instead of being prosecuted

NORRIS, Christopher   1 Feb 1702/3 G85r freed by patrimony   4 Apr 1709 G164r of Old Change; his apprentice George Green is freed   6 Sep 1714 G221v Richard Wild is bound to him   3 Dec 1716 G245v Henry Revle is bound to him

NORRIS, Edward   3 Oct 1709 G171r bound to John Bradshaw, 7 years

NORRIS, Thomas   6 Feb 1692/3 F183v petitions for £50 of Norton bequest money; referred as Court disapproves of the names of one of his sureties   13 Mar 1692/3 F185r petition accepted   6 May 1695 F223v Moses Gregory is bound to him   24 Oct 1695 (W) William Downing to be a witness against him for printing Oxford primer illegally   6 Jul 1702 G78r his apprentice Moses Gregory is freed   2 May 1709 G165r elected to cloathing   4 Jul 1709 G167v cloathed. William Norris, his son, is bound to him   4 Dec 1710 G185v bookseller on London Bridge; to be served with a copy of the writ of execution against Benjamin Harris   13 Mar 1711/12 G198r to be proceeded against if he does not pay remaining £10 of Livery fine   7 Jun 1714 G219r Master, Wardens and Clerk to attend the Commissioners of the Stamp Office and request them to summon Norris before them concerning his printing and publishing of Dr John Partridge's Prophecy   2 Aug 1714 G221r Master and Wardens to resolve the differences between S.C. and him   7 Feb 1714/15 G224v elected to Martin Boddington's £80 share   7 May 1716 G239v elected First Renter Warden   21 Jun 1716 G240v receives his charge from Upper Warden   8 Jan 1716/17 G246r Francis Rhodes is turned over to him from Richard Ware

NORRIS, William   4 Jul 1709 G167v bound to Thomas his father, 7 years

NORTH, George   7 Apr 1701 G58v bound to Alexander Bosvile, 7 years

NORTH, John   5 Jul 1680 E101v debate re. £10 stopped from his dividend for not becoming Renter Warden to be deferred until next Court   2 Aug 1680 E102r dividend, which had been stopped for his failure to accept office of Renter Warden, paid; discharged from all other offices and charges in consideration of his presenting plate worth over £20 to S.C.   1 Mar 1687/8 F97v expelled from Livery by order of Lord Mayor   8 Nov 1697 G1r of Dublin, deceased; his £80 share disposed of to Awnsham Churchill

NORTH, Mrs   3 Feb 1700/1 G55v of Ireland; her £80 share disposed of to John Ray. A discharge to be obtained from herself and her present husband on payment of the money

NORTHCOTT/NORTHCOT, Richard   4 Oct 1686 F64v elected to Livery   8 Nov 1686 F67r cloathed

NORTHCOTT, Thomas   4 Oct 1686 (W) on original list of new Livery members, though not in the end chosen

NORTHEY, Sir Edward   4 May 1702 G70v Attorney General; to be attended by Master and Wardens and given 5 guineas as a retainer   9 Jun 1707 G142v opinion that Dr Harrison and his wife should be proceeded against at law   8 Dec 1709 G172v to give advice whether Parker's Ephemeris is a calendar or not   13 Jan 1709/10 G173v opinion concerning the Copyright Bill read

See also ATTORNEY GENERAL

NORTMAN, John, snr – see following entry

NORTMAN, John, jnr   13 Jun 1715 G229v son of John; bound to Bartholomew Baker, 7 years

NORTON'S BEQUEST   5 Feb 1682/3 E163v no part to be put out in future without three good securities. Edward Evett granted £100 loan on good surety   4 Aug 1684 F21v John Marlow's request to retain £50 loan for three more years is granted   26 Mar 1685/6 F54r Henry Faithorne to be granted £50 if his securities are approved   2 May 1687 F82v Edward Evett to repay £50 at Midsummer and £50 at Michaelmas   5 Dec 1692 F183r Daniel Gregory's petition for £100 loan referred to committee   6 Feb 1692/3 F183v Thomas Norris's petition for £50 referred as Court disapproves of one of his securities   13 Mar 1692/3 F185r Daniel Gregory's petition rejected and Thomas Norris's accepted   4 Dec 1693 F196v Philip Cholmley's request for £50 deferred as Court does not approve of surety   3 Jun 1695 F225r committee to inspect the records for this and the agreement with St Faith's about a bequest made to it

See also ST FAITH'S

NORTON, [   ]   29 Jul 1700 G43v advertisement in the Gazette that his patents are to be sold in view of his bankruptcy. Decided that it is in S.C.'s interests to purchase them. Committee to deal   4 Nov 1706 G136r Master, Wardens and Stock-keepers to settle affair of his printing the grammar   7 Jun 1708 G153r Master, Wardens and Stock-keepers to settle matter of his printing the grammar at Oxford and Cambridge

NORTON, Ann   4 Feb 1683/4 F8v lately a pensioner; 10s paid for her funeral   26 Mar 1684 F11r deceased; Dorothy Lambert is elected to her 10s pension

NORTON, Elizabeth   22 Mar 1715/16 G238r elected to Deborah Godman's pension

NORTON, John   4 Jul 1681 E116r committee to inspect the wills of William Norton and himself   1 Aug 1681 E117r Lilly to inform Court of the contents of the wills of William and John Norton which are not to be found in S.C. records

NORTON, Mrs   1 Sep 1712 G203r John Baskett, printer at Oxford, requesting the £30 paid to S.C. by her   6 Oct 1712 G204r her £30 p.a. paid to Baskett

NORTON, Roger, snr   18 Apr 1680 E99r to audit barge accounts with John Macock   28 Mar 1680 E99r to audit Renter Wardens' accounts   7 Jun 1680 E100r has audited barge accounts   2 Aug 1680 E102v authorised to audit Wardens' accounts   11 Oct 1680 E104v promises to pay a proportionable part of the expense for management of the Printing Act   1 Mar 1680/1 E107v elected Stock-keeper for Assistants with Edward Brewster   2 May 1681 E110v with John Towse, chosen to audit Renter Warden Godfrey Head's accounts. With John Towse, to ascertain the value of the S.C. ground cut off to widen Ave Maria Lane, for amelioration money   4 Jul 1681 E115v and Towse, desired to continue efforts to secure amelioration money. Assigned £80 share by Whitlock in trust for S.C. to secure payment of £50 loan within 1 year   21 Feb 1681/2 E144v competes unsuccessfully for Master in place of Thomas Vere who has died in office   1 Mar 1681/2 E145v elected Stock-keeper for Assistants with Henry Herringman   6 Mar 1681/2 E146v takes over chair while Samuel Mearne submits his disagreement with Robert Scott over a warehouse to the Court   27 Mar 1682 E149r chosen to audit Renter Wardens' accounts   3 Apr 1682 E151r committee to negotiate

with him and Henry Hills re. charge for Customs House seizure of books   1 Jul 1682
E154v competes unsuccessfully for Master   1 Mar 1682/3 E164v elected Stock-keeper
for Assistants with Robert Horne   26 Mar 1683 E166v appointed to audit Renter
Wardens' accounts with Edward Brewster   4 Jun 1683 E170r chosen Master for the
day in place of Samuel Mearne, deceased   25 Jun 1683 E171r 'in loco Magistri'   30
Jun 1683 F1r elected Master   2 Jul 1683 F2r John Macock is elected Stock-keeper in
his place, left vacant on becoming Master   5 Jul 1684 F19r re-elected as Master; Richard
Royston and John Macock also in competition   7 May 1685 (W) confirmed as
member of new Livery   3 May 1686 F55v he and John Macock to estimate a fair price
for the 2 presses of John Mayo, Simon Hinch, Baldwin and John Palmer, to be sold to
Henry Hills jnr   7 Jun 1686 F56r reports that the presses are worth £9   3 Jul 1686
F58v stands unsuccessfully for Master. Among those chosen to audit Renter Wardens'
accounts. With others, tells Court that Simon Miller wishes to be excused Under
Wardenship and dismissed from Assistants   4 Oct 1686 F64r registers dissent from
other auditors of Warden's accounts as he objects to cakes and ale being charged to S.C.
and not Wardens   2 Jul 1687 F85v elected Master   6 Aug 1688 F105r surviving
signatory of the original deed of conveyance of St Martin's Ludgate   11 Oct 1688
F108v restored to Assistants   27 Nov 1688 F110v restored as Assistant but competes
unsuccessfully for former office of Master   26 Mar 1689 F116r chosen to audit Renter
Wardens' accounts with William Rawlins   1 Jul 1689 F120v to re-execute conveyance
to present Court members   7 Oct 1689 F125r assigns [Sir Thomas Browne], 'Urn
Burial or [i.e. 'and'?] the Garden of Cyrus' and [Hamon L'Estrange], 'The Alliance of
Divine Offices' to Charles Broome   5 May 1690 F134v to represent Master at St
Austin's church on 6 May to hear Lamb's sermon and dine at the Hall   5 Jul 1690
F138r among those chosen to audit Warden's accounts. Competes unsuccessfully for
Master   6 Apr 1691 F152r gives his name to agreement compiled with Oxford. Among
those chosen to audit Renter Wardens' accounts   7 Sep 1691 F159v Cambridge com-
mittee asked to negotiate with him re. number of grammars printed at Cambridge   1
Feb 1691/2 F164v agrees to pay £30 p.a. to S.C. for not printing his grammar at
Oxford as he did to Peter Parker and Thomas Guy, and is indemnified re. Oxford. His
part in concluding Oxford agreement is detailed   7 Mar 1691/2 F166v Mrs Harris
promises to give him a full account of her printing his Accidence and Grammar. Indemnified by transfer of mortgage of Stock estate against engagement with Oxford   2 May
1692 F170v declaration of trust re. Oxford endorsed on counterpart of mortgage
indenture from S.C. to Norton and others   7 Nov 1692 F182r William Miller complains
of Norton suing him over printing a book he claims is his; both are told to take legal
advice   18 Sep 1693 F191v to be indemnified from any payment to Oxford as long as
he pays S.C. £30 p.a.   6 Jul 1695 F229v among those chosen to audit Warden's
accounts   4 May 1696 F242r chosen to audit Renter Wardens' accounts with Capt.
William Phillipps   6 Jul 1696 F246v added to comprinting committee. Among those
chosen to audit Warden's accounts   3 Aug 1696 F246v acquaints Court that George
Hopper is dead   3 May 1697 F261v chosen to audit Renter Wardens' accounts with
Edward Brewster   13 Apr 1698 G6r added to Oxford committee   2 May 1698 G7r
consents to order that John Garrett should deliver two leases to the Clerk   6 Jun 1698
G8r asked Court to consider rent of Mrs Mills' house   4 Jul 1698 G10v Henry Mortlock
attempting to gain release for them both from bond to Oxford University of £2000   7
Oct 1698 G15r appointed to Goldsmiths' lights committee   6 Mar 1698/9 G22r to
accompany Mrs Isted to consult Counsel re. writings belonging to the S.C.   5 Jun 1699
G25v his son William Norton is freed by patrimony   2 Oct 1699 G31v his apprentice
John Stubbs is freed

NORTON, Roger, jnr   4 Feb 1711/12 G196v freed by patrimony

NORTON, William (I) 4 Jul 1681 E116r committee to inspect the wills of John Norton and himself 1 Aug 1681 E117r Lilly to inform Court of the contents of William and John Norton's wills not to be found in S.C. records

NORTON, William (II) 5 Jun 1699 G25v freed by Roger Norton by patrimony 7 Aug 1699 G29r cloathed. Daniel Rogers is bound to him 8 Nov 1703 G97r Rex Kempton is bound to him

NORWOOD, Nathaniel 4 Feb 1705/6 G127v bound to William Norwood, 7 years

NORWOOD, William 6 Dec 1703 G99v freed by John Newton 4 Feb 1705/6 G127v Nathaniel Norwood is bound to him

NOST, William 2 Dec 1700 G54r freed by James Orme and William Redmaine

NOTT, James 3 Dec 1705 G126r freed by Francis Leach

NOTT, William 3 Mar 1689/90 F130v the bond in which he is involved for £50 due to S.C. is to be delivered into legal hands since Arthur Jones has failed to pay

NOTTAGE/NOTTIGE, Joshua 6 Dec 1703 G99v bound to John Darby, 7 years 6 Aug 1711 G193r freed by John Darby

NOWELL, Christopher 3 May 1708 G152v bound to Richard Sare, 7 years 3 Oct 1709 G171r turned over from Richard Sare to Maurice Atkins

NOWELL/NOEL/NOELL, Nathaniel, snr 3 Jun 1689 F119v excused cloathing 7 Nov 1692 F181v of Duck Lane; summoned to be cloathed 5 Dec 1692 F183r excused cloathing 12 Nov 1694 F215r his son Nathaniel is bound to him 3 Jun 1695 F225r excused cloathing 2 Aug 1697 F265r excused cloathing for some time 4 Jul 1698 G11r cloathed 4 Aug 1701 G63v John Wilcox is bound to him 6 Jul 1702 G78r his son and apprentice Nathaniel Nowell is freed 4 Feb 1705/6 G127r elected to Thomas Simpson's £40 share. Promises to pay his Renter Warden's fine 26 Mar 1706 G130r fined for First Renter Warden 1 Apr 1706 G130v request for S.C. to take £200 and pay an annuity for his wife's life refused 7 Oct 1706 G135r petition desiring S.C. to take £200 and allow himself and his wife an annuity refused 5 Mar 1710/11 G187v deceased; his £40 share disposed of to James Knapton

NOWELL, Nathaniel, jnr 12 Nov 1694 F215r son of Nathaniel Nowell; bound to his father 6 Jul 1702 G78r freed by his father 3 Nov 1707 G146v to be summoned to next Court to take cloathing 5 Jul 1708 G154r elected to cloathing 2 Aug 1708 G156v Clerk to acquaint him that he will be proceeded against if he refuses cloathing 6 Sep 1708 G157r Clerk to call on him to request payment of Livery fine 4 Oct 1708 G158r cloathed 8 Nov 1708 G158v Charles Davis is bound to him 7 Mar 1708/9 G162r his apprentice John Wilcox is freed 5 Apr 1714 G217v excused office of Renter Warden for one year 26 Mar 1716 G238v excused office of Renter Warden for one year 26 Mar 1717 G248v fined for First Renter Warden

NOY, Charles 6 Nov 1699 G33r bound to John Gerrard, 7 years

NUTHALL, Mary 21 Jun 1706 G132v elected to Thomas Spicer alias Helder's pension; to be paid 15s per quarter 24 Mar 1709/10 G176v deceased; Elizabeth Burrows is given her pension

NUTT, Edward 1 Aug 1709 G169v bound to William Freeman, 7 years

NUTT, Elizabeth 2 Jul 1716 G242r William White turned over to her from Peter Tanner 12 Nov 1716 G244v Timothy Hattersley is bound to her

NUTT, John 7 Oct 1698 G14v granted lease of S.C.'s house, formerly in the possession of Mrs Whitlock. To let Mrs Burrows have the same rooms that she occupied in Mrs Whitlock's lifetime 5 Dec 1698 G16v required to return draft of lease   7 Feb 1698/9 G2ov lease to him of S.C.'s house in Stationers' Court for 11 years at £16 p.a. sealed   7 Apr 1701 G58r cloathed   5 Apr 1703 G88r to take lease of Nicholas Hooper's house. Henry Million to have all rooms except ground floor   3 May 1703 G89r lease of house in Amen Corner lately in occupation of Charles Lewis sealed   7 Aug 1704 G111r Thomas Johnson is bound to him   5 Feb 1704/5 G114v petition of Henry Million concerning   2 Apr 1705 G118v petition of Million against John Nutt's attempt to turn Million out of a room in his house   26 Mar 1706 G130r fined for First Renter Warden   3 Mar 1706/7 G139r William Cole is bound to him   6 Oct 1707 G145v printer; William Hunter is bound to him   3 Oct 1709 G171r elected into Mrs Milbourne's £40 share   7 Nov 1709 G172r printer; John Bird is bound to him   1 Jun 1713 G210v Robert Ryley is bound to him   1 Feb 1713/14 G215v competes unsuccessfully for James Roberts' £80 share. Elected to Mrs Wray's £80 share. His £40 share disposed of to William Innys   6 Feb 1715/16 G236r his apprentices William Hunter and Richard Harbin are freed   2 Jul 1716 G242r Robert Ryley turned over from him to William Hunter

NUTT, Thomas, snr – see following entry

NUTT, Thomas, jnr   8 Aug 1715 G232r son of Thomas; bound to Owen Lloyd, 7 years

NUTTHEAD, Susanna   20 Dec 1693 F197r deceased; her pension voted to Thomas Westwey

NYE, Henry (I)   6 Sep 1697 F267r petitions asking for relief; ordered to come to next pension Court   28 Sep 1697 F267v liveryman in reduced circumstances; petitions for relief and is given 30s   20 Dec 1711 G196r to have 30s from Poor Box

NYE, Henry (II)   26 Mar 1706 G130r scrivener; question about who Thomas Rawson, his servant, is

OADES, James   3 Jul 1682 E155r cloathed   11 Apr 1690 F133v elected Assistant Renter Warden   5 May 1690 F135r sworn in as Renter Warden   25 Jun 1691 F155v to appear with John Harding at next Court to pay the balance of their Renter Wardens' accounts   6 Aug 1694 F211r petition for the £160 share assigned to him by bankruptcy commissioner in a commission of bankruptcy against Henry Clarke, deceased, is adjourned   10 Sep 1694 F212r exhibits a petition similar to that he put forward on 6 August; committee appointed   3 Apr 1699 G24r Robert Hodges is bound to him   8 Apr 1700 G39r Edward Dawgs is bound to him   4 Sep 1704 G112r William Oades is bound to him   4 Feb 1705/6 G127v Charles Cade is bound to him

OADES, William   4 Sep 1704 G112r bound to James Oades, 7 years

OAKE/OAKES, Joseph   1 Jul 1695 F228r servant to Isaac Frith; freed   6 Jun 1698 G8v Thomas Hudson is bound to him   1 Aug 1698 G13r cloathed   12 Nov 1711 G195r to be summoned to next Court day to explain non-payment of Livery fine   7 Dec 1713 G215r now in good circumstances. Warden and Clerk to take his bond for payment of his Livery fine   1 Mar 1713/14 G216v Master and Wardens to decide how to proceed over his non-payment of Livery fine

OAKES, David   3 Jul 1699 G27v freed by John Heptingstall

See also OAKE

OBSERVATIONS ON TIME SACRED AND PROFANE (by 'N.B., Philomath')   5 Feb 1704/5 G114v complaint against Daniel Browne, William Davis and Thomas Slater for printing this, which contains S.C.'s calendar   5 Mar 1704/5 G116v books and plates to be delivered to Warehousekeeper

OCKOULS, Richard   10 Sep 1705 G123r formerly a goldsmith in 'Lumbard [i.e. Lombard?] Street', bequest to S.C.

ODELL, Abraham   4 Feb 1694/5 F217r son of William Odell, Newport Pagnell, fell-monger; bound to Robert Limpany, from last Michaelmas

ODELL, Benjamin   9 Jun 1707 G142v bound to Benjamin Motte, 8 years   3 Apr 1710 G178v turned over from Benjamin Motte to Edward Midwinter   1 Dec 1712 G205v turned over to James Rawlins   8 Aug 1715 G232r freed by Elizabeth Rawlins

ODELL, William   4 Feb 1694/5 F217r fellmonger of Newport Pagnell; his son Abraham is bound to Robert Limpany, from last Michaelmas

OGDEN, John   7 Oct 1706 G135r bound to Benjamin Beardwell, 7 years

OGSTON, James   4 Jun 1705 G120v bound to John Humphreys

OLDNER, George   6 May 1717 G250v John Callowe is turned over to him from John Clarke

OLIVER, [   ]   6 Jul 1696 F245v to be negotiated with over lights in S.C. garden   7 Sep 1696 F248r Lord Mayor to resolve differences between him, S.C. and Mills, the surveyor on lights

OLIVER, Benjamin   4 Mar 1716/17 G248r son of Thomas; bound to James Brookes, 7 years

OLIVER, Francis   5 Dec 1692 F183r elected into the pension of Jane Evance, deceased   20 Dec 1693 F197r deceased; his pension voted to Benjamin Thrale

OLIVER, Thomas   4 Mar 1716/17 G248r his son Benjamin is bound to James Brookes, 7 years

ONLEY/ONLY, William   16 Oct 1697 F269r printer; to be prosecuted for printing counterfeit books and almanacks   22 Jun 1698 G9v general release from S.C.   5 Sep 1698 G14v his apprentice Follensby Thackery is freed   8 May 1699 G24v printer; Stock-keepers to deduct from monies due to him from S.C. a sum due from him on bond to S.C.   5 Jun 1699 G25r order of last Court day concerning monies due from him to be suspended, as Samuel Briscoe is requesting remittance of the £10 Livery fine for which Onley acted as surety   3 Jun 1700 G40v has behaved 'very contumaciously to the Court'. To be employed by the Stock-keepers no more, nor to have any English Stock work   7 Aug 1704 G111r Greene Hudson is bound to him   1 Oct 1711 G195r deceased; his apprentice Greene Hudson is given freedom by his administratrix

ORD, William   3 Apr 1682 E150v cloathed   6 Aug 1683 F3r widow allowed to have bond for Livery fine cancelled 'in regard he was but lately called on the Livery'

ORIALL, [   ]   22 Jun 1698 G9v general release from S.C.

ORIGINES ANGLICANIS [i.e. John Inett, *Origines Anglicanae*]   4 Sep 1710 G183v negotiations between S.C. and Oxford re. this

ORME, James   2 Dec 1700 G54r and William Redmaine. Their apprentice William Nost is freed   5 May 1702 G88r his apprentice Robert Knell is freed   3 May 1703 G89v William Antrobus is bound to him   4 Mar 1705/6 G129r William Antrobus is turned over from him to John Matthews

ORME, Mary   22 Jun 1699 G25v deceased; John Dooley is given her pension

ORNATUS AND ARTECIA   5 Sep 1681 E129v (by Emmanuel Ford); assigned by Thomas Vere to John Clarke snr

OSBORNE/OSBOURNE, Charles   5 Feb 1693/4 F198v servant to William Parsons; freed   4 Feb 1694/5 F217r Roger Millert is bound to him   7 Feb 1697/8 G3v Samuel Butler is bound to him   2 Jul 1705 G121v his apprentice Samuel Butler is freed

OSBORNE/OSBORN/OSBURN, John (I)   6 Sep 1703 G94v bound to Thomas Guy, 7 years   1 Sep 1712 G203r freed by Thomas Guy   5 Oct 1713 G214r excused cloathing for one year 14 Mar 1714/15 G226r elected to cloathing 19 Jun 1716 G240v Thomas Longman is bound to him

OSBORNE, John (II) 7 Sep 1713 G213v son of John; bound to William Osborne, 7 years

OSBORNE, Samuel 5 May 1701 G59v bound to Nathaniel Hiller, 7 years 7 Jun 1708 G153v freed by Nathaniel Hiller 5 Sep 1715 G232v Robert Eggellton is bound to him

OSBORNE, Thomas 5 Jul 1703 G92r freed by William Powell. John Curson is bound to him 3 Jul 1710 G182r Gray's Inn, stationer; Joseph Dryer is bound to him 2 Oct 1710 G184v his apprentice John Curson is freed 7 Sep 1713 G213v Leake Jackman is bound to him

OSBORNE, William 5 Feb 1704/5 G115r freed by Samuel Bridge 7 Sep 1713 G213v John Osborne is bound to him

OTWAY/OTTWAY, Arthur 13 Mar 1692/3 F185r elected to Livery; summons to be sent to his home at Cheshunt, Hertfordshire 7 Jun 1694 F208v has long record of disobedience re. Livery; elected and summoned when he fails to turn up to special Court 10 Sep 1694 F212r summoned re. cloathing 12 Nov 1694 F214v Clerk to take legal action against him for failing to be cloathed

OVERTON, John 26 Mar 1685 F32r elected First Renter Warden 1 Jun 1685 F38v asks Court to choose another Renter Warden since he is not on the Livery; Under Warden to sue him for £40 penalty of refusal 3 Aug 1685 F42r Lord Mayor upholds his decision not to serve as Renter Warden, since he was left off the Livery for opposing the government 13 Oct 1687 F91v sworn in as Assistant, fined for Renter Warden 9 Jan 1687/8 F97r elected to Dorman Newman's £40 share 7 Oct 1689 F125r elected to Thomas Dring's £80 share 3 Jul 1693 F189v competes unsuccessfully for the late Henry Twyford's £160 share 8 Apr 1695 F220r competes unsuccessfully for the late John Clarke's £160 share 6 May 1695 F222v competes unsuccessfully for Henry Mortlock's £160 share 2 Dec 1695 F237r name in margin 2 Mar 1701/2 G67v Benjamin Browne is bound to him 7 Dec 1702 G83v his apprentice Philip Overton is freed. John Marlow is bound to him 13 Apr 1713 G208v deceased; his £80 share is disposed of to Christopher Bateman 5 Dec 1715 G235v his apprentice John Marlow is freed by his executor

OVERTON, Nathaniel – see following entry

OVERTON, Philip 2 Dec 1695 F237r son of Nathaniel Overton; bound to his father 7 Dec 1702 G83v freed by John Overton 5 May 1712 G199v cloathed 7 Dec 1713 G215r owing £10 of Livery fine 5 Jul 1714 G220v to be sued for non-payment of £10 of his Livery fine

OVID 8 Nov 1686 F66v 'Notes on Ovid' by 'Menelius' [i.e. John Minellius]; this with all other foreign and domestic notes on S.C. books to be entered to Master in trust for S.C. 18 Mar 1687/8 F79v Gregor Bersmann's edition of Ovid among books in catalogue annexed to the Oxford agreement 4 Sep 1688 F106v Freeman Collins owns to printing the 'Metamorphoses with Menelius' notes' (see above), a Stock book, for Thomas Dring and Abel Swale 1 Sep 1690 F142r Court agrees to buy the Epistles 'Englished by Mr. S. [i.e. Wye Saltonstall] with cuts' from Henry Mortlock and Benjamin Tooke 6 Oct 1690 F143r Epistles to be entered in trust for S.C. 2 Mar 1690/1 F150v Richard Wild accused of importing 'Farnaby upon Ovid' [i.e. Thomas Farnaby's edition of the *Metamorphoses*?], a Stock book 2 Mar 1695/6 F239v Abel Swale is discovered to be printing Ovid's 'Metamorphoses in Usum Delphini' for his own use, but submits to fine 1 Apr 1706 G130v committee to consider matter of books of Ovid and Terence printed for Willymott; printers to be summoned to attend next meeting of Stock-keepers

OWEN, [ ] 20 Dec 1693 F197r lawyer for St Martin's Ludgate over drainage dispute

OWEN, John, snr – see following entry

OWEN, John, jnr 12 Nov 1716 G244v son of John; bound to Elizabeth Grover, 7 years

OXFORD, Bishop of (Anthony Sparrow, d. 18 May 1685; William Lloyd, confirmed 4 Jul 1685) 5 Oct 1685 F45r his letters to be written in a register (Liber A, 160–165) See also OXFORD UNIVERSITY

OXFORD UNIVERSITY 28 Mar 1680 E98r contract of Oxford farmers for 8000 psalters in large and 7000 in small 12mo on payment of £360 overruled; S.C. resolves to print them 5 Jul 1681 E116v committee set up to negotiate with Oxford men 21 Feb 1681/2 E145r committee set up to deal with Oxford printers 'for this present quarter only' 16 Jan 1684/5 F28v bill in Chancery to be drawn up against University 29 Apr 1685 F33r Peter Parker and Thomas Guy, 'farmers of the University of Oxford's privileges for printing', to be prosecuted by S.C. John Lilly requests that some members of the Parker and Guy committee treat with the Bishop of Oxford 21 Jul 1685 F41r committee to negotiate with Bishop of Oxford re. agreement between S.C. and University 3 Aug 1685 F41v draft agreement with Bishop of Oxford, on behalf of University, and letter explaining that the agreement excludes books bought from Seamour, approved by Court 18 Aug 1685 F42v Under Warden and Lilly to answer Bishop of Oxford's letter, altering the expressions in agreement between S.C. and Oxford University as he suggests. Oxford committee augmented 22 Aug 1685 F43r Bishop of Oxford sent revised draft agreement, made by a 3-year covenant rather than a grant at Henry Pollexfen's suggestion, with list of books covered 12 Sep 1685 F44v Bishop of Oxford desires alteration in draft of agreement; proviso added and approved 5 Oct 1685 F45r agreement between S.C. and Oxford University sealed 7 Dec 1685 F47v workmen printers complain of the irregularities used by farmers of Oxford privileges 18 Mar 1686/7 F79v consideration to be given to whether list of books annexed to Oxford agreement should be reprinted 4 Sep 1688 F106v although Oxford has comprinted on S.C. because of their non-payment of 1½ yrs' rent, Treasurer will not pay it in full because of clause in articles 1 Oct 1688 F107r Vice-Chancellor, Gilbert Ironside, petitions Crown re. S.C.'s and King's Printers' alleged encroachment on University privileges. (W) petition and *quo warranto* order 3 Nov 1688 F109r Counsel at Law advises, re. comprinting and rent, that new articles should be drawn up to be sent to Oxford with the money; agreed 20 Dec 1688 F112r letter to Vice-Chancellor re. differences between S.C. and Oxford over almanacks is read and approved 4 Feb 1688/9 F112v Vice-Chancellor refers the difference with S.C. wholly to Parker and Guy; committee to consult with them, lawyers, Archbishop of Canterbury and Bishop of London 6 Mar 1688/9 F115r agreement reached with Parker and Guy and new articles drawn up between S.C. and University 5 Jun 1690 F136r Benjamin Tooke given £10 compensation for breaking his arm three years ago while travelling to Oxford on S.C. business 6 Apr 1691 F152r Master and Wardens report that, in their own names and those of Roger Norton and John Bellinger, they have compiled an agreement with Oxford University 22 Dec 1691 F164r Master, Wardens, Henry Mortlock, Bellinger and Norton to be indemnified by S.C. re. the agreement with Oxford now concluding 1 Feb 1691/2 F164v Master describes the agreement made between S.C. and Oxford on printing privileges in detail. (W) two earlier versions of agreement. Roger Norton pays £30 p.a. for not printing his grammar at Oxford to S.C. instead of Oxford 1 Mar 1691/2 F166r committee appointed to manage business relating to

Oxford privileges 7 Mar 1691/2 F166v transfer of mortgage of Stock estate completed to indemnify S.C. members against engagement with Oxford and Sir Henry Seamour 2 May 1692 F170r declaration of trust from Master, Henry Mortlock and John Bellinger approved; endorsed on mortgage indenture counterpart. Court agrees to borrow £1000 @ 5% p.a. from the executors of George Pawlett or others for administering Oxford business. Master and Wardens to take advice from Assistants concerning printing materials and proposed treaty with King's Printers 27 May 1692 F171r Court called specially to approve bond of £1200 penalty to Margaret Royston for money for 'Oxford affair' 4 Jul 1692 F174r committee to be revived and augmented by Thomas Bassett, Robert Clavell and Henry Mortlock. Workmen printers' petition against Robert Elliott being employed at Oxford referred to Oxford committee 6 Jul 1692 F174r Oxford committee orders Clerk to make a copy of free workmen printers' petition for Treasurer. Committee orders Treasurer to provide paper for Book of Common Prayer in folio 1 Aug 1692 F176v a friend of Henry Mortlock's lends S.C. £250 @ 5% p.a. for use of Oxford privileges 21 Nov 1692 F182r committee appointed to go to Oxford 25 Nov 1692 F182v charges of printing at Oxford estimated at ca. £3059 14s 4½d; Christmas dividends deferred until first Monday in February to assist with payment 6 Feb 1692/3 F183v legal advice to be taken over possibility of increasing number of English Stock shares for down payment to meet costs of printing at Oxford. Committee report that they are not empowered to buy 1500 folio Common Prayer books from King's Printers; power granted 13 Mar 1692/3 F184v Oxford committee augmented; to consider ways to raise money for dividends and carry on Oxford printing 3 Apr 1693 F186r a copy of proposals for raising money to pay dividends and carry on printing at Oxford ordered for every S.C. member 12 Jun 1693 F188v committee to have power to negotiate with King's Printers re. printing at Oxford 18 Sep 1693 F191v Roger Norton to be saved harmless from any payment to Oxford so long as he pays S.C. £30 p.a. List of books that S.C. and agents must not comprint on at Oxford 13 Apr 1694 F202v committee chosen at special Court to go to Oxford 7 May 1694 F203r Master tells Court of committee's satisfactory negotiations with Vice-Chancellor 17 May 1695 F224r 450 of 'Gibson's Portus Julus' [i.e. William Somner, *Julii Caesaris Portus Iccius*, ed. & intro. by Edmund Gibson] at 10d per book sent from Oxford; committee to take advice about selling them 7 Oct 1695 F233v committee to wait upon the Vice-Chancellor and delegates (W) and endeavour to get off what is rated above 4s per pound on the last cargo of books that came from Ireland, i.e. Dr Wallis's, Dr Hyde's and Mr Gibson's 24 Oct 1695 F234r printers to return 30 of the 'Oxford Antiquities' [i.e. White Kennett, *Parochial Antiquities ... in ... Oxford*] to Oxford, begin a quarto Bible by 1 Jan 1696 and settle debts, except for a disputed £150 8 Jun 1696 F243r committee appointed to travel there 6 Jul 1696 F246v committee to go to Oxford as soon as possible 1 Mar 1696/7 F255r committee to go to Oxford on S.C.'s account 7 Aug 1697 F266r letters from Thomas about the treaty are read, with the Master's answer; committee appointed to travel to Oxford 6 Sep 1697 F266v committee present proposals to Court as advised by Vice-Chancellor; deferred until University's answer is received 8 Nov 1697 G1r committee to meet to discuss treaty between University and S.C. 26 Mar 1698 G5v letters concerning treaty between University and S.C. read. Committee to go to Oxford and agree the treaty 13 Apr 1698 G6r University has refused to abate part of the payment of £200 formerly made by S.C. to the University. Committee to draw up new version of Articles between S.C. and the University concerning comprinting at 18 Apr 1698 G7r report from Oxford committee that amendments have been made to the Articles. Master and Wardens to go to Counsel with the revised Articles and then to Oxford 7 Jun 1698 G9r report that one part of the Articles has been sealed by Convocation and other part is being sent to be sealed by members of S.C. Members of S.C. to have the same security as was given to parties to former Articles   4 Jul 1698 G1ov Mortlock requests release from bond from Norton and himself to Oxford University of £2000 penalty. Mrs Isted also requests release from bond entered into by her husband which has expired. Counter-security of John Bellinger concerning comprinting superseded by new Articles   4 Sep 1699 G30r copy of Oxford Articles to be entered in a book in the warehouse for the use of the Stock-keepers   6 Jul 1700 G43r committee to go to Oxford concerning affairs between S.C. and the University   6 Oct 1701 G64v letters from Vice-Chancellor to Treasurer   23 Jul 1702 G79r half a year's rent to Oxford not paid by Benjamin Tooke   3 Aug 1702 G79v bond from Capt. William Phillipps to pay £100 rent due to   25 Mar 1703 G86v Articles between S.C. and University concerning printing there expired. Members of Table to go to Oxford to renew contract   5 Apr 1703 G87v report of proceedings at   22 Apr 1703 G88v letter from Vice-Chancellor re. agreement concerning S.C.'s printing there. S.C. answer that they cannot agree with Vice-Chancellor's proposal, but tenants are willing to give £50 to be excused from taking the books suggested   9 Sep 1706 G134v agreement with John Baskett over printing Clarendon   17 Jul 1708 G155v committee to go to Oxford to renew privilege of printing at   2 Aug 1708 G156r agreement reached between University and Oxford committee concerning printing at Oxford   4 Sep 1710 G183v tenants of Oxford to try to prevail with the delegates for S.C. to take only 100 of Dr Inett's 'Origines Anglicanis' [i.e. *Origines Anglicanae*] at the price set   10 Sep 1711 G193v grant privilege given to them by the S.C., due to expire Lady Day twelvemonth, to some other person from the Company. Committee to deal with granting of these privileges to protect English Stock   4 Aug 1712 G202v committee appointed to settle matter in difference between John Baskett and Williams re. printing there. Committee to consider rent to be paid by S.C. to the University of Oxford or their grantees after the expiry of the lease   1 Sep 1712 G203r report of committee who have met Baskett and Williams concerning printing at Oxford University. Ordered that when agreement is made, S.C. will be obliged not to let or make use of Cambridge privilege for 7 years and the Psalms will be kept at the usual price   6 Oct 1712 G204r agreement with Baskett concerning printing at

— OXFORD STOCK   10 Apr 1693 F186r Court subscribes to proposals but various amendments proposed; to be engrossed again before Stock partners subscribe to it   8 May 1693 F188r all those expecting benefit from proposals to subscribe to them before 27 May. Order to be printed for partners so far not subscribing   26 Jun 1693 F189r committee set up to draw up articles for management of Oxford affair, for the English Stock printers to sign   7 Aug 1693 F190r new stock to pay University rent of £200 p.a. and perform other matters comprised in Oxford articles. No English Stock books to be printed by new Stock partners at Oxford   6 May 1695 F222r dispute about accounts between English Stock and Oxford Stock to be settled by committee   17 May 1695 F224r committee appointed to advise about selling the impressions which Oxford articles oblige S.C. to take from Oxford   5 Sep 1698 G14r account of Oxford Stock to be made up for next Court day   4 Dec 1699 G33v £50 paid by S.C. to Thomas Guy and Peter Parker to be placed in account of   3 Jun 1700 G40r committee to dispose of Oxford books in the warehouse   1 Jul 1700 G41r committee to meet again about Oxford books   17 Apr 1701 G59r committee unable to dispose of Oxford books to any advantage so Samuel Buckley to dispose of them overseas   5 May 1701 G59v Articles between Buckley and S.C. concerning Oxford books   7 Sep 1702 G8or English Stock indebted to it   3 May 1703 G89r Master reports that he has written to Vice-Chancellor. Accountant to be employed to assist Stock-keepers   7 Mar 1708/9 G161v accounts with English Stock to be settled   4 Apr 1709 G163v state of account with English Stock discussed and adjusted by Court. Oxford Stock to pay capitation tax but not land tax

OXFORD AND CAMBRIDGE UNIVERSITIES 7 Nov 1687 F94v books to be brought in to S.C. for Vice-Chancellors of both universities under revived Printing Act 1 Feb 1691/2 F165r £300 to be borrowed from a friend of Samuel Lowndes towards paying Universities for stock. Order to send copies of all books published to their libraries revived 7 Aug 1693 F190r Master and Wardens to take legal advice re. transferring interest in printing materials to new Stock partners 28 Sep 1693 F192r total charges, amounting to £2097 3s 5d, to be engrossed and annexed as a schedule to the indenture approved at last Court 6 Oct 1693 F193r deed sealed and executed by John Bellinger and Henry Mortlock as trustees for S.C.; deposited with Treasurer until counterpart sealed 24 Oct 1693 F193v subscribers sign co-partnership articles; deed to remain with Clerk until they have all signed 5 Oct 1696 F250v committee to consult with Vice-Chancellors re. Printing Act 7 Jun 1708 G153r Master, Wardens and Stock-keepers to settle matter concerning printing of grammar there by Norton

See also ENGLISH STOCK: relations with Oxford Stock; GUY, Thomas; HOMER; KING'S PRINTERS; PARKER, Peter; PRINTING ACT; WARDENS

OXFORD ANTIQUITIES – see PAROCHIAL ANTIQUITIES

OXFORDSHIRE FEAST 3 Oct 1715 G233v Hall not to be let for this event under 5 guineas

PACKMAN, Joseph 1 Sep 1701 G64r bound to Ralph Snow, 7 years

PACQUET OF ADVICE – see CURTIS, Langley; PLAYFORD, John

PADBURY, Anne 26 Sep 1712 G203v daughter of John; bound to Christopher Browne, 7 years

PADBURY, John – see preceding entry

PAGE, Thomas 5 Mar 1715/16 G237r for some years out of his apprenticeship and living outside the freedoms of the City, made free by Warden Richard Mount. Cloathed. Promises to pay his Renter Warden's fine when required. To be admitted to next £80 share that shall fall vacant and the next £160 share after all members of the Table shall have £160 shares, in consideration of his coming into the freedom so voluntarily 26 Mar 1716 G238v fined for First Renter Warden 2 Jul 1716 G241v elected to John Taylor's £80 share in accordance with order of 5 Mar 1715

PAGET, George 6 Sep 1703 G95r signature as witness to the signature of Thomas Feilder

PAGITT, [Eusebius] 3 Jul 1682 E155v half of his 'History of the Bible' assigned by Simon Miller to Edward Brewster

PAINE, [ ] 6 Aug 1694 F211r late member of S.C. Churchwarden of St Faith's complains that charity money given by him and Lamb was not distributed 10 Sep 1694 F212r it appears that Paine never did give any money to St Faith's

PAINE, Charles, snr – see following entry

PAINE, Charles, jnr 2 Dec 1695 F237v son of Charles Paine of Woollavington, Somerset, clerk; bound to John James from 2 April 1692

PAINTER 20 Dec 1704 G115v bill to be paid by Joseph Collyer 3 Dec 1705 G125v bill for painting palisado pales to be paid 6 Oct 1712 G204r bill to be paid by Under Warden 7 Feb 1714/15 G225r bill to be paid

PAKEMAN, Mrs (I) 2 Jun 1684 F16r deceased; her £320 share voted to James Cotterell

PAKEMAN, Mrs (II) 25 Jun 1684 F18v of Moorfields; affirms her son was bound to the trade and her husband was freed of the Clothworkers, and she is a pensioner. Submitted herself to S.C. pleading great poverty; referred

PALFREY, George   1 Mar 1682/3 E164v one of the sureties for James Vade's £50 loan; granted a month's grace after Midsummer day next

PALMER, Herbert – see MEMORIALS OF GODLINESS

PALMER, John   22 Dec 1685 F48v petition of John Mayo, Baldwin, Simon Hinch and John Palmer   1 Feb 1685/6 F50v his petition with Mayo and Hinch rejected as being 'the direct contrary to their former confession'

PALMER, Richard   2 Aug 1708 G156v bound to William Mears, 7 years

PALMER, Samuel   7 Jun 1708 G153v bound to Benjamin Motte, 7 years   8 Aug 1715 G232r freed by Anne Motte   1 Apr 1717 G249v John Grimston is bound to him

PALMER, William   4 Mar 1705/6 G128v of Crooked Lane; evidence of Gilbert Beauchamp that he sold counterfeit copies of psalters at Bristol fair   1 Apr 1706 G130v committee to consider matter of counterfeit psalms sold by him

PAMPHLETS   6 Nov 1682 E159v committee appointed to enquire into all scandalous pamphlets printed against Government   9 Feb 1691 F149r Robert Stephens gives Court a list of those who have failed to enter pamphlets in Entry Book of Copies

See also ILLEGAL PRINTING

PAPE, Nicholas   22 Jun 1705 G120v elected to John Lowndes' pension

See also following entry

PAPE, Thomas   3 Jun 1695 F225v son of Nicholas Pape; freed by patrimony

PAPER   1 Nov 1689 F125v paper patentees offer to sell S.C. 28/400 shares of their patent right stock and estate; deferred for consideration by all   4 Nov 1689 F126r S.C. not to purchase any shares in the patent right of the papermaking patentees   5 Jul 1690 F138r committee to consider ways of raising money to supply Stock with paper   8 Jul 1690 F139r some of £1500 borrowed by Stock to go towards 3000 reams of paper for coming year and paper bills from Capt. Edward Darrell and others   5 Oct 1696 F250v entry to be made when any of S.C.'s paper is delivered to members or others

See also ACTS OF PARLIAMENT

PAPERS – see ARCHIVES

PARDOE, Mary   20 Dec 1716 G246r elected to Elizabeth Slate's pension

PARISMUS   6 Apr 1696 F241v Matthew Wootton complains that William Thackery has printed or appropriated his 'Parismus' [by Emmanuel Ford]; deferred

PARKER, Andrew   5 Dec 1709 G172r of Inner Temple Lane, stationer; freed by Robert Podmore. Thomas Hadduck is bound to him   4 Sep 1710 G183v cloathed   4 Feb 1711/12 G196v Robert Podmore is turned over to him   6 Sep 1714 G221v his apprentice Richard Berry is freed   4 Mar 1716/17 G248r Manwaring Davis is bound to him

PARKER, Edmund   7 Feb 1703/4 G101v freed by Thomas Guy   3 Dec 1705 G126r Henry Allestree is bound to him   2 Dec 1706 G136v cloathed   5 Sep 1709 G170r elected to Elinor Smith's £40 share   2 Mar 1712/13 G207r George Price is bound to him   26 Mar 1713 G207v fined for First Renter Warden   5 Oct 1713 G214r Thomas Hutchinson is bound to him

PARKER, George   2 Jun 1701 G60r to be prosecuted by S.C. for printing, publishing and selling a double Ephemeris   14 Mar 1703/4 G104r examined concerning his printing of the Ephemerides without S.C.'s leave   23 Mar 1703/4 G104r to be proceeded against on his bond to the S.C.   3 Apr 1704 G105r double Ephemeris printed for him by Bridge. To pay a fine of 4 guineas to Warehousekeeper   5 Dec 1709 G172r to be sued on his bond for publishing a calendar in his Ephemeris for this year   4 Dec 1710

G185v Clerk has refused to enter his Ephemeris. Gave evidence before the Court. To be proceeded against upon his bond

PARKER, Henry   7 Feb 1703/4 G101v bound to Edmund Powell, 7 years   5 Feb 1710/11 G188r freed by Edmund Powell   1 Apr 1717 G249v John Cuxon turned over to him from Richmond

PARKER, John (I)   8 Nov 1697 G1v bound to John Harding

PARKER, John (II)   2 Aug 1714 G221r his son Samuel is bound to Robert Elmes, 7 years

PARKER, James   5 May 1712 G199v his son Thomas is bound to John Bradshaw, 7 years

PARKER, Leonard   3 Feb 1700/1 G55v freed by Samuel Scott

PARKER, Peter, snr   4 Sep 1682 E157v Thomas Pierrepont assigns him 'The English Gardener'   13 Oct 1687 F92r elected Assistant Renter Warden instead of Gabriel Cox and summoned to next Court   17 Oct 1687 F92v fined for Assistant Renter Warden   1 Mar 1687/8 F97v expelled from Livery by order of Lord Mayor   11 Oct 1688 F108v restored to Livery   13 Mar 1692/3 F184v Ralph Simpson complains Parker has printed [William] Dyer's works and reads assignment; committee to inspect register book   2 Apr 1694 F202v Henry Nelme, his apprentice, freed   22 Jun 1698 G9v general release from S.C.   4 Jul 1698 G11r his son Peter Parker is freed   5 May 1701 G61v bill in Chancery against him and Edwards for illegally printing and publishing S.C.'s calendar   7 Jul 1701 G61v served with subpoena to answer a Bill in Chancery for printing and publishing S.C.'s Calendar. Matter to be discharged on his paying the charges of the prosecution and giving bond of £40 not to publish any more of S.C.'s copies   4 Aug 1701 G63r desires a remittance of charges in Chancery. To pay 50s and give a bond with £40 penalty not to print any more of S.C.'s almanacks   6 Oct 1707 G145v to be proceeded against in Chancery for printing and selling counterfeit psalms and almanacks   1 Aug 1709 G169v almanack to be received by S.C. for this year on reasonable terms   7 Jul 1712 G201v William Thackery's £80 share, mortgaged to him for £75, disposed of and mortgage and interest repaid

See also following entry

PARKER (Peter) and GUY (Thomas)   4 Aug 1684 F22v request that the 5 quarters' rent due to Oxford should be set against the Stock books given them; balance to be paid by S.C. to them. Court agrees. Parker and Guy to indemnify S.C. for claims of rent from Oxford University   1 Sep 1684 F23v John Bellinger tells Court that Parker and Guy are printing 25,000 books of psalms in Oxford; committee appointed to negotiate   6 Oct 1684 F24v committee appointed to deal with their printing of S.C. psalms   11 Oct 1684 F25r request re. psalms to make the same agreement with S.C. as the King's Printers have. S.C. decides to sue as they have broken their contracts with S.C. and printed without licence   25 Dec 1684 (W) letter to Master requesting payment for rent. If this is not paid, and Parker and Guy are not permitted to print psalms on the same terms as the King's Printers, their forebearance re. not printing the psalms will not continue beyond 25 Mar   16 Jan 1684/5 F28v committee meeting. Henry Pollexfin, the S.C. counsel, is asked to proceed to a joynder in demurrer against Parker and Guy. Counsel's advice should be taken to draw up a bill in Chancery against Parker and Guy and Oxford University for printing of almanacks   26 Mar 1685 F32r their letter referred to the appropriate committee. (W) Copy of their letter   29 Apr 1685 F33r Committee meeting. Lawsuit commenced against them, and John Lilly requests that some members treat with the Bishop of Oxford to resolve matter in difference   21 Jul 1685 F41r Godfrey Head to be summoned for casting letters for. Committee vote not to sue

Oxford re. psalms, to see Bishop of Oxford and to come to agreement without King's Printers   3 Aug 1685 F42r Godfrey Head tells Court that its order re. type has been revoked   7 May 1688 F101r letter read objecting to S.C.'s complaints about them to Crown; Court thanks Master and Wardens and begs them to prosecute   23 Sep 1688 (W) Oxford printers; defended in Gilbert Ironside's petition   4 Feb 1688/9 F112r Vice-Chancellor of Oxford refers dispute re. almanacks to them and a committee is chosen to negotiate with them   6 Mar 1688/9 F115r detailed agreement resolving dispute is approved and sealed. (W) note of agreement written by Thomas Dring   1 Jul 1689 F120v Treasurer to pay them Oxford's quarterly rent; committee to negotiate with them   6 Apr 1691 F152r committee chosen to negotiate with them re. 'the sale of such parcels of Psalms as they shall desire'. Court allows Thomas Bradyll to sue them for printing [William] Dyer's works   1 Feb 1691/2 F164v mentioned as making it impossible for S.C. to negotiate with Oxford under its own name. Under new agreement Roger Norton to pay £30 to S.C. rather than Parker and Guy for not printing grammar   21 Nov 1692 F182r Court summoned to hear of 'amicable end' to differences between Parker and Guy and S.C. and consider how further money may be raised for Oxford; referred   6 Mar 1698/9 G21v declaration against Henry Mortlock and Thomas Dring in relation to affairs of S.C. Subpoena to be taken out against Parker and Guy by Clerk at the S.C.'s suit   20 Oct 1699 G32r articles between Guy and Parker on the one part and Mortlock and Dring, Master, Wardens and Assistants on the other read. £60 demanded by Guy and Parker for their satisfaction. Committee to adjust and settle   4 Dec 1699 G33v agreement that S.C. should pay them £50, they executing a discharge to and for Mortlock and the administrator of Thomas Dring and the Master and Wardens. The £50 to be placed in the account of the Oxford Stock

PARKER, Peter, jnr   22 Jun 1698 G9v general release from S.C.   4 Jul 1698 G11r freed by his father, Peter Parker   4 Dec 1710 G185v to be served with a copy of the writ of execution against Benjamin Harris

PARKER, Richard (I)   26 Mar 1686 F54r elected waterman   4 Apr 1687 F81v elected waterman

PARKER, Richard (II)   19 Nov 1695 F236r freed and cloathed   26 Mar 1709 G162v fined for First Renter Warden   6 Feb 1709/10 G175r elected to John Heptingstall's £40 share   9 Apr 1716 G239r deceased; his £40 share disposed of to Bernard Lintott

PARKER, Samuel (I)   6 Nov 1710 G184r son of William; bound to John Senex, 7 years

PARKER, Samuel (II)   2 Aug 1714 G221r son of John; bound to Robert Elmes, 7 years

PARKER, Thomas (I)   8 Apr 1695 F221r servant to Miles Flesher; freed

PARKER, Thomas (II)   5 May 1712 G199v son of James; bound to John Bradshaw, 7 years

PARKER, William, snr   6 Nov 1710 G184r his son Samuel is bound to John Senex, 7 years

See also following entry

PARKER, William, jnr   5 May 1712 G199v son of William; bound to Ralph Simpson, 7 years

PARKHURST, Priscilla   5 Oct 1713 G214r her apprentice Parkhurst Smith is freed   1 Feb 1713/14 G216r memorandum agreed with her about Thomas Parkhurst's legacy to the S.C.

PARKHURST, Thomas   1 Mar 1679/80 E97v elected Stock-keeper for Livery   4 Jul 1681 E116r voted that time should be taken to consider whether he, Simon Miller and others should be made Assistants   8 May 1682 E152v assigned Dr [John] Lightfoot's

'Harmony of the Scriptures' [i.e. *Scripture Harmonies*] by Simon Miller. Assignment from Mrs Maxwell to him of Christopher Wase's 'Methodi Practica[e] Specimen' confirmed 13 Oct 1687 F91v sworn in as Assistant. Elected into William Cooper's place as Stock-keeper 5 Dec 1687 F95r Court mitigates his £8 fine for trying to force his way on to the Court to £5 since he is candidate for a £160 share. Submits to his £5 fine being detained out of his next dividend but asks that his precedency in Court will not be affected. Elected to the late Mrs Waterson's £160 share 9 Jan 1687/8 F96v to pay the £5 which was not in fact deducted from his last dividend 7 May 1688 F101r money for his Livery dinner to be added to the 29 May collation 30 Jun 1688 F103r competes unsuccessfully for Under Warden 4 Feb 1688/9 F112v re-elected Assistant 6 May 1689 F117r ranked first of Assistants never elected as Master or Warden 1 Jul 1689 F120v voted not to restore to him the £5 fine he had incurred through trying to force himself on to the Court 6 Jul 1689 F121v elected Under Warden 2 Dec 1689 F127r competes unsuccessfully for the late Ralph Smith's £320 share 5 Jun 1690 F135v re-appointed Assistant 7 Jul 1690 F139r competes unsuccessfully for the late Dorothy Thrale's £320 share 25 Sep 1690 F143r committee to treat with Smith, Benjamin Motte and him re. their printing of Lucius [Annaeus] Florus, Justin and [William] Barton's Psalms 6 Oct 1690 F143v committee required to reach agreement with him and report 4 Jul 1691 F156v fined for second year of Under Warden 4 Jul 1692 F173v chosen to audit late Warden's accounts 6 Nov 1693 F194v complaint that he and James Astwood have printed 1000 sheets of metrical psalms; these are sent for and the formes distributed. Committee to look into precedents for what action to take against them 4 Dec 1693 F195r under byelaw he forfeits share for printing psalms, with money going to poor; when he comprinted Scotch psalms with Dorman Newman he was fined £10 and paid £30 for liberty to sell the impression 9 May 1694 F204v competes unsuccessfully for Upper Warden. Allowed to fine for 1 year's Upper Wardenship to preserve his seniority 30 Jun 1694 F209v competes unsuccessfully for Master. Fined for second year of Upper Warden 6 May 1695 F222r competes unsuccessfully for Mrs Bellinger's £320 share when she remarries. Asks Court to consider report of 3 December 1693 re. his printing part of the Psalms; fined £5, to be put in the Poor Box 3 Jun 1695 F224v complains that his payment to the poor of St Martin's Ludgate has been omitted from Warden's accounts; committee appointed 1 Jul 1695 F227r refused permission to go on printing the psalms he was recently fined for beginning 3 Aug 1696 F246v elected to the £320 share of Mrs Wilkinson, lately remarried 30 Sep 1696 F249v allowed to print Richard Mayo's 'Exposition of the Catechism', paying what Robert Clavell does for Dr Isham's, i.e. 6s 8d for 500. Comes to Court after 11 a.m. and forfeits his half-crown to the Poor Box 26 Mar 1697 F258v he and Robert Clavell successfully request that Jonathan Robinson be excused the Renter Wardenship next year 7 Jun 1697 F263r Richard Burrowes is bound to him 3 Jul 1697 F263v competes unsuccessfully for Master 2 Aug 1697 F265v his apprentice Ralph Smith is freed 7 Mar 1697/8 G5r his apprentice Robert Halsey is freed 10 Jan 1698/9 G18v added to committee to consider Printing Act 3 Jul 1699 G26v to be given John Simms's Assistant's share as surety for a loan of an extra £20 to him 5 Jul 1701 G61v competes unsuccessfully for Master 9 Feb 1701/2 G67r has lent Simms £300 to pay off mortgagees of Assistant's share. Took assignment of these mortgages 15 Jul 1703 G93r elected Master 7 Feb 1703/4 G101v his apprentice Nathaniel Cliff is freed 12 Jun 1704 G107v his apprentice Richard Burrough is freed 6 Nov 1704 G113r agrees to lend S.C. £100 4 Dec 1704 G113v bond to S.C. sealed 16 Oct 1705 G124v to attend Lord Mayor re. Renter Wardens' unwillingness to provide dinner 3 Feb 1706/7 G137r £25 mortgage to him of Mrs Miller's share in English Stock. Following her death, to be repaid together with the remainder of the overplus of her share as he alleges more money is due to him   5 Jul 1707 G143r competes unsuccessfully for Master   6 Oct 1707 G145v Parkhurst Smith is bound to him   7 Mar 1708/9 G162r his apprentice Daniel Jackson is freed   9 Feb 1712/13 G206r deceased; legacy to S.C. of £50 accepted   1 Feb 1713/14 G215v clause from his will concerning legacy of Bibles and psalms to be given to the poor of the S.C. entered in Court book   4 Oct 1714 G222r his executor, Holden, disposes of John Simms's Assistant's share mortgaged to him

PARKINS/PARKINES, Abraham   2 Oct 1699 G31v bound to Thomas Hodgkins   4 Nov 1706 G136r freed by Thomas Hodgkins   6 Jun 1709 G165v of Wapping; Thomas Crump is bound to him

PARLIAMENT   7 Dec 1685 F47v Benjamin Harris lists those with whom he printed the proceedings of the Westminster Parliament

See also ACTS OF PARLIAMENT, HOUSE OF COMMONS, HOUSE OF LORDS

PARMER, [   ]   5 Jun 1710 G180r excused cloathing

PAROCHIAL ANTIQUITIES (by White Kennett)   24 Oct 1695 F234r printers to return 30 of the 'Oxford Antiquities' [i.e. *Parochial Antiquities … in … Oxford*] to Oxford

PARREY, John   3 Oct 1709 G171r bound to Dryden Leach, 7 years

PARRIS, Robert   10 Sep 1694 F212v freed by Thomas Sawbridge, deceased

PARROTT, Richard   6 Aug 1716 G242v son of William; bound to Susanna Collins, 7 years

PARROTT, William – see preceding entry

PARRY, John   2 Jul 1716 G242r turned over from Dryden Leach to Thomas Parry

PARRY/PERRY, Thomas   5 May 1701 G59v bound to John Bullard, 7 years   7 Sep 1702 G80v turned over from John Bullard to Francis Leach   5 Jul 1708 G155r freed by Dryden Leach   24 May 1716 G240r Henrietta Maria Germa is bound to him   2 Jul 1716 G242r John Parry is turned over to him

PARSELL, Nathaniel   2 Aug 1703 G94r bound to Thomas Meade   6 Oct 1712 G204v freed by Matthew Jenour

PARSONS/PARSON, Henry   11 Nov 1700 G46v freed by Ebenezer Tracy   8 Nov 1703 G97r William Horner is bound to him   1 Dec 1707 G147r cloathed   6 Dec 1708 G159v of London Bridge; George Bourne is bound to him   7 May 1711 G190v his apprentice William Horner is freed   2 Jul 1711 G192v Samuel Storey is bound to him   7 Jul 1712 G201v received his charge as Renter Warden from Warden Deputy Collins   4 Oct 1714 G222v elected to Thomas Varnam's £40 share   11 Jul 1716 G242r James Taylor is bound to him   8 Jan 1716/17 G246r his apprentice George Bourne is freed   4 Feb 1716/17 G246v Samuel Tyler is bound to him

PARSONS, Joseph – see following entry

PARSONS, Samuel   10 Sep 1716 G243r son of Joseph; bound to John Walthoe, 7 years

PARSONS, William   2 Nov 1691 F162r cloathed and promises fine   5 Feb 1693/4 F198v his apprentice Charles Osborne is freed   6 Oct 1701 G65r his apprentice Samuel Hadson is freed (turned over)

PARTERIDGE, [   ]   16 Jun 1684 F17v from near Charing Cross and free of the Haberdashers' Company; declares himself willing to be translated to S.C.

PARTRIDGE, Dr John   7 Jul 1709 G168r committee to meet concerning difference between S.C. and himself relating to his almanack for the year ensuing   24 Jul 1709

G168v letter to Awnsham Churchill from him concerning almanack read. Committee to consider the matter   17 Dec 1709 G173r his 'Letter to a Member of Parliament ... Touching his Almanack for ... 1710' considered by Court. Committee to prepare an answer   22 Dec 1709 G173r Clerk to draw up order overruling demur put in by Partridge and John Darby   14 May 1713 G210r committee to settle differences between himself and Darby and S.C.   1 Jun 1713 G210r John Sprint, a friend of him and Darby, has insisted that he should have £150 for his almanack. Committee to agree to give him £100 for this year and Sprint and Darby to agree on allowance for future years   7 Sep 1713 G213r time and manner of payment to him pursuant to the order of 1 June is the responsibility of Richard Mount and Darby   5 Mar 1715/16 G237v letter read from his executors concerning the allowance to him for his almanack and order of 1 June 1713; matter referred to Stock-keepers

See also ALMANACKS

PASHAM, Thomas   2 May 1681 E111v ordered to repay £20 loan money at the next Court, one of his sureties being dead   6 Jun 1681 E112v to continue £20 loan until next Michaelmas on different surety

PASSENGER, Mrs   12 Apr 1692 F169r deceased; her £160 share voted to Richard Simpson

PASSENGER, Thomas (I)   5 Sep 1681 E129v assigned [Edmund Wingate's] 'The Use of the Rule of Proportion in Arithmetic and Geometry' by Dorothy Stephens   7 Nov 1681 E137v voted the £40 share which James Collins forfeited by mortgaging it without permission, to make his share up to £80   1 Mar 1682/3 E164v elected Stock-keeper for Livery with Samuel Lowndes   19 Dec 1683 F7r complaint re. his sale of 'The Art of Wheedling' [i.e. Richard Head, *Proteus Redivivus*] deferred until next Court   3 Mar 1683/4 F10r elected Stock-keeper for Yeomanry in William Shrewsbury's stead (note in margin claims this was an error)   7 Apr 1684 F14r on the list of loyal Assistants presented to the Crown   2 Jun 1684 F15v promises to fine for Renter Warden   11 May 1685 F34v his name on the Livery list is vetoed by the Lord Mayor. Committee to tell Lord Mayor that the Secretaries of State's accusations against him have been disproved   20 May 1685 F35v approved as liveryman by Lord Mayor   12 Oct 1687 F91r among those chosen to audit Warden's accounts. Competes unsuccessfully for Under Warden   5 Dec 1687 F95v elected to the late Mrs Brewster's £160 share   1 Mar 1687/8 F97v displaced as Assistant by order of Crown and expelled from Livery by order of Lord Mayor   20 Dec 1688 F112r deceased; legacy of 40s to S.C. poor paid into Poor Box

PASSENGER, Thomas (II)   12 Jun 1693 F188v cloathed

PASTON, William   3 Feb 1706/7 G137v desiring £200 owed to him by the S.C. to be paid in March   26 Mar 1707 G140r Warden Israel Harrison to pay off his bonds of £200

PATEN, John   2 Jun 1712 G200v John Brind is bound to him

PATEN, William – see PAYTON, William

PATENTS   21 Jun 1700 G41r three old patents and one new one delivered into Court by Clerk and put in chest

PATENTS PRINTING HOUSE   29 Jul 1700 G43v committee to enquire of Mr Bell, one of the Commissioners for bankruptcy, concerning this and other things previously in the possession of Norton which are being disposed of

PATRICK, John – see PSALMS

PATRICK, Symon – see DISCOURSE

PATTENDEN, Thomas   3 Dec 1694 F216r deceased; Matthew Duckett is elected to his pension

PATTISON, Francis   6 Oct 1701 G65r bound to Richard George, 7 years   12 Nov 1705 G125r turned over from Richard George to William Sheffield   3 Mar 1706/7 G139r turned over from Richard George to Richard Smith   4 Oct 1708 G158r freed by Robert Smith

PAUL, Samuel   3 Nov 1707 G146v bound to George Mortimer, 7 years   8 Aug 1715 G232r freed by George Mortimer. Arthur Middleton is bound to him

PAVIOUR   7 Nov 1681 E137r to be paid for paving the courtyard before the Hall and the Treasurer's house   7 Nov 1709 G171v bill to be paid

PAWLETT, Blanche   1 Oct 1683 F3v she and George Pawlett, wife and son of Robert Pawlett, given leave to prosecute S.C. members dealing in books entered to him   2 Jul 1688 F104r deceased; her £40 share is voted to Stephen Bateman

PAWLETT, Edmund   15 Apr 1692 F170r bookseller of Chancery Lane; admitted to freedom by redemption on paying £5. Cloathed and promises payment of fine

PAWLETT/PAWLITT, George   1 Oct 1683 F3v he and Blanche Pawlett, son and wife of Robert Pawlett, given leave to prosecute S.C. members dealing in his books   1 Mar 1685/6 F51r cloathed   1 Mar 1687/8 F97v expelled from Livery by order of Lord Mayor   11 Oct 1688 F108v restored to Livery   12 Apr 1692 F169r deceased; leaves £5 to S.C. poor   2 May 1692 F170v deceased; Court offers to borrow £1000 from executors @ 5% p.a. for administration of Oxford business

PAWLETT, Robert (I)   26 Mar 1681 E108r elected Assistant Renter Warden   11 Apr 1681 E109v fined for Assistant Renter Warden   6 Nov 1682 E160r request to prosecute any S.C. members with dealings in books entered to him is granted   2 Jul 1683 F2v competes unsuccessfully for Ann Godbid's £80 share   1 Oct 1683 F3v deceased; his wife Blanche and son George are given leave to prosecute S.C. members dealing in his books

PAWLETT, Robert (II)   4 Dec 1704 G114r freed by redemption. Cloathed

PAWLITT – see PAWLETT

PAXTON, Mrs   2 Dec 1689 F127v deceased; her £160 share is voted to Dorman Newman

PAYBODY, Edmund   2 Nov 1702 G83r bound to Emmanuel Matthews, 7 years   2 Jul 1711 G192v freed by Emmanuel Matthews

PAYNE, Benjamin   5 Dec 1698 G17r bond from S.C. for £100 at 5% sealed   13 Apr 1702 G70r bond to be repaid   4 May 1702 G70v bond from S.C. repaid

PAYNE, Philip, snr – see following entry

PAYNE, Philip, jnr   4 Dec 1693 F197r son of Philip Payne, deceased, haberdasher of London; bound to Elyphall Jay for 7 years, freed from 6 November last

PAYNE, Thomas   4 Jul 1709 G167v bound to Thomas Shelmerdine, 7 years

PAYNE, [William]   7 Aug 1699 G28r his 'Sermons' are among the books requested to be assigned to Samuel Sprint and J. Nicholson

PAYTON, Sir Robert   6 Mar 1688/9 F114v Mrs Curtis claims that he and Sir William Waller ordered her to print unlicensed pamphlets

PAYTON/PATEN, William   12 Jun 1704 G107v bound to John Brookes, 7 years   2 Jun 1712 G200v freed by John Brookes

PEACH, Henry   5 Oct 1702 G81v apprentice of Richard Janeway, who was turned over to John Franknell, is now turned over to (blank)   4 Sep 1704 G112r ex-apprentice of Richard Janeway, freed by Joseph Hazard

PEACOCK, Daniel, snr   26 Mar 1686 F54r elected First Renter Warden   3 May 1686 F55r sworn in as First Renter Warden   7 Jun 1686 F57v elected to Richard Simpson's £40 share but swearing-in deferred in view of counsel's opinion on disposal of Samuel Hoyle's share to Simpson   5 Jul 1686 F60v sworn into his share   7 Feb 1686/7 F70v elected to William Cooper's £80 share   1 Mar 1687/8 F97v expelled from Livery by order of Lord Mayor   11 Oct 1688 F108v restored to Livery   7 Mar 1697/8 G4v his £80 share to be disposed of to Thomas Snowden   5 Sep 1698 G14r see following entry

PEACOCK, Daniel, jnr   5 Sep 1698 G14r freed by patrimony. Cloathed

PEACOCK, John   6 Jul 1713 G212v his son William is bound to John Lowen, 7 years

PEACOCK, Dean   9 Sep 1706 G134v bound to Robert Elmes, 7 years   1 Feb 1713/14 G216r freed by Robert Elmes

PEACOCK, Richard   7 Oct 1698 G15r bound to Ichabod Dawkes, 7 years

PEACOCK, Thomas   1 Jun 1702 G71v bound to Ann Snowden, 7 years   1 Aug 1709 G169v freed by Ann Snowden

PEACOCK, William   6 Jul 1713 G212v son of John; bound to John Lowen, 7 years

PEALE, [ ]   2 Nov 1691 (W) freed by John Clomley

PEARSON, John   1 Feb 1691/2 (W) his apprentice William Perkins is freed by William Wild

PEARSON, John, Bishop of Chester   3 Feb 1695/6 F238v assignment of 'Pierson's Holy Creed' [i.e. *An Exposition of the Creed*] to Bennett Griffin entered

PEARSON/PIERSON, William   8 May 1693 F188r when John Hippinstall comes in to free him he is fined 30s for having bound Pearson with a foreign indenture   5 Dec 1698 G17r William Johnson is bound to him   6 Oct 1701 G64v cloathed; G65r Henry Blyth is bound to him   6 Mar 1703/4 G103v Jacob Foden is turned over to him   3 Dec 1705 G126r William Johnson is freed by him   4 Feb 1705/6 G127v George Fabian is bound to him   3 Feb 1706/7 G138r printer; James Horton is bound to him   5 Jul 1708 G155r his apprentice Jacob Foden is freed   1 Dec 1712 G205v John Grainger is bound to him   13 Apr 1713 G208v his apprentice George Fabian is freed. Thomas Whitmarsh is bound to him   6 Dec 1714 G224r Isaac Buckley is bound to him

PEDDAR – see PETHER

PEDLARS – see ACTS OF PARLIAMENT

PEIRCE, Timothy   1 Mar 1687/8 F97v expelled from Livery by order of Lord Mayor

PEIRSON, Elizabeth   3 Dec 1694 F216r deceased; James Gray elected to her pension

PIERSON, William – see PEARSON, William

PIERSON'S HOLY CREED – see PEARSON, John, Bishop of Chester

PELE, John   4 Dec 1710 G186r bound to Daniel Browne, 7 years

PELLIN, Rev.   3 May 1680 E100r application to make a door from St Martin's Ludgate into S.C. garden accepted; one key to be kept by him and one by S.C.

PELLIPAR   9 Feb 1690/1 F148r copy of letter to Skinners' Company from Edward Cary, late tenant of Pellipar, is read re. Irish troubles stopping dividends   6 Jul 1691 F157r clerk of Skinners sends S.C. a memorial from Edward Cary setting forth his losses caused by Irish disturbances

PEMBERTON, Sergeant   19 Dec 1683 F7r committee to consult with him or other counsel re. validity, force and power of byelaw concerning disobedient Stock partners

PEMBERTON, Sir Francis   5 Aug 1689 F122v to be consulted by John Lilly re. Richard Chiswell's complaint about unqualified shareholders   7 Dec 1696 F254v gives opinion that leave should be given Thomas Bassett to make a second mortgage and thereby mortgage his £320 share up to its full value

PEMBERTON, John   3 Jun 1700 G40v bound to William Rogers, 7 years   7 Jul 1707 G143v freed by William Rogers   5 Jun 1710 G180r cloathed   5 Feb 1710/11 G187r of Fleet Street, bookseller; Rutter is bound to him   7 May 1716 G240r Henry Cole is bound to him

PEMBROKE, Thomas Herbert, 8th Earl of   11 Jun 1694 F209r Court to wait upon him re. his desire for a Latin-English interlineary Aesop, discussed with Awnsham Churchill

PEN – see PENN

PENDRED, James   3 Jun 1700 G40v freed by Henry Perris

PENFOLD, Thomas   5 Feb 1699/1700 G35r John Delander is bound to him

PENFORD, Thomas   4 Jun 1694 F208r cloathed   3 Feb 1695/6 F239r Court refuses to discharge him, John Sparkes and John Gerrard from S.C. so they can take up freedom of the Ironmongers' Company

PENGELLY, Serjeant   3 Oct 1715 G233v advice to be taken by Clerk on suit against John England

PENN/PEN, John   2 May 1681 E111r to retain £100 loan money for another 3 years   8 May 1682 E152r Court grants his request to retain £100 loan for 3 more years, with sureties Robert Hollinghurst and John Croft   3 Dec 1683 F6v to propose an alternative surety to Croft the goldsmith, who had 'gone aside'   3 Nov 1684 F25v elected to William Shrewsbury's £40 share   7 May 1685 (W) confirmed as member of new Livery   7 Feb 1686/7 F70v competes unsuccessfully for the late Mary Symons's £80 share   16 Mar 1686/7 F79r to be summoned on 4 April for the election of Renter Wardens   2 May 1687 F82v elected Second Renter Warden. Elected to the late Edward Horton's £80 share   22 Jun 1687 F85r elected First Renter Warden   8 Apr 1695 F220r elected to the late Mary Kirton's £160 share   7 Aug 1699 G29r stationer; his apprentice William Harvey is freed   4 Dec 1699 G34r John Ford is bound to him   6 May 1700 G39v Richard Green is bound to him   7 Apr 1701 G58v William Shaw is bound to him   3 May 1703 G89v his apprentice Owen Lloyd is freed   8 May 1704 G106v Henry Litchfeild is bound to him   4 Dec 1704 G114r James Steward is turned over to him   2 Apr 1705 G118v his apprentice Edward Jones is freed   12 Nov 1705 G125r John Burnell is bound to him   2 Aug 1708 G156v bookbinder; David Samuel is bound to him   4 Dec 1710 G186r his apprentice William Shaw is freed

PENN, John (II)   2 Aug 1697 F265v bound to Edward Powell   7 Aug 1704 G111r freed by Edward Powell   3 Mar 1711/12 G197r excused from cloathing   5 Oct 1713 G214r cloathed. Richard Reeve is bound to him

PENNSYLVANIA   3 Aug 1685 F42r Godfrey Head tells Court that a Quaker has ordered him to cast type to send to Pennsylvania

PENSIONS   7 Aug 1682 E156v committee considering Clerk's duties re. pension notes (for some years last past omitted) to report at next Court   1 Feb 1685/6 F51r committee revived to consider the Clerk's remuneration for entering pension notes

PEPPER, Robert   1 Oct 1716 G244r apprentice of William Sandys; freed by Richard Simpson

PEPPER'S ALMANACK – see ALMANACKS

PERE, John   1 Feb 1691/2 (W) freed by Christopher Hussey   2 Oct 1693 F193r excused cloathing on grounds of inability   11 Nov 1695 F235r excused cloathing

PERIPONT – see PIERREPONT

PERKINS, Francis 20 Oct 1699 G32r bound to William Rawlins, 7 years 8 May 1704 G106v turned over to William Botham 7 Aug 1704 G111r turned over to John Brudnell

PERKINS, John 6 Dec 1708 G159v bound to Thomas Mew, 7 years

PERKINS, William 1 Feb 1691/2 (W) freed by William Wild

PERO, John 26 Mar 1701 G58r his apprentice Benjamin Price is freed

PERRIS/PERRYS, Henry 6 Mar 1698/9 G21v excused cloathing for 6 months 4 Sep 1699 G30r to be summoned next Court day to take cloathing 2 Oct 1699 G31r cloathed 3 Jun 1700 G40v his apprentice James Pendred is freed 26 Mar 1706 G130r excused office of Renter Warden for the year 3 Feb 1706/7 G138r ironmonger; Jeremiah Lammas is bound to him 3 Mar 1706/7 G139r his apprentice Jeremiah Lammas is turned over to Thomas Holden 26 Mar 1709 G162v fined for First Renter Warden

PERRY, Richard 4 Oct 1708 G158r bound to Thomas Bullock, 8 years

PERRY, Thomas – see PARRY, Thomas

PERRYS – see PERRIS

PERSIUS FLACCUS, Aulus 7 Apr 1690 F133r Abel Swale accuses Thomas Dring of printing the Satires of Juvenal and Persius, his copy; dispute referred to committee 5 Jun 1699 G25r Walford's request that a caveat be entered against re-entering copies in the register granted 3 Jul 1699 G27r paper from Nicholson and Timothy Child concerning copyright for printing. Richard Chiswell, Robert Clavell and Samuel Sprint's interest in Satires. Reference before Treasurer to be expedited 7 Aug 1699 G29r extension of period of reference before Treasurer

PERSIVELL, William 5 Sep 1709 G170r bound to James Read, 7 years

PERSONS, Robert, et al. 5 Mar 1693/4 F200v Court to negotiate with Awnsham Churchill re. damasked paper of 'Doleman about the English Succession' [i.e. the pseudonymous publication by Robert Persons and others]

PESTELL, Thomas 21 Jun 1706 G132v citizen and merchant of London; two bonds from S.C. to him sealed, totalling £300 3 Mar 1706/7 G139r bond from S.C. for payment of £100 and interest cancelled 5 Feb 1710/11 G187r to be allowed 6% for the £200 due to him on S.C.'s bond

PETHER/PEDDAR, John 1684–1699 Cook 3 May 1697 F261v urges repayment of £4 10s owed to him by Capt. John Williams on his fellow ex-Renter Warden, John Darby. S.C. to use money from Mrs Anne Williams' share to pay Darby and hence Pether 7 Jun 1697 F262v to be paid £4 10s from dividend of Capt. Williams's widow 8 Nov 1697 G2r S.C.'s cook; Mrs Williams petitions that her dividend may not be stopped on account of any claims made by him 5 Jun 1699 G25r Treasurer to pay him £4 due from Capt. Williams when Renter Warden 2 Oct 1699 G31r cook, deceased

PETHER, Susannah 7 Nov 1715 G234v widow of S.C.'s cook. Letter asserting that racks and spits in the kitchen of the Hall were the property of Stephens the late cook

PETTY, Mrs 5 Jul 1708 G154v Clerk to demand her rent arrears

PEWTERER 6 Oct 1712 G204r bill to be paid by Under Warden

PHELPS, William 3 Nov 1701 G65r bound to Robert Smith, 7 years 7 Feb 1703/4 G101v formerly turned over to Edmund Powell, now turned over to Francis Leach 1 Mar 1707/8 G150r turned over from Francis Leach to Isaac Cleave

PHILLIPPS, John, snr – see following entry

PHILLIPPS, John, jnr   1 Oct 1694 F213v son of John Phillipps snr, late silk-throwster of London; bound to John Shrimpton

PHILLIPPS/PHILLIPS, Joshua   7 May 1688 F101r John Baker assigns to Joseph Watts and him Joseph Glanvill's 'An Earnest Invitation to the ... Lord's Supper', 7th edn   3 Jun 1689 F119r cloathed   27 Mar 1704 G105r elected Assistant Renter Warden   20 Apr 1705 G199r late Renter Warden; unwilling to deliver book of quarterage to Clerk, only promising to deliver it on penalty of being summoned before the Lord Mayor with Ralph Simpson

PHILLIPPS, Richard, snr – see following entry

PHILLIPPS/PHILLIPS, Richard, jnr   4 Jun 1694 F208v son of Richard Phillipps, tallow-chandler of London; bound to Thomas Warren   5 Aug 1706 G134r freed by Thomas Warren

PHILLIPPS/PHILLIPS, William, Capt.   3 Feb 1679/80 E96v elected to Mrs Griffin's £80 share   11 Apr 1681 E110r fined for Renter Warden   7 Apr 1684 F14r on the list of loyal Assistants presented to the Crown. (W) letter from Richard Graham and Burton recommending him as an Assistant loyal to the Crown   7 May 1685 (W) confirmed as member of new Livery   26 Jun 1685 F38v to be added to auditors of Renter Wardens' accounts   2 Nov 1685 F45v elected to John Bellinger's £160 share   3 Jul 1686 F59v among those chosen to audit Renter Wardens' accounts   4 Oct 1686 F64r reports that the Warden's accounts are correct, contrary to Roger Norton's view   2 Jul 1687 F85v among those chosen to audit Warden's accounts; competes unsuccessfully for Under Warden   11 Oct 1688 F108v restored to Livery   4 Feb 1688/9 F112v re-elected Assistant   6 May 1689 F116v ranked fifth of Assistants never elected as Master or Warden   5 Jun 1690 F135v re-elected Assistant   5 Jul 1690 F138r competes unsuccessfully for Under Warden   4 Jul 1691 F156v among those chosen to audit Renter Wardens' accounts   2 Jul 1692 F172v elected Under Warden   7 Nov 1692 F181v competes unsuccessfully for the late Mrs Man's £320 share   1 Jul 1693 F189r re-elected Under Warden   2 Jul 1694 F210r augments drain committee negotiating with St Martin's Ludgate   1 Oct 1694 F213v Richard Mawson, his apprentice, is freed   4 Mar 1694/5 F218r is added to drain committee   6 Jul 1695 F229v competes unsuccessfully for Upper Warden; allowed to fine for 1 year's service as Upper Warden to preserve his seniority   7 Oct 1695 F233v elected Stock-keeper in place of William Rawlins, now Upper Warden   4 May 1696 F242r chosen to audit Renter Wardens' accounts with Roger Norton   4 Jul 1696 F245r competes unsuccessfully for Upper Warden but is elected when William Rawlins fines; he too is allowed to fine   6 Jul 1696 F245v competes unsuccessfully for Stock-keeper's position left vacant by the appointment of Henry Mortlock as Master   3 Aug 1696 F248v competes unsuccessfully for the £320 share of Mrs Wilkinson, lately remarried   5 Oct 1696 F250r delivers to Court the vouchers &c. he has in his possession; these are ordered to be put in the chest   1 Mar 1696/7 F255r chosen Stock-keeper for Assistants with William Rawlins   3 Jul 1697 F263v competes unsuccessfully for Master   5 Jul 1697 F264v among those chosen to audit Warden's accounts   1 Mar 1697/8 G4r Stock-keeper for the Assistants   7 Jun 1698 G9r party to Articles with University of Oxford   1 Mar 1698/9 G21r elected Stock-keeper for Assistants   6 Mar 1698/9 G22r to accompany Mrs Isted to Counsel re. writings belonging to S.C.   3 Jul 1699 G26v auditor of Master and Wardens' accounts   1 Mar 1699/1700 G36r elected Stock-keeper for Assistants   6 Jul 1700 G41v elected Master   3 Feb 1700/1 G54v elected to Mrs Mearne's Assistant's share. His Livery share disposed of to Thomas Clarke   5 Jul 1701 G61v elected Master   4 Jul 1702 G76v elected Master. Excused from providing a buck for the venison feast as he has already served for two years   23 Jul 1702 G79r offers to lend S.C. £100 to enable them to pay half a year's rent to the University of Oxford which Benjamin Tooke has refused to pay   3 Aug 1702 G79v offers to lend S.C. £200 to repay money due to Mrs Webb. Bond from S.C. of £200 sealed, to pay £100 rent to University of Oxford for English Stock   7 Sep 1702 G80v bond from S.C. of £400 sealed   27 Mar 1703 G86v £200 lent by him from Mrs Royston's money to be repaid by bond of Mrs Webb   3 May 1703 G89r gives 10s to Thomas Hooper   7 Jun 1703 G90r thanks of the Court to be given for his great care and good services to the S.C.   2 Aug 1703 G93v delivers two cases and the opinions of the Attorney General thereon relating to Tooke   6 Sep 1703 G94v to meet John Gadbury the almanack-maker   4 Oct 1703 G95v has met Gadbury but no agreement reached. Two bonds from him of £300 discharged   21 Oct 1703 G96r instructed to answer letter from Vice-Chancellor of Cambridge University   6 Dec 1703 G99v accounts (as Master?) audited   7 Feb 1703/4 G101r added to committee considering John Hayes's account re. Cambridge affairs   2 Mar 1703/4 G102v elected Stock-keeper for Assistants. To take Counsel's advice re. John Bradford's plea   14 Mar 1703/4 G104r to take Counsel's advice re. Ephemerides   3 Apr 1704 G105v auditor of late Renter Wardens' accounts   30 Jun 1704 G108r reports on negotiations with Benjamin Tooke. Chosen to be arbitrator for S.C. in the case   3 Jul 1704 G109v auditor of late Master and Wardens' accounts   5 Feb 1704/5 G114v Clerk's bill for proceedings in Chancery referred to him   1 Mar 1704/5 G116r elected Stock-keeper for Assistants   2 Apr 1705 G118v auditor of late Renter Wardens' accounts   2 Jul 1705 G121v auditor of late Master and Wardens' accounts   6 Aug 1705 G122r to assist with election dinner   8 Dec 1705 G126v signatory to Articles with University of Cambridge   4 Feb 1705/6 G127v Clerk's two bills referred to him   19 Feb 1705/6 G128r to speak to [William] Willymott, the editor of Terence   1 Mar 1705/6 G128v elected Stock-keeper for Assistants   1 Apr 1706 G130v auditor of late Renter Wardens' accounts   5 Aug 1706 G133v auditor of late Master and Wardens' accounts   1 Mar 1706/7 G138v elected Stock-keeper for Assistants   5 May 1707 G141v auditor of late Renter Wardens' accounts   5 Jul 1707 G143r competes unsuccessfully for Master   7 Jul 1707 G143v auditor of late Master and Wardens' accounts   4 Aug 1707 G144r to meet Members of the House of Commons re. Act of Parliament   3 Dec 1707 G148r signs re. not taking Clarendon   1 Mar 1707/8 G149v to adjust Clerk's bill for law charges   26 Mar 1708 G151r to be added to committee re. Clarendon in octavo   3 May 1708 G152v auditor of late Renter Wardens' accounts   5 Jul 1708 G154v auditor of late Renter Wardens' accounts   17 Jul 1708 G155v grant from University of Oxford to him, Henry Mortlock and Robert Andrews read. Ordered to go down to Oxford. Articles of agreement between University of Oxford and Mortlock, Andrews and himself read   7 Feb 1708/9 G160v to adjust and order payment of Clerk's bill for law charges   1 Mar 1708/9 G161r elected Stock-keeper for Assistants   4 Apr 1709 G164r auditor of Renter Wardens' accounts   6 Jun 1709 G165r added to Morphew committee. To attend Sir Peter King   4 Jul 1709 G167r ordered to meet Jackson, an officer of the Commissioners of the Sewers, in order to consider how a drain may be made into the common sewer. Ordered to meet Benjamin Tooke to settle account. Auditor of late Master and Wardens' accounts   1 Aug 1709 G169r elected Master. Ordered that he be excused from the charge of a buck and from all other charges incident to him as Master   6 Feb 1709/10 G175v S.C. to pay 6% for the monies due to him on bond   3 Jul 1710 G181v elected Master. Thanks of Court given to him for his good and faithful services   30 Jun 1711 G192r elected Master   15 Jul 1712 G202r agrees to be Master on great persuasion   13 Apr 1713 G208r deceased

See also PHILLIPS

PHILLIPS, John (I)   8 Apr 1700 G39r bound to Edmund Beresford, 7 years   7 Jul 1707 G143v freed by John Beresford   4 Sep 1710 G183v cloathed   6 Aug 1711 G193r Edward Simons is bound to him

PHILLIPS, John (II)   3 Mar 1711/12 G197r his son Ralph is bound to Robert Stephenson

PHILLIPS, Philip   7 Feb 1708/9 G160v bound to John Doleman, 7 years

PHILLIPS, Ralph   3 Mar 1711/12 G197r son of John; bound to Robert Stephenson
See also PHILLIPPS

PHILMOTT, John   3 May 1708 G152v bound to Ann Snowden, 8 years   4 Sep 1710 G183v turned over from Ann Snowden to William Hurt   3 May 1714 G219r turned over to Samuel Keimer   6 May 1717 G250v freed by Samuel Keimer

PHILPOT, John   9 Sep 1700 G45r freed by Thomas Grover

PHILPOTT, James   7 Feb 1698/9 G20v bound to Thomas Ilive, 7 years

PHILPOTT, John   3 Jun 1706 G132v freed by Jane Ilive

PHILLPOTT, [   ] – see PHILMOTT, John

PHILPOTT/PHILLPOT/PHILLPOTT/PHILPOT, Thomas   8 Nov 1703 G97r bound to James Roberts, 7 years   10 Sep 1711 G194r freed by James Roberts

PICKARD, John   2 Aug 1703 G94r freed by James Rawlins   3 Jul 1710 G182r cloathed

PICKARD, Samuel – see following entry

PICKARD, Thomas   12 Nov 1716 G244v son of Samuel; bound to Nathan Firth, 7 years

PIERCE, William   1 Feb 1696/7 F255r re-summoned re. cloathing   22 Jun 1697 F263r cloathed and promises fine at two six-monthly intervals   2 Aug 1697 F265v William Monins is bound to him

PIERREPONT/PERIPONT, Thomas   4 Sep 1682 E157v assigns 'The English Gardener' to Peter Parker   7 Feb 1686/7 F70v asks to dispose of his £80 share to William Rogers but is told to surrender it to the Master first (W) letter of surrender; Rogers is duly elected   1 Mar 1687/8 F97v expelled from Livery by order of Lord Mayor

PIERSON, [   ]   5 Oct 1702 G81r to be summoned to Court to answer charges
See also PEARSON

PIGG, John, snr – see following entry

PIGG, John, jnr   3 Jun 1695 F226r son of John Pigg, merchant taylor of London; bound to Ralph Snow

PILKINTON, Sir Thomas   2 Dec 1689 (W) Lord Mayor of London

PINCHORNE, Abraham   5 Mar 1715/16 G237v freed by John Buchanan

PINFOLD, Thomas   5 Feb 1704/5 G115r bound to Ralph Snow, 7 years

PIRACY   9 Sep 1700 G44v committee to consider letter proposing an agreement to be signed by members of S.C. to prevent piracy and printing of particular persons' copies

PITT, Moses   5 Jul 1686 F60v assigns 'Poetical Histories' [by Pierre Gautruche] to Thomas Guy

PITTARD, Charles   4 Jul 1698 G11r bound to Alexander Bosvile, 'turnover', 7 years

PLACE, Edward   1 Dec 1701 G66r freed by his father John Place by patrimony. Cloathed   2 Aug 1703 G94r Edward Price is bound to him   26 Mar 1708 G150v fined for First Renter Warden   4 Sep 1710 G183v of Holborn, stationer; John Smith is bound to him

PLACE, John   12 Jun 1684 F17r his former apprentice Richard Sare to take freedom   30 Sep 1684 F24r is elected to the £40 share that William Rawlins surrenders, making him a £80 stockholder in all   2 Mar 1684/5 F31v elected Stock-keeper for Yeomanry with Samuel Roycroft   7 May 1685 (W) confirmed as member of new Livery   22 Jun 1687 F85r elected Second Renter Warden and asks for time until next Court to consider it   4 Jul 1687 F86r fined for Second Renter Warden   11 Oct 1688 F108v restored to Livery   1 Mar 1694/5 F217v elected Stock-keeper for Yeomanry with John Rogers   4 Mar 1694/5 F218r sworn in as Stock-keeper   3 Feb 1695/6 F239r elected to Dorothy Dring's £160 share, she having remarried   2 Mar 1695/6 F239v takes partner's oath   4 May 1696 F242v elected as Assistant and summoned   8 Jun 1696 F243r sworn in as Assistant. Thomas Cater, his apprentice, is freed   1 Apr 1697 F260v to ask booksellers, printers and paper-manufacturers of Holborn for money towards Paper Act test case   3 Jul 1697 F263v competes unsuccessfully for Under Warden   5 Jul 1697 F264r competes unsuccessfully for Under Warden   10 Jan 1698/9 G18v added to committee to consider Printing Act   3 Apr 1699 G24r auditor of Renter Wardens' accounts   1 Mar 1699/1700 G36r elected Stock-keeper for Assistants   5 Jul 1701 G61v competes unsuccessfully for Under Warden   1 Dec 1701 G66r his son, Edward Place, is freed   6 Jul 1702 G77v fined for Under Warden. Auditor of late Renter Wardens' accounts   5 Jul 1703 G91v fined for Under Warden to preserve seniority   6 Mar 1703/4 G103v deceased; his £160 share disposed of to Brabazon Aylmer

PLASTERER   4 Sep 1704 G111v bill to be paid   10 Sep 1705 G123r bill to be paid by Joseph Collyer   4 Oct 1708 G158r bill referred to Master and Wardens for payment   7 Feb 1714/15 G225r bill to be paid

PLATE   2 Aug 1680 E102r John North discharged from all offices and charges on presenting a piece of plate to S.C. worth over £20   6 Jun 1681 E112v silver bowl presented to S.C. from Mrs Martin in discharge of her deceased husband's legacy of £20   3 Apr 1682 E151r Henry Herringman as Thomas Newcomb's executor awards S.C. a silver bowl in discharge of Newcomb's legacy   4 Dec 1682 E160v plate chest to be moved from a room by the Court Room and placed in the Warden's room 'in the new parlour'; 3 new locks to be made   7 Feb 1686/7 F71r Richard Royston's widow presents two silver candlesticks. Under Warden brings in a pair of silver snuffers and a silver snuffer box bought by S.C. for Royston's candlesticks   6 Jul 1689 F121v Susan Latham's executors present a silver trencher to S.C.   1 Aug 1692 F176v John Macock's executors present a silver cup to pair George Sawbridge's gift; it is 1 oz lighter and they pay 6s to Poor Box   2 Nov 1696 F252r details and weight of S.C. plate to be entered in a book   10 Feb 1703/4 G102r silver flagon to be purchased for S.C. with Herringman's gift of £20   14 Mar 1703/4 G104r Herringman's gift of a silver flagon produced in Court. Ordered to be put with rest of S.C.'s plate and inscribed   4 Aug 1707 G144v silver flagon, gift of William Rawlins, deceased, brought into Court by Charles Harper and taken into custody of Warden

PLAUTUS   18 Mar 1686/7 F79v among books in catalogue annexed to Oxford agreement

PLAYFORD, Henry   1 Mar 1685/6 F51r cloathed   1 Mar 1687/8 F97v expelled from Livery by order of Lord Mayor   11 Oct 1688 F108v restored to Livery   27 Mar 1693 F185r fined for First Renter Warden   8 May 1693 F187v is paid £512 10s and bond cancelled; money raised by entering into another bond with Edward Fenwick   5 Mar 1693/4 F200v fined £5 for printing metrical psalms; points out that to teach people to sing psalms well ought to help sale of Stock books   22 Jun 1694 F209r pays £10 for the privilege of printing 1000 of part of the Psalms of David in metre   4 Feb 1694/5 F217r John Cullin is bound to him   8 Apr 1695 F220v competes unsuccessfully for James Taylor's £40 share   6 May 1695 F222v competes unsuccessfully for Samuel Smith's £40 share   7 Oct 1695 F233v competes unsuccessfully for Benjamin Motte's £40 share   2 Nov 1696 F252r allowed to print 1500 psalms with music on payment of £15 but to give 10s to the Poor Box since he has already begun (W) 'it appearing he did not do it clandestinely, but through inadvertency'   7 Dec 1696 F252v elected to Isaac Cleave's £40 share   7 Feb 1697/8 G3v and Samuel Sprint to have leave to print an impression of 2000 psalms with Playford's musical notes   2 May 1698 G7v his apprentice Edward Conduit is freed   2 Mar 1701/2 G67v John Baker is bound to him. His apprentice John Cullin is freed   5 Oct 1702 G81r to be summoned to Court to answer charges   2 Nov 1702 G82v Samuel Sprint informs Court that Playford has paid S.C. for one impression of psalms printed for him by Heptingstall without leave of the Court and was willing to pay for the other   1 Dec 1707 G147v stationer; William Walker is bound to him

See also PSALMS

PLAYFORD, John (I)   25 Aug 1680 E103r he and Langley Curtis admonished for printing 'The Pacquet of Advice' anonymously under new byelaw; appends his name   20 Jun 1681 E113r Crown mandate that he should become an Assistant   5 Sep 1681 E129r competes unsuccessfully for Thomas Vere's £160 share   22 Dec 1681 E141r elected to Richard Clarke's £160 share   7 May 1683 E169v S.C. to give him a bond on common seal for £200 at 5% p.a. for six months (W) £100   25 Jun 1683 E171r delivers £200 bond to be cancelled and lends S.C. £200 more; bond for payment of £410 on 21 Dec sealed   7 Apr 1684 F13v on the list of loyal Assistants presented to the Crown   4 Jul 1685 F39r ordered to fine for Under Warden because of want of choice for Upper Warden   6 Jul 1685 F40r fined for 2 years' Under Warden   2 Nov 1685 F45v competes unsuccessfully for the late James Cotterell's £320 share. Request to assign his £160 share to his son, who would then fine for Livery, is refused   1 Feb 1686/7 F50r competes unsuccessfully for the late Mrs Sawbridge's £320 share   26 Mar 1686 F54v pays 12d charity for being absent from Court without leave of Master. Request again refused to grant his £160 share to his son and surrender his right to a £320 share   3 Jul 1686 F59r excused Upper Wardenship on account of 'infirmity of body'   7 Feb 1686/7 F70v deceased; his £160 share is voted to William Cooper

PLAYFORD, John (II)   5 Jul 1680 E101v cloathed   7 May 1683 E169v Ann Godbid's request to elect him to her £80 share deferred; committee to discuss whether his Vade Mecum has harmed stock   2 Jun 1683 (W) committee's initial view that Vade Mecum not prejudicial   4 Jun 1683 E170v committee concludes the Vade Mecum is prejudicial to the English Stock in the sale of almanacks and wishes legal advice to be taken   2 Jul 1683 F2r elected to Ann Godbid's £80 share   6 May 1685 F34r deceased; his £80 share is voted to Edward Horton

PLAYFORD, John (III)   12 Jun 1693 F188v given a bond of £800 penalty for payment of £400 plus interest at 5% by 23 Dec 1693

PLAYFORD, Mrs   7 Feb 1686/7 F70r interrogated about her right to print contrary to Act of Parliament and forbidden to continue; promises to give over trade

PLINY (Gaius Plinius Caecilius Secundus/Pliny the Younger)   18 Mar 1686/7 F79v his 'Epistolae' among books in catalogue annexed to Oxford agreement

PLUCKNETT, Brook   1 Jun 1702 G71v bound to Thomas Simpson, 7 years

PLUMBER   4 Dec 1704 G113v bill to be paid by Joseph Collyer   7 Jul 1707 G143v bill of £8 14s 9d to be settled by Master and Wardens   2 May 1709 G164v bill of £2 12s 5d to be paid by Under Warden

PLUMER, Michael   5 Aug 1689 F122r excused cloathing on plea of juniorship and inability

POCOCK, Richard   1 Oct 1705 G124r freed by Ichabod Dawkes

PODMORE, Robert   10 Sep 1694 F212r allowed to defer cloathing for a year   11 Nov 1695 F235r cloathed   7 Jun 1697 F263r Andrew Barker is bound to him   6 Nov 1704 G113r John Berry is bound to him   26 Mar 1707 G139v elected Assistant Renter Warden   7 Apr 1707 G140r fined for Assistant Renter Warden   4 Aug 1707 G144v stationer; Richard Berry is bound to him   5 Dec 1709 G172r his apprentice Andrew Parker is freed   7 May 1711 G190v of the Temple, stationer; James Wreathcock is bound to him   4 Feb 1711/12 G196v Richard Berry is turned over from him to Andrew Parker   4 Oct 1714 G222v John Foulkes is bound to him

POET LAUREATE – see TATE, Nahum

POETAE MINORES   3 Jun 1700 G40v committee to examine S.C. register books re. right to copy   2 Jun 1701 G60v S.C. has printed Awnsham Churchill's copy of this by mistake

POETICAL HISTORIES (by Pierre Gautruche)   5 Jul 1686 F60v assigned from Moses Pitt to Thomas Guy

POINTING, Henry   7 May 1694 F203v printer and servant of Thomas Moore for seven years; refused freedom on grounds that he was bound by foreign indenture at a scrivener's   9 May 1694 F204v submits a petition to be freed, seconded by several workmen printers contrary to their normal policy; he is freed

POLE, Francis – see following entry

POLE, Richard   9 May 1694 F204v son of Francis Pole of St Giles's Cripplegate, baker; bound to John Wilde, 7 years

POLLEXFIN, Henry   16 Jan 1684/5 F28v asked to proceed to a joynder in demurrer against Parker and Guy at a committee meeting   22 Aug 1685 F43r draft agreement with Oxford altered at his suggestion to be a 3-year covenant, not a grant

POLITEUPHUIA – see WIT'S COMMONWEALTH

POMFERT, Robert   3 Oct 1709 G171r bound to Jeffrey Wale, 7 years

POMFRETT, Joseph   7 Sep 1702 G80v bound to Benjamin Johnson, 7 years   1 Oct 1711 G194v freed by Benjamin Johnson. Charles Eareson is bound to him   4 Mar 1716/17 G248r George Houghton is bound to him

PONDAR – see PONDER

PONDER, [ ]   6 Feb 1681/2 E144r committee appointed to treat with him, Symons and Skinner re. their Chancery case against S.C.

PONDER, Nathaniel   3 Nov 1679 E95r William English, his apprentice, is freed   26 Mar 1684 F11v elected Second Renter Warden   2 Jun 1684 F15v re-elected as Renter Warden   7 Jul 1684 F20r request to bind an apprentice with intent to turn him over to a bookseller in the country refused   3 Aug 1685 F41v to pay with Christopher Wall the balance on the Renter Wardens' accounts to Ambrose Isted   13 Oct 1687 F91v sworn in as Assistant   5 Dec 1687 F96r elected to Nathaniel Ranew's £40 share   5 Mar 1687/8 F98v committee formed about his debt to S.C.   6 Aug 1688 (W) half Yeomanry share to be disposed of if he does not pay for it by next Court day   3 Nov 1688 F109v forgiven a £20 debt to John Leigh in trust for S.C. in consideration of a present he has recently made to S.C.   15 Apr 1692 F169v assigns to Jacob Tonson [Bulstrode Whitlock's] 'Memorials of English Affairs'   4 Jul 1692 F173v resigns his £40 share to S.C. requesting that James Taylor be elected to it; this is done   5 Feb 1693/4 F198v his son George is freed by patrimony   2 May 1698 G7v petition asking for relief. Given 10s from Poor Box   22 Jun 1698 G9r petition asking for relief. To be given 10s from Poor Box and to be given Anne Haddock's pension   27 Sep 1698 G13v pension to be increased 10s so that henceforth he receives 20s quarterly   22 Jun 1699 G26v deceased; Mary Brockett given his pension

PONDER, Robert   5 Feb 1693/4 F198v son of Nathaniel Ponder; freed by patrimony   7 Dec 1713 G215r Adrian Crownefeild is bound to him

POOLE, Benjamin   14 Mar 1711/12 G198r answer of S.C. to bill in Chancery brought by himself and John Stowe relating to share of £160 belonging to Mrs Mary Cooper   7 Feb 1714/15 G224v money due to him from Mrs Carr   6 Feb 1715/16 G236r commissioned to sell Mrs Cooper's stock. To be visited by Clerk to resolve the matter   5 Mar 1715/16 G237r agreed to seal a writing with Mrs Cooper authorising the S.C. to dispose of her stock

POOLE, Edward   3 Feb 1695/6 F239r his apprentice Thomas Minton is freed   6 Jun 1698 G8v Jerman Bowden is bound to him

POOLE, Jacob   7 Apr 1701 G58v bound to Henry Skelton, 7 years   7 May 1705 G120r turned over from Henry Skelton to Daniel Shellswell   3 May 1708 G152v freed by Daniel Shellswell

POOLE, Richard   4 Aug 1701 G63v freed by John Wilde

POOLER, [   ]   3 Nov 1707 G146v and others in arrears with Livery fines to be called on by Clerk

POOLER, Haynes/Heames   1 Mar 1702/3 G86r freed by Humphrey Pooler, patrimony   4 Jun 1705 G120v Thomas Bush is bound to him   5 Aug 1706 G134r cloathed

POOLER, Henry   13 Apr 1702 G70r Thomas Somervile is bound to him (NB: 'Henry' apparently crossed out, 'Humphrey' substituted)

POOLER, Humphrey   16 Mar 1686/7 F79r to be summoned on 4 April for the election of Renter Wardens   4 Apr 1687 F81r elected Second Renter Warden; asked to appear at next Court   1 Mar 1687/8 F97v expelled from Livery by order of Lord Mayor   11 Oct 1688 F108v restored to Livery   1 Feb 1691/2 (W) his apprentices Richard Trow and Robert Elmes are freed   7 Jun 1697 F263r Joseph Brookeland and Richard Hooke are bound to him   6 May 1700 G39v William Stonall is bound to him   1 Mar 1702/3 G86r his son Haynes is freed by patrimony.

See also preceding entry

POOR   Paid – 1 Dec 1679 E95v; 19 Dec 1679 E96v; 23 Jun 1680 E100v; 30 Sep 1680 E104v; 26 Mar 1681 E108r; 5 Jul 1681 E116v; 22 Dec 1681 E141v; 27 Mar 1682 E149r; 26 Jun 1682 E154r; 4 Oct 1682 E159r; 20 Dec 1682 E162v; 26 Mar 1683 E166r; 25 Jun 1683 E171r; 1 Oct 1683 F3r; 19 Dec 1683 F6v; 26 Mar 1684 F11r; 25 Jun 1684 F18r; 30 Sep 1684 F24r; 20 Dec 1684 F27r; 26 Mar 1685 F32r; 26 Jun 1685 F38v; 5 Oct 1685 F45r; 22 Dec 1685 F48r; 26 Mar 1686 F54v; 3 Jul 1686 F58r; 4 Oct 1686 F64v; 20 Dec 1686 F69r; 23 Mar 1686/7 F80r; 3 Oct 1687 F89r; 20 Dec 1689 F128r; 26 Mar 1690 F131r; 25 Jun 1690 F136v; 25 Sep 1690 F142v; 19 Dec 1690 F147v; 4 Apr 1691 F151r; 25 Jun 1691 F155v; 5 Oct 1691 F161r; 22 Dec 1691 F163v; 23 Mar 1691/2 F167r; 23 Jun 1692 F172r; 26 Sep 1692 F179v; 19 Dec 1692 F183r; 27 Mar 1693 F185r; 21 Jun 1693 F188v; 28 Sep 1693 F191v; 26 Mar 1694 F201v; 22 Jun 1694 F209r; 28 Sep 1694 F212v; 20 Dec 1694 F216r; 21 Mar 1694/5

F219r; 21 Jun 1695 F226v; 12 Dec 1695 F238r; 26 Mar 1696 F241r; 30 Jun 1696 F243v; 30 Sep 1696 F249v; 22 Dec 1696 F253v; 27 Mar 1697 F259v; 22 Jun 1697 F263r; 28 Sep 1697 F267v; 22 Dec 1697 G2v; 26 Mar 1698 G5r; 22 Jun 1698 G9r; 27 Sep 1698 G13v; 19 Dec 1698 G17v; 27 Mar 1699 G22v; 22 Jun 1699 G25v; 27 Sep 1699 G30v; 19 Dec 1699 G34v; 26 Mar 1700 G38r; 21 Jun 1700 G40v; 26 Sep 1700 G45v; 20 Dec 1700 G54r; 26 Mar 1701 G57v; 19 Jun 1701 G61r; 20 Dec 1701 G66r pension court (no specific mention of poor being paid); 24 Mar 1701/2 G68r; 22 Jun 1702 G76r; 28 Sep 1702 G80v pension court (as above); 18 Dec 1702 G84r pension court (as above); 25 Mar 1703 G86v; 23 Jun 1703 G90v; 28 Sep 1703 G95r; 20 Dec 1703 G100r pension court (as above); 23 Mar 1703/4 G104r pension court (as above); 22 Jun 1704 G108r; 27 Sep 1704 G112r; 20 Dec 1704 G115v; 23 Mar 1704/5 G117r; 22 Jun 1705 G120v; 27 Sep 1705 G123v; 20 Dec 1705 G126r; 21 Mar 1705/6 G129v pension court (as above); 21 Jun 1706 G132v; 27 Sep 1706 G135r; 20 Dec 1706 G137r; 21 Jun 1707 G143r; 18 Dec 1707 G148r; 23 Mar 1707/8 G150r; 22 Jun 1708 G153v; 22 Dec 1708 G159v; 23 Jun 1709 G166r; 28 Sep 1709 G170v; 22 Dec 1709 G173r; 24 Mar 1709/10 G176v; 23 Jun 1710 G180v; 27 Sep 1710 G184r; 20 Dec 1710 G186r; 23 Mar 1710/11 G188v; 23 Jun 1711 G191v; 28 Sep 1711 G194r; 20 Dec 1711 G195v; 24 Mar 1711/2 G198r; 23 Jun 1712 G200v; 26 Sep 1712 G203v; 19 Dec 1712 G205v; 21 Mar 1712/3 G207v; 20 Jun 1713 G210v; 28 Sep 1713 G213v; 22 Dec 1713 G215v; 24 Mar 1713/4 G217r; 23 Jun 1714 G219v; 24 Sep 1714 G221v; 23 Dec 1714 G224r; 22 Mar 1714/5 G226v; 22 Jun 1715 G229v; 27 Sep 1715 G233r pension court (as above); 22 Dec 1715 G235v; 22 Mar 1715/6 G238r; 21 Jun 1716 G240v; 27 Sep 1716 G243v; 20 Dec 1716 G246r; 21 Mar 1716/7 G248r

7 Nov 1681 E138r poor register to be brought up to date with quarterly distributions from 7 October 1673, and to be maintained by Clerk   22 Jun 1687 F85r paid £41 2s 6d in all   20 Dec 1687 F96r paid a total of £40 15s   26 Mar 1688 F100r paid a total of £42   25 Jun 1688 F102r paid a total of £43   1 Oct 1688 F108r paid a total of £43 5s   19 Dec 1688 F111r paid a total of £41 15s   26 Mar 1689 F115v paid £43 12s 6d   1 Jul 1689 F120r paid a total of £43   4 Dec 1693 F195r receive money from Thomas Parkhurst's share, forfeited for comprinting. Paid   27 Sep 1695 F232v all charity money whatsoever bestowed by S.C. to be entered in pension book

See also ST AUSTIN'S, ST FAITH'S, ST MARTIN'S LUDGATE

POOR BOX   3 Dec 1683 F6r John Bellinger gives 20s to Poor Box on account of his failure to dine with Sir William Pritchard, late Lord Mayor   7 Apr 1690 F133r Elizabeth Prosser, widow of Enoch, given 5s from Poor Box   6 Jun 1692 F172r John Harris admitted to freedom of S.C. on paying £1 to Poor Box   3 Oct 1692 F180r Joseph Watts pays 5s fine to the Poor Box for printing catechisms illegally   24 Oct 1693 F193v Roger Clavell freed and cloathed on paying 2 guineas to the Poor Box   6 May 1695 F223r Thomas Parkhurst's fine of £5 for printing psalms goes in Poor Box   2 May 1698 G7v Nathaniel Ponder given 10s from Poor Box   22 Jun 1698 G9r Nathaniel Ponder given 10s from Poor Box   3 Jul 1699 G27r Anne Williams given 10s from Poor Box   3 May 1703 G89r Thomas Hooper paid £5 from Poor Box   2 Aug 1703 G94r John Hunter pays 2 guineas and other usual fees into it for freedom by redemption   4 Sep 1704 G112r 20s paid into it for Archibald Asburne's freedom by redemption   2 Apr 1705 G118r Tace Sowle pays fine into Poor Box for binding an apprentice by foreign indenture   1 Dec 1707 G147r 40s paid to by Samuel Brimlicombe   5 Sep 1709 G170r all persons coming into the Court after the minutes read to forfeit a shilling to the Poor Box   2 Jul 1711 G192v payment of 30s from it to release John Vousden from prison   6 Aug 1711 G193r John Wickins to be given 30s from Poor Box   1 Oct 1711 G194v John Amery to be given 20s from Poor Box   9 Feb 1712/13 G206r 40s from it to be used to pay Abel Swale's rent   20 Jun 1713 G210v upon all pension days, members of the table coming after 10 o'clock to Court to forfeit 1s to Poor Box   3 May 1714 G218v Philip Monckton given 40s from Poor Box   4 Oct 1714 G222v John Hartley given a guinea from Poor Box. Abel Swale to have 10s from Poor Box   26 Mar 1715 G227r members of Table coming to any Court after the sitting of the Court to forfeit one shilling to Poor Box

PORTER   9 Feb 1690/1 F148v on the news of Philip Briggs's death several people are nominated for porter but the choice is adjourned   2 Mar 1690/1 F150r Nicholas Hooper voted porter by a show of hands; John Whitlock and William Hawkins also in competition. Voted that the porter should be disenfranchised from S.C. to render him capable of being a witness   12 Apr 1692 F168v petitions for post brought into Court but the post is decided to be unnecessary   4 Oct 1714 G222r Edward Stiles chosen as porter to English Stock on death of Adam Winch

PORTON, Henry   7 Apr 1701 G58v bound to Nicholas Boddington, 7 years   6 Mar 1703/4 G103v turned over to William Bateman   3 Apr 1704 G106r turned over to William Bateman   2 Aug 1708 G156v freed by Nicholas Boddington   7 May 1716 G240r Thomas Downham is bound to him

PORTUS ICCIUS (by William Somner) – see GIBSON, Edmund

PORVIS, Sir Thomas   30 Jun 1696 F243v counsel retained for S.C. in general, and in particular re. comprinting

POST-BOY   4 Dec 1710 G185v advertisement to be placed in 'Post-Boy' and 'Post-Man' re. Benjamin Harris' illegal publication of almanack

POST-MAN – see preceding entry

POSTERNE, William   5 Aug 1700 G44r of Hertfordshire; bond from S.C. of £400 at 5% interest sealed

POSY OF GODLY PRAYERS – see ROSARY OF GODLY PRAYER

POULTER/POUULTER, Edward   7 Apr 1701 G58v bound to Abel Roper, 7 years   4 Feb 1705/6 G127v turned over from Abel Roper to John Hodges

POWELL, David   2 Mar 1712/13 G207r his son Joshua is bound to William Humphreys, 7 years

POWELL, Ebenezer   5 Apr 1714 G218r son of Joseph; bound to Ebenezer Tracey, 7 years

POWELL, Edmund   12 Nov 1694 F214v servant to Macock and turned over to Benjamin Motte; freed   8 Nov 1703 G97r David Griffith is bound to him   7 Feb 1703/4 G101v Henry Parker is bound to him. William Phelps turned over from him to Francis Leach. Thomas Spencer is turned over to him   5 Mar 1704/5 G116v cloathed. John Woolfe is bound to him. Thomas Spencer is turned over from him to William Downing   7 Mar 1708/9 G162r of Blackfriars; Benjamin Eve is bound to him   5 Feb 1710/11 G188r his apprentice Henry Parker is freed   9 Apr 1711 G189v of Blackfriars, printer; Richard Bell is bound to him   7 May 1711 G190v of Blackfriars, printer; Randoll Letour is bound to him   1 Sep 1712 G203r John Harwell is bound to him   4 Oct 1714 G222v his apprentice John Woolfe is freed   1 Oct 1716 G244r the apprentice Richard Bell is turned over from 'Edward' [i.e. Edmund?] Powell to Thomas Sharpe

POWELL, Edward   2 Oct 1682 E158r Richard Janeway confesses to printing 'The Letter about Abhorrers and Addressers' for Powell, and accuses him of failing to indemnify him. Powell denies that he promised to indemnify Janeway, and claims he employed him to sell the 'Letter about Abhorrers' for an unnamed Welshman   4 Oct 1682 E159r Richard Janeway produces his receipt   2 Aug 1697 F265v John Penn is bound to him   4 Jul 1698 G11r his apprentice James Wiltshire is freed   5 Aug 1700

G45r not permitted to bind an apprentice because he already has one and is not of the Livery. Alleges that he is not in a position to accept the Livery   5 May 1701/2 G59v James Steward turned over to him from William Shrewsbury   7 Aug 1704 G111r his apprentice John Penn is freed

See also POWELL, Edmund

POWELL, George   3 Jun 1689 F119v excused cloathing   2 Apr 1694 F202v William Hurt is bound to him, 7 years

POWELL, Joseph   5 Apr 1714 G218r his son Ebenezer is bound to Ebenezer Tracey, 7 years

POWELL, Joshua   2 Mar 1712/13 G207r son of David; bound to William Humphreys, 7 years   28 Sep 1713 G213v turned over from William Humphreys to William Scott

POWELL, Nicholas   2 Dec 1706 G136v turned over from Thomas Mead to Matthew Jenour

POWELL, Robert, snr – see following entry

POWELL, Robert, jnr   11 Nov 1695 F236r son of Robert Powell snr of Malmsbury, Wiltshire, tailor; bound to John Heptingstall for eight years   3 Jul 1704 G110r freed by John Heptingstall

POWELL, Samuel   16 Jan 1710/11 G186v bound to James Holland, 7 years

POWELL, William   5 Jul 1703 G92r his apprentice Thomas Osborne is freed

POWER, John – see following entry

POWER, William   1 Dec 1712 G205v son of John; bound to Robert Knaplock, 7 years

POWIS, Sir Thomas   19 Mar 1696/7 F257v lawyer; his name is suggested as a possible second opinion on the Paper Act

POWLE, William   25 Jun 1684 F18v trading in Gray's Inn; did not serve all his time with Richard Tonson, his master, and he and Tonson are ordered to appear at the next Court   7 Jul 1684 F20r Tonson owns to having discharged Powle while he still had a year of his time to serve   3 Jun 1689 F119r allowed until next Court to consider cloathing   3 Apr 1704 G105v of Gray's Inn, former servant to Tonson. Clerk to search at Chamberlain's office to discover whether free of the City

PRATT, John   7 Aug 1699 G29r bound to Thomas Dalton, 7 years   5 Feb 1704/5 G115r turned over from Thomas Dalton to Anne Morris

PRAYER BOOK   1 Oct 1688 F107r Vice-Chancellor of Oxford petitions Crown re. S.C. and King's Printers encroaching on printing of Book of Common Prayer   6 Jul 1692 F174r Oxford committee orders Treasurer to provide paper for printing Book of Common Prayer in folio   6 Feb 1692/3 F184r power granted to Oxford committee to buy 1500 folio Books of Common Prayer from King's Printers

PRESENT STATE OF ETHIOPIA   7 Mar 1708/9 G162r Aaron Hills granted right to print 'The History of Aethiopia' [i.e. *The Present State of Ethiopia*], apparently compiled by him

PRESTON, Richard Graham, Viscount   9 Feb 1690/1 F148r Samuel Heyrick allowed to print 'The Trials of the Lord Preston and the late [John] Ashton' in S.C. kitchen

PRICE, [ ]   2 Aug 1697 F265r writes to Master on behalf of the Bishop of Worcester re. Meredith bequest   4 Oct 1714 G222v sheet almanack called 'Dublin's Calendar' produced in Court by him

PRICE, Benjamin   26 Mar 1701 G58r freed by John Pero

PRICE, Charles   6 Sep 1697 F267r freed by John Leake

PRICE, Daniel   2 Mar 1712/13 G207r his son George is bound to Edmund Parker, 7 years

PRICE, Edward   7 Oct 1695 F234r servant to John Redmaine jnr; freed   2 Aug 1703 G94r bound to Edward Place

PRICE, George   2 Mar 1712/13 G207r son of Daniel; bound to Edmund Parker, 7 years

PRICE, John   11 Nov 1700 G46v bound to Henry Lloyd, 7 years   18 Dec 1702 G84r turned over from Henry Lloyd to Thomas Arne

PRICE, Samuel, snr – see following entry

PRICE, Samuel, jnr   22 Dec 1715 G235v son of Samuel; bound to James Roberts, 7 years

PRICE, William   18 Feb 1706/7 G138r bound to William Sayes, 7 years

PRICHARD, Charles   7 Nov 1709 G172r bound to John Walthoe, 7 years

PRICHARD, Susanna   26 Jun 1682 E154r admitted to 5s pension in place of Cassandra Johnson

See also PRITCHARD

PRICKETT, William   6 Jul 1702 G78r Mary Shepperd is bound to him   7 Sep 1702 G80v Martha Haxby is bound to him

PRIMER   7 Jun 1680 E100v signatures of stock primer assigned to various people   22 Dec 1685 F48v petition of John Mayo, Baldwin, John Palmer and Simon Hinch   6 Aug 1688 F104v Widow Flesher made to dispose of her one sheet of the primer to a printer willing to buy the type from her   7 Apr 1690 F132v Thomas Moore's £50 bond to be put in suit against him after his allegedly printing the Old Primer without a licence   24 Oct 1695 F234v William Downing's nut and spindle, taken from him for printing the Oxford primer, are returned on his promising good behaviour

PRINCE, Lydia   2 Aug 1708 G156v bound to Daniel Realy, 7 years

PRINTERS   26 Aug 1684 (W) proceedings against unfree printers to be deferred until the City Charter is renewed; byelaw of the City that no freeman shall be allowed to print except those that are free of S.C.

See also ENGLISH STOCK

PRINTERS, FREE WORKMEN   7 Dec 1685 F47v petition of free workmen printers complaining of unfair competition from aliens, irregularities of farmers of Oxford privileges and unlawful printing houses   22 Dec 1685 F49r committee consulting with Sir Roger L'Estrange re. their petition decide to send Crown an abbreviated version   5 Mar 1687/8 F99r petition complaining of masters binding supernumerary apprentices, &c.   4 Jul 1692 F174r workmen printers' petition read against S.C. employing Robert Elliott at Oxford; referred to Oxford committee   6 Jul 1692 F174r Clerk to make a copy of the free workmen printers' petition for the Treasurer   9 May 1694 F204v they second Henry Pointing's petition to be freed   19 Mar 1696/7 F257v seeking advice on whether or not duty is payable on their paper under the new Act

JOURNEYMEN PRINTERS – see APPRENTICES

PRINTING   17 Aug 1681 E125r byelaw requires printers to put their name or that of a bookseller to each book, pamphlet, portrait or picture published

PRINTING ACT – see ACTS OF PARLIAMENT

PRINTING, ILLEGAL   6 Jun 1681 E112r committee to investigate Bradyll's breach of the byelaw concerning a press in a hole   20 Jun 1681 E113r mandate re. press control from Charles II read   7 Aug 1682 E156r leave granted to Henry Herringman and Robert Scott to prosecute persons printing or selling books not in the Register   10 Jun 1684 F16v printers, booksellers, bookbinders and dealers in books operating outside S.C. to be summoned to next Court under powers granted by the new charter   16 Jun 1684 F17r illegal traders appear in Court and their cases are considered   4 Aug 1684 F22r new clause in loan bonds re. debtors and sureties not having dealings in seditious literature or illegally in Stock books   29 Jan 1684/5 F29r 6 rules re. licensing drawn up by Court and Roger L'Estrange   17 Feb 1684/5 F30v L'Estrange desires Court to list dealers in books not among their freemen, so Crown through Lord Mayor can coerce them   6 May 1685 F33v letter from Lord Sunderland ordering a complete list of bookdealers outside S.C. and a report for Roger L'Estrange   20 May 1685 F35v Lord Mayor to see Master and Wardens re. bookdealers outside S.C. and their entry of or translation to it   22 May 1685 F37v committee re. translations report; dispute over which company should pay fees; dealers to be freed at Guildhall next Tuesday   1 Jun 1685 F38v translation committee to appear next day at the Court of Aldermen   7 Dec 1685 F47v free workmen printers' petition read complaining about foreigners, unlawful printing houses at York and Chester, and irregularities of farmers of Oxford privileges   8 Nov 1686 F66v Dorman Newman to be summoned for printing the calendar of the S.C. almanack   6 Dec 1686 F68v Newman refuses to give satisfaction re. illegal printing of S.C.'s calendar   4 Apr 1687 F80v Salter denies printing music books outside S.C. and explains that his ex-master forced him to buy them   30 Jun 1688 F102v Henry Hills re-elected Master specifically to continue 'the good Work of regulating Printing'   4 Aug 1690 F141r Wilkins asks pardon for printing 'A Memorial Extracted out of the Modest Enquiry' without licence; to show at the next court his warrant to print in Wallis' absence   1 Sep 1690 F142r Clerk to make an alphabetical list of Stock books to make checking on comprinting easier   6 Apr 1691 F152v Joshua Coniers, John Back and Thomas James summoned re. the two latter printing a copy belonging to the former   6 Jun 1692 F171v private press discovered in house of Thomas Topham and William Anderson in Shoreditch; landlord to be prosecuted   5 Mar 1693/4 F200v Court to negotiate with Awnsham Churchill re. damasked paper of 'Doleman [i.e. Robert Persons et al.] concerning the English Succession'   3 Dec 1694 F215v Court refers Ichabod Dawkes's complaint about a press at Chester, possibly producing seditious pamphlets, to a Secretary of State   24 Oct 1695 F234v William Downing's nut and spindle taken from him for printing the Oxford primer are returned on his promising good behaviour   2 Mar 1695/6 F239v Abel Swale is discovered to be printing the Metamorphoses for his own use, but submits to fining; committee to consider   6 Apr 1696 F241v Matthew Wootton complains that William Thackery has printed or appropriated part of [Emmanuel Ford's] 'Parismus'; consideration deferred   8 Jun 1696 F243r committee appointed to consult about proceeding against comprinters   30 Jun 1696 F243v Attorney General, Solicitor General and Sir Thomas Porvis to be retained for S.C. in general and in particular re. comprinting   6 Jul 1696 F246v committee augmented   3 Aug 1696 F246r Master tells Court he and Wardens have been 'at pains' over comprinting   5 Oct 1696 F250v solicitor to take out attachments against all those who have not answered S.C.'s comprinting bill   17 Oct 1696 F251r Robert Stephens discovers a press in Distaff Lane printing almanacks for 1697   2 Aug 1697 F265r committee to treat with Mumford re. his printing psalms   6 Sep 1697 F267r committees re. comprinting to be revived   16 Oct 1697 F269r Charles Browne and William Only to be prosecuted in the Court of Exchequer for printing and binding counterfeit books and almanacks   28 Oct 1697 F267r Master outlines measures to discourage counterfeit almanacks   9 Sep 1700 G44v committee to consider letter proposing an agreement to be signed by members of S.C. to prevent piracy and printing of particular persons' copies   7 Jul 1701 G62r committee to consider illegal printing of S.C.'s copies   25 Jul 1701 G62v meeting of committee to consider illegal printing of S.C.'s psalms   1 Aug 1709 G169v Master and Wardens to go into printing houses suspected of printing S.C.'s copies and almanacks

See also ALMANACKS, CATECHISMS, CHESTER, ENGLISH STOCK: STOCK BOOKS, PSALMS, SEDITIOUS PRINTING, YORK

PRINTING, OVERSEAS – see CUSTOMS HOUSE, PSALMS

PRINTING, SEDITIOUS   6 Nov 1682 E159v committee appointed to inquire into anti-Government pamphlets and consider methods of suppression   4 Dec 1682 E160v committee for suppressing scandalous pamphlets records new byelaw to that effect; Common Hall called for on 6 Dec to confirm it   6 Dec 1682 E161v byelaw against seditious literature copied out   3 Mar 1683/4 F9v King Charles II's letter re. electing certain S.C. members to the Court of Assistants to assist in stamping out seditious printing. Court agree to letter and William Cooper, Christopher Wilkinson and William Shrewsbury fine for Renter Warden so they are eligible   4 Aug 1684 F22r persons taking loans on bond from S.C. not to print or otherwise be involved in treasonable, seditious or scandalous books and pamphlets   1 Sep 1684 F23r the French booksellers John Boileau, Barnardi, Bernard and Bureau are reported for dealing in scandalous books   20 Dec 1684 F27v Crown expresses desire to have libels suppressed via Roger L'Estrange   3 Nov 1685 (W) address to all Mayors, Sheriffs &c. to assist S.C. in searching out seditious printing   9 Mar 1695/6 F240r House of Lords orders S.C. to search for a 1695 Jacobite pamphlet

See also MONMOUTH ROUTED, RAREE-SHOW

PRITCHARD, Sir William   5 Feb 1682/3 E163r S.C. to dine as a corporation with Pritchard, the present Lord Mayor   3 Dec 1683 F6r John Bellinger gives 20s to Poor Box on account of his failure to dine with Sir William Pritchard, late Lord Mayor

See also PRICHARD

PROCTER, [   ]   3 May 1686 F55v to be paid £60 due to him from English Stock

PROCTOR, [   ]   1 Apr 1697 F263v to speak to the cardmakers about the money needed for a Paper Act test case

PROGNOSTICATIONS   22 Aug 1685 F43r Master to head deputation to persuade Archbishop of Canterbury to license prognostications

PROPER, Elizabeth   23 Dec 1714 G224r elected to Elizabeth Andrews's pension

PROPRIETORS OF LIGHTS   8 Jun 1691 F154v allowed at Master's request to meet in Court room twice a week

PROSODIA – see GRAMMAR

PROSSER, Enoch – see following entry

PROSSER, Elizabeth   7 Apr 1690 F133r widow of Enoch; given 5s out of Poor Box

PROTESTANT RESOLUTION (by William Sherlock)   6 Apr 1685 F32v assigned by Robert Horne to Abel Swale

PROTESTANT'S TUTOR   7 Sep 1685 F44r Benjamin Harris to be summoned re. printing this   5 Oct 1685 F45r Benjamin Harris assures Court he has printed no copies of this since 1682

PROTEUS REDIVIVUS – see ART OF WHEEDLING

PROTHER, [   ]   5 Dec 1692 F182v stationer; granted the £200 due to him for paper sold to S.C.

PRYOR, Thomas 1 Sep 1707 G145r bound to John Marshall, 7 years

PSALMS 7 Jun 1680 E100v signatures of Stock 12mo psalms and Stock psalter assigned to various people 5 Feb 1682/3 E163v impression of psalter and primer to be printed with the Roman letter as well as the English 1 Sep 1684 F23v John Bellinger tells Court that Peter Parker and Thomas Guy are printing 25,000 books of psalms in Oxford 11 Oct 1684 F25r at meeting of Parker and Guy committee they request to make the same agreement with S.C. as King's Printers have for printing psalms 21 Jul 1685 F41r S.C. voted not to sue Oxford re. printing S.C.'s psalms 3 Aug 1685 F42r Godfrey Head tells Court that Parker and Guy's order re. type for psalms has been revoked 1 Aug 1687 F87r Thomas Mathew licensed to print 2000 metrical psalms with music under certain itemised conditions 5 Sep 1687 F88r owner of prohibited psalms printed overseas, seized by Master and Wardens at the Customs House, to be prosecuted 6 Aug 1688 F104v Widow Flesher is made to dispose of 2 sheets of the psalter to a printer willing to buy the type from her 1 Oct 1688 F107r Vice-Chancellor of Oxford petitions Crown re. S.C. and King's Printers encroaching on University printing of singing psalms 3 Mar 1689/90 F131r Thomas Mathew asks S.C. to relieve him of 1600 out of an edition of 2000 metrical psalms with musical notes 'at the rate they stand him in for paper & printing' 7 Jul 1690 F139r Mathew's request again turned down, but Court advises him to ask Everingham his printer to get them subscribed for him 6 Apr 1691 F152r committee chosen to negotiate with Parker and Guy re. sale of consignments of psalms 6 Nov 1693 F194v Thomas Parkhurst and James Astwood are alleged to have printed 1000 sheets of metrical psalms 4 Dec 1693 F195r Thomas Parkhurst forfeits share for comprinting on metrical psalms and previously on Scotch psalms with Dorman Newman 5 Mar 1693/4 F200v Henry Playford fined £5 for printing metrical psalms with music despite his plea that he is indirectly helping Stock sales 22 Jun 1694 F209r Henry Playford pays £10 for the privilege of printing 1000 of part of the Psalms of David in metre in the same volume as before 24 Oct 1694 F214r Master and Wardens to decide whether to purchase for £100 a moiety of a new metrical version of the psalms 6 May 1695 F223r Thomas Parkhurst, re. report of 3 December 1693, is fined £5 for printing part of the psalms 1 Jul 1695 F227r Thomas Parkhurst is refused permission to continue printing psalms he was fined for beginning 2 Nov 1696 F252r Henry Playford allowed to print 1500 psalms with music on payment of £15 but to pay 10s to the Poor Box as he has already begun 2 Aug 1697 F265r committee to treat with Mumford re. his printing psalms 6 Sep 1697 F267r leave given to Mumford to print a version of the psalms in the name of the S.C., paying a small acknowledgement 7 Feb 1697/8 G3v Samuel Sprint granted permission for himself and Playford to print 1 Aug 1698 G13r Samuel Sprint given leave to print an impression of 2 Jun 1701 G60v S.C.'s psalms printed by Benjamin Motte without permission using Kebell White's name 7 Jul 1701 G62r S.C.'s psalms and books printed by Motte without permission. Committee to look into precedents of action taken against those printing 1 Jun 1702 G71r 'The Child's Psalter' and 'A Psalter for Children', copyright of S.C., printed without permission 2 Nov 1702 G82v Samuel Sprint informs Court that Playford has paid S.C. for one impression of psalms printed for him by Heptingstall without leave of the Court and is willing to pay for the other 19 Feb 1705/6 G128r counterfeit psalters and psalms sold by James Drinkell without S.C.'s permission 4 Mar 1705/6 G128v counterfeit psalms sold by Drinkell and William Palmer 1 Apr 1706 G130v committee to consider matter of counterfeit psalters and '[First Book for Children, or the] Complete Schoolmistress' sold to Gilbert Beauchamp at Bristol fair 6 May 1706 G131v affidavit from Jackson declaring he has no counterfeit psalters 6 Oct 1707 G145v Charles Browne, Elizabeth Blair, Button and his mother and Gwillam to be prosecuted for printing and selling counterfeit psalms and almanacks   3 Oct 1709 G171r Capt. John Williams to have an impression of Psalms in folio at 14d per book   1 Sep 1712 G203r John Baskett's proposed terms for printing at Oxford to be considered by committee   6 Oct 1712 G204r folio and quarto; amounts paid by John Baskett to English Stock in exchange for privilege to print

— BARTON'S PSALMS (by William Barton)   6 Jun 1681 E113r articles between S.C. and Edward Barton re. psalms to be sealed   25 Sep 1690 F143r committee to treat with Thomas Parkhurst, Smith and Benjamin Motte re. printing of Lucius Florus, Justin and Barton's Psalms   6 Oct 1690 F143v committee required to reach agreement re. Barton's Psalms and report   7 Sep 1696 F248v deed whereby William Barton or heirs are to be paid £10 if his version of the psalms has sold well is inquired into   5 Oct 1696 F250v Barton to be paid £10 for metrical psalms

— PATRICK'S PSALMS   5 Oct 1691 F161v John Patrick's metrical translation is to be printed by Luke Meredith; matter referred to Cambridge committee   7 Dec 1691 F163r Luke Meredith fined 2d per book for 2 impressions of 1500 and 2000 respectively of Dr Patrick's psalms   12 Apr 1692 F168v Luke Meredith begs to be excused the 2d fine per book for printing 3500 of Dr Patrick's psalms   7 Jun 1714 G219v printed by Awnsham Churchill

— PEARL PSALMS   28 Mar 1680 E99r contract agreed with King's Printers re. printing them

— SELECT PSALMS   7 Mar 1708/9 G162r printed by John Heptingstall without S.C.'s leave   2 May 1709 G164v printed by Mrs Baldwin without S.C.'s leave

— TATE AND BRADY (NEW VERSION OF DAVID'S PSALMS)   6 May 1698 G7v articles of agreement between Nahum Tate, Nicholas Brady and the Master and Wardens relating to them read and sealed   4 Dec 1699 G34r S.C. decides not to accept Tate's offer of shares in the copy   5 Feb 1699/1700 G35r Tate and Brady granted rights to print   6 May 1700 G39r Court has not accepted Tate's offer of shares   19 Jul 1700 G43r Tate offers his remaining shares to S.C.; accounts to be drawn up to assist S.C. in its decision   5 Aug 1700 G44r S.C. decides not to purchase Tate's share   7 Apr 1701 G58r Tate to be given copy of the orders of Court relating to   4 Aug 1701 G63r Tate's proposal to sell S.C. his remaining shares in   2 Aug 1703 G93v complaint that James Rawlins is illegally printing   8 Nov 1703 G97r Tate's proposal to sell his interest in to S.C.   4 Sep 1704 G111v Brady requesting S.C. to buy shares in   4 Dec 1704 G113v profit on them paid to Brady   5 Feb 1704/5 G114v settlement of Benjamin Tooke's affairs in relation to left to Master, Wardens and Stock-keepers   7 May 1705 G119v accounts   28 May 1706 G131v Brady's unauthorised printing of them   4 Nov 1706 G135v Tate's proposal to sell his third part to S.C.   3 Mar 1706/7 G139r answer to Tate's request for S.C. to purchase his whole property in the Psalms and Chauntry's 20 shares in them to be deferred until next Court day   26 Mar 1707 G140r Court rejects proposal from Chauntry to buy his 20 shares in   7 Mar 1708/9 G161v Thomas Harrison's request to print at Cambridge refused   23 Jun 1709 G166r Thomas Harrison granted permission to print 1000   5 Dec 1709 G172r Master informs S.C. that they were printed privately   20 Dec 1711 G196r Tate to prosecute Baker for printing   2 May 1715 G228v Master, Wardens and Stock-keepers to consider Tate's request to borrow £25 against his share of the Psalms

PULLER, [   ], snr   3 Dec 1705 G125v desires that his son be excused for six months from taking the cloathing

PULLER, [   ], jnr   3 Dec 1705 G125v excused cloathing for six months at the request of his father   6 May 1706 G131r to be summoned to take cloathing next Court day

PULLER, Mrs 5 Sep 1698 G14r to have 6% interest on £500 bond from S.C. 6 Jul 1700 G43r to receive money due from the S.C. which she has requested 19 Jul 1700 G43r clerk to write to her re. payment 5 Aug 1700 G44r agrees to receive her money when the Court pays the same

PULLEYNE, James 4 Apr 1709 G164r cloathed 7 Dec 1713 G215r owing £5 of Livery fine

PULLEYNE, Octavian 19 Dec 1698 G17v cloathed

PUMP 6 Dec 1680 E105v George Sawbridge, Treasurer and S.C. workmen to view ground re. making a pump 30 Sep 1684 F24r and well to be dug in Stationers' Court near Awnsham Churchill's back door for the inhabitants of Ave Maria Lane and Stationers' rents

PUNCHARD, John – see following entry

PUNCHARD, Thomas 6 May 1717 G250v son of John; bound to Henry Morley, 7 years

PUREFOY, George 3 Mar 1689/90 F130v the bond in which he is involved for £50 due to S.C. is to be delivered into legal hands because of Arthur Jones not paying

PURSER, John 3 Apr 1710 G178v bound to William Redmaine, 7 years

PYKE, Francis 4 Sep 1699 G30v bound to Jasper Roberts 1 Jun 1702 G71v turned over to Robert Tooke 4 Nov 1706 G136r freed by Roberts

QUAKERS 3 Aug 1685 F42r Godfrey Head tells Court that a Quaker has ordered him to cast type to be sent to Pennsylvania 3 Nov 1690 F146r as a Quaker, Joseph Usquhart refuses to take oath of freedom; given until next Court to consider

QUARLES, Francis 11 Apr 1681 E109v a moiety of his 'Emblems' assigned by (Francis?) Egglesfeild to Samuel Mearne 7 Apr 1690 F133r his 'Argalus and Parthenia' assigned by Thomas Burdikin, executor of the late Thomas Rookes, to William Freeman

QUARTERAGE 6 Mar 1698/9 G22r Renter Wardens to collect arrears of 3 Jun 1700 G40r Clerk to make out note of arrears of 21 Jun 1700 G40v members who refuse to pay arrears to be summoned to Court of Conscience 2 Jun 1701 G60v place to be made in lobby for Renter Wardens to collect 12 Jun 1704 G107r names of those with quarterage arrears to be sought by Clerk and members to be summoned to appear before Court of Conscience 20 Apr 1705 G119r Clerk attempting to recover quarterage book from Renter Wardens 9 Apr 1711 G189v Renter Wardens to have 2 shillings in the pound of quarterage collected abroad instead of expenses for doing so 5 Apr 1714 G218r committee to consider method for recovering arrears

QUARTERN BOOKS 6 Mar 1698/9 G22r motion by Richard Chiswell re. double quartern books that usual allowance is too great 14 Jun 1711 G191v quartern books in all almanacks to be allowed as formerly

QUEEN – see CROWN

QUEVEDO, Francisco de 3 Jul 1693 F189v Roger L'Estrange's translation of de Quevedo's 'Visions' assigned by Henry Herringman to John Hindmarsh and Richard Sare

QUILT, George 1 Aug 1687 F86v his wife pays Under Warden £20 of a £50 loan due from the late John Marlow for whom Quilt was a surety

QUILT, Mrs – see preceding entry

QUINNEY, John 3 Nov 1701 G65r John Williams is bound to him

QUINTUS CURTIUS 18 Mar 1686/7 F79v among books in catalogue annexed to Oxford agreement

QUINTUS HORATIUS FLACCUS – see HORACE

QUIRKE, Thomas   4 Aug 1707 G144v bound to Brabazon Aylmer, 7 years

QUO WARRANTO   26 Mar 1684 F11v subpoena served on S.C.   27 Mar 1684 F12v petition against   1 Oct 1688 F107r request to Crown that *quo warranto* process of 23 September (order in W) might be withdrawn and S.C. settle difference with Oxford printers directly   2 Jun 1690 F135v reversal of this

See also CROWN

RADFORD, John   4 May 1702 G71r bound to Benjamin Mynds, 7 years

RADFORD, Robert – see following entry

RADFORD, William   6 May 1695 F223v son of Robert Radford; bound to his father for eight years

RAIKES, Robert   1 Oct 1705 G124r bound to John Barber, 7 years   1 Dec 1712 G205v freed by John Barber

RAINBOW COFFEE HOUSE   2 Jul 1694 F210v appointed as a meeting-place to discuss Sedgwick's title to £80 awarded him in a statute of bankruptcy against Adiel Mill

RAINES, Aaron   7 Aug 1704 G111r freed by Joseph Ray

RAINSFORD, Cornelius   7 Aug 1704 G111r bound to Robert Whitledge, 8 years   9 Feb 1712/13 G206v freed by Robert Whitledge   7 Feb 1714/15 G225r Joseph Jeffryes is bound to him   2 May 1715 G228v Dickinson Sharp turned over to him from Robert Whitledge

RAINSFORD, Robert   8 Nov 1686 F67r competes unsuccessfully to be bargemaster's mate

RALEIGH, Sir Walter   26 Mar 1683 E167v 'The Trial and Arraignment of Sir Walter Raleigh' [i.e. John Shirley's *Life*, which includes the trial and arraignment?] assigned to G. [George?] Dawes by Benjamin Sherley

RANCE, James/John   7 Jul 1701 G62r to be bound to Lewis Thomas although both at Oxford; bound (under the name of John) to Lewis Thomas, 7 years

RANCE, John – see preceding entry

RANDALL, Elizabeth   23 Jun 1692 F172r deceased; Richard Butler is admitted to her 20s share   3 Feb 1695/6 F239r Thomas Harding, her ex-apprentice, is freed

RANDALL, James   3 Jul 1686 F58r elected to a 20s pension

RANDALL, John (I)   4 Jun 1694 F208r servant to Benjamin Johnson; freed

RANDALL, John (II)   2 Mar 1701/2 G67v freed by Isaac Frith

RANDALL/RANDELL/RANDOLL, Richard   1 Feb 1691/2 F165r of Newcastle upon Tyne; cloathed   12 Apr 1692 F168v of Newcastle upon Tyne; writes asking to be excused cloathing on grounds of poverty; Court to investigate and John Lilly to delay suit   5 Feb 1699/1700 G35r of Newcastle; elected to cloathing   8 Apr 1700 G38v Clerk to write and acquaint him that the Court does not accept his excuse for not accepting the cloathing   6 May 1700 G39r of Newcastle; Court to proceed against him to accept cloathing unless he makes an affidavit before the Mayor of that place that he is not worth £500   3 Jun 1700 G40r of Newcastle; Clerk to inform him that the Court does not dispose of any share or stock to anyone who is not on the Livery   9 Sep 1700 G44v of Newcastle; summoned to appear at the S.C.'s suit for his refusal of the Livery   2 Jun 1701 G60v of Newcastle; to be proceeded against for non-payment of his Livery fine   26 Jun 1702 G77r Clerk to enter proceedings and judgement of suit against him in Court Book   6 Jul 1702 G77r of Newcastle; verdict against him for non-payment of

Livery fine to be entered into Court Book by Lilly (G72r-G75r). Request that he may be remitted part of costs granted. To pay £50 only   26 Mar 1706 G130r of Newcastle; to be sent for on next occasion of choosing Renter Wardens   26 Mar 1712 G198v elected First Renter Warden   7 Apr 1712 G198v excused office of First Renter Warden for a year   26 Mar 1715 G227r of Newcastle upon Tyne; elected Assistant Renter Warden. Clerk to inform him of this   4 Apr 1715 G227v of Newcastle; Clerk to write to him again requesting an answer   2 May 1715 G228r of Newcastle; excused office of Renter Warden for a year

RANDOLL, John (I)   3 Aug 1702 G79v James Taylor is bound to him   5 Mar 1704/5 G116v cloathed   7 Nov 1709 G172r his apprentice James Taylor is freed   26 Mar 1713 G208r excused from office of First Renter Warden for a further year   2 May 1715 G228v Miles Townsend turned over to him from John Fletcher

RANDOLL, John (II)   1 Sep 1701 G64r bound to Samuel Cooke, 7 years   6 Nov 1704 G113r turned over to Nathaniel Dancer   3 Nov 1712 G205r freed by Nathaniel Dancer

See also RANDALL

RANDS/RAND, [ ]   3 Mar 1683/4 F10v Court reject Samuel Hoyle's request to mort-gage his £80 share to Rands to satisfy debt to Rands's wife, formerly Widow Kendall (sic), as Rands is not a S.C. member   7 Jun 1686 F57r complains that his wife, formerly Widow Kendon, has not been paid by Samuel Hoyle for her £80 share; Court was to have disposed of it for cash but disposal deferred on receipt of counsel's opinion   1 Mar 1687/8 F98r husband of Widow Kendon; demands refund and interest for his wife's £80 share which the Court pays, deducting 6 months' interest   15 Jun 1688 F102r 'Sergeant at Mace'; his wife's £80 share is the cause of a bill of complaint drawn up by Samuel Hoyle

RANDS, Mrs – see KENDON/KENDALL, Alice

RANEW, Nathaniel   26 Mar 1681 E108r elected First Renter Warden   5 Dec 1681 E139r partner of Dorman Newman, who did not provide a dinner   13 Oct 1687 F91v sworn in as Assistant   5 Dec 1687 F94v together with Edward Brewster, complains about Thomas Bassett and Henry Harefinch. Elected to Henry Mortlock's £40 share. Elected to Thomas Parkhurst's £80 share   9 Jan 1687/8 F97r Bassett to be summoned to answer Brewster's and Ranew's complaint   5 Mar 1687/8 F99r he and Brewster allowed to sue Bassett for an alleged moiety of the 'Turkish History' which Bassett has recently reprinted   4 Feb 1688/9 F112v re-elected Assistant   6 May 1689 F117r ranked twelfth of Assistants never elected as Master or Warden. He and Dorman Newman ordered to pay the charge of £24 not paid when they were Renter Wardens   1 Jul 1689 F120v to pay Renter Warden's charges before next Court or be fined for disobedience   5 Aug 1689 F122r he and Dorman Newman given until next Court to prepare an account of their charges as Renter Wardens   7 Oct 1689 F124r submits with Newman to Court's decision, 'their Renter Warden's dinners being insufficient'   5 Jun 1690 F135v re-elected Assistant   3 Aug 1691 F158v elected to the late George Calvert's £160 share   1 Mar 1692/3 F184v elected Stock-keeper for Assistants with Henry Mortlock   13 Mar 1692/3 F184v augments committee of 1 March 1692 considering ways to raise money for dividends and carry on Oxford printing   3 Apr 1693 F185v as a co-proprietor of the English Josephus, complains that Roger L'Estrange's new translation will affect his sales   13 Apr 1713 G208v deceased; his £160 share disposed of to Thomas Simpson

RANSHAW, Francis, snr – see following entry

RANSHAW, Francis, jnr   3 May 1714 G219r son of Francis; bound to Daniel Browne, 7 years

RAPER, Philip   7 Apr 1707 G141r bound to Margaret Wild, 7 years

RAPIER, [   ]   20 Dec 1693 F197r churchwarden of St Martin's Ludgate; engages with S.C. over drainage dispute

RAREE-SHOW (attr. Stephen College)   11 Apr 1681 E110r Astwood clears Benjamin Harris of asking for this to be printed

RAVEN, Joseph   5 Feb 1693/4 F198v cloathed   6 Aug 1694 F211v John Briggs is bound to him   8 Apr 1700 G39r Richard Chroskill is bound to him   7 Aug 1704 G110v to print almanack. Copperplate to be delivered to Joseph Collyer by Sturt

RAVEN'S ALMANACK – see ALMANACKS

RAW, Judith   7 Apr 1707 G140v deceased; her £160 share disposed of to Capt. Edward Darrell

RAW, Thomas   5 Feb 1682/3 E163v granted £50 of Tyler's bequest   1 Mar 1682/3 E164r £50 loan from Tyler's bequest repealed on account of misbehaviour in several points   7 Jan 1683/4 F8r competes unsuccessfully for Henry Herringman's £160 share   2 Jun 1684 F16r elected to Thomas Cotterell's £160 share   1 Mar 1687/8 F97v expelled from Livery by order of Lord Mayor

RAWLEIGH – see RALEIGH, Sir Walter

RAWLINGS, William   2 May 1681 E111r fined for Renter Warden

See also RAWLINS, William

RAWLINS, Bartholomew   6 Jun 1709 G165v bound to John Lenthall, 7 years

RAWLINS, Elizabeth   8 Aug 1715 G232r her apprentice Benjamin Odell is freed

RAWLINS, James   2 Jul 1694 F210v Fulke Cleaver jnr is bound to him   12 Nov 1694 F214v cloathed   7 Feb 1698/9 G20v Daniel Sell is bound to him   6 Jul 1702 G78r William Wilkins is bound to him   2 Nov 1702 G83r Thomas Hinton is bound to him   2 Aug 1703 G93v answers complaint that he is illegally printing an impression of Tate and Brady's Psalms. His apprentice John Pickard is freed   8 May 1704 G106v John Henson is bound to him   4 Aug 1707 G144v William Wilkins turned over from him to John Humphreys   26 Mar 1708 G150v fined for First Renter Warden   28 Sep 1709 G170v summoned to attend next Court   4 Feb 1711 G196v Richard Ryley, son of Daniel, is bound to him   7 Apr 1712 G199r competes unsuccessfully for John Lawrence's £80 share   1 Sep 1712 G203r his apprentice John Henson is freed   1 Dec 1712 G205v Benjamin Odell turned over to him   3 May 1714 G219r George Newbolt is bound to him   6 Feb 1715/16 G236r deceased; George Newbolt is turned over from him to James Roberts

RAWLINS, John   12 Apr 1708 G152r bound to Thomas Bradyll, 7 years

RAWLINS, William   30 Sep 1684 F24r surrenders £40 share; his request (letter in W) that it go to John Place is granted   13 Oct 1687 F91v sworn in as Assistant   5 Dec 1687 F96r elected into the late George Wells's £80 share   5 Mar 1687/8 F99r to lend Master, Henry Hills, £300 on the transfer of his £320 share, to pay Katherine Sawbridge to whom it is mortgaged   2 Apr 1688 F100r chosen to audit Renter Wardens' accounts with John Macock   30 Jun 1688 F103r among those chosen to audit Renter Wardens' accounts   4 Feb 1688/9 F112v re-elected Assistant   26 Mar 1689 F116r chosen to audit Renter Wardens' accounts with Roger Norton   6 May 1689 F116v ranked sixth of Assistants never elected as Master or Warden   2 Dec 1689 F127v elected to Robert Scott's £160 share   5 May 1690 F135r chosen to audit Renter Wardens' accounts with Thomas Bassett   5 Jun 1690 F135v re-elected Assistant   5 Jul 1690 F138r among those chosen to audit Warden's accounts   6 Apr 1691 F152v Master to supervise Clerk drawing up a mortgage of Thomas Bassett's £320 share to Rawlins   4

Jul 1692 F173v chosen to audit Renter Wardens' accounts   26 Mar 1694 F201v elected
Stock-keeper at special meeting   30 Jun 1694 F209v elected Under Warden but fines
on account of ill-health and business taking him out of town frequently   2 Jul 1694
F210r elected Stock-keeper as replacement for John Simms, now Master. Among those
chosen to audit Warden's accounts   20 Dec 1694 F216r Court agrees that he should
receive Thomas Bassett's next dividend on his £320 share as it is mortgaged to him   1
Mar 1694/5 F217v elected Stock-keeper for Assistants with Charles Harper   8 Apr
1695 F220r appointed auditor for Renter Wardens' accounts with Edward Brewster   6
Jul 1695 F229r elected Upper Warden   7 Oct 1695 F233v Capt. William Phillipps is
elected Stock-keeper in his place now he is Upper Warden   3 Feb 1695/6 F238v Henry
Mortlock is appointed to audit Warden's accounts in his stead   4 Jul 1696 F245r elected
Upper Warden and fined   6 Jul 1696 F245v added to comprinting committee. Elected
into Stock-keeper's place left vacant by the election of Henry Mortlock as Master; sworn
in   3 Aug 1696 F248r Thomas Bassett, now bankrupt, is found to have had his stock
mortgaged to Rawlins for a long time; deferred as Rawlins is in the country   7 Sep 1696
F248v was assigned Bassett's share as surety for £250 plus interest; shows Court
accounts; Court orders Treasurer to check dividends for Commissioner of Bankruptcy   30 Sep 1696 F249v occupies warehouse once used by Mrs Royston; she demands
satisfaction for boards, &c., left behind   5 Oct 1696 (W) asked to ensure that minutes
which Clerk has neglected to enter are entered by next Court day   1 Feb 1696/7 F254v
moves for committee to be appointed inquiring what rights S.C. has to copies and at
what rates they were purchased   1 Mar 1696/7 F255r elected Stock-keeper for Assistants with Capt. William Phillipps   3 Jul 1697 F263v competes unsuccessfully for
Master   8 Nov 1697 G1r to be added to committee to meet the Vice-Chancellor of
Oxford to settle details of treaty between University and S.C.   13 Apr 1698 G6r added
to the Oxford committee. Request that Thomas Bassett's share mortgaged to him for
£250 be disposed of, as neither interest nor the capital sum has been paid   2 Jul 1698
G10r auditor of Master and Wardens' accounts   1 Aug 1698 G13r excused from
auditing Master and Wardens' accounts because out of town   20 Oct 1699 G32r Francis
Perkins is bound to him   5 Aug 1700 G44r Nicholas Smith is bound to him   4 Jul
1702 G76v fined for Master   18 Dec 1702 G84r elected to Margaret Royston's £320
share. His £160 share disposed of to Samuel Sprint. Pays fine of 5 guineas for Master to
Warden Robert Andrews   3 Jul 1703 G91r elected Master   5 Jul 1703 G91v letter
from him concerning serving as Master   15 Jul 1703 G93r excused from office of
Master as he has fined the previous year   6 Dec 1703 G99r loan from him of £250 on
assignment of Thomas Bassett's Assistant's share repaid   2 Mar 1703/4 G103r to take
advice of Counsel re. John Bradford's plea   5 Aug 1706 G133v remainder of his fine
for Master paid by Charles Harper   5 May 1707 G141v deceased; his Assistant's share
disposed of to Richard Chiswell   4 Aug 1707 G144v gift of silver flagon to S.C.

RAWSON, Thomas   12 Sep 1692 F179r summoned to show why he should not be
cloathed   7 Nov 1692 F181v elected into Livery and summoned   5 Dec 1692 F183r
cloathed   26 Mar 1706 G130r servant of Henry Nye, scrivener; question as to his status

RAY, [   ]   2 Aug 1680 E102v to have 10s for gloves on presenting plate to S.C.

RAY, Joseph   3 Feb 1700/1 G55v of Ireland; elected to Mrs North's £80 share.
Cloathed. Not to be elected Renter Warden nor be at any further charge of offices in the
S.C. during abode in Ireland   7 Aug 1704 G111r his apprentice Aaron Raines is freed

RAYMENT, James   1 Jun 1702 G71v his apprentice William Taylor is freed

RAYMENT, Jane   7 May 1694 F204r William Taylor is bound to her   3 Jun 1700
G40v Thomas James is bound to her   4 Feb 1705/6 G127v Thomas James is turned
over from her to Owen Lloyd

RAYMENT, William   3 Feb 1695/6 F239r James Goodwin, his apprentice, is freed

RAYNARD, John   3 Nov 1690 (W) was refused permission to be bound to Robert Lamburne until it appeared Lamburne was not a printer, bookseller or bookbinder   6 Sep 1708 G157v bound to Richard Bassill, 7 years   6 May 1717 G250v freed by Richard Bassill

RAYNOLDS, Daniel   7 Aug 1704 G111r freed by John Richardson

RAYNSFORD, Robert   26 Mar 1686 F54r elected waterman   4 Apr 1687 F81v elected waterman

REA, [John]   6 Feb 1681/2 E144r his 'Flora: Seu de Florum Cultura' assigned by Richard Marriott to Robert Boulter

READ, Alexander   1 Aug 1681 E117v his 'Anatomy' assigned to Thomas Flesher by Benjamin Thrale   7 Dec 1685 F48r 'Read's Works: or a Treatise of Chirurgery to be Improved by Dr Richard Browne' [i.e. *Chirurgorum Comes: Or the Whole Practice of Chirurgery?*], assigned by Thomas Flesher to Edward Jones

READ, Emmanuel   2 Oct 1699 G31v bound to William Hawes

READ, George   6 Nov 1699 G33r cloathed   4 Dec 1699 G34r Christopher Hardie is bound to him   6 Nov 1704 G113r John Cox is bound to him   26 Mar 1708 G150v elected First Renter Warden   12 Apr 1708 G151v fined for Assistant Renter Warden   3 May 1708 G152v banker; William Mayer is bound to him   4 Feb 1711/12 G196v his apprentice John Cox is freed

READ, Henry   1 Dec 1707 G147v bound to Charles Walkden, 7 years

READ, James   7 May 1694 F203v son of Robert Read of St Andrew's Holborn, labourer; bound to Jeremiah Wilkins   7 Jul 1701 G62r freed by Jeremiah Wilkins   4 Dec 1704 F114r Francis Thorne is bound to him   1 Sep 1707 G145r printer; John Dutton is bound to him   5 Sep 1709 G170r printer; cloathed. William Persivell is bound to him   4 Jun 1711 G191r of Whitefriars, printer; Richard Mathard is bound to him   4 Jul 1715 G231r John Benson turned over to him from William Heathcott   5 Sep 1715 G232v John Dutton is freed by him   5 Dec 1715 G235v William Read is bound to him   26 Mar 1717 G248v fined for Assistant Renter Warden

READ, John   2 Mar 1701/2 G67v bound to Samuel Drury, 7 years   6 Mar 1703/4 G103v turned over to Thomas Shelmerdine   7 Mar 1708/9 G162r freed by Thomas Shelmerdine

READ, Robert   7 May 1694 F203v of St Andrew's Holborn, labourer; his son James is bound to Jeremiah Wilkins

READ, William, snr – see following entry

READ, William, jnr   5 Dec 1715 G235v son of William; bound to James Read, 7 years

READING, Francis   3 Nov 1707 G146v bound to Margaret Bennett, 7 years   4 Jul 1709 G167v turned over from Margaret Bennett to Thomas Howlatt

REALY, Daniel   2 Aug 1708 G156v printer; Lydia Prince is bound to him

REASON, William   3 Aug 1702 G79v bound to John Meakins, 7 years   7 Nov 1709 G172r freed by John Meakins   13 Jun 1715 G229v Richard Goulston is bound to him

RECORD, [Robert]   15 Apr 1692 F170r his 'Arithmetic' is assigned, with its appendix by John Howkins, to William Freeman by Elizabeth Flesher

REDDROPP, John   3 Nov 1712 G205r son of Richard; bound to Dryden Leach, 7 years

REDDROPP, Richard – see preceding entry

REDMAIN, [ ]   1 Mar 1679/80 E97r petitions and is paid money 'to supply his present necessities'   7 Jun 1680 E100v assigned signatures N and O of stock psalter and signature E of stock Child's Guide

REDMAINE, Daniel   9 Feb 1707/8 G149r freed by patrimony

REDMAINE/REDMAYNE, Edmund   6 Mar 1698/9 G22r bound to William Redmaine, 8 years   9 Feb 1707/8 G149r freed by patrimony

REDMAINE, Elizabeth   3 May 1697 F262r John Flory, her apprentice, is freed

REDMAINE, Francis   3 Nov 1712 G205r son of John; bound to Roger Redmaine, 7 years

REDMAINE, John (I)   1 Aug 1681 E117v assigned [Thomas à Kempis, attrib.] 'The Imitation of Christ or the Christian's Pattern' by John Clarke   5 Feb 1682/3 E163v granted £50 of Tyler's bequest   6 Jun 1687 F84r has paid in his £50 loan from Tyler's Bequest   1 Jul 1700 G41v his apprentice Jonathan Cotton is freed, although he has quarterage arrears because he is very poor

REDMAINE, John (II), jnr (sic)   7 Oct 1695 F234r his apprentice Edward Price is freed

REDMAINE, John (III)   3 Nov 1712 G205r his son Francis is bound to Roger Redmaine, 7 years

REDMAINE, Mary   7 Aug 1710 G183r of Addle Hill, printer; Thomas Eaton is bound to her   22 Dec 1713 G215v given Elizabeth Thraile's pension   22 Mar 1714/15 G226v given Ursula Dukes' pension. Sarah Dryng given her pension   29 Sep 1715 G233r elected to Anne Minds' pension. Thomas Mills given her pension

REDMAINE, Mrs   6 Aug 1688 F106r Warden ordered to see that she discontinues her lawsuit against Richard Butler if he repays debt   12 Nov 1694 F214v summoned by Bennett over entering caveats against Dr Richard Busby's 'Rudimentum Grammaticae' and 'Rudimentum Anglo-Latinum'   3 Dec 1694 F215v Busby's works are entered to Bennett with a salvo

See also REDMAINE, Elizabeth

REDMAINE, Roger   8 Nov 1708 G158v freed by patrimony   3 Nov 1712 G205r Francis Redmaine is bound to him

REDMAINE/REDMAYNE, Samuel   3 May 1714 G219r freed by patrimony   4 Mar 1716/17 G248r Samuel Wade is bound to him

REDMAINE/REDMAYNE, William   7 Sep 1691 F160r of Yarmouth; cloathed and to be informed of this by post   4 Jul 1692 F173r excused cloathing on the grounds that he has recently sustained many losses   6 Mar 1698/9 G22r Edmund Redmaine is bound to him   5 Jun 1699 G25v Samuel Copson is bound to him   2 Dec 1700 G54r Edward Bird is bound to him. William Nost, apprentice of Redmaine and James Orme, is freed   4 Aug 1707 G144v printer; John Hitchcock is bound to him   1 Aug 1709 G169v Thomas Thompson is turned over to him from Thomas Ilive   22 Dec 1709 G173r elected to Margaret Driver's pension   3 Apr 1710 G178v printer, of Jowen Street; John Purser is bound to him   23 Jun 1710 G180v elected to Richard Lilly's pension. James Flowrey is given his pension   20 Dec 1711 G196r deceased; Martha Widows is given his pension

REDMAN, Edward   6 Jun 1692 F171v pleads that his uncle William is unable to pay Livery fine; proceedings stayed until next Court

REDMAN, William   6 Jun 1692 F171v his nephew Edward pleads that William Redman is unable to pay his Livery fine; proceedings stayed until next Court

REDMAYNE – see REDMAINE

REEVE, Henry   6 Mar 1698/9 G22r bound to John Everington (i.e. Everingham?)   1 Sep 1707 G145r freed by Elinor Everingham

REEVE, Richard, snr – see following entry

REEVE, Richard, jnr   5 Oct 1713 G214r son of Richard; bound to John Penn, 7 years

REEVE/REEVES, Thomas   4 Aug 1707 G144v bound to Richard Bruges   6 Sep 1714 G221v freed by Richard Bruges

REGISTER BOOK/ENTRY BOOK OF COPIES   30 Mar 1680/1 E108v list of S.C. register books &c. delivered by Lilly to the new Clerk   4 Apr 1687 F81v Clerk to enter assignments and makings-over in margin of Entry Book of Copies and to keep a waste register to be read at Court before being entered, and to be recompensed for this   2 May 1687 F82r Master and Wardens to take legal advice about Waste Register   9 Feb 1690/1 F149r Robert Stephens gives Court a list of those who have failed to enter pamphlets in Entry Book of Copies   6 Jul 1691 F157r committee to read Waste Register Book; books entered there before every Court to be copied up by the Clerk every Court day. Book to remain in Warden's chest when the Clerk is not copying entries from it   7 Dec 1691 F162v committee to consider methods of entering more efficiently   4 Mar 1694/5 F218v committee appointed to inspect register   26 Mar 1697 F259v Master, Wardens and Assistants permitted to search without fees   13 Apr 1698 G6v in future any re-entry of copies arising from assignment to be cross-referenced with original entry   5 Jun 1699 G25r caveat to be entered concerning re-entering of Juvenal and Persius at request of Walford   3 Jun 1700 G40v committee to inspect re. right to the copy of the 'Poetae Minores'   4 Mar 1705/6 G129r committee to consider proposal that money arising from the registering of private members' copies should be applied for supporting their rights thereto   18 Apr 1710 G178v for entering of copies of books pursuant to Act of Parliament. Committee to consider most proper method of keeping

REGISTER OF THE COMPANY'S WRITINGS   2 May 1698 G7r state of S.C.'s lands and estate in Ireland to be entered in

REHEARSAL (by George Villiers, 2nd Duke of Buckingham)   1 Dec 1690 F147r Thomas Dring produces in Court William Cadman's assignment of half of this to him, and Francis Saunders renounces claim to it

RENT   8 Nov 1686 F66v printed summonses to be served on all S.C. tenants to pay rent quarterly on a set day to Treasurer   5 Sep 1687 F88r Walter Davis asks for his rent to be lowered and repairs carried out before he takes out a new lease   3 Feb 1706/7 G137v state of all to be prepared   3 Mar 1706/7 G139r Clerk to demand arrears of rent

RENTER WARDENS   26 Mar 1680 E98r Thomas Goreing elected First Renter Warden, Godfrey Head elected Assistant Renter Warden   26 Mar 1681 E108r Nathaniel Ranew elected First Renter Warden, Robert Pawlett elected Assistant Renter Warden   11 Apr 1681 E109v Pawlett fined, George Copping fined, Richard Chiswell fined; E110r Simpson fined, Capt. William Phillipps fined; E110v Gabriel Cox excused, George Dawes elected [Assistant Renter Warden]   2 May 1681 E110v Dawes fined; E111r William Rawlins fined, Dorman Newman elected [Assistant Renter Warden]   17 Aug 1681 E125v byelaw   27 Mar 1682 E149r Gabriel Cox elected First Renter Warden, Thomas Spicer alias Helder elected Assistant Renter Warden   3 Apr 1682 E149v Cox pleads inability to serve on account of debts incurred through recusancy, Spicer/Helder chosen First Renter Warden, Samuel Heyrick elected Assistant Renter Warden   8 May 1682 E152r Heyrick accepts post 26 Mar 1683 E166r Samuel Hoyle and Adam Felton elected Renter Wardens   4 Jun 1683 E170r audit of accounts passed; balance to be paid to Under Warden   25 Oct 1683 F4r because of Hoyle's having 'gone aside' and not being likely to make the usual provision for Lord Mayor's Day, Second Renter Warden Adam

Felton is elected First Renter Warden for the remainder of the year. Hoyle to be sent a letter ordering him to settle accounts with Samuel Lowndes and Adam Felton and deliver the Renter Warden's books to them. (W) letter from Master and Wardens to Hoyle mentioning 'trouble fallen upon you'   26 Mar 1684 F11v Christopher Wall elected First Renter Warden, William Richardson excused, Nathaniel Ponder elected Assistant Renter Warden   2 Jun 1684 F15v Wall and Ponder re-elected as Renter Wardens   26 Mar 1685 F32r John Overton elected First Renter Warden, John Richardson elected Assistant Renter Warden   6 Apr 1685 F32v Richardson sworn in   1 Jun 1685 F38v Overton asks Court to choose another Renter Warden since he is not on the Livery; Under Warden to sue him for £40 penalty of refusal   6 Jul 1685 F40r Richardson allowed to fine for Assistant Renter Warden by reason of commands to attend his Majesty's service. (W) letter from Richardson to the Master; F40v Bennett Griffin elected in place of Richardson   3 Aug 1685 F42r Lord Mayor upholds Overton's decision not to serve as Renter Warden, since he was left off the Livery for opposing the government; F42v Griffin elevated to First Renter Warden in place of Overton; Charles Harper fined; John Leigh fined; John Amery fined; Adiel Mill accepts   26 Mar 1686 F53v William Whitwood excused for this year and promises to hold or fine next year; William Crooke fined; Obadiah Blagrave fined; F54r Daniel Peacock elected First Renter Warden, Thomas Sawbridge elected Assistant Renter Warden   3 May 1686 F55r Peacock and Sawbridge sworn in   4 Oct 1686 F64v William Whitwood to be placed after those who have served or fined as Renter Warden or will do so, in order of Livery   11 Oct 1686 F66r Renter Wardens to list all who are in arrears to S.C. for quarterage and by what amount   16 Mar 1686/7 F79r Whitwood and Humphrey Pooler to be summoned on 4 April for the election of Renter Wardens   4 Apr 1687 F81r William Richardson set aside from choice due to ill health; Whitwood elected First Renter Warden, Pooler elected Assistant Renter Warden; the latter is out of town so is re-summoned   2 May 1687 F82v Thomas Clarke elected First Renter Warden, John Penn elected Assistant Renter Warden   22 Jun 1687 F85r Clarke fined, Penn elevated to First Renter Warden in his place; Thomas Newcomb and Henry Hills fined; John Place elected but given till next court to consider   4 Jul 1687 F86r Place fined, George Wells elected Assistant Renter Warden   12 Oct 1687 F91v Wells displaced from livery and is thus unable to serve; Gabriel Cox elected   7 Nov 1687 F94r all fines for the office to be recorded by the Clerk   26 Mar 1688 F99v Roger L'Estrange writes asking for Joseph Bennet to be excused Renter Wardenship and court excuses him for this year; Thomas Hodgkins elected First Renter Warden; James Astwood pleads inability to serve or fine, so is excused for present year; Robert Roberts elected Assistant Renter Warden   26 Mar 1689 F115v John Harding elected First Renter Warden but pleads inability to serve, and the court will inquire into this; Robert Andrews and Capt. Samuel Roycroft fined; Thomas Milbourne excused on promise to serve next year; Joseph Bennet chosen First Renter Warden   6 May 1689 F117r Harding excused on condition he serves next year; Bennet excused this year; Thomas Snowden elected First Renter Warden, Matthew Gilliflower elected Assistant Renter Warden   29 May 1689 F118v Gilliflower fined; Thomas Minshall elected Assistant Renter Warden   26 Mar 1690 F131v John Harding elected First Renter Warden, Thomas Milbourne elected Assistant Renter Warden   7 Apr 1690 F132v Harding sworn in, Milbourne excused this year, James Astwood chosen; petition of John Harding, Brabazon Aylmer and Samuel Keeble to increase number of Renter Wardens and reduce individual cost is rejected   8 Apr 1690 F133r Astwood fined, Brabazon Aylmer fined, Thomas Lacy chosen   11 Apr 1690 F133v Thomas Lacy, Robert Everingham and William Marshall fined; Capt. John Williams out of town and excused this year on Thomas Bassett's request; F134r James Oades chosen   5 May 1690 F134v Oades sworn in; John Harding refuses Renter Warden's book and office; the byelaws re. forfeiture are read against him   22 Oct 1690 F144v to be fined £50 for not providing Lord Mayor's dinner despite Harding's request to fine for office instead   25 Oct 1690 F145r do not appear at a Court called to discuss whether they should be admitted to a fine instead of giving a dinner   3 Nov 1690 F145v apologise for non-appearance and say they have deposited £20 in lieu of dinner with Treasurer; excused increase of fine to £24   4 Apr 1691 F151r Israel Harrison elected First Renter Warden, Samuel Keeble elected Assistant Renter Warden; both fined; Jasper Harmer elected First Renter Warden; Joseph Knight elected Assistant Renter Warden and fined; William Warter elected Assistant Renter Warden and summoned   6 Apr 1691 F151v Harmer and Warter fined, Freeman Collins elected First Renter Warden; Capt. Edward Darrell, Henry Bonwick and Abel Swale fined; Joseph Hindmarsh elected Assistant Renter Warden   20 Apr 1691 F152v Hindmarsh fined; William Terry excused for this year; Thomas Bradyll elected Assistant Renter Warden   4 May 1691 F153v Bradyll fined; Lawrence Hatsell fined; William Baker elected Assistant Renter Warden   8 Jun 1691 F154v to stop paying salaries to Clerk, Beadle, under-Beadle, &c., which are to be paid by Wardens instead   5 Oct 1691 F161r in response to their complaint, voted that next Lord Mayor's Day the 'Clerk's man' and Beadle should seat Livery in order of rank   26 Mar 1692 F167v Henry Million elected First Renter Warden; George Downes, Thomas Milbourne, Capt. John Williams, Thomas Flesher and John Wickings all excused; William Terry elected Assistant Renter Warden   12 Apr 1692 F168v Million excused; Terry fined; Daniel Browne and William Hensman fined; John Miller elected First Renter Warden; F169r Benjamin Motte fined; Jacob Tonson elected Assistant Renter Warden and summoned   15 Apr 1692 F169v Tonson fined, Isaac Cleave and William Rogers fined, Edward Jones elected Assistant Renter Warden   27 Mar 1693 F185r Henry Million fined for First Renter Warden; Thomas Milbourne and Capt. John Williams excused; Henry Playford fined; F185v William Freeman elected First Renter Warden; Samuel Smith fined; Timothy Goodwin chosen Assistant Renter Warden   3 Apr 1693 F185v Freeman and Goodwin fined, James Crayle elected First Renter Warden; F186r Francis Saunders fined, Charles Broome elected Assistant Renter Warden and summoned; Crayle appears in court and fined; Broome elected First Renter Warden, Richard Bentley elected Assistant Renter Warden   10 Apr 1693 F186v Broome fined, Bentley elevated to First Renter Warden, Richard Sare elected Assistant Renter Warden and summoned; Bentley appears in court and fined; Sare elevated to First Renter Warden; James Adamson elected Assistant Renter Warden   2 Oct 1693 F193r John Dormer pays them 10s and thus is deemed to have discharged his arrears of quarterage, 'he being a poor man'   26 Mar 1694 F201v voted that Thomas Milbourne should not be a Renter Warden; Capt. John Williams and George Castle elected and summoned   2 Apr 1694 F202r Williams sworn in; Castle fined; John Darby elected Assistant Renter Warden and summoned; Renter Wardens henceforward to go round houses collecting quarterage 'according to ancient custom' and pay salaries to the Clerk and Beadle out of this   7 May 1694 F203r John Darby sworn in   26 Mar 1695 F219v William Horton and John Heptingstall elected and summoned   11 Nov 1695 F235v Master tells Court that he has been unable to bring the late Renter Wardens, John Darby and John Williams, to account; Court leaves it to him and Wardens   26 Mar 1696 F241r Oliver Elliston and John Baskett elected and sworn in   26 Mar 1697 F258v Jonathan Robinson excused, Nicholas Boddington and Thomas Dalton chosen; Boddington appears and is sworn in as Assistant Renter Warden   27 Mar 1697 F260r Dalton excused as out of town; William Wild elected First Renter Warden   1 Apr 1697 F260v Wild sworn in   4 Oct 1697 F268r not to invite more than six people each to dinner next Lord Mayor's Day   26 Mar 1698 G5r John Leake elected First Renter Warden and Luke Meredith Assistant Renter Warden   6 Mar 1698/9 G22r to collect arrears of quarterage   27

Mar 1699 G22v John Wild fined, Benjamin Bound elected Assistant Renter Warden. Thomas Dalton fined, Edward Limpany elected First Renter Warden 3 Apr 1699 G23v committee to consider precedence 20 Oct 1699 G32r Limpany and Bound, Renter Wardens, told that they may provide their own provisions for dinner on Lord Mayor's Day if they please, but S.C. will use their own cook 26 Mar 1700 G38r John Arden fined, Awnsham Churchill elected First Renter Warden. Robert Vincent elected Assistant Renter Warden 8 Apr 1700 G39r Awnsham Churchill fined for First Renter Warden, John Walthoe elected Assistant [i.e. First?] Renter Warden 3 Jun 1700 G40r to be allowed 10s for collecting quarterage 1 Jul 1700 G41r to be fined 2s 6d for late attendance and to forfeit a half-crown apiece 2 Dec 1700 G47v agreement entered into by members of S.C. re. holding the office. No party to agreement to be elected to share in English Stock or employed by Stock-keepers 3 Feb 1700/1 G55r committee to treat with those who have entered into agreement concerning holding of office 3 Mar 1700/1 G56v report from committee to meet those who have entered into Renter Wardens' agreement. For the future only five persons permitted to fine 26 Mar 1701 G57v Thomas Cockerill, John Sprint, Henry Kift, William Sussex, James Roberts and Benjamin Tooke jnr fined, John Lawrence elected. Thomas Bennett elected Assistant Renter Warden 7 Apr 1701 G58r committee could not come to agreement with representatives of the Renter Wardens who insisted on having the accustomed fines for Renter Warden lessened 2 Jun 1701 G60v convenient place to be made in the lobby for their better accommodation for receiving quarterage 26 Mar 1702 G68v Benjamin Walford, Thomas Horne and Thomas Mercer fined; Gilham Hills elected First Renter Warden; Charles Burdett elected Assistant Renter Warden 13 Apr 1702 G70r Gilham Hills to be excused for one year, Charles Burdett fined, Matthew Wootton elected First Renter Warden. Christopher Bateman elected Assistant Renter Warden 27 Mar 1703 G86v John Darby jnr and Martin Boddington fined, John Taylor elected First Renter Warden, Joseph Marshall fined, Richard Marshall elected Assistant Renter Warden 27 Mar 1704 G105r Thomas Benskin, Thomas Beaver, Daniel Midwinter and John Marshall fined, Ralph Simpson elected First Renter Warden, Joshua Phillipps elected Assistant Renter Warden 12 Jun 1704 G107r to attend Court of Conscience 26 Mar 1705 G117v James Brooks, Thomas Simpson and John Usborne fined, George Mortimer elected First Renter Warden, Samuel Manship elected Assistant Renter Warden 20 Apr 1705 G119r refuse to hand over book of quarterage 10 Sep 1705 G123v to provide dinner for Lord Mayor's Day according to bill of fare taken from late Cook's books 1 Oct 1705 G124r to provide dinner for Lord Mayor's Day according to Cook's bill of fare 16 Oct 1705 G124r to be compelled to provide dinner for Lord Mayor's Day like that provided when John Lawrence and Thomas Bennett were Renter Wardens 26 Mar 1706 G130r a 'great part' of the Livery list read and names of potential Renter Wardens identified. John Nicholson, Nathaniel Nowell, Richard Wilkins and John Nutt fined, Robert Elmes and Henry Perris excused for one year, John Gerrard elected First Renter Warden, George Littlebury elected Assistant Renter Warden 9 Sep 1706 G134v Christopher Wilkinson fined 26 Mar 1707 G139v Robert Knaplock, John Brooks, Ralph Smith and Christopher Wilkinson fined, Obadiah Smith elected First Renter Warden 7 Apr 1707 G140r Smith fined, Christopher Browne elected First Renter Warden, Robert Podmore fined, Capt. John Williams elected Assistant Renter Warden 5 May 1707 G141v Christopher Browne receives his charge from the Warden 26 Mar 1708 G150v William Mount, Edward Place and James Rawlins fined for First Renter Warden 12 Apr 1708 G151v John Hunt fined, Henry Rhodes elected First Renter Warden. George Read fined, John Clarke elected Assistant Renter Warden 8 Oct 1708 G158v Jacob Tonson fined for First Renter Warden. To pay half of what they usually pay to Watermen Music Whifflers 26 Mar

1709 G163r Ebenezer Tracy excused for one year; William Bowyer, Emmanuel Matthews, Richard Parker and Henry Perris fined, George Grafton elected First Renter Warden, Abel Roper elected Assistant Renter Warden   27 Mar 1710 G177r John Mayo excused, Ebenezer Tracy and Robert Whitledge fined for First Renter Warden, John Barber fined for Assistant Renter Warden   3 Apr 1710 G178r George Strachan excused, Samuel Crouch elected First Renter Warden, James Taylor fined, James Knapton elected Assistant Renter Warden   26 Mar 1711 G189r ordered that no more than five persons may fine for Renter Warden in any one year and that the fifth fine shall be applied to the two persons holding the office provided they make a dinner on Lord Mayor's Day. Philip Barrett excused, George Mortlock and Lewis Thomas fined, John Mayo elected First Renter Warden. Benjamin Wilde and Thomas Wilmer fined, Roger Clavell elected Assistant Renter Warden   9 Apr 1711 G189v orders of 26 March to be suspended. To have two shillings in the pound for expenses for quarterage collected abroad. Not to have the 10s usually allowed for expenses   3 Mar 1711/12 G197r part of fifth fine to be paid towards the charge of the dinner on Lord Mayor's Day   26 Mar 1712 G198v Richard Randall elected First Renter Warden, Christopher Coningsby fined. Philip Barrett excused for one year, John Francks elected Assistant Renter Warden   7 Apr 1712 G198v Randall asks to be excused First Renter Warden, George Strahan elected   5 May 1712 G199v John Francks excused Assistant Renter Wardenship for one year. Andrew Bell elected   2 Jun 1712 G200r George Strahan fined for First Renter Warden   23 Jun 1712 G200v Arthur Bettesworth fined for Assistant Renter Warden   7 Jul 1712 G201v Henry Parsons receives his charge as   26 Mar 1713 G207v Ichabod Dawkes, John Beresford, Thomas Shermandine and John Randoll excused for one year. Philip Barrett and Edmund Parker fined, Thomas Lewis elected First Renter Warden. Charles Walkden fined, Joseph Downing elected Assistant Renter Warden   4 May 1713 G209v James Holland and Maurice Atkins excused for one year, Thomas Lewis fined for First Renter Warden, Jonah Bowyer elected Assistant Renter Warden   26 Mar 1714 G217r Benjamin Sprint, Robert Elmes and John Beresford fined for First Renter Warden. Owen Lloyd, James Round and Thomas Shermandine excused. John Wyatt elected First Renter Warden. Samuel Briscoe excused Assistant Renter Warden   5 Apr 1714 G217v William Holland, Joseph Watts, Nathaniel Nowell and William Hill all excused for a year and James Holland elected Assistant Renter Warden   1 Nov 1714 G223r thanked for handsome entertainment on Lord Mayor's Day and for their cheerful performance of their office on that occasion   26 Mar 1715 G227r William Hill and Thomas Shelmerdine excused for one year, Owen Lloyd fined, James Round elected First Renter Warden   4 Apr 1715 G227v William Holland ordered to attend next Court day and take office of Renter Warden or pay fine   2 May 1715 G228r James Round fined, Thomas Varnum elected First Renter Warden. Richard Randall excused, Bernard Lintott elected Assistant Renter Warden   26 Mar 1716 G238v Dryden Leach and Thomas Page fined, Nathaniel Nowell excused, William Holland elected First Renter Warden, Thomas Norman elected Assistant Renter Warden   9 Apr 1716 G239r William Holland excused, William Taylor fined for First Renter Warden   7 May 1716 G239v Thomas Norris elected First Renter Warden, Thomas Norman excused and James Bissell elected Assistant Renter Warden   4 Jun 1716 G240r James Bissell excused, Samuel Clarke elected Assistant Renter Warden   26 Mar 1717 G248v William Mears excused for one year, Nathaniel Nowell fined for First Renter Warden. James Read fined for Assistant Renter Warden   1 Apr 1717 G249v Richard Harris, William Innys and Fisher Mount fined, Joseph Hazard elected First Renter Warden. John Buchanan fined. Thomas Norman elected Assistant Renter Warden

RENTER WARDENS' ACCOUNTS   2 May 1681 E110v accounts of Renter Warden Godfrey Head audited by Roger Norton and John Towse   26 Mar 1683 E166v

audited   4 Jun 1683 E170r audited   26 Mar 1684 F11v audited   26 Mar 1685 F32r
audited   4 Jul 1685 F40r Robert Horne, Capt. John Baker, Henry Clarke and Simon
Miller elected to audit Renter Wardens' accounts   3 Aug 1685 F41v audited   25 Sep
1690 F143r auditors deliver them to Court and they are passed   1 Aug 1692 F177r
auditors report the balance to be £26 6s 1d; ordered to be paid by them (Freeman
Collins and William Baker)   3 Jul 1693 F189v Christopher Wilkinson and Samuel
Lowndes, auditors for Renter Wardens John Miller and Edward Jones, report a £19 2s
2d balance to be paid by them   3 Apr 1699–1717 audited annually

REVLE, Henry, snr – see following entry

REVLE, Henry, jnr   3 Dec 1716 G245v son of Henry; bound to Christopher Norris, 7
years

REYLEY, Daniel   19 Dec 1712 G205v elected to Grace Middlewright's pension

REYNER, Christopher – see following entry

REYNER, William   6 Sep 1714 G221v son of Christopher; bound to Anne Motte, 8
years

REYNOLDS, Mary   20 Dec 1693 F197r elected to the pension of Margaret Crowther,
deceased   22 Mar 1714/15 G226v Clare Clifford is given her pension

REYNOLDS, Matthew   5 Feb 1699/1700 G35r freed by Robert Roberts

RHODES, Francis   8 Jan 1716/17 G246r turned over from Richard Ware to Thomas
Norris

RHODES, Henry – see RODES, Henry

RHODES, John   4 Feb 1705/6 G127v bound to John Darby, 7 years

RHODES, Matthew   5 Mar 1704/5 G117r query whether his apprentice Batterton is
free

RHODES, Thomas   26 Mar 1680 E98r his apprentice John Fenn is freed

RICHARDS, Daniel   10 Sep 1711 G194r freed by patrimony

RICHARDS, Mary   1 Aug 1709 G169v William Underwood is bound to her   6 Jul
1713 G212r fined 40 shillings for binding an apprentice by foreign indenture. Her
apprentice William Wyatt is freed   6 Aug 1716 G242v her apprentice William Underwood is freed

RICHARDS, Richard   2 Dec 1689 F128r supplicates for freedom by redemption;
voted that he should pay £5

RICHARDS, Samuel   3 Oct 1692 (W) freed by Charles Harper

RICHARDSON, [   ]   19 Dec 1679 E96r given allowance of 30s towards repairs of
S.C.'s house, deductable from rent, in addition to £3 8s 11d already allowed   2 May
1681 E111v his complaint referred to next Court   4 Sep 1682 E157r pipe and funnel
from the Clerk's garret to the 'house of Office' to be separate from Richardson's   3 Jun
1695 F225r excused cloathing

RICHARDSON, Daniel   7 Oct 1689 F124v S.C. demised a house in Ave Maria Lane to
him of which William Woolley is the assignee

RICHARDSON, Edmund/Edward   4 Oct 1697 F268v Robert Smith is bound to
him   4 Sep 1699 G30r elected to cloathing   5 Mar 1704/5 G117r his apprentice Robert
Smith is freed   2 Apr 1705 G118v his former apprentice Francis Faram is freed   3 Jun
1706 G132v Henry Shepherd is bound to him   5 Jul 1708 G155r bookbinder; John
Blyzard is bound to him   6 Dec 1714 G224r John Wardell is bound to him

RICHARDSON, Edward – see preceding entry

338

RICHARDSON, Israel, Mrs   8 Nov 1703 G97r widow of John Richardson; disposes of her husband's £100 share (*sic*) to Thomas Beaver

RICHARDSON, James, snr – see following entry

RICHARDSON, James, jnr   10 Sep 1694 F212v son of James Richardson, apothecary of London; bound to Edward Brewster   6 Oct 1701 G65r freed by Edward Brewster   4 Dec 1710 G186r to have £10 from loan money on giving surety

RICHARDSON, John (I)   26 Mar 1685 F32r elected Assistant Renter Warden   6 Apr 1685 F32v sworn in as Renter Warden   7 May 1685 (W) confirmed as member of new Livery   6 Jul 1685 F40r allowed to fine for Assistant Renter Warden by reason of commands to attend his Majesty's service. (W) letter from Richardson to the Master   13 Oct 1687 F91v printer; sworn in as Assistant   1 Mar 1687/8 F98v elected Stock-keeper for Assistants with John Towse   11 Oct 1688 F108v (described as 'Capt.') restored to Livery   4 Feb 1688/9 F112v printer; re-elected Assistant   6 May 1689 F117r printer; ranked eleventh of Assistants never elected as Master or Warden   2 Dec 1689 F127v competes unsuccessfully for Robert Scott's £160 share   7 Jul 1690 F139r competes unsuccessfully for Thomas Bassett's £160 share   9 Feb 1690/1 F149r elected to the late Susanna Leigh's £160 share   2 Jul 1694 F210r among those chosen to audit Warden's accounts   4 Jul 1696 F245r elected Under Warden   7 Sep 1696 F248v produces deed by which S.C. are obliged to pay William Barton and his heirs £10 if Barton's version of the psalms sells well   3 Jul 1697 F263v comes second in competition for Under Warden   5 Jul 1697 F264r elected Under Warden and fined for second year   27 Mar 1699 G22v requests that his son William be permitted to fine for Assistant Renter Warden   7 Aug 1704 G111r his apprentice Daniel Raynolds is freed   3 Jun 1706 G132v his apprentice Robert Whiskin is freed by Thomas Willimer

RICHARDSON, John (II)   20 Dec 1689 F128v cloathed, paying £10 towards the fine

RICHARDSON, John (III)   4 Feb 1705/6 G127v bound to Thomas Horne, 7 years   3 May 1714 G219r freed by Thomas Horne

RICHARDSON, Katherine   8 Nov 1703 G97r widow of William Richardson; declares an interest in John Richardson's £100 share (*sic*) and consents to its being surrendered   8 May 1704 G106r £40 share disposed of to Thomas Wilmer

RICHARDSON, Samuel   1 Jul 1706 G133r bound to John Wild, 7 years   13 Jun 1715 G229v freed by John Wild

RICHARDSON, Thomas   7 Mar 1697/8 G5r freed by William Hunt

RICHARDSON, William (I)   26 Mar 1684 F11r bookbinder; excused from Renter Wardenship for a year   4 Oct 1686 F64v to be placed in order of Livery after those who have served or fined as Renter Warden or will do so   16 Mar 1686/7 F79r to be summoned on 4 April for the election of Renter Wardens   4 Apr 1687 F81r set aside from Renter Warden nominations because of illness   20 Dec 1689 F128v cloathed, paying £10 towards the fine   11 Nov 1695 F234v elected to the late James Adamson's £40 share and summoned   19 Nov 1695 F236r takes partner's oath   2 Dec 1695 F237r clerk of Putney; given a bond on English Stock of £600 penalty for payment of £307 10s by 3 June 1696   27 Mar 1699 G22v fined for Assistant Renter Warden, at his father John Richardson's request   2 Oct 1699 G31v Thomas Stocker is bound to him   5 May 1701 G59v William Mewes is bound to him   5 Oct 1702 G81v his apprentice Richard Gunney is freed   2 Apr 1705 G118v his apprentice Francis Faram, previously turned over to Edmund Richardson and Thomas Horne, is freed   6 May 1706 G131r desiring £300 due to him from the S.C.   3 Jun 1706 G132r £300 to be taken in by the S.C. to pay him off   21 Jun 1706 G132v bond from S.C. of £300 cancelled

339

RICHARDSON, William (II) 7 Jul 1707 G143v bound to Thomas Hodgkins

RICHARDSON, William (III) 6 Jun 1709 G165v bound to Thomas Wilmer, 7 years

RICHMOND, David 3 Jun 1700 G40v bound to John Mayo, 7 years 9 Jun 1707 G142v freed by John Mayo 7 Feb 1714/15 G225r John Cuxon is bound to him 1 Apr 1717 G249v John Cuxon is turned over from him to Henry Parker

RICHMOND, Peter 11 Jun 1694 F209r Thomas Todd, turned over to him, is freed but fined 2s 6d for turning him over outside Stationers' Hall 8 Apr 1700 G39r William Collyer is bound to him 11 Nov 1700 G46v his apprentice Samuel Staines is freed

RIDGE, Thomas 4 Dec 1710 G186r bound to John Brookes 6 Oct 1712 G204v turned over to Edward Rowe

RISDELL, John – see following entry

RISDELL, William 22 Dec 1713 G215v son of John; bound to Thomas Francklyn, 7 years

RITCH, Sir Peter 2 Aug 1686 F61r will report re. mount from the committee for City Lands

RIVER WATER 7 Oct 1700 G46r S.C. to pay for it to be laid into house leased to Charles Lewis

RIVINGTON, Charles 6 Oct 1707 G145v turned over from Emmanuel Matthews to Awnsham Churchill 4 Sep 1710 G183v freed by Emmanuel Matthews

RIVINGTON, John 6 Aug 1716 G242v son of Thurstan; bound to Francis Jeffreys, 7 years

RIVINGTON, Thurstan – see preceding entry

RIX, [ ] 8 Nov 1680 E105r cloathed

RIX, John 26 Mar 1684 F11r liveryman and prisoner at the King's Bench; given 10s charity 3 Dec 1684 F26v prisoner; to be given 20s

RIX, Mary 27 Sep 1698 G13v elected to pension of Thomas Egglesfeild, deceased; Anne Crouch is given her pension 22 Jun 1699 G25v deceased; Richard Lilly is given her pension

ROBERTS, Hugh 5 Jul 1703 G92r bound to Isaac Gunn, 7 years

ROBERTS, James 1 Jul 1695 F227v cloathed 26 Mar 1701 G57v fined for First Renter Warden 1 Mar 1702/3 G85v elected to Samuel Keeble's £40 share 8 Nov 1703 G97r Thomas Philpott is bound to him 6 May 1706 G131v Edward Walker is bound to him 3 Feb 1706/7 G137v competes unsuccessfully for Mrs Collins's £80 share 5 Mar 1707/8 G141v competes unsuccessfully for Mrs Brown's £80 share 24 Jul 1709 G168v summoned to attend next Court 1 Aug 1709 G169r attends Court and is heard by it 4 Dec 1710 G186r of Stationers' Court, printer; William Waters is bound to him 10 Sep 1711 G194r his apprentice Thomas Philpott is freed 3 Mar 1711/12 G197r elected to John Walthoe's £80 share. His £40 share is disposed of to William Mears 1 Feb 1713/14 G215v elected to his mother's £160 share. His £80 share is disposed of to Whitledge 14 Mar 1714/15 G226r his apprentice John Shillingford is freed 22 Dec 1715 G235v Samuel Price is bound to him 6 Feb 1715/16 G236r George Newbolt is turned over to him from James Rawlins

ROBERTS, Jasper 6 May 1695 F223r son of Robert Roberts; freed by patrimony 7 Feb 1698/9 G20r cloathed 5 Jun 1699 G25v Thomas Welton is bound to him 4 Sep 1699 G30v Francis Pyke is bound to him 7 Apr 1701 G58v Stephen Harrott is bound to him 7 Jul 1701 G62r Henry Cartwright is bound to him 6 Jul 1702 G78r deceased;

his apprentice Henry Cartwright is turned over to Samuel Buckley   3 Aug 1702 G79v deceased; his apprentice Stephen Harcourt is turned over to Benjamin Tooke

ROBERTS, John (I)   7 Jun 1708 G153v his apprentice George Wells is freed

ROBERTS, John (II)   12 Apr 1708 G152r bound to Freeman Collins, 8 years   7 May 1716 G240r freed by Susanna Collins

ROBERTS, Mary   26 Mar 1702 G68v lease from S.C. to her of two houses fronting the Hall sealed   9 Feb 1707/8 G149r John Shillingford is bound to her   1 Feb 1713/14 G215v deceased; her £160 share passed to James Roberts, her son

ROBERTS/ROBERT, Robert   7 Jun 1686 F56r printer and substitute for John Macock; reports that the presses of John Mayo, Baldwin, Simon Hinch and John Palmer are worth £9   26 Mar 1688 F99v elected Assistant Renter Warden   2 Dec 1689 F127v elected to Samuel Sprint's £40 share   4 Aug 1690 F141v does not appear; ordered that he should be suspended from printing until a further Court order   1 Sep 1690 F142r debate re. his non-appearance; deferred in Master's absence to next Friday at 3 p.m.   5 Sep 1690 F142v Court decides to fine him £3 for printing unlicensed pamphlet illegally   8 Jun 1691 F154r tenant of S.C.; appears to confirm that he printed a first impression of 1500 of Dr Williams's Catechism   4 Jul 1692 F173v elected to Richard Chiswell's £80 share   4 Jun 1694 F208v John Barrisse is bound to him   6 May 1695 F223r his son Jasper is freed by patrimony   7 Feb 1698/9 G20v Christopher Norbury is bound to him   1 Mar 1698/9 G21r elected Stock-keeper for Livery   7 Aug 1699 G29r Joseph Whitehead is bound to him   4 Dec 1699 G34r his apprentice James Styles is freed; William Johnson is bound to him   5 Feb 1699/1700 G35r his apprentices Matthew Reynolds and Neville Simmons are freed   1 Mar 1699/1700 G36r elected Stock-keeper for Livery   8 Apr 1700 G39r John Talbot is bound to him   6 May 1700 G39r takes oath of Assistant   11 Nov 1700 G46v house to be viewed by Master and Wardens in order for lease to be taken   3 Feb 1700/1 G54v house to be repaired and lease renewed. Competes unsuccessfully for Capt. William Phillipps's £160 share. Elected to Mrs Gellebrand's £160 share. His £80 share is disposed of to Timothy Goodwin   3 Mar 1700/1 G57r John Cleeve is bound to him   5 May 1701 G59r George Wells is bound to him   2 Jun 1701 G60v his apprentice John Barrisse is freed   1 Sep 1701 G63v bills for work to his house to be settled by Master and Wardens   9 Feb 1701/2 G67r deceased; lease which was to have been made to him of his house to be made to his wife and administratrix   4 Mar 1705/6 G129r his apprentice Christopher Norbury is freed   9 Jun 1707 G142v his apprentice John Talbot is freed

ROBERTS, William   6 Dec 1708 G159v bound to Ann Downing, 7 years

ROBINS, Elizabeth   3 May 1697 F262r bound to Elizabeth Anson

ROBINSON, [   ]   6 Nov 1683 F4v Henry Herringman to enter a list of books bought from him for 40s

ROBINSON, Francis   4 May 1691 F153r Gilbert Wharton appears to answer for the non-payment of a £20 bond for which Robinson is partly responsible

ROBINSON, Jonathan   29 May 1689 F118v cloathed   3 Jun 1689 F119r among those petitioning against hawkers; admitted onto the committee dealing with the problem   26 Mar 1697 F258v on the request of Robert Clavell and Thomas Parkhurst, excused Renter Wardenship for the year ensuing   5 Jun 1699 G25v his apprentice John King is freed   6 Nov 1699 G33r Thomas Atkinson is bound to him   3 Jun 1706 G132v Samuel Rogers is bound to him

ROBINSON, Joseph   1 Mar 1702/3 G86r bound to Edward Midwinter, 7 years   3 Mar 1706/7 G139r turned over from Edward Midwinter to Richard Janeway   6 Mar 1709/10 G176v freed by Richard Janeway

ROBINSON, Katharine   22 Jun 1715 G229v deceased; Elizabeth Tough is given her pension

ROBINSON, Mrs   4 Feb 1716/17 G246v widow of Jonathan Robinson; her apprentice Samuel Rogers is freed

ROBINSON, Ranew/Rany/Raney   5 Jul 1714 G220v freed by patrimony. Cloathed   2 Aug 1714 G221r Charles Motte is turned over to him   1 Oct 1716 G244r elected to William Leybourne's £40 share

ROBINSON, Timothy   3 May 1680 E99v of Greenwich; pays £5 of his bond and 10s for charges; Gilbert Wharton to pay the rest   4 May 1691 F153r Wharton appears to answer for the non-payment of a £20 bond for which Robinson is partly responsible   8 Jun 1691 F154r is shown in Warden's accounts to have paid £5 towards the debt of Francis Robinson, Wharton and himself which is then discharged

ROBINSON, Underhill   1 Sep 1707 G145r bound to William Sayes, 7 years   4 Oct 1714 G222v freed by William Sayes

ROCHESTER, [John Wilmot, Earl of]   1 Dec 1690 F146v Jacob Tonson to be summoned re. Francis Saunders's complaint that he has printed Rochester's poems See also SODOM

ROCK, William   2 Aug 1686 F61v smith; to be paid out of the money allotted to John Mayo for his confiscated press, for which he made the ironwork

ROCKALL, [   ]   4 Dec 1683 F197r William Gray is bound to him

ROCKALL, Abel   7 Jul 1701 G62r and Robert Whitledge; their apprentice William Gray is freed   7 Apr 1707 G141r bookbinder; Nathaniel Bullock is bound to him   6 Oct 1712 G204v John Kingman is bound to him   7 Jun 1714 G219v his apprentice Nathaniel Bullock is freed

ROCKALL, William   6 Feb 1709/10 G175v bookbinder; Benjamin Littleboy is bound to him

ROCKWELL, William   2 Nov 1702 G83r Francis White is bound to him

RODDAM, John   10 Sep 1711 G194r son of Robert; bound to Joseph Harper, 7 years

RODDAM, Robert – see preceding entry

RODES, George   5 Sep 1687 F88r petitions to have his Livery fine refunded since he has had no benefit of it and is now very poor; granted £4 charity

RODES/RHODES, Henry   26 Mar 1680 E98r freed by redemption   1 Sep 1684 F23r Benjamin Thrale assigns to him 'Coffee House Jests' [by William Hickes]   3 Dec 1684 F27r Simon Neale assigns to him 'The Whole Duty of a Communicant' by John Gauden, late Bishop of Exeter   29 May 1689 F118v cloathed   4 Sep 1699 G30v William Russell is bound to him   1 Mar 1702/3 G86r Richard Strouhton is bound to him   12 Apr 1708 G151v elected First Renter Warden   7 Jun 1708 G153v bookseller; Henry Booth is bound to him

ROGERS, [   ]   1 Apr 1697 F263v to ask booksellers, printers and paper manufacturers in Fleet Street and Temple Bar within for money towards Paper Act test case

ROGERS, Daniel   7 Aug 1699 G29r bound to William Norton, 7 years   7 Aug 1704 G111r turned over to James Dover   9 Sep 1706 G134v freed by James Dover

ROGERS, George   26 Mar 1686 F54r elected waterman   4 Apr 1687 F81v elected waterman

ROGERS, Henry (I)   25 Jun 1684 F18r of Westminster Hall and former apprentice of Richard Firbank, a S.C. member; freed after paying a self-determined fine of 4 guineas   4 Oct 1686 (W) on original list of new livery members, though not in the end chosen

ROGERS, Henry (II)   4 Jun 1716 G240v his son John is bound to John Beresford, 7 years

ROGERS, John (I)   1 Mar 1694/5 F217v elected Stock-keeper for Yeomanry with John Place   9 Feb 1707/8 G148v of Shrewsbury, bookseller; bill in Chancery to be brought against him   3 May 1708 G152v not to be proceeded against further for selling sham almanacks   22 Jun 1708 G153v granted privilege of printing Welsh Almanacks   5 Jul 1708 G155r to have exclusive privilege of printing Welsh Almanack for 3 years

ROGERS, John (II)   1 Feb 1713/14 G216r son of William; bound to Hammond Bankes, 7 years

ROGERS, John (III)   4 Jun 1716 G240v son of Henry; bound to John Beresford, 7 years

ROGERS, Samuel   3 Jun 1706 G132v bound to Jonathan Robinson, 7 years   4 Feb 1716/17 G246v freed by Jonathan Robinson's widow

ROGERS, William, snr (I)   1 Mar 1685/6 F51r cloathed   7 Feb 1686/7 F70v Thomas Pierrepont, wishing to dispose of his £80 share to Rogers, is told that one usually surrenders it first; Rogers is elected to it   1 Mar 1687/8 F98v elected Stock-keeper for Yeomanry with John Miller   1 Mar 1688/9 F113v elected Stock-keeper for Yeomanry with Samuel Keeble   3 Jun 1689 F119r among those petitioning against hawkers; admitted to the committee dealing with the problem   1 Mar 1691/2 F165v elected Stock-keeper for Yeomanry with Brabazon Aylmer   15 Apr 1692 F169v fined for Assistant Renter Warden   1 Mar 1693/4 F199v elected Stock-keeper for Yeomanry with Daniel Browne   5 Mar 1693/4 F200v Edmund Herringman jnr is bound to him, 7 years   4 Mar 1694/5 F219r Benjamin Tooke jnr, his apprentice, freed   1 Mar 1696/7 F255v elected Stock-keeper for Yeomanry with Isaac Cleave   1 Apr 1697 F263v to ask booksellers, printers and paper manufacturers in Fleet Street and Temple Bar within for money towards Paper Act test case   3 Jun 1700 G40v John Pemberton is bound to him   2 Mar 1703/4 G102v elected Stock-keeper for Livery   1 Mar 1705/6 G128v elected Stock-keeper for Livery   7 Jul 1707 G143v his apprentice John Pemberton is freed   1 Mar 1707/8 G149v summoned as partner of English Stock   25 Mar 1708 G150r elected Assistant   4 Jul 1709 G167r auditor of late Master and Wardens' accounts   6 Feb 1709/10 G175r elected to Robert Andrews's £160 share. His £80 share disposed of to John Heptingstall   18 Apr 1710 G178v of Fleet Street; his son, William Rogers, is bound to him   2 Jul 1711 G192v auditor of late Master and Wardens' accounts   6 Oct 1712 G204r deceased; his £160 share disposed of to Robert Knaplock

ROGERS, William (II)   4 Feb 1705/6 G127v bound to John Fowell, 7 years

ROGERS, William, jnr (III)   18 Apr 1710 G178v bound to his father, William Rogers

ROGERS, William (IV)   1 Feb 1713/14 G216r his son John is bound to Hammond Bankes, 7 years

ROLLES/ROLLS, Nathaniel   5 Aug 1695 F231r does not appear on summons; elected into Livery and resummoned   11 Nov 1695 F235r appears and refuses cloathing   1 Feb 1696/7 F255r excused cloathing

ROOKE, [   ]   22 Sep 1680 E104r assignment to George Sawbridge to be entered

ROOKES, Mary   7 Apr 1690 F133r executrix of Thomas Rookes for whom Thomas Burdikin as her executor assigns Francis Quarles' 'Argalus and Parthenia' to William Freeman

ROOKES, Thomas – see preceding entry

ROOPER – see ROPER

ROPER, [ ] (I)   11 Apr 1681 E110v deceased; substitute to be found for him as surety to Sir Joseph Seamour   2 May 1681 E111r Francis Tyton and Henry Herringman to stand as substitutes for Roper and Martin

ROPER, [ ] (II)   3 Aug 1616 F246v Mrs Wilkinson is lately remarried to Roper; her £320 share is voted to Thomas Parkhurst

ROPER, Abel   3 Jun 1689 F119v excused cloathing   12 Apr 1692 F169r excused cloathing for the present   5 Mar 1693/4 F200v cloathed   5 Jul 1697 F264v elected to Mrs Thompson's £80 share   5 Sep 1698 G14v Richard Mendall is bound to him   7 Apr 1701 G58v Edward Poulter is bound to him   8 Nov 1703 G97r John Isted is freed by him   1 Oct 1705 G124r Peter Edwards is bound to him   4 Feb 1705/6 G127v Edward Poulter turned over from him to John Hodges   1 Dec 1707 G147v bookseller; Edward Beardwell is bound to him   6 Dec 1708 G159v of Fleet Street; Edward King is bound to him   26 Mar 1709 G163r elected Assistant Renter Warden   28 Sep 1709 G170v summoned to next Court to attend his duty

ROPER, Mrs   7 Jan 1683/4 F7v deceased; her £320 share voted to Henry Herringman

ROSARY OF GODLY PRAYER [i.e. Nicholas Themylthorpe, *The Posy of Godly Prayers*]   11 Apr 1681 E109v retained by Dorothy Thrale when she assigns all her late husband's other copies to her son Benjamin

ROSE, Acquilla   6 Feb 1709/10 G175v bound to Edward Saunders, 7 years

ROSE, Richard   1 Sep 1707 G145r bound to James Brookes, 9 years

ROSE, Thomas   6 Sep 1703 G95r signs as witness to signature of Thomas Feilder

ROTHWELL, Andrew   5 Jul 1680 E101v given one-off charity payment of £10   3 Dec 1683 F6v given 40s charity; his case to be considered at next pension Court, and to be admitted to the next pension vacant   22 Jun 1697 F263v deceased; Mary Godwin elected to his pension

ROTHWELL, John   7 Aug 1699 G28r clerk; petition requesting a contribution of the Court in his present circumstances dismissed by them as not their concern

ROTHWELL, Mary   27 Mar 1682 E149r deceased; Matthew Morris admitted to her pension

ROUND, Charles   1 Apr 1706 G131r bound to Edward Bell, 7 years

ROUND, James   3 Dec 1694 F215v son of John Round of Stratford-upon-Avon, gentleman; bound to Brabazon Aylmer   2 Mar 1701/2 G67v freed by Brabazon Aylmer   5 Jul 1708 G154v cloathed   26 Mar 1714 G217v excused from office of Renter Warden for a year   26 Mar 1715 G227r elected First Renter Warden   2 May 1715 G228r fined for First Renter Warden

ROUND, John – see preceding entry

ROUND, Thomas   7 Feb 1708/9 G160v bound to James Dover, 7 years

ROUSE, Isaac – see following entry

ROUSE, John   5 Jul 1714 G220v son of Isaac; bound to William Dew, 7 years

ROWE, Edward   6 Oct 1712 G204v Thomas Ridge is turned over to him

ROWLAND, William   6 Mar 1709/10 G176v bound to Jacob Tonson, 7 years

ROWSE, Thomas   12 Nov 1705 G125r freed by Gilham Hills

ROYAL ALMANACK – see ALMANACKS

ROYCROFT, [ ]   7 Jun 1680 E100v assigned signatures J and K of stock psalter and signature B of stock 12mo psalms

ROYCROFT/ROYSCROFT/RYCROFT, Capt. Samuel 6 Jun 1681 E112r Stock-keepers for Assistants to rectify differences between him and Evan Tyler 6 Feb 1681/2 E143v elected to the late Sarah Adams's £40 share 3 Apr 1682 E151v Court accepts his offer of £25 in hand and £75 in 6 months (highest bidder) to print [Foxe's] Book of Martyrs, providing he specifies on the title page it is printed for S.C. 8 May 1682 E153r articles and amendments with S.C. re. Book of Martyrs sealed; ordered to pay £5. To print Sheet B of Saunders's Almanack for the year ensuing 2 Jul 1683 F2r Ralph Holt complains that Roycroft is printing Sheet B of Saunders's Almanack with Holt's type; matter deferred till end of year 7 Jul 1684 F20v Ralph Holt reminds Court of his dispute with Roycroft re. Sheet B of Saunders's Almanack; Holt is allowed to print it for next year 2 Mar 1684/5 F31v elected Stock-keeper for Yeomanry with John Place 7 May 1685 (W) confirmed as member of new Livery 7 Dec 1685 F48r articles with S.C. re. [Foxe's] Book of Martyrs referred to Treasurer 3 Jul 1686 F59v to be summoned re. Holt's complaint against him 5 Jul 1686 F60v appears; quarrel referred to Master, Wardens and Stock-keepers 11 Oct 1688 F108v restored to Livery 26 Mar 1689 F115v fined for Assistant Renter Warden 2 Dec 1689 F127v elected to Dorman Newman's £80 share 1 Mar 1689/90 F129v elected Stock-keeper for Livery with John Miller 8 Apr 1695 F220r elected to the late John Clarke's £160 share. Summoned to next Court to be sworn in 6 May 1695 F222v takes partner's oath 2 Mar 1695/6 F240r elected Stock-keeper for Livery with Samuel Sprint 4 May 1696 F242v elected Assistant and summoned 8 Jun 1696 F243r sworn in as Assistant 6 Jul 1696 F245v sworn in as Stock-keeper for Livery 3 Jul 1697 F263v competes unsuccessfully for Under Warden 5 Jul 1697 F264r competes unsuccessfully for Under Warden; tells Court that Richard Simpson wishes to fine for Under Warden 2 Jul 1698 G10r auditor of Master and Wardens' accounts 1 Aug 1698 G13r excused from auditing Master and Wardens' accounts because out of town. Assignment to Roycroft from Benjamin Motte of a moiety of Dr [Thomas] Comber's 'Companion to the Temple', parts 1–2, read and ordered to be entered 5 Jul 1703 G92r auditor of Master and Wardens' accounts 1 Jul 1704 G109v fined for Under Warden 3 Jul 1704 G109v auditor of late Master and Wardens' accounts 5 Feb 1704/5 G114v Clerk's bill for proceedings in Chancery referred to him 30 Jun 1705 G121r fined for Under Warden to preserve seniority 6 Jul 1706 G133v competes unsuccessfully for Upper Warden 9 Jun 1707 G142v added to committee re. Cambridge affairs convened on 5 Aug last 5 Jul 1707 G143r competes unsuccessfully for Upper Warden 3 Jul 1708 G154r elected Upper Warden and not permitted to fine 2 Jul 1709 G166v fined for second year of Upper Warden 1 Aug 1709 G169r question put whether, as he has served for one year as Upper Warden and fined for the other, he should be put in nomination for Master. Granted 6 Feb 1709/10 G175r candidate for Robert Scott's £320 share but resigns his claims thereto in respect of seniority 3 Jul 1710 G181v fined for Master in order to preserve his seniority 9 Apr 1711 G189v auditor of late Renter Wardens' accounts 7 May 1711 G190r elected to the late Richard Chiswell's Assistant's share. His £160 share disposed of to Timothy Goodwin 30 Jun 1711 G192r competes unsuccessfully for Master 15 Jul 1712 G202r competes unsuccessfully for Master 24 Apr 1713 G209r signatory to S.C.'s notes to Thomas Guy

ROYDEN, Charles 6 Nov 1710 G185r his son John is bound to Thomas Hughes, 7 years

ROYDEN, George 2 Nov 1702 G83r complaint that his master, John Darby snr, refuses to make him free 1 Mar 1702/3 G86r freed by John Darby 4 Sep 1704 G112r excused cloathing for some time. Thomas Maplesden is bound to him

ROYDEN/ROYDON, John (I) 3 Jul 1704 G110r William Cooke is turned over to him from Henry Morris 3 Dec 1705 G126r William Cooke is turned over from him to Benjamin Beardswell

ROYDEN, John (II)   6 Nov 1710 G185r son of Charles; bound to Thomas Hughes, 7 years

ROYSCROFT – see ROYCROFT

ROYSTON, [   ]   1 Sep 1701 G64r his warehouse to be repaired and paper for use of English Stock to be brought into it   6 Feb 1709/10 G175r S.C. to pay his legatees 6% on the £1000 due to them on bond from the S.C.

ROYSTON, Margaret   1 Sep 1690 F142r given a bond of £800 penalty for the payment of £410 by 1 March next   27 May 1692 F171r bond of £1200 penalty for £615 to be paid on 27 November 1692 approved; money to be put towards 'Oxford affair'   30 Sep 1696 F249v committee to view the 'boards and other goods' left when she moved out of the warehouse, as she wants compensation   22 Dec 1696 F253v to be paid £6 16s for goods left in her two warehouses   10 Jan 1698/9 G18v motion of Bennett Griffin that Richard Chiswell should receive her £40 dividend money as he maintains and provides for her in her present circumstances. Matter adjourned to next Court   7 Feb 1698/9 G20v her son-in-law Chiswell to receive her £40 dividend money   3 Aug 1702 G79r committee to deal with her affairs   18 Dec 1702 G84r deceased; her £320 share disposed of to William Rawlins   27 Mar 1703 G86v deceased; £200 lent by Master from her estate to be repaid by S.C.   5 Apr 1703 G88r £200 due to her estate to be paid by Joseph Collyer   3 Dec 1716 G245r deceased; £1000 principal due on two bonds to her paid

ROYSTON, Richard   21 Feb 1681/2 E144v competes unsuccessfully for Master in place of Thomas Vere who has died in office   8 May 1682 E152v 7-year lease sealed with S.C. for the use of the warehouse by the stairs, on which he has already laid out £20   1 Jul 1682 E154v competes unsuccessfully for Master   2 May 1683 E169r S.C. warehouse is let to him   7 May 1683 (W) to pay 12d to Poor Box for coming after the Court had sat   30 Jun 1683 F1r competes unsuccessfully for Master   7 Apr 1684 F13v on the list of loyal Assistants presented to the Crown   5 Jul 1684 F19r competes unsuccessfully for Master   7 May 1685 (W) confirmed as member of new Livery   2 Nov 1685 F46r to be summoned to answer Robert Scott, George Wells and Richard Bentley's complaint that he has printed their 'Life of Dr. Hammond' [by John Fell]   7 Dec 1685 F47v Wells and Bentley accuse him of printing their 'Life of Dr. Hammond'; deferred   1 Feb 1685/6 F50v allowed further time to discuss the difference between him, Wells and Bentley re. Dr Hammond's 'Life'   3 May 1686 F55v refuses to make allowance for his £320 share to be forfeited for printing Stock books without permission; share to be disposed of if he does not come to agreement   7 Jun 1686 F56v sum of damages, £54 9s, commuted to £20 on consideration of services, but he is not granted any further allowance for work on the school book patent for S.C.   3 Jul 1686 F58v stands unsuccessfully for Master   20 Dec 1686 F69r deceased; his £5 gift to S.C. poor is distributed

See also ROYSTON, [   ], and following entry

ROYSTON, Widow   7 Feb 1686/7 F71r presents 2 silver candlesticks to S.C. as the legacy of Richard Royston

RUCK, William, snr – see following entry

RUCK, William, jnr   12 Nov 1694 F215r son of William Ruck of Sellinge, Kent, yeoman; bound to Charles Spicer, alias Helder

RUDIMENTUM ANGLO-LATINUM – see GRAMMARS

RUDIMENTUM GRAMMATICAE – see GRAMMARS

RUES/RUE, Abraham   6 Nov 1710 G185r son of John; bound to Thomas Harrison, 7 years   1 Feb 1713/14 G216r turned over from Thomas Harrison to John Harrison

RUES, John – see preceding entry

RUGG, Elizabeth   1 Dec 1707 G147v freed by Isaac Cleave

RULE OF PROPORTION – see USE OF THE RULE

RUMBALL, Edmund   5 Jun 1699 G25v freed by Richard Bentley. Stephen Butcher is bound to him

RUMBALL, Elizabeth   3 Jun 1706 G132v Michael Stapleton is bound to her

RUSH, John   12 Nov 1705 G125r bound to Edward Maddoc, 7 years   9 Apr 1711 G189v turned over from Edward 'Haddocks' [i.e. Maddoc] to Dryden Leach

RUSSELL, Jonathan, snr – see following entry

RUSSELL, Jonathan, jnr   13 Jun 1715 G229v son of Jonathan; bound to Benjamin Motte, 7 years

RUSSELL, William   4 Sep 1699 G30v bound to Henry Rodes, 7 years

RUTTER, [   ]   5 Feb 1710/11 G187r bound to John Pemberton, 7 years

RUTTER, Thomas   7 Feb 1708/9 G160v bound to Robert Elmes, 7 years

RYCROFT – see ROYCROFT

RYDER'S ALMANACK – see ALMANACKS

RYLEY, Christopher   1 Jun 1713 G210v his son Robert is bound to John Nutt, 7 years

RYLEY, Daniel   24 Sep 1714 G222r deceased; Ann Fowell is given his pension
See also following entry

RYLEY, Richard   4 Feb 1711/12 G196v son of Daniel; bound to James Rawlins, 7 years

RYLEY, Robert   1 Jun 1713 G210v son of Christopher; bound to John Nutt, 7 years   2 Jul 1716 G242r turned over from John Nutt to William Hunter

RYMES, Aron   7 May 1705 G120r Charles Bell is bound to him

SABIN, Elizabeth   23 Mar 1686/7 F80r elected into the late Ursula Barker's 40s pension

SACKETT, George   5 May 1701 G59v freed by Nathaniel Sackett

SACKETT, Nathaniel   5 Feb 1693/4 F198v servant to John Southby; freed   5 May 1701 G59v his apprentice George Sackett is freed

SACKFEILD, John (I)   4 Sep 1704 G112r bound to Richard Crosskill, 7 years   10 Sep 1711 G194r freed by Richard Crosskill. John Sackfeild is bound to him   6 Jul 1713 G212v John Hughes is bound to him   5 Sep 1715 G232r elected to cloathing because he was coming to bind a second apprentice. James Hopkins is bound to him   4 Mar 1716/17 G248r John Arnold is bound to him

SACKFEILD, John (II)   1 Oct 1711 G194v son of Robert; bound to John Sackfeild snr

SACKFIELD, Robert – see previous entry

SADDLERS' COMPANY   16 Jun 1684 F17v Samuel Holford of the Saddlers' declares himself willing to be translated to S.C.   7 May 1694 F203v Holford is allowed to defer his acceptance of livery until next monthly Court to sever ties with Saddlers   4 Jun 1694 F208r Samuel Holford refuses cloathing on the grounds that he is liable to be called to the Livery of the Saddlers

SADUCISMUS TRIUMPHATUS – see GLANVILL, Joseph

SAFYER, Edward, snr – see following entry

SAFYER, Edward, jnr   7 Jun 1714 G219v son of Edward; bound to John Berrisford

ST AUSTIN'S   7 May 1688 F101r united to St Faith's; William Lamb's anniversary sermon was preached there by Dr Moore   5 May 1690 F134v Roger Norton to represent Master at Lamb's sermon at St Austin's church and dinner on 6 May, accompanied by those not going to Court of Aldermen (W) those who attend dinner but not sermon to forfeit £12 (sic) apiece   7 Dec 1691 F163r Court is doubtful as to whether its 12 poor get 1d and 1d's worth of bread from Randall Taylor and order a baker to see to the bread

ST BARTHOLOMEW'S HOSPITAL   23 Dec 1714 G224r place available for Elizabeth Andrews

ST CECILIA'S DAY   6 Nov 1693 F194r Hall not to be let for St Cecilia's Day for under £5   7 Nov 1698 G16r Hall to be used for St Cecilia's Day feast   8 Nov 1699 G33r Hall to be used for St Cecilia's Day feast   11 Nov 1700 G46r Hall to be used for St Cecilia's Day feast

ST FAITH'S   3 Nov 1679 E94v agreement concluded re. moiety paid to 6 poor freemen of the parish or their widows   1 Dec 1679 E95r draft of deed re. parish poor to be engrossed by Clerk   19 Dec 1679 E96r previous agreement re. 3s per week for parish poor to be continued; agreement to be sealed   2 May 1681 E111r Clerk to advise with John Lilly re. churchwarden's demands for William Lamb's bequest of 2s per week and that from S.C.   6 Jun 1681 E112r arrears of Lamb's bequest demanded by churchwardens of St Faith's; referred to committee   4 Feb 1683/4 F8r churchwardens demand arrears of Lamb's charity; committee set up to report to next Court   1 Mar 1683/4 F9r Lamb's charity judged to be discontinued in the parish of St Faith's since the church burnt down, but continued in St Austin's   6 Aug 1694 F211r churchwarden complains that charity money given by Paine and Lamb, late members of S.C., was not distributed; committee appointed   10 Sep 1694 F212r committee report that all Lamb's money has been distributed while Paine never did leave any money to St Faith's   3 Jun 1695 F225r committee to inspect records for Norton's will and an agreement with St Faith's about a bequest made to it   1 Jul 1695 F227r the dispute over deduction of taxes out of the 3s charity that S.C. pay them per week is referred to Sir Bartholomew Shore   5 Aug 1695 F230r agreement between S.C. and St Faith's to be produced at next Court   7 Oct 1695 F233r articles of agreement re. Norton bequest made; Clerk to copy them for churchwardens   8 Apr 1700 G38v charity from Lamb to poor persons of the parish   4 Aug 1701 G63r churchwardens desiring benefit of Lamb's gift   1 Sep 1701 G64r Lamb's gift to be paid once a year from Michaelmas next   6 Oct 1701 G64v weekly payment of Lamb's gift to continue as before

See also ST AUSTIN'S

ST JAMES'S WESTMINSTER   7 Mar 1708/9 G162r 'Select Psalms' for use in

ST MARTIN'S LUDGATE   28 Mar 1680 E99r exchange of ground with them agreed to   6 Aug 1688 F105r deed of conveyance of this, a Stock estate; signatories listed   1 Oct 1688 F107v conveyance of ground and houses in area to new feoffees sealed   6 May 1689 F117v churchwardens ask for £6 towards the charge of making three screens for the three doors of the church and are paid £3   1 Jul 1689 F120v conveyance of land in area to be cancelled and made out to present Court members. Surviving feoffees to execute this and be indemnified by S.C.   5 Aug 1689 F122v conveyance from surviving feoffees to present Assistants sealed   20 Dec 1693 F197r committee appointed to discuss the danger to the burial vaults of St Martin's Ludgate of S.C.'s rainwater trench. Repairs to be made by next Lady Day   5 Feb 1693/4 F198r new drain required. Committee to consider division of costs between S.C. and St Martin's Ludgate as latter claim they cannot afford cost of drain (£20-£30)   5 Mar 1693/4 F200r committee agree to defray half the drain cost and for a double agreement to be drawn up if St

Martin's accept the terms   2 Jul 1694 F210r drain committee revived; John Bellinger and William Phillipps added to it   6 Aug 1694 F211r committee report that they and the churchwardens have agreed to defray the cost of the drains equally   4 Mar 1694/5 F218r drain committee revived and augmented by Capt. William Phillipps and Bennett Griffin   3 Jun 1695 F224v committee to investigate Thomas Parkhurst's complaint that his payments to St Martin's poor were omitted from Warden's accounts   6 Sep 1703 G95r S.C.'s agreement with St Martin's Ludgate for making a drain in the S.C.'s garden   26 Mar 1709 G163r committee to consider proposal to make a vault under the S.C.'s garden   4 Apr 1709 G163v S.C. would agree to proposal to make a vault under the S.C.'s garden for 50 guineas   1 Oct 1711 G194v churchwardens permitted to make a vault under S.C.'s garden but S.C. does not accept 50 guineas offered; committee to settle   2 Nov 1711 G195r grant from S.C. to Rector and churchwardens for making a vault read and sealed   5 Dec 1715 G235v Master and Wardens to consider churchwardens' request to lay river water into pipe belonging to S.C. in the garden

ST PAUL'S   6 Jun 1681 E112v committee considering arrears due to the Chamber of London for St Paul's preachers to give directions for payment   7 Nov 1681 E138r letter from City Solicitor re. £115 arrears to preachers of St Paul's Cross; S.C. decided to borrow £100 on common seal to pay for this   5 Dec 1681 E139v Evan Tyler to enter into a bond for £100 with S.C. to enable them to pay off preachers' arrears   4 Feb 1705/6 G127r stands for S.C. for Queen's visit there   5 Aug 1706 G134r carpenter's bill for stands for Queen's visit there

ST THOMAS THE APOSTLE   1 Sep 1701 G64r churchwardens request S.C. to take £100 belonging to the poor of the parish on bond at 5%   4 Sep 1701 G64r bond from S.C. of £100 to minister and churchwardens sealed   9 Feb 1707/8 G148v S.C.'s bond of £50 to churchwardens

SALE, John   4 Oct 1703 G96r bound to John Science, 7 years

SALISBURY/SALUSBURY, John   5 Aug 1689 F122r given until next Court to decide about cloathing   1 Aug 1692 F177r refuses cloathing without good reason; Court elects him nevertheless and orders his prosecution for £40 under byelaw   7 Jun 1694 F208v has long record of disobedience re. Livery; elected, and when he refuses to turn up, summoned to special Court   10 Sep 1694 F212r summoned re. cloathing   1 Oct 1694 F213r has disobeyed many summonses for cloathing and is ordered to be summoned before Lord Mayor   5 Oct 1694 F213v Master and Wardens asked to decide whether S.C. should pay the legal fees over Salusbury's being summoned   3 Mar 1700/1 G57r and John Nicholson. Their apprentice Samuel Ballard is freed

SALISBURY, Thomas   3 Jun 1689 F119r cloathed

SALLUST   18 Mar 1686/7 F79v in 24mo; among books in catalogue annexed to Oxford agreement

SALTER, [ ]   4 Apr 1687 F80v denies printing music books outside S.C. and explains that his ex-master had forced him to buy them. Has ca. 150 books

SALTER, George   7 Mar 1697/8 G5r bound to Joshua Silvester   4 Jun 1705 G120v freed by Joshua Silvester. John Wale is bound to him

SALTMARSH, [ ]   20 Dec 1693 F197r churchwarden of St Martin Ludgate; engages with S.C. over drainage dispute

SALTMARSH, John   6 Mar 1698/9 G22r bound to William Crosse, 7 years   3 Feb 1706/7 G138r freed by William Crosse   3 Mar 1706/7 G139r James Askew is bound to him

SALTONSTALL, Wye   1 Sep 1690 F142r Court agrees to buy his translation of Ovid's Epistles from Henry Mortlock and Benjamin Tooke

SALUSBURY – see SALISBURY

SAMUEL, David   2 Aug 1708 G156v bound to John Penn, 7 years

SANDERS'S ALMANACK [i.e. Saunders's Almanack] – see ALMANACKS

SANDERS, Theodorus   9 Jun 1707 G142v bound to Joseph Marshall, 7 years   2 Aug 1714 G221r freed by Joseph Marshall

SANDYS, Oliver – see following entry

SANDYS, William   1 Oct 1716 G244r son of Oliver; bound to Robert Pepper, 7 years

SANGAR, Egbard/Egbert/Egbar/Egbart   6 Mar 1698/9 G22r bound to Mary Tonson, 7 years   3 Mar 1706/7 G139r freed by Mary Tonson   5 Jun 1710 G180r summoned to cloathing   3 Jul 1710 G182r cloathed   3 Mar 1711/12 G197r John Harrindine is bound to him   1 Sep 1712 G203r John Norcock is bound to him   13 Apr 1713 G208v John Norcock turned over from him to Daniel Browne

SARE, Richard   16 Jun 1684 F17r of Holborn and ex-apprentice of John Place, a member of S.C.; his freedom to be taken at next Court   6 Sep 1686 F62r Crown approval of him as the new Treasurer is recommended by Bridgeman and Sir Roger L'Estrange; meeting planned with latter   4 Oct 1686 F64v elected to Livery   8 Nov 1686 F67r accepts cloathing   28 Feb 1686/7 F72r lately cloathed; his Livery fine remitted 'as a respect from this Court to Sir Roger L'Estrange'   3 Apr 1693 F185v to print the new translation of Josephus by Roger L'Estrange   10 Apr 1693 F186v elected Assistant Renter Warden and summoned, then elected First Renter Warden when Richard Bentley fines   3 Jul 1693 F190r Henry Herringman assigns to him and John Hindmarsh Don [Francisco de] Quevedo's 'Visions', made English by Roger L'Estrange   4 Dec 1693 F196r competes unsuccessfully for £40 share declined by Abel Swale; asks to have 'Letters Writ by a Turkish Spy' entered to himself and Joseph Hindmarsh; assignment from John Leake read   1 Apr 1697 F260v to ask booksellers, printers and paper manufacturers of Holborn for money towards Paper Act test case   2 Aug 1697 F265v Thomas Levens, his apprentice, is freed   7 Aug 1699 G29r Richard Williamson is bound to him   25 Mar 1708 G150v competes unsuccessfully for place as Assistant   3 May 1708 G152v Christopher Nowell is bound to him   3 Oct 1709 G171r Christopher Nowell is turned over from him to Maurice Atkins   3 Jul 1710 G182r of Gray's Inn, bookseller; James Best is bound to him   6 Oct 1712 G204v John Cox is bound to him   6 Sep 1714 G221v William Harris is bound to him   2 May 1715 G228r letter from him to Awnsham Churchill read

SARGEANT, Widow   5 Sep 1681 E131r paid 10s charity

SARSON, John   7 Feb 1714/15 G225r his son William Sarson is turned over to him from George Strahan

SARSON/SERSON, William   7 Aug 1710 G183r bound to George Strahan, 7 years   3 Aug 1713 G213r turned over from George Strahan to Thomas Bickerton   7 Feb 1714/15 G225r turned over from George Strahan to John Sarson, his father

SATIRES – see JUVENAL, PERSIUS

SATTERTHWAIT, Widow   3 Aug 1691 F158v remarries; her £40 share voted to William Baker

SATTERTWAITE/SCHATTERTWAITE/SHATTERTWAITE, Humphrey   20 Jun 1681 E113v elected Assistant   5 Sep 1681 E129r elected to John Bellinger's £40 share

SAUNDERS'S ALMANACK – see ALMANACKS

SAUNDERS, Edward   4 Jun 1694 F208v son of Richard Saunders of Wendress, Gloucestershire, husbandman; bound to Tace Cheese   3 Nov 1701 G65r freed by Tace

Cheese and Tace Sowle   6 Feb 1709/10 G175v printer; Acquilla Rose is bound to him   4 Sep 1716 G242v John Huggonson is bound to him

SAUNDERS, Francis   1 Mar 1685/6 F51v cloathed   1 Mar 1687/8 F97v expelled from Livery by order of Lord Mayor   11 Oct 1688 F108v restored to Livery   1 Dec 1690 F146v complains that Tonson has printed his 'Poems of Rochester'; Tonson is summoned. Saunders renounces his claim to half of [Buckingham's] 'The Rehearsal' when Thomas Dring produces William Cadman's assignment of it to him   3 Apr 1693 F186r fined for Assistant Renter Warden   6 Apr 1696 F241v elected to the late Joseph Knight's £40 share   7 Sep 1696 F249r payment for Knight's share, voted to Saunders in April 1696, stopped until his debt to S.C. is paid   3 May 1697 F262r his £40 share to be disposed of if he does not pay for it in full before next Court day   4 Sep 1699 G30r his £40 share disposed of to Robert Limpany

SAUNDERS, George   3 Jul 1699 G26v deceased; Samuel Browne to receive money due on assignment of John Simms's Assistants' share, formerly assigned to Saunders, whose executrix is now married to Browne

SAUNDERS, Henry   4 Jul 1716 G240v his son Timothy is bound to Theodore Saunders

SAUNDERS, Lovett   7 Aug 1699 G29r bound to George Littlebury, 7 years

SAUNDERS, Richard (I)   4 Jun 1694 F208v of Wendress, Gloucestershire, husband-man; his son Edward is bound to Tace Cheese

SAUNDERS, Richard (II), author of *Apollo Anglicanus* (Saunders's Almanack) – see ALMANACKS

SAUNDERS, Samuel   4 Oct 1703 G96r turned over to John England

SAUNDERS, Theodore   4 Jun 1716 G240v Timothy Saunders is bound to him   10 Sep 1716 G242v excused cloathing for one year

SAUNDERS, Thomas   2 Dec 1700 G54r bound to Isaac Gunn, 7 years

SAUNDERS, Timothy   4 Jun 1716 G240v son of Henry; bound to Theodore Saunders, 7 years

SAVAGE, Samuel   6 Nov 1704 G113r bound to Charles Bates, 7 years   2 Dec 1706 G136v turned over from Charles Bates to Alexander Milbourne   6 Oct 1712 G204r freed by Alexander Milbourne

SAVORY, Edward   5 Jul 1697 F264v bound to William Whitehead

SAWBRIDGE, [ ]   4 Nov 1706 G136r precedents to be searched to see what was done by Court upon his being elected Sheriff of London   2 Dec 1706 G136v precedents for being elected Master when also elected Sheriff of London reported   9 Jun 1707 G142r Henry Hills's £320 share, mortgaged to him and assigned to Mrs Mearne, sold to Charles Harper

SAWBRIDGE, George (I)   5 Mar 1679/80 E98r 'after a long debate' it is voted that the Stock-keepers check through his accounts for mistakes by 26 March   28 Mar 1680 E98v debate on accounts to be resumed before next Court   7 Jun 1680 E100r Clerk to copy Sawbridge's accounts and his answer to them, and deliver them to the old Stock-keepers for the next Court   3 Jul 1680 E101r stands unsuccessfully for Master   5 Jul 1680 E101v Widow Husbands's Livery share mortgaged to him for £30   2 Aug 1680 E102v authorised to audit Wardens' accounts   22 Sep 1680 E104r assignment from Rooke to be entered. Takes chair while Mrs Legatt's £320 share is voted to the Master   6 Dec 1680 E105v ordered to view ground with Treasurer and S.C. workmen re. making a pump   6 Jun 1681 E112v committee to investigate his accounts   7 Nov

1681 E137r Leybourne accused of mortgaging his £80 share to him without Court's consent 6 Feb 1681/2 E142v committee to inspect his accounts 6 Mar 1681/2 E146v deceased; drew up an agreement when Treasurer, whereby Mrs Lilly has to be paid £20 for the use of her husband's almanack 20 Mar 1681/2 E148r meeting of committee re. his accounts; concluded that his estate owes the Stock £158 16s 1½d plus £417 17s 2d received for use of the English Stock 3 Apr 1682 E150v committee reports on its findings. Edward Brewster's plea that his administratrix be reimbursed for paper is dismissed; Stock books to be examined concerning his account 7 Aug 1682 E156r committee to draw up account between S.C., King's Printers and Sawbridge's estate before next Court 4 Sep 1682 E157v committee, including Robert Scott, to meet before next Court, to accept discharge of account from administratrix and report 7 Mar 1682/3 E165r committee report that £158 16s 1½d is owing to S.C., and ask for this to be paid by his relict and S.C. papers handed in 6 Aug 1683 F2v see Mrs Sawbridge 1 Aug 1692 F176v John Macock's executors present a silver cup to S.C. designed to pair Sawbridge's gift

SAWBRIDGE, George (II) 4 Aug 1690 F141v cloathed and promises payment of fine 3 May 1703 G89v James Johnson is bound to him 5 Feb 1704/5 G114v complaint that he had printed 'The Traveller's and Chapman's Daily Instructor' containing S.C.'s calendar. All books to be delivered to Warehousekeeper under threat of prosecution in Chancery 5 Mar 1704/5 G116v to send calendars in the 'Traveller's and Chapman's Daily Instructor' to Warehousekeeper or be made party to S.C.'s bill in Chancery 6 Aug 1705 G122v his apprentice Thomas Bickerton is freed 4 Feb 1705/6 G127v John Wilford is bound to him 3 Oct 1709 G171r of Little Britain, bookseller; Thomas Davis is bound to him 7 May 1711 G190v of Little Britain, bookseller; William Cuthbert is bound to him 2 Jul 1716 G242r Richard Crosse is bound to him

SAWBRIDGE, Hannah 7 Nov 1681 E137r to negotiate with Leybourne before next Court to disprove allegations of his mortgaging his £80 share to George Sawbridge 5 Dec 1681 E140v Edward Brewster tells Court that Leybourne's account with her is not finished; granted respite until next Court 2 May 1683 E169r S.C. warehouse let to her at £5 p.a. 6 Aug 1683 F2v bond for £512 10s to be sealed and delivered to her as administratrix to George Sawbridge; general releases to be drawn up 1 Oct 1683 F4r bond from S.C. of £512 10s at £1000 penalty and general release from S.C. to her is signed 25 Jun 1684 F18v John Towse desires on her behalf that the old £500 bond at 5% be cancelled and a new one drawn up; this is done 5 Oct 1685 F45r to be summoned to answer the complaints of Ralph Smith's widow and Fisher re. printing their copy 1 Feb 1685/6 F50r deceased; her £320 share voted to Ambrose Isted 26 Mar 1686 F53v deceased; Widow Thrale transfers her mortgage of her £320 share from her executors to Edward Brewster 5 Jul 1686 F60v bond entered into with Thomasine Fish to raise £500 due on bond to her executors 2 Aug 1686 F61r bond cancelled 1 Mar 1689/90 F129v Master, as executor to her, has an interest in Cambridge printing for 3½ years which he offers to S.C. for £100 p.a.

SAWBRIDGE, Isaac – see following entry

SAWBRIDGE, Katherine 1 Aug 1687 F87r widow of Isaac Sawbridge, wine cooper; Court grants Henry Hills snr permission to mortgage his £320 share to her 5 Mar 1687/8 F99r Master to pay off the mortgage of his £320 share to her by remortgaging it to William Rawlins 7 Dec 1691 F162v Hoyle demands interest on Hills's £360 share mortgaged to Widow Sawbridge for £300 7 Oct 1695 F233v deceased; Benjamin Motte elected to her £80 share

SAWBRIDGE, Thomas (I) 1 Mar 1681/2 E145v elected Stock-keeper from Yeomanry with Benjamin Tooke 8 May 1682 E153r objections to Charles Spicer, Thomas

Williams's executor, assigning books to Sawbridge and Benjamin Tooke held until next Court   4 Sep 1682 E157v assignment to him and Benjamin Tooke to be entered   5 Feb 1682/3 E163r voted to Robert Horne's £80 share   1 Mar 1682/3 E164v elected Stock-keeper for Yeomanry with William Crooke   2 Jul 1683 F1v to pay ready money for shares before next Court on pain of forfeiting them, under the terms of Tyler's will   6 Aug 1683 F2v pays part of share money; his and Godfrey Head's appeal to the Table results in the order of last Court being deferred to next Court   6 Nov 1683 F4v disposal of his and Godfrey Head's shares to be deferred to next Court   7 May 1685 (W) confirmed as member of the new Livery   1 Mar 1685/6 F52r elected Stock-keeper for Livery with Obadiah Blagrave   26 Mar 1686 F54r elected Assistant Renter Warden   3 May 1686 F55r sworn in as Renter Warden   8 Nov 1686 F67r committee to treat with his administrators for interest in Cambridge printing   19 Nov 1686 F67r committee re. buying his interest in Cambridge printing could not take place as his administrator Edward Brewster failed to turn up   1 Mar 1689/90 F129v as administrator to him, Master has an interest in Cambridge printing for another 3½ years; offers this to S.C. at £100 p.a.

SAWBRIDGE, Thomas (II)   1 Mar 1685/6 F51v cloathed   1 Mar 1687/8 F97v order from Lord Mayor that he should be restored to the Livery. Summoned to next Court to be nominated for Assistant   5 Mar 1687/8 F99r elected Assistant despite not appearing   26 Mar 1688 F99v sworn in as Assistant   4 May 1691 F153v to attend auditing of Renter Wardens' accounts   10 Sep 1694 F212v deceased; his apprentice Robert Parris is freed

For all Sawbridge entries, see also CAMBRIDGE, KING'S PRINTERS

SAWTELL, Edward   7 Jul 1712 G201v son of Thomas; bound to Henry Mortlock, 7 years

SAWTELL, Thomas – see preceding entry

SAY, Edward   27 Sep 1710 G184r bound to Benjamin Motte, 7 years   5 Mar 1710/11 G188r bound to Anne Motte, 7 years

SAYES, William   9 Sep 1700 G45r freed by William Whitwood   6 Nov 1704 G113r excused cloathing for 6 months   5 Feb 1704/5 G115r cloathed. James Ayrey is turned over to him from James Willshire. William Collyer is turned over from him to James Willshire   18 Feb 1706/7 G138r printer; William Price is bound to him   5 May 1707 G142r Samuel Aris is turned over from him to Daniel Bridge   1 Sep 1707 G145r printer; Underhill Robinson is bound to him   6 Jul 1713 G212v James Watts is bound to him   4 Oct 1714 G222v his apprentice Underhill Robinson is freed

SAYWELL, John   7 Feb 1698/9 G20v bound to Thomas Snowden, 7 years   4 Mar 1705/6 G129r freed by Thomas Snowden

SCHATTERTWAITE – see SATTERTWAITE

SCHOFEILD – see SCOFEILD

SCHOOL BOOK PATENT   17 Aug 1681 E127r byelaw   7 Jun 1686 F56v Richard Royston is not allowed money back from his sum of damages for work done in renewing School Book Patent   7 Jun 1714 G219r S.C.'s rights to the printing of school books to be investigated

SCIENCE, John, snr (I) – see following entry

SCIENCE, John, jnr (II)   19 Nov 1695 F236v son of the late John Science snr of Tetsworth, Oxfordshire, yeoman; bound to John Science   7 Dec 1702 G83v freed by John Science

SCIENCE/SCYENCE, John (III)   19 Nov 1695 F236v John Science jnr is bound to him   22 Jun 1698 G9v general release from the S.C. for himself and his wife is

sealed   7 Dec 1702 G83v his apprentice John Science is freed   4 Oct 1703 G96r John
Sale is bound to him   8 Nov 1703 G97r Edmund Scofeild is turned over to him   3
Nov 1712 G205r his apprentice Edmund Scofeild is freed

SCIENCE, Thomas   16 Oct 1716 G244r freed by patrimony

SCOFEILD, Edmund   6 Nov 1699 G33r bound to Fish Bramston, 7 years   8 Nov
1703 G97r turned over to John Science   3 Nov 1712 G205r freed by John Science

SCOTCH PSALMS – see PSALMS

SCOTT, Robert (I)   3 Feb 1679/80 E96v summoned to next general Court   3 May
1680 E99v S.C. to appeal against his subpoena against them   7 Jun 1680 E100r Court
decides not to answer or bring a crossbill against his bill; Master (Samuel Mearne)
protests   6 Sep 1680 E103v charges for suit in Chancery against S.C. to be investigated   8 Nov 1680 E105r Jonathan Edwin's £40 and 40s for his charges to be paid to
him forthwith by the Treasurer   20 Jun 1681 E113r Crown mandate that he should
become an Assistant   4 Jul 1681 E116r consideration of Mrs Martin's request that her
late husband's copies go to him and to George Wells to be deferred until next Court   7
Nov 1681 E137v succeeds in negotiating a low assignment fee of 50s for those books 'of
little or no value' assigned to him by Mrs Martin and enters 361 books in the
register   21 Feb 1681/2 E145r altercation between him and Henry Clarke as to whose
right is greater for Francis Tyton's £160 share; Scott voted into it   6 Mar 1681/2
E146v lengthy outline of his disagreement with Samuel Mearne over a warehouse   3
Apr 1682 E150v difference between Samuel Mearne, Henry Herringman and himself
and partner concerning assignment of copies by Mrs Kirton   8 May 1682 E153r
among sureties for the payment of Sir Joseph Seamour's annuity; indemnified by
S.C.   3 Jul 1682 E155v among those indemnified from liability to Sir Joseph Seamour
in the demise of the Hall and tenements. Difference with Samuel Mearne involving Henry
Herringman re. books entered to Mearne in 1673 to be resolved before next Court   7
Aug 1682 E156r with Herringman, granted leave to prosecute persons printing books
not in register. No meeting held with Mearne and Herringman re. difference over copies;
agreed that the entry of copies by Mearne be null and void   4 Sep 1682 E157v co-opted
onto Sawbridge committee. To be added, with Ambrose Isted, to committee re. Lilly and
Clerk's duties as to byelaws and pension notes   2 May 1683 E169r S.C. warehouse
formerly let to Gellebrand is let to him   7 Apr 1684 F13v on the list of loyal Assistants
presented to the Crown   2 Jun 1684 F16r competes unsuccessfully for the late Widow
Pakeman's £320 share   2 Mar 1684/5 F31v elected Stock-keeper for Assistants with
John Bellinger   26 Mar 1685 F32r with John Bellinger, appointed to audit Renter
Wardens' accounts   7 May 1685 (W) confirmed as member of the new Livery   1 Jun
1685 F38r out of England so Ambrose Isted is appointed to audit Renter Wardens'
accounts   4 Jul 1685 F39r ordered to fine for Under Warden because of want of choice
for Upper Warden   5 Oct 1685 F45r promises to fine for 2 years' Under Warden   2
Nov 1685 F46r complains with George Wells and Richard Bentley that Royston has
printed their 'Life of Dr. Hammond' [by John Fell]   1 Feb 1685/6 F50r competes
unsuccessfully for the late Mrs Sawbridge's £320 share   26 Mar 1686 F54v pays 12d
charity for being absent from Court without leave of Master   3 Jul 1686 F59r fined for
2 years' Upper Warden on account of going abroad next year   2 Jul 1687 F85v competes
unsuccessfully for Master   11 Oct 1688 F108v restored to Assistants   6 Jul 1689
F121v among those chosen to audit Wardens' accounts   2 Dec 1689 F127r elected to
the late Ralph Smith's £320 share   3 Mar 1689/90 F130r John Starkey claims his place
as an Assistant is just below Robert Scott instead of as Junior Assistant   9 Feb 1690/1
F149r wishes to fine for Master on account of extreme deafness to preserve seniority;
voted he should pay 5 guineas rather than 10   2 Nov 1691 F162r he, Thomas Dring

and Abel Swale to pay 2d per book for printing 3000 Virgils without a licence   7 Dec 1691 F162v fine reduced to 1d per book through Dring's intervention   22 Dec 1691 F163v letter from him read demanding relief from the order of the last Court for himself, Dring and Swale; not granted   1 Feb 1691/2 F164v his part in concluding Oxford agreement is detailed   7 Mar 1691/2 F166v mentioned on indenture transferring Stock estate to S.C. members being indemnified against engagements with Oxford   5 Sep 1692 F178r to be summoned re. general complaints about him and for illegal importations   3 Oct 1692 F180v Samuel Smith to make affirmation that he imported S.C.'s copies   3 Jul 1693 F189v competes unsuccessfully for Master   3 Jul 1697 F263v competes unsuccessfully for Master   6 Feb 1709/10 G175r deceased; his £320 share disposed of to Robert Andrews

SCOTT, Robert (II)   7 Mar 1697/8 G5r bound to John Mecham

SCOTT, Samuel   3 Feb 1700/1 G55v his apprentice Leonard Parker is freed

SCOTT, William   4 Aug 1701 G63v bound to Gilham Hills, 7 years   1 Aug 1709 G169v freed by Gilham Hills   28 Sep 1713 G213v Joshua Powell is turned over to him from William Humphreys   5 Sep 1715 G232v William Jackson is bound to him   10 Sep 1716 G243r William Jackson is turned over from him to John Watts

SCRIPTURAL CATECHISM   7 Aug 1699 G28r among the books assigned to Samuel Sprint and J. [i.e. John?] Nicholson

SCRIPTURE HARMONIES – see HARMONY OF THE SCRIPTURES

SCRIVENERS   4 Jun 1683 E170v Thomas Dawkes is fined 10s for having bound his apprentice, William Spire, at a scrivener's   3 Dec 1684 F26v Smith complains that some S.C. members have bound supernumerary apprentices at scriveners   5 Mar 1687/8 F99r free workmen printers claim that some masters bind supernumerary apprentices at scriveners   2 Apr 1688 F100v free workmen printers complain that David Mallett has bound a supernumerary apprentice there

SCYENCE – see SCIENCE

SEALE/SEILE, Elizabeth   30 Sep 1696 F249v admitted to the pension of her late husband Thomas   20 Dec 1701 G66r deceased; Mary Spurdance is given her pension

SEALE, Thomas   26 Mar 1684 F11r elected into the 7s 6d pension of Elizabeth Evans, she having lately married

See also preceding entry

SEAMOUR/SEAMOR/SEYMOUR, Sir Joseph   7 Mar 1680/1 E108r his business to take place at next Court   11 Apr 1681 E110v request to have two Court members named to stand as surety for S.C. in place of Roper and Martin, deceased, deferred   2 May 1681 E111r Francis Tyton and Henry Herringman asked to stand as surety to him for S.C. instead of Roper and Martin, deceased   5 Sep 1681 E129r Francis Tyton, Thomas Vere, Thomas Newcomb and Henry Herringman indemnified from engagement to him on S.C.'s behalf   7 Nov 1681 E138v Thomas Newcomb to have custody of indentures and other writings relating to Seamour   8 May 1682 E153r his request for the Master, John Towse, Edward Brewster and Robert Scott to stand surety for the payment of his annuity granted   3 Jul 1682 E155v demise of Hall and tenements made to Master and Wardens with Edward Brewster and Robert Scott indemnifying them from engagement to Seamour to be sealed   3 Aug 1685 F41v letter from Bishop of Oxford explaining that the agreement excludes books bought from Seamour is read to Court   22 Dec 1691 F164r securities for payment of his annuity of £100 to be summoned to next Court   1 Feb 1691/2 F164v his part in concluding Oxford agreement is detailed   7 Mar 1691/2 F166v transfer of mortgage of Stock estate completed to indemnify S.C. members against engagement with Seamour and Oxford

SEARLE, James   3 Feb 1700/1 G55v bound to John Marsh, 7 years   7 Jun 1708 G153v freed by John Marsh. Augustus Hitchcock is bound to him

SECRETARIES OF STATE   7 Dec 1685 F47v Court to ask them a favour re. not prosecuting Benjamin Harris for being in possession of copies of 'English Liberties'   22 Dec 1685 F49v Benjamin Harris informed that S.C. has negotiated with them and has delayed but possibly not rescinded action against him   5 Mar 1685/6 F52v committee meeting resolves to apply to Secretary of State re. unlicensed aliens selling books   12 Oct 1687 F90v Master to ask Secretary of State why William Cooper was displaced from the Assistants but not the Livery   6 Aug 1688 F104v Widow Holt and Widow Thompson asked to apply to the Secretary of State for a licence to print   6 Mar 1688/9 F114v Lord Shrewsbury; supplies Robert Stephens with a search warrant for Mrs Curtis's printing house; Secretary of State to be consulted re. outcome   3 Dec 1694 F215v Ichabod Dawkes's complaint about an illegal press at Chester is referred to one of the Secretaries of State

See also ALMANACKS

SEDGELEY/SEDGLEY, Henry   4 Apr 1709 G164r bound to Henry Kifft, 7 years   7 May 1716 G240r freed by the executor of Mrs Kifft

SEDGWICK, [   ]   2 Jul 1694 F210r appears on behalf of Anthony Nelme, a S.C. tenant, to ask for money for a drainpipe. Demands £80 for a share assigned to him in Adiel Mill's statute of bankruptcy; committee to attend him at agreed meeting-place   6 Jun 1698 G8v request that he might take down wainscotting in Nelme's house refused. Demands £80 share formerly belonging to Adiel Mill on behalf of his wife. No action taken as suit in Chancery against S.C. brought by himself and his wife

SEDGWICK, Dina   27 Sep 1699 G30v to be given Mary Bateson's pension

SEELE, Elizabeth   22 Mar 1714/15 G238r Rebecca Hull is given her pension

SEGUIN, James   26 Jun 1684 (W) letter from the Duke of Buckingham requesting his freedom

SEILE, Elizabeth – see SEALE, Elizabeth

SEILE, Reuben, snr – see following entry

SEILE, Reuben, jnr   6 May 1695 F223r son of Reuben Seile snr; freed by patrimony

SELECT OBSERVATIONS   3 Oct 1692 F180v [John Hall's] 'Select Observations on English Bodies of Eminent Persons on Desperate Diseases' assigned by Benjamin Shirley to William Marshall

SELL, Daniel   7 Feb 1698/9 G20v bound to James Rawlins, 7 years

SELLER, Abednego – see INFALLIBLE

SELLER, John   26 Mar 1686 F53r merchant-taylor; asks Court about his right to sell mathematical books. His son is freed by patrimony and he is asked to translate   3 Jun 1689 F119v excused cloathing

SELLERS, John   3 Jun 1689 F119v excused cloathing

SELLS, William   1 Dec 1707 G147v bound to Owen Lloyd, 7 years

SENDALL, Richard   5 Aug 1700 G44r bound to Benjamin Motte, 7 years

SENECA, Lucius Annaeus   1 Aug 1687 F87r his 'Morals' assigned by Roger L'Estrange to Richard Bentley, Jacob Tonson and Joseph Hindmarsh

SENEX, John, snr – see following entry

SENEX, John, jnr   5 Aug 1695 F232r son of John Senex snr of Ludlow, gentleman; bound to Robert Clavell from   1 Jul 1695   4 Mar 1705/6 G129r freed by Robert

Clavell   6 May 1706 G131v William Lathbury is bound to him   6 Nov 1710 G185r bookseller; Samuel Parker is bound to him   1 Feb 1713/14 G216r Ephraim Chambers is bound to him   5 Dec 1715 G235v Thomas Gregory Warren is bound to him

SENTENTIAE – see HOOLE, Charles

SERJEANT, John, snr – see following entry

SERJEANT, John, jnr   6 Oct 1712 G204v son of John; bound to Edmund Calverley, 7 years

SERJEANT, Nicholas – see following entry

SERJEANT, William   22 Dec 1715 G235v son of Nicholas; bound to John Baskett, 7 years

SERSON – see SARSON

SEVERAL WEIGHTY QUERIES – see HERACLITUS

SEWERS, COMMISSIONERS OF   4 Jul 1709 G167r Capt. William Phillipps to consult with Mr Jackson, officer of this body

SEYMOUR – see SEAMOUR

SHARP/SHARPE, Dickinson/Dickonson   4 Aug 1712 G202v son of William; bound to Robert Whitledge, 7 years   2 May 1715 G228v turned over from Robert Whitledge to Cornelius Rainsford

SHARP/SHARPE, William   4 Aug 1712 G202v his son Dickinson is bound to Robert Whitledge, 7 years

SHARPE, George   3 Jul 1704 G110r bound to William Holland, 7 years   1 Feb 1713/14 G216r freed by William Holland

SHARPE, John   7 Oct 1695 F234r servant to Thomas Snowden; freed

SHARPE, Thomas   1 Sep 1707 G145r bound to John Hartley, 7 years   1 Mar 1713/14 G216v turned over from John Hartley to John Matthews   7 Nov 1715 G234v freed by Mary Matthews   1 Oct 1716 G244r to be summoned to take cloathing next Court day; Richard Bell is turned over to him from Edmund Powell   3 Dec 1716 G245v cloathed

SHARPEY, Thomas   7 May 1705 G120r bound to John Clarke, 7 years   2 Mar 1712/13 G206v complaint that his master, John Clarke, would not make him free although he had served the term of his indenture   7 Dec 1713 G214v freed by John Clarke

SHARPLESSE, [ ]   2 Mar 1690/1 F150v married name of Widow Harefinch; husband to be prosecuted since she continues to print despite Sharplesse not being free of S.C.

SHATTERTWAITE – see SATTERTWAITE

SHAW, John   6 May 1700 G39v bound to John Francknell, 7 years   2 Mar 1701/2 G67v bound to George Strange, 7 years

SHAW, William   7 Apr 1701 G58v bound to John Penn, 7 years   4 Dec 1710 G186r freed by John Penn   1 Sep 1712 G203r Benjamin Barrett is turned over to him from Richard Davis   2 Aug 1714 G221r his apprentice Benjamin Barrett is freed

SHAWLER, Edward, snr – see following entry

SHAWLER, Edward, jnr   21 Jun 1695 F226v son of the late Edward Shawler, distiller of London; bound to John Tuckey   1 Mar 1702/3 G86r turned over from Joseph Tokey (alternative spelling of Tuckey?) and freed by Francis Leak

SHEERES/SHERES, [ ]   25 Jun 1684 F18v of the Strand; owns that he wants 'a year of his time' and alleges himself a freeman's son; complains at £5 fine and is referred   7 Jul 1684 F21r refuses to pay £5 fine for freedom; forbidden to trade

SHEFFIELD/SHEFFEILD, William   6 Dec 1697 G2r bound to Medriach Mead   2 Aug 1703 G94r turned over to Edward Hawkins (repeated under 6 Sep 1703, G94v)   6 Aug 1705 G122v freed by Edward Hawkins   12 Nov 1705 G125r Francis Pattison turned over to him from Richard George

SHELL, George   2 Dec 1700 G54r his apprentice Robert Smith is freed   2 Jun 1701 G60v William Backhouse is bound to him   4 Sep 1704 G112r Gwin Needham is bound to him   7 Jun 1707 G143v Gwin Needham turned over from him to Hannah Clarke

SHELL, Millicent   22 Mar 1715/16 G238r elected to Patience Ghent's pension   21 Mar 1716/17 G248r elected to Sarah Dickens's pension. William Hawkins is given her pension

SHELLSWELL/SHELSWELL, Daniel   7 May 1705 G120r Jacob Poole is turned over to him from Henry Skelton   3 May 1708 G152v his apprentice Jacob Poole is freed

SHELLEY/SHELLY, Benjamin   3 Mar 1700/1 G57r bound to William Horton (repeated under 26 Mar 1701, G58r)   8 May 1704 G106v turned over from William Horton to John Grantham

SHELLY, Samuel   2 Jul 1705 G121v bound to George Marshall, 7 years

SHELMARDINE/SHELMERDINE/SHERMANDINE, Thomas   7 Feb 1703/4 G101r cloathed   6 Mar 1703/4 G103v John Read turned over to him   7 Mar 1708/9 G162r his apprentice John Read is freed   4 Jul 1709 G167v Thomas Payne is bound to him   26 Mar 1713 G207v excused office of Renter Warden for one year   1 Jun 1713 G210v John Mills is bound to him   26 Mar 1714 G217v excused office of Renter Warden for one year   26 Mar 1715 G227r excused office of First Renter Warden for one year

SHELSWELL – see SHELLSWELL

SHENTON, John   7 Apr 1701 G58v bound to Benjamin Beardwell, 7 years

SHEPHARD/SHEPARD, [   ]   5 Oct 1696 (W) committee chosen to inspect his lease in Ave Maria Lane   2 Nov 1696 (W) reported that Shephard paid about £33 p.a. for his house and Woolley paid about £24 p.a.   4 Sep 1699 G29v in possession of S.C.'s house in Ave Maria Lane leased by William Woolley

SHEPHERD, Henry   3 Jun 1706 G132v bound to Edmund Richardson, 7 years

SHEPHERD, James   7 Feb 1714/15 G225r son of Thomas; bound to John Lilly, 7 years

SHEPHERD, Thomas (I) – see preceding entry

SHEPHERD, Thomas (II)   10 Sep 1694 F212v Samuel Hodgson is bound to him
See also preceding entry

SHEPPARD, Thomas   6 Feb 1692/3 F184r cloathed and promises payment of fine
See also SHEPHERD, Thomas

SHEPPERD, Mary   6 Jul 1702 G78r bound to William Prickett, 7 years

SHERLEY, Benjamin   26 Mar 1683 E167v assigns G. [i.e. George?] Dawes 'A View of [the] Admiral Jurisdiction' [i.e. John Godolphin, *Synegoros Thalassos*] and 'The Life, Trial and Arraignment of Sir Walter Raleigh'
See also SHIRLEY, Benjamin

SHERLOCK, Dr   5 Dec 1692 F183r writes on Mrs Draper's behalf to Court re. S.C. tenement

SHERLOCK, Richard – see CATECHISMS

SHERLOCK, William – see PROTESTANT RESOLUTION

SHERMANDINE, Thomas – see SHELMARDINE, Thomas

SHERMENDINE, [ ]   1 Dec 1701 G65v excused from cloathing

See also SHERMANDINE, Thomas

SHERRINGTON, [ ]   3 Nov 1679 E94v order for prosecution given against his widow and her husband   1 Dec 1679 E95r two bonds owned by him to be given to his widow upon payment to the poor of £10 20s

SHILFOX, David   1 Jun 1702 G71v bound to Israel Harrison jnr

SHILLINGFORD/SHILLINGSFORD, John   9 Feb 1707/8 G149r bound to Mary Roberts, 7 years   14 Mar 1714/5 G226r freed by James Roberts

SHILTON, John   2 Aug 1714 G221r freed by Mrs Everingham

SHIPTHORP, John   3 Jun 1706 G132v freed by John Wild

SHIPWRIGHT   7 Dec 1685 F47r his bill to be compared with former bills and discussed at next Court   22 Dec 1685 F49r his bill for barge for last Lord Mayor's Day to be paid   4 Oct 1703 G95v his bill for trimming the barge to be paid   2 Oct 1704 G112v bill to be paid   12 Nov 1705 G124v bill of £3 10s to be paid   1 Dec 1707 G147r to be paid for cleaning the barge   4 Dec 1710 G186r his bill for trimming the barge to be paid   7 Dec 1713 G215r bill to be paid   12 Nov 1716 G244v bill to be paid

SHIRLEY, Benjamin   3 Oct 1692 F180v assigns [John Hall's] 'Select Observations … on Desperate Diseases' and [James Cooke's] 'Marrow of Chirurgery' to William Marshall

See also SHERLEY, Benjamin

SHIRLEY, John – see RALEIGH, Sir Walter

SHORE/SHORES, Sir Bartholomew   8 Oct 1690 F144v Counsel at Law for Crown; John Lilly to take his advice re. drawing up case against hawkers   1 Jul 1695 F227r to be consulted re. dispute over whether taxes should be deducted from the 3s charity paid weekly to St Faith's

SHORTER, Daniel   12 Apr 1708 G152r bound to Thomas Mead, 7 years

SHORTER, John   7 Dec 1691 F163r writing-school master; to be paid 15s for a present made to S.C., 'the types and figures of Christ in a lackered [i.e. lacquered] frame'

SHORTHARELL, John   12 Dec 1695 F238r servant to Richard Hunt; freed

SHOTWELL, Joseph   1 Aug 1692 (W) is freed by executrix of Richard Andrews   12 Sep 1692 F179r of Clerkenwell and newly made free of Richard Andrews's executors; name given to Lord Chamberlain

SHOWER, [John]   7 Aug 1699 G28r 'Shower on Eternity' [i.e. John Shower, *Serious Reflections on Time and Eternity*] among books assigned to Samuel Sprint and J. [i.e. John?] Nicholson

SHOWER, Sir Bartholomew   19 Mar 1696/7 F257v gives legal opinion to S.C. re. Paper Act

SHREWSBURY, Charles Talbot, Earl of (Duke from 1694) – see SECRETARY OF STATE

SHREWSBURY, William   6 Feb 1681/2 E143v elected to John Simms's £40 share   1 Mar 1683/4 F9r elected Stock-keeper for Yeomanry with Walter Kettleby   3 Mar 1683/4 F9v elected Assistant in response to request from Crown as a reward for stamping out seditious printing. Thomas Passenger elected Stock-keeper for Yeomanry in his stead (note in margin claims this was an error). Fined for Renter Warden so he is eligible for Court   7 Apr 1684 F14r on the list of loyal Assistants presented to the Crown   2 Jun 1684 F16r to continue as Stock-keeper for Yeomanry until next election

despite being made an Assistant   3 Nov 1684 F25v elected to the late Robert Stephens's
£80 share   7 May 1685 (W) confirmed as a member of the new Livery   5 Mar 1685/6
F52v at committee meeting about stall booksellers   11 Oct 1688 F108v restored to
Livery   6 May 1689 F117r ranked fifteenth of Assistants never elected as Master or
Warden   5 Jun 1690 F135v re-elected Assistant   7 Nov 1692 F181v elected to
Christopher Wilkinson's £160 share   3 Jul 1697 F264r competes unsuccessfully for
Under Warden   5 Jul 1697 F264r competes unsuccessfully for Under Warden; allowed
to pay a £5 fine for a year to preserve his seniority   6 Jun 1698 G8r fined for first year
as Under Warden   10 Jan 1698/9 G18v added to committee to consider Printing
Act   3 Jul 1699 G26v auditor of Master and Wardens' accounts   6 Jul 1700 G43r
fined for second year as Under Warden   9 Sep 1700 G45r James Steward is bound to
him   5 May 1701/2 G59v James Steward turned over from him to Edward Powell   6
Mar 1703/4 G103v competes unsuccessfully for Henry Herring-man's £320 share   1
Jul 1704 G109r declines to fine for Upper Warden to preserve his seniority   5 Jul 1707
G143r competes unsuccessfully for Upper Warden   1 Sep 1707 G145r deceased; his
£160 share is disposed of to Nicholas Boddington   1 Dec 1707 G147v bond of £100
to S.C. is repaid

SHRIMPTON, John   1 Oct 1694 F213v John Phillipps jnr is bound to him

SHUCKBURGH, John   5 Jul 1714 G220v son of Richard; bound to Jonah Bowyer, 7
years

SHUCKBURGH, Richard – see preceding entry

SIDELIUS MANUAL [a work by Andreas or Fridericus Sidelius?]   18 Mar 1686/7
F79v among books in catalogue annexed to Oxford agreement

SIDNEY, Henry   9 Jun 1707 G142v bound to Thomas Brewer, 7 years

SILVER – see PLATE

SILVESTER/SYLVESTER, Joshua   8 Nov 1697 G1v made free   7 Mar 1697/8 G5r
George Salter is bound to him   6 Nov 1699 G32v excused from cloathing   1 Sep 1701
G64r excused from cloathing   4 Jun 1705 G120v his apprentice George Salter is
freed   5 Apr 1714 G217v excused from cloathing

SILVESTER, Thomas, snr – see following entry

SILVESTER, Thomas, jnr   4 Apr 1715 G227v son of Thomas; bound to Samuel
Ashurst, 7 years

SIMMONS, Neville   5 Feb 1699/1700 G35r freed by Robert Roberts

SIMMS, Edward   7 Nov 1715 G234v son of Richard; bound to Thomas Lingard, 7
years

SIMMS/SIMS, John   6 Feb 1681/2 E143v elected to John Bellinger's £80 share   3 Mar
1683/4 F9v elected Assistant in response to Crown's request as a reward for stamping
out seditious printing   26 Mar 1684 F11v sworn into Court of Assistants   7 Apr 1684
F14r on the list of loyal Assistants presented to the Crown   2 Jun 1684 F16r competes
unsuccessfully for Thomas Cotterell's £160 share   7 May 1685 (W) confirmed as
member of the new Livery   1 Jun 1685 F38r elected to John Wright's £160 share   3
Jul 1686 F59v elected Under Warden; Beadle asked to inform him as he is out of
town   5 Jul 1686 F60r allowed to fine for 2 years' Under Warden on account of living
out of town   12 Oct 1687 F91r competes unsuccessfully for Upper Warden   30 Jun
1688 F103r elected Upper Warden   7 Oct 1689 F124r his and Benjamin Tooke's
Wardens' accounts reveal that wine was presented to the Lord Chancellor in the middle
of the Oxford dispute   5 Jun 1690 F135v re-appointed Assistant   5 Jul 1690 F138r
competes unsuccessfully for Upper Warden   4 May 1691 F153v chosen to audit

Renter Wardens' accounts in place of Thomas Bassett, the latter going out of town 4 Jul 1691 F156v among those chosen to audit Renter Wardens' accounts 2 Jul 1692 F172v elected Upper Warden 4 Jul 1692 F173v elected to the £320 share of John Macock, deceased 1 Mar 1693/4 F199v elected Stock-keeper for Assistants with Samuel Lowndes 4 Jun 1694 F208r among those chosen to audit Renter Wardens' accounts 30 Jun 1694 F209v elected Master 2 Jul 1694 F210r William Rawlins is elected Stock-keeper in his stead 6 Jul 1695 F229r re-elected Master 6 Jul 1696 F245v added to comprinting committee. Competes unsuccessfully for Stock-keeper's position left vacant by the appointment of Henry Mortlock as Master 5 Oct 1696 F250r substitutes for Edward Brewster on Cambridge committee when Brewster is ill; (W) asked to ensure that minutes which Clerk has neglected to enter are entered by next Court day 2 Nov 1696 (W) says he received no summons to enter minutes 3 Jul 1697 F263v competes unsuccessfully for Master 5 Jul 1697 F264v among those chosen to audit Warden's accounts 13 Apr 1698 G6r added to Oxford committee 1 Aug 1698 G13r auditor of Master and Wardens' accounts 5 Sep 1698 G14r to examine repairs required to barge 1 Mar 1698/9 G21r elected Stock-keeper for Assistants 6 Mar 1698/9 G21v reports from barge and barge house committee that barge found to be in a bad condition 3 Jul 1699 G26v permitted to use his Assistant's share as surety for further loan of £20 from Parkhurst. Simms to have notice that Court ordered that Samuel Browne (to whom the share was assigned for £100) should have money due on the assignment 27 Jul 1699 G27v Beadle not to leave any more summons for him to attend Court as an Assistant 9 Feb 1701/2 G67r mortgages on his Assistant's share to be assigned to Thomas Parkhurst who lent him £300 to pay off mortgages 5 Mar 1704 G116v discharged from being an Assistant because he has been a prisoner of the Fleet for three years (lately discharged by virtue of an Act of Parliament for relief of poor prisoners for debts) 4 Oct 1714 G222r deceased; his Assistant's share, mortgaged to Parkhurst, disposed of to Awnsham Churchill

SIMMS, Richard 7 Nov 1715 G234v his son Edward is bound to Thomas Lingard, 7 years

SIMONS, Edward 6 Aug 1711 G193r son of Katherine; bound to John Phillips, 7 years

SIMONS, Katherine – see preceding entry

SIMONS, Neville 7 Jun 1680 E100v his apprentice John Kidgell is freed

SIMPSON, [ ] 11 Apr 1681 E110r fined for Renter Warden

SIMPSON/SYMPSON, Benjamin 3 Apr 1699 G24r freed by Warden Richard Simpson 6 Jul 1702 G77v elected to Thomas Yates's £40 share in English Stock 3 Dec 1716 G245v Robert Fillimore is bound to him

SIMPSON, Israel 2 Apr 1705 G118v bound to Robert Everingham, 8 years 5 Sep 1715 G232v freed by Elinor Everingham

SIMPSON/SYMPSON/SYMPON, Ralph 16 Jun 1684 F18r to be granted £50 from Tyler Bequest if his sureties are approved 25 Jun 1684 F18v sureties approved 6 May 1689 F117v allowed to continue his £50 loan if he finds a new surety in place of Richard Dawson, deceased, and pays it before September 29 May 1689 F118v cloathed 13 Mar 1692/3 F184v complains that Peter Parker has printed [William] Dyer's works, and reads assignment; committee formed to inspect register book 4 Feb 1694/5 F217r William Middleton is bound to him 7 Jul 1701 G62r Nathan Crosley is bound to him 9 Feb 1701/2 G67r William Mathews (Meadows) is bound to him 4 Oct 1703 G96r his apprentice William Middleton is freed 27 Mar 1704 G105r elected First Renter Warden 20 Apr 1705 G119r Joshua Phillips unwilling to deliver quarterage book to desk, only promising to on penalty of being summoned before the Lord Mayor together with Simpson   7 Feb 1708/9 G160v James Davenport is bound to him   4 Apr 1709 G164r his apprentice William Meadows is freed   5 May 1712 G199v William Parker is bound to him

SIMPSON, Richard   7 Jun 1686 F57r elected to Samuel Hoyle's £80 share, though swearing-in suspended in view of Counsel's opinion   5 Jul 1686 F60v sworn in to his share   28 Feb 1686/7 F76v re-admitted into the Livery on apologizing for his 'miscarriage in Poleing [i.e. polling?]'   1 Mar 1687/8 F97v order from Lord Mayor that he should be restored to the Livery. Summoned to next Court to be nominated for Assistant   5 Mar 1687/8 F99r Samuel Hoyle claims the £80 share that was disposed of to Simpson on 7 June 1686. Elected Assistant   4 Feb 1688/9 F112v re-elected Assistant   6 May 1689 F117r ranked twelfth of Assistants never elected as Master or Warden   5 Jun 1690 F135v re-elected Assistant   12 Apr 1692 F169r elected to the late Mrs Passenger's £160 share. Shown on examination of S.C.'s and Haberdashers' records to be senior to Richard Chiswell   10 Sep 1694 F212r takes over from Richard Chiswell as auditor for the Warden's accounts since the latter is out of town   7 Oct 1695 F234r his apprentice Henry Chawblin is freed   4 Jul 1696 F245r competes unsuccessfully for Under Warden   6 Jul 1696 F245v among those chosen to audit Warden's accounts   3 Jul 1697 F263v competes unsuccessfully for Under Warden   5 Jul 1697 F264r fined for Under Warden   2 Jul 1698 G10r elected Under Warden and not permitted to fine   10 Jan 1698/9 G18r complaint that he had put his name to 'The Life of John Milton and his Works'. Court declares its dislike of entering the book and orders him to take more care in future   3 Apr 1699 G24r his apprentice Benjamin Simpson is freed   1 Jul 1700 G41r alternative member of committee to raise subscription for new barge bottom   6 Jul 1700 G42v elected Upper Warden   5 Jul 1701 G61v elected Upper Warden   5 Apr 1703 G88r auditor of late Renter Wardens' accounts   6 Mar 1703/4 G103v elected to Mrs Herringman's £320 share. His £160 share disposed of to Thomas Bennett   1 Jul 1704 G109r elected Master   7 Aug 1704 G111r Thomas Waples is bound to him   30 Jun 1705 G121r elected Master   20 Dec 1706 G137r Thomas Ferrour is bound to him   5 May 1707 G141v auditor of late Renter Wardens' accounts   5 Jul 1707 G143r competes unsuccessfully for Master   9 Apr 1711 G189v auditor of late Renter Wardens' accounts   12 Nov 1711 G195r his apprentice Thomas Waples is freed   7 Jul 1712 G201v John Jennings is bound to him   24 Apr 1713 G209r signatory to S.C.'s notes to Thomas Guy   4 Jul 1713 G211r acquaints Court that John Baskett wishes to fine for Upper Warden   3 May 1714 G218v signs note to Guy   1 Oct 1716 G244r his apprentice Robert Pepper is freed   21 Feb 1716/17 G246v conveyance of trusteeship of Hall, &c., from him

SIMPSON/SYMPSON, Thomas   2 Dec 1695 F237r cloathed   2 Jun 1701 G60v William Woolley is bound to him   1 Jun 1702 G70v Brook Plucknett is bound to him   26 Mar 1705 G117v fined for first Renter Warden   3 Dec 1705 G125v elected to John Sprint's £40 share   4 Feb 1705/6 G127r elected to Deputy Collins' £80 share   3 Feb 1706/7 G138r John William Bryan turned over to him from Oliver Elliston   2 Aug 1708 G156v his apprentice William Woolley is freed   13 Apr 1713 G208v elected to the late Nathaniel Ranew's £160 share. His £80 share disposed of to Ralph Smith   2 May 1715 G228v elected Assistant   5 Mar 1715/16 G237v signed note for payment to Thomas Guy   2 Jul 1716 G241v auditor of late Master and Wardens' accounts   21 Feb 1716/17 G246v trusteeship of S.C.'s property conveyed to him

SIMS, Samuel   1 Feb 1702/3 G85r turned over from Samuel Clark to Joseph Hind

See also SIMMS, SYMS

SKEELS – see STEELE

SKELTON, Henry   2 Dec 1695 F237v Robert Spencer jnr is bound to him   7 Apr 1701 G58v Jacob Poole is bound to him   7 May 1705 G120r Jacob Poole is turned over from him to Daniel Shellswell   4 Jun 1705 G120v his apprentice John Taunton, alias Collins, is freed

SKINNER, [   ]   6 Feb 1681/2 E144r committee appointed to treat with him, Ponder and Symons re. their Chancery case against S.C.

SKINNER, Edward   6 Mar 1709/10 G176v bound to Henry Carter, 7 years

SKINNER, Jonathan   13 Jun 1715 G229v son of Thomas; bound to William Harvey, 7 years

SKINNER, Thomas – see preceding entry

SKINNERS' COMPANY   9 Feb 1690/1 F148r letter sent to them from Edward Cary, late tenant of Pellipar; S.C. had received dividends from Pellipar until Irish troubles   6 Jul 1691 F157r their Clerk sends memorial from Edward Cary setting forth his losses in Ireland; committee appointed to negotiate with Skinners and others   10 Oct 1692 F181r ask S.C. to appoint a committee to meet at Skinners' Hall re. Irish plantation to hear tenants' proposals; committee appointed

SLADE, Elizabeth   27 Sep 1715 G233r elected to Anne Fowell's pension

SLATE, Elizabeth   20 Dec 1716 G246r deceased; Mary Pardoe is given her pension

SLATER, [   ]   3 Nov 1707 G146v Joseph Collyer to deliver to him plates of an almanack, once they have been defaced

SLATER, Thomas   5 Feb 1704/5 G114v complaint against him for printing 'Observations on Time Sacred and Profane' containing S.C.'s calendar   5 Mar 1704/5 G116v and Daniel Browne; to send copies of [N.B. Philomath, *pseud*.] 'Observations on Time Sacred and Profane' to Warehousekeeper or be party to bill in Chancery

SLATTER, James   3 Jul 1699 G27v bound to Benjamin Motte, 7 years   3 Feb 1706/7 G138r freed by Benjamin Motte

SMALSHAW/SMALLSHAW, James   7 Feb 1698/9 G20r pays fine of 30s because he was bound by foreign indenture. Freed by Thomas Whitledge   24 Sep 1714 G222r elected to Bridget Thomas's pension

SMART, [   ]   26 Mar 1681 E108v John Lilly's bill for business concerning Smart to be paid

SMART, John   4 May 1702 G70v permission granted to print 'A Table or an Account of Time for 200 Years' [i.e. *Tables of Time Calculated for Two Hundred Years?*]

SMART, Richard   6 Jun 1681 E112v given 40s charity

SMELT, Matthew   29 Sep 1710 G184r made a pensioner with 7s 6d a quarter   24 Mar 1711/12 G198r deceased; Clement Williams is given his pension

SMITH   12 Jun 1693 F188v £2 1s 1d bill for work on the Hall to be paid   5 Apr 1703 G88r bill for work on the Hall to be paid   2 Oct 1704 G112v bill to be paid   3 Feb 1706/7 G137v bill to be paid   4 Oct 1708 G158r bill referred to Master and Wardens for payment   6 Mar 1709/10 G176r bill for work on the Hall to be paid

SMITH, [   ]   3 Dec 1684 F26v complains that several S.C. members, on being refused supernumerary apprentices, have bound some at the scriveners   25 Sep 1690 F143r committee appointed to treat with Thomas Parkhurst, Benjamin Motte and Smith re. printing Lucius [Annaeus] Florus, Justin and [William] Barton's Psalms   6 Oct 1690 F143v committee required to reach agreement with him and report   12 Nov 1694 F214v involved in dispute over printing Horace   7 Dec 1696 (W) writing master, cloathed   1 Apr 1697 F260v to ask booksellers, printers and paper manufacturers of St Paul's Churchyard for money towards Paper Act test case

SMITH, Abraham   3 Oct 1692 (W) a foreigner, made free on payment of 2 guineas to the Poor Box

SMITH, Charles   13 Apr 1698 G6v bound to Charles Harper, 7 years   4 Jun 1705 G120v freed by Charles Harper   4 Apr 1709 G164r Thomas Mayhew is turned over to him from Andrew Mayhew

SMITH, Elinor/Eleanor   8 May 1693 F187v Mrs Newcomb complains she has not been paid a £40 debt by Mrs Smith; Court orders her £40 share to be disposed of   12 Jun 1693 F188v allowed to mortgage her £40 share to Samuel Sprint   5 Sep 1709 G170r deceased; her £40 share disposed of to Edmund Parker

See also SMITH, Francis

SMITH, Elizabeth   7 Feb 1708/9 G160v of Ludgate Street; John Hopkins is bound to her

SMITH, Francis   11 Apr 1681 E110r the printer Astwood clears him of asking for 'A Raree-Show' to be printed   21 Feb 1681/2 E145r his sureties are asked to find someone to undertake his £50 bond to S.C. since he is no longer resident in the City or suburbs   2 Oct 1682 E158r Richard Janeway confesses to printing 'Merlin Revived' for Francis Smith's youngest son Samuel, and 'Ignoramus Justices' [i.e. Edmund Whitaker, *Ignoramus Justices*, or the anonymous *Ignoramus Justice*?] for Smith's wife   7 Jul 1684 F21r given leave to sue Downing, a S.C. member, alleged to have had dealings in a book of his since 7 Oct 1681   7 Dec 1685 F47v in Benjamin Harris's partnership for printing the proceedings of the Westminster Parliament   1 Mar 1687/8 F97v expelled from Livery by order of Lord Mayor   11 Oct 1688 F108v restored to Livery   8 May 1693 F187v his widow is complained of by Mrs Newcomb for refusing to pay a £40 debt

See also SMITH, Elinor

SMITH, Hannah   5 Aug 1695 F231v Samuel Babbington is bound to her   22 Jun 1704 G108r given Anne Monday's pension   24 Mar 1711/12 G198r elected to Amy Hunt's pension. Anne Ferry is given her pension   19 Dec 1712 G205v deceased; Grace Middlewright is given her pension

SMITH, Henry   2 Aug 1708 G156v freed by patrimony   3 Oct 1709 G171r bound to Samuel Clarke, 7 years   5 Apr 1714 G218r turned over from Samuel Clarke to Arthur Bettesworth

SMITH, James   6 May 1706 G131v bound to William Wilkins, 7 years   7 Apr 1712 G199r turned over from William Wilkins to William Sparkes   9 Apr 1716 G239r turned over from Daniel Mead to James Holland

SMITH, Jeremiah   7 Feb 1708/9 G160v freed by James Dover

SMITH, John (I)   16 Jun 1684 F17r of Covent Garden and ex-apprentice of Magnus, a member of S.C.; freed   1 Mar 1699/1700 G36r elected Stock-keeper for Yeomanry

SMITH, [John] (II)   7 Aug 1699 G28r clockmaker; an assignment of 'Smiths Clock-work' [i.e. *Horological Disquisitions*] to Samuel Sprint and J. [i.e. John?] Nicholson by James Crayle and others is read, but order for entry deferred until next Court day

SMITH, John (III)   5 Aug 1700 G44r freed by Samuel Darker

SMITH, John (IV)   2 Mar 1701/2 G67v bound to Thomas Cope, 7 years

SMITH, John (V)   4 Sep 1710 G183v bound to Edward Place, 7 years

SMITH, Marmaduke   7 Feb 1714/15 G225r son of William; bound to John Grantham, 7 years

SMITH, Mrs (I)   8 Nov 1703 G97r deceased; her £40 share disposed of to Joseph Marshall

SMITH, Mrs (II)   6 Dec 1708 G159r widow of Samuel Smith; dividend money to be stopped and share disposed of to pay Samuel Smith's debts, unless she pays £80 for the share by next monthly Court

SMITH, Mrs (III)   5 Oct 1685 F45r widow of Ralph Smith; complains that Mrs Sawbridge has printed her copy

SMITH, Nicholas   5 Aug 1700 G44r bound to William Rawlins, 7 years   5 Jul 1703 G92r turned over to Richard Janeway   6 Oct 1707 G145v freed by Richard Janeway

SMITH, Obadiah, snr   6 Jul 1691 F157v of 'Dantry' [i.e. Daventry]; Clerk to inform him of his election to cloathing and obtain his £20 Livery fine by post   26 Mar 1706 G130r of Daventry, Northants; to be sent for on next choosing of Renter Wardens   26 Mar 1707 G139v Clerk to inform him that he has been elected First Renter Warden   7 Apr 1707 G140v to fine for First Renter Warden   26 Mar 1708 G151r his son Obadiah Smith is freed

SMITH, Obadiah, jnr   26 Mar 1708 G151r freed by patrimony

SMITH, Parkhurst   6 Oct 1707 G145v bound to Thomas Parkhurst, 7 years   5 Oct 1713 G214r freed by Mrs Parkhurst

SMITH, Ralph (I)   30 Jun 1683 F1r competes unsuccessfully for Master   5 Oct 1685 F45r his widow complains that Mrs Sawbridge has printed her copy

SMITH, Ralph (II)   7 May 1685 (W) confirmed as a member of the new Livery   7 Dec 1685 F47v in Benjamin Harris's partnership for printing the proceedings of the Westminster Parliament   1 Mar 1687/8 F97v displaced as Assistant by order of Crown and expelled from Livery by order of Lord Mayor   6 Aug 1688 F105r surviving signatory of the original deed of conveyance of St Martin's Ludgate   1 Jul 1689 F120v to re-execute conveyance to present Court members   2 Dec 1689 F127r deceased; his £320 share voted to Robert Scott

SMITH, Ralph (III)   2 Aug 1697 F265v freed by Thomas Parkhurst   1 Dec 1701 G66r excused cloathing until next Court day   2 Mar 1701/2 G67v cloathed   26 Mar 1707 G139v fined for First Renter Warden   7 Apr 1707 G141r elected to Richard Wilkins' £40 share   13 Apr 1713 G208v elected to Thomas Simpson's £80 share. His £40 share disposed of to John Usborne

SMITH, Richard   3 Mar 1706/7 G139r Francis Pattison turned over to him from Richard George   5 Jul 1708 G155r bound to George Croome, 7 years

SMITH, Robert (I)   16 Jun 1684 F17v of Bow Lane and free of the Merchant Taylors' Company; declares himself willing to be translated to S.C.   3 Nov 1701 G65r William Phelps is bound to him   4 Oct 1708 G158r his apprentice Francis Pattison is freed

SMITH, Robert (II)   4 Oct 1697 F268v bound to Edmund Richardson   5 Mar 1704/5 G117r freed by Edmund Richardson

SMITH, Robert (III)   2 Dec 1700 G54r freed by George Shell

SMITH, Robert (IV)   6 Sep 1714 G221v son of William; bound to John Brookes, 7 years

SMITH, Robert Lowden   12 Nov 1705 G125r bound to Robert Knaplock, 7 years   1 Dec 1712 G205v freed by Robert Knaplock

SMITH, Samuel   3 Jul 1682 E155r petition for £100 loan rejected; decided that he is more fit to be called onto the livery   2 Oct 1682 E158r son of Francis Smith; Richard Janeway confesses to printing 'Merlin Revived' for him   4 Oct 1686 F64v elected to livery   8 Nov 1686 F67r excused cloathing   2 Mar 1690/1 F150v to be summoned on the charge of importing Stock books   1 Feb 1691/2 F165r summoned to next Court to answer the complaint of Walter Kettleby   12 Apr 1692 F169r elected to Stephen

Bateman's £40 share 26 Jul 1692 F175v to be summoned 5 Sep 1692 F177v summoned to answer Thomas Dring's complaint about importing Ciceros; committee appointed 3 Oct 1692 F180r re. his difference with Dring, committee present their award and order; approved and entered; reference to Liber A. To be summoned to next Court to affirm that Robert Scott has imported several of S.C.'s books 27 Mar 1693 F185v fined for Assistant Renter Warden 6 May 1695 F222v elected to Thomas Cockerell's £80 share 13 Apr 1698 G6v complaint that he, Henry Mortlock and Robert Clavell have comprinted copy of Horace, in breach of S.C. byelaws 4 Jul 1698 G11r Jeffrey Wale is bound to him 1 Dec 1701 G66r his apprentice Samuel Buckley is freed 22 Jun 1704 G108r Jonathan Baldwine is bound to him 6 Dec 1708 G159r deceased; unless his widow pays £80 for the share by the next monthly Court, her dividend money will be stopped and the share disposed of to pay his debts

SMITH, Thomas (I) 13 Mar 1692/3 F185r Robert Everingham appears to have Thomas Smith freed and is fined for binding him with foreign indenture

SMITH, Thomas (II) 4 Oct 1697 F268v bound to Thomas Beaver 4 May 1702 G70v turned over from Thomas Beaver to Bernard Lintott

SMITH, Thomas (III) 4 Aug 1701 G63v bound to Thomas Bradyll

SMITH, William (I) 4 Mar 1688/9 F114r chosen as butler to S.C. after a commendatory certificate from the Lord Mayor, Sir John Chapman, has been read

SMITH, William (II) 7 Nov 1698 G16r freed by Henry Carter

SMITH, William (III) 2 Dec 1700 G54r freed by James Astwood and John Darby snr

SMITH, William (perhaps to be identified with II or III?) 5 Mar 1704/5 G117r James Cooper is turned over to him from Thomas Leigh 12 Nov 1716 G244v Thomas Fox is bound to him

See also WILLIAMS, William

SMITH, William (IV) 7 Apr 1707 G141r bound to Joshua Gilbert, 7 years 16 Oct 1716 G244r freed by Joshua Gilbert

SMITH, William (V) 7 Feb 1714/15 G225r his son Marmaduke is bound to John Grantham, 7 years

SMITH, William (VI) 6 Sep 1714 G221v his son Robert is bound to John Brookes, 7 years

SMITH'S CLOCKWORK – see SMITH, John

SMYTHIES, [William] 3 Nov 1684 F26r Roger L'Estrange complains that John Southby has libelled him in registered books, esp. half a sheet attached to 'Smithies sermon' [i.e. Smythies' *The Spirit of Meekness* or *The Unworthy Non-Communicant*?]

SMYTHERS, William 5 Jul 1703 G92r freed by Thomas Milbourne

SNAPES, [ ] 6 Mar 1703/4 G103v letter to be considered at next pension court

SNELL, George 2 Dec 1700 G47v 10s accepted as payment of his quarterage arrears in respect of his low condition

SNELL, John 8 Jan 1716/17 G246r son of Josias, is bound to Elizabeth Milbourne, 7 years

SNELL, Josias – see preceding entry

SNODEN, SNODHAM – see SNOWDEN

SNOW, [ ] 7 Aug 1699 G28r and three other door-keepers of the House of Lords paid 3 guineas by the Treasurer for their attendance in relation to Act of Parliament for laying duty on paper

SNOW, Joseph   3 Dec 1711 G195v freed by his father, Richard Snow

SNOW, Ralph   8 Apr 1695 F221v servant to Richard Lilley; freed   3 Jun 1695 F226r
John Pigg is bound to him   1 Feb 1696/7 F255r resummoned re. cloathing   3 May
1697 F261v cloathed and promises fine at two six-monthly intervals; F262r John Clarke
is bound to him   5 Dec 1698 G16v to be prosecuted for non-payment of Livery fine   6
Mar 1698/9 G22r to be proceeded against for non-payment of Livery fine   1 Sep 1701
G64r Joseph Packman is bound to him   1 Feb 1702/3 G85r Thomas Franklin is
bound to him   3 Apr 1704 G106r John Coulter is bound to him   2 Oct 1704 G112v
Abraham Fitter is bound to him   5 Feb 1704/5 G115r Thomas Pinfold is bound to
him   2 Apr 1705 G118v his apprentice John Clarke is freed   6 Sep 1708 G157v writing
master; Philip Dorey is bound to him   2 Oct 1710 G184v of Moorfields, writing master;
Zachary Chambers is bound to him   7 Apr 1712 G199r Lewis Cappell is bound to
him   5 Oct 1713 G214r William Underhill is bound to him

SNOW, Richard   3 Dec 1711 G195v frees his son Joseph. Remitted 12s 6d of his quarterage; this is to be entered as paid to him in the next pension papers

SNOWDEN/SNOWDON, Ann   1 Jun 1702 G71v Thomas Peacock is bound to
her   7 May 1705 G120r Thomas Davis is bound to her   3 May 1708 G152v printer;
John Philmott is bound to her   6 Jun 1709 G165v Henry Lebrand is turned over to her
from Bryan Mills   1 Aug 1709 G169v her apprentice Thomas Peacock is freed   4 Sep
1710 G183v John Philmott is turned over from her to William Hurt

SNOWDEN/SNODEN, George   4 Feb 1683/4 F8v petition for £50 of Tyler's bequest
to be considered at next Court   3 Mar 1683/4 F11r petition deferred until next Court

SNOWDEN, Mary   27 Sep 1710 G184r deceased; Mary Chandler is given her pension

SNOWDEN/SNODEN/SNODHAM/SNOWDON, Thomas (I)   3 Feb 1679/80 E96v
cloathed   5 Dec 1681 E140v printer; to have George Lloyd, son of Samuel Lloyd, turned
over to him from Robert Stephens   6 May 1689 F117r elected First Renter Warden   2
Dec 1689 F127v elected to 'Major' [i.e. Capt. Samuel] Roycroft's £40 share   7 Dec
1691 F163r summoned to next Court to explain why he and Thomas Minshall have
not made up their Renter Wardens' accounts and paid Warden the balance   6 May
1695 F223v John Cluer is bound to him   1 Jul 1695 F228r John Huntley is bound to
him   7 Oct 1695 F234r John Sharpe, his apprentice, is freed   7 Mar 1697/8 G4v elected
to Daniel Peacock's £80 share   7 Nov 1698 G16r his son Thomas is freed by patrimony   7 Feb 1698/9 G20v Thomas Saywell is bound to him   4 Mar 1705/6 G129r his
apprentice Thomas Saywell is freed

SNOWDEN, Thomas (II)   7 Nov 1698 G16r freed by Thomas Snowden, patrimony

SNOWDON, Mary   18 Dec 1707 G148r elected to Katherine Hall's pension

SNOWDON, William   4 May 1702 G71r his apprentice John Cluer is freed
See also SNOWDEN

SODOM OR THE QUINTESSENCE OF DEBAUCHERY [attr. John Wilmot, Earl of
Rochester]   7 Oct 1689 F125r Benjamin Crayle and Joseph Streeter to be prosecuted
for publishing this

SOLICITOR GENERAL   30 Jun 1696 F243v to be retained for S.C. both in general
and re. comprinting in particular

SOLICITOR IN PARLIAMENT – see ALLEN, [   ]

SOLLARS, Robert   7 Oct 1698 G15r bond to S.C. to be put in suit   7 Nov 1698
G15v promised payment of £20 due on his bond in 3 months' time   3 Apr 1699 G23r
to be sued upon his bond for not complying with repeated promises   5 Jun 1699 G25r
Clerk to request him to pay the remaining £10 of his Livery fine   7 Aug 1699 G28r

Clerk to ask him for speedy payment of Livery fine   4 Sep 1699 G29v Court agrees to postponement of the remaining £10 due from him until next term

SOLLERS, Robert   24 Jun 1682 E154r cloathed

SOMERSCALES, Rebecca   20 Dec 1716 G246r Christopher Thomas is turned over to her from John Buchanan

SOMERVILE, Thomas   13 Apr 1702 G70r bound to Humphrey [substituted for Henry] Pooler, 7 years

SOMNER, William – see GIBSON, Edmund

SOULES – see SOWLE

SOUTHBY, John   3 Nov 1684 F26r Roger L'Estrange complains that Southby has libelled him in registered books, esp. half a sheet attached to 'Smithies sermon' [i.e. William Smythies' *The Spirit of Meekness* or *The Unworthy Non-Communicant?*]. S.C. has no powers to prosecute because he registered the copies in accordance with the byelaw   5 Aug 1689 F122r given until next Court to decide about cloathing   12 Sep 1692 F179r summoned to show why he should not be cloathed   3 Oct 1692 F180v cloathed   5 Feb 1693/4 F198v his apprentice Nathaniel Sackett is freed

SOUTHBY, William   6 Oct 1712 G204v freed by patrimony

SOUTHWOOD, Thomas   16 Jun 1684 F17v of Princes Street; owns himself 'a Gentleman's Servingman and never bred to the trade', so the Master and Wardens are to suppress him

SOWLE/SOULES, Andrew   7 May 1688 F100v of Holiday Yard in Creed Lane; Mrs Humphreys tells Court she has sold her press and type to him   4 Aug 1690 F141v summoned for printing the same unlicensed pamphlet as Robert Roberts; Robert Stephens to take him before Lord Chief Justice   7 Oct 1695 F234r his daughter Tace is freed   5 Dec 1698 G17r his apprentice Thomas Martyn is freed

SOWLE, Jane   7 Mar 1708 G162r of Leadenhall Street; Moses Carter is bound to her

SOWLE, Tace   7 Oct 1695 F234r daughter of Andrew Sowle; freed   5 Jul 1697 F264v George Bond is bound to her   3 Nov 1701 G65r and Tace Cheese. Their apprentice Edward Saunders is freed   5 Oct 1702 G81v Edmund Bourne is bound to her   4 Sep 1704 G112r John Mongar is bound to her   2 Apr 1705 G118v fined 2 guineas for making free Andrew Hind who was bound by a foreign indenture. Her apprentice George Bond is freed

SPACKMAN, Richard, snr – see following entry

SPACKMAN, Richard, jnr   5 Apr 1714 G218r son of Richard; bound to Samuel Keimer, 7 years   7 Nov 1715 G234v turned over from Samuel Keimer to William Bowyer

SPARKE, John   2 Oct 1693 F193r summoned re. cloathing

SPARKES, John   4 Dec 1693 F196v cloathed   3 Dec 1694 F216r Thomas Boucher is bound to him   3 Feb 1695/6 F239r Court refuses to discharge him, John Gerrard and Thomas Penford from S.C. so they can take up freedom of the Ironmongers' Company

SPARKES, William   2 May 1698 G7v Edward Lewis is bound to him   7 Feb 1703/4 G101v Christopher Chapman is bound to him   7 May 1705 G120r his apprentice Edward Lewis is freed   3 Dec 1711 G195v James Hookes is bound to him   7 Apr 1712 G119r James Smith is turned over to him from William Wilkins

SPARKS, John   4 May 1702 G71r Richard Harle is bound to him

SPARROW, Anthony – see OXFORD, Bishop of

SPEED, [   ]   4 May 1691 F153v to be summoned to next Court

SPEED, Thomas 5 Apr 1714 G217v excused cloathing for one year 13 Jun 1715 G229r summoned to take cloathing 4 Jul 1715 G231r cloathed. Obtains discount for prompt payment of the fine

SPENCER, Joseph 1 Oct 1694 F213v cook of Istleworth, Middlesex; his son Thomas is bound to John Franke

SPENCER, Robert, Earl of Sunderland – see SUNDERLAND

SPENCER, Robert, snr – see following entry

SPENCER, Robert, jnr 2 Dec 1695 F237v son of Robert Spencer snr, St John's Wapping, Middlesex, 'malsman' [i.e. maltster?]; bound to Henry Skelton

SPENCER, Thomas (I) 1 Oct 1694 F213v son of Joseph Spencer, Istleworth, Middlesex, cook; bound to John Franke

SPENCER, Thomas (II) 7 Nov 1698 G16r bound to William Horton, 7 years 7 Feb 1703/4 G101v turned over to Edmund Powell 5 Mar 1704/5 G117r turned over from William Horton to Edmund Powell and from him to William Downing 5 May 1707 G142r freed by William Downing

SPICER/SPYCER, Charles, alias HELDER 8 May 1682 E153r Thomas Williams's executor; objections to his assigning books to Benjamin Tooke and Thomas Sawbridge held over until next Court 24 Jun 1682 E154r cloathed 2 Mar 1684/5 F31r alias Helder; to be summoned to explain non-payment of Livery fine 26 Mar 1685 (W) proceedings against him to be stopped 6 Apr 1685 F32v his request that he should be struck out of Livery and remitted his fine, paying legal fees, is granted 12 Nov 1694 F215r alias Helder; William Ruck is bound to him 5 Sep 1698 G14v alias Helder; Edward Grubb is bound to him 1 Jun 1702 G71v alias Helder; his apprentice William Buck is freed 7 Sep 1702 G80v alias Helder; Eliazar Duncombe is bound to him 6 Jul 1713 G212v his son Thomas is bound to Mary Spicer, his mother, 7 years

SPICER, Mary, alias HELDER 2 Aug 1708 G156v William Gibson is bound to her 26 Sep 1712 G203v her apprentice Eleazar Duncombe is freed 6 Jul 1713 G212v alias Helder; her son, Thomas Spicer, alias Helder, is bound to her 8 Aug 1715 G232r alias Helder; Thomas Boorman is bound to her 7 May 1716 G240r her apprentice William Gibson is freed

SPICER, Steward 3 Oct 1709 G171r bound to Edward Head, 7 years 6 Oct 1712 G204v turned over to Mary Head

SPICER, Thomas, alias HELDER (I) 27 Mar 1682 E149r alias Helder; elected Assistant Renter Warden 3 Apr 1682 E149v alias Helder; elected First Renter Warden 1 Oct 1683 F3v elected to Henry Clarke's £80 share 7 May 1685 (W) confirmed as a member of the new Livery 23 Mar 1686/7 F80r allowed to mortgage his £80 share to John Towse for £40 17 Oct 1687 F93r John Towse moves that he should be made an Assistant but it is carried in the negative 1 Mar 1687/8 F97v expelled from Livery by order of Lord Mayor 11 Oct 1688 F108v restored to Livery 1 Feb 1702/3 G85r surrenders £80 share to Benjamin Browne 22 Jun 1705 G120v alias Helder; elected to Hannah Chapman's pension 21 Jun 1706 G132v alias Helder, deceased; Mary Nuthall is given his pension

SPICER, Thomas, alias HELDER (II) 6 Jul 1713 G212v alias Helder; son of Charles; bound to Mary Spicer, his mother, 7 years

SPIKEMAN, Edward 7 Nov 1709 G172r bound to Robert Whitledge, 7 years

SPILLER, [ ] 4 Dec 1710 G185v to be served with a copy of the writ of execution against Benjamin Harris

SPILLER, Nathaniel   7 Feb 1703/4 G101r together with William Spiller, to pay money due on a penal bond within a fortnight

SPILLER, William   7 Feb 1703/4 G101r together with Nathaniel Spiller, to pay money due on a penal bond within a fortnight   6 Mar 1703/4 G103r to meet Master and Wardens to decide manner of payment of debt to S.C.   12 Jun 1704 G107r house to be assigned by him to S.C.   7 Aug 1704 G110v house judged unsuitable as a surety and money due to the S.C. to be paid forthwith   12 Nov 1705 G124v Clerk to write to him concerning debt due to S.C. If not paid, to be proceeded against at law   4 Feb 1705/6 G127v to be proceeded against at law for money due to S.C.

SPIRE, William   4 Jun 1683 E170v freed; his master, Thomas Dawkes, is fined 10s for having bound Spire by foreign indenture at a scrivener's

SPONGE, James, snr – see following entry

SPONGE, James, jnr   12 Nov 1716 G244v son of James; bound to Lorrain Whitledge, 7 years

SPRINGALL, John   7 Feb 1708/9 G160v bound to Lewis Thomas, 7 years

SPRINT, Benjamin   8 Apr 1700 G39r bound to John Sprint, 7 years   1 Mar 1707/8 G149v made free by brother John Sprint, as executor of his father Samuel. Cloathed   26 Mar 1714 G217r fined for First Renter Warden   4 Mar 1716/17 G247v elected to John Wyatt's £40 share

SPRINT, John   4 Mar 1694/5 F219r son of Samuel Sprint; freed by patrimony   3 Jun 1695 F225r cloathed   3 Aug 1696 F246v elected to Jacob Tonson's £40 share after his father Samuel declines Thomas Parkhurst's £160 share and requests this   7 Sep 1696 F249r sworn in as partner   8 Apr 1700 G39r Benjamin Sprint is bound to him   26 Mar 1701 G57v fined for Renter Warden   1 Mar 1702/3 G86r elected Stock-keeper for Yeomanry   2 Mar 1703/4 G102r elected Stock-keeper for Yeomanry   1 Mar 1704/5 G116r elected Stock-keeper for Yeomanry   3 Dec 1705 G125v elected to John Hayes's £80 share   1 Mar 1705/6 G128v elected Stock-keeper for Yeomanry   1 Mar 1706/7 G138v elected Stock-keeper for Livery   3 Dec 1707 G148r 'signed' re. not taking Clarendon   1 Mar 1707/8 G149v his brother Benjamin Sprint is freed. Elected Stock-keeper for Livery   25 Mar 1708 G150v elected Assistant in second ballot   1 Mar 1708/9 G161r elected Stock-keeper for Assistants   4 Jul 1709 G167r to meet Benjamin Tooke snr to settle account   3 Oct 1709 G171r books held in co-partnership with Chapman   1 Mar 1709/10 G176r elected Stock-keeper for Assistants   13 Aug 1711 G193v to assist Master, Wardens and Stock-keepers for this year in the management of Stock affairs   4 Feb 1711/12 G196r to receive £5 from Warden Daniel Browne to buy books to put Abel Swale into business   1 Mar 1711/12 G197v elected Stock-keeper for Assistants   2 Jun 1712 G200r elected to Thomas Hodgkins's £160 share. His £80 share disposed of to John Leake   7 Jul 1712 G201v auditor of late Master and Wardens' accounts   6 Oct 1712 G204r signs report of Baskett committee   2 Mar 1712/13 G207r elected Stock-keeper for Assistants   24 Apr 1713 G209r signatory to S.C.'s notes to Thomas Guy   4 May 1713 G209v auditor of Renter Wardens' accounts   1 Jun 1713 G210v to determine what allowance Partridge should have for his almanack in future   1 Mar 1713/14 G216v elected Stock-keeper for Assistants   3 May 1714 G218v signs note to Guy   3 Jul 1714 G220r competes unsuccessfully for Under Warden   2 Aug 1714 G221r auditor of late Master and Wardens' accounts   1 Mar 1714/15 G225v elected Stock-keeper for Assistants   2 Jul 1715 G230r elected Under Warden   30 Jun 1716 G241r elected Under Warden   3 Dec 1716 G245r requests committee who audited his accounts as Warden to re-inspect them, as a great error has been committed by them   21 Feb 1716/17 G246v new trustee of S.C.'s property

SPRINT, Samuel   17 Oct 1687 F92v fined for Assistant Renter Warden   1 Mar 1687/
8 F98r summoned to next Court to be nominated to Assistants   5 Mar 1687/8 F99r
elected Assistant   3 Jun 1689 F119r George Downes mortgages his £40 share to him
for £40   2 Dec 1689 F127v elected to William Rawlins's £80 share   1 Mar 1689/90
F129v elected Stock-keeper for Yeomanry with Thomas Hodgkins   2 Mar 1690/1
F150v elected Stock-keeper for Livery with Charles Harper   1 Mar 1691/2 F165v
elected Stock-keeper for Livery with Thomas Cockerell   1 Mar 1692/3 F184r elected
Stock-keeper for Livery with William Crook   13 Mar 1692/3 F184v sworn in as Stock-
keeper   12 Jun 1693 F188v Eleanor Smith is allowed to mortgage her £40 share to
him   1 Mar 1694/5 F217v elected Stock-keeper for Livery with Brabazon Aylmer and
summoned to take Stock-keeper's oath   4 Mar 1694/5 F219r his son John is freed by
patrimony   8 Apr 1695 F220v sworn in as Stock-keeper   2 Mar 1695/6 F240r elected
Stock-keeper for Livery with Capt. Samuel Roycroft   4 May 1696 F242v elected as
Assistant and summoned. Takes Stock-keeper's oath   8 Jun 1696 F243r sworn in as
Assistant   3 Aug 1696 F246v declines to compete for Thomas Parkhurst's £160 share
and asks instead that his son John compete for Jacob Tonson's £40 share   3 Jul 1697
F263v competes unsuccessfully for Under Warden   5 Jul 1697 F263r competes unsuc-
cessfully for Under Warden. Among those chosen to audit Warden's accounts   7 Feb
1697/8 G3v Court consents to his request to print impression of 2000 psalms with
Henry Playford's musical notes   1 Aug 1698 G13r appointed auditor of Master and
Wardens' accounts. Given leave to print an impression of Playford's musical psalms   10
Jan 1698/9 G18v added to committee to consider Printing Act   3 Apr 1699 G24v
auditor of Renter Wardens' accounts   3 Jul 1699 G27r interested in the copy and right
of printing the Satires of Juvenal and Persius   7 Aug 1699 G28r assignment to him and
J. [John?] Nicholson of 'Shower on Eternity' [i.e. John Shower, *Serious Reflections on
Time and Eternity*], 'Letter to a Deist by [Edward] Stillingfleet', 'Scriptural Catechism'
[by R.E.?], 'Smith's Clockwork' [i.e. John Smith, *Horological Disquisitions*], part of
[anon.], 'Bachelor's Directory', 'Treatise of Prayer and Thanksgiving' [possibly
Benjamin Whichcote, *A Compendium of Devotion, Containing a Treatise of Prayer and
Thanksgiving*], 'Burgers Divirs Logic English' [i.e. a translation of Franco Burgersdijck,
Institutionum Logicarum], 'Sturmey of Reproofe' [unidentified], 'Paynes Sermons' [by
William Payne?] and 'Letter' [i.e. *A Letter from Dr P.— to the Bishop of R.—?*] &c. by
James Crayle and others read, but order for entry deferred until next Court day. Consents
to postponement of consideration of reference before Tooke re. printing of Juvenal and
Persius until next Court day   1 Jul 1700 G41r alternative member of committee to
raise subscriptions towards new barge bottom   6 Jul 1700 G43r takes oath as Under
Warden   26 Mar 1701 G57v requests that his son John be allowed to fine for Renter
Warden   5 Jul 1701 G61v elected Under Warden   6 Jul 1702 G77v elected Stock-
keeper for Assistants in place of Walter Kettleby   2 Nov 1702 G82v informs Court
that John Playford has paid S.C. for one impression of Psalms printed for him by John
Heptingstall without leave of the court, and is willing to pay for the other   18 Dec 1702
G84r elected to William Rawlins's £160 share. Henry Bonwick is elected to his £80
share   27 Mar 1703 G86v informs Court that John Darby jnr wishes to fine for First
Renter Warden   7 Jun 1703 G90v given thanks of Court and 3 guineas for his attendance in warehouse after removal of Benjamin Tooke   23 Jun 1703 G91r to inform
Daniel Blague that S.C. will allow him an annuity   23 Mar 1703/4 G104v to decide how
to direct payment of £5 charity money to Thomas Yates and his family   1 Jul 1704
G109r elected Upper Warden   30 Jun 1705 G121r elected Upper Warden   7 Apr
1707 G140v deceased; his £160 share disposed of to John Baskett

SPURDANCE, Edward   5 Oct 1685 F45r given 5s charity in response to petition   23
Mar 1686/7 F80r deceased; his widow Mary is elected into the quarterly charity
formerly received by him

SPURDANCE, Henry   1 Feb 1702/3 G85r freed by patrimony

SPURDANCE, Mary   23 Mar 1686/7 F80r elected into the quarterly charity of her deceased husband Edward   20 Dec 1701 G66r elected to Elizabeth Seile's pension. Mary Mawson is given her pension   18 Dec 1707 G148r deceased; Mary Collins is given her pension

SPYCER, [   ]   28 Oct 1697 F267r herald painter; to make a City streamer at the cost of £5 and deliver it by 3 November   7 Feb 1697/8 G3v herald painter; bill for making escutcheons for the S.C.

See also SPICER

SQUIBB, William   3 Mar 1700/1 G57r bound to John Worrell, 7 years

STAFFORD, Thomas   1 Feb 1702/3 G85r bound to Henry Danverse, 7 years

STAGG, John   5 Sep 1709 G170r bound to Richard Humphreys, 7 years

STAINES, Samuel   11 Nov 1700 G46v freed by Peter Richmond

STALL BOOKSELLERS   6 Jul 1685 F40v committee set up re. their suppression   5 Mar 1685/6 F52v Wardens to entreat Archbishop of Canterbury and Bishop of London not to license stall booksellers; application to be made to Secretary of State about aliens selling books without a licence. At committee meeting, names and places of stall book-sellers to be listed, and a check made as to which ones are members of S.C. Wardens to advise with Counsel as to whether unlicensed persons can 'utter or sell' books from stalls or shops   14 Mar 1686/7 F78v committee meeting decides that their names should be given to the Court and a check made as to which are S.C. members. Counsel's advice to be taken as to whether brokers or joiners or others not free of S.C. may utter or sell books old or new. (W) Committee decides that application may be made to Secretary of State about aliens selling books without a licence   [   ] May 1686 (W) further meeting of committee. To request bishops not to license haberdashers or foreigners to sell books 'and acquaint them with the mischiefs thereof'   7 May 1688 F101v several freed; ordered as a 'disencouragement' that this will not happen henceforth   6 Aug 1688 F104v Foreman is summoned for being a stall bookseller and defends himself by saying that he was bred to the trade

STAMPING OF PAPER – see STAMP ACT

STAMP OFFICE   10 Jul 1711 G192v Master and Wardens have attended Commis-sioners of Stamp Office re. stamping of almanacks   10 Sep 1711 G193v Commissioners of Stamp Office have agreed to take a bond from the S.C. for paying the duties on the stamping of almanacks   7 Jun 1714 G219r Thomas Norris to be summoned before Commissioners re. his printing and publishing Dr John Partridge's Prophecy

STANDFAST, Richard   11 Nov 1695 F235v servant to William Freeman; freed   9 Apr 1716 G239r John Ayshford is bound to him

STANNARD, John, snr – see following entry

STANNARD, John, jnr   6 Aug 1694 F211v son of John Stannard of Simpson, Bucks, clerk; bound to George Littlebury

STANTON, Isaac   1 Oct 1694 F213v servant to William Baker; freed

STAPLES, Robert   6 Jul 1702 G78r bound to John Matthews, 7 years   6 Oct 1712 G204v freed by John Matthews   14 Mar 1714/15 G226r Thomas Bryan is bound to him

STAPLETON, Michael   3 Jun 1706 G132v bound to Elizabeth Rumball, 7 years

STARKEY, John   1 Aug 1681 E117v in response to his letter, 'The Company think themselves not Obliged to take notice of any such Papers as that is'   12 Nov 1683 F5r

Thomas Bassett's collusion with him to force himself onto Court of Assistants   19 Dec
1683 F7r dividend to remain with Treasurer for time being, since he is 'at present under
some trouble' ((W) seizure of his goods on his Majesty's account?)   3 Nov 1684 F26r
Braburne the attorney to be summoned to explain why Starkey's £80 share cannot be
disposed of, he 'being under outlawry'   3 Dec 1684 F26v disposal of his stock to be
deferred   20 Dec 1684 F27v Braburne the attorney's brother alleges that Starkey's £80
share was settled upon his wife on her marriage (W) committee to consult with Lord
Chief Justice re. stock of John Starkey and Nathaniel Thompson, both being outlawed   3 Feb 1684/5 F30r Samuel Hoyle and Counsel at Law petition Court to dispose
of Starkey's share and pay the money to his wife; granted   5 Dec 1687 F95r fined £8
for trying to force his way onto Court   1 Mar 1687/8 F97v expelled from Livery by
order of Lord Mayor   4 Feb 1688/9 F113r to be given Francis Maidstone's bond to be
cancelled on giving discharge for his stock. Bond was to indemnify S.C. on payment of
Starkey's £80 share to Maidstone's wife   3 Feb 1689/90 F129r asks to become an Assistant; he is voted in   3 Mar 1689/90 F130r refuses Junior Assistant's place and claims
one below Robert Scott; committee to scrutinise precedents and take legal advice   3 Apr
1690 F131v committee meeting decides after discussing precedence based on seniority
and hearing legal advice that he is a Junior Assistant   7 Apr 1690 F132r Court confirms findings of committee and informs Starkey himself of them   5 May 1690 F134v
mistakenly cited in the margin against an entry relating to an Aldermen's dinner   5 Jun
1690 F136r when precedence has been worked out, disagrees with it and threatens to
seek remedy before the Lord Mayor   25 Jun 1690 F136v committee financed by Warden
and authorised by Assistants to consider order of Lord Mayor re. petition of Starkey
and others. S.C.'s answer to his petition given in full   15 Jul 1690 F140r Beadle tells
Court that he tore to pieces 'in great wrath and indignation' his summons to Court for
soliciting troop money   2 Mar 1690/1 F150r ((W) deceased) Richard East has £4
deducted from his stock dividend for having colluded with him

See also following entry

STARKEY, Mrs   20 Dec 1684 F27v Braburne the attorney's brother alleges that Starkey's £80 share was settled upon his wife on her marriage   26 Mar 1686 F53v appears
with Francis Maidstone and demands share; Court discontinues demand for legal fees
on her pleading poverty and dependants

STARR, John   6 Dec 1714 G224r freed by William Kitchener

STATIONERS' COMPANY   5 Apr 1714 G218r committee to consider state and affairs
of

— BOOKS   7 Jul 1701 G62r index to Court books started by John Lilly to be continued   27 Mar 1703 G87r books to be kept in the room behind the Court Room of
the Hall   5 Jul 1714 G220r committee to consider carrying on book and settling it

— BYELAWS   2 Aug 1680 E102v 1000 copies of new one to be printed and delivered
to every member of S.C. 'dealing in Books'; Clerk to be paid   6 Jun 1681 E112r committee to go to Counsel about the byelaw concerning 'a press in a hole' breached by
Bradyll   20 Jun 1681 E113v committee set up to inspect byelaws and create others
where necessary   4 Jul 1681 E116r new one to be delivered to every member of S.C.   1
Aug 1681 E117v draft byelaws, rules and ordinances recorded   17 Aug 1681 E125r
agreed at a Common Hall re. printing of names, the election of Renter Wardens,
property, power to search, schoolbooks, patent rights, Livery   5 Oct 1681 E131r new
ordinances and byelaws concerning English Stock including those concerning the poor
and the choice of Treasurer and Stock-keepers   5 Dec 1681 E140r new ones concerning
the Corporation to be hung up in Hall   7 Aug 1682 E156v committee considering
demerits of John Lilly and Clerk (sic) in 'attending drawing engrossing & getting passed'

the recent byelaws to report at next Court. Their printing and distribution to be discussed at some future date   4 Sep 1682 E157r to be printed and distributed to S.C. members   6 Dec 1682 E161v against seditious literature, re. entering names in registers   2 Jul 1683 (W) byelaws to be read again at next Court   19 Dec 1683 F7r committee to consult with Sergeant Pemberton and others re. application of byelaw concerning disobedient Stock partners   7 Jul 1684 F20v committee considering the demerits of John Lilly's and Clerk's work on the byelaws revived and augmented, to report at next Court   1 Feb 1685/6 F51r committee revived to consider Clerk's remuneration for passing byelaws   20 Dec 1686 F69v committee appointed to peruse byelaws concerning Treasurer and alter them if necessary   14 May 1694 F205r agreed at Common Hall   7 Feb 1698 G20r James Smalshaw was bound to Thomas Whitledge by foreign indenture, contrary to the byelaws   7 Aug 1699 G28v disobeyed by former Renter Wardens John Leake and Luke Meredith   4 Dec 1699 G34r Herbert Walwyn to be sued for failing to accept cloathing   6 May 1700 G39v forbidding a freeman to bind more than one apprentice unless he accepts cloathing   21 Jun 1700 G41r last byelaws of S.C. delivered into Court by Clerk and put in chest   3 Nov 1701 G65r Wellington to be prosecuted for importing Company's books contrary to them

— COPIES – see ENGLISH STOCK

— COURT   2 Jul 1683 F2r no member of Court to sit at Table without his gown   3 Jul 1686 F59v no-one to presume to dine on Court days in S.C. parlour without an invitation   12 Oct 1687 F91r first new Court takes place after the elections forced upon S.C. by the Royal order   6 Aug 1688 F105v the whole Court, listed, have the Stock estate of St Martin's Ludgate conveyed to them in trust for S.C.   27 Nov 1688 F109v those who were Master, Wardens and Assistants on the day the *quo warranto* was served, 26 Mar 1684, are summoned and take their chairs to supervise elections of new officers. Ordered that those who have already served or fined for Master, Wardens and Renter Wardens will not have to do so again   3 Dec 1688 F111r committee to inspect transactions made by those who have been Masters, Wardens and Assistants since 3 October 1687   4 May 1691 F153r order to wear gowns suspended until the beginning of winter on account of the heat   21 Nov 1692 F182r described as meeting in the dining parlour   5 Dec 1692 F182v orders of 7, 21 and 25 November referred to a committee to amend the wording before being entered in Court book   7 May 1694 F204r special assembly to approve revised ordinances cannot be held because the Upper Warden, Thomas Bassett, does not appear   30 Jun 1694 F209v thanks retiring Master and Wardens   4 May 1696 F242r if any Assistant or Renter Warden arrives at Court after 11 a.m., their half-crown dinner money will be forfeited to the Poor Box   5 Oct 1696 (W) John Simms, William Rawlins and Samuel Lowndes asked to ensure that minutes which Clerk has neglected to enter are entered by next Court day   2 Nov 1696 (W) minutes not yet entered as Simms says they have received no summons to do so   7 Dec 1696 F253r minutes taken in Court to be read every Court day before the Court rises   1 Mar 1696/7 F255r orders of Court not entered by Christopher Grandorge passed and ordered to be entered   8 Apr 1700 G39r any person chosen into any office of the Court to have notice of this in summons to next Court

— DEBTS   7 Dec 1696 (W) book to be obtained in which to set down debts of S.C.

— PROPERTY   17 Aug 1681 E126v byelaw   2 Oct 1682 E158v defect in partition wall between Robert Everingham's and Clerk's houses, and any others, to be referred to committee

See also ENGLISH STOCK

STATIONERS' COURT – see HALL

STEEL, Richard   5 May 1707 G142r bound to Thomas Huse, 7 years

See also STEELE

STEELE, Elizabeth   27 Sep 1710 G184r given Priscilla Mosse's pension

STEELE, Jane   1 Sep 1712 G203r freed by Thomas Elliott, patrimony   5 Sep 1715 G232v Charles Fox is bound to her

STEELE/SKEELS/STEEL, Robert   4 Jun 1694 F208v Samuel Illidge is bound to him   7 Nov 1698 G16r William Burscoe is bound to him   1 Dec 1701 G66r Edward Browne is turned over to him from William Baker, deceased   1 Jun 1702 G71v his apprentice Samuel Illidge is freed   5 Oct 1702 G81v William Burscoe is turned over from him to Samuel Illidge   7 Oct 1706 G135r his apprentice Edward Bourn is freed   1 Dec 1707 G147v bookseller; John Neal is bound to him   2 Oct 1710 G184v of Little Britain, bookbinder; William Giles is bound to him

STEEVENS, [ ]   25 Aug 1680 E103v paid 40s for pains taken re. passing byelaw

STEEVENS, Rowland   3 May 1708 G152v bound to John Barber, 7 years

STELBY, Isaac   6 Mar 1709/10 G176v bound to Job King, 7 years

STEPHENS, [ ]   22 Sep 1680 E104r assignment to John Williams to be entered   26 Mar 1701 G57v competes unsuccessfully for cook

STEPHENS, Charles (I)   8 Nov 1703 G97r bound to Benjamin Bound, 7 years   4 Dec 1710 G186r freed by Benjamin Bound

STEPHENS, Charles (II)   4 Dec 1710 G186r of Forster Lane, ironmonger; Samuel Stephens is bound to him

STEPHENS, Christopher   4 Dec 1693 F196v carpenter of Henley-upon-Thames; his son William is bound to Robert Stephens

STEPHENS, Daniel   5 Jul 1703 G92r bound to John Doleman, 7 years   5 Jul 1714 G220v freed by John Doleman

STEPHENS, Dorothy   5 Sep 1681 E129v assigns to Thomas Passenger [Edmund Wingate's] 'The Use of the Rule of Proportion in Arithmetic and Geometry'

STEPHENS, Francis   6 Mar 1703/4 G103v bound to Sarah Holt, 7 years   6 Aug 1711 G193r freed by Sarah Holt

STEPHENS, Joel   3 Oct 1709 G171r bound to Thomas Beaver

STEPHENS, John (I)   1 Feb 1702/3 G85r of St Martin's Le Grand; printed an almanack, 'The Tradesman's or Shopkeeper's Companion', without permission of the S.C.   5 Apr 1703 G88r Job Thompson is bound to him

STEPHENS, John (II)   9 Feb 1707/8 G149r bound to Benjamin Webster, 7 years   6 Oct 1712 G204v turned over to John Noone   6 Sep 1714 G221v turned over to Mark Forster   14 Mar 1714/15 G226r freed by Mark Forster

STEPHENS, Mrs (I)   1 Mar 1682/3 E164v her bond not to be called in with others as it is secured by the Stock   12 Nov 1683 F5r disposes of her £320 share to Henry Hills

STEPHENS, Mrs (II)   7 Nov 1715 G234v widow of the late cook; granted claim for £7 for racks and spits in the kitchen of the Hall which had belonged to her husband

STEPHENS, Nathaniel   26 Mar 1702 G68v competes unsuccessfully for cook   27 Mar 1703 G87v competes unsuccessfully for cook

STEPHENS, Richard   7 Dec 1702 G83v bound to William Stephens, 7 years

STEPHENS, Robert (I)   3 Mar 1683/4 F10r allowed to mortgage his £80 share to Henry Clarke for £70 plus interest, having discharged his mortgage to Samuel Mearne, deceased   3 Nov 1684 F25v deceased; his £80 share voted to William Shrewsbury

STEPHENS/STEVENS, Robert (II)   3 Jan 1680/1 E106r to be paid gratuity of £5   5
Sep 1681 E129v pays £8 1s charges in an indictment   5 Dec 1681 E140v to receive
George Lloyd, son of Samuel Lloyd, late Stationer, as apprentice with intention of turning
him over to Thomas Snowden   2 Oct 1682 E158v cloathed   1 Mar 1682/3 E165r
Court grants his request to be struck out of the Livery and have his £20 Livery fine
repaid him   3 Dec 1683 F6v to appear at next Court with Francis Egglesfeild to answer
Charles Mearne's complaint   19 Dec 1683 F7r in response to petition, granted £8 for
services done to the benefit of the English Stock   16 Jun 1684 F18r petitions for a salary
as recompense for his services 'in preventing Piracy upon the English Stock'; referred to
next Court   25 Jun 1684 F18v petition re-read; ordered that he should be paid 40s   6
Mar 1688/9 F114v Messenger of the Press; accuses Mrs Curtis and Leach of printing
unlicensed pamphlets   26 Mar 1689 F116r supplicates for the Messenger of the Press's
salary; granted £10 quarterly   7 Oct 1689 F125r to prosecute Benjamin Crayle and
Joseph Shooter for printing and publishing 'Sodom or the Quintessence of Debauchery'
[attr. John Wilmot, Earl of Rochester]. To be paid 30s for seizing 'Hickeringale's' pamphlet [i.e. a publication by Edmund Hickeringill?]   7 Apr 1690 F132v to be paid £3 for
discovering Thomas Moore's printing of the Old Primer, a Stock book   4 Aug 1690
F141v to take Andrew Sowle before the Lord Chief Justice, Sir John Holt, for printing
an unlicensed pamphlet   5 Sep 1690 F142v to be paid £5 for discovering Gaines's
press   9 Feb 1690/1 F149r gives Court a list of those who have failed to enter pamphlets   22 Dec 1691 F164r given letter of attorney empowering him to take possession of
the goods of those Stock tenants in arrears   1 Feb 1691/2 F165r to give at next Court
a list of all printers in and about London specifying which are not qualified according to
the Act   7 Mar 1691/2 F166r Messenger of the Press; to visit York with Wardens to
investigate illegal supernumerary printers comprinting Stock books and seize those
found   12 Apr 1692 F168v petitions for 'gratification' for attendance at Court and
waiting on Wardens weekly at Customs House; to be paid £5 plus 20s a quarter   6 Jun
1692 F171v told of illegal press in Shoreditch by Robert Stephens (sic), a constable in
Shoreditch; reimbursed for informant's reward and told to keep £5 earned from prosecuting landlord   26 Sep 1692 F179v henceforth to be paid quarterly 'in the Pension
notes' the 20s per quarter granted him at the Court of 12 April 1692   8 May 1693
F188r to be given £5 for discovering Anderton's press   28 Sep 1693 F191v allowed
free access to registers in Clerk's presence, as requested by the Bishop of London and the
Archbishop of Canterbury   4 Dec 1693 F196v William Stephens is bound to him   2
Apr 1694 F202r his petition to be lent £100 is deferred until he can propose surety   17
Oct 1696 F251r discovers press in Distaff Lane belonging to Roger Bradley, working on
a sheet almanack for 1697; they had printed 20 reams in red when raided   2 Aug 1697
F265v Daniel and Samuel Freeman, his apprentices, are freed   4 Oct 1697 F268v salary
of £10 paid him annually by the Wardens to be paid by the Treasurer in future   7 Feb
1698/9 G20r account of disbursements for work done in the building of several warehouses in S.C.'s garden to be examined by a committee   3 Apr 1699 G23r lease to be
granted to him by S.C. of three warehouses built by himself   7 Aug 1699 G28v his two
bills and bill of charges for wainscotting the back room behind the Court room to be
referred to a committee for settlement   4 Sep 1699 G30r bills to be paid on giving
receipt of all accounts due from S.C.   8 Apr 1700 G39r to ensure that no boys play in
the S.C.'s garden and that no pigeons are kept there   6 Jul 1700 G43r his apprentice
William Framewell is freed   1 Dec 1701 G66r his apprentice William Stephens is
freed   2 Mar 1701/2 G67v competes unsuccessfully for Treasurer   2 Nov 1702 G83r
granted lease from S.C. on warehouses he had built on S.C.'s land   1 Feb 1702/3 G85r
lease of warehouses sealed. S.C. to have warehouse they now possess at same rent as
formerly   1 Mar 1702/3 G86r competes unsuccessfully for Warehousekeeper   8 Nov

1703 G97r reprimanded for giving out names of persons to be summoned to be Assistants   3 Apr 1704 G106r John Hill is bound to him   10 Sep 1705 G123r Warehousekeeper; wicket he had made through door on south side of Hall without permission of Court to be nailed up   21 Mar 1705/6 G129v Messenger of the Press; employed by S.C. to attend at Custom House when Act of Parliament concerning printing was in force. Allowed to discontinue this as Act no longer in force   9 Sep 1706 G134v to go to Cambridge concerning S.C.'s printing house affairs there   1 Mar 1706/7 G138v competes unsuccessfully for Warehousekeeper   6 Oct 1707 G145v to prepare an account of printing letters and materials for committee on Cambridge affairs   7 Nov 1709 G171v an apprentice turned over to him from William King   1 Mar 1709/10 G176r competes unsuccessfully for Warehousekeeper   1 Mar 1710/11 G187v competes unsuccessfully for Warehousekeeper   1 Mar 1711/12 G197v competes unsuccessfully for Warehousekeeper   7 Apr 1712 G198v surrenders his £80 share and requests that John Barber be elected to it   19 Dec 1712 G206r his apprentice Robert White is freed   2 Mar 1712/13 G207r competes unsuccessfully for Warehousekeeper   1 Mar 1713/14 G217r competes unsuccessfully for Warehousekeeper   7 Feb 1714/15 G225r Master, Wardens and Stock-keepers to settle with him matter relating to warehouses   1 Mar 1714/15 G225v competes unsuccessfully for Warehousekeeper   1 Mar 1715/16 G236v competes unsuccessfully for Treasurer   4 Jun 1716 G240v John May is bound to him   1 Mar 1716/17 G247r competes unsuccessfully for Warehousekeeper   26 Mar 1717 G248v competes unsuccessfully for Beadle

STEPHENS, Robert (III)   6 Jun 1692 F171v constable in Shoreditch; discovers an illegal press to his namesake and is paid 40s by Court

STEPHENS, Robert (IV)   5 Apr 1703 G88r bound to John England, 7 years

STEPHENS, Rowland   2 May 1709 G165r bound to Ichabod Dawkes, 7 years

STEPHENS, Samuel   4 Dec 1710 G186r bound to Charles Stephens, 7 years

STEPHENS/STEVENS, William   4 Dec 1693 F196v son of Christopher Stephens of Henley-upon-Thames, carpenter; bound to Robert Stephens for 8 years from 1 December   1 Dec 1701 G66r freed by Robert Stephens   7 Dec 1702 G83v Richard Stephens is bound to him   4 Feb 1711/12 G196v John Milner is turned over from him to John Ellis   9 Feb 1712/13 G206v John Meeres is bound to him   4 Jun 1716 G240v William Hinckley is bound to him

See also STEVENS

STEPHENSON, Robert   3 Mar 1711/12 G197r freed by John England. Ralph Phillips is bound to him

STEVENS, [ ]   5 Aug 1706 G133v cook; bill for breakfast and dinner for S.C. on last day Queen went to St Paul's to be referred to Master and Wardens

STEVENS, John   7 Nov 1715 G234v Henry Amey is bound to him

STEVENS, William, snr – see following entry

STEVENS/STEPHENS, William, jnr   8 Apr 1695 F221r son of William Stevens snr; freed by patrimony   4 Nov 1706 G136r brazier; John Milner is bound to him   8 Nov 1708 G158v brazier; Thomas Street is bound to him

See also STEPHENS

STEVENSON, Christopher   12 Nov 1705 G125r bound to Thomas Tebb, 7 years   4 Mar 1716/17 G247v freed by Thomas Tebb

STEWARD, James   22 Jun 1698 G9v general release from S.C. sealed   9 Sep 1700 G45r bound to William Shrewsbury, 7 years   5 May 1701 G59v turned over from

William Shrewsbury to Edward Powell   7 Feb 1703/4 G101v turned over to Samuel Illidge   4 Dec 1704 G114r turned over to John Penn

STILES, Edward, snr – see following entry

STILES, Edward, jnr   1 Mar 1713/14 G216v son of Edward; bound to John Hooke, 7 years   4 Oct 1714 G222r elected porter to English Stock at salary of £5   26 Mar 1715 G227r competes unsuccessfully for Beadle   26 Mar 1716 G238v competes unsuccessfully for Beadle

STILLINGFLEET, Edward, Bishop of Worcester   2 Aug 1697 F265r Price writes to the Master on the Bishop's behalf re. Meredith bequest   7 Aug 1699 G28r his 'Letter to a Deist' assigned to Samuel Sprint and J. [John?] Nicholson

STILLINGFLEET, Edward   7 Feb 1708/9 G160v bound to Henry Mortlock, 7 years

STILTON, John   2 Mar 1701/2 G67v bound to Robert Everingham, 7 years

STOAKS, Theophilus   3 Mar 1706/7 G139r bound to Robert Limpany, 7 years

STOCKER, Thomas   2 Oct 1699 G31v bound to William Richardson

STOCK-KEEPERS   1 Mar 1680/1 E107v Roger Norton and Edward Brewster for Assistants, William Miller and Robert Clavell for Livery, Benjamin Tooke and Charles Harper for Yeomanry   1 Mar 1681/2 E145v Roger Norton and Henry Herringman for Assistants, Robert Clavell and Thomas Dring for Livery, Benjamin Tooke and Thomas Sawbridge for Yeomanry   1 Mar 1682/3 E164v Roger Norton and Robert Horne for Assistants, Thomas Passenger and Samuel Lowndes for Livery, William Crooke and Thomas Sawbridge for Yeomanry   2 Jul 1683 F2r John Macock in place of Roger Norton   1 Mar 1683/4 F9r Edward Brewster and John Bellinger for Assistants, Samuel Lowndes and Samuel Heyrick for Livery, Walter Kettleby and William Shrewsbury for Yeomanry   30 Sep 1684 F24r to decide number of impression of the new almanack, Merlinus Rusticus   2 Mar 1684/5 F31v John Bellinger and Robert Scott for Assistants, Obadiah Blagrave and George Wells for Livery, John Place and Samuel Roycroft for Yeomanry   6 Jul 1685 F40v Robert Clavell in place of John Bellinger   1 Mar 1685/6 F52r John Towse and John Baker for Assistants, Thomas Sawbridge and Obadiah Blagrave for Livery, John Amery and William Whitwood for Yeomanry   5 Jul 1686 F60v William Cooper in place of John Baker   1 Mar 1686/7 F77r John Towse and William Cooper for Assistants, William Crooke and George Wells for Livery, Miles Flesher and Robert Andrews for Yeomanry   1 Mar 1687/8 F98v John Towse and John Richardson for Assistants, Charles Harper and Miles Flesher for Livery, William Rogers and John Miller for Yeomanry   1 Mar 1688/9 F113v John Bellinger and Thomas Dring for Assistants, Bennett Griffin and Richard Tonson for Livery, William Rogers and Samuel Keeble for Yeomanry   7 Oct 1689 F124r to be paid 2s when summoned on business in lieu of dinners which were discontinued because of S.C.'s debt   1 Mar 1689/90 F129v detailed account of proceedings previous to election of Stock-keepers. John Bellinger and Henry Mortlock for Assistants, Capt. Samuel Roycroft and John Miller for Livery, Samuel Sprint and Thomas Hodgkins for Yeomanry   7 Jul 1690 F138v Christopher Wilkinson in place of Henry Mortlock   2 Mar 1690/1 F150v John Bellinger and Christopher Wilkinson for Assistants, Samuel Sprint and Charles Harper for Livery, Thomas Cockerell and Brabazon Aylmer for Yeomanry   22 Dec 1691 F164r to meet on first and third Wednesday in every month to examine Treasurer's accounts and conduct other Stock business   1 Mar 1691/2 F165v John Bellinger and Christopher Wilkinson for Assistants, Thomas Cockerell and Samuel Sprint for Livery, Brabazon Aylmer and William Rogers for Yeomanry   1 Mar 1692/3 F184r Henry Mortlock and Nathaniel Ranew for Assistants, Samuel Sprint and William Crooke for Livery, Israel Harrison and Daniel Browne for Yeomanry   6 Nov 1693 F194v one bill

for the purchase of Stock paper to be kept by them and regular entries made   1 Mar
1693/4 F199v John Simms and Samuel Lowndes for Assistants, William Crooke and
Freeman Collins for Livery, Daniel Browne and William Rogers for Yeomanry   26 Mar
1694 F201v Henry Mortlock, William Rawlins and Thomas Dring elected Stock-keepers
at a special meeting   2 Jul 1694 F210r William Rawlins and Richard Chiswell to act for
Assistants as John Simms and Samuel Lowndes have been elected Master and Warden
respectively   1 Mar 1694/5 F217v William Rawlins and Charles Harper for Assistants,
Samuel Sprint and Brabazon Aylmer for Livery, John Place and John Rogers for Assis-
tants   7 Oct 1695 F233v Capt. William Phillipps in place of William Rawlins   2 Mar
1695/6 F240r Edward Brewster and Henry Mortlock for Assistants, Samuel Sprint and
Samuel Roycroft for Livery, Benjamin Motte and Timothy Goodwin for Yeomanry   6
Jul 1696 F245r William Rawlins in place of Henry Mortlock   1 Mar 1696/7 F255r
William Phillipps and William Rawlins for Assistants, Thomas Hodgkins and Brabazon
Aylmer for Livery, William Rogers and Isaac Cleave for Yeomanry   1 Mar 1697/8 G4r
John Heptingstall and Isaac Cleave for Yeomanry, Brabazon Aylmer and Daniel Browne
for Livery, Robert Andrews and William Phillipps for Assistants   5 Sep 1698 G14r to
be given notice that accounts of Oxford Stock are to be made up for the next Court
day   1 Mar 1698/9 G21r William Phillipps and John Simms for Assistants, Robert
Roberts and Israel Harrison for Livery, William Freeman and Timothy Goodwin for
Yeomanry   4 Sep 1699 G30r Oxford articles to be entered into a book for Stock-
keepers' use   1 Mar 1699/1700 G36r William Phillipps and John Place for Assistants,
Isaac Cleave and Robert Roberts for Livery, John Smith and Thomas Bennett for Yeo-
manry   3 Jun 1700 G40v William Onely not to be employed by them any longer   1
Mar 1700/1 G56r Henry Mortlock and Walter Kettleby for Assistants, Brabazon
Aylmer and Isaac Cleave for Livery, Thomas Bennett and William Freeman for Yeoman-
ry   2 Mar 1701/2 G67v Walter Kettleby and Henry Mortlock for Assistants, Brabazon
Aylmer and [ ] Jones for Livery, Thomas Cockerell and Henry Bonwick for Yeoman-
ry   1 Jun 1702 G71r have examined accounts of English Stock and discovered that the
Stock has received a great prejudice. Note of monies and charges entered by Treasurer to
be taken by Warden after every Court and delivered to them   6 Jul 1702 G77v Samuel
Sprint elected in place of Walter Kettleby. To meet again to examine Benjamin
Tooke   23 Jul 1702 G79r Tooke has refused to deliver warehouse and books to
them   1 Mar 1702/3 G85v Robert Clavell and Charles Harper for Assistants, Henry
Bonwick and Thomas Bennett for Livery, [ ] Wild and John Sprint for Yeomanry   3
May 1703 G89r accountant to be employed to assist them in keeping accounts of
English and Oxford Stocks   15 Jul 1703 G93r Tooke had attended and been made
aware of the resolutions of the Court concerning him   8 Nov 1703 G96v to consider
terms for Dr John Gadbury printing Ephemerides   6 Dec 1703 G99v to appoint some
more work to Ichabod Dawkes. To give an account of the Stock work of the S.C. in the
several printers' hands by next Court day   20 Dec 1703 G100r to compute charge for
Dr John Gadbury printing 500 copies of Ephemerides   2 Mar 1703/4 G102v Robert
Clavell and William Phillipps for Assistants, William Rogers and Thomas Bennett for
Livery, John Nicholson and John Sprint for Yeomanry   3 Apr 1704 G105v letter
concerning printing at Cambridge to be referred to them   6 Nov 1704 G113r members
of committee to dispose of foreign books of the S.C.   5 Feb 1704/5 G114v to settle
affairs of Tooke   1 Mar 1704/5 G116r Henry Mortlock and William Phillipps for
Assistants, Deputy Collins and Thomas Bennett for Livery, John Nicholson and John
Sprint for Yeomanry   1 Mar 1705/6 G128v William Phillipps and Thomas Bennett for
Assistants, William Rogers and William Freeman for Livery, John Sprint and Robert
Knaplock for Yeomanry   1 Apr 1706 G131r printers of Ovid and Terence to attend
their next meeting   4 Nov 1706 G135v Henry Mortlock elected   1 Mar 1706/7

G138v Henry Mortlock and William Phillipps for Assistants, William Freeman and John Sprint for Livery, Benjamin Walford and Robert Knaplock for Yeomanry   1 Dec 1707 G147r to decide whether to take Baskett's Clarendon in folio   3 Dec 1707 G148r committee and meeting of   1 Mar 1707/8 G149v Israel Harrison and Henry Mortlock for Assistants, John Sprint and William Freeman for Livery, Robert Knaplock and Richard Mount for Yeomanry   1 Mar 1708/9 G161r John Sprint and William Phillipps for Assistants, Matthew Wootton and John Walthoe for Livery, Wilkins and Daniel Midwinter for Yeomanry   7 Mar 1708/9 G161v of English and Oxford Stocks to settle accounts between the two stocks   1 Aug 1709 G169v Henry Mortlock elected in place of William Phillipps   1 Mar 1709/10 G175v John Sprint and Henry Mortlock for Assistants, Richard Wilkins and Matthew Wootton for Livery, Timothy Child and Daniel Midwinter for Yeomanry   5 Jun 1710 G180r to deal with Walthoe about his printing of Justin   1 Mar 1710/11 G187v Henry Mortlock and Nicholas Boddington for Assistants, Richard Wilkins and Matthew Wootton for Livery, Daniel Midwinter and Christopher Bateman for Yeomanry   14 Jun 1711 G191v opinion that half the number of almanacks usually printed should be produced   1 Mar 1711/12 G197v John Sprint and Robert Knaplock for Assistants, Daniel Midwinter and Richard Wilkins for Livery, Timothy Child and James Knapton for Yeomanry   2 Mar 1712/13 G207r candidates for Stock-keeper for Livery and Yeomanry initially selected by all partners before Assistants make the final choice. Robert Knaplock and John Sprint for Assistants, Daniel Midwinter and Richard Wilkins for Livery, Timothy Child and James Knapton for Yeomanry   1 Mar 1713/14 G216v Robert Knaplock and John Sprint for Assistants, Daniel Midwinter and Richard Wilkins for Livery, Timothy Child and James Knapton for Yeomanry   1 Mar 1714/15 G225v Robert Knaplock and John Sprint for Assistants, Daniel Midwinter and Richard Wilkins for Livery, Timothy Child and James Knapton for Yeomanry   4 Jul 1715 G231r Nicholas Boddington to be summoned to their meeting to assist them if they think fit   1 Mar 1715/16 G236v Daniel Midwinter and Nicholas Boddington for Assistants, Martin Boddington and Richard Wilkins for Livery, Timothy Child and John Wyatt for Yeomanry   5 Mar 1715/16 G237v letter concerning allowance to Dr John Partridge for his almanacks to be referred to   1 Mar 1716/17 G247r Daniel Midwinter and Richard Mount for Assistants, Martin Boddington and Richard Wilkins for Livery, Timothy Child and John Wyatt for Yeomanry

See also ENGLISH STOCK, TREASURER

STOCKLEY, Joseph   7 Oct 1700 G46r bound to Thomas James, 7 years

STOKER, Luke   2 Jun 1712 G200v John Bradley turned over to him from George Harris

STOKES, John, snr – see following entry

STOKES, John, jnr   6 May 1695 F223v son of John Stokes of Melton Mowbray, mercer; bound to Joseph Hindmarsh

STONALL, William   6 May 1700 G39v bound to Humphrey Pooler, 7 years

STONE, Peter   6 Sep 1686 F62v deceased; Henry Clarke jnr ordered to find a new surety for his £50 loan from Tyler bequest   6 Jun 1687 F84v deceased; Henry Clarke is asked for his widow's consent to become bound for his surety in Stone's stead

See also STONE, Widow

STONE, Richard   1 Mar 1687/8 F97v expelled from Livery by order of Lord Mayor

STONE, Widow   1 Aug 1687 F87v does not wish to be a surety; Clarke binds John Fearne instead   1 Oct 1688 F107v discharged from her bond re. Henry Clarke's loan

See also STONE, Peter

STOREY, Samuel   2 Jul 1711 G192v son of Walter; bound to Henry Parsons, 7 years

STOREY, Walter – see preceding entry

STOUGHTON, Aram/Aaron   7 Apr 1707 G141r bound to Samuel Clarke, 7 years   3 May 1714 G219r freed by Samuel Clarke

STOWE, John   13 Mar 1711/12 G198r S.C.'s answer to his and Benjamin Poole's bill in Chancery concerning Mrs Mary Cooper's £160 share

STRACY, Edward   26 Mar 1702 G68v Hall to be let to him for 2 months for 40 guineas for sale of household goods

STRAHAN, George   7 Sep 1702 G80v freed by Joseph Hindmarsh   7 Dec 1702 G83v John Lewis turned over to him from David Edwards   5 Apr 1703 G88r to be summoned to next Court to take cloathing   3 May 1703 G89v excused cloathing   8 May 1704 G106v summoned to take cloathing   4 Sep 1704 G111v cloathed   27 Mar 1710 G177r elected First Renter Warden   3 Apr 1710 G178r excused office of First Renter Warden for one year   7 Aug 1710 G183r of Cornhill, bookseller; William Sarson is bound to him   7 Apr 1712 G198v elected Renter Warden. To be given notice to attend next Court   5 May 1712 G199v not permitted to be excused from office of Renter Warden on account of his losses   2 Jun 1712 G200r fined for Renter Warden   3 Aug 1713 G213r William Sarson is turned over from him to Thomas Bickerton   7 Feb 1714/15 G225r William Sarson is turned over from him to John Sarson

STRAINGE, Elizabeth   24 Sep 1714 G222r elected to Jane Mawson's pension   20 Dec 1716 G246r deceased; Thomas Machell is given her pension

STRAINGE, Johanna   23 Jun 1710 G180v elected to Anne Crawford's pension. Hester Ferris is given her pension   22 Dec 1713 G215v deceased; Elizabeth Thrale is given her pension

STRANGE, George   2 Mar 1701/2 G67v John Shaw is bound to him

STRANGE NEWS   2 Oct 1682 E158r Richard Janeway confesses to printing 'Strange News from Hick's Hall' for R. Harbottle

STREET, Thomas   8 Nov 1708 G158v bound to William Stephens, 7 years

STREETE, George – see following entry

STREETE, Richard   6 May 1695 F223v son of George Streete of Guildford, draper; bound to John Bradshaw

STREETER, Joseph   7 Oct 1689 F125r he and Benjamin Crayle to be punished by Robert Stephens for printing and publishing 'Sodom or the Quintessence of Debauchery' [attr. John Wilmot, Earl of Rochester]

STRODE, William   26 Mar 1697 F258v competes unsuccessfully to replace Christopher Grandorge as Clerk

STROUHTON, Richard   1 Mar 1702/3 G86r bound to Henry Rodes, 7 years

STUBBS, John   2 Oct 1699 G31v freed by Roger Norton

STURMEY OF REPROOF   7 Aug 1699 G28r unidentified book; assigned to Samuel Sprint by J.[John?] Nicholson

STURT, [ ]   7 Aug 1704 G111r to deliver copperplate of Raven's or London Almanack to Joseph Collyer

STYLES, Edward   4 Jul 1709 G167v Peter Styles, his son, is bound to him

STYLES, James   4 Dec 1699 G34r freed by Robert Roberts

STYLES, Peter   4 Jul 1709 G167v bound to his father Edward, 7 years

SUCKLING, [ ]   7 May 1716 G240r his daughter Henrietta Maria Germa is bound to Thomas Parry, 7 years

SUDWORTH, William   6 Dec 1697 G2r bound to Robert Everingham   5 Feb 1704/5 G115r freed by Robert Everingham

SUETONIUS   18 Mar 1686/7 F79v among books in catalogue annexed to Oxford agreement

SUNDERLAND, Robert Spencer, Earl of   17 Dec 1684 (W) letter recommending S.C. to communicate with Surveyor of the Press re. 'preventing intolerable liberties'   2 Jan 1684/5 (W) letter from Roger L'Estrange to Master and Wardens requesting delivery of 'the enclosed' (S.C.'s petition) to the Earl of Sunderland   29 Jan 1684/5 F29r has signed Crown order referring suppression of seditious books to L'Estrange   6 May 1685 F33v sends letter ordering a complete list of bookdealers outside S.C. so they can be turned over, and a report for L'Estrange   21 May 1685 (W) royal command to L'Estrange, signed by Sunderland, renewing regulations concerning licensing and restriction of number of presses   7 Mar 1708/9 G161v one of Her Majesty's principal Secretaries of State. Signatory of assign manual granting Aaron Hills the sole printing of the 'History of Ethiopia' [i.e. *The Present State of Ethiopia*]

SUNKY, Dowsett   12 Nov 1694 F214v servant to Thomas Brockett; freed

SURBUTT, Widow   5 Sep 1687 F87v deceased; her £160 share voted to Christopher Wilkinson

SURVEYOR OF THE PRESS – see L'ESTRANGE, Roger

SUSSEX, Giles   7 Feb 1686/7 F70r competes unsuccessfully for Daniel Peacock's £40 share   16 Jun 1691 F155r petitions Lord Mayor re. his non-election as Assistant; Court agrees to appear before the Court of Aldermen in obedience to their order   25 Jun 1691 F155v Assistants vote down the opinion of the Lord Mayor in declaring that Sussex should not be elected an Assistant   18 Jul 1692 F174v Master and Wardens summoned to Guildhall concerning their refusal to submit Giles Sussex to Court   26 Jul 1692 F175r Court vote down mayoral order; committee appointed to safeguard S.C. rights   28 Jul 1692 F175v reasons why he should not be admitted to the Court copied out in full   1 Aug 1692 F176v proceedings in Sussex case to be entered in register; Court thank Master and Wardens for maintaining S.C. rights   7 May 1694 F203v his servant John Gatfeild is freed. His son and servant William is freed   6 Aug 1694 F211v Thomas Arnold is bound to him

SUSSEX, William   7 May 1694 F203v son and servant of Giles Sussex; freed   5 Sep 1698 G14r elected to cloathing   7 Oct 1698 G15r to be summoned to next Court day to take cloathing   7 Nov 1698 G16r cloathed   26 Mar 1701 G57v fined for Renter Warden   4 May 1702 G71v his apprentice Thomas Arnold is freed   18 Dec 1702 G84r elected to Henry Bonwick's £40 share

SUTTON, William   3 Jun 1706 G132v bound to John Franks, 7 years

SWAILE – see SWALE

SWAILS, Mrs   6 Jul 1702 G77v to have 20s a year for her chamber rent

SWALE/SWAILE/SWALLE, Abel   7 Nov 1681 E138r declines cloathing; given time to consider his decision   24 Jun 1682 E154r cloathed   6 Apr 1685 F32v Robert Horne assigns him various theological books, itemised   4 Sep 1688 F106v Freeman Collins admits to printing the Metamorphoses, a Stock book, for Swale and Thomas Dring; told to negotiate with them   11 Oct 1688 F108v restored to Livery   7 Apr 1690 F133r complains that Thomas Dring has printed his Satires of Juvenal and Persius; Court asks them to refer dispute to committee   6 Apr 1691 F152r fined for Assistant

Renter Warden 2 Nov 1691 F162r with Robert Scott and Dring fined 2d per copy for printing Virgil without a licence 7 Dec 1691 F162v fine reduced to 1d per book through Dring's intervention 22 Dec 1691 F163v Scott asks for relief from last Court order on his behalf; not granted 3 Jul 1693 F189v elected to Thomas Lacy's £40 share 4 Dec 1693 F196r declines to accept his £40 share which is put up for election 2 Mar 1695/6 F239v committee formed on Samuel Heyrick's information that Swale is printing the Metamorphoses, but will submit to fining 7 Sep 1702 G80v Liveryman; his wife Mary's petition is read and consideration of it is deferred till next Court 7 Feb 1703/4 G101v Warden Robert Andrews to answer his letter 6 Mar 1703/4 G103v letter to be considered at next Pension Court 6 Sep 1708 G157r petition for relief to enable him to go to Ireland. 40s to be given now and £3 in Ireland 5 Mar 1710/11 G188r to be paid £3 30s now and another 30s when he comes to Chester on the way to Ireland. The £3 and 40s he had before to be put in the pension papers 4 Feb 1711/12 G196r £5 from charity account to purchase books to put him in business 3 Mar 1711/12 G197r Warden Daniel Browne to pay the remainder of the £5 for his use, as in the order of 4 February 9 Feb 1712/13 G206r to be given 50s from Poor Box for rent and clothes. To be recorded in next pension papers 4 Oct 1714 G222v to have 10s from Poor Box

See also following entry

SWALE/SWAILE, Mary 7 Sep 1702 G80v wife of Abel; petition read but consideration thereof referred to next Court 28 Sep 1702 G80v admitted to a 20s pension in place of Thomas Hodgkinson, deceased

See also preceding entry

SWALLE – see SWALE

SWEETING, [ ] 4 Aug 1684 F21v his will to be searched for in the Prerogative Office by the Clerk and a copy taken and recorded in S.C.'s register

SWEETING'S FEAST – see FEASTS

SWEETING, Lewes 1 Mar 1707/8 G150r bound to Isaac Cleave, 8 years

SWIFT AND SECRET MESSENGER – see WILKINS, John, Bishop of Chester

SYLVESTER – see SILVESTER

SYMONS, [ ] 6 Feb 1681/2 E144r committee appointed to treat with him, Ponder and Skinner re. their Chancery case against S.C.

SYMONDS, Bryan 5 Jun 1710 G180v bound to Thomas Bradyll, 7 years

SYMONDS, Henry 2 Dec 1695 F237v son of John Symonds of Dorchester, Dorset, gentleman; bound to John Baskett

SYMONDS, John – see preceding entry

SYMONS, Mary 7 Feb 1686/7 F70v deceased; her £80 share voted to William Whitwood

SYMPSON – see SIMPSON

SYMS, Henry 1 Sep 1701 G64r bound to Samuel Clarke, 7 years

See also SIMMS, SIMS

SYNEGOROS THALASSIOS – see VIEW OF ADMIRAL JURISDICTION

SYSTEMA HORTICULTURA [by John Worlidge] 4 Dec 1699 G33v assigned by Richard Hargrave to William Freeman

TABLE OR AN ACCOUNT OF TIME FOR 200 YEARS 4 May 1702 G70v John Smart granted permission to print

TACITUS, Cornelius 18 Mar 1686/7 F79v his works among books in catalogue annexed to Oxford agreement

TALBOT, John 8 Apr 1700 G39r bound to Robert Roberts, 7 years 9 Jun 1707 G142v freed by Robert Roberts

TALBOTT, Richard 5 Apr 1703 G88r bound to Isaac Cleave, 7 years

TANNER, Peter 5 Apr 1703 G88r freed by George Grafton, to whom he had been turned over from Felton 4 Oct 1703 G96r Francis Zouch is bound to him 4 May 1713 G209v his apprentice Francis Zouch is freed 7 Feb 1714/15 G225r John King is turned over to him from William Harvey 2 Jul 1716 G242r William White is turned over from him to Elizabeth Nutt

TANNER, Richard 1 Dec 1712 G205v freed by patrimony; William White is bound to him

TATE, Nahum 6 May 1698 G7v Articles of agreement between him and Nicholas Brady and the Master and Wardens and commonalty of the Mystery of Stationers relating to the New Version of David's Psalms read and sealed 6 Jun 1698 G8v correction of mistakes in two parts of the Articles lately executed 4 Dec 1699 G34r Court decides not to accept his offer of 20 shares in the copy of the New Version of the Psalms 5 Feb 1699/1700 G35r request granted to himself and Brady for a thousand of the New Version of the Psalms in 12mo and one hundred in octavo 6 May 1700 G39r Court does not accept his offer of shares in the New Version of the Psalms 19 Jul 1700 G43r proposal that S.C. should buy the remainder of his shares in the New Version of the Psalms 5 Aug 1700 G44r decision of Court not to purchase his shares 7 Apr 1701 G58r desiring copies of Court orders relating to New Version of the Psalms 4 Aug 1701 G63r proposal to sell S.C. his remaining shares in the New Version of the Psalms 8 Nov 1703 G97r proposal to sell S.C. his interest in the New Version of the Psalms to be considered 28 May 1706 G131v Brady alleges Tate has done wrong to him 4 Nov 1706 G135v proposal to sell his third part of the New Version of the Psalms to the S.C.; committee to treat with him 3 Mar 1706/7 G139r answer to his request to sell New Version of the Psalms deferred until next Court day 20 Dec 1711 G196r did not consent to impression of New Version of the Psalms printed by Baker. Willing to contribute to cost of prosecuting a suit against him 2 May 1715 G228v Master, Wardens and Stock-keepers to consider his request to borrow £25 against his share of the New Version of the Psalms 4 Jul 1715 G230v Master, Wardens and Stock-keepers to consider his request to borrow £30 upon an assignment of his salary as Poet Laureate

See also BRADY, Dr Nicholas; PSALMS

TATE/TEATE, Thomas 6 Nov 1704 G113r bound to John Buchanan 2 Jun 1712 G200v freed by John Buchanan 5 Sep 1715 G232v Joseph Luke is bound to him

TAUNTON, John 4 Jun 1705 G120v alias Collins; freed by Henry Skelton

TAUNTON, Thomas 4 Jul 1715 G231r son of William; bound to Richard Bruges, 7 years

TAUNTON, William – see preceding entry

TAYLER – see TAYLOR

TAYLOR, [ ] 23 Mar 1679/80 E98r 25s of George Bales's money remaining in Taylor's hands to be made up to 40s, paid to Under Warden and paid off 10s quarterly 6 Sep 1680 E103v schedule to be made of Bendigle's goods in his custody 24 Oct 1695 (W) Master to call on him to demand the £10 p.a. left to one Bruce, and after her decease to S.C. to buy Bibles to be given to the hospital 11 Nov 1695 (W) said deceased did not order payment for Bibles until Michaelmas next. Formerly Mr Crayle's man; cloathed

TAYLOR, Bartholomew   6 Jul 1702 G78r bound to Thomas Yeates, 7 years   6 Jul 1713 G212v freed by Elizabeth Yate

TAYLOR, Henry   3 Jul 1699 G27v bound to John Baskett, 7 years

TAYLOR/TAYLER, James (I)   1 Sep 1684 F23v William Whitwood is allowed to switch the mortgage of his £40 share from Mrs Mearne to Taylor   4 Jul 1692 F173v elected to Nathaniel Ponder's £40 share at Ponder's request   8 Apr 1695 F220r cloathed. Admitted into William Whitwood's £80 share at Whitwood's request   26 Mar 1706 G130r of Chatham; to be sent for on next occasion of choosing Renter Wardens   27 Mar 1710 G177r elected Assistant Renter Warden   3 Apr 1710 G178r fined for Assistant Renter Warden   6 Aug 1711 G193r John Loveday is bound to him

TAYLOR, James (II)   3 Aug 1702 G79v bound to John Randoll, 7 years   7 Nov 1709 G172r freed by John Randoll

TAYLOR, James, snr (III — possibly to be identified with I or II) – see following entry

TAYLOR, James, jnr (IV)   11 Jul 1716 G242r son of James; bound to Henry Parsons, 7 years

TAYLOR/TAYLER, John (I)   29 May 1689 F118v cloathed   6 Jun 1698 G8v William Taylor is bound to him   4 May 1702 G70v J. Hodgkins printed for him 'An Ephemerides of the Celestial Motions for 6 Years' containing a calendar which was copyright of the S.C. Not permitted to sell any more of the said books   27 Mar 1703 G87r elected First Renter Warden   12 Jun 1704 G107r to give names of those with quarterage arrears   6 Aug 1705 G122r Thomas Bradyll's share mortgaged to him   10 Sep 1705 G123r Thomas Bradyll's share mortgaged to him as surety for loan   4 Mar 1705/6 G129r his apprentice William Taylor is freed   2 Jun 1712 G200r competes unsuccessfully for John Sprint's £80 share   6 Oct 1712 G204r elected to Robert Knaplock's £80 share   2 May 1715 G228v elected Assistant   5 Mar 1715/16 G237v signs note for payment to Thomas Guy   2 Jul 1716 G241v elected to Benjamin Tooke's £160 share. His £80 share disposed of to Thomas Page   4 Feb 1716/17 G246v to be new trustee of S.C.'s property   21 Feb 1716/17 G246v trust of S.C.'s property conveyed to him as new trustee

TAYLOR, John (II)   7 May 1694 F204r of Harlow; his son William is bound to Jane Rayment, widow

TAYLOR, John (III)   4 Aug 1701 G63v bound to John Freer, 7 years

TAYLOR, John (IV — possibly to be identified with I)   6 Dec 1714 G224r his son Joseph is bound to Margaret Wild, 7 years

TAYLOR, Jonathan   6 Jun 1709 G165v bound to William Taylor, 7 years   4 Jul 1709 G167v turned over from William Taylor to Samuel Hoole   2 Jul 1716 G242r freed by William Taylor

TAYLOR, Joseph   6 Dec 1714 G224r son of John; bound to Margaret Wild, 8 years

TAYLOR/TAYLER, Randall   1680–1691 Beadle   2 May 1681 E111v £50 loan to be held over for a year   6 Jun 1681 E112v on account of death and insolvency of his trustees, Court accepts his £80 share as surety for £50 loan   20 Jun 1681 E114r signs disenfranchisement. Surrenders £80 share; John Whitlock is admitted to it   8 May 1682 E153v complaints about his behaviour give rise to a list of orders and rules for the Beadle   26 Mar 1683 E166v with John Whitlock, his son-in-law, granted permission to continue Whitlock's £50 loan a year longer   3 Mar 1683/4 F10v arrears of £30 for rent were discharged in consideration that, as Beadle, he surrendered his £80 share; his rent reduced to £8 p.a.   2 Nov 1685 F46r salary to be given to charity because of his misbehaviour; Taylor entreats Master's pardon   1 Feb 1685/6 F51r Beadle, paid his quarterly salary, due at Christmas, on receipt of better reports about his behaviour   7 Jun 1686 F56r fined £10, 6 months' salary, for being rude to the Master at Tyler dinner; ordered that he be sacked for the next offence. Anyone pleading for Taylor to pay £20 (sic) to the poor from dividends   7 Feb 1686/7 F70v petitions to be excused rent; Court orders him to pay arrears as they forgave him £34 on 3 Mar 1683 and lowered rent by £8 p.a.   7 Mar 1686/7 F78r £8 docked from his salary for misdemeanours paid into the Poor Box   4 Apr 1687 F81r re-elected Beadle; orders re. his rude behaviour (8 May 1682) are read to him   6 Aug 1688 F105r apologises for behaviour on barge and asks for £10 fine to be remitted; Court remits him £12 of his £32 rent arrears   26 Mar 1690 F131v warned that his salary will be suspended unless he regularly summons those receiving quarterly charity   7 Apr 1690 F132v 2 years in arrears with rent; warned he will be suspended from office for six months if he does not pay before next Court   7 Sep 1691 F159v lease to continue for no longer than he is Beadle to S.C.   7 Dec 1691 F163r Court doubts whether he pays 1d and 1d's worth of bread to the 12 poor of St Austin's each week and orders that a baker see to the bread   26 Mar 1692 F168r Nicholas Hooper elected Beadle after presenting petition complaining of Taylor's and Jonathan Whitlock's abuses of him   7 Aug 1693 F190v offered freedom now he no longer needs as Beadle to be disenfranchised from S.C.; given time to consider   4 Sep 1693 F191r to have rent of Stock tenement increased from £8 to £16 p.a. if he does not yield up 3 copies of all his books by Michaelmas

TAYLOR, Richard   2 May 1698 G7v bound to Benjamin Johnson, 7 years   7 Jun 1708 G153r freed by Hester Johnson   6 Feb 1709/10 G175v bookbinder; Henry White is bound to him

TAYLOR, Thomas   5 Aug 1700 G44r bound to John Walthoe, 7 years   7 Sep 1713 G213v freed by John Walthoe

TAYLOR, William (I)   7 May 1694 F204r son of John Taylor of Harlow; bound to Jane Rayment, widow   1 Jun 1702 G71v freed by James Rayment   6 Oct 1707 G145v bookseller; Nevinson Baker is bound to him   5 Jul 1708 G154v cloathed   6 Jun 1709 G165v of St Paul's Churchyard; Jonathan Taylor is bound to him   4 Jul 1709 G167v Jonathan Taylor turned over from him to Samuel Hoole   3 Jul 1710 G182r of Paternoster Row, bookseller; Thomas Janny is bound to him   9 Feb 1712/13 G206v William Graves is bound to him   10 Nov 1713 G214v James Lacy is bound to him   9 Apr 1716 G239r fined for Renter Warden   7 May 1716 G239v elected to Mrs Everingham's £80 share at her request   4 Jun 1716 G240v Thomas Hillyard is bound to him   2 Jul 1716 G242r his apprentice Jonathan Taylor is freed

TAYLOR/TAYLER, William (II)   6 Jun 1698 G8v bound to John Taylor, 7 years   4 Mar 1705/6 G129r freed by John Taylor

TEALE, Thomas   4 Oct 1714 G222r Thomas Barnes is bound to him

TEATE – see TATE

TEBB, Thomas   11 Jun 1694 F209r turned over to Peter Richmond and freed   8 Nov 1697 G1r Thomas Hobbs is bound to him   4 Dec 1704 G114r his apprentice Thomas Hobbs is freed   12 Nov 1705 G125r Christopher Stevenson is bound to him   4 Mar 1716/17 G247v his apprentice Christopher Stevenson is freed

TEBBATT, [   ]   8 Apr 1700 G38v Churchwarden of St Faith's; acquaints Court that Lamb's charity has not been fully applied for some time

TEGG, Edward – see following entry

TEGG, William   11 Nov 1695 F236r son of Edward Tegg of Pangbourne, yeoman; bound to Robert Jole

TELES, [   ]   19 Dec 1692 F183r deceased; his/her pension voted to Robert Cox

386

TEONGE, George 6 May 1706 G131v of Warwick; question as to whether he is fit for the Livery

TEONGE, Thomas 5 Aug 1695 F231v servant to Evan Tyler; freed 3 Apr 1699 G24r Joshua Gilbert is bound to him 6 May 1706 G131v his apprentice Joshua Gilbert is freed

TERENCE (Publius Terentius Afer) 4 Sep 1688 F106r a Stock book; Benjamin Motte is fined £10 for printing it 2 Mar 1690/1 F150v Richard Wild confesses to importing ca. 150 of 'Menelius [i.e. John Minellius] upon Terence', a Stock book 6 Apr 1691 F152r Richard Wild to be prosecuted for importing Terence without a licence 6 Jul 1691 F157v Richard Wild fined £9 1s for importing 181 copies of Minellius upon Terence and selling ca. 50 4 Feb 1705/6 G127v Mead to give explanation for printing without S.C.'s permission 19 Feb 1705/6 G128r discussion of Mead's printing of [William] Willymott's edition of Terence 1 Apr 1706 G130v committee to consider Terence and Ovid printed for Willymott

TERRELL, Edward 7 Feb 1703/4 G101v freed by John Vasey

TERRILL/TERRIL, Edward 3 Jul 1704 G110r William Hollis is bound to him 7 Aug 1704 G111r John Fletcher is turned over to him

See also TERRELL

TERRY, William 1 Mar 1687/8 F97v expelled from Livery by order of Lord Mayor 11 Oct 1688 F108v restored to Livery 20 Apr 1691 F152v about to be elected Assistant Renter Warden until some members inform Court that he is in Holland for several months 26 Mar 1692 F167v elected Assistant Renter Warden and summoned 12 Apr 1692 F168v fined for First Renter Warden 6 Dec 1697 G2r competes unsuccessfully for Peter Maplesden's £40 share

THACKARY – see THACKERY

THACKERY, Follensby 5 Sep 1698 G14v freed by William Onely

THACKERY, Thomas 6 Aug 1694 F211r son of William Thackery; freed by patrimony

THACKERY/THACKARY, William (I) 1 Mar 1682/3 E156r Humphrey Baker's 'Arithmetic' assigned to Thackery and John Wright by Elizabeth Thomas, administratrix of Edward Thomas 3 Feb 1684/5 F30r Mary Cole's Livery share is mortgaged to him for £80 13 Oct 1687 F91v sworn in as Assistant and fined for Renter Warden 7 May 1694 F203v elected Assistant and summoned 6 Aug 1694 F211r his son Thomas is freed by patrimony. Sworn in as Assistant 3 Dec 1694 F215v competes unsuccessfully for Dorman Newman's £160 share, fallen vacant because of Newman's bankruptcy 4 Feb 1694/5 F217r assigns [Emmanuel Ford's] 'History of Parismus' and five other books to William Wilde 6 Apr 1696 F241v Matthew Wootton's complaint that Thackery has printed or appropriated part of 'Parismus' deferred. To produce a list of warehouse books belonging to that co-partnership by which he is claiming right to disputed premises 4 May 1696 F242r no summons to be given him in future to attend the Court as an Assistant 13 Apr 1698 G6v assignment from him to Jonah Deacon and John Wilde of several copies or books to be entered in Register book 7 Jul 1712 G201v granted request for his mortgaged £80 share to be disposed of to James Brookes 20 Jun 1713 G210v given Alice Briggs's pension 24 Mar 1713/14 G217r deceased; Elizabeth Thrale is given his pension

THACKERY, William (II) 9 Feb 1707/8 G149r freed by patrimony

THANKSGIVING DAY 4 Sep 1704 G112r Master and Wardens to take care of the standing of the Assistants and Livery on 1 Jul 1706 G133r music to be paid for the same as last year 1 Dec 1707 G147r carpenter's bill for S.C. stand 2 Aug 1708 G156v Master and Wardens to provide dinner and entertainment 6 Jul 1713 G212r no member of S.C. to be admitted to S.C.'s stand on that day or to dinner without his Livery gown and no other person to be admitted to S.C.'s stand on that day

THEAK, John 5 Dec 1698 G17r bound to Robert Tristram, 8 years

THEORY … OF PHYSIC [unidentified; possibly Michael Ettmüller, *Etmullerus Abridged: or, A Complete System of the Theory and Practice of Physic*] 7 Dec 1685 F48r a third of this is assigned by Thomas Flesher to Edward Jones

THIRLBY, John 7 Dec 1691 F163r cloathed

THOMAS, [ ] 7 Aug 1697 F266r writes several times to Master re. Oxford treaty 26 Mar 1698 G5v of Oxford; letter from him reporting that a meeting of the delegates has debated the Treaty between the S.C. and the University 7 Jun 1698 G9r of Oxford; letter from him to Master saying that one part of Articles between the University and some members of the Table has been sealed and the other will be sent to London to be sealed

See also THOMAS, Lewis

THOMAS A KEMPIS – see IMITATION OF CHRIST

THOMAS, Bridget 23 Jun 1710 G180v elected to Widow Cox's pension 24 Sep 1714 G222r deceased; James Smalshaw is given her pension

THOMAS, Christopher 18 Nov 1715 G234v son of Thomas; bound to John Buchanan, 7 years 20 Dec 1716 G246r turned over from John Buchanan to Rebecca Somerscales

THOMAS, Edward 1 Mar 1682/3 E165r his administratrix, Elizabeth Thomas, assigns Humphrey Baker's 'Arithmetic' to John Wright and William Thackery

THOMAS, Elizabeth (I) 1 Mar 1682/3 E165r administratrix of Edward Thomas; assigns Humphrey Baker's 'Arithmetic' to John Wright and William Thackery 1 Feb 1685/6 F50r widow and administratrix of Edward Thomas; allowed to mortgage her £80 share to John Towse for £20 4 May 1702 G70v deceased; her £80 share is disposed of to Awnsham Churchill

THOMAS, Elizabeth (II) 8 Nov 1708 G158v Richard Loader is turned over from her to John Bennett

THOMAS, James 12 Jun 1704 G107v his apprentice Charles Garrett is freed

THOMAS, John 24 Mar 1701/2 G68r bound to Medriach Mead, 8 years

THOMAS, Lewis 7 Oct 1698 G11r elected to cloathing. Elected to Mrs Whitlock's £80 share 22 Dec 1698 G17v cloathed 6 Jul 1700 G43r John Garrett is bound to him 7 Jul 1701 G62r of Oxford; James (alias John) Rance is bound to him 22 Apr 1703 G88v of Oxford; Master to write to him by way of an answer to the Vice-Chancellor concerning profits from the S.C.'s printing in Oxford 5 Feb 1704/5 G115r Charles Combes is bound to him 2 Apr 1705 G118r of Oxford; to be presented with Clarendon's History for good service to S.C. relating to buying of said book 3 Jun 1706 G132v his apprentice Stephen Bryan is freed 5 Jul 1708 G155r John Bull is bound to him 17 Jul 1708 G155v of Oxford; letter from him concerning S.C.'s agreement with University of Oxford 7 Feb 1708/9 G160v of Oxford; John Springall is bound to him 26 Mar 1711 G189r fined for First Renter Warden 4 Feb 1711/12 G196v Morris Thomas is bound to him 1 Feb 1713/14 G216r John Hill is bound to him

See also THOMAS, [ ]

THOMAS, Morris 4 Feb 1711/12 G196v son of Timothy; bound to Lewis Thomas, 7 years

THOMAS, Thomas   18 Nov 1715 G234v his son Christopher is bound to John Buchanan, 7 years

THOMAS, Timothy   4 Feb 1711/12 G196v his son Morris is bound to Lewis Thomas, 7 years

THOMASON, George   5 Dec 1681 E140r Thomas Newcomb is allowed to enter 88 books 'of little value' assigned to him by Thomason at a lower rate than usual

THOMPSON, [ ]   1 Mar 1679/80 E97r fined for printing Welsh Almanack illegally   16 Jun 1684 F17v a tailor whose wife trades in books at Westminster Hall; submits to S.C. for further consideration

THOMPSON, Cyprian   5 Dec 1698 G17r bound to Robert James, 7 years

THOMPSON, George   5 Sep 1692 (W) freed by Mary Crooke, widow   12 Sep 1692 F179r of Addle Hill and newly made free of Mary Crooke; name sent to Lord Chamberlain

THOMPSON, Job   5 Apr 1703 G88r bound to John Stephens, 7 years

THOMPSON, Lawrence   9 Sep 1700 G45r bound to William Downing, 7 years   1 Dec 1707 G147v freed by Ann Downing

THOMPSON, Mary   6 Aug 1694 F211v James Bostock is bound to her   13 Apr 1702 G69v William Wise is turned over from her to Jeremiah Wilkins

THOMPSON, Mrs   5 Jul 1697 F264v surrenders her £80 share; Abel Roper is elected to it

THOMPSON, Nathaniel   20 Dec 1684 (W) committee to consult with Lord Chief Justice re. stock of Nathaniel Thompson and John Starkey, both being outlawed   7 Feb 1686/7 F71v to be summoned re. not freeing his apprentice William Newbolt; if he does not appear Newbolt is to be freed at the next Court   7 Mar 1686/7 F78r does not appear and Newbolt is freed   1 Mar 1687/8 F97r deceased; his mortgage to the late John Leigh of his £80 share for £80 plus interest, now possessed by his wife, is presented to Court by Leigh's widow

THOMPSON, Thomas   1 Mar 1707/8 G150r bound to Thomas Ilive, 7 years   1 Aug 1709 G169v turned over from Thomas Ilive to William Redmaine

THOMPSON, Widow   26 Mar 1685 F32r given 7s 6d charity   6 Aug 1688 F104v ordered to stop printing, but may apply to the Secretary of State for a licence

THOMPSON, William   4 Mar 1705/6 G129r bound to Francis Leach, 7 years

THORN, William   7 Oct 1700 G46r bound to Richard Wellington, 7 years

THORNCOMB, Andrew   3 Nov 1684 F26r request for £50 loan deferred

THORNCOMB/THORNCOMBE, Thomas   1 Sep 1701 G64r bound to Hugh Newman, 7 years   8 May 1704 G106v turned over to Thomas Hodgkins

THORNE, Francis   4 Dec 1704 G114r bound to James Read, 7 years

THOROSON, Robert   6 Sep 1697 F267r freed by Edward Evetts

THRAILE – see THRALE

THRALE/THRAYLE, Benjamin   11 Apr 1681 E109v assigned his late father's copies by his mother Dorothy, except for 'The Rosary of Godly Prayer' [i.e. Nicholas Themylthorpe, *The Posy of Godly Prayers*]   1 Aug 1681 E117r assigns Dr [Alexander] Read's 'Manual of Anatomy or Dissection of the Body' to Thomas Flesher   1 Sep 1684 F23r assigns 'Coffee House Jests' to Henry Rodes   20 Dec 1686 F69v heir to last surviving feoffee of Wood Street; ordered that he convey it to other feoffees in trust for S.C.   2 May 1687 F83r seals indenture of conveyance of Wood Street estate with his mother

Dorothy and his wife Elizabeth   20 Dec 1693 F197r elected into the pension of Francis Oliver, deceased   23 Jun 1709 G166r deceased; Elizabeth, his widow, is given his pension

THRALE, Dorothy   11 Apr 1681 E109v her late husband's copies entered to her son, Benjamin Thrale, except for 'The Rosary of Godly Prayer' [i.e. Nicholas Themylthorpe, *The Posy of Godly Prayers*]   26 Mar 1686 F53v allowed to transfer the mortgage of her £320 share from Hannah Sawbridge's executors to Edward Brewster for £100 and interest   2 May 1687 F83r seals indenture of conveyance of Wood Street estate with her son Benjamin and his wife Elizabeth   5 Jun 1690 F136r deceased; before disposing of her £320 share, Court elect committee re. entitlement to shares of those not involved in trade   7 Jul 1690 F138v share disposed of by balloting to Thomas Bassett

THRALE/THRAILE/THRAYLE, Elizabeth   2 May 1687 F83r seals indenture of conveyance of Wood Street estate with her husband Benjamin and his mother Dorothy   23 Jun 1709 G166r elected to her late husband Benjamin's pension   22 Dec 1713 G215v elected to Johanna Strainge's pension. Mary Redmaine is given her pension   24 Mar 1713/14 G217r elected to William Thackery's pension. Mary Crump is given her pension

THRALE, James   2 May 1687 F83r heir of Richard Thrale (deceased). His heir is Benjamin Thrale

THRALE, Mrs   1 Dec 1679 E95v assignment to Brewster entered

THRALE, Richard   2 May 1687 F83r last surviving feoffee of Wood Street estate, now deceased

THRAYLE – see THRALE

THURLOE, John   1 Feb 1702/3 G85r bound to Christopher Coningsby, 7 years

THUROGOOD, Theophilus   1 Dec 1707 G147v bound to Mary Danvers, 7 years

THURSFEILD [i.e. John Trussell?] – see DANIEL, Samuel

THYNNE, [Henry Frederick or James]   7 Nov 1687 F94r under the Printing Act requests a copy of every book printed for the King's Library, including those printed before the last Act expired

TIDMARSH, Samuel   4 Oct 1686 (W) on original list of new livery members, though not finally chosen

TILLY, John   2 Apr 1705 G118v bound to John Heptingstall, 7 years   7 Apr 1712 G199r freed by John Heptingstall

TIPPER, [   ]   5 Jun 1710 G180r proposal for printing a monthly book. Court agrees to try it for a month or two

TITCHBORNE, John   3 Jul 1699 G27v freed by William Harris

TITUS LIVIUS – see LIVY

TOAKE, Andrew   2 Dec 1706 G136v and Baxter to examine and correct all classical authors belonging to the English Stock

TODD, Douglas   22 Jun 1699 G25v deceased; Sara Lovell is given his pension

TODD, William   4 Dec 1710 G186r bound to Elizabeth Grover, 7 years

TOFT, George   6 May 1695 F224r son of Joshua Toft of Godalming, clothier; bound to John Brookes

TOFT, Joshua – see preceding entry

TOKEFEILD, [   ]   3 Nov 1679 E94v given one-off charity payment of £5

TOKEFEILD/TOKEFIELD/TOOKEFIELD, George   2 May 1681 E111v ordered that he should have £4 charity if he is really in the Charterhouse as a pensioner   5 Oct 1681

E131r his note on Westbrooke's bond to S.C. shows it has already been cancelled   3 Apr 1682 E151r his petition and begging letter put out of Court   4 Sep 1682 E157r begging letter returned without answer   5 Feb 1682/3 E163r on reception of another begging letter, ordered that no more papers are to be received from him   4 May 1691 F153r former Clerk. A receipt in his hand is produced by Gilbert Wharton for part payment of a £20 bond   26 Mar 1695 F219v competes unsuccessfully for Clerk   26 Mar 1696 F241r competes unsuccessfully for Clerk

TOKEY, Joseph   1 Mar 1702/3 G86r Edward Shawler turned over from him to Francis Leak

See also TUCKEY, John

TOLAND, John – see SIMPSON, Richard

TOMKINS, Samuel   6 Feb 1715/16 G236r son of Thomas; bound to Robert Elmes, 7 years

TOMKINS, Thomas – see preceding entry

TOMLINS, Margaret   20 Dec 1687 F96r widow; leave granted her to mortgage her £80 share to John Towse for £50   7 Apr 1707 G141r deceased; her £80 share disposed of to Richard Wilkins

TOMLINSON, Enoch   22 Jun 1698 G9v general release from S.C. sealed

TONSON, Jacob (I)   4 Dec 1682 E160v assigned one fifth of [Mézeray's] 'History of France' by William Cadman   4 Oct 1686 F64v elected to Livery   8 Nov 1686 F67r summoned re. cloathing   6 Dec 1686 F68v to be sued for refusal of cloathing and non-attendance at Court   20 Dec 1686 F69v appears, apologises and is cloathed   1 Aug 1687 F87r assigned part of '3 Translations or Books' by Sir Roger L'Estrange   1 Mar 1687/8 F97v expelled from Livery by order of Lord Mayor   11 Oct 1688 F108v restored to Livery   1 Dec 1690 F146v to answer complaint made by Francis Saunders that he printed Lord Rochester's poems   12 Apr 1692 F169r elected Assistant Renter Warden and summoned   15 Apr 1692 F169v fined for Assistant Renter Warden. He is assigned [Bulstrode Whitlock's] 'Memorials of the English Affairs' by Nathaniel Ponder   10 Oct 1692 F181r summoned for having given out 'reflecting speeches of this Company'   4 Dec 1693 F196r elected to £40 share declined by Abel Swale and ordered to pay at same time as those elected on 3 July   5 Feb 1693/4 F198v sworn into £40 share   3 Feb 1695/6 F239r competes unsuccessfully for John Place's £80 share   3 Aug 1696 F246v elected to the £80 share of George Hopper, deceased   5 Oct 1696 F251r sworn in to Yeomanry share   3 May 1697 F262r John Allen, his apprentice, is freed   3 May 1708 G152r elected Assistant   7 Jun 1708 G153r added to committee re. Benjamin Harris arrears   8 Nov 1708 G158v elected to Capt. Edward Darrell's £160 share. His £80 share is disposed of to his nephew Jacob Tonson   1 Aug 1709 G169v Thomas Wall is bound to him   30 Jun 1711 G192r competes unsuccessfully for Under Warden   2 Mar 1712/13 G207r permitted to fine for first year of Under Warden to preserve his seniority to William Freeman   4 Jul 1713 G211r fined for second year of Under Warden and first and second years of Upper Warden   7 Jun 1714 G219r has attended Stock-keepers concerning his printing several copies belonging to S.C.   5 Dec 1715 G235r dividend to be stopped until such time as he and his son give satisfaction to S.C. for printing S.C.'s copies   30 Jun 1716 G241r elected Master but permitted to fine

TONSON, Jacob (II)   6 Sep 1708 G157r freed by patrimony; cloathed   8 Nov 1708 G158v elected to his uncle Jacob Tonson's £80 share. Elected Renter Warden   3 Mar 1711/12 G197r Isaac Miller is bound to him   7 Mar 1708/9 G162r of Gray's Inn; Edward Lathbury is bound to him   4 Apr 1709 G164r Samuel Watkins is bound to him   6 Mar 1709/10 G176v bookseller; William Rowland is bound to him

TONSON, Mary   6 May 1694/5 F223v Samuel Mabbatt is bound to her   6 Mar
1698/9 G22r Egbert Sangar is bound to her   10 Sep 1705 G123v Henry Yemes is
bound to her   4 Mar 1705/6 G129r her apprentice William Wyse is freed by David
Edwards   3 Mar 1706/7 G139r her apprentice Egbert Sangar is freed   3 Nov 1712
G205r her apprentice Henry Yemes is freed

TONSON, Richard   7 Feb 1680/1 E107r cloathed   25 Jun 1684 F18v ordered to
appear at next Court on account of William Powle, an ex-apprentice, not serving all his
time   7 Jul 1684 F20r owns that he discharged William Powle while he still had a year
of his time to serve   2 May 1687 F83r elected to John Penn's £40 share   11 Oct 1688
F108v restored to Livery   1 Mar 1688/9 F113v elected Stock-keeper for Livery with
Bennett Griffin   3 Apr 1704 G105v Powle is described as a former servant to him

TOOK, [ ]   3 Mar 1700/1 G57r as executor to William Baker, granted freedom to
William Baker jnr

TOOKE, Benjamin, snr   1 Mar 1679/80 E97r competes unsuccessfully for Treasurer   1
Mar 1680/1 E107v elected Stock-keeper for Yeomanry with Charles Harper   1 Mar
1681/2 E145v elected Stock-keeper from Yeomanry with Thomas Sawbridge   8 May
1682 E153r consideration of objections to Charles Spicer, Thomas Williams's executor,
assigning books to Tooke and Thomas Sawbridge held over until next Court   7 Aug
1682 E156r elected to the £40 share of Widow Greene, deceased, to make up £80 with
his other share   4 Sep 1682 E157v assignment to him and Thomas Sawbridge to be
entered   1 Mar 1683/4 F9r Richard Dutton's son Baptist is discharged from apprenticeship to Tooke   7 Apr 1684 F14r on the list of loyal Assistants presented to the
Crown   2 Jun 1684 F15v promises to fine for Renter Warden   7 May 1685 (W)
confirmed as member of new Livery   7 Sep 1685 F44r to be summoned with Richard
Chiswell and Waterson re. printing a Stock book, 'Daniel and Thursfeild's History' [i.e.
Samuel Daniel & John Trussell, *History of England*]   26 Mar 1686 F54v pays 12d
charity for being absent from Court without Master's leave   9 Jan 1687/8 F69v lame
and out of town, so does not deduct £5 each from the dividends of Thomas Parkhurst,
Henry Mortlock and William Miller   1 Mar 1686/7 F77r stands for Warehousekeeper
and declares that he will give up his place on the Court if elected; duly elected   1687–
1702 Warehousekeeper/Treasurer   7 Mar 1686/7 F78r proposed sureties to be
accepted   2 May 1687 F82v he and Walter Kettleby each to pay £25 to defray a £50
loan to John Wallis   6 Jun 1687 F84r he and Kettleby given till Michaelmas to pay
Wallis's loan   3 Oct 1687 F89v awarded £5 over and above his quarterly salary   1
Mar 1687/8 F97v order from Lord Mayor that he should be restored as an Assistant
and to the Livery. Re-elected Treasurer. Salary to be increased by £20 to £100 p.a.   26
Mar 1688 F99v sureties' bonds for his faithful service to S.C. are presented in
Court   30 Jun 1688 F103r elected Under Warden   6 Aug 1688 F104r Treasurer's
bond and sureties, usually held by Under Warden, delivered to Upper Warden since
Tooke himself is Under Warden   7 Oct 1689 F124r his and Simms's Wardens' accounts
reveal that wine was presented to the Lord Chancellor in the middle of the Oxford
dispute   5 Jun 1690 F136r given £10 compensation for having broken his arm while
travelling to Oxford on S.C. business three years ago   13 Jun 1690 (W) confirms
receipt of £10 from Warden Parkhurst   7 Jul 1690 F139r elected to Thomas Bassett's
£160 share   1 Sep 1690 F142r sells three books to Court for same price that he and
Henry Mortlock paid for them   4 Dec 1690 F147v becomes obliged to Cambridge on
behalf of S.C. for the payment of £100 p.a. for university privileges   6 Jul 1696 F246r
to officiate as Clerk in witnessing indentures, &c., during Christopher Grandorge's
incapacity and to receive fees for Grandorge's use   22 Dec 1697 G2v Treasurer.
Treatment of exchequer notes and pistoles taken in for the use of the S.C.   6 Jun 1698
G8v Bartholomew Barker is bound to him   1 Mar 1698/9 G21r elected Treasurer.

Brother, Randall Tooke, and Thomas Carpenter as sureties   1 Mar 1699/1700 G36r elected Treasurer. His brother, Randall Tooke, and Thomas Carpenter are given as sureties   8 Apr 1700 G39r to help ensure that no boys play in S.C. garden and that no pigeons are kept there   3 Jun 1700 G40r acquaints Court that £100 is due to Mrs Tucker and £100 to Mr Baker by bond from S.C. Says that his brother would lend the S.C. £200. To pay Lilly cost of suit taxed against Robert Everingham concerning Act for laying a duty upon paper   1 Mar 1700/1 G56r elected Treasurer. Gives Randall Tooke and Thomas Carpenter as sureties   1 Dec 1701 G65v to be paid £50 for his moiety of copy and impression of 'Gradus ad Parnassum' entered before he became a servant of the S.C.   9 Feb 1701/2 G66v appears desiring more money for his moiety of 'Gradus ad Parnassum'. No more money granted   2 Mar 1701/2 G67v elected Treasurer. Proposes the same persons for sureties as last year   26 Mar 1702 G69r copy of his instrument for assigning his interest in his moiety of 'Gradus ad Parnassum' to the S.C.   6 Jul 1702 G77v given copy of charge against him concerning accounts of English Stock. Does not give satisfactory answers to the charge   14 Jul 1702 G78r discussion by Court of charges against him   16 Jul 1702 G78v has paid English Stock printers more than he has accounted for. To be suspended from post of Treasurer. To make up his accounts with Stock-keepers and deliver up warehouse, books and monies   23 Jul 1702 G79r refuses to deliver up warehouse and books to Stock-keepers. Refuses to pay £100 due to University of Oxford from the S.C.   3 Aug 1702 G79v Attorney General to be consulted by S.C. over his case   7 Sep 1702 G80r reading of opinion of Attorney General on his case to be adjourned until next Court   5 Oct 1702 G81v opinion of Attorney General read. To be discharged from S.C.'s service and to deliver up possession of house and warehouse   9 Oct 1702 G82r further debate by Court. No more rent to be paid to him by tenants of English Stock   12 Jul 1703 G92v opinion of Attorney General read. To be sent for concerning his accounts and securities   15 Jul 1703 G93r Court informed that he has attended Stock-keepers and been acquainted with resolutions of Court   2 Aug 1703 G93v opinions of Attorney General on. Committee to settle accounts and affairs   20 Oct 1703 G96v report from committee to consider his affairs. Draft of document produced to be delivered to him   8 Nov 1703 G96v and his sureties put on bail   30 Jun 1704 G108r desiring suit between S.C. and himself to be settled by means of negotiators   20 Jul 1704 G110r bond of arbitration between S.C. and himself, Thomas Carpenter and Randall Tooke of £1000 penalty sealed   4 Dec 1704 G113v Dr Nicholas Brady to be paid for profit of an impression of Tate and Brady's Psalms not brought to account by Tooke   5 Feb 1704/5 G114v affairs relating to Tate and Brady's Psalms to be left to Master, Wardens and Stock-keepers   7 May 1705 G119v to meet Thomas Bennett concerning accounts of Tate and Brady's Psalms   22 Jun 1705 G120v suit against him   9 Sep 1706 G134v his apprentice Bartholomew Baker is freed   3 May 1708 G152v Clerk to make enquiries of him concerning order between S.C. and Thomas Jones about printing Welsh almanack   2 Aug 1708 G156r dividend of Mrs Eversden received by him to be allowed to her in the arrears due from her rent   4 Jul 1709 G167r to be met by Capt. William Phillipps and John Sprint to settle accounts; £10 received by him from Brunt for rent not accounted for   2 Jul 1716 G241v deceased; his £160 share disposed of to John Taylor

TOOKE, Benjamin, jnr   4 Mar 1694/5 F219r servant to William Rogers; freed   3 Jun 1695 F225r cloathed   3 Feb 1700/1 G55v elected to Timothy Goodwin's £40 share   26 Mar 1701 G57v fined for Renter Warden   3 Aug 1702 G79v Stephen Harcourt is turned over to him   2 Aug 1703 G94r his apprentice William Tooke is freed   9 Sep 1706 G134v competes unsuccessfully for William Hensman's £80 share   7 Apr 1707 G140v elected to Capt. Edward Darrell's £80 share. His £40 share disposed of to John Walthoe   6 Sep 1714 G221v William Willymott's letter to him re. printing of Corderius to be dealt with by Master, Wardens and Stock-keepers   7 Feb 1714/15 G224v competes unsuccessfully for £160 share

TOOKE, Randall/Randolph   7 Nov 1692 F181v citizen and saller (*sic*) of London; given a bond of £400 penalty for payment of £205 by 8 May 1693   1 Mar 1698/9 G21r surety for his brother Benjamin as Treasurer   1 Mar 1699/1700 G36r surety for his brother Benjamin as Treasurer   3 Jun 1700 G40r bond from S.C. of £400 penalty to pay £205 on 4 December sealed   1 Mar 1700/1 G56r surety for Benjamin Tooke as Treasurer   7 Jul 1701 G62r citizen and saller of London. Bond from S.C. to him of £200 penalty to pay £102 10s   20 Jul 1704 G110r arbitrator on behalf of Benjamin Tooke   22 Dec 1708 G159v £300 to be repaid to him   24 Dec 1708 G160r Court called for the purpose of sealing bonds with which to pay off his bond   4 Apr 1709 G164r deceased; £200 bond taken up by S.C. to pay that sum to his executors. Advance of £40 to be paid

TOOKE/TOOK, Robert   1 Jun 1702 G71v Francis Pyke is turned over to him   5 Sep 1709 G170r printer, of Broadstreet; Samuel Kent is bound to him

TOOKE, William   2 Aug 1703 G94r freed by Benjamin Tooke

TOOKEFEILD – see TOKEFEILD

TOOKEY, Robert   1 Jun 1702 G71v Thomas Darrack is bound to him   6 Jun 1709 G165v his apprentice Thomas Darrack is freed

TOPHAM, [ ]   4 Aug 1707 G144v committee to meet him, Compton and other MPs in order to get an Act of Parliament for securing copyright

TOPHAM, Thomas   6 Jun 1692 F171v private press discovered in his and William Anderson's house; landlord to be prosecuted

TOPLADY, Alice   18 Jul 1690 F140v widow; S.C. gives her a bond to pay £205 by 18 Jan with a £400 penalty

TOPLADY, Mrs   7 Nov 1692 F181v is paid £205 and bond cancelled; money raised by entering into another bond with Randall Tooke

TOUGH, Elizabeth   22 Jun 1715 G229v elected to Katharine Robinson's pension

TOUGH, Joseph   6 Mar 1703/4 G103v freed by Sarah Holt

TOWER LIBERTY/LITTLE TOWER HILL/TOWER PRECINCT   27 Mar 1704 G104v bond to S.C. of £100   5 Feb 1704/5 G115r Richard Mount to pay £10 more on bond from poor of Little Tower Hill to S.C.   7 Jun 1708 G153r upon payment of a further £10 by churchwardens, new bond can be prepared by S.C. to pay £5 p.a. to the poor there   4 Oct 1708 G158r bond for yearly payment of £5 to poor of Liberty of Great and Little Tower Hill sealed. Old bond cancelled

TOWN CLERK   6 May 1685 F33v Clerk ordered to carry list of bookdealers outside S.C. to Town Clerk   12 Oct 1687 F91r Clerk to give him account of elections after membership revision, with names of restored and remaining Livery   7 Nov 1687 F94r subsequently approves William Cooper as Assistant, member of Livery and Stock-keeper   5 Dec 1687 F95r delivers commission from Crown confirming the several choices of officers for the London companies   26 Mar 1691/2 F167v Clerk to return precept read at last Court to Town Clerk   4 Jul 1692 F173r to be sent list of S.C. freemen and Liverymen not free of the City

See also CROWN; LONDON, LORD MAYOR OF

TOWNSEND, John, snr – see two following entries

TOWNSEND, John, jnr   7 Jul 1712 G201v son of John; bound to Hannah Mayo, 7 years

TOWNSEND, Miles   2 Jun 1712 G200v son of John; bound to John Fletcher, 7 years   2 May 1715 G228v turned over from John Fletcher to John Randoll

TOWSE, John   3 Jul 1680 E101v stands unsuccessfully for Under Warden   2 May 1681 E110v elected, with Roger Norton, to audit Renter Warden Godfrey Head's accounts. With Roger Norton, to ascertain the value of the S.C. ground cut off to widen Ave Maria Lane, for amelioration money   2 Jul 1681 E115v elected Under Warden   4 Jul 1681 E115v and Norton desired to continue efforts to secure amelioration money   6 Mar 1681/2 E147v to organise a dinner on behalf of Thomas Vere, who died shortly after admission to a £320 share, and be reimbursed by executors   8 May 1682 E153r among sureties for the payment of Sir Joseph Seamour's annuity; indemnified by S.C.   1 Jul 1682 E155r fined for Under Warden   4 Sep 1682 E157r to be paid £5 for a buck out of Thomas Vere's part in Stock. To be paid £6 13s 4d by Thomas Newcomb's executors for election dinner   5 Feb 1682/3 E163r elected to Evan Tyler's £320 share   30 Jun 1683 F1v elected Upper Warden   7 Apr 1684 (W) on list of loyal Assistants presented to Crown   25 Jun 1684 F18v on Hannah Sawbridge's behalf desires an old £500 bond to be cancelled and a new one drawn up; this is done   5 Jul 1684 F19r fined for his second year as Upper Warden   7 May 1685 (W) confirmed as a member of the new Livery   1 Feb 1685/6 F50r Elizabeth Thomas is allowed to mortgage her £80 share to him for £20   1 Mar 1685/6 F52r elected Stock-keeper for Assistants with John Baker   3 May 1686 F55v among those chosen to audit Renter Wardens' accounts   3 Jul 1686 F58v stands unsuccessfully for Master   6 Sep 1686 F62r tells Court that Peter Stone, surety of Henry Clarke jnr's for a £50 loan from Tyler Bequest, is dead   1 Mar 1686/7 F77r elected Stock-keeper for Assistants with William Cooper   7 Mar 1686/7 F78r Godfrey Head is allowed to mortgage his £80 share to Towse for a sum of £60   23 Mar 1686/7 F80r Thomas Spicer alias Helder is allowed to mortgage his £80 share to him for £40   4 Apr 1687 F81r among those chosen to audit Warden's accounts   2 Jul 1687 F85v among those chosen to audit Warden's accounts   1 Aug 1687 F87v debate concerning precedency between Towse, Henry Herringman and John Bellinger referred to next Court   5 Sep 1687 F88v resolved that Towse should be fined £5 for not having served as Master, and then take precedence of Herringman and Bellinger   12 Oct 1687 F90v competes unsuccessfully for Master and among those chosen to audit Warden's accounts   17 Oct 1687 F93r moves that Thomas Spicer alias Helder should be made an Assistant; motion defeated   20 Dec 1687 F96r Margaret Tomlins mortgages her £80 share to him for £50   1 Mar 1687/8 F98v elected Stock-keeper for Assistants with John Richardson   30 Jun 1688 F103r among those chosen to audit Renter Wardens' accounts   27 Nov 1688 F110v restored to Assistants and elected Master   6 Jul 1689 F121r competes unsuccessfully for Master   7 Oct 1689 F124r claims precedency over Henry Herringman and John Bellinger; confusion discovered over order of 5 Sep 1687. Deferred   2 Dec 1689 F127r Widow Crooke mortgages her £80 share to him for £70 plus interest   1 Feb 1691/2 F164v his part in concluding Oxford agreement is detailed. Requests that Anthony Baskervile should have 6 months longer to pay his Livery fine and succeeds in halting prosecution for that duration   7 Mar 1691/2 F166v with other S.C. feoffees, executes transfer of mortgage of Stock estate to indemnify S.C. members re. Oxford

TOWSE, Mrs   8 Oct 1708 G158v deceased; Assistant's share disposed of to Capt. Edward Darrell

TOY, Humphrey   22 Dec 1681 E141v deceased; Millicent Dennis is given his pension

TRACEY/TRACY, Ebenezer   11 Nov 1700 G46v cloathed and his apprentice Henry Parson is freed   5 May 1707 G142r bookseller; Thomas Cox is bound to him   26 Mar 1709 G163r excused from serving as Renter Warden this year   27 Mar 1710

G177r fined for First Renter Warden   4 Dec 1710 G185v to be served with a copy of the writ of execution against Benjamin Harris   19 Dec 1712 G206r elected to Thomas Lacy's £80 share   5 Apr 1714 G218r his son(?) John is bound to him. Ebenezer Powell is bound to him

TRACEY, John   5 Apr 1714 G218r son of Ebenezer(?); bound to his father, 7 years

TRACEY, William   11 Nov 1695 F235r excused cloathing

See also TRACY

TRACY, Edward   26 Mar 1700/1 G38r Ann Wood is bound to him

TRANTUM, Richard   5 Oct 1713 G214r son of Thomas; bound to William Chapman, 7 years

TRANTUM, Thomas – see preceding entry

TRAVELL, John   2 May 1709 G164v bricklayer; to view Morphew's house   2 Jul 1709 G166v bricklayer; to be employed on repairs to Morphew's house

TRAVELLER'S AND CHAPMAN'S DAILY INSTRUCTOR   5 Feb 1704/5 G114v to be delivered to Joseph Collyer by George Sawbridge   5 Mar 1704/5 G116v S.C.'s calendars therein to be delivered to Joseph Collyer by George Sawbridge

TRAVERS, Mary   1 Aug 1692 (W) is freed by Francis Leach, having been bound by foreign indenture   12 Sep 1692 F179r newly made free of Francis Leach; name sent to Lord Chamberlain

TREADWELL, John   15 Nov 1703 G97v of Norwich; bill in Chancery to be brought against him concerning sham almanacks

TREASURER/WAREHOUSEKEEPER   1679–1686 John Leigh   8 Nov 1680 E105r to pay Robert Scott 40s for charges over and above £40 of Jonathan Edwin's money   6 Dec 1680 E105v to view ground with George Sawbridge and S.C. workmen re. making a pump   1 Mar 1685/6 F51v to pay no money henceforth without order of Court   8 Sep 1686 F63r Sir Roger L'Estrange's letter re. election of Treasurer and S.C.'s response is given   11 Oct 1686 F65r Court vote to select a Treasurer *pro tempore*. (W) Reference to recommendation of Bridgeman and L'Estrange being 'contrary to inclinations and intentions of the generality of partners' and fears that disobliging L'Estrange might undermine 'the whole Stock and privileges' held from Crown   12 Oct 1686 F66r all Stock-keepers decline to be Treasurer, at a special meeting, except Obadiah Blagrave who is elected   20 Dec 1686 F69v committee appointed to peruse byelaws concerning Treasurer and alter them if necessary   7 Feb 1686/7 F70r orders, rules and directions re. the post read; Thomas Dring or any other Assistant to have a copy; given a week for complaints   21 Feb 1686/7 F71v Thomas Bassett and Dring's objections to proposed duties of Treasurer to be presented to whole Court   28 Feb 1686/7 F72v name to be changed to Warehousekeeper; alterations to orders presented and approved   1687–1702 Benjamin Tooke   1 Mar 1686/7 F77r candidates make protestations and the new orders are read; Benjamin Tooke is elected. (W) Court at next meeting to consider repealing the order of 28 February 1686/7 under which the Treasurer is to be called Warehousekeeper   23 Mar 1686/7 F80r to be given schedule of wainscots, partitions, shelves, dressers and moveables in Warehousekeeper's house, compiled by Clerk; Clerk to take schedule of wainscots, partitions, shelves, dressers and other moveables in house before Tooke moves in   30 May 1687 F83r Obadiah Blagrave is voted £70 gratuity for acting as *pro tempore* Warehousekeeper   4 Jul 1687 F86r ordered £5 over and above quarterly salary   1 Aug 1687 F87r to deliver to Thomas Mathew as many copies of the Psalms he has printed as he requires   20 Dec 1687 F96r to have £5 over and above quarterly salary   3 Nov 1688 F109r Nathaniel Ponder is forgiven a debt of £20 to the late Treasurer John Leigh in trust for S.C. in consideration of a recent present to S.C. To print and publish advertisements against counterfeit almanacks   6 May 1689 F117v Samuel Jewell and Thomas Caister are appointed his sureties and the Clerk is ordered to draw up their bond to S.C.   7 Oct 1689 F124v to pay himself and Stock-keepers 2s per meeting in lieu of dinners, stopped because of S.C. debts   15 Jul 1690 F140r to go to houses of members soliciting subscriptions towards troops for Crown   1 Sep 1690 F142r to make a rental of the Stock estate for every Court day; Clerk to do this for Corporation estate under Treasurer's rental   16 Jun 1691 F155v ordered to deliver house in Amen Corner to Nicholas Hooper in good repair   7 Sep 1691 F159v empowered to give tenants notice of renewal of leases and serve 6 months' notice on those not renewing   22 Dec 1691 F163v to send written account of all receipts and payments made on Stock account to Master's or Upper Warden's house every Saturday   13 Apr 1693 F187r to make Oxford proposals available for remaining English Stock members to subscribe to them   6 Oct 1693 F193r deed for new Stock at Oxford and Cambridge deposited with him until a counterpart is sealed   6 Nov 1693 F194v 1 bill for the purchase of Stock paper to be kept by him and to be entered regularly   20 Dec 1694 F216r door between Hall and Treasurer's house to be temporarily opened for the more convenient carrying of dividends out of the Hall   15 Feb 1694/5 F217r to finance Master and Wardens re. Printing Act   3 Jun 1695 F225v Nicholas Hooper is ordered to pay rent arrears to Treasurer before his petition for rent abatement can be considered   5 Aug 1695 F230v committee appointed to investigate a complaint that the Treasurer has been engaging in trade contrary to Court orders   11 Nov 1695 F235v Court indemnifies him against a 'sudden Fall of Guineas' in receiving money for almanacks   3 Feb 1695/6 F239r to make a note of all borrowings and receipts from S.C.   1 Apr 1697 F260v to be paid moneys donated towards a Paper Act test case   4 Oct 1697 F268r to draw up accounts with Beadle of all matters between them relating to S.C. before next Court. To pay Robert Stephens's salary of £10 in the future instead of the Wardens. To pay Nicholas Hooper's bill of 15s 8d   7 Mar 1697/8 G4v to pay herald painters   26 Mar 1698 G5v has paid Warden Bennett Griffin £50 given by executors of Knight to poor of S.C.   13 Apr 1698 G6r to have a copy of the Court's order concerning Thomas Bassett's share in the English Stock   22 Jun 1698 G9v bond to him of £30 from Henry Nelme   4 Jul 1698 G11r to pay Thomas Fox's and John Lilly's bills   1 Aug 1698 G11v to pay Warden Richard Simpson £100 due from English Stock to Corporation   5 Sep 1698 G14r to make up Mrs Eversden's and the Beadle's accounts with S.C. for next Court day   7 Oct 1698 G15r to pay Clerk's bill for soliciting in Chancery   5 Jun 1699 G25r to pay John Pether £4 due to him from Capt. John Williams when Renter Warden, and to deduct this from Mrs Williams's dividend money   3 Jul 1699 G27v dispute over rights of printing the Satires of Juvenal and Persius referred to him   7 Aug 1699 G28r to pay John Lilly's bill. To pay doorkeepers at House of Lords for their attendance in relation to Act of Parliament for laying duty on paper. Matter of Juvenal and Persius extended until next monthly Court   4 Sep 1699 G30r to pay Clerk's bill for charges in Chancery   2 Oct 1699 G31v to be paid £60 fine for Sir William Woolley's lease   6 Nov 1699 G32v acquaints Court of George Horne's desire to surrender his £40 share   4 Dec 1699 G34r allows Bennett Griffin 36 shillings for printing of [Charles] Hoole's 'Sententiae'   8 Apr 1700 G39r to ensure that no boys play in S.C.'s garden nor pigeons be kept there   1 Jul 1700 G41r not to pay Renter Wardens their half crowns apiece because of late attendance   19 Jul 1700 G43r to prepare account of the profit of the New Version of the Psalms to assist in decision of whether or not to buy Nahum Tate's remaining shares   7 Oct 1700 G46r to pay Clerk's bill of charges in Chancery for prosecuting John Bradford and Dennis   20 Dec 1700 G54r to deduct arrears of quarterage and other monies owning from English Stock dividends   7 Apr

1701 G58v to give John Wilkins £5 from pension money   19 May 1701 G60r to pay
Samuel Buckley £30   2 Jun 1701 G60v to request Benjamin Motte to deliver illegally
printed psalms to the Warehouse   7 Jul 1701 G62r opinion given on Motte   4 Sep
1701 G64r bond from S.C. to Minister and Churchwardens of parish of St Thomas the
Apostle delivered to him   6 Oct 1701 G64v letters from Vice-Chancellor of Oxford
University. Treasurer to attend Master and Henry Mortlock when they go to
Oxford   1 Dec 1701 G65v to pay dividends on English Stock   13 Apr 1702 G70r S.C.'s
bond to Joseph Cole is delivered to him   4 May 1702 G70v has brought bond from
S.C. to Benjamin Payne into Court. 10s to be paid to him by John Smart for printing 'A
Table or an Account of Time'. Opinion given on infringement of S.C.'s copyright by
Thomas Hodgkins in printing the Ephemerides   1 Jun 1702 G71r opinion heard in
debate concerning printing of the Ephemerides. Questioned concerning assets of English
Stock. Note of monies and charges entered into cheque book for which he is accountable
to be taken by Warden after every Court and delivered by him to the Stock-keepers   16
Jul 1702 G78v Tooke suspended from office   9 Oct 1702 G82r salary to be no more
than £60 in future, but to have same house as Tooke, the late Treasurer, rent free   1702–
1703 Joseph Collyer   15 Oct 1702 G82r Joseph Collyer elected. Required to find
sureties   26 Oct 1702 G82v proposes John Guy and Christopher Hussey as sureties
and bond drawn up   2 Nov 1702 G82v Joseph Collyer takes oath of Warehouse- keeper
and, with sureties, enters into bond with S.C.   1703 onwards see WARE-HOUSE-
KEEPER

TREASURY   2 Dec 1689 F128r letter from the Lords of the Treasury re. loan to Crown
is read to Court

TREATISE OF PRAYER AND THANKSGIVING [i.e. Benjamin Whichcote, *A Compendium of Devotion, Containing a Treatise of Prayer and Thanksgiving?*]   7 Aug
1699 G28r assigned to Samuel Sprint by J. [John?] Nicholson

TREBY, Sir George   1 Feb 1680/1 E106v to be consulted by a deputation re. Act of
Parliament

TRENCH, [   ]   26 Jun 1682 E154v bond for £200 and interest to S.C. cancelled;
another bond taken out to John Godden to pay for it

TRENCHFIELD/TRENSHFEILD, Caleb   6 Apr 1685 (W) his 'A Cap of Grey Hairs' to
be entered by Warsall

TRENT, Henry   4 Apr 1715 G227v son of John; bound to William Chapman, 7 years

TRENT, John – see preceding entry

TRESARE, Thomas   3 Apr 1704 G106r bound to Hugh Meere, 7 years

TREVETT, [   ]   3 Nov 1690 F145v to be summoned to next Court re. painting list of
benefactors   1 Dec 1690 F146v to be paid 1d for each letter of title, 12d per name
thereafter and 10s per japanned panel, and to cover charge of removing panels

TRIAL AND ARRAIGNMENT OF SIR WALTER RALEIGH – see RALEIGH, Sir
Walter

TRICKETTS, Philip – see following entry

TRICKETTS, William   4 Mar 1716/17 G248r son of Philip, is bound to Ralph
Arnold, 7 years

TRIGG – see GADBURY & TRIGG

TRINDER, Henry   20 Dec 1686 F69r dispute between S.C. and Henry Hills re. Catholic
Almanack to be referred to him at Middle Temple if not decided by 15 Jan

TRINDER/TRINTER, Sargeant   5 Aug 1689 F122v to be consulted by John Lilly re.
Richard Chiswell's complaint about unqualified shareholders

TRISTRAM, Robert   5 Dec 1698 G17r John Theak is bound to him

TROPHIES   2 Aug 1680 E102v herald painter to repair and amend them   8 Nov 1680 E105r Jeremiah Wright, the herald painter, to be paid for

TROTMAN, John   5 Sep 1709 G170r bound to Robert Willoughby, 7 years

TROW, Richard   1 Feb 1691/2 (W) freed by Humphrey Pooler   1 Jul 1695 F227v cloathed

TRUSSELL, John – see DANIEL, Samuel

TUCKER, Joseph   5 Dec 1698 G16v desires payment of £100 of the £200 due to him from the S.C.

TUCKER, Mrs   3 Jun 1700 G40r £100 lent to S.C. to be repaid

TUCKEY, John   3 Jun 1695 F226v Edward Shawler jnr is bound to him
See also TOKEY, Joseph

TUCKYER, Roger   2 May 1698 G7v bound to Elizabeth Miller, 7 years

TULCE, Sir Henry   3 Dec 1683 F6v S.C. to dine as a corporation with Sir Henry Tulce, the present Lord Mayor

TULLY'S OFFICES/TULLY'S WORKS – see CICERO, Marcus Tullius

TURFORD, Thomas   6 May 1700 G39v bound to Emmanuel Matthews, 7 years

TURKISH HISTORY   5 Mar 1687/8 F99r lately reprinted by Thomas Bassett; Edward Brewster and Nathaniel Ranew claim a moiety of it and are allowed to sue

TURKISH SPY [attr. Giovanni Paolo Marana]   4 Dec 1693 F196r Richard Sare and Joseph Hindmarsh are assigned 'Letters Writ by a Turkish Spy' in 8 vols 12mo; assignment from John Leake read

TURNER, [   ]   6 Aug 1688 F106r Warden ordered to see that he discontinues his lawsuit against Richard Butler

TURNER, Adam   23 Mar 1707/8 G150r given Jane Curtis's pension   23 Jun 1709 G166r deceased; Richard Mills is given his pension

TURNER, Anthony   1 Feb 1713/14 G216r his son Thomas is bound to Anne Jones, 7 years

TURNER, Beatrice   25 Mar 1702 G86v given Elizabeth Andrews's pension. Mary Haddock is given her pension   27 Sep 1710 G184r deceased; James Flowrey is given her pension

TURNER, Benjamin   4 Jun 1716 G240v son of John; bound to his father (?), 7 years

TURNER, John (I)   6 May 1706 G131v bound to William Keeble, 7 years   1 Aug 1709 G169v turned over from William Keeble to Thomas Hodgkin   1 Jun 1713 G210v freed by Thomas Hodgkin

TURNER, John (II)   4 Jun 1716 G240v his son(?) Benjamin Turner is bound to him

TURNER, Thomas (I)   2 Mar 1701/2 G67v freed by Henry Kifft

TURNER, Thomas (II)   2 Oct 1704 G112v bound to Benjamin Harris, 7 years

TURNER, Thomas (III)   1 Feb 1713/14 G216r son of Anthony; bound to Anne Jones, 7 years

TURNER, Sir William   22 Dec 1685 F48v has committed John Palmer and Simon Hinch to the Counter

TURNER, William   4 Jul 1698 G11r freed by Catherine Madoc   5 Sep 1698 G14v Joshua Worrall is bound to him   3 May 1703 G89r cloathed   10 Sep 1705 G123v Thomas Agerton is bound to him

TURVEY, Robert   5 Mar 1693/4 F200v son of William Turvey; freed by patrimony

TURVEY, William – see previous entry

TUTLE, Joseph   1 Mar 1702/3 G86r his apprentice John England is freed

TWEDY/TWEDDY, James   2 Aug 1697 F265v bound to John Marsh   6 Nov 1704 G113r freed by Widow Marsh

TWIN, Edward   2 Oct 1710 G184v bound to Thomas King, 7 years

TWITTY, George   7 Oct 1706 G135r bound to Agar Warren, 7 years

TWYFORD, Henry   22 Sep 1680 E104r elected to John Macock's £160 share; disposal of his £80 share deferred   11 Oct 1680 E104v Bennett Griffin elected to a moiety of his £80 share   6 Dec 1680 E105v John Leigh, the Treasurer, elected to a moiety of Twyford's £80 share   4 Feb 1683/4 F8v pays 1s to Poor Box for coming in late to Court   7 Apr 1684 F13v on the list of loyal Assistants presented to the Crown   2 Jun 1684 F16r competes unsuccessfully for the late Widow Pakeman's £320 share   5 Jul 1684 F19v competes unsuccessfully for Under Warden   7 May 1685 (W) confirmed as a member of the new Livery   4 Jul 1685 F39r ordered to fine for Under Warden because of want of choice for Upper Warden   1 Feb 1685/6 F50v on John Williams's plea, £10 of Twyford's dividend, retained as a fine for two years' Under Warden, is restored but he loses status   1 Mar 1687/8 F97r mortgage to the late John Leigh of his £160 share for payment of £50 plus interest is presented to Court by Leigh's widow. Displaced as Assistant by order of Crown and expelled from Livery by order of Lord Mayor   3 Jul 1693 F189v deceased; Charles Harper is elected to his £160 share

TWYNNE/TWYNE, John   24 Mar 1713/14 G217r elected to Isaac Lane's pension   22 Mar 1714/15 G226v elected to Isaiah Ward's pension. Mary Ward is given his pension

TYLER, [ ]   1 Mar 1679/80 E97r elected Stock-keeper for Assistants   28 Mar 1679/ 80 E99r to audit Renter Wardens' accounts   7 Jun 1680 E100v assigned signature C of Stock 12mo psalms and signatures C and D of Stock psalter

See also TYLER, Evan

TYLER, Evan   6 Jun 1681 E112r Assistants and Stock-keepers to rectify differences between him and Capt. Samuel Roycroft   5 Dec 1681 E139v to receive S.C. bond for £100 to pay arrears for preachers of St Paul's; thanked for his 'voluntary and ready offer'   22 Dec 1681 E141r bond between him and S.C. for £100 sealed for one year at £200 penalty and 6% interest   6 Feb 1681/2 E142r 'loco Magistri qui tunc languebat'. Bond for £300 with penalty of £600 to pay £309 in August 1682 sealed; delivered to Tyler on his payment of £200 cash and deliverance of a £100 bond   5 Feb 1682/3 E162v deceased; the £40 dividend of his £320 share to be paid to his executors, and his will and codicil to be entered in S.C. register. His £320 share disposed of to John Towse   3 Dec 1683 F5v executors' demands for interest on Tyler's money in S.C. hands due up to the day of his death to be considered by Lilly   5 Aug 1695 F231v Thomas Teonge, his apprentice, is freed

(EVAN) TYLER'S BEQUEST   5 Feb 1682/3 E163v John Redmaine, John Wallis and Thomas Raw each granted £50   1 Mar 1682/3 E164r John Heptingstall and William Freeman each granted £50. Thomas Raw's £50 loan repealed on account of 'misbe-haviour in several points'   7 Mar 1682/3 E165v the interest from his £120, with S.C. at the time of his death, to provide £7 4s for a yearly collation on 29 May for Court and guests. Money to be held by S.C. (W) placed with English Stock   26 Mar 1683 E166v John Egglesfeild and Josiah Blare each granted £50. Dinner to be held in barge every 29 May for Master, Wardens and Assistants and either one holder of Livery share or two holders of Yeomanry shares   2 Apr 1683 E168r John Egglesfeild's surety not approved   4 Jun 1683 E170v Blare's surety to be inquired into. William Abington granted £50   2 Jul 1683 F1v Thomas Sawbridge and Godfrey Head to pay ready money for shares before next Court or forfeit them under the terms of the will   12 Nov 1683 F5v dinner to be had on 30 November, having been omitted on 29 May last   4 Feb 1683/4 F8v George Snowden's petition for £50 to be considered at next Court   3 Mar 1683/4 F11r Arthur Jones to be granted £50 if his securities are approved   16 Jun 1684 F18r Francis Leach and Ralph Simpson each to be granted £50 if their securities are approved   25 Jun 1684 F18v Francis Leach's and Ralph Simpson's securities approved   4 Aug 1684 F21v Henry Clarke jnr to be granted £50 (had requested £100) if his securities are approved. Thomas Moore to be granted £50 if his securities are approved   6 May 1685 F34r feast to be kept on 29 May   3 May 1686 F55v commemoration feast to be held on 29 May in barge   6 Sep 1686 F62v Henry Clarke jnr has to find a new surety for his £50 loan, Peter Stone being dead   4 Apr 1687 F81r John Wallis's petition to work out his £50 loan is rejected and motion to sue him deferred until next Court   2 May 1687 F82r John Heptingstall to repay his £50 loan by 1 August. William Freeman repays £50 loan. Benjamin Tooke and Walter Kettleby to repay John Wallis's £50 loan. Feast to be held on 30 May; any member arriving late to be fined 12d   6 Jun 1687 F84r John Redmaine has repaid his £50 loan. Henry Clarke asked to procure Mrs Stone's assent to becoming his surety in place of her late husband Peter   7 May 1688 F101r Court determine to augment this with any extra money from Lamb's charity. Dinner to be held on 29 May. Master, Wardens, Assistants and their wives to go by water in S.C.'s barge to dine at Chelsea   1 Oct 1688 F107v Francis Leach and Henry Clarke are given 6 months longer to repay their loans   6 May 1689 F118r collation to be held on 29 May   7 Apr 1690 F132v £8 6s 8d to be spent on a dinner for the Court on 6th May in commemoration of Lamb and Tyler   4 May 1691 F153r feast to be held on Friday 29 May   6 Jul 1691 F157v Benjamin Johnson to be granted £50 if his securities are approved; unusually full addresses are given   7 Sep 1691 F160r Benjamin Johnson's securities approved   2 May 1692 F170v dinner to be held on 26 May instead of 29 May, a Sunday   4 May 1696 F242v debate deferred until next Court when it is ordered his will should be read   3 May 1697 F261v money from Tyler bequest to be applied to election dinner to take place on 10 August. Moore given more time to pay back £50 loan if Court approves of his new surety   7 Jun 1697 F262v Clerk to call on Thomas Moore re. new surety

TYLER, James – see following entry

TYLER, Samuel   4 Feb 1716/17 G246v son of James; bound to Henry Parsons, 7 years

TYTON, Francis   3 Jul 1680 E101v elected Under Warden   2 May 1681 E111r asked to stand as surety for S.C. to Sir Joseph Seamour, with Henry Herringman   4 Jul 1681 E116r committee authorised to audit his accounts as Warden   1 Aug 1681 E117r to give in his Warden's accounts and deliver to new Under Warden all S.C. writings, papers and keys in his custody   5 Sep 1681 E128v promises to give in Warden's accounts in a fortnight. Seals an indenture of demise of the Hall and tenements to Sir Joseph Seamour   3 Oct 1681 E130r his Warden's accounts to be entered into S.C. register   22 Dec 1681 E141v to be paid £4 6s 8d out of Richard Clarke's stock, money laid out for deceased in the year they were Wardens together   6 Feb 1681/2 E142r replaces Thomas Newcomb, deceased, as Upper Warden   21 Feb 1681/2 E144v elected to the £320 share of Thomas Vere, deceased   1 Jul 1682 E154v elected Upper Warden   30 Jun 1683 F1r his 1 year's normal service and 6 months' substitution for the late Thomas Newcomb as Upper Warden to count as 2 years   6 Nov 1683 F4v comes in late and pays 1s to Poor Box

TYTON, Widow 3 Oct 1692 F180r deceased; her £320 share is voted to Robert Clavell

UNDER BEADLE 8 Jun 1691 F154v salary to be paid by Wardens instead of Renter Wardens

See also PORTER

UNDER WARDEN – see WARDENS

UNDERHILL, George 6 Nov 1710 G185r son of Thomas; bound to Joseph Bush, 7 years 6 Jul 1713 G212v turned over from Joseph Bush to Marshall

UNDERHILL, Mrs 11 Apr 1681 E109v assigns [Herbert Palmer's] 'The Memorials of Godliness and Christianity' to Samuel Crouch

UNDERHILL, Thomas 6 Nov 1710 G185r his son George is bound to Joseph Bush, 7 years

UNDERHILL, William, snr – see following entry

UNDERHILL, William, jnr 5 Oct 1713 G214r son of William; bound to Ralph Snow, 7 years

UNDERWOOD, William 1 Aug 1709 G169v bound to Mary Richards, 7 years 6 Aug 1716 G242v freed by Mary Richards

UNIVERSITIES – see OXFORD AND CAMBRIDGE

UPPER WARDEN – see WARDENS

URN-BURIAL [i.e. Sir Thomas Browne, *Hydriotaphia*] 7 Oct 1689 F125r Roger Norton assigns to Charles Broome 'Urn-burial or the Garden of Cyrus' (*sic*)

URRY, Thomas 6 May 1700 G39v bound to Freeman Collins

USBOURNE/USBORNE, John 7 Feb 1698/9 G20r cloathed 3 Jul 1704 G110r Samuel Hall is bound to him 26 Mar 1705 G117v fined for First Renter Warden 7 Jul 1712 G201v John Lowe is bound to him 13 Apr 1713 G208v elected to Ralph Smith's £40 share. Lary Hawes is bound to him

USE OF THE RULE OF PROPORTION [by Edmund Wingate] 5 Sep 1681 E129v assigned to Thomas Passenger by Dorothy Stephens

USQUHART, Joseph 3 Nov 1690 F146r a Quaker who refuses to take oath of freedom; given to next Court to consider

VADE, James 2 May 1681 E111v his surety to come to next Court, where it will be decided whether to call in or continue his loan 6 Jun 1681 E112v to appear at next Court with sureties as they are out of town 4 Jul 1681 E116r appears with sureties; new 3-year bond to be drawn up for £50 loan 1 Mar 1682/3 E164v George Palfrey, one of his sureties for a £50 loan, is granted a month's grace to repay after Midsummer day next

VADE MECUM 7 May 1683 E170r committee to discuss whether this, a book of John Playford's, has harmed Stock

VALENTINE, Edward 8 Nov 1703 G97r freed by Timothy Goodwin

VANDEPUT/VANDERPUT, Sir Peter 1 Feb 1685/6 F50r voluntarily lowers his rent on the bargehouse to £10 p.a.

VARNAM/VARNUM, Thomas 7 May 1694 F203v servant of Thomas Guy; freed 5 Jun 1710 G180r cloathed 7 May 1711 G190r elected to Daniel Midwinter's £40 share 3 Mar 1711/12 G197r Jeremiah Batley is turned over to him from Thomas Guy 4 Oct 1714 G222v elected to John Heptingstall's £80 share 2 May 1715 G228r elected First Renter Warden 4 Jul 1715 G230v read his charge as Assistant Renter

Warden (sic) by the Upper Warden   6 May 1717 G250r elected Assistant as he is heir at law of Thomas Guy, to whom Guy intended to dispose a considerable estate

VASEY, John (I)   5 Jul 1703 G92r Matthew Jenkinson is bound to him   7 Feb 1703/4 G101v his apprentice Edward Terrell is freed

VASEY, John (II)   7 Aug 1704 G111r bound to John Matthews, 7 years   4 Apr 1709 G164r turned over from John Matthews to George James

See also VEASEY, Joseph

VAUGHAN, John   11 Nov 1695 F235v servant to John Whitlock; freed

VAULTS   26 Mar 1683 E167v Thomas Allen, vintner, to dig out a vault in S.C. court at his own expense, making good all damage, to be leased from S.C.   2 Apr 1683 E168r committee to inquire into dimensions of Thomas Allen's intended vault   26 Mar 1709 G163r minister, churchwardens and council of St Martin's Ludgate wish to make a vault under the S.C.'s garden   2 Nov 1711 G195r grant sealed from S.C. to rector and churchwardens of St Martin's Ludgate for making a vault under the S.C.'s garden

VEASEY, Joseph [i.e. John Vasey]   6 Oct 1712 G204v freed by George James

VEAZY, Mary   7 Nov 1709 G172r John Holloway is bound to her   1 Apr 1717 G249v her apprentice John Holloway is freed

VERE, Lawrence   6 Aug 1694 F211v servant to Freeman Collins; freed

VERE, Thomas   3 Jul 1680 E101r fined for second year of Upper Warden   3 Jan 1680/1 E106r Dorman Newman to be questioned by a committee about his complaint against Vere seizing the [Westminster] Assembly's Catechisms as Warden   7 Feb 1680/1 E107r and Samuel Mearne to search for the Bishop of London's order for damasking the Assembly's Catechism   7 Mar 1680/1 E107v to bring, together with Mearne, the Bishop of London's order for damasking the Assembly's Catechism to the next Court   2 Jul 1681 E115r elected Master   5 Sep 1681 E129r Widow Crooke's £320 share voted to him, after his hinting that it was his prerogative. Seals an indenture of demise of the Hall and tenements to Sir Joseph Seamour. Assigns to John Clarke snr, of Little St Bartholomew's, one third of [John Booker's] 'The Dutch Fortune Teller', half of [Emmanuel Ford's] 'Ornatus and Artecia', and others   21 Feb 1681/2 E144v deceased; Samuel Mearne is elected Master in his place   6 Mar 1681/2 E147v executors to fund a dinner, organized by John Towse, which Vere himself was unable to give on admission to his £320 share   7 Aug 1682 E156v his executor Ephraim Cooley makes an assignment to Jonah Deacon   4 Sep 1682 E157r John Towse to be paid £5 for a buck out of Vere's part in Stock

VERNON, John   26 Sep 1712 G203v freed by William Barker

VIEW OF THE ADMIRAL JURISDICTION [i.e. John Godolphin, *Synegoros Thalassios*]   26 Mar 1683 E167v assigned to [George] Dawes by Benjamin Sherley

VILLIERS, George, 2nd Duke of Buckingham – see BUCKINGHAM

VINCENT, [ ]   1 Feb 1691/2 F165r he and Keeble summoned to next Court to answer Edward Brewster's complaint against them   7 Mar 1691/2 F166v he and Keeble submit to arbitration on Edward Brewster's complaint of them printing books belonging to King's Printers

VINCENT, Richard   6 Dec 1714 G224r his son William is bound to George Mortimer, 7 years

VINCENT, Robert (I)   20 Dec 1689 F128v cloathed, promising payment of fine   3 Dec 1694 F216r Robert Henning is bound to him   26 Mar 1698 G5r competes unsuccessfully for Renter Warden   5 Feb 1699/1700 G35r John Crofts is bound to him   26

Mar 1700 G38r elected Assistant Renter Warden 6 May 1700 G39v elected to Mrs Hindmarsh's £40 share 1 Jul 1700 G41v Renter Warden, excused fine of 2s 6d having attended on Saturday last on S.C. business 4 May 1702 G71r his apprentice Robert Kemp is freed 6 Jul 1702 G78r John Fowler is bound to him 3 Mar 1706 G139r his apprentice John Crofts is freed 6 Dec 1708 G159v of Fleet Street; his son Robert Vincent is bound to him 1 Aug 1709 G169v his apprentice John Fowler is freed 6 Feb 1709/10 G175r competes unsuccessfully for William Freeman's £80 share 7 May 1711 G190r competes unsuccessfully for Timothy Goodwin's £80 share, elected to Mrs Eversden's £80 share, his £40 share disposed of to Hazard 2 Mar 1712/13 G207r Robert Ward is bound to him 1 Apr 1717 G249v his son Robert is freed

VINCENT, Robert (II) 6 Dec 1708 G159v bound to his father Robert, 7 years 1 Apr 1717 G249v freed by his father, Robert

VINCENT, William 6 Dec 1714 G224r son of Richard; bound to George Mortimer, 7 years

VINCOMB, Thomas 7 May 1705 G120r freed by Thomas [no other name given]

VINEY, David – see following entry

VINEY, Robert 6 Feb 1715/16 G236r son of David; bound to William Gray, 7 years

VIRGIL 4 Sep 1688 F106v Thomas Bradyll fails to appear to answer the charge of printing Virgil with 'Menelius's' [i.e. John Minellius's] notes, a Stock book 7 Apr 1690 F133r Thomas Dring to compensate English Stock for printing Virgil, a Stock book 2 Nov 1691 F162r Robert Scott, Thomas Dring and Abel Swale fined 2d per book for printing 3000 Virgils without a licence 7 Dec 1691 F162v fine reduced to 1d per book 2 Jul 1705 G121v S.C. to buy Virgil with Minellius's notes from Bradyll

VIRTUE AND CONSTANCY 3 May 1686 F55v Joshua Conyers complains that Dennison has printed the ballad 'Virtue and Constancy Rewarded' as 'Love and Constancy United'

VISIONS 3 Jul 1693 F190r 'Don Quevedo's Visions made English', by Roger L'Estrange, is assigned by Henry Herringman to John Hindmarsh and Richard Sare

VOUSDEN, John 2 Jul 1711 G192v prisoner in Wood Street Compter for fees of 30s. 30s to be taken from Poor Box to pay his fees

WADE, Edward 7 Feb 1703/4 G101v bound to Samuel Heyrick, 7 years

WADE, Samuel 4 Mar 1716/17 G248r son of William; bound to Samuel Redmaine, 7 years

WADE, William (I) 4 Aug 1701 G63r comes to be made free but letter from Thomas James opposes this 1 Sep 1701 G64r freed by Thomas James

WADE, William (II) 4 Mar 1716/17 G248r his son Samuel is bound to Samuel Redmaine, 7 years

WAGSTAFF, [ ] 1 Aug 1681 E117r Clerk to inquire at his office re. City order for not building near City wall

WAILES, Mary – see WALES, Mary

WAINHOUSE/WAYNHOUSE, Isaac 6 Mar 1709/10 G176v bound to Charles Hawkins, 8 years 5 Apr 1714 G218r turned over from Charles Hawkins to Robert Whitledge

WALDWIN – see WALWIN

WALE/WALL/WHALEY, Jeffrey 4 Jul 1698 G11r bound to Samuel Smith, 7 years 5 Jul 1703 G92r freed by redemption and cloathed 6 Mar 1703/4 G103v William

Crompton is bound to him   12 Nov 1705 G125r Charles Biddulph is bound to him   4 Aug 1707 G144r notice of meeting of his creditors. Debtor to English Stock for £55. Master and Wardens to deal with this   3 Oct 1709 G171r Robert Pomfert is bound to him

WALE, John   4 Jun 1705 G120v bound to George Salter

WAILES/WALES, Mary   26 Mar 1700 G38r elected to Friswid Bolter's pension   27 Sep 1705 G123v married; Robert Harrison is given her pension

WALFORD, B. —   12 Nov 1694 F214v involved in dispute over printing Horace   5 Jun 1699 G25r requests a caveat to be entered in the Register against the re-entering of copies of Juvenal and Persius; ordered accordingly

WALFORD, Benjamin (I)   2 Oct 1693 F192v cloathed   3 Feb 1695/6 F239r elected to John Place's £80 share   2 Mar 1695/6 F239v takes partner's oath   5 May 1701 G59v Benjamin Walford is bound to him   26 Mar 1702 G68v fined for Renter Warden   1 Jun 1702 G71r William Innys is bound to him   1 Mar 1706/7 G138v elected Stock-keeper for Yeomanry   3 May 1708 G152r of Paul's Churchyard; elected Assistant   17 Jul 1708 G155v ordered to go to Oxford   5 Feb 1708/9 G160v William Noble is bound to him   6 Jun 1709 G165v his apprentice William Innys is freed   3 Jul 1710 G182r William Noble is turned over from him to William Innys

WALFORD, Benjamin (II)   5 May 1701 G59v bound to Benjamin Walford, 7 years

WALKDEN, Charles   5 Jun 1699 G25v bound to John Brook, 7 years   21 Jun 1706 G132v freed by John Brook. Cloathed   1 Dec 1707 G147v stationer; Henry Read is bound to him   7 Jun 1708 G153v stationer; John Andrew Holloway is bound to him   5 May 1712 G199r John Andrew Holloway is turned over from him to John Darby   26 Mar 1713 G208r fined for Assistant Renter Warden   6 Jul 1713 G212v Stiles Lupert is bound to him

WALKER, [ ]   6 Oct 1697 F269r to act as attorney when Charles Browne and William Onley are prosecuted in the Court of Exchequer for illegal printing

WALKER, Cuthbert   7 Apr 1712 G199r son of Joseph; bound to Humphrey Child

WALKER, Edward   6 May 1706 G131v bound to James Roberts, 7 years

WALKER, George   26 Mar 1695 F219v competes unsuccessfully for cook   26 Mar 1696 F241r competes unsuccessfully for cook   26 Mar 1698 G5v competes unsuccessfully for cook   27 Mar 1699 G23r competes unsuccessfully for cook   2 Oct 1699 G31r elected cook   20 Oct 1699 G32r the cook, called in to give evidence concerning another cook being brought in to prepare dinner on Lord Mayor's Day. Chosen cook for the occasion and given keys of kitchen

WALKER, James   7 Jun 1697 F263r Joseph Bedcock is bound to him   2 Oct 1699 G31v Abraham Dickson is bound to him   2 Nov 1702 G83r Richard Child is bound to him   5 Aug 1706 G134r Richard Joyner is bound to him   7 Jun 1708 G153v his apprentice Abraham Dickson is freed

WALKER, John   3 Nov 1712 G205r Jarvis Adams is turned over to him

WALKER, Joseph   9 Feb 1690/1 F148v cloathed and promises fine   7 Apr 1712 G199r his son Cuthbert is bound to Humphrey Child

WALKER, Robert   3 Jul 1699 G27v bound to Thomas Mead, 7 years   2 Dec 1706 G136v freed by Thomas Mead

WALKER, Samuel   2 Aug 1703 G94r freed by Samuel Heyrick   8 Nov 1703 G97r Thomas Belsoe is bound to him

WALKER, Thomas (I)   1700–1704 cook

WALKER, Thomas (II) 6 Mar 1703/4 G103v bound to Richard Humphreys, 7 years 4 Sep 1704 G112r turned over from Richard Humphreys to James Hazard 4 Aug 1712 G202v freed by Joseph Hazard 4 Jun 1716 G240v William Adley is bound to him

WALKER, William 1 Dec 1707 G147v bound to Henry Playford, 7 years

WALKWOODS, David 5 Mar 1710/11 G188r bound to Stephen Gilbert, 7 years

WALL, Christopher 26 Mar 1684 F11v elected First Renter Warden 2 Jun 1684 F15v re-elected as Renter Warden 3 Aug 1685 F41v to pay with Nathaniel Ponder the balance on the Renter Wardens' accounts to Ambrose Isted

WALL, Thomas (I) 6 Jul 1691 F157v at Bristol; Clerk to inform him of his cloathing and to obtain his £20 fine by post 7 Mar 1691/2 F166v Court refuse Ball's request that Wall of Bristol should not be prosecuted for non-payment of his Livery fine 26 Mar 1692 F167v Ball pays Wall's Livery fine and Court abate £5 of it

WALL, Thomas (II) 1 Aug 1709 G169v bound to Jacob Tonson, 7 years
See also WALE

WALLDROM, William 7 Feb 1708/9 G160v bound to Thomas Grover, 7 years

WALLER, Sir William 6 Mar 1688/9 F114v Mrs Curtis claims that he and Sir Robert Payton ordered her to print unlicensed pamphlets

WALLIS, [ ] 4 Aug 1690 F141r Wilkins is summoned for printing 'A Memorial Extracted out of the Modest Enquiry' without licence; to show at next court his warrant to print in Wallis' absence

WALLIS, Dr 17 May 1695 F224r 420 of his books at £1 16s per book sent from Oxford to S.C.; committee to take advice about selling them 7 Oct 1695 (W) committee seeking a reduction from Oxford in cost of books on the last cargo that came from Ireland, including Dr Wallis's

WALLIS, John 5 Feb 1682/3 E163v granted £50 of Tyler bequest 2 Mar 1684/5 F31r consideration of petition to work out his £50 loan suspended until next Court 4 Apr 1687 F81r his petition to work out his £50 loan from Tyler bequest is rejected and motion to sue him deferred until next Court 2 May 1687 F82v Benjamin Tooke and Walter Kettleby to pay £25 each to repay his £50 loan from Tyler bequest

WALLIS, Peter 7 Apr 1701 G58v freed by Thomas Minshall 1 Dec 1701 G66r William Hart is bound to him 2 Aug 1714 G221r John Curghey is turned over to him

WALLSALL/WALLSSALL/WALSHALL, Samuel 9 Feb 1701/2 G67r his apprentice John Green is freed 24 Mar 1713/14 G217r elected to William Barlow's pension 24 Sep 1714 G222r deceased; Isaiah Ward is given his pension

WALMSLEY, Mary 5 Oct 1685 F45r given £1 charity in response to petition

WALROND, Henry – see following entry

WALROND, William 2 Dec 1695 F237r son of Henry Walrond of Abbott Soyle, Somerset, gentleman; bound to Freeman Collins

WALSHALL – see WALLSALL

WALTER, John 5 Feb 1704/5 G115r freed by Philip Brooksby

WALTHOE/WALTHO, John, snr (I) 16 Jun 1684 F17v of Chancery Lane and ex-apprentice of George Dawes, a member of S.C.; is freed 5 Aug 1689 F122r excused cloathing on plea of juniority and inability 7 Nov 1692 F181v cloathed and promises payment of fine 20 Dec 1694 F216r competes unsuccessfully for the £40 share that Charles Browne has refused 4 Sep 1699 G30v Kingsmill Grove is bound to him 8

Apr 1700 G39r elected Assistant [i.e. First?] Renter Warden   6 May 1700 G39v his apprentice John Walthoe is freed   1 Dec 1701 G66r Edward Benson is bound to him   1 Feb 1702/3 G84v and Daniel Browne will pay only one guinea as acknowledgement to S.C. for printing the 'Abridgement of the Book of Martyrs'. Master to determine the matter   1 Mar 1702/3 G86r Thomas Ward is bound to him   1 Mar 1706/7 G138v and Timothy Goodwin to be paid £30 towards fees and charges of Copyright Bill due to Jodrell   7 Apr 1707 G140v elected to Benjamin Tooke jnr's £40 share   1 Mar 1707/8 G149v and Goodwin to bring an account of the subscriptions relating to the Copyright Act to next Court   12 Apr 1708 G152r returns an account of monies disbursed re. Copyright Act   3 May 1708 G152v elected to the late Mrs Garthwaite's £80 share   1 Mar 1708/9 G161r elected Stock-keeper for Livery   7 Mar 1708/9 G162r his son John is bound to him   7 Nov 1709 G172r Charles Prichard is bound to him   5 Jun 1710 G180r has printed Justin with notes; Stock-keepers to treat with him about disposal   1 Oct 1711 G194v to give John Amery 20s from Poor Box   3 Mar 1711/12 G196v has acquired Amery's £160 share. To give bond to pay him £5 for cloathing, £12 p.a. in quarterly payments and £5 towards his funeral. His £80 share disposed of to James Roberts   6 Jul 1713 G212v Leonard Corbin is bound to him   7 Sep 1713 G213v his apprentice Thomas Taylor is freed   2 May 1715 G228v elected Assistant   4 Jul 1715 G231r auditor of Master and Wardens' accounts. Clerk's bill referred to him   5 Dec 1715 G235v James Crokatt is bound to him   5 Mar 1715/16 G237v signed note for payment to Thomas Guy   30 Jun 1716 G241r competes unsuccessfully for Under Warden   2 Jul 1716 G242r auditor of late Master and Wardens' accounts. His son, John Walthoe, is freed   10 Sep 1716 G243r Samuel Parsons is bound to him   4 Feb 1716/17 G246v to be new trustee of S.C.'s property   21 Feb 1716/17 G246v trust of S.C.'s property conveyed to him as new trustee   4 Mar 1716/17 G247v to pay Clerk's bill   6 May 1717 G250v auditor of Renter Wardens' accounts

WALTHOE, John (II)   6 May 1700 G39v freed by John Walthoe

WALTHOE, John, jnr (III)   7 Mar 1708/9 G162r bound to his father John, 7 years   2 Jul 1716 G242r freed by his father, John

WALTHOE, Thomas   3 Apr 1704 G106r bound to Edward Jones, 7 years

WALTHUS, Susanna   22 Dec 1708 G159v Robert Harris is given her pension

WALTON, Daniel – see following entry

WALTON, John   5 Apr 1714 G218r son of Daniel; bound to Susannah Battersby, 7 years

WALTON, Lancelot   6 Dec 1697 G2r bound to Henry Bonwick

WALWYN/WALDWIN/WALWIN, Herbert   6 Jun 1698 G8v freed by Thomas Cockerell, excused cloathing for some time   6 Mar 1698/9 G21v excused cloathing for six months   4 Sep 1699 G30r to be summoned to next Court day to take cloathing   6 Nov 1699 G32v refuses to accept cloathing   4 Dec 1699 G34r to be sued and prosecuted according to byelaws for refusal to accept cloathing   4 Mar 1699/1700 G36v to be proceeded against for refusal to accept cloathing   8 Apr 1700 G38v to be summoned before Lord Mayor for non-acceptance of cloathing   1 Dec 1701 G66r cloathed

WAPLES, Thomas   7 Aug 1704 G111r bound to Richard Simpson, 7 years   12 Nov 1711 G195r freed by Richard Simpson

WAPSHOTT, [   ]   3 Mar 1706/7 G139r ejectment to be brought to avoid his lease for non-payment of rent   3 Nov 1707 G146v lease cancelled; 5 houses formerly let to him now leased to Samuel Brunts

WARBOYSE, Edward   4 Oct 1703 G96r bound to Thomas Grover, 7 years

WARD, [ ] 26 Jan 1703/4 G100v alehouse-keeper of the Red Lion, St Martin's Le Grand; defendant to S.C.'s Bill in Chancery

WARD, Aaron 6 Nov 1710 G185r son of John; bound to Samuel Ballard, 7 years

WARD, Edward 2 Apr 1694 F202v his apprentice Samuel Crabtree is freed 7 Feb 1697/8 G3v his apprentice John Mecham is freed

WARD, Isaiah (I) 24 Sep 1714 G222r elected to Samuel Wallsall's pension 22 Mar 1714/15 G226v elected to Robert Harrison's pension. John Twynne is given his pension

WARD, Isaiah (II) 7 Apr 1712 G199r turned over to John Heptingstall 5 Sep 1715 G232v freed by John Heptingstall

WARD, John 6 Nov 1710 G185r his son Aaron is bound to Samuel Ballard, 7 years

WARD, Josiah 5 Jul 1708 G155r bound to Edward Midwinter, 7 years

WARD, Mary 22 Mar 1714/15 G226v elected to John Twyne's pension

WARD, Richard, snr – see following entry

WARD, Richard, jnr 6 Aug 1711 G193r son of Richard; bound to Sarah Holt, 7 years

WARD, Robert, snr – see following entry

WARD, Robert, jnr 2 Mar 1712/13 G207r son of Robert; bound to Robert Vincent, 7 years

WARD, Thomas 1 Mar 1702/3 G86r bound to John Walthoe 6 Oct 1712 G204v freed by patrimony

WARD, William 7 Mar 1697/8 G5r bound to Thomas Bennett 4 Jun 1705 G120v freed by Thomas Bennett 3 Dec 1716 G245v bookseller of Nottingham; elected to cloathing

WARDELL, John 6 Dec 1714 G224r son of Thomas; bound to Edmund Richardson, 7 years

WARDELL, Thomas – see preceding entry

WARDENS 7 Sep 1685 F44r not henceforth to lay out more than 40s on Hall repairs without leave or Court order 5 Mar 1686/7 F52v at committee meeting about stall booksellers 8 Jun 1691 F154v to take over the paying of Clerk's, Beadle's and Under-Beadle's salaries from Renter Wardens 3 Apr 1693 F186r committee to consider motion that Wardens should receive Wood Street rents 20 Oct 1699 G32r have met Thomas Guy and Peter Parker in an attempt to accommodate 4 Jul 1713 G211v elected by hands rather than by ballot box this time 3 Oct 1715 G232v to have only one guest ticket in future for Lord Mayor's Day and 10th of August

— ACCOUNTS 25 Aug 1680 E103v audited version of Thomas Newcomb's accounts to be entered in S.C. register 3 Jul 1682 E155v committee to audit them 4 Sep 1682 E157v audited accounts to be entered in register 2 Jul 1683 F2r committee set up to audit them 1 Oct 1683 F3r audited accounts to be entered in register 5 Jul 1684 F19v audited 1 Sep 1684 F23v audited accounts to be registered and signed 26 Jun 1685 F38v Capt. William Phillipps to be added to the auditors 7 Sep 1685 F43v Warden James Cotterell's accounts audited and signed; to be entered by Clerk in Warden's account book. Balance to be paid, and bonds, &c., to be delivered up and listed 4 Oct 1686 F64r account signed by three assenting auditors, excluding Roger Norton, to be registered 2 Jul 1687 F85v John Towse, Henry Hills, Capt. William Phillipps and Thomas Dring are elected to audit them 7 Oct 1689 F124r auditors report that £50 was paid to Sir Basil Firebrasse for wine presented to late Lord Chancellor in middle of Oxford dispute 7 Dec 1691 F162v delivered up by auditors and ordered to be entered in register, then delivered to Under Warden. Committee to consider question raised by auditors of whether there should be a check on all S.C. accounts   7 Nov 1692 F182r approved and entered; auditors present   4 May 1702 G70v money borrowed for English Stock for which the Common Seal of the S.C. was used to be charged to   9 Oct 1702 G82r delivered to Under Warden   7 Jun 1703 G90v delivered into Court by Robert Andrews   6 Dec 1703 G99v signed off

— UNDER WARDEN   5 Jul 1679 E88r Thomas Newcomb elected   3 May 1680 E99v to raise money required by Lord Chief Justice for new byelaw charges   3 Jul 1680 E101v Francis Tyton elected   2 Aug 1680 E102v to receive at next pension Court the 20s he paid to Widow Sly, a prisoner in Ludgate   2 Jul 1681 E115v John Towse elected   1 Jul 1682 E155r Henry Hills elected   30 Jun 1683 F1v Henry Hills elected   6 Nov 1683 F4v to prosecute those who will not pay Renter Wardens' and Livery fines   5 Jul 1684 F19v James Cotterell elected   2 Mar 1684/5 F31v to dispose of 1 guinea in charity   4 Jul 1685 F39r several people fine for Under Warden because of a lack of candidates for Upper Warden; F39v Ambrose Isted elected   3 Jul 1686 F59v John Simms elected, but out of town   5 Jul 1686 F60r Simms allowed to fine for 2 years' Under Warden; F60v Robert Clavell elected   2 Jul 1687 F85v Thomas Bassett elected   12 Oct 1687 F91r Christopher Wilkinson elected   7 Nov 1687 F94r all fines for the office to be recorded by the Clerk   30 Jun 1688 F103r Benjamin Tooke elected   6 Aug 1688 F104r Treasurer's bond and sureties to be held by Upper rather than Under Warden since the Treasurer, Tooke, is Under Warden   27 Nov 1688 F110v Robert Clavell elected   6 Jul 1689 F121v Thomas Parkhurst elected   2 Jun 1690 F135r Henry ('Deputy') Clarke elected for rest of year   5 Jul 1690 F138r Henry Mortlock elected   4 Jul 1691 F156v Henry Mortlock elected   2 Nov 1691 F161v only he and tenants of warehouses to have keys to Hall precincts   22 Dec 1691 F163v Upper Warden to keep separate accounts for Stock and Corporation on Court days as 'check and charge' to Under Warden and Treasurer   2 Jul 1692 F172v Capt. William Phillipps elected   26 Jul 1692 F175v to receive S.C. keys from Thomas Bassett   3 Apr 1693 F186r committee to consider his motion that the Wardens receive Wood Street rents   1 Jul 1693 F189r Capt. William Phillipps elected   30 Jun 1694 F209v Samuel Lowndes elected   6 Jul 1695 F229v Samuel Lowndes elected   4 Jul 1696 F245r John Richardson elected   2 Nov 1696 (W) bills and bonds delivered to him to be recorded   17 Mar 1696/7 F257r to disburse legal fees re. Paper Act   3 Jul 1697 F263v George Copping elected   5 Jul 1697 F264r Copping fines; F264v Bennett Griffin elected   2 Aug 1697 F265r committee to settle the account usually delivered to every Under Warden when he begins the office. Tells Court that Christopher Grandorge has drawn £30 from him that he is not entitled to   4 Oct 1697 F268r tells Court that some members have offered to fine for Under Warden in exchequer notes; ordered to be paid in cash. Bill from Nicholas Hooper to Upper Warden for £5 10s 3d allowed and ordered to be paid by Under Warden   6 Dec 1697 G2r ordered to pay Loftus the shipwright's bill for cleaning the barge   26 Mar 1698 G5v £5 paid to him for the poor by Treasurer from Joseph Knight's executors   2 Jul 1698 G10r Richard Simpson elected   1 Aug 1698 G11v Tooke to pay him £100 due from English Stock to the Corporation   10 Jan 1698/9 G18v added to committee to consider Printing Act   1 Jul 1699 G26r Richard Chiswell fined for second year and Charles Harper elected   2 Oct 1699 G31r to reimburse Warden Samuel Heyrick the 12s 6d paid to Christopher Grandorge   4 Mar 1699/1700 G36v to pay bricklayer's bill of £7 for repairing the tiling of part of the Hall   3 Jun 1700 G40r to pay Warner the painter's bill   6 Jul 1700 G41v Charles Harper fined for second year, Bennett Griffin fined for second year, Walter Kettleby fined for second year, William Shrewsbury fined for second year. Samuel Sprint elected   15 Nov 1700 G47r £100 borrowed for payment of workman's bills delivered to him by Clerk   5 Jul 1701 G61v Samuel Sprint elected 20 Dec 1701 G66v quarterage paid to him by James Holland and David Edwards 4 Jul 1702 G76v letter to him from William Rawlins asking to fine for Master. Receives fine for Upper Warden from George Copping. Robert Andrews elected 6 Jul 1702 G77v John Place fined. To pay 40s or 50s to five musicians for playing at the Election Dinner 9 Oct 1702 G82r Warden's accounts delivered to him 2 Nov 1702 G82v bond of Joseph Collyer to S.C. delivered to him 18 Dec 1702 G84r William Rawlins pays 5 guineas' fine for Master to him 1 Mar 1702/3 G86r to oversee bequest of schoolbooks and Bibles to tenants of Kempsey Manor in Worcestershire from Meredith's will 25 Mar 1703 G86v to go to Oxford re. renewing Act 5 Apr 1703 G87v report that he has been at Oxford. To pay smith's bill for work done about the Hall 7 Jun 1703 G90v delivers Warden's book of accounts into Court 3 Jul 1703 G91v Robert Andrews elected 5 Jul 1703 G91v John Place fined 2 Aug 1703 G93v reports from Cambridge committee 6 Sep 1703 G94v to meet John Gadbury the almanack maker 4 Oct 1703 G95v has met Gadbury. To pay shipwright's bill 7 Feb 1703/4 G101r money due on a penal bill from William and Nathaniel Spiller to be paid to him. To reply to Abel Swale's case and representation 10 Feb 1703/4 G102r to purchase silver flagon for S.C. with Henry Herringman's gift 2 Mar 1703/4 G103r to take counsel's advice re. Bradford's plea 14 Mar 1703/4 G104r Thomas Wilmer paid fine for cloathing to him. To take counsel's advice re. Ephemerides. Produced in Court silver flagon which was Herringman's gift 3 Apr 1704 G105v to ensure that more leather buckets are provided in Hall 12 Jun 1704 G107r to view the house to be assigned by William Spiller to S.C. 15 Jun 1704 G107v to pay carpenter's bill 1 Jul 1704 G109v Capt. Samuel Roycroft fined, Thomas Clarke elected 3 Jul 1704 G109v Clarke fined, Thomas Hodgkins elected 4 Sep 1704 G112r 20s paid to him for Archibald Asburne to be made free by redemption 6 Nov 1704 G113r to pay interest due to Edward Littleton 4 Dec 1704 G113v to pay glazier's bill of £2 8s 3d. To adjust and order payment of bricklayer's bill 20 Dec 1704 G115v to order payment of painter's bill 5 Feb 1704/5 G114v (minutes copied before those of 20 Dec 1704) to settle affairs of Tooke. Clerk's bill for affairs in Chancery referred 5 Mar 1704/5 G117r to pay the butler £3 of his bill of £4 4s 2 Apr 1705 G118r to ensure books which were the gift of Christopher Meredith are sent to Kempsey school. To pay carpenter's bills. Carpenter's and joiner's bills referred to him. Tace Sowle's 2-guinea fine paid to him 22 Jun 1705 G120v to oversee painting of pales in garden 30 Jun 1705 G121r Capt. Samuel Roycroft fined, Thomas Hodgkins elected 2 Jul 1705 G121v Thomas Clarke fined. To deal with Thomas Bradyll 6 Aug 1705 G122r to be responsible for election dinner 16 Oct 1705 G124v to attend Lord Mayor to compel Renter Wardens to provide dinner 12 Nov 1705 G124v to pay shipwright's bill of £3 10s 3 Dec 1705 G125v to settle painter's bill. To pay glazier's bill 4 Feb 1705/6 G127r carpenter's bill referred to him for payment. Clerk's two bills referred. To pay Clerk's bill relating to the Corporation; G128v to send Bibles to poor people of Kempsey 6 May 1706 G131r bond from Joseph Collyer and his sureties delivered to him by Clerk 6 Jul 1706 G133v Israel Harrison elected 3 Feb 1706/7 G137v to adjust and order payment of carpenter's and smith's bills 26 Mar 1707 G140r money from bonds to Mrs Ellen Mace and Ambrose Dickins paid to him in order to repay bonds of £200 to William Paston 4 Aug 1707 G144r Awnsham Churchill fined, Israel Harrison fined for second year, Deputy Collins elected 1 Dec 1707 G147r to adjust carpenter's bill for stands for Thanksgiving Day 1 Mar 1707/8 G149v to adjust Clerk's bill for law charges 26 Mar 1708 G150v William Mount's fine for First Renter Warden is paid to him 3 Jul 1708 G154r Freeman Collins elected 6 Sep 1708 G157r to pay money to Awnsham Churchill for Abel Swale 8 Nov 1708 G158v ordered to pay for the watermen, music and whifflers 7 Feb 1708/9 G160v to adjust and order payment of Clerk's bill for law charges 2 May 1709 G164v

to examine and pay plumber's bill   6 Jun 1709 G165r to attend Sir Peter King   23 Jun
1709 G166r ordered to pay glazier's bill   2 Jul 1709 G166v John Baskett elected. Daniel
Browne competes unsuccessfully   1 May 1710 G179r suggests to Court that S.C.
should contribute towards charges for obtaining the late Act of Parliament. Auditor of
late Renter Wardens' accounts   1 Jul 1710 G181r John Baskett elected, Daniel Browne
competes unsuccessfully   3 Jul 1710 G181v Capt. Samuel Roycroft's fine for office of
Master has been paid to him; G182r John Baskett takes oath   7 Aug 1710 G182v
Israel Harrison's fine for Upper Warden has been paid to him   4 Dec 1710 G185v to
pay shipwright's bill   30 Jun 1711 G192r Daniel Browne elected   2 Jul 1711 G192v
to oversee payment of 30s from Poor Box to release John Vousden from prison   4 Feb
1711/12 G196r to leave £5 in hands of John Sprint to buy books for Abel Swale   3
Mar 1711/12 G197r to pay the remainder of the £5 to and for Swale; to pay John
Matthews £10 towards the charge of the dinner on Lord Mayor's Day   5 Jul 1712
G201r William Freeman elected   6 Oct 1712 G204r to pay bills of pewterer, painter
and printers   9 Feb 1712/13 G206r to accept legacy of Thomas Parkhurst. To pay
Swale's rent with 40s from the Poor Box   2 Mar 1712/13 G207r Jacob Tonson fined
for first year   4 May 1713 G209v note for payment of Thomas Lewis's fine for Renter
Warden delivered to him. To consider rent on Carter's house   4 Jul 1713 G211r Court
agrees to allow members to fine for two years in order to provide choice of candidates
for Upper Warden. William Freeman, Jacob Tonson and Daniel Browne fined for second
year. Nicholas Boddington and Timothy Goodwin fined for first and second year. John
Lawrence fined for first year and is elected for second year. Richard Mount fined for
first year   3 May 1714 G218v signs note to Thomas Guy   3 Jul 1714 G220r Richard
Mount elected   13 Jun 1715 G229r to let John Hartley have 40s towards paying fees
and being discharged from prison   2 Jul 1715 G230r John Sprint elected   4 Jul 1715
G230v letter to him from Nahum Tate desiring to borrow £30 upon an assignment of
his salary as Poet Laureate   7 Nov 1715 G234v ordered to pay Mrs Stephens £7 for the
racks and spits in S.C.'s kitchen which belonged to her husband   5 Dec 1715 G235r
Clerk has delivered to him a bond from John England for payment of his Livery fine   4
Jun 1716 G240v auditor of late Renter Wardens' accounts   30 Jun 1716 G241r John
Sprint elected   1 Oct 1716 G244r to take care that Bargemaster has a new livery against
the next Lord Mayor's day   4 Mar 1716/17 G247v to pay Clerk's bill
— UPPER WARDEN   5 Jul 1679 E87v Thomas Vere elected   3 Jul 1680 E101r
Richard Clarke elected   2 Jul 1681 E115r Thomas Newcomb elected   6 Feb 1681/2
E142r Francis Tyton elected   1 Jul 1682 E154v Francis Tyton elected   30 Jun 1683
F1r Francis Tyton's 6 months' service as substitute for the late Thomas Newcomb, with
1 year's normal service, to count as 2 years; F1v John Towse elected   5 Jul 1684 F19v
Henry Hills elected   4 Jul 1685 F39r several Assistants permitted to fine for two years'
Under Warden as only one candidate for Upper Warden; F39v John Bellinger elected   3 Jul 1686 F59r Capt. John Baker elected   2 Jul 1687 F85v Capt. John Baker elected   12 Oct 1687 F90v Edward Brewster elected   30 Jun 1688 F103r John Simms
elected   6 Aug 1688 F104r Treasurer's bond and sureties to be held by Upper rather
than Under Warden since the Treasurer, Benjamin Tooke, is Under Warden   27 Nov
1688 F110v 'Major' John Baker elected   26 Mar 1689 F116r Ambrose Isted elected   6
Jul 1689 F121r Ambrose Isted elected   2 Jun 1690 F135r Ambrose Isted elected   5
Jul 1690 F138r Henry ('Deputy') Clarke elected   4 Jul 1691 F156v Thomas Bassett
elected   2 Jul 1692 F172v John Simms elected   1 Jul 1693 F189r Thomas Bassett
elected   9 May 1694 F204v Henry Mortlock elected   30 Jun 1694 F209v Henry
Mortlock elected   6 Jul 1695 F229r William Rawlins elected   4 Jul 1696 F245r Samuel
Heyrick elected   3 Jul 1697 F263r Samuel Lowndes elected   8 Nov 1697 G1r reports
from committee appointed to treat with Awnsham Churchill re. printing Aesop's

Fables   7 Mar 1697/8 G4r baker who serves the S.C. with bread for a benefactor's gift to give Warden a quarterly receipt for money paid to him   7 Jun 1698 G9r party to Articles with University of Oxford   2 Jul 1698 G10r Samuel Lowndes elected   5 Sep 1698 G14r to examine repairs required to barge   7 Oct 1698 G14v to reimburse [John] Barrow [jnr?] the 15s paid for the barge road   27 Mar 1699 G23r gives Renter Wardens their charge   1 Jul 1699 G26r Samuel Heyrick elected   4 Sep 1699 G30r to pay Robert Stephens's and Clerk's bills. Asked to demand from Christopher Grandorge writings in his custody belonging to S.C.   2 Oct 1699 G31r to pay Barnes the bricklayer and Atwood the carpenter 10s each for viewing S.C.'s houses. Reports that he has received writings belonging to S.C. from Grandorge on payment of 12s 6d   3 Jun 1700 G40r to pay workman's bills   6 Jul 1700 G42v Richard Simpson elected   7 Oct 1700 G45v Nicholas Hooper's quarterly bills to be entered in the Warden's instructions usually given to him at his entrance into that office   2 Dec 1700 G47v to pay Adam Winch 2s for every Court day attended   26 Mar 1701 G57v reads Renter Wardens their charge   5 Jul 1701 G61v Richard Simpson elected   6 Oct 1701 G64v informs Court that William Horton wishes to dispose of his stock   1 Jun 1702 G71v has received 10s in part-payment for use of Hall for a funeral. Note of monies and charges entered by Treasurer in the cheque book to be taken up by him after every Court and delivered to the Stock-keepers   4 Jul 1702 G76v George Copping fined. Walter Kettleby elected   7 Sep 1702 G80r to pay for barge to be trimmed   3 Jul 1703 G91r Richard Chiswell and George Copping fined. Walter Kettleby elected   2 Aug 1703 G94r John Hunter's redemption fees paid to him   6 Sep 1703 G94v to meet John Gadbury the almanack maker   2 Mar 1703/4 G103r to take counsel's advice re. John Bradford's plea   14 Mar 1703/4 G104r to take counsel's advice re. Ephemerides   1 Jul 1704 G109r Charles Harper and Robert Andrews fined. Samuel Sprint elected   2 Oct 1704 G112v to pay shipwright's bill   4 Dec 1704 G114r to adjust and order payment of bricklayer's bill   20 Dec 1704 G115v to order payment of painters' bill   5 Feb 1704/5 G114v (minutes copied before those of 20 Dec 1704) to settle affairs of Tooke. Clerk's bill for Chancery referred to him   2 Apr 1705 G118r carpenter's and joiner's bills referred to him   22 Jun 1705 G120v to oversee painting of pales in garden   30 Jun 1705 G121r Charles Harper fined. Samuel Sprint elected   2 Jul 1705 G121v to deal with Thomas Bradyll   6 Aug 1705 G122r reports from his meeting with Bradyll and John Taylor. To be responsible for election dinner   16 Oct 1705 G124v to attend Lord Mayor to compel Renter Wardens to provide dinner   12 Nov 1705 G124v to pay shipwright's bill   3 Dec 1705 G125v to settle painter's bill   4 Feb 1705/6 G127r carpenter's bill referred for payment. Clerk's two bills referred   6 Jul 1706 G133v Robert Andrews elected and takes oath   9 Sep 1706 G134v to be paid Christopher Wilkinson's fine for Renter Warden   4 Nov 1706 G135v to pay Loftus for fitting up S.C.'s barge   3 Feb 1706/7 G137v to order payment of carpenter's and smith's bills   26 Mar 1707 G140r to be paid 3 guineas for use of Hall   5 Jul 1707 G143r Robert Andrews elected and takes oath   1 Dec 1707 G147r to pay carpenter's bill. To pay shipwright's bill for cleansing the barge   1 Mar 1707/8 G149v to adjust Clerk's bill for law charges   3 May 1708 G152r Renter Wardens receive charge from   3 Jul 1708 G154r Capt. Samuel Roycroft is elected   7 Feb 1708/9 G160v to adjust and order payment of Clerk's bill for law charges   6 Jun 1709 G165v Grafton, Renter Warden, receives charge from; G166r to attend Sir Peter King   2 Jul 1709 G166v Thomas Hodgkins elected and takes oath   6 Mar 1709/10 G176v to pay smith's bill for work done on Hall   1 May 1710 G179r auditor of Renter Wardens' accounts   3 Jul 1710 G181v Thomas Clarke fined, Deputy Collins elected. James Knapton, Renter Warden, receives his charge from   7 Aug 1710 G182r Thomas Hodgkins and Thomas Clarke fined for second year. Israel Harrison fined for first year   30 Jun 1711 G192r Israel Harrison elected   5 Jul 1712 G201r Deputy Collins elected   7 Jul 1712 G201v Henry Parsons, Renter Warden, receives charge from   26 Sep 1712 G203v Andrew Bell, Renter Warden, receives charge from   6 Oct 1712 G204r signs report of Baskett committee   2 Mar 1712/13 G206v Israel Harrison acting Upper Warden in place of Freeman Collins, deceased, until usual time for election   13 Apr 1713 G208r Joseph Downing, Assistant Renter Warden, receives charge from   4 May 1713 G209v to consider rent on Carter's house. Jonah Bowyer receives his charge as Assistant Renter Warden from the Warden   4 Jul 1713 G211r John Baskett only person qualified to be elected – fined for two years. Daniel Browne, William Freeman, Timothy Goodwin and Jacob Tonson fined for two years. Nicholas Boddington elected   7 Sep 1713 G213r amounts owing to Master and Wardens in respect of English Stock to be paid to Warden by Joseph Collyer   7 Dec 1713 G215r to pay bills of bricklayer, carpenter and shipwright insofar as they were for work done for the Corporation. To call upon Joseph Oake re. payment of Livery fine. To call upon Philip Overton, John Lenthall, James Pulleyne, James Bissell and Christopher Coningsby to inform them that if they do not pay Livery fines they will be proceeded against   5 Apr 1714 G217v gives charges to Renter Wardens   3 May 1714 G218v to give Philip Monckton 40s out of Poor Box   3 Jul 1714 G220r Nicholas Boddington elected   13 Jun 1715 G229r Bernard Lintott receives charge as Assistant Renter Warden from him   2 Jul 1715 G230r casting vote chooses John Baskett as Master. Richard Mount elected as the only person eligible   4 Jul 1715 G230v reads charge to Thomas Varnam as Assistant Renter Warden. To view houses of Mrs Everingham and Mrs Davies   8 Aug 1715 G231v reports that committee appointed to view houses of Mrs Everingham and Mrs Davies has found that they are in indifferent repair   9 Apr 1716 G239r to write to enquire of circumstances of Henry Brickwood   7 May 1716 G239v reported that he has heard Brickwood's circumstances are very good   6 Jun 1716 G240v auditor of late Renter Wardens' accounts   21 Jun 1716 G240v Thomas Norris receives his charge as Renter Warden and Samuel Clarke his charge as Assistant Renter Warden from Upper Warden   30 Jun 1716 G241r byelaws for choice of Warden read. Richard Mount elected (no-one else eligible to stand)   2 Jul 1716 G241v fines for Master paid to him   12 Nov 1716 G244v to pay shipwright's bill   3 Dec 1716 G245r suggests that committee which audited his late accounts should re-inspect them as Warden Sprint has found an error   4 Mar 1716/17 G247v to pay Clerk's bill   26 Mar 1717 G248v acquaints Court that James Read wishes to fine for Assistant Renter Warden   6 May 1717 G250r bond from Collyer and his sureties delivered to him. Informs Court that Guy would be a considerable benefactor to the S.C. and the poor thereof

WARE, Richard   8 Jan 1716/17 G246r Francis Rhodes is turned over from him to Thomas Norris

WAREHOUSES   6 Mar 1681/2 E146v ordered after disagreement that no S.C. member may use a warehouse without a lease from Master, Wardens and Assistants and that they are let to highest bidder   8 May 1682 E152v committee report that the value of the warehouse by the stairs is £6 p.a.; 7-year lease sealed with Richard Royston who has already spent £20 on it   20 Apr 1683 E169r committee to ascertain how many warehouses are in S.C.'s possession to be let, and how many are let and to whom   2 May 1683 E169r committee report that one warehouse is let to Mrs Sawbridge, one to Richard Royston, one to Robert Scott and one to John Williams, all at £5 p.a.   7 May 1683 E169v committee report deferred   2 Nov 1691 F161v only Under Warden and tenants of warehouses to have keys to Hall precincts   7 Aug 1693 F190r committee appointed to assist Master and Wardens re. building warehouses on land behind Hall   28 Sep 1693 F192r report from committee to oversee building of warehouse in S.C.'s garden   2 Oct 1693 F192v warehouse to be only one storey high   4 Dec 1693 F195r building costs of warehouse to be paid for by the Corporation rather than the English

Stock, and Warden to pay ground rent to City and workmen   30 Sep 1696 F249v Mrs
Royston asks satisfaction for boards, &c., left when she moved out of the warehouse
now occupied by William Rawlins, Charles Harper and others   22 Dec 1696 F253v
Mrs Royston is paid £6 16s for boards which she left in her warehouses   5 Dec 1698
G16v committee to assess repairs of Awnsham Churchill's warehouse and others   7
Feb 1698/9 G20r disbursements for building in S.C.'s garden   7 Aug 1699 G28v com-
mittee to assess repairs of Awnsham Churchill's warehouse   4 Sep 1699 G30r copy of
Oxford Articles to be entered in a book there for the use of the Stock-keepers   3 Jun
1700 G40r committee to sell Oxford books there   2 Jun 1701 G60v copies of S.C.'s
psalms printed by Benjamin Motte to be brought to Treasurer's warehouse   1 Jun
1702 G71r impression of works printed for the S.C. to be delivered there   1 Feb 1702/3
G85r S.C. to rent warehouse from Robert Stephens at the same rent as formerly

See also ENGLISH STOCK

WAREHOUSEKEEPER (before 1703, see TREASURER)   1703–1717 Joseph Collyer   5 Apr 1703 G88r to receive money from Mrs Webb's bond in order to pay Mrs
Royston and to pay £200 due to Mrs Royston's estate from S.C.   7 Jun 1703 G90r to
have charge of bond from S.C. to a friend of the Master   6 Sep 1703 G94v letter to him
from John Gadbury read. To pay Allen's bill   20 Oct 1703 G96v to receive lease from
University of Cambridge to Feild   15 Nov 1703 G97v letter from Dr Gadbury concerning the Ephemerides. To attend him   6 Dec 1703 G99r to be indemnified from damages
arising from bond made by him with University of Cambridge on behalf of S.C.   20
Dec 1703 G100r to pay Mrs Miller £5 of her dividend for board and lodging   14 Mar
1703/4 G104r to pay for Elizabeth Lightfoot's burial   23 Mar 1703/4 G104v to pay
£5 out of charity money to Thomas Yates   3 Apr 1704 G105v to receive bond from
S.C. to James Crane and John Keeblebutter. George Parker to pay him a fine for printing
the Ephemerides   12 Jun 1704 G107r to pay Allen's bill   7 Aug 1704 G111r copperplate of Raven's Almanack to be delivered to him   4 Sep 1704 G111v to pay plasterer's
bill. To pay William Bowyer's salary   4 Dec 1704 G113v to pay plumber's, glazier's and
bricklayers' bills. To pay Dr Nicholas Brady a share of the profit from an impression of
Tate and Brady's Psalms in octavo. To have a gratuity for his faithful service to the S.C.
for this year   20 Dec 1704 G115v (minute copied after that of 5 Feb 1704/5) to pay
painter's bill   5 Feb 1704/5 G114v George Sawbridge to deliver copies of 'The Traveller's and Chapman's Daily Instructor' to him. Daniel Browne, William Davis and Thomas
Slater to deliver copies of [N.B., Philomath], 'Observations on Time Sacred and Profane',
to him. To pay Clerk's bill for proceedings in Chancery   5 Mar 1704/5 G116v George
Sawbridge to deliver S.C.'s calendars in 'The Traveller's and Chapman's Daily Instructor'
to him. Browne and Slater to deliver to him books and plates relating to 'Observations
on Time'   2 Apr 1705 G118r to pay joiner's bill   10 Sep 1705 G123r to pay those
employed in procuring the small London Plate Almanack. To pay those who printed
advertisements opposing Maydwell's projects to exhibit his Bill in Parliament. To pay
plasterer's bill for English Stock   3 Dec 1705 G125v to pay Daniel Blague 25 shillings
per quarter. To be allowed the same gratuity as last year   4 Feb 1705/6 G127v to pay
Clerk's bill relating to English Stock   6 May 1706 G131r bond from Collyer and
sureties delivered by Clerk to Warden Thomas Hodgkins. To pay monies arising from
Mrs Miller's share to Mrs Isted who has a mortgage thereof   28 May 1706 G132r to
pay £50 loan to Dr Brady   3 Jun 1706 G132r to answer letter from John Hayes of
Cambridge. To withhold payment for John Arden's share because of infancy of legatee,
Thomas Asgall   21 Jun 1706 G133r to pay Clerk 40 shillings for his advance of monies
to William Richardson   4 Nov 1706 G136r to pay money for Arden's £40 share to
Asgall   2 Dec 1706 G136v gives report of accounts of English Stock. To have same
gratuity (£20) this year as last   3 Feb 1706/7 G137r requests directions of Court

concerning payment of remainder of Mrs Miller's money   1 Mar 1706/7 G138v to pay Timothy Goodwin and John Walthoe money towards fees and charges of Bill in Parliament   1 Sep 1707 G145r to give answer of Master, Wardens and Stock-keepers to Samuel Farley   10 Oct 1707 G146r to pay Gellebrand his 10 guineas   3 Nov 1707 G146v to deliver plates of an almanack to Slater   18 Dec 1707 G148r to have a £20 gratuity this year, as last   9 Feb 1707/8 G148v to have a present of £20. To use bond to churchwardens of St Thomas the Apostle to pay off bond to Mrs Fisher   1 Mar 1707/8 G149v to pay Clerk's bill for law charges   7 Jun 1708 G153r to prepare account of rent arrears of Awnsham Churchill, Mrs Mills and Mrs Eversden. Clerk has delivered to him account of arrears of rent due to English Stock   5 Jul 1708 G154v to settle account with Mrs Eversden. To make up the account of Mrs Mills   4 Oct 1708 G158r to prepare an account of rent due to the English Stock at Michaelmas last   6 Dec 1708 G159r responsible for settlement of Mrs Mills' rent arrears   22 Dec 1708 G159v to have a present of £20 for good and faithful services   7 Feb 1708/9 G160v to have a present of £20 for his services, but 'not to be a precedent for the future'   4 Apr 1709 G164r to pay Clerk £40 advance of £200 to pay off Randall Tooke's bond   6 Jun 1709 G165v to pay retaining fee to Sir Peter King as S.C.'s counsel   7 Jul 1709 G168r speaks to Court re. Dr John Partridge's almanack   7 Nov 1709 G171v to pay bills of workmen   22 Dec 1709 G173r to pay Mrs Anne Blague her husband's share for the quarter   6 Feb 1709/10 G175r to have a gratuity of £20 for his service   2 Oct 1710 G184v to pay Roger Higgins interest on bond from S.C.   4 Dec 1710 G186r presents statement of accounts of English Stock   20 Dec 1710 G186v to have a gratuity of £20 for his year's service   1 Mar 1710/11 G187v to pay money to Abel Swale   23 Mar 1710/11 G188v to be paid one guinea by William Bowyer   9 Apr 1711 G189v to pay Clerk's bill   1 Oct 1711 G194v to be indemnified for drawing up a note for the repayment of Thomas Guy's loan to the S.C.   20 Dec 1711 G196r to have usual gratuity of £20   3 Mar 1711/12 G197r to have a further gratuity of £20 for extraordinary services   7 Apr 1712 G199r to give John Baskett a note for payment with interest in October next   2 Jun 1712 G200r to pay Clerk's two bills and gratuity   1 Dec 1712 G205v S.C.'s bond received by him for delivery to Thomas Guy   19 Dec 1712 G205v to pay workmen's bills for repairing Carter's house. To have the usual gratuity of £20 for care in affairs of English Stock   7 Sep 1713 G213r to pay English Stock amounts appearing mistakenly in Corporation accounts   5 Oct 1713 G213v no longer required to pay disbursements of English Stock as he has already paid sums on account of the Corporation   7 Dec 1713 G214v to get in money due to English Stock for almanacks, &c. To have a gratuity of £20 for the year. To make payments for work done for English Stock; bricklayer's, carpenter's and shipwright's bills   3 May 1714 G218v note drawn on him for payment of the printers renewed   4 Oct 1714 G222r to pay carpenter's bill   6 Dec 1714 G223v to have same gratuity (£20) as last year   7 Nov 1715 G234r standing order for the future that he is to have the same fees on alienation of shares in English Stock as upon other persons being elected into them   5 Dec 1715 G235r to obtain all monies due to English Stock. To have usual gratuity of £20   5 Mar 1715/16 G237v notes drawn on him signed by members of the Table   3 Dec 1716 G245r bonds from S.C. to Mary Green delivered to her   20 Dec 1716 G246r to have usual gratuity of £20   6 May 1717 G250r Clerk delivers his bond and sureties to Warden John Sprint

WARNE, Philip   3 Oct 1715 G233v son of Roger; bound to Thomas Harbin, 7 years

WARNE, Roger – see preceding entry

WARNER, [   ]   3 Jun 1700 G40v the painter; bill of £7 13s 9d to be paid by Warden Charles Harper

WARR, James   6 Mar 1703/4 G103v freed by Thomas Weaver

WARRALL, John   3 Mar 1700/1 G57r 15s of quarterage arrears to be remitted

WARREN, [   ]   30 Sep 1680 E104v articles between S.C., Knowles and Warren for building to be sealed

WARREN, Agar   5 Dec 1698 G17r bound to Robert Elmes, 7 years   3 Jun 1706 G132v freed by Robert Elmes   7 Oct 1706 G135r George Twitty is bound to him

WARREN, James   2 Aug 1686 F61v joiner; to be paid out of the money John Mayo is allotted for his confiscated press, which he himself made

WARREN, Thomas   4 Jun 1694 F208v Richard Phillipps jnr is bound to him   1 Sep 1701 G64r Edward Ince is bound to him   5 Aug 1706 G134r his apprentice Richard Phillipps is freed   7 Feb 1708/9 G160v his apprentice Edward Ince is freed   1 Oct 1711 G194v Robert Hubbard is bound to him

WARREN, Thomas Gregory   5 Dec 1715 G235v bound to John Senex, 7 years

WARRETT, Thomas   1 Mar 1702/3 G86r bound to Stephen Keys, 7 years

WARSALL, [   ]   6 Apr 1685 (W) copy of 'A Cap of Grey Hairs' by Caleb Trenchfield to be entered by him

WARTER, Mrs   7 Nov 1715 G234r widow of William Warter; her £40 share disposed of to her son-in-law John Lenthall

WARTER, William (I)   24 Jun 1682 E154r cloathed   1 Mar 1687/8 F97v expelled from Livery by order of Lord Mayor   11 Oct 1688 F108v restored to Livery   4 Apr 1691 F151r elected Assistant Renter Warden and ordered to be summoned   6 Apr 1691 F151v elected First Renter Warden instead of Assistant Renter Warden; fined   1 Mar 1691/2 F165v elected to Brabazon Aylmer's £40 share   12 Nov 1694 F215r Sarah Marshall is bound to him   4 Feb 1694/5 F217r John Kingsley, his apprentice, is freed   7 Mar 1697/8 G5r Ambrose Newton is bound to him   4 Sep 1699 G30v John Lenthall is bound to him   5 Feb 1699/1700 G35r his apprentice John Evitt is freed   1 Mar 1702/3 G85v competes unsuccessfully for Mrs Holt's £80 share   5 Mar 1704/5 G117r competes unsuccessfully for Judith Webb's £80 share   2 Jul 1705 G121v Charles Baldwin is bound to him   5 Aug 1706 G134r William Hinckly is bound to him   9 Sep 1706 G134v his apprentice John Lenthall is freed

WARTER, William (II)   4 Jul 1698 G11r freed by patrimony

WARWICKSHIRE GENTLEMEN   2 Nov 1702 G83r Hall let to them for annual feast

WASE, Christopher   8 May 1682 E152v assignment of his 'Methodi Practica[e] Specimen' from Mrs Maxwell to Thomas Parkhurst confirmed

WASTE REGISTER BOOK – see ENTRY BOOK OF COPIES

WATERMEN   8 Nov 1708 G158v to be paid half of what is usually paid by Under Warden and Renter Wardens (30s and 20s respectively)

WATERS, William   4 Dec 1710 G186r bound to James Robert, 7 years

WATERSON, [   ]   7 Sep 1685 F44r to be summoned with Benjamin Tooke and Richard Chiswell re. printing a Stock book, 'Daniel and Thursfield's History' [i.e. Samuel Daniel & John Trussell, *History of England*]   2 Nov 1685 F45v to be summoned after Court finds that the 'History' is entered for 5 March 1619   7 Dec 1685 F47v asked to prove previous title to 'History' to avert legal proceedings   1 Feb 1685/6 F51r to be summoned   1 Mar 1685/6 F52r to be re-summoned
See also following entry

WATERSON, Mrs   11 Oct 1680 E104v assignment to Simon Miller to be entered   3 May 1686 F55r she and her sons disobey summons to explain title to [Samuel] Daniel and [John] Trussell's 'History [of England]'; ordered that their dividends should be sequestered if they do not attend next Court   7 Feb 1686/7 F71r Mills tells Court that the 'History' was entered to Mr Waterson; Master replies that this may vindicate her and Clerk ordered to search   1 Mar 1686/7 F77v Court satisfied that she has title to the 'History' and orders that her dividend should be paid   5 Dec 1687 F95v deceased; her £160 share is vacant but her youngest son's offer to take it up and fine for Renter Warden &c. is refused

WATTIS, John   3 May 1708 G152v bound to John Leake, 7 years

WATKINS, Joseph   6 Aug 1711 G193r bound to Richard Watkins, his brother, 7 years

WATKINS, Richard   31 Jan 1710/11 G186v freed by John Baskett   6 Aug 1711 G193r his brother Joseph is bound to him

WATKINS, Samuel   4 Apr 1709 G164r bound to Jacob Tonson, 7 years

WATSON, Arthur   6 May 1689 F117v deceased; Henry Hills jnr is ordered to find a new surety for the rest of his £100 loan

WATSON, Francis   4 Feb 1705/6 G127v freed by Francis Leach   7 Feb 1714/15 G225r his son Thomas is bound to him

WATSON, James   3 Oct 1709 G171r bound to William Bowyer, 7 years

WATSON, John   4 Oct 1708 G158r bound to William Chapman, 7 years

WATSON, Robert   2 Jul 1709 G166v glazier; to be employed on repairs to Morphew's house

WATSON, Thomas   7 Feb 1714/15 G225r son of Francis; bound to his father, 7 years

WATSON, William   7 Aug 1699 G29r freed by Henry Carter

WATT, James   1 Feb 1702/3 G85r bound to Henry Kifft, 7 years

WATT, John   7 Jul 1701 G62r of London, merchant; bond from S.C. to him for payment of £1025 10s sealed   6 Feb 1709/10 G175v S.C. to pay his executors 6% on the £1000 due to them on bond

WATTS, [ ]   7 Jul 1690 F138v given licence to print an impression of 750 of the Church Catechism for 30s

WATTS, James, snr – see following entry

WATTS, James, jnr   6 Jul 1713 G212v son of James; bound to William Sayes for 7½ years

WATTS, John   7 Oct 1698 G15r bound to Robert Everingham, 7 years   9 Jun 1707 G142v freed by William Watts   9 Feb 1707/10 G149r bookseller; Benjamin Young is bound to him   7 Dec 1713 G214v cloathed   2 Jul 1716 G242r Thomas Adams is bound to him   10 Sep 1716 G243r William Jackson is turned over to him from William Scott

WATTS, Joseph   7 May 1688 F101r John Baker assigns to Joshua Phillipps and him Joseph Glanvill's 'An Earnest Invitation to the ... Lord's Supper', 7th edn   3 Jun 1689 F119r cloathed   1 Aug 1692 F177r summoned with Henry Bonwick to explain why they have printed Thomas Jekyll's Catechism illegally   3 Oct 1692 F180r has printed 750 church catechisms; ordered to pay 30s for permission to print and sell them and 5s fine to the Poor Box   5 Apr 1714 G217v excused office of Renter Warden for one year

WATTS, William   4 Jul 1698 G11r bound by Adam Hampton, 7 years   7 Feb 1698/9 G20v freed by Benjamin Crayle   9 Jun 1707 G142v his apprentice John Watts is freed

WAYMAN, William   26 Mar 1686 F54r elected waterman   4 Apr 1687 F81v elected waterman

WAYNHOUSE – see WAINHOUSE

WEADEN, Luke   5 Jul 1703 G92r freed by Hannah Clarke

WEAVER, Thomas   6 Mar 1703/4 G103v his apprentice James Warr is freed

WEAVERS' COMPANY   3 Dec 1684 F26v James Cole is allowed to be translated to the Weavers' on a contribution to the Poor Box and promise of further charity to poor of S.C.

WEBB, Elizabeth   25 Jun 1684 F18v of Westminster Hall; submits to a three-guinea fine and is ordered to be freed at next Court   7 Jul 1684 F20r pleads against fine on account of 'mean trade' and this is confirmed; two guineas are remitted and she is freed

WEBB, George   1 Sep 1707 G145r bound to John Crofts, 7 years

WEBB, Judith   5 Mar 1679/80 E97v bond to her of £400 penalty for payment of £200 at 5% entered into   4 Feb 1683/4 (W) Capt. John Williams to assign his £160 share to her for £100 at 6%   3 Mar 1683/4 F10v Williams mortgages his £160 share to Mrs Webb for £100 plus interest   1 Mar 1691/2 F166r Williams transfers the mortgage of his £160 share from her to John Bellinger   23 Mar 1691/2 F167r of Hammersmith; given bond of £1000 penalty for payment of £12 10s on 24 Sep 1692 and £500 plus £12 10s on 24 March 1692/3   3 Aug 1702 G79r requests payment of £200 of £500 due to her on bond from S.C.   7 Sep 1702 G80v £200 of her bond paid   5 Oct 1702 G81v bond from S.C. for payment of £307 10s sealed. Old bond for £500 cancelled   27 Mar 1703 G86v bond from S.C. for £200 to be drawn up   5 Apr 1703 G88r bond from S.C. to pay £285 sealed   7 Aug 1704 G110v S.C. to take a further £100 from her on bond and to transfer the whole to her kinswoman, Mary Mason of London   4 Sep 1704 G111v two bonds from S.C. of £300 and £200 cancelled   5 Mar 1704/5 G117r deceased; her £80 share disposed of to William Freeman

WEBSTER, Benjamin   4 Mar 1694/5 F219r name in margin   7 Oct 1700 G46r and Daniel Browne; their apprentice Amos Coppleton is freed   9 Feb 1707/8 G149r bookbinder; John Stephens is bound to him

WEBSTER, John   1 May 1710 G179v bound to Thomas Wild, 7 years

WEBSTER, Margaret   20 Jun 1713 G210v elected to Mrs Yates' pension. Isaac Lane is given her pension   1 Mar 1713/14 G216v replaces Mrs Battersby as cleaner of the Hall

WEEDEN/WEEDON, Cavendish   20 Dec 1701 G66v granted use of Hall twice a week for a year for the performance of divine music

WEEDON, Alexander – see following entry

WEEDON, Richard   2 Nov 1713 G214v son of Alexander; bound to Robert Harman, 7 years   31 Aug 1716 G242v turned over from Robert Harman to Thomas Atkins

WEEKES, John   5 Mar 1704/5 G117r his apprentice Anthony Barber, who was turned over to Alexander Boswell, is freed

WEILDY, Joseph   6 Jul 1691 F157v carpenter of Houndsditch; proposed as surety by Benjamin Johnson for £50 loan from Tyler Bequest   23 Sep 1691 F161r John Marshall substituted for him as surety

WELCHMAN – see WELSHMAN

WELL AND PUMP   3 Nov 1684 F25v Treasurer to pay £5 towards charge thereof, as a good supply of water for the Hall and 'ready help in case of fire'
See also PUMP

WELLBANK, Christopher   6 Dec 1708 G159v bound to Thomas Cope, 8 years

WELLINGTON, [ ]   7 Jun 1697 F263r cloathed, promising to fine at two six-monthly intervals   8 May 1699 G24v to be sued for remaining £10 of his Livery fine   3 Nov 1701 G65r to be prosecuted for importing S.C.'s books contrary to the byelaws   9 Feb 1701/2 G67r answer to Bill in Chancery against him and Minshall

WELLINGTON, Richard   7 Oct 1700 G46r William Thorn is bound to him   9 Feb 1707/8 G149r bookseller; James Fishwick is bound to him

WELLS, Ann   11 Oct 1686 F65v given bond for £307 10s; to discharge £300 bond due to Emmanuel Blake

WELLS, Elizabeth   20 Dec 1701 G66r elected to John Dooly's pension   23 Mar 1710/11 G188v deceased; William Barlow is given her pension

WELLS, George (I)   4 Jul 1681 E116r consideration of Mrs Martin's request that her late husband's copies be assigned to him and to Robert Scott to be deferred until next Court   5 Dec 1681 E140v elected to Widow Kirby's £40 share   22 Dec 1681 E141r elected to John Playford's £80 share   2 Mar 1684/5 F31v elected Stock-keeper for Livery with Obadiah Blagrave   7 May 1685 (W) confirmed as member of new Livery   2 Nov 1685 F46r complains with Robert Scott and Richard Bentley that Royston has printed their 'Life of Dr. Hammond' [by John Fell]   7 Dec 1685 F47v on behalf of himself and Bentley, accuses Royston of printing their 'Life of Dr. Hammond'; consideration deferred until next Pension Court   1 Feb 1685/6 F50v Royston is allowed further time to discuss his differences with Wells and Bentley   1 Mar 1686/7 F77r elected Stock-keeper for Livery with William Crooke   4 Jul 1687 F86r elected Assistant Renter Warden   12 Oct 1687 F91v displaced from the Livery and so cannot serve as Assistant Renter Warden; Gabriel Cox elected in his place   5 Dec 1687 F96r deceased but corpse not yet interred; voted to dispose of his £80 share just the same

WELLS, George (II)   5 May 1701 G59v bound to Robert Roberts   7 Jun 1708 G153v freed by John Roberts

WELLS, John   6 Jul 1713 G212v his son Whiteborne is bound to William Botham, 7 years

WELLS, Mrs   6 Dec 1708 G159r £300 due to her from S.C. to be paid within three months

WELLS, Whiteborne   6 Jul 1713 G212v son of John; bound to William Botham, 7 years

WELLS, William   9 Feb 1707/8 G149r bound to John Grantham   2 Nov 1713 G214v turned over from John Grantham to Thomas Hodgkins

WELSHMAN/WELCHMAN, Samuel   1 Oct 1705 G124r Samuel Holmes is bound to him   12 Nov 1705 G124v excused cloathing for three months   2 Oct 1710 G184v cloathed   1 Oct 1711 G194v Nathaniel Capell is bound to him   1 Jun 1713 G210v his apprentice Samuel Holmes is freed

WELTON, Thomas   5 Jun 1699 G25v bound to Jasper Roberts, 8 years

WEST, John   28 Oct 1697 (W) bound to Samuel Manship, 7 years   5 Apr 1703 G88r turned over to George Bryant

WESTBROOKE, [ ]   5 Oct 1681 E131r bond for £12 to be cancelled since a note on it in George Tokefeild's hand shows it has been paid

WESTWAY, Thomas   20 Dec 1693 F197r elected into the pension of Susanna Nutthead, deceased

WHALEY – see WHALLEY, WALE

WHALLEY, [John]   4 Dec 1710 G185v Awnsham Churchill to write to his correspondent in Ireland concerning Whalley's sending over his almanacks for the next year to be printed by S.C.

WHARTON, Gilbert   3 May 1680 E99v to pay a proportion of a bond   4 May 1691 F153r appears to answer for non-payment of £20 bond taken out by himself and others; produces receipt for £13 and ordered to pay remaining £7 and legal fees   8 Jun 1691 F154r pays 40s, the remaining sum due on bond of Francis and Timothy Robinson and himself. General release from S.C. to be prepared   3 Aug 1691 F158r his general release to be entered in Bond Book

WHEELER, John   5 Oct 1702 G81v bound to Thomas Franklin, 7 years

WHIFFLERS   8 Nov 1708 G158v to be paid half of what they are usually paid by Under Warden and Renter Wardens (30s and 20s respectively)

WHIPP, Elinor   23 Mar 1703/4 G104r elected to Elizabeth Lightfoote's pension

WHISKIN, Robert   3 Jun 1706 G132v apprentice of John Richardson, freed by Thomas Willimer

WHITAKER, Edmund – see IGNORAMUS JUSTICO

WHITCRAFT, Charles   6 Feb 1715/16 G236r freed by John Ford

WHITE, Bernard   2 Jul 1687 F85v surrenders £80 share to Court. (W) letter surrendering share   4 Jul 1687 F86r £80 share disposed of to William Hensman

WHITE, Francis   2 Nov 1702 G83r bound to William Rockwell, 7 years   5 Apr 1703 G88r turned over to Robert Whitledge

WHITE, Henry   6 Feb 1709/10 G275v bound to Richard Taylor, 7 years

WHITE, Kebell   2 Jun 1701 G60v his name used by Benjamin Motte in illegal printing of S.C.'s psalms

WHITE, Mrs   7 Jun 1680 E100v assigned printing of Stock ABC, signatures E and F of Stock primer and signatures L and M of Stock psalter   2 Apr 1683 E168r asks to make over her £160 share to Richard Chiswell as she could sell it to him for £180; Court decides she is better off mortgaging it for £150   20 Apr 1683 E168v her petition to surrender her £160 share for ready money accepted; Capt. John Baker is voted into it

WHITE, Robert   19 Dec 1712 G206r freed by Robert Stephens   1 Feb 1713/14 G216r John Mitchell is bound to him

WHITE, Roger   1 Dec 1712 G205v his son William is bound to Richard Tanner, 7 years

WHITE, Samuel   6 Dec 1697 G2r freed by Henry Crispe

WHITE, Thomas   6 Nov 1699 G33r bound to William Haddon, 7 years   7 Jul 1707 G143v his apprentice William Haddon is freed   1 Dec 1707 G147v shoemaker; Jacob Crow is bound to him   9 Feb 1707/8 G149r shoemaker; Henry Barnsley is bound to him

WHITE alias MARSHALL, William (I)   5 Aug 1700 G44r William White alias Marshall freed by him by patrimony

WHITE alias MARSHALL, William (II)   5 Aug 1700 G44r freed by William White alias Marshall by patrimony

WHITE, William (III)   1 Dec 1712 G205v son of Roger; bound to Richard Tanner, 7 years   2 Jul 1716 G242r turned over from Peter Tanner to Elizabeth Nutt

WHITECROFT, Charles   3 May 1708 G152v bound to Benjamin Mind, 7 years

WHITEHEAD, Daniel   5 Apr 1714 G218r his son William is bound to Samuel Austin, 7 years

WHITEHEAD, Joseph   7 Aug 1699 G29r bound to Robert Roberts, 7 years

WHITEHEAD, William (I)   5 Jul 1697 F264v Edward Savory is bound to him   9 Feb 1701/2 G67r John Dell is bound to him

WHITEHEAD, William (II)   5 Apr 1714 G218r son of Daniel; bound to Samuel Austin, 7 years

WHITEHEART, Roger   2 May 1715 G228v Richard Mansell is bound to him

WHITEYATE, Roger   7 Aug 1704 G111r bound to Robert Jole, 7 years

WHITFEILD, [   ]   26 Mar 1709 G163r Minister of St Martin's Ludgate, together with Churchwardens and Common Councilmen of the parish, to meet with S.C. committee concerning their wish to make a vault into the ground of the S.C.'s garden   1 Oct 1711 G194v committee to meet him and churchwardens of St Martin's Ludgate concerning plans for making a burial vault

WHITLEDGE, [   ]   7 Oct 1698 G15r requested until next Court day to consider whether or not to take cloathing   7 Dec 1702 G83v summoned to take cloathing   3 May 1708 G152v to have a lease of Garrett's house for 21 years at £25 p.a.   6 Jun 1709 G165v stone cutters in passage between his house and that of Mrs Everingham to be viewed by Morphew committee and repairs ordered   2 Jul 1709 G166v masonry work on passage between his house and Mrs Everingham's to be carried out by Harbin   7 Nov 1709 G171v mason's bill for work on passage by his house to be paid by Joseph Collyer   1 Feb 1713/14 G216r elected to James Roberts's £80 share. His share disposed of to Thomas Brewer

WHITLEDGE, Bowen/Bonen   6 Oct 1707 G145v bound to Robert, his father, 7 years   1 Nov 1714 G223r son of Robert, freed by his father. Cloathed

WHITLEDGE, Lawrence   1 Aug 1709 G169v freed by Robert Whitledge, patrimony

WHITLEDGE/WHITLIDGE, Lorrain   1 Jun 1702 G71v bound to John Baldry, 7 years   12 Nov 1716 G244v James Sponge is bound to him

WHITLEDGE/WHITLIDGE, Robert   4 Feb 1694/5 F217r James Holland, his apprentice, is freed   2 Mar 1695/6 F240r Daniel Whitlidge, his apprentice, is freed   3 Jul 1699 G27v Francis Bennett is bound to him   3 Mar 1700/1 G57r cloathed   7 Jul 1701 G62r and Thomas Norman's apprentice Jasper Hazard is freed. Robert Whitledge and Abel Rockall's apprentice William Gray is freed   5 Apr 1703 G88r cloathed. Francis White is turned over to him   7 Aug 1704 G111r Cornelius Rainsford is bound to him   4 Dec 1704 G113v elected to Thomas George's £40 share   3 Mar 1706/7 G139r his apprentice Francis Bennett is freed   6 Oct 1707 G145v bookseller; Bowen, his son, is bound to him   2 Aug 1708 G156r stationer; his apprentice Charles Hawkins is freed. Richard Baldwin is bound to him   1 Aug 1709 G169v Lawrence Whitledge is freed by him by patrimony   7 Nov 1709 G172r bookseller; Edward Spikeman is bound to him   27 Mar 1710 G177r fined for First Renter Warden   5 Mar 1710/11 G187v lease of his house in Ave Maria Lane for 19 years at £35 p.a. sealed   4 Aug 1712 G202v Dickinson Sharp is bound to him   9 Feb 1712/13 G206v his apprentice Cornelius Rainsford is freed   5 Apr 1714 G218r Isaac Wainhouse is turned over to him from Charles Hawkins   1 Nov 1714 G223r his son, Bowen, is freed   2 May 1715 G228v Dickinson Sharp is turned over from him to Cornelius Rainsford   7 May 1716 G240r his apprentice Richard Baldwin is freed

WHITLEDGE, Thomas   5 Aug 1695 F231v William Lucas jnr is bound to him   7 Feb 1698/9 G20r deceased in a poor condition. James Smalshaw was bound to him by foreign indenture, contrary to the byelaws of the S.C. Smalshaw is freed on payment of a 30-shilling fine   2 Aug 1703 G94r his apprentice William Lucas is freed

WHITLEDGE/WHITLIDGE, Daniel   2 Mar 1695/6 F240r servant to Robert Whitledge; freed

WHITLIDGE – see WHITLEDGE

WHITLOCK, [ ]   5 Jul 1680 E102r to be prosecuted if he does not bring in to the next Court the money due to S.C.   4 Jul 1681 E115v assigns £80 share to Roger Norton in trust for S.C. to secure repayment of £50 loaned to him by Randall Taylor within one year

WHITLOCK, Bulstrode   15 Apr 1692 F169v entry of an assignment of his 'Memorials of the English Affairs' from Nathaniel Ponder to Jacob Tonson

WHITLOCK, James   26 Mar 1682/3 E166v Randall Taylor's son-in-law; allowed to continue his £50 loan a year longer

WHITLOCK, John   20 Jun 1681 E114r elected to Randall Taylor's £80 share   2 Mar 1690/1 F150r competes unsuccessfully for porter   3 Dec 1694 F215v asks Court about leasing the Stock property he lives in; Court leaves it to Master, Wardens and Stock-keepers   26 Mar 1695 F219v competes unsuccessfully for Beadle   1 Jul 1695 F227v cloathed   5 Aug 1695 F231v Daniel Winchester jnr is bound to him for eight years   11 Nov 1695 F235r John Vaughan, his servant, is freed

WHITLOCK, Jonathan   26 Mar 1692 F168r son-in-law of Randall Taylor; Nicholas Hooper presents petition complaining of Taylor's and Whitlock's abuses of him

WHITLOCK, Mrs   3 Feb 1695/6 F238v petition rejected to have her late husband John's £10 Livery fee refunded to help with bringing up her several small children   5 Oct 1696 F250v to have £7 deducted from her rent for repair of her house, and to take a lease for 7 years from last Christmas at £16 p.a.   7 Oct 1698 G14v deceased; John Nutt to take a lease on the house which she rented from S.C. Her £80 share disposed of to Lewis Thomas

WHITMARSH, Nicholas – see following entry

WHITMARSH, Thomas   13 Apr 1713 G208v son of Nicholas; bound to William Pearson, 7 years

WHITMORE, Thomas   8 Nov 1703 G97r bound to John Collyer, 7 years

WHITTINGHAM, [ ]   8 Nov 1697 G1v married to Widow Fox; requests £100 due to him in the right of his wife on bond from S.C.

WHITTYATE, Roger   7 Jul 1712 G201v freed by Thomas Franklin

WHITWOOD, William   3 Nov 1679 E95r Robert Hanch, his apprentice, is freed   1 Sep 1684 F23v allowed to switch the mortgage of his £40 share from Mrs Mearne to James Tayler for £35   3 Dec 1684 F27r assigns a moiety of 'No Jest Like a True Jest, Being … the Merry Life of Capt. James Hind' to Jonah Deacon   1 Mar 1685/6 F52r elected Stock-keeper for Yeomanry with John Amery   26 Mar 1686 F53v excused Renter Wardenship on promise to hold it or fine for it next year   4 Oct 1686 F64v to be placed after those who have served or fined as Renter Warden or will do so, in order of Livery   7 Feb 1686/7 F70v competes unsuccessfully for William Cooper's £80 share. Elected to the late Mary Symons's £80 share   16 Mar 1686/7 F79r to be summoned on 4 April for the election of Renter Wardens   4 Apr 1687 F81r elected First Renter Warden   2 May 1687 F82v fined for Renter Warden   1 Mar 1687/8 F97v expelled from Livery by order of Lord Mayor   11 Oct 1688 F108v restored to Livery   1 Sep 1690 F142r Henry Mortlock and Benjamin Tooke sell three books to Court for the same price that Whitwood charged them   6 Oct 1690 F143r assignment from him to Warden and Treasurer of three books to be entered in trust for S.C.   7 May 1694 F203v elected Assistant and summoned   4 Jun 1694 F208r sworn in as Assistant   8 Apr 1695 F220v allowed to admit James Taylor into his £80 share   5 Feb 1699/1700 G35r debtor; consideration of his request to be re-admitted to the Court of Assistants deferred   9 Sep 1700 G45r his apprentice William Sayes is freed

WHOLE DUTY OF A COMMUNICANT   3 Dec 1684 F27r Simon Neale assigns 'The Whole Duty of a Communicant' [by John Gauden, late Bishop of Exeter] to Henry Rodes

WICKELL, Samuel   1 Oct 1711 G194v bound to Dryden Leach, 7 years

WICKINGS, John   26 Mar 1692 F167v set aside for a year from serving or fining for Renter Warden

WICKINS, John   8 May 1682 E152r cloathed   6 Aug 1711 G193r to be given 30s from the Poor Box

WICKS, [   ]   2 Jul 1709 G166v Clerk to request his rent arrears

WIDOWS/WYDDOWERS/WYDDOWES, Martha   27 Sep 1710 G184r elected to Hester Ferrys's pension   20 Dec 1711 G196r elected to William Redmaine's pension. John Newton is given her pension   22 Mar 1715/16 G238r elected to Elizabeth Miller's pension. Deborah Godman is given her pension

WIGGINS, Thomas   4 Jul 1698 G11r bound to John Matthews, 7 years   10 Sep 1705 G123v freed by John Matthews

WIGLEY, William   3 Mar 1700/1 G57r bound to John Leake, 7 years   12 Apr 1708 G152r freed by John Leake

WILCOX/WILCOCKS, John (I)   4 Sep 1699 G29v equity of redemption of Susanna Miller's £160 share, mortgaged to Mrs Isted for £120, to be mortgaged to him   1 Dec 1701 G66r mortgagee of equity of redemption of Susanna Miller's share   6 Dec 1703 G99v mortgage on Mrs Miller's stock to be secured by payment of overplus of her dividend after payment of Mrs Isted's interest, after deduction of £5 for her board and lodging   20 Dec 1703 G100r receives overplus of Mrs Miller's dividend

WILCOX, John (II)   4 Aug 1701 G63v bound to Nathaniel Nowell, 7 years   7 Mar 1708/9 G162r freed by Nathaniel Nowell

WILD, [   ]   1 Mar 1702/3 G86r elected Stock-keeper for Yeomanry

WILD/WILDE, Benjamin   13 Apr 1698 G6v bound to his father, William, 7 years   27 Sep 1704 G112r son of William; freed by patrimony and cloathed   4 Apr 1709 G164r elected to his mother's £80 share   26 Mar 1711 G189r fined for Assistant Renter Warden

WILD, Edward   1 Mar 1687/8 F97v expelled from Livery by order of Lord Mayor

WILD, James   6 Sep 1714 G221v his son Richard is bound to Christopher Norris, 7 years

WILD/WILDE/WYLD/WYLDE, John   9 May 1694 F204v cloathed. Richard Pole is bound to him   7 Mar 1697/8 G4v elected to Elizabeth Brooke's £80 share   13 Apr 1698 G6v and John Deacon. Assignment from William Thackery of copies to be entered in Register Book   27 Mar 1699 G22v fined for Assistant Renter Warden   6 May 1700 G39v Francis Clare is bound to him   4 Aug 1701 G63v his apprentice Richard Poole is freed   4 May 1702 G70v not permitted to bind an apprentice as he has two already   3 Jun 1706 G132v his apprentice John Shipthorp is freed   1 Jul 1706 G133r Samuel Richardson is bound to him   3 Nov 1707 G146v his apprentice Francis Clare is freed   3 Oct 1709 G171r of Aldersgate Street, printer; John Littler is bound to him   5 Mar 1710/11 G188r of Aldersgate Street, printer; John Holmes is bound to him   6 Oct 1712 G204v Thomas Dowing is bound to him   13 Jun 1715 G229v his apprentice Samuel Richardson is freed

WILD/WILDE/WYLDE, Margaret   8 Apr 1700 G39r William Davy is bound to her   4 Feb 1705/6 G127v Thomas Branson is bound to her   7 Apr 1707 G141r stationer;

Philip Raper is bound to her   3 Nov 1707 G146v her apprentice William Davy is freed   1 Feb 1713/14 G216r Thomas Windsor is bound to her   6 Dec 1714 G224r Joseph Taylor is bound to her

WILD, Mrs   4 Apr 1709 G164r disposes of her £80 share to her son Benjamin

WILD, Richard (I)   2 Mar 1690/1 F150v confesses to importing ca. 150 copies of 'Menelius [i.e. John Minellius] upon Terence', a Stock book. Also accused of importing '[Thomas] Farnaby upon Ovid and Juvenal'. Promises to appear at next Court with a written account   6 Apr 1691 F152r to be prosecuted for importing Terence without a licence   6 Jul 1691 F157v confesses to importing 181 and selling ca. 50 of Minellius upon Terence, in ignorance that it was a Stock book; fined 12d per book

WILD, Richard (II)   6 Sep 1714 G221v son of James; bound to Christopher Norris, 7 years

WILD, Seth   4 Dec 1699 G34r bound to John Marsh, 7 years   7 Apr 1707 G141r freed by John Marsh

WILD, Thomas   1 May 1710 G179v of Aldersgate Street, printer; John Webster is bound to him

WILD/WILDE/WYLD, William (I)   29 May 1689 F118v cloathed   18 Jun 1689 F120r formerly freed of the Cutlers' Company; to take his place in Livery according to the date of his City freedom   1 Feb 1691/2 (W) his apprentice William Perkins is freed   4 Feb 1694/5 F217r William Thackery assigns him [Emmanuel Ford's] 'The History of Parismus' and five other books   27 Mar 1697 F260r elected Renter Warden   1 Apr 1697 F260v sworn in as First Renter Warden   5 Jul 1697 F264v elected to Stephen Bateman's £80 share and sworn in   16 Oct 1697 F269r Edward Dykes, his apprentice, is freed   13 Apr 1698 G6v his son Benjamin is bound to him   7 Nov 1698 G16r Benjamin Butler is bound to him   27 Sep 1704 G112r his son Benjamin is freed by patrimony   4 Feb 1705/6 G127v his apprentice Benjamin Butler is freed

WILD, William (II)   5 Aug 1689 F122r excused cloathing on grounds of juniorship and inability

WILDE – see WILD

WILDER, Richard   6 May 1706 G131v bound to Hannah Clarke, 7 years   5 Jul 1714 G220v freed by Hannah Clarke

WILDGOOSE, Elizabeth   4 Oct 1686 F64v deceased; Ann Haddock is admitted to her 40s pension

WILFORD, John   4 Feb 1705/6 G127v bound to George Sawbridge, 7 years

WILFORD, Joseph   3 May 1708 G152v his apprentice John Martin is freed   5 Jul 1708 G154v of Walthamstow, Essex; elected to cloathing

WILKINS, [ ]   4 Aug 1690 F141r asks pardon for printing without licence 'A Memorial Extracted out of the Modest Enquiry'; to bring to next court his warrant to print in Mr Wallis's absence   7 Jun 1697 F262v excused cloathing for present on request of some Court members   7 Oct 1700 G46r cloathed   1 Mar 1708/9 G161r elected Stock-keeper for the Yeomanry   1 Mar 1709/10 G176v elected Stock-keeper for the Livery   1 Mar 1710/11 G187v elected Stock-keeper for the Livery   1 Mar 1711/12 G197v elected Stock-keeper for the Livery   2 Mar 1712/13 G207r elected Stock-keeper for the Livery   1 Mar 1713/14 G216v elected Stock-keeper for the Livery   3 May 1714 G218v has printed 'Exposition of Mrs Lewis of the Catechism' [i.e. John Lewis, *The Church Catechism Explain'd*] and paid an acknowledgement for so doing to the S.C.   1 Mar 1714/15 G225v elected Stock-keeper for the Livery   1 Mar 1715/16 G236v elected Stock-keeper for the Livery   1 Mar 1716/17 G247r elected Stock-keeper for the Livery

See also WILKINS, Richard

WILKINS, Jeremiah   7 May 1694 F203v James Read is bound to him   7 Feb 1697/8 G3v John Atkins is bound to him   7 Apr 1701 G58v his apprentice Anne Boddily is freed   7 Jul 1701 G62r his apprentice James Read is freed   13 Apr 1702 G69v William Wise is turned over to him from Mary Thompson   23 Mar 1704/5 G117r his apprentice John Atkins is freed

WILKINS, John   7 Apr 1701 G58v petition requesting repayment of his Livery fine. £5 to be paid out of next quarterly pension money

WILKINS, John, Bishop of Chester   4 Sep 1693 F191r Court questions John Gellebrand's right to assign Wilkins's '[Mercury: or the] Swift and Secret Messenger' to Richard Baldwyn

WILKINS, Jonathan   3 Nov 1679 E95r freed by Dorman Newman

WILKINS, Richard   4 Feb 1705/6 G127v elected to John Arden's £40 share   26 Mar 1706 G130r fined for Renter Warden   4 Nov 1706 G136r Royston Meredith is turned over to him from Thomas Bennett   7 Apr 1707 G140v competes unsuccessfully for John Baskett's £80 share. Elected to Margaret Tomlins's £80 share. His £40 share disposed of to Ralph Smith   4 May 1713 G209v his apprentice Royston Meredith is freed

WILKINS, William (I)   6 May 1706 G131v part of quarterage arrears remitted as he had kept his mother-in-law, a pensioner of S.C. James Smith is bound to him   7 Apr 1712 G199r James Smith is turned over from him to William Sparkes   4 Oct 1714 G222v Thomas Hood is turned over from Anne Motte to him   8 Aug 1715 G232r Nicholas Blandford is bound to him

WILKINS, William (II)   6 Jul 1702 G78r bound to James Rawlins, 7 years   4 Aug 1707 G144v turned over from James Rawlins to John Humphreys   1 Feb 1713/14 G216r freed by William Humphreys

WILKINSON, [   ]   1 Mar 1679/80 E97v elected Stock-keeper for Yeomanry

WILKINSON, Adam   26 Mar 1698 G5v competes unsuccessfully for Beadle

WILKINSON, Christopher (I)   21 Feb 1681/2 E145r competes unsuccessfully for the £80 share of Mrs Harward, deceased   4 Dec 1682 E160v assigned one fifth of [Mézeray's] 'History of France' by William Cadman   3 Mar 1683/4 F9v elected Assistant in response to Crown's request as a reward for stamping out seditious printing. Fined for Renter Warden so he is eligible for Court   7 Apr 1684 F14r on the list of loyal Assistants presented to the Crown   2 Jun 1684 F16r elected to Thomas Raw's £80 share   7 May 1685 (W) confirmed as member of new Livery   7 Feb 1686/7 F70v competes unsuccessfully for the late John Playford's £160 share   5 Sep 1687 F87v elected to the late Widow Surbutt's £160 share   12 Oct 1687 F91r elected Under Warden   30 Jun 1688 F103r fined for second year of Under Warden   2 Jul 1688 F103v given £10 to be laid out by him with the advice of Stephen Bateman for William Jacob's relief   6 Aug 1688 F106r tells Court that he and Bateman have laid out £10 for Jacob's relief   27 Nov 1688 F110v among those chosen to audit Renter Wardens' accounts   5 Jun 1690 F135v re-appointed Assistant   7 Jul 1690 F138v elected Stock-keeper in place of Henry Mortlock, now Under Warden   2 Mar 1690/1 F150v elected Stock-keeper for Assistants with John Bellinger   1 Mar 1691/2 F165v elected Stock-keeper for Assistants with John Bellinger   4 Jul 1692 F173v chosen to audit Warden's accounts   7 Nov 1692 F181v elected to the late Mrs Man's £320 share   3 Apr 1693 F186r auditor of Renter Warden's accounts with Samuel Lowndes   3 Jul 1693 F189v with Samuel Lowndes, reports that the balance of the late Renter Wardens' accounts is £19 2s 2d   6 Aug 1694 F211v his son Christopher is freed by patrimony

WILKINSON, Christopher (II)   6 Aug 1694 F211v son of Christopher Wilkinson; freed by patrimony   1 Jul 1695 F227v cloathed   2 Aug 1697 F265v competes unsuccessfully for William Hill's £40 share   7 Mar 1697/8 G4v elected to Thomas Snowden's £40 share   9 Feb 1701/2 G67r competes unsuccessfully for Mrs Baker's £80 share   4 Feb 1705/6 G127r competes unsuccessfully for Deputy Collins's £80 share   9 Sep 1706 G134v desires not to be put in nomination for Renter Warden in future and fined. Elected to William Hensman's £80 share. His £40 share disposed of to Daniel Midwinter   26 Mar 1707 G139v fined for First Renter Warden   7 May 1711 G190r competes unsuccessfully for Capt. Samuel Roycroft's £160 share

WILKINSON, Mrs   3 Aug 1696 F246v lately remarried to Roper; her £320 share voted to Thomas Parkhurst

WILLIAMS, [ ]   8 May 1693 F187v on Mrs Newcomb's behalf complains that Eleanor Smith has not paid £40 debt; Court orders her £40 share to be disposed of   10 Sep 1711 G194r committee to meet John Baskett and Williams to ensure English Stock is protected despite privilege being granted by Oxford University to another person   1 Oct 1711 G194v no agreement reached with Baskett and Williams concerning English Stock   4 Aug 1712 G202v committee appointed to settle differences between S.C., Baskett and Williams concerning printing at Oxford   1 Sep 1712 G203r report from committee who had met Baskett and Williams concerning printing at Oxford

WILLIAMS, Alice   25 Jun 1690 F136v elected to the late Anne Napper's 40s pension   22 Jun 1694 F209v deceased; Mrs Jacob elected to her pension

WILLIAMS, Anne   2 Nov 1696 F251v widow of John Williams; petitions that her next dividend may not be stopped to pay her £12 9s debt to S.C.; only 40s stopped   3 May 1697 F261v debt incurred by her husband John is gradually being discharged on the account of her share   7 Jun 1697 F262v money due to S.C. and £4 10s due to John Pether to be deducted from her dividend   6 Dec 1697 G2r petitions requesting that her dividend should not be stopped on account of a debt due to S.C. from her late husband, John, or any claim of Pether, the S.C.'s cook, deferred to next Pension Court   22 Dec 1697 G2v only 30s to be deducted from her dividend in view of her mean condition   7 Feb 1698/9 G20r widow of John Williams; requests that the remainder of her dividend money may be paid to her. Warden to pay her 40s which will be stopped out of her next dividend money   3 Apr 1699 G23v petition requesting allowance of further money from her dividend. Account to be prepared for next Court. Meanwhile, Treasurer to let her have 20s for her subsistence   5 Jun 1699 G25r £4 due to Pether from her late husband when Renter Warden to be deducted from her next dividend money   3 Jul 1699 G27r to receive 10s from the Poor Box   3 Mar 1706/7 G139r William Gillison is bound to her   1 Sep 1707 G145r deceased; her £160 share is disposed of to Richard Mount
See also WILLIAMS, John

WILLIAMS, Clement   24 Mar 1711/12 G198r elected to Matthew Smelt's pension   23 Dec 1714 G224r Edward Davenport is given his pension   27 Sep 1716 G243v discharged from the list of pensioners as now a pensioner in Dulwich Hospital

WILLIAMS, John (I)   22 Sep 1680 E104r assignment from Mrs Stephens to be entered   7 Mar 1680/1 E108r cloathed   5 Feb 1682/3 E163r resigns his £160 share, requesting Court to elect his son Capt. John Williams to it; this is accordingly done. (W) Letter to this effect

WILLIAMS, John (II)   2 May 1692 F171r cloathed   27 Mar 1693 F185r voted that he should not be elected First Renter Warden   4 Sep 1699 G30r his son John Williams is freed by patrimony   2 Jun 1701 G60v Roger Hodges is bound to him   7 Sep 1702 G80v George Barton is bound to him   6 Aug 1705 G122v William Gilbert is bound to him 1 Aug 1709 G169v his apprentice Roger Hodges is freed 3 Dec 1711 G195v William Aldersey is bound to him 8 Aug 1715 G232r John Arno is bound to him 1 Apr 1717 G249v Thomas Baskett is bound to him

WILLIAMS, John (III) 4 Sep 1699 G30r freed by John Williams, patrimony 2 Oct 1699 G31r has petitioned for loan of £50, part of monies usually lent to young traders. S.C. to consider what monies they can call in

WILLIAMS, John (IV) 3 Nov 1701 G65r bound to John Quinney, 7 years

WILLIAMS, John (V) – see following entry

WILLIAMS, John (VI) 4 Aug 1712 G202v son of John; bound to John Harding, 7 years

WILLIAMS, John, Dr – see CATECHISMS

WILLIAMS, Capt. John (I) 5 Feb 1682/3 E163r elected to his father's £160 share at his father's request 2 May 1683 E169r S.C. warehouse let to him for £5 p.a. 4 Feb 1683/4 (W) to assign his £160 share to Mrs Judith Webb for £100 at 6% 3 Mar 1683/4 F10v allowed to mortgage his £160 share to Mrs Webb for £100 plus interest, having discharged his mortgage to Samuel Mearne, deceased 7 May 1685 (W) confirmed as member of new Livery 1 Feb 1685/6 F50v pleads his father-in-law Henry Twyford's inability to serve S.C. through old age 11 Oct 1688 F108v restored to Livery 11 Apr 1690 F133v suggested for Assistant Renter Warden but set aside at the request of Thomas Bassett for living out of town 4 Aug 1690 F141v Beadle to ensure that he pays rent due for storing books in S.C. cellar before he removes them 1 Sep 1690 F142r summoned to next Court re. his payment for cellar rent 1 Mar 1691/2 F166r allowed to transfer the £150 mortgage of his £160 share from Mrs Webb to John Bellinger 26 Mar 1692 F167v set aside for a year from serving or fining for Renter Warden 2 May 1692 F170v allowed to continue using buttery under Hall as warehouse on backdated payment of 50s p.a. 6 Feb 1692/3 F184r John Bellinger asks that Williams's £160 share be disposed of at next Court to satisfy a debt to him of £150 26 Mar 1694 F201v elected Renter Warden and summoned 2 Apr 1694 F202r accepts post of First Renter Warden 11 Nov 1695 F235v Master tells Court that he has been unable to bring the late Renter Wardens John Darby and Williams to account 3 May 1697 F261v has died in poverty; his fellow ex-Renter Warden John Darby is being pressed for £4 10s which Williams owed John Pether. S.C. to pay him from Williams's estate

See also WILLIAMS, Anne

WILLIAMS, Capt. John (II) 7 Apr 1707 G141r elected Assistant Renter Warden 3 Oct 1709 G171r to have an impression of the Psalms of David in folio at 14d per book

WILLIAMS, Philip 4 Jun 1716 G240v his son William is bound to John Lenthall, 7 years

WILLIAMS, Thomas 8 May 1682 E153r objections to his executor Charles Spicer assigning books to Benjamin Tooke and Thomas Sawbridge deferred until next Court

WILLIAMS, William (I) 6 Jul 1702 G78r bound to George Butter, 7 years

WILLIAMS, William (II – possibly a mistake for SMITH, William) 1 Oct 1705 G124r James Cooper is turned over from him to Francis Leach

WILLIAMS, William (III) 4 Jun 1716 G240v son of Philip; bound to John Lenthall, 7 years

WILLIAMSON, John 1 Mar 1679/80 E97r frees James Gilbertson 7 Feb 1680/1 E107r to have the first £50 of loan money coming in from either James Collins or Jonathan Edwin 'he giving good security'

WILLIAMSON, Richard   7 Aug 1699 G29r bound to Richard Sare, 7 years

WILLIAMSON, Robert   8 Apr 1695 F221r servant to William Barker; freed   6 May 1695 F223v John Griffin is bound to him   2 Oct 1699 G31v William Doleman is bound to him

WILLIMER, Thomas   3 Jun 1706 G132v his apprentice Robert Whiskin is freed

WILLIS, [   ]   16 Jun 1684 F17r his former apprentice Roger Neild to be freed

WILLIS, John, snr – see following entry

WILLIS, John, jnr   6 Aug 1694 F211v son of John Willis of South Hinksey, Berkshire, gentleman; bound to Samuel Briscoe for 7 years from 8 August

WILLIS, William   6 Jul 1691 F157v cloathed and summoned to next Court re. fine

WILLMER/WILMER/WILLMOR, Thomas   14 Mar 1703/4 G104r freeman of Saddlers' Company; made free and cloathed   8 May 1704 G106r elected to Katherine Richardson's £40 share   7 Aug 1704 G111r Thomas Collyer is bound to him   4 Aug 1707 G144v printer; Richard Berrisford is bound to him   3 May 1708 G152v printer; Jacob Francis is bound to him   5 Jul 1708 G155r his apprentice William Mewes is freed   6 Jun 1709 G165v William Richardson is bound to him   26 Mar 1711 G189r fined for Assistant Renter Warden   1 Oct 1711 G195r his apprentice Thomas Collyer is freed   13 Jun 1715 G229v Stephen Lee and Humphrey King are bound to him

WILLOUGHBY/WILLOWBY, Robert   5 Sep 1698 G14v bound to Edward Hawkins   5 Oct 1702 G81v turned over from Edward Hawkins to Mark Forster   4 Mar 1705/6 G129r freed by Mark Forster   5 Sep 1709 G170r of Fleet Street, bookbinder; John Trotman is bound to him   12 Nov 1711 G195r Gabriel Ballden is bound to him

WILLSHIRE/WILSHIRE/WILTSHERE, James   5 Jul 1703 G92r James Ayrey is bound to him   4 Sep 1704 G112r Charles Knock is bound to him   5 Feb 1704/5 G115r James Ayrey turned over from him to William Sayes. William Collyer turned over to him from William Sayes

WILLYMOTT, William   19 Feb 1705/6 G128r letter to Henry Mortlock concerning the printing of his edition of Terence by Mead   1 Apr 1706 G130v committee to consider matter of books of Ovid and Terence printed for him   6 Sep 1714 G221v letter to Benjamin Tooke concerning printing of 'Corderius' [i.e. Mathurin Cordier] referred to Master, Wardens and Stock-keepers

WILMER, WILLMOR – see WILLMER

WILMOT, John, Earl of Rochester – see ROCHESTER

WILSHERE, Upton   27 Apr 1710 G178v bound to John Wind, 7 years

WILSHIRE – see WILLSHIRE

WILSON, Ebenezer   13 Jun 1715 G229v his son John is bound to John Darby, 7 years

WILSON, Elizabeth   9 Oct 1702 G82r of St Dunstan's in the West; bond from S.C. of £1000 penalty for payment of £512 10s sealed

WILSON, Henry   7 Jul 1707 G143v bound to John Wyatt

WILSON, John   13 Jun 1715 G229v son of Ebenezer; bound to John Darby, 7 years

WILSON, Robert   2 Jul 1694 F210v servant to Christopher Lingard; freed. Lingard is fined 2s 6d for not turning him over at the Hall

WILSON, Thomas   4 Jun 1705 G120v bound to Daniel Mead

WILTSHERE, James   1 Sep 1712 G203r his apprentice William Collyer is freed

WILTSHIRE, James   4 Jul 1698 G11r freed by Edward Powell

WINCH, Adam   3 Oct 1687 F89r elected to Thomasine Cupper's 20s pension   2 Dec 1700 G47v has been illegally demanding money of persons coming to be made free. Warden to pay him 2s for every Court day attended, but required to cease this practice   26 Mar 1701 G57v competes unsuccessfully for Beadle   26 Mar 1702 G68v competes unsuccessfully for Beadle   4 May 1702 G71r John Bennett is bound to him   18 Dec 1702 G84r elected to Katherine Bowyer's pension   27 Mar 1704 G105r competes unsuccessfully for Beadle   26 Mar 1705 G117v competes unsuccessfully for Beadle   26 Mar 1706 G130v competes unsuccessfully for Beadle   26 Mar 1707 G140r competes unsuccessfully for Beadle   26 Mar 1708 G151r competes unsuccessfully for Beadle   26 Mar 1709 G163r competes unsuccessfully for Beadle   27 Mar 1710 G177v competes unsuccessfully for Beadle   26 Mar 1711 G189r competes unsuccessfully for Beadle   26 Mar 1713 G208r competes unsuccessfully for Beadle   24 Sep 1714 G222r deceased; Mary Crump is given his pension   4 Oct 1714 G222r porter to English Stock, deceased

WINCHESTER, Daniel, snr – see following entry

WINCHESTER, Daniel, jnr   5 Aug 1695 F231v son of Daniel Winchester of Windsor, wheelwright; bound to John Whitlock, 8 years

WIND, John   8 Nov 1703 G97r freed by Henry Collins   27 Apr 1710 G178v of Great St Helen's, packer; Upton Wilshere is bound to him   7 Aug 1710 G183r packer; excused cloathing for the present

WINDSOR, Thomas   1 Feb 1713/14 G216r son of William; bound to Margaret Wild, 7 years

WING, John   4 May 1702 G70v author of 'Ephemerides of the Celestial Motions for Six Years'

WINGRAVE, George   2 Aug 1703 G94r bound to Edward Davis

WINGATE, Edmund   5 Sept 1681 E129v his 'Use of the Rule of Proportion in Arithmetic and Geometry' assigned to Thomas Passenger by Dorothy Stephens

WINSLOW, [   ]   1 Mar 1702/3 G86r of Worcestershire; requesting that school books and Bibles given to tenants of Kempsey Manor should be sent

WISE, William   13 Apr 1702 G69v turned over from Mary Thompson to Jeremiah Wilkins   3 Jul 1710 G182r John Bagnall is turned over to him from Andrew Hind

WIT'S COMMONWEALTH [i.e. Nicholas Ling, *Politeuphuia. Wit's Commonwealth*]   15 Apr 1692 F17or assigned to William Freeman by Elizabeth Flesher

WOLLAME/WOOLLAME, Robert   15 Nov 1703 G97v of Norwich; bill in Chancery to be brought against him concerning sham almanacks   26 Jan 1703/4 G100v of Norwich; throws himself on S.C.'s mercy but required to give a full answer to S.C.'s bill in Chancery against him   7 Feb 1703/4 G101v answer to S.C.'s bill in Chancery   10 Feb 1703/4 G102r required to give further answers to S.C.'s bill in Chancery

WOLLEY – see WOOLLEY

WOOD, Ann   26 Mar 1700 G38r bound to Edward Tracy, 7 years

WOOD, Nicholas   8 Nov 1703 G97r bound to Thomas Dalton, 7 years

WOOD, Philip   2 Dec 1695 F237r servant to Alexander Milbourne; freed   2 Mar 1701/2 G67v John Hellam is bound to him

WOOD, Thomas   2 May 1698 G7v bound to Bennett Griffin, 7 years   9 Feb 1707/8 G149r freed by Christian Griffin   5 Mar 1715/16 G237v cloathed

WOOD, William   3 Apr 1704 G106r bound to Mary Curtis, 7 years   4 Jun 1711 G191r freed by Mary Curtis

WOOD STREET   20 Dec 1686 F69v Benjamin Thrale is heir to its last surviving feoffee; ordered that the estate be conveyed to other feoffees in trust for S.C.   2 May 1687 F83r indenture consenting to conveyance from Dorothy Thrale, and from Benjamin Thrale and his wife Elizabeth, heirs to last feoffees, of S.C.'s houses in Great Wood Street and Friars Alley is sealed   3 Apr 1693 F186r committee to consider motion that the Wardens should receive Wood Street rents

WOODFALL, Abraham   26 Mar 1685 F32r given 2s 6d charity

WOODFALL, Henry   2 Jun 1701 G60v bound to John Darby   5 Jul 1708 G155r freed by John Darby

WOODWARD, John   4 Jun 1711 G191r bound to Hannah Clarke, 7 years

WOODWARD, Thomas   2 Jul 1705 G121v bound to Matthew Wootton, 7 years   3 Nov 1712 G205r freed by Matthew Wootton   6 May 1717 G250v to be summoned to take cloathing

WOOLFE, John   5 Mar 1704/5 G117r bound to Edmund Powell, 7 years   4 Oct 1714 G222v freed by Edmund Powell

WOOLLAME – see WOLLAME

WOOLLY, Francis   6 Jul 1702 G78r bound to John Grantham, 7 years

WOOLLEY/WOLLEY/WOOLLY, William (I)   7 Oct 1689 F124v assignee of Daniel Richardson to whom S.C. demised a house in Ave Maria Lane; request to renew the lease for 21 years refused   5 Oct 1696 F251r committee to inquire into his desire to renew the lease of his house in Ave Maria Lane which is within 3 years of expiring   2 Nov 1696 (W) reported that Shephard paid about £33 p.a. for the house and Woolley paid about £24 p.a.   5 Jul 1697 F264v comes to Court to renew his lease and is asked to return next Court day   2 Aug 1697 F265r asks again to renew lease; committee to view his house and others 'which Mr. Mills holds of this company'   6 Sep 1697 F266v Court offers to renew lease on his paying a fine of £60, subsequently reduced to £50; given until next Court to consider   7 Aug 1699 G28v terms of lease renewed from S.C. for 21 years   4 Sep 1699 G29v proposing different terms for his lease   2 Oct 1699 G31v lease of house in Ave Maria Lane sealed   8 Nov 1703 G97r refused request for changes to terms of lease

WOOLLEY/WOOLLY, William (II)   2 Jun 1701 G60v bound to Thomas Simpson   2 Aug 1708 G156v freed by Thomas Simpson

WOOTTON/WOOTON/WOTTON/WOTON, Matthew   7 Oct 1689 F125r cloathed   12 Nov 1694 F214v complains on behalf of himself, Richard Chiswell, &c., that Henry Mortlock and others have printed Horace; matter left to Mortlock   6 Apr 1696 F241v complains that William Thackery has printed or appropriated his 'Parismus' [by Emmanuel Ford]; decision deferred   26 Mar 1698 G5r competes unsuccessfully for Renter Warden   3 Apr 1699 G24r his apprentice Richard Greenaway is freed   7 Aug 1699 G29r Arthur Collins is bound to him   13 Apr 1702 G70r elected First Renter Warden   2 Jul 1705 G121v Thomas Woodward is bound to him   6 Oct 1707 G145v Arthur Collins is freed by him   3 May 1708 G152v elected to John Walthoe's £40 share   1 Mar 1708/9 G161r Stock-keeper for Livery   6 Feb 1709/10 G175r elected to William Freeman's £80 share   1 Mar 1709/10 G176r elected Stock-keeper for Livery   1 Mar 1710/11 G187v elected Stock-keeper for Livery   10 Sep 1711 G194r bookseller; Nathan Drake is bound to him   3 Nov 1712 G205r his apprentice Thomas Woodward is freed   13 Apr 1713 G208v competes unsuccessfully for Nathaniel Ranew's £160 share   22 Dec 1713 G215r elected to Thomas Clarke's £160 share. His £80 share disposed of to John Darby   2 May 1715 G228v elected Assistant   5 Mar 1715/16 G237v signs note for payment to Guy   4 Feb 1716/17 G246v to be new trustee of

S.C.'s property 21 Feb 1716/17 G246v trust of S.C.'s property conveyed to him as new trustee

WORCESTER, BISHOP OF – see STILLINGFLEET, Edward

WORKMEN 11 Nov 1700 G46v £100 to be borrowed on Corporation's account to pay workmens' and other bills

WORLIDGE, John – see SYSTEMA HORTICULTURA

WORRALL, John, snr 5 Dec 1709 G172r of Warwick Court, bookbinder; his son John is bound to him 3 Aug 1713 G213r his son Thomas is bound to Robert Gostlin, 7 years

WORRALL, John, jnr 5 Dec 1709 G172r bound to John, his father, 7 years

WORRALL, Joshua 5 Sep 1698 G14v bound to William Turner 5 Mar 1710/11 G188r freed by Christopher Bateman

WORRALL, Thomas 3 Aug 1713 G213r son of John; bound to Robert Gostlin, 7 years

WORRELL, John 3 Mar 1700/1 G57r William Squibb is bound to him

WOSALD, Jane 23 Jun 1711 G191v to be discharged from having any further relief from the S.C.

WOTON/WOTTON – see WOOTTON

WRAY, Elizabeth 1 Feb 1713/14 G215v deceased; her £80 share disposed of to John Nutt. Her dividend to revert to English Stock as she died before Dividend Day

WREATHCOCK, James 7 May 1711 G190v bound to Robert Podmore, 7 years

WRIGHT, [ ] 7 Dec 1685 F47v in Benjamin Harris's partnership for printing the proceedings of the Westminster Parliament 28 Oct 1697 F269v herald painter; to make the King's banner at the cost of £10 and to deliver it by 3 November 7 Feb 1697/8 G3v herald painter; bill for making escutcheons to be paid only when he has made banner good 7 Mar 1697/8 G4v to be paid £9 10s and no more as he has not done his work as well as he ought to have done

WRIGHT, Elinor 3 Feb 1700/1 G55v arrears of quarterage to be remitted on account of poverty. John Wright, her son, is bound to her 7 Mar 1708/9 G162r her apprentice John Wright is freed

WRIGHT, Elizabeth 21 Mar 1694/5 F219r elected into the pension of Eleanor Golding, deceased 23 Mar 1704/5 G117r deceased; Robert Chowne is given her pension

WRIGHT, George (I) 6 Aug 1694 F211v of Brandon, Suffolk, clerk; his son John is bound to Robert Elmes

WRIGHT, George (II) 13 Jun 1715 G229v son of Robert; bound to Sarah Cliff, 7 years

WRIGHT, Henry 8 Apr 1695 F221r son of Richard Wright of Nottingham, gentleman; bound to Henry Mortlock 6 Jul 1702 G78r freed by Henry Mortlock

WRIGHT, Jeremiah 8 Nov 1680 E105r to be paid £15 for his work as herald painter

WRIGHT, John (I) 1 Mar 1682/3 E165r Elizabeth Thomas, administratrix of Edward Thomas, assigns Baker's 'Arithmetic' to Wright and William Thackery 1 Jun 1685 F38r deceased; his widow's £160 share is voted to John Simms on her remarriage

WRIGHT, John (II) 5 Dec 1687 F95r fined £8 for trying to force his way on to Court

WRIGHT, John (III) 6 Aug 1694 F211v son of George Wright of Brandon, Suffolk, clerk; bound to Robert Elmes

WRIGHT, John (IV)   3 Feb 1700/1 G55v bound to his mother, Elinor Wright, 7 years   7 Mar 1708/9 G162r freed by Elinor Wright

WRIGHT, Mrs   1 Jun 1685 F38r widow of John Wright, now remarried; her £160 share voted to John Simms

WRIGHT, Richard   8 Apr 1695 F221r of Nottingham, gentleman; his son Henry is bound to Henry Mortlock, 7 years

WRIGHT, Robert (I)   26 Mar 1685 F32r elected into the 40s pension of Francis Church, deceased; given 2s 6d charity   9 Mar 1696 F241r deprived of pension when it is discovered he is not free of S.C.

WRIGHT, Robert (II)   13 Jun 1715 G229v his son George is bound to Sarah Cliff, 7 years

WRITINGS   1 Jul 1695 F227r catalogue of all S.C. writings to be taken, in the presence of the Master and one of the Wardens

WYATT, John, snr   12 Sep 1692 F179r summoned to show why he should not be cloathed   3 Oct 1692 F180v to be summoned to cloathing   5 Dec 1692 F183r cloathed   1 Jul 1695 F228v Thomas Clement jnr is bound to him   9 Sep 1700 G45r George Baynam is bound to him   7 Jul 1707 G143v Henry Wilson is bound to him   1 Sep 1712 G203r his son John is bound to him   3 Nov 1712 G205r his apprentice Thomas Glenister is freed   13 Apr 1713 G208v elected to Christopher Bateman's £40 share   5 Apr 1714 G217v receives charge as First Renter Warden   7 Feb 1714/5 G225r competes unsuccessfully for Mary Jones's £80 share   1 Mar 1715/16 G236v elected Stock-keeper for Yeomanry   1 Mar 1716/17 G247r elected Stock-keeper for Yeomanry   4 Mar 1716/17 G247v elected to Mrs Cleave's £80 share. His £40 share disposed of to Benjamin Sprint

WYATT, John, jnr   1 Sep 1712 G203r bound to John, his father, 7 years

WYATT, Richard   6 Oct 1707 G145v freed by William Holland

WYATT, William   6 Jul 1713 G212v freed by Mary Richards (he was bound by a foreign indenture)   3 Aug 1713 G213r John Harrindine is bound to him

WYDDOWES – see WIDOWS

WYLD, [ ]   10 Sep 1716 G243r writing master, excused cloathing for some time See also WILD

WYLDE – see WILD

WYND, John   2 Dec 1706 G136v Daniel Davis is bound to him

WYNNE, John   4 Feb 1711/12 G196r ordered to take cloathing at next Court   7 Apr 1712 G198v cloathed

WYSE, William   4 Mar 1705/6 G129r apprentice to Mary Tonson; freed by David Edwards

XENOPHON   5 Jul 1703 G92r committee appointed to sell books of Xenophon from Oxford

YARNES, Benjamin   12 Nov 1705 G125r Bezaleel Creek is turned over to him from Edward Hawkins

YATE, Elizabeth   20 Dec 1710 G186v elected to Anne Bramstone's pension   6 Jul 1713 G212v her apprentice Bartholomew Taylor is freed

YATES, John Thomas   3 May 1703 G89r bound to Robert King, 7 years

YATES, Joseph   5 May 1707 G142r bound to Sarah, his mother, 7 years

YATES, Mrs   20 Jun 1713 G210v elected to Robert Chowne's pension. Margaret Webster is given her pension

YATES, Sarah   5 May 1707 G142r mason; her son Joseph is bound to her

See also preceding entry

YATES, Thomas   3 Jun 1689 F119r cloathed   4 May 1691 F153r George Downes surrenders his £40 share and the Court elects Yates into it at Downes's request   2 Dec 1695 F237r John Flinstone, his apprentice, is freed   4 Jul 1698 G11r William Banks is bound to him   6 Jul 1702 G77v his £40 share is surrendered and disposed of to Benjamin Simpson   27 Mar 1703 G87v petition as candidate for Beadle not read as he had previously entered into an agreement and confederacy prejudicial to S.C.   2 Aug 1703 G94r petition for part of Livery fine to be restored to him on account of poverty, being a prisoner in Ludgate   6 Mar 1703/4 G103v petition to be considered at next Pension Court   23 Mar 1703/4 G104v to be paid £5 from charity money

YATES, William   7 Feb 1708/9 G160v bound to John How, 7 years

YEATES, Thomas   6 Jul 1702 G78r Bartholomew Taylor is bound to him

YEATS, William   6 Aug 1716 G242v freed by John How

YEMES, Henry   10 Sep 1705 G123v bound to Mary Tonson, 7 years   3 Nov 1712 G205r freed by Mary Tonson

YEO, Philip   7 Jul 1701 G62r bound to Awnsham Churchill, 7 years

YEOMANRY   15 Jul 1690 F140r Livery and Yeomanry, some abstaining, subscribe towards raising horse and dragoons for the Crown

YORK   7 Dec 1685 F47v workmen printers complain of illegal printing house there   7 Jun 1686 F57v master printers allege in petition (copy in W) that York's three illegal presses are printing books belonging to S.C. members; Master asks for proof   2 Jul 1688 F103v Master and Wardens to take legal advice re. regulating printing in York and elsewhere   7 Mar 1691/2 F166r Wardens and Robert Stephens to visit York to investigate illegal supernumerary printers comprinting Stock books and seize the books

YORKE, William   5 Jul 1703 G92r bound to James Holland, 7 years   7 Feb 1703/4 G101v Christopher Harris is bound to him   3 May 1708 G152v oatmeal man; his apprentice Robert Hale is freed; Henry Merryman is bound to him   4 Oct 1708 G158r of Gravel Lane, Wapping; William Nicholls is bound to him

YOUNG, Benjamin   9 Feb 1707/8 G149r bound to John Watts, 7 years

YOUNGE, Richard   2 Jul 1694 F210v fined 2s 6d when his apprentice William Lillingston is freed, for not turning him over at the Hall

ZOUCH, Francis   4 Oct 1703 G96r bound to Peter Tanner, 7 years   4 May 1713 G209v freed by Peter Tanner